THIRD EDITION

POETRY

An Introduction

Michael Meyer

University of Connecticut

BEDFORD / ST. MARTIN'S   Boston ◆ New York

FOR BEDFORD / ST. MARTIN'S

Developmental Editor: Aron Keesbury
Production Editor: Stasia Zomkowski
Production Supervisor: Joe Ford
Marketing Manager: Brian Wheel
Editorial Assistant: Joshua Levy
Production Assistant: Thomas P. Crehan
Copyeditor: Jane Zanichkowsky
Text Design: Claire Seng-Niemoeller
Cover Design: Donna Lee Dennison
Cover Art: Paul Klee, "Park bei Lu(zern)," 1938. © 2000 Artists Rights Society (ARS), New York/VG Bild-Kunst, Bonn.
Composition: Stratford Publishing Services, Inc.
Printing and Binding: Haddon Craftsmen, Inc.

President: Charles H. Christensen
Editorial Director: Joan E. Feinberg
Editor in Chief: Karen S. Henry
Director of Marketing: Karen Melton
Director of Editing, Design, and Production: Marcia Cohen
Managing Editor: Elizabeth M. Schaaf

Library of Congress Control Number: 00-106484

For information, write: Bedford/St. Martin's
75 Arlington Street, Boston, MA 02116
(617-399-4000)

ISBN: 0-312-25076-2

Acknowledgments

Diane Ackerman. "A Fine a Private Place" from *Jaguar of Sweet Laughter* by Diane Ackerman. Copyright © 1991 by Diane Ackerman. Reprinted by permission of Random House, Inc.

Virginia Hamilton Adair. "Dirty Old Man" from *Beliefs and Blasphemies* by Virginia Hamilton Adair. Copyright © 1998 by Virginia Hamilton Adair. Reprinted by permission of Random House, Inc.

Anna Akhmatova. "Lot's Wife" from *Anna Akhmatova, Selected Poems,* trans. from the Russian by Richard McKane. Copyright © 1967 by Richard McKane, Bloodaxe Books, Ltd.

Claribel Alegría. "I Am Mirror" from *Sobrevito* by Claribel Alegría. Reprinted by permission of the author.

Paula Gunn Allen. "Hoop Dancer" from *Shadow Country* by Paula Gunn Allen, University of California Publication in American Indian Series © 1982. Reprinted with permission of the University of California Press.

Acknowledgments and copyrights are continued at the back of the book on pages 704–12, which constitute an extension of the copyright page. It is a violation of the law to reproduce these selections by any means whatsoever without the written permission of the copyright holder.

For My Wife
Regina Barreca

Preface for Instructors

Poetry: An Introduction, Third Edition, is drawn from the widely adopted *Bedford Introduction to Literature*. This third edition of *Poetry* has many distinctive features that have already been class-tested in hundreds of literature courses and carefully revised over five editions of the larger book. With its balance of classic and contemporary, traditional, and multicultural works, along with its in-depth treatment of selected poets, its provocative secondary materials, and its pervasive concern with critical reading, thinking, and writing, *Poetry* addresses all the requirements of the contemporary poetry course.

Poetry: An Introduction reflects the assumptions that understanding enhances the enjoyment of literature and that reading literature offers a valuable and unique means of apprehending life in its richness and diversity. The book also reflects the hope that the selections included will encourage students to become lifelong readers of imaginative literature. Designed to accommodate a variety of teaching styles, this rich collection of 453 poems (115 of them new) represents a wide range of periods, nationalities, ethnicities, and voices. Each selection has been carefully chosen for its appeal to students today and for its usefulness in demonstrating the effects, significance, and pleasures of poetry. To enhance these selections, this edition includes many images and photographs of selected poets. Also new to this edition is a separate chapter consisting of concise biographies of selected poets that provide valuable background information.

Poetry for Today's Course

Poetry: An Introduction, Third Edition, is designed for the introductory poetry course as it is taught today, which varies — from school to school and from instructor to instructor — more than ever before. Even the traditional course emphasizing the elements of poetry and a broad range of works from the Western canon is changing in response to important developments in literary studies and, more generally, in higher education and in American society. The course is now viewed by many teachers as an opportunity to supplement classics of Western literature with the work of writers previously excluded from the traditional canon. Increasingly, it now also serves as an introduction to the discipline of literary study, a challenging development that brings to the undergraduate classroom important trends in literary theory and provocative new readings of both familiar and unfamiliar texts. Finally, Introduction to Poetry is now frequently taught as a second course in composition in which the critical thinking and writing that students do are as important as the reading that they do. The third edition of *Poetry: An Introduction* responds to these developments with distinctive features that address the needs of instructors who teach a traditional course but who are also concerned about canonical issues, literary theory, and writing about literature.

Flexible, Teachable Organization

To be flexible enough to support a number of teaching styles, and yet to still hold on solidly to a framework for understanding poetry, *Poetry: An Introduction* is divided into four principal parts that may be taught consecutively or in any order you prefer. Part One of the book — the first eleven chapters — is devoted to the elements of poetry; Part Two consists of six chapters that feature a variety of approaches to poetry; Part Three discusses strategies for critical thinking and writing; and Part Four is a collection of poems from 75 authors.

The Elements of Poetry

The first ten chapters of the book are devoted to the elements of poetry, including such matters as diction, tone, images, figures of speech, symbols, sounds, rhythm, and poetic forms. Each of these chapters begins with a focused discussion of the particular elements, interspersed with examples of poetry that are especially effective in helping students to identify the elements and understand how they contribute to the effects and meanings of a poem. Each chapter then concludes with several "poems for further study," each accompanied by questions for critical thinking and writing.

New to this edition is the eleventh chapter, "Combining the Elements of Poetry," which guides students through the sometimes complex process of synthesizing their new understanding of poetic elements into a more complete appreciation of the whole poem. In addition, this chapter follows a student through every stage of the process of combining the elements into a sample explication.

Critical, Cultural, and Thematic Case Studies

Building on the success of the "Critical Case Study" of T. S. Eliot's "The Love Song of J. Alfred Prufrock," which enhances the poem with readings from a variety of critical perspectives, Part Two of *Poetry: An Introduction* adds three other chapters that place poetry within multiple contexts. A new "Cultural Case Study" presents Julia Alvarez's "Queens, 1963" along with relevant historical and cultural documents (a television script, photographs, advertisements, and an interview with the poet herself), inviting students to practice cultural criticism by asking new questions of the text. A second new chapter clusters several poems around two different poetic themes: poems about love and poems about teaching and learning. Finally, a third new chapter presents brief biographies of selected poets that add richness and depth to students' understanding of the poems by those authors. These chapters model, in a student-friendly and insightful way, the various approaches to poetry that have become a staple of the introductory class. Perhaps more important, they give students the opportunity to approach poetry from a rich variety of angles, use a number of sources to think critically about poems, and write their own papers.

Selected Major Authors Treated in Depth

Also appearing in Part Two of the book is the popular in-depth coverage of Robert Frost, Emily Dickinson, and Langston Hughes. With thirty-nine poems by Dickinson, twenty-two by Frost, and twenty-nine by Hughes, the third edition now presents these poets in newly organized chapters that highlight a particular context for each poet. Frost's poems are presented in the context of his biography, Hughes's in the context of the culture in which they were written, and Dickinson's in the context of her body of work.

Substantial introductions provide useful biographical and critical information about each of these important writers. A selection of "Perspectives" — excerpts from letters, journals, and critical commentaries — follows each writer's works to provide a context for discussion and writing. "Considerations for Critical Thinking and Writing" follow both selections and "Perspectives"; these questions encourage critical thinking and provide stimulating opportunities for student essays.

In addition, "Two Complementary Critical Readings" on a particular work by each of the three major authors offer students examples of the variety of approaches they can take in reading and writing about poetry. The two readings on Dickinson, for instance, focus on the eroticism of "Wild Nights — Wild Nights!" and its relationship to nineteenth-century popular sensationalist literature. By reading commentaries from two critics who argue competing ideas about one text or who illuminate different aspects of that text, students can see immediately that there is no single way to read a work of literature, an important and necessary step for learning how to formulate their own critical approaches in their essays.

Critical Thinking and Writing

Part Three of *Poetry: An Introduction* builds on the introductory material on reading poetry in Chapter 1 and the genre-specific writing assignments and questions for responsive reading in Chapter 2 by including a wealth of critical thinking and writing coverage in a group of four chapters. Chapter 19, "Critical Strategies for Reading," deepens the introductory discussion of active reading by focusing on the different reading strategies employed by contemporary literary theorists. This chapter, which can be assigned at any point in the course, introduces students to a wide variety of major contemporary theoretical approaches — formalist, biographical, psychological, historical (including literary history criticism, Marxist criticism, new historicist criticism, and cultural criticism), gender strategies (including feminist criticism and gay and lesbian criticism), mythological, reader-response, and deconstructionist. In brief examples the approaches are applied in analyzing Robert Frost's "Mending Wall" and other works, so that students will have a sense of how to use these strategies in their own reading and writing. A selected bibliography for the approaches concludes this important chapter.

The next two chapters — Chapter 20, "Reading and Writing," and Chapter 21, "The Literary Research Paper" — discuss and illustrate the writing process while offering models of the different types of papers usually assigned in an introductory course, including explication, analysis, and comparison-contrast. Chapter 22, "Taking Essay Examinations," helps students to hone their writing skills in preparation of midterms and final exams. Throughout the book are a total of eight sample papers that provide concrete, accessible models for a wide range of assignments.

In addition — though the emphasis in this text is on critical reading and understanding rather than on critical terminology — terms such as *symbol, irony,* and *metaphor* are defined and illustrated to equip students with a basic working vocabulary for discussing and writing about poetry. When first defined in the text, these terms appear in boldface type. An "Index of Terms" appears inside the back cover of the book for easy reference, and a "Glossary of Literary Terms" provides concise explanations of more than one hundred terms central to the study of poetry.

The Collection and Albums of Contemporary and World Poetry

Part Four of *Poetry: An Introduction* consists of a wide-ranging collection of 130 poems. Arranged alphabetically by author, the poems in the collection represent different periods and nationalities and include classic and contemporary voices as diverse as Maya Angelou, William Blake, E. E. Cummings, John Donne, Marianne Moore, Pat Mora, Christina Georgina Rossetti, Walt Whitman, and William Butler Yeats.

Included in the collection is an album of contemporary selections that offers some of the most interesting and lively poems published in the last decade or so, including works by Martín Espada, Deborah Garrison, Donald Hall, Jane Hirshfield, Linda Hogan, Mary Oliver, and Ronald Wallace. Biographical information about the album authors is included in the text to introduce instructors and students to these important but, perhaps, unfamiliar writers. Moreover, many contemporary poets are included throughout *Poetry*.

In addition, an album of world literature offers students a sampling of poems from other cultures, including the work of Claribel Alegría (El Salvador), Faiz Ahmed Faiz (Pakistan), Xu Gang (China), Wole Soyinka (Nigeria), Wislawa Szymborska (Poland), and Tomas Transtromer (Sweden), among others. More than a third of the poems in this edition are by women and minority writers and writers from other cultures. Related to the multicultural emphasis of *Poetry* is a section in Chapter 3, "Word Choice, Word Order, and Tone," on poetry in translation that provides different translations of a poem that helps students to understand the significance of a translator's choices concerning diction and tone. These poems in translation encourage students to explore the nuances of poetic language as well as larger issues related to translation.

"Connections to Other Selections" consist of questions that link the selections in the albums of contemporary and world literature to more traditional selections in the text. For example, Linda Hogan's "Hunger" is linked with Emily Dickinson's "'Heaven' — is what I cannot reach!" and Wole Soyinka's "Future Plans" is connected to Dylan Thomas's "The Hand That Signed the Paper." These questions provide engaging writing opportunities and provocative topics for class discussion. "Connections to Other Selections" questions also appear after many of the works in the chapters on the elements of poetry.

Perspectives on Literature

This popular feature has been revised in ways that make the third edition's seventy "Perspectives" — journal notes, letters, classic and contemporary theoretical essays, interviews, and student responses — even more useful for class discussion and student writing. "Perspectives" are included in five different places in the text: in the chapters treating major authors in depth; in Chapter 15, "A Critical Case Study" on T. S. Eliot's "The Love Song of J. Alfred Prufrock"; in Chapter 16 (new), "A Cultural Case Study" on Julia Alvarez's "Queens, 1963"; at the end of Chapter 19, on literary theory; and, finally, throughout the text's discussion chapters. Individual "Perspectives" in these chapters follow the works to which they refer and, in many cases, discuss a poem in terms of the element of literature for which it serves as an illustration to teach students how to think critically and write effectively about poetry.

Connections between "Popular" and "Literary" Culture

Poetry: An Introduction, Third Edition, draws carefully on examples from popular culture to explain the elements of poetry, inviting students to make connections between what they already know and what they will encounter in subsequent selections. Comparisons between popular culture and more canonical literary selections offer excellent writing opportunities, and suggestions are provided after each popular culture example. The examples include greeting card verse and contemporary song lyrics, such as Bruce Springsteen's "Streets of Philadelphia" and Saundra Sharp's "It's the Law: A Rap Poem."

Resources for Teaching POETRY: AN INTRODUCTION, *Third Edition*

This thorough and practical instructor's manual — about 400 pages long — discusses every selection, suggests answers to the questions posed in the text, provides suggestions for connections to other selections, and includes teaching tips from instructors who have taught from previous editions. The manual also offers commentary and writing assignments for the collection of poems, an appendix, "Suggested Thematic Units for Discussion and Writing," including questions, and an annotated list of videos, films, recordings, and online resources related to the works of literature in the text.

Literature Aloud

An audio ancillary, either on CD or audiocassette, offers recordings of selected classic and contemporary poems from the book, and is available to instructors who adopt the third edition of *Poetry: An Introduction*. The audio features the work of poets treated in depth (Dickinson, Frost, and Hughes), and poems that serve as good examples of the elements of poetry discussed in the book — read by the poets themselves or by famous entertainment personalities.

Robert Frost: Poems, Life, Legacy

This comprehensive CD-ROM on the life and works of Robert Frost includes searchable text of his poetry, audio performances of Frost reading sixty-nine of his finest poems, over 1,500 pages of biography and literary criticism, and a new documentary film narrated by Richard Wilbur. It is available to qualified adopters of *Poetry: An Introduction,* Third Edition.

LitLinks and Companion Web Site

Because researching literary topics on the Web can be a daunting task for an undergraduate, Bedford/St. Martin's has compiled LitLinks — research links annotated to show students what kinds of information about a work, its author, or literary period they'll find on each site. LitLinks are organized alphabetically by author within five genres (fiction, poetry, drama, the essay, and literary criticism), and include links and brief biographies for almost every author included in the book. In addition to LitLinks, a Web site for *Poetry: An Introduction,* Third Edition, provides additional online resources for instructors and students who use the book. Both can be accessed at <http://www.bedfordstmartins.com>.

Acknowledgments

This book has benefited from the ideas, suggestions, and corrections of scores of careful readers who helped transform various stages of an evolving manuscript into a finished book and into subsequent editions. I remain grateful to those I have thanked in prefaces of *The Bedford Introduction to Literature,* particularly to the late Robert Wallace of Case Western Reserve University. I would also like to give special thanks to Ronald Wallace of the University of Wisconsin and William Henry Louis of Mary Washington College. In addition, many instructors who have used *Poetry: An Introduction* responded to a questionnaire on the book. For their valuable comments and advice I am grateful to Dibaker Barua, Golden West College; Alan Brownley, Anne Arundel Community College; Nancy Butterworth, University of South Carolina, Columbia; Helen Dayan, Hillsborough Community College; Deborah Edson, Tidewater Community College; Tara Hart, Howard Community College; Robert Holtzclaw, Middle Tennessee State University; Katherine Purcell, Trident Technical College; Henry Sloth, Anne Arundel Community College; and Vlatka Velcic, Austin Peay State University.

I am also indebted to those who cheerfully answered questions and generously provided miscellaneous bits of information. What might have seemed to them like inconsequential conversations turned out to be important leads. Among these friends and colleagues are Raymond Anselment, Ann Charters, Irving Cummings, William Curtin, Margaret Higonnet, Patrick Hogan, Lee Jacobus, Greta Little, George Monteiro, Brenda Murphy, Joel Myerson, Thomas Recchio, William Sheidley, Milton Stern, Kenneth Wilson, and the dedicated reference librarians at the Homer Babbidge Library, University of Connecticut.

I continue to be grateful for what I have learned from teaching my students and for the many student papers I have received over the years that I have used in various forms to serve as good and accessible models of student writing. I am particularly indebted to Jill McDonough for her excellent work on the third edition of *Resources for Teaching Poetry: An Introduction.*

At Bedford Books, my debts once again require more time to acknowledge than the deadline allows. Charles H. Christensen and Joan Feinberg initiated this project and launched it with their intelligence, energy, and sound advice. Karen Henry, Kathy Retan, and Alanya Harter tirelessly steered earlier editions through rough as well as becalmed moments; their work was as first-rate as it was essential. Aron Keesbury splendidly carried on that tradition as developmental editor for this third edition; his solid contributions and poetic sensibilities made this project a pleasure. With the help of Donna Ashley, Josh Levy oversaw *Resources for Teaching Poetry: An Introduction* with clear-headed intelligence as well as enthusiasm, and Amy Thomas deftly arranged permissions. The difficult tasks of production were skillfully managed by Stasia Zomkowski. Jane Zanichkowsky provided careful copyediting, and Janet Cocker and Jocelyn Humelsine did more than meticulous proofreading. I thank all of the people at Bedford Books — including Donna Dennison who designed the cover, and Richard Cadman, the marketing manager — who helped to make this formidable project a manageable one.

Finally, I am grateful to my sons Timothy and Matthew for all kinds of help, but mostly I'm just grateful they're my sons. And for making all the difference, I thank my wife, Regina Barreca.

Brief Contents

CRITICAL THINKING AND WRITING 479

A COLLECTION OF POEMS 587

An extensive collection of 130 poems, including albums of world and contemporary poetry.

Contents

5. Figures of Speech   114

Simile and Metaphor   115

Other Figures   119

Poems for Further Study   123

9. Poetic Forms   223

Some Common Poetic Forms   223

Sonnet   226

Villanelle   232

Sestina   234

Epigram   237

Limerick   238

Haiku   240

Elegy   240

15. Critical Case Study: T. S. Eliot's "The Love Song of J. Alfred Prufrock"   404

16. Cultural Case Study: Julia Alvarez's "Queens, 1963"   420

17. Two Thematic Case Studies 433

18. Biographies of Selected Poets 451

CRITICAL THINKING AND WRITING 479

19. Critical Strategies for Reading 481

Glossary of Literary Terms   687

INTRODUCTION

Reading
Imaginative Literature

THE NATURE OF LITERATURE

Literature does not lend itself to a single tidy definition because the making of it over the centuries has been as complex, unwieldy, and natural as life itself. Is literature everything that has been written, from ancient prayers to graffiti? Does it include songs and stories that were not written down until many years after they were recited? Does literature include the television scripts from *Friends* as well as Shakespeare's *King Lear*? Is literature only writing that has permanent value and continues to move people? Must literature be true or beautiful or moral? Should it be socially useful?

Although these kinds of questions are not conclusively answered in this book, they are implicitly raised by the poems included here. No definition of literature, particularly a brief one, is likely to satisfy everyone because definitions tend to weaken and require qualification when confronted by the uniqueness of individual works. In this context it is worth recalling Herman Melville's humorous use of a definition of a whale in *Moby-Dick* (1851). In the course of the novel Melville presents his imaginative and symbolic whale as inscrutable, but he begins with a quotation from Georges Cuvier, a French naturalist who defines a whale in his nineteenth-century study *The Animal Kingdom* this way: "The whale is a mammiferous animal without hind feet." Cuvier's description is technically correct, of course, but there is little wisdom in it. Melville understood that the reality of the whale (which he describes as the "ungraspable phantom of life") cannot be caught by isolated facts. If the full meaning of the whale is to be understood, it must be sought on the open sea of experience, where the whale itself is, rather than in exclusionary definitions. Facts and definitions are helpful; however, they do not always reveal the whole truth.

Despite Melville's reminder that a definition can be too limiting and even comical, it is useful for our purposes to describe literature as a fiction consisting of carefully arranged words designed to stir the imagination. Stories, poems, and plays are fictional. They are made up—imagined— even when based on actual historic events. Such imaginative writing differs from other kinds of writing because its purpose is not primarily to transmit facts or ideas. Imaginative literature is a source more of pleasure than of information, and we read it for basically the same reasons we listen to music or view a dance: enjoyment, delight, and satisfaction. Like other art forms, imaginative literature offers pleasure and usually attempts to convey a perspective, mood, feeling, or experience. Writers transform the facts the world provides—people, places, and objects—into experiences that suggest meanings.

Consider, for example, the difference between the following factual description of a snake and a poem on the same subject. Here is *Webster's Ninth New Collegiate Dictionary* definition:

> any of numerous limbless scaled reptiles (suborder Serpentes or Ophidia) with a long tapering body and with salivary glands often modified to produce venom which is injected through grooved or tubular fangs.

Contrast this matter-of-fact definition with Emily Dickinson's poetic evocation of a snake in "A narrow Fellow in the Grass":

A narrow Fellow in the Grass
Occasionally rides—
You may have met Him—did you not
His notice sudden is—

The Grass divides as with a Comb—   5
A spotted shaft is seen—
And then it closes at your feet
And opens further on—

He likes a Boggy Acre
A floor too cool for Corn—   10
Yet when a Boy, and Barefoot—
I more than once at Noon
Have passed, I thought, a Whip lash
Unbraiding in the Sun
When stooping to secure it   15
It wrinkled, and was gone—

Several of Nature's People
I know, and they know me—
I feel for them a transport
Of cordiality—   20

But never met this Fellow
Attended, or alone
Without a tighter breathing
And Zero at the Bone—

The dictionary provides a succinct, anatomical description of what a snake is, while Dickinson's poem suggests what a snake can mean. The definition offers facts; the poem offers an experience. The dictionary would probably allow someone who had never seen a snake to sketch one with reasonable accuracy. The poem also provides some vivid subjective descriptions — for example, the snake dividing the grass "as with a Comb" — yet it offers more than a picture of serpentine movements. The poem conveys the ambivalence many people have about snakes — the kind of feeling, for example, so evident on the faces of visitors viewing the snakes at a zoo. In the poem there is both a fascination with and a horror of what might be called snakehood; this combination of feelings has been coiled in most of us since Adam and Eve.

That "narrow Fellow" so cordially introduced by way of a riddle (the word *snake* is never used in the poem) is, by the final stanza, revealed as a snake in the grass. In between, Dickinson uses language expressively to convey her meaning. For instance, in the line "His notice sudden is," listen to the *s* sound in each word and note how the verb *is* unexpectedly appears at the end, making the snake's hissing presence all the more "sudden." And anyone who has ever been surprised by a snake knows the "tighter breathing / And Zero at the Bone" that Dickinson evokes so successfully by the rhythm of her word choices and line breaks. Perhaps even more significant, Dickinson's poem allows those who have never encountered a snake to imagine such an experience.

A good deal more could be said about the numbing fear that undercuts the affection for nature at the beginning of this poem, but the point here is that imaginative literature gives us not so much the full, factual proportions of the world as some of its experiences and meanings. Instead of defining the world, literature encourages us to try it out in our imaginations.

THE VALUE OF LITERATURE

Mark Twain once shrewdly observed that a person who chooses not to read has no advantage over a person who is unable to read. In industrialized societies today, however, the question is not who reads, because nearly everyone can and does, but what is read. Why should anyone spend precious time with literature when there is so much reading material available that provides useful information about everything from the daily news to personal computers? Why should a literary artist's imagination compete for attention that could be spent on the firm realities that constitute everyday life? In fact, national best-seller lists much less often include collections of stories, poems, or plays than they do cookbooks and, not surprisingly, diet books. Although such fare may be filling, it doesn't stay with you. Most people have other appetites too.

Certainly one of the most important values of literature is that it nourishes our emotional lives. An effective literary work may seem to speak directly to us, especially if we are ripe for it. The inner life that good writers reveal in their characters often gives us glimpses of some portion of ourselves. We can be moved to laugh, cry, tremble, dream, ponder, shriek, or rage with a character by simply turning a page instead of turning our lives upside down. Although the experience itself is imagined, the emotion is real. That's why the final chapters of a good adventure novel can make a reader's heart race as much as a 100-yard dash or why the repressed love of Hester Prynne in *The Scarlet Letter* by Nathaniel Hawthorne is painful to a sympathetic reader. Human emotions speak a universal language regardless of when or where a work was written.

In addition to appealing to our emotions, literature broadens our perspectives on the world. Most of the people we meet are pretty much like ourselves, and what we can see of the world even in a lifetime is astonishingly limited. Literature allows us to move beyond the inevitable boundaries of our own lives and culture because it introduces us to people different from ourselves, places remote from our neighborhoods, and times other than our own. Reading makes us more aware of life's possibilities as well as its subtleties and ambiguities. Put simply, people who read literature experience more life and have a keener sense of a common human identity than those who do not. It is true, of course, that many people go through life without reading imaginative literature, but that is a loss rather than a gain. They may find themselves troubled by the same kinds of questions that reveal Daisy Buchanan's restless, vague discontentment in F. Scott Fitzgerald's *The Great Gatsby:* "What'll we do with ourselves this afternoon?" cried Daisy, "and the day after that, and the next thirty years?"

Sometimes students mistakenly associate literature more with school than with life. Accustomed to reading it in order to write a paper or pass an examination, students may perceive such reading as a chore instead of a pleasurable opportunity, something considerably less important than studying for the "practical" courses that prepare them for a career. The study of literature, however, is also practical because it engages you in the kinds of problem solving important in a variety of fields, from philosophy to science and technology. The interpretation of literary texts requires you to deal with uncertainties, value judgments, and emotions; these are unavoidable aspects of life.

People who make the most significant contributions to their professions — whether in business, engineering, teaching, or some other area — tend to be challenged rather than threatened by multiple possibilities. Instead of retreating to the way things have always been done, they bring freshness and creativity to their work. F. Scott Fitzgerald once astutely described the "test of a first-rate intelligence" as "the ability to hold two opposed ideas in the mind at the same time, and still retain the ability to function." People with such intelligence know how to read situations, shape questions, interpret details, and evaluate competing points of view. Equipped with a healthy respect for facts, they also understand the value of pursuing hunches and exercising their imaginations. Reading literature encourages a suppleness of mind that is helpful in any discipline or work.

Once the requirements for your degree are completed, what ultimately matters are not the courses listed on your transcript but the sensibilities and habits of mind that you bring to your work, friends, family, and, indeed, the rest of your life. A healthy economy changes and grows with the times; people do too if they are prepared for more than simply filling a job description. The range and variety of life that literature affords can help you to interpret your own experiences and the world in which you live.

To discover the insights that literature reveals requires careful reading and sensitivity. One of the purposes of a college introduction to literature class is to cultivate the analytic skills necessary for reading well. Class discussions often help establish a dialogue with a work that perhaps otherwise would not speak to you. Analytic skills can also be developed by writing about what you read. Writing is an effective means of clarifying your responses and ideas because it requires you to account for the author's use of language as well as your own. This book is based on two premises: that reading literature is pleasurable and that reading and understanding a work sensitively by thinking, talking, or writing about it increase the pleasure of the experience of it.

Understanding its basic elements — such as point of view, symbol, theme, tone, and irony is a prerequisite to an informed appreciation of literature. This kind of understanding allows you to perceive more in a literary work in much the same way that a spectator at a tennis match sees more if he or she understands the rules and conventions of the game. But literature is not simply a spectator sport. The analytic skills that open up literature also have their uses when you watch a television program or film and, more important, when you attempt to sort out the significance of the people, places, and events that constitute your own life. Literature enhances and sharpens your perceptions. What could be more lastingly practical as well as satisfying?

THE CHANGING LITERARY CANON

Perhaps the best reading creates some kind of change in us: we see more clearly; we're alert to nuances; we ask questions that previously didn't occur to us. Henry David Thoreau had that sort of reading in mind when he remarked in *Walden* that the books he valued most were those that caused him to date "a new era in his life from the reading." Readers are sometimes changed by literature, but it is also worth noting that the life of a literary work can also be affected by its readers. Melville's *Moby-Dick,* for example, was not valued as a classic until the 1920s, when critics rescued the novel from the obscurity of being cataloged in many libraries (including Yale's) not under fiction but under cetology, the study of whales. Indeed, many writers contemporary to Melville who were important and popular in the nineteenth century—William Cullen Bryant, Henry Wadsworth Longfellow, and James Russell Lowell, to name a few—are now mostly unread; their names appear more often on elementary schools built early in this century than in anthologies. Clearly, literary reputations and what is valued as great literature change over time and in the eyes of readers.

Such changes have accelerated during the past thirty years as the literary *canon*—those works considered by scholars, critics, and teachers to be the most important to read and study—has undergone a significant series of shifts. Writers who previously were overlooked, undervalued, neglected, or studiously ignored have been brought into focus in an effort to create a more diverse literary canon, one that recognizes the contributions of the many cultures that make up American society. Since the 1960s, for example, some critics have reassessed writings by women who had been left out of the standard literary traditions dominated by male writers. Many more female writers are now read alongside the male writers who traditionally populated literary history. This kind of enlargement of the canon also resulted from another reform movement of the 1960s. The civil rights movement sensitized literary critics to the political, moral, and aesthetic necessity of rediscovering African American literature, and more recently Asian and Hispanic writers have been making their way into the canon. Moreover, on a broader scale the canon is being revised and enlarged to include the works of writers from parts of the world other than the West, a development that reflects the changing values, concerns, and complexities of the past several years, when literary landscapes have shifted as dramatically as the political boundaries of eastern Europe and the former Soviet Union.

No semester's reading list—or anthology—can adequately or accurately echo all the new voices competing to be heard as part of the mainstream literary canon, but recent efforts to open up the canon attempt to sensitize readers to the voices of women, minorities, and writers from all over the world. This development has not occurred without its urgent advocates or passionate dissenters. It's no surprise that issues about race, gender, and class often get people off the fence and on their feet (these controversies are discussed further in Chapter 19, "Critical Strategies for Reading"). Although what we regard as literature—whether it's called great, classic, or canonical—continues to generate debate, there is no question that such controversy will continue to reflect readers' values as well as the writers they admire.

The Elements
of Poetry

1

Reading Poetry

READING POETRY RESPONSIVELY

Perhaps the best way to begin reading poetry responsively is not to allow yourself to be intimidated by it. Come to it, initially at least, the way you might listen to a song on the radio. You probably listen to a song several times before you hear it all, before you have a sense of how it works, where it's going, and how it gets there. You don't worry about analyzing a song when you listen to it, even though after repeated experiences with it you know and anticipate a favorite part and know, on some level, why it works for you. Give yourself a chance to respond to poetry. The hardest work has already been done by the poet, so all you need to do at the start is listen for the pleasure produced by the poet's arrangement of words.

Try reading the following poem aloud. Read it aloud before you read it silently. You may stumble once or twice, but you'll make sense of it if you pay attention to its punctuation and don't stop at the end of every line where there is no punctuation. The title gives you an initial sense of what the poem is about.

MARGE PIERCY (B. 1936)

The Secretary Chant   1973

My hips are a desk.
From my ears hang
chains of paper clips.
Rubber bands form my hair.
My breasts are wells of mimeograph ink.   5
My feet bear casters.
Buzz. Click.
My head is a badly organized file.

9

My head is a switchboard
where crossed lines crackle.   10
Press my fingers
and in my eyes appear
credit and debit.
Zing. Tinkle.
My navel is a reject button.   15
From my mouth issue canceled reams.
Swollen, heavy, rectangular
I am about to be delivered
of a baby
Xerox machine.   20
File me under W
because I wonce
was
a woman.

What is your response to this secretary's chant? The point is simple enough — she feels dehumanized by her office functions — but the pleasures are manifold. Piercy makes the speaker's voice sound mechanical by using short bursts of sound and by having her make repetitive, flat, matter-of-fact statements ("My breasts . . . My feet . . . My head . . . My navel"). "The Secretary Chant" makes a serious statement about how such women are reduced to functionaries. The point is made, however, with humor since we are asked to visualize the misappropriation of the secretary's body — her identity — as it is transformed into little more than a piece of office equipment, which seems to be breaking down in the final lines, when we learn that she "wonce / was / a woman." Is there the slightest hint of something subversive in this misspelling of "wonce"? Maybe so, but the humor is clear enough, particularly if you try to make a drawing of what this dehumanized secretary has become.

The next poem creates a different kind of mood. Think about the title, "Those Winter Sundays," before you begin reading the poem. What associations do you have with winter Sundays? What emotions does the phrase evoke in you?

ROBERT HAYDEN (1913–1980)

Those Winter Sundays   *1962*

Sundays too my father got up early
and put his clothes on in the blueblack cold,
then with cracked hands that ached
from labor in the weekday weather made
banked fires blaze. No one ever thanked him.   5

I'd wake and hear the cold splintering, breaking.
When the rooms were warm, he'd call,
and slowly I would rise and dress,
fearing the chronic angers of that house,

Speaking indifferently to him, 10
who had driven out the cold
and polished my good shoes as well.
What did I know, what did I know
of love's austere and lonely offices?

Does the poem match the feelings you have about winter Sundays? Either way your response can be useful in reading the poem. For most of us Sundays are days at home; they might be cozy and pleasant experiences or they might be dull and depressing. Whatever they are, Sundays are more evocative than, say, Tuesdays. Hayden uses that response to call forth a sense of missed opportunity in the poem. The person who reflects on those winter Sundays didn't know until much later how much he had to thank his father for "love's austere and lonely offices." This is a poem about a cold past and a present reverence for his father — elements brought together by the phrase "Winter Sundays." *His* father? You may have noticed that the poem doesn't use a masculine pronoun; hence the voice could be a woman's. Does the sex of the voice make any difference to your reading? Would it make any difference about which details are included or what language is used?

What is most important about your initial readings of a poem is that you ask questions. If you read responsively, you'll find yourself asking all kinds of questions about the words, descriptions, sounds, and structures of a poem. The specifics of those questions will be generated by the particular poem. We don't, for example, ask how humor is achieved in "Those Winter Sundays" because there is none, but it is worth asking what kind of tone is established by the description of "the chronic angers of that house." The remaining chapters in this part will help you to formulate and answer questions about a variety of specific elements in poetry, such as speaker, image, metaphor, symbol, rhyme, and rhythm. For the moment, however, read the following poem several times and note your response at different points in the poem. Then write down a half dozen or so questions about what produces your response to the poem. To answer questions, it's best to know first what the questions are, and that's what the rest of this chapter is about.

JOHN UPDIKE (B. 1932)

Dog's Death 1969

She must have been kicked unseen or brushed by a car.
Too young to know much, she was beginning to learn
To use the newspapers spread on the kitchen floor
And to win, wetting there, the words, "Good dog! Good dog!"

We thought her shy malaise was a shot reaction. 5
The autopsy disclosed a rupture in her liver.
As we teased her with play, blood was filling her skin
And her heart was learning to lie down forever.

Monday morning, as the children were noisily fed
And sent to school, she crawled beneath the youngest's bed.   10
We found her twisted and limp but still alive.
In the car to the vet's, on my lap, she tried

To bite my hand and died. I stroked her warm fur
And my wife called in a voice imperious with tears.
Though surrounded by love that would have upheld her,   15
Nevertheless she sank and, stiffening, disappeared.

Back home, we found that in the night her frame,
Drawing near to dissolution, had endured the shame
Of diarrhoea and had dragged across the floor
To a newspaper carelessly left there. *Good dog.*   20

Here's a simple question to get started with your own questions: what would its effect have been if Updike had titled the poem "Good Dog" instead of "Dog's Death"?

THE PLEASURE OF WORDS

The impulse to create and appreciate poetry is as basic to human experience as language itself. Although no one can point to the precise origins of poetry, it is one of the most ancient of the arts, because it has existed ever since human beings discovered pleasure in language. The tribal ceremonies of peoples without written languages suggest that the earliest primitive cultures incorporated rhythmic patterns of words into their rituals. These chants, very likely accompanied by the music of a simple beat and the dance of a measured step, expressed what people regarded as significant and memorable in their lives. They echoed the concerns of the chanters and the listeners by chronicling acts of bravery, fearsome foes, natural disasters, mysterious events, births, deaths, and whatever else brought people pain or pleasure, bewilderment or revelation. Later cultures, such as the ancient Greeks, made poetry an integral part of religion.

Thus, from its very beginnings, poetry has been associated with what has mattered most to people. These concerns — whether natural or supernatural — can, of course, be expressed without vivid images, rhythmic patterns, and pleasing sounds, but human beings have always sensed a magic in words that goes beyond rational, logical understanding. Poetry is not simply a method of communication; it is a unique experience in itself.

What is special about poetry? What makes it valuable? Why should we read it? How is reading it different from reading prose? To begin with, poetry pervades our world in a variety of forms, ranging from advertising jingles to song lyrics. These may seem to be a long way from the chants heard around a primitive campfire, but they serve some of the same purposes. Like poems printed in a magazine or book, primitive chants, catchy jingles, and popular songs attempt to stir the imagination through the carefully measured use of words.

Although reading poetry usually makes more demands than does the kind of reading used to skim a magazine or newspaper, the appreciation of poetry comes naturally enough to anyone who enjoys playing with words. Play is an important element of poetry. Consider, for example, how the following words appeal to the children who gleefully chant them in playgrounds:

> I scream, you scream
> We all scream
> For ice cream.

These lines are an exuberant evocation of the joy of ice cream. Indeed, chanting the words turns out to be as pleasurable as eating ice cream. In poetry, the expression of the idea is as important as the idea expressed.

But is "I scream . . ." poetry? Some poets and literary critics would say that it certainly is one kind of poem because the children who chant it experience some of the pleasures of poetry in its measured beat and repeated sounds. However, other poets and critics would define poetry more narrowly and insist, for a variety of reasons, that this isn't true poetry but merely **doggerel,** a term used for lines whose subject matter is trite and whose rhythm and sounds are monotonously heavy-handed.

Although probably no one would argue that "I scream . . ." is a great poem, it does contain some poetic elements that appeal, at the very least, to children. Does that make it poetry? The answer depends on one's definition, but poetry has a way of breaking loose from definitions. Because there are nearly as many definitions of poetry as there are poets, Edwin Arlington Robinson's succinct observations are useful: "poetry has two outstanding characteristics. One is that it is undefinable. The other is that it is eventually unmistakable."

This comment places more emphasis on how a poem affects a reader than on how a poem is defined. By characterizing poetry as "undefinable," Robinson acknowledges that it can include many different purposes, subjects, emotions, styles, and forms. What effect does the following poem have on you?

WILLIAM HATHAWAY (B. 1944)

Oh, Oh   1982

My girl and I amble a country lane,
moo cows chomping daisies, our own
sweet saliva green with grass stems.
"Look, look," she says at the crossing,
"the choo-choo's light is on." And sure   5
enough, right smack dab in the middle
of maple dappled summer sunlight
is the lit headlight — so funny.
An arm waves to us from the black window.
We wave gaily to the arm. "When I hear   10

trains at night I dream of being president,"
I say dreamily. "And me first lady," she
says loyally. So when the last boxcars,
named after wonderful, faraway places,
and the caboose chuckle by we look   15
eagerly to the road ahead. And there,
poised and growling, are fifty Hell's Angels.

Hathaway's poem serves as a convenient reminder that poetry can be full of surprises. Even on a first reading there is no mistaking the emotional reversal created by the last few words of this poem. With the exception of the final line, the poem's language conjures up an idyllic picture of a young couple taking a pleasant walk down a country lane. Contented as "moo cows," they taste the sweetness of the grass, hear peaceful country sounds, and are dazzled by "dappled summer sunlight." Their future together seems to be all optimism as they anticipate "wonderful, faraway places" and the "road ahead." Full of confidence, this couple, like the reader, is unprepared for the shock to come. When we see those "fifty Hell's Angels," we are confronted with something like a bucket of cold water in the face.

But even though our expectations are abruptly and powerfully reversed, we are finally invited to view the entire episode from a safe distance — the distance provided by the delightful humor in this poem. After all, how seriously can we take a poem that is titled "Oh, Oh"? The poet has his way with us, but we are brought in on the joke too. The terror takes on comic proportions as the innocent couple is confronted by no fewer than *fifty* Hell's Angels. This is the kind of raucous overkill that informs a short animated film produced some years ago titled *Bambi Meets Godzilla:* you might not have seen it, but you know how it ends. The poem's good humor comes through when we realize how pathetically inadequate the response of "Oh, Oh" is to the circumstances.

As you can see, reading a description of what happens in a poem is not the same as experiencing a poem. The exuberance of "I scream . . ." and the surprise of Hathaway's "Oh, Oh" are in the hearing or reading rather than in the retelling. A *paraphrase* is a prose restatement of the central ideas of a poem in your own language. Consider the difference between the following poem and the paraphrase that follows it. What is missing from the paraphrase?

ROBERT FRANCIS (1901–1987)

Catch   *1950*

Two boys uncoached are tossing a poem together,
Overhand, underhand, backhand, sleight of hand, every hand,
Teasing with attitudes, latitudes, interludes, altitudes,
High, make him fly off the ground for it, low, make him stoop,
Make him scoop it up, make him as-almost-as-possible miss it,   5
Fast, let him sting from it, now, now fool him slowly,

Anything, everything tricky, risky, nonchalant,
Anything under the sun to outwit the prosy,
Over the tree and the long sweet cadence down,
Over his head, make him scramble to pick up the meaning,   10
And now, like a posy, a pretty one plump in his hands.

Paraphrase: A poet's relationship to a reader is similar to a game of catch. The poem, like a ball, should be pitched in a variety of ways to challenge and create interest. Boredom and predictability must be avoided if the game is to be engaging and satisfying.

A paraphrase can help us achieve a clearer understanding of a poem, but, unlike a poem, it misses all the sport and fun. It is the poem that "outwit[s] the prosy" because the poem serves as an example of what it suggests poetry should be. Moreover, the two players — the poet and the reader — are "uncoached." They know how the game is played, but their expectations do not preclude spontaneity and creativity or their ability to surprise and be surprised. The solid pleasure of the workout — of reading poetry — is the satisfaction derived from exercising your imagination and intellect.

That pleasure is worth emphasizing. Poetry uses language to move and delight even when it includes a cast of fifty Hell's Angels. The pleasure is in having the poem work its spell on us. For that to happen, it is best to relax and enjoy poetry rather than worry about definitions of it. Pay attention to what the poet throws you. We read poems for emotional and intellectual discovery — to feel and to experience something about the world and ourselves. The ideas in poetry — what can be paraphrased in prose — are important, but the real value of a poem consists in the words that work their magic by allowing us to feel, see, and be more than we were before. Perhaps the best way to approach a poem is similar to what Francis's "Catch" implies: expect to be surprised; stay on your toes; and concentrate on the delivery.

A SAMPLE ANALYSIS

Tossing Metaphors Together in "Catch"

The following sample paper on Robert Francis's "Catch" was written in response to an assignment that asked students to discuss the use of metaphor in the poem. Notice that Chris Leggett's paper is clearly focused and well organized. His discussion of the use of metaphor in the poem stays on track from beginning to end without any detours concerning unrelated topics (for a definition of **metaphor**, see p. 116). His title draws on the central metaphor of the poem, and he organizes the paper around four key words used in the poem: "attitudes, latitudes, interludes, altitudes." These constitute the heart of the paper's four substantive paragraphs, and they are effectively framed by introductory and concluding paragraphs. Moreover, the transitions between paragraphs clearly indicate that the author was not merely tossing a paper together.

Chris Leggett

Professor Lyles

English 203-1

November 9, 20--

Tossing Metaphors Together in "Catch"

The word "catch" is an attention getter. It usually means something is about to be hurled at someone and that he or she is expected to catch it. "Catch" can also signal a challenge to another player if the toss is purposefully difficult. Robert Francis, in his poem "Catch," uses the extended metaphor of two boys playing catch to explore the considerations a poet makes when "tossing a poem together." Line 3 of "Catch" enumerates these considerations metaphorically as "attitudes, latitudes, interludes, [and] altitudes." While regular prose is typically straightforward and easily understood, poetry usually takes great effort to understand and appreciate. To exemplify this, Francis presents the reader not with a normal game of catch with the ball flying back and forth in a repetitive and predictable fashion, but with a physically challenging game in which one must concentrate, scramble, and exert oneself to catch the ball, as one must stretch the intellect to truly grasp a poem.

The first consideration mentioned by Francis is attitude. Attitude, when applied to the game of catch, indicates the ball's pitch in flight, upward, downward, or straight. It could also describe the players' attitudes toward each other or toward the game in general. Below this literal level lies attitude's meaning in relation to poetry. Attitude in this case represents a poem's tone. A poet may "teas[e] with attitude" by experimenting with different tones to achieve the desired mood. The underlying tone of "Catch" is a playful one, set and reinforced

by the use of a game. This playfulness is further rein-
forced by such words and phrases as "teasing," "outwit,"
and "fool him."

Considered also in the metaphorical game of catch is
latitude, which, when applied to the game, suggests the
range the object may be thrown--how high, how low, or how
far. Poetic latitude, along similar lines, concerns a
poem's breadth, or the scope of topic. Taken one level
further, latitude suggests freedom from normal restraints
or limitations, indicating the ability to go outside the
norm to find originality of expression. The entire game of
catch described in Francis's poem reaches outside the nor-
mal expectations of something being merely tossed back and
forth in a predictable manner. The ball is thrown in al-
most every conceivable fashion, "overhand, underhand . . .
every hand." Other terms describing the throws--such as
"tricky," "risky," "fast," "slowly," and "Anything under
the sun"--express endless latitude for avoiding predict
ability in Francis's game of catch and metaphorically in
writing poetry.

During a game of catch the ball may be thrown at dif-
ferent intervals, establishing a steady rhythm or a bro-
ken, irregular one. Other intervening features, such as
the field being played on or the weather, could also af
fect the game. These features of the game are alluded to
in the poem by the use of the word "interludes." "Inter-
lude" in the poetic sense represents the poem's form,
which can similarly establish or diminish rhythm or en-
hance meaning. Lines 6 and 9 respectively show a broken
and a flowing rhythm. Line 6 begins rapidly as a hard toss
that stings the catcher's hand is described. The rhythm of
the line is immediately slowed, however, by the word "now"
followed by a comma, followed by the rest of the line. In

contrast, line 9 flows smoothly as the reader visualizes the ball flying over the tree and sailing downward. The words chosen for this line function perfectly. The phrase "the long sweet cadence down" establishes a sweet rhythm that reads smoothly and rolls off the tongue easily. The choice of diction not only affects the poem's rhythmic flow but also establishes through connotative language the various levels at which the poem can be understood, represented in "Catch" as altitude.

While "altitudes" when referring to the game of catch means how high an object is thrown, in poetry it could refer to the level of diction, lofty or down-to-earth, formal or informal. It suggests also the levels at which a poem can be comprehended, the literal as well as the interpretive. In Francis's game of catch the ball is thrown either high to make the player reach, low to make him stoop, or over his head to make him scramble, implying that the player should have to exert himself to catch it. So too, then, should the reader of poetry put great effort into understanding the full meaning of a poem. Francis exemplifies this consideration in writing poetry by giving "Catch" not only an enjoyable literal meaning concerning the game of catch but also a rich metaphorical meaning--reflecting the process of writing poetry. Francis uses several phrases and words with multiple meanings. The phrase "tossing a poem together" can be understood as tossing something back and forth or the process of constructing a poem. While "prosy" suggests prose itself, it also means the mundane or the ordinary. In the poem's final line the word "posy" of course represents a flower, while it is also a variant of the word "poesy," meaning poetry, or the practice of composing poetry.

Leggett 4

Francis effectively describes several considerations to be taken in writing poetry in order to "outwit the prosy." His use of the extended metaphor in "Catch" shows that a poem must be unique, able to be comprehended on multiple levels, and a challenge to the reader. The various rhythms in the lines of "Catch" exemplify the ideas they express. While achieving an enjoyable poem on the literal level, Francis has also achieved a rich metaphorical meaning. The poem offers a good workout both physically and intellectually.

Before beginning your own writing assignment on poetry, you should review Chapter 2, "Writing about Poetry," and Chapter 20, "Reading and Writing," which provides a step-by-step overview of how to choose a topic, develop a thesis, and organize various types of writing assignments. If you are using outside sources in your paper, you should make sure that you are familiar with the conventional documentation procedures described in Chapter 21, "The Literary Research Paper."

WOLE SOYINKA (B. 1934)

Telephone Conversation

1960

The price seemed reasonable, location
Indifferent. The landlady swore she lived
Off premises. Nothing remained
But self-confession. "Madam," I warned,
"I hate a wasted journey — I am African."   5
Silence. Silenced transmission of
Pressurized good-breeding. Voice, when it came,
Lipstick coated, long gold-rolled
Cigarette-holder pipped. Caught I was, foully.
"HOW DARK?" . . . I had not misheard . . . "ARE YOU LIGHT   10
OR VERY DARK?" Button B. Button A. Stench
Of rancid breath of public hide-and-speak.
Red booth. Red pillar-box. Red double-tiered
Omnibus squelching tar. It *was* real! Shamed

By ill-mannered silence, surrender   15
Pushed dumbfoundment to beg simplification.
Considerate she was, varying the emphasis —
"ARE YOU DARK? OR VERY LIGHT?" Revelation came.
"You mean — like plain or milk chocolate?"
Her assent was clinical, crushing in its light   20
Impersonality. Rapidly, wave-length adjusted,
I chose. "West African sepia" — and as afterthought,
"Down in my passport." Silence for spectroscopic
Flight of fancy, till truthfulness clanged her accent
Hard on the mouthpiece. "WHAT'S THAT?" conceding   25
"DON'T KNOW WHAT THAT IS." "Like brunette."
"THAT'S DARK, ISN'T IT?" "Not altogether.
Facially, I am brunette, but madam, you should see
The rest of me. Palm of my hand, soles of my feet
Are a peroxide blonde. Friction, caused —   30
Foolishly madam — by sitting down, has turned
My bottom raven black — One moment madam!" — sensing
Her receiver rearing on the thunderclap
About my ears — "Madam," I pleaded, "wouldn't you rather
See for yourself?"   35

    The conversation that we hear in this traditional English telephone box evokes serious racial tensions as well as a humorous treatment of them; the benighted tradition represented by the landlady seems to be no match for the speaker's satiric wit.

    Poets often remind us that beauty can be found in unexpected places. What is it that Elizabeth Bishop finds so beautiful about the "battered" fish she describes in the following poem?

ELIZABETH BISHOP (1911–1979)

The Fish   *1946*

I caught a tremendous fish
and held him beside the boat
half out of water, with my hook
fast in a corner of his mouth.
He didn't fight.   5
He hadn't fought at all.
He hung a grunting weight,
battered and venerable
and homely. Here and there
his brown skin hung in strips   10
like ancient wall-paper,
and its pattern of darker brown
was like wall-paper:
shapes like full-blown roses

stained and lost through age.   15
He was speckled with barnacles,
fine rosettes of lime,
and infested
with tiny white sea-lice,
and underneath two or three   20
rags of green weed hung down.
While his gills were breathing in
the terrible oxygen
— the frightening gills,
fresh and crisp with blood,   25
that can cut so badly —
I thought of the coarse white flesh
packed in like feathers,
the big bones and the little bones,
the dramatic reds and blacks   30
of his shiny entrails,
and the pink swim-bladder
like a big peony.
I looked into his eyes
which were far larger than mine   35
but shallower, and yellowed,
the irises backed and packed
with tarnished tinfoil
seen through the lenses
of old scratched isinglass.   40
They shifted a little, but not
to return my stare.
— It was more like the tipping
of an object toward the light.
I admired his sullen face,   45
the mechanism of his jaw,
and then I saw
that from his lower lip
— if you could call it a lip —
grim, wet, and weapon-like,   50
hung five old pieces of fish-line,
or four and a wire leader
with the swivel still attached,
with all their five big hooks
grown firmly in his mouth.   55
A green line, frayed at the end
where he broke it, two heavier lines,
and a fine black thread
still crimped from the strain and snap
when it broke and he got away.   60
Like medals with their ribbons
frayed and wavering,
a five-haired beard of wisdom
trailing from his aching jaw.

I stared and stared   65
and victory filled up
the little rented boat,
from the pool of bilge
where oil had spread a rainbow
around the rusted engine   70
to the bailer rusted orange,
the sun-cracked thwarts,
the oarlocks on their strings,
the gunnels — until everything
was rainbow, rainbow, rainbow!   75
And I let the fish go.

CONSIDERATIONS FOR CRITICAL THINKING AND WRITING

1. FIRST RESPONSE. Which lines in this poem provide especially vivid details of
   the fish? What makes these descriptions effective?

2. How is the fish characterized? Is it simply a weak victim because it "didn't
   fight"?

3. Comment on lines 65–76. In what sense has "victory filled up" the boat,
   given that the speaker finally lets the fish go?

The speaker in Bishop's "The Fish" ends on a triumphantly joyful
note. The *speaker* is the voice used by the author in the poem; like the nar-
rator in a work of fiction, the speaker is often a created identity rather than
the author's actual self. The two should not automatically be equated.
Contrast the attitude toward life of the speaker in "The Fish" with that of
the speaker in the following poem.

PHILIP LARKIN (1922–1985)

A Study of Reading Habits   *1964*

When getting my nose in a book
Cured most things short of school,
It was worth ruining my eyes
To know I could still keep cool,
And deal out the old right hook   5
To dirty dogs twice my size.

Later, with inch-thick specs,
Evil was just my lark:
Me and my cloak and fangs
Had ripping times in the dark.   10
The women I clubbed with sex!
I broke them up like meringues.

Don't read much now: the dude
Who lets the girl down before

The hero arrives, the chap   15
Who's yellow and keeps the store,
Seem far too familiar. Get stewed:
Books are a load of crap.

What the speaker sees and describes in "The Fish" is close if not identi-
cal to Bishop's own vision and voice. The joyful response to the fish is clearly
shared by the speaker and the poet, between whom there is little or no dis-
tance. In "A Study of Reading Habits," however, Larkin distances himself
from a speaker whose sensibilities he does not wholly share. The poet — and
many readers — might identify with the reading habits described by the
speaker in the first twelve lines, but Larkin uses the last six lines to criticize
the speaker's attitude toward life as well as reading. The speaker recalls in
lines 1–6 how as a schoolboy he identified with the hero, whose virtuous
strength always triumphed over "dirty dogs," and in lines 7–12 he recounts
how his schoolboy fantasies were transformed by adolescence into a fascina-
tion with violence and sex. This description of early reading habits is pleas-
antly amusing, because many readers of popular fiction will probably recall
having moved through similar stages, but at the end of the poem the
speaker provides more information about himself than he intends to.

As an adult the speaker has lost interest in reading because it is no
longer an escape from his own disappointed life. Instead of identifying
with heroes or villains, he finds himself identifying with minor characters
who are irresponsible and cowardly. Reading is now a reminder of his fail-
ures, so he turns to alcohol. His solution, to "Get stewed" because "Books
are a load of crap," is obviously self-destructive. The speaker is ultimately
exposed by Larkin as someone who never grew beyond fantasies. Getting
drunk is consistent with the speaker's immature reading habits. Unlike the
speaker, the poet understands that life is often distorted by escapist fan-
tasies, whether through a steady diet of popular fiction or through alco-
hol. The speaker in this poem, then, is not Larkin but a created identity
whose voice is filled with disillusionment and delusion.

The problem with Larkin's speaker is that he misreads books as well as
his own life. Reading means nothing to him unless it serves as an escape
from himself. It is not surprising that Larkin has him read fiction rather
than poetry because poetry places an especially heavy emphasis on lan-
guage. Fiction, indeed any kind of writing, including essays and drama, re-
lies on carefully chosen and arranged words, but poetry does so to an even
greater extent. Notice, for example, how Larkin's deft use of trite expres-
sions and slang characterizes the speaker so that his language reveals
nearly as much about his dreary life as what he says. Larkin's speaker
would have no use for poetry.

What is "unmistakable" in poetry (to use Robinson's term again) is its
intense, concentrated use of language — its emphasis on individual words
to convey meanings, experiences, emotions, and effects. Poets never simply
process words; they savor them. Words in poems frequently create their

own tastes, textures, scents, sounds, and shapes. They often seem more sensuous than ordinary language, and readers usually sense that a word has been hefted before making its way into a poem. Although poems are crafted differently from the ways a painting, sculpture, or musical composition is created, in each form of art the creator delights in the medium. Poetry is carefully orchestrated so that the words work together as elements in a structure to sustain close, repeated readings. The words are chosen to interact with one another to create the maximum desired effect, whether the purpose is to capture a mood or feeling, create a vivid experience, express a point of view, narrate a story, or portray a character.

Here is a poem that looks quite different from most *verse,* a term used for lines composed in a measured rhythmical pattern, which are often, but not necessarily, rhymed.

ROBERT MORGAN (B. 1944)

Mountain Graveyard   1979

for the author of "Slow Owls"

Spore Prose

stone	notes
slate	tales
sacred	cedars
heart	earth
asleep	please
hated	death

Though unconventional in its appearance, this is unmistakably poetry because of its concentrated use of language. The poem demonstrates how serious play with words can lead to some remarkable discoveries. At first glance "Mountain Graveyard" may seem intimidating. What, after all, does this list of words add up to? How is it in any sense a poetic use of language? But if the words are examined closely, it is not difficult to see how they work. The wordplay here is literally in the form of a game. Morgan uses a series of *anagrams* (words made from the letters of other words, such as *read* and *dare*) to evoke feelings about death. "Mountain Graveyard" is one of several poems that Morgan has called "Spore Prose" (another anagram) because he finds in individual words the seeds of poetry. He wrote the poem in honor of the fiftieth birthday of another poet, Jonathan Williams, the author of "Slow Owls," whose title is also an anagram.

The title, "Mountain Graveyard," indicates the poem's setting, which is also the context in which the individual words in the poem interact to provide a larger meaning. Morgan's discovery of the words on the stones of a graveyard is more than just clever. The observations he makes among the silent graves go beyond the curious pleasure a reader experiences in finding the words *sacred cedars,* referring to evergreens common in cemeteries, to consist of the same letters. The surprise and delight of realizing the connection between heart and earth is tempered by the more sober recognition that everyone's story ultimately ends in the ground. The hope that the dead are merely asleep is expressed with a plea that is answered grimly by a hatred of death's finality.

Little is told in this poem. There is no way of knowing who is buried or who is looking at the graves, but the emotions of sadness, hope, and pain are unmistakable — and are conveyed in fewer than half the words of this sentence. Morgan takes words that initially appear to be a dead, prosaic list and energizes their meanings through imaginative juxtapositions.

The following poem also involves a startling discovery about words. With the peculiar title "l(a," the poem cannot be read aloud, so there is no sound, but is there sense, a *theme,* a central idea or meaning, in the poem?

E. E. CUMMINGS (1894–1962)

l(a
1958

l(a

le
af
fa

ll

s)
one
l

iness

CONSIDERATIONS FOR CRITICAL THINKING AND WRITING

1. FIRST RESPONSE. Discuss the connection between what appears inside and outside the parentheses in this poem.
2. What does Cummings draw attention to by breaking up the words? How do this strategy and the poem's overall shape contribute to its theme?
3. Which seems more important in this poem — what is expressed, or the way it is expressed?

Although "Mountain Graveyard" and "l(a" do not resemble the kind of verse that readers might recognize immediately as poetry on a page, both are actually a very common type of poem, called the *lyric,* usually a brief poem that expresses the personal emotions and thoughts of a single speaker. Lyrics are often written in the first person but sometimes — as in "Spore Prose" and "l(a" — no speaker is specified. Lyrics present a subjective mood, emotion, or idea. Very often they are about love or death, but almost any subject or experience that evokes some intense emotional response can be found in lyrics. In addition to brevity and emotional intensity, lyrics are also frequently characterized by their musical qualities. The word *lyric* derives from the Greek word *lyre,* meaning a musical instrument that originally accompanied the singing of a lyric. Lyric poems can be organized in a variety of ways, such as the sonnet, elegy, and ode (see Chapter 9), but it is enough to point out here that lyrics are an extremely popular kind of poetry with writers and readers.

The following anonymous lyric was found in a sixteenth-century manuscript.

ANONYMOUS

Western Wind   *c. 1500*

Western wind, when wilt thou blow,
The small rain down can rain?
Christ, if my love were in my arms,
And I in my bed again!

This speaker's intense longing for his lover is characteristic of lyric poetry. He impatiently addresses the western wind that brings spring to England and could make it possible for him to be reunited with the woman he loves. We do not know the details of these lovers' lives because this poem focuses on the speaker's emotion. We do not learn why the lovers are apart or if they will be together again. We don't even know if the speaker is a man. But those issues are not really important. The poetry gives us a feeling rather than a story.

A poem that tells a story is called a ***narrative poem.*** Narrative poetry may be short or very long. An ***epic,*** for example, is a long narrative poem on a serious subject chronicling heroic deeds and important events. Among the most famous epics are Homer's *Iliad* and *Odyssey,* the Old English *Beowulf,* Dante's *Divine Comedy,* and John Milton's *Paradise Lost.* More typically, however, narrative poems are considerably shorter, such as the following poem, which tells the story of a child's memory of her father.

REGINA BARRECA (B. 1957)

Nighttime Fires   *1986*

When I was five in Louisville
we drove to see nighttime fires. Piled seven of us,
all pajamas and running noses, into the Olds,
drove fast toward smoke. It was after my father
lost his job, so not getting up in the morning   5
gave him time: awake past midnight, he read old newspapers
with no news, tried crosswords until he split the pencil
between his teeth, mad. When he heard

the wolf whine of the siren, he woke my mother,
and she pushed and shoved 10
us all into waking. Once roused we longed for burnt wood
and a smell of flames high into the pines. My old man liked
driving to rich neighborhoods best, swearing in a good mood
as he followed fire engines that snaked like dragons
and split the silent streets. It was festival, carnival. 15

If there were a Cadillac or any car
in a curved driveway, my father smiled a smile
from a secret, brittle heart.
His face lit up in the heat given off by destruction
like something was being made, or was being set right. 20
I bent my head back to see where sparks
ate up the sky. My father who never held us
would take my hand and point to falling cinders that
covered the ground like snow, or, excited, show us
the swollen collapse of a staircase. My mother 25
watched my father, not the house. She was happy
only when we were ready to go, when it was finally over
and nothing else could burn.
Driving home, she would sleep in the front seat
as we huddled behind. I could see his quiet face in the 30
rearview mirror, eyes like hallways filled with smoke.

This narrative poem could have been a short story if the poet had wanted to say more about the "brittle heart" of this unemployed man whose daughter so vividly remembers the desperate pleasure he took in watching fire consume other people's property. Indeed, a reading of William Faulkner's famous short story "Barn Burning" suggests how such a character can be further developed and how his child responds to him. The similarities between Faulkner's angry character and the poem's father, whose "eyes [are] like hallways filled with smoke," are coincidental, but the characters' sense of "something . . . being set right" by flames is worth comparing. Although we do not know everything about this man and his family, we have a much firmer sense of their story than we do of the story of the couple in "Western Wind."

Although narrative poetry is still written, short stories and novels have largely replaced the long narrative poem. Lyric poems tend to be the predominant type of poetry today. Regardless of whether a poem is a narrative or a lyric, however, the strategies for reading it are somewhat different from those for reading prose. Try these suggestions for approaching poetry.

SUGGESTIONS FOR APPROACHING POETRY

1. Assume that it will be necessary to read a poem more than once. Give yourself a chance to become familiar with what the poem has to offer.

Like a piece of music, a poem becomes more pleasurable with each encounter.

2. Pay attention to the title; it will often provide a helpful context for the poem and serve as an introduction to it. Larkin's "A Study of Reading Habits" is precisely what its title describes.

3. As you read the poem for the first time, avoid becoming entangled in words or lines that you don't understand. Instead, give yourself a chance to take in the entire poem before attempting to resolve problems encountered along the way.

4. On a second reading, identify any words or passages that you don't understand. Look up words you don't know; these might include names, places, historical and mythical references, or anything else that is unfamiliar to you.

5. Read the poem aloud (or perhaps have a friend read it to you). You'll probably discover that some puzzling passages suddenly fall into place when you hear them. You'll find that nothing helps, though, if the poem is read in an artificial, exaggerated manner. Read in as natural a voice as possible, with slight pauses at line breaks. Silent reading is preferable to imposing a te-tumpty-te-tum reading on a good poem.

6. Read the punctuation. Poems use punctuation marks — in addition to the space on the page — as signals for readers. Be especially careful not to assume that the end of a line marks the end of a sentence, unless it is concluded by punctuation. Consider, for example, the opening lines of Hathaway's "Oh, Oh":

> My girl and I amble a country lane,
> moo cows chomping daisies, our own
> sweet saliva green with grass stems.

Line 2 makes little or no sense if a reader stops after "own." Keeping track of the subjects and verbs will help you find your way among the sentences.

7. Paraphrase the poem to determine whether you understand what happens in it. As you work through each line of the poem, a paraphrase will help you to see which words or passages need further attention.

8. Try to get a sense of who is speaking and what the setting or situation is. Don't assume that the speaker is the author; often it is a created character.

9. Assume that each element in the poem has a purpose. Try to explain how the elements of the poem work together.

10. Be generous. Be willing to entertain perspectives, values, experiences, and subjects that you might not agree with or approve. Even if baseball bores you, you should be able to comprehend its imaginative use in Francis's "Catch."

11. Try developing a coherent approach to the poem that helps you to shape a discussion of the text. See Chapter 19, "Critical Strategies for Reading," to review formalist, biographical, historical, psychological, feminist, and other possible critical approaches.

12. Don't expect to produce a definitive reading. Many poems do not resolve all the ideas, issues, or tensions in them, and so it is not always possible to drive their meaning into an absolute corner. Your reading will explore rather than define the poem. Poems are not trophies to be stuffed and mounted. They're usually more elusive. And don't be afraid that a close reading will damage the poem. Poems aren't hurt when we analyze them; instead, they come alive as we experience them and put into words what we discover through them.

A list of more specific questions using the literary terms and concepts discussed in the following chapters begins on page 47. That list, like the suggestions just made, raises issues and questions that can help you to read just about any poem closely. These strategies should be a useful means for getting inside poems to understand how they work. Furthermore, because reading poetry inevitably increases sensitivity to language, you're likely to find yourself a better reader of words in any form — whether in a novel, a newspaper editorial, an advertisement, a political speech, or a conversation — after having studied poetry. In short, many of the reading skills that make poetry accessible also open up the world you inhabit.

You'll probably find some poems amusing or sad, some fierce or tender, and some fascinating or dull. You may find, too, some poems that will get inside you. Their kinds of insights — the poet's and yours — are what Emily Dickinson had in mind when she defined poetry this way: "If I read a book and it makes my whole body so cold no fire can ever warm me, I know that it is poetry. If I feel physically as if the top of my head were taken off, I know that it is poetry." Dickinson's response may be more intense than most — poetry was, after all, at the center of her life — but you too might find yourself moved by poems in unexpected ways. In any case, as Edwin Arlington Robinson knew, poetry is, to an alert and sensitive reader, "eventually unmistakable."

POETRY IN POPULAR FORMS

Before you try out these strategies for reading on a few more poems, it is worth acknowledging that the verse that enjoys the widest readership appears not in collections, magazines, or even anthologies for students, but in greeting cards. A significant amount of the personal daily mail delivered in the United States consists of greeting cards. That represents millions of lines of verse going by us on the street and in planes over our heads. These verses share some similarities with the poetry included in this anthology, but there are also important differences that indicate the need for reading serious poetry closely rather than casually.

The popularity of greeting cards is easy to explain: just as many of us have neither the time nor the talent to make gifts for birthdays, weddings, anniversaries, graduations, Valentine's Day, Mother's Day, and other holidays, we are unlikely to write personal messages when cards conveniently say them for us. Although impersonal, cards are efficient and convey an important message no matter what the occasion for them: I care. These greetings are rarely serious poetry; they are not written to be. Nevertheless, they demonstrate the impulse in our culture to generate and receive poetry.

In a handbook for greeting-card freelancers, a writer and past editor of such verse began with this advice:

> Once you determine what you want to say—and in this regard it is best to stick to one basic idea—you must choose your words to do several things at the same time:
>
> 1. Your idea must be expressed as a complete idea; it must have a beginning, a middle, and an end.
> 2. There must be coherence in your verse. Every line must be linked logically and smoothly with its neighbors.
> 3. Your expressions . . . must be conversational. High-flown language rarely comes off successfully in greeting-card writing.
> 4. You must write with emphasis—and something else: enthusiasm. It's necessary to create interest in that all-important first line. From that point on, writing your verse is a matter of developing your idea and bringing it to a peak of emphasis in the last line. Occasionally you will find that you have shot your wad too early in the verse, and whatever you say after that point sounds like an afterthought.
> 5. You must do all of the above and at the same time make everything come out right in the meter-and-rhyme department.[1]

This advice is followed by a list of approximately fifty of the most frequently used rhyme sounds accompanied by rhyming words, such as *love, of, above* for the sound *uv*. The point of these prescriptions is that the verse must be written so that it is immediately accessible—consumable—by both the buyer and the recipient. Writers of these cards are expected to avoid any complexity.

Compare the following greeting-card verse with the poem that comes after it. "Magic of Love," by Helen Farries, has been a longtime favorite in a major greeting-card company's "wedding line"; with different endings it has been used also in valentines and friendship cards.

HELEN FARRIES

Magic of Love   *date unknown*

There's a wonderful gift that can give you a lift,
It's a blessing from heaven above!
It can comfort and bless, it can bring happiness —
It's the wonderful MAGIC OF LOVE!

[1]Chris Fitzgerald, "Conventional Verse: The Sentimental Favorite," *The Greeting Card Writer's Handbook*, ed. H. Joseph Chadwick (Cincinnati: Writer's Digest, 1975): 13, 17.

Like a star in the night, it can keep your faith bright,   5
Like the sun, it can warm your hearts, too —
It's a gift you can give every day that you live,
And when given, it comes back to you!

When love lights the way, there is joy in the day
And all troubles are lighter to bear,   10
Love is gentle and kind, and through love you will find
There's an answer to your every prayer!

May it never depart from your two loving hearts,
May you treasure this gift from above —
You will find if you do, all your dreams will come true,   15
In the wonderful MAGIC OF LOVE!

JOHN FREDERICK NIMS (1913–1999)

Love Poem   *1947*

My clumsiest dear, whose hands shipwreck vases,
At whose quick touch all glasses chip and ring,
Whose palms are bulls in china, burs in linen,
And have no cunning with any soft thing

Except all ill-at-ease fidgeting people: 5
The refugee uncertain at the door
You make at home; deftly you steady
The drunk clambering on his undulant floor.

Unpredictable dear, the taxi drivers' terror,
Shrinking from far headlights pale as a dime   10
Yet leaping before red apoplectic streetcars —
Misfit in any space. And never on time.

A wrench in clocks and the solar system. Only
With words and people and love you move at ease.
In traffic of wit expertly maneuver   15
And keep us, all devotion, at your knees.

Forgetting your coffee spreading on our flannel,
Your lipstick grinning on our coat,
So gaily in love's unbreakable heaven
Our souls on glory of spilt bourbon float.   20

Be with me, darling, early and late. Smash glasses —
I will study wry music for your sake.
For should your hands drop white and empty
All the toys of the world would break.

CONSIDERATIONS FOR CRITICAL THINKING AND WRITING

   1. FIRST RESPONSE. Read these two works aloud. How are they different? How the same?

2. To what extent does the advice to would-be greeting-card writers apply to each work?
3. Compare the two speakers. Which do you find more appealing? Why?
4. How does Nims's description of love differ from Farries's?

In contrast to poetry, which transfigures and expresses an emotion or experience through an original use of language, the verse in "Magic of Love" relies on *clichés,* ideas or expressions that have become tired and trite from overuse, such as describing love as "a blessing from heaven above." Clichés anesthetize readers instead of alerting them to the possibility of fresh perceptions. They are used to draw out **stock responses,** predictable, conventional reactions to language, characters, symbols, or situations; God, heaven, the flag, motherhood, hearts, puppies, and peace are some often-used objects of stock responses. Advertisers manufacture careers from this sort of business.

Clichés and stock responses are two of the major ingredients of sentimentality in literature. **Sentimentality** exploits the reader by inducing responses that exceed what the situation warrants. This pejorative term should not be confused with *sentiment,* which is synonymous with *emotion* or *feeling.* Sentimentality cons readers into falling for the mass murderer who is devoted to stray cats, and it requires that we not think twice about what we're feeling because those tears shed for the little old lady, the rage aimed at the vicious enemy soldier, and the longing for the simple virtues of poverty might disappear under the slightest scrutiny. The experience of sentimentality is not unlike biting into a swirl of cotton candy; it's momentarily sweet but wholly insubstantial.

Clichés, stock responses, and sentimentality are generally the hallmarks of weak writing. Poetry—the kind that is unmistakable—achieves freshness, vitality, and genuine emotion that sharpen our perceptions of life.

Although the most widely read verse is found in greeting cards, the most widely *heard* poetry appears in song lyrics. Not all songs are poetic, but a good many share the same effects and qualities as poems. Consider these lyrics by Bruce Springsteen about Philadelphia, the City of Brotherly Love.

BRUCE SPRINGSTEEN (B. 1949)

Streets of Philadelphia 1993

I was bruised and battered and I couldn't tell
What I felt
I was unrecognizable to myself
I saw my reflection in a window I didn't know
My own face   5
Oh brother are you gonna leave me
Wastin' away
On the streets of Philadelphia

I walked the avenue till my legs felt like stone
I heard the voices of friends vanished and gone   10
At night I could hear the blood in my veins
Black and whispering as the rain
On the streets of Philadelphia

Ain't no angel gonna greet me
It's just you and I my friend   15
My clothes don't fit me no more
I walked a thousand miles
Just to slip this skin

The night has fallen, I'm lyin' awake
I can feel myself fading away   20
So receive me brother with your faithless kiss
Or will we leave each other alone like this
On the streets of Philadelphia

CONSIDERATIONS FOR CRITICAL THINKING AND WRITING

1. FIRST RESPONSE. Characterize Philadelphia in this song lyric. What sort of life is described by the speaker? Which images seem especially evocative to you?

2. Why is there almost no punctuation in these lines? How do you make sense of the lines in the absence of conventional punctuation?

3. What kind of mood is evoked by the language of this song? How does your reading of "Streets of Philadelphia" compare with listening to Springsteen singing it (available on his *Greatest Hits*, a Columbia CD)?

4. Explain whether you think this song can be accurately called a narrative poem.

SAUNDRA SHARP (B. 1942)

It's the Law: A Rap Poem   *1991*

You can learn about the state of the U.S.A.
By the laws we have on the books today.
The rules we break are the laws we make
The things that we fear, we legislate.

We got laws designed to keep folks in line   5
Laws for what happens when you lose your mind
Laws against stealing, laws against feeling,
The laws we have are a definite sign
That our vision of love is going blind.
(They probably got a law against this rhyme.)   10
Unh-hunh . . . . .

We got laws for cool cats & laws for dirty dogs
Laws about where you can park your hog
Laws against your mama and your papa, too
Even got a law to make the laws come true.   15

It's against the law to hurt an ol' lady,
It's against the law to steal a little baby,
The laws we make are what we do to each other
There is no law to make brother love brother
Hmmm   20

Now this respect thang is hard for some folks to do
They don't respect themselves so they can't respect you
This is the word we should get around —
These are the rules: we gonna run 'em on down.
Listen up!:   25

It ain't enough to be cute,
It ain't enough to be tough
You gotta walk tall
You gotta strut your stuff

You gotta learn to read, you gotta learn to write.   30
Get the tools you need to win this fight
Get your common sense down off the shelf
Start in the mirror . . . . Respect your Self!

When you respect yourself you keep your body clean
You walk tall, walk gentle, don't have to be mean   35
You keep your mind well fed, you keep a clear head
And you think 'bout who you let in your bed —
Unh-hunh . . . . . .

When you respect yourself you come to understand
That your body is a temple for a natural plan,   40
It's against that plan to use drugs or dope —
Use your heart and your mind when you need to cope . . .
It's the law!

We got laws that got started in '86
And laws made back when the Indians got kicked   45
If we want these laws to go out of favor
Then we've got to change our behavior

Change what!? you say, well let's take a look
How did the laws get on the books? Yeah.
I said it up front but let's get tougher   50
The laws we make are what we do to each other

If you never shoot at me then I don't need
A law to keep you from shooting at me, do you see?
There's a universal law that's tried and true
Says Don't do to me —   55
What you don't want done to you
Unh-hunh!
Don't do to me —
What you don't want done to you
It's the law!   60

CONSIDERATIONS FOR CRITICAL THINKING AND WRITING

1. FIRST RESPONSE. According to this rap poem, what do laws reveal "about the state of the U.S.A."?

2. How are the "laws" different from the "rules" prescribed in the middle stanzas of the poem?

3. What is the theme of this rap poem?

PERSPECTIVE

ROBERT FRANCIS (1901–1987)

On "Hard" Poetry   *1965*

When Robert Frost said he liked poems hard he could scarcely have meant he liked them difficult. If he had meant difficult he would have said he didn't like them easy. What he said was that he didn't like them soft.

Poems can be soft in several ways. They can be soft in form (invertebrate). They can be soft in thought and feeling (sentimental). They can be soft with excess verbiage. Frost used to advise [writers] to squeeze the water out of a poem. He liked poems dry. What is dry tends to be hard, and what is hard is always dry, except perhaps on the outside.

Yet though hardness here does not mean difficulty, some difficulty naturally goes with hardness. A hard poem may not be hard to read but is hard to write. Not too hard, preferably. Nor so hard to write that there is no flow in the writer. But hard enough for the growing poem to meet with some healthy resistance. Frost often found this healthy resistance in a tight rhyme scheme and strict meter. There are other ways of getting good resistance, of course.

And in the reader too, a hard poem will bring some difficulty. Preferably not too much. Not enough difficulty to completely baffle him. Ideally a hard poem should not be too hard to make sense of, but hard to exhaust its meaning and its beauty.

"What I care about is the hardness of the poems. I don't like them soft, I want them to be little pebbles, but placed where they won't dislodge easily. And I'd like them to be little pebbles of precious stone — precious, or semiprecious" (interview with John Ciardi, *Saturday Review*, March 21, 1959).

Here is hard prose talking about hard poetry. Frost was never shrewder or more illuminating. Here, as well as in anything else he ever said, is his flavor.

What contemporary of his can you imagine saying this or anything like it?

In 1843 Emerson jotted in his journal: "Hard clouds and hard expressions, and hard manners, I love."

From The Satirical Rogue on Poetry

CONSIDERATIONS FOR CRITICAL THINKING AND WRITING

1. What is the distinction between "hard" and "soft" poetry?

2. Given Francis's brief essay and his poem "Catch" (p. 14), write a review of Helen Farries's "Magic of Love" (p. 30) as you think Francis would.

3. Explain whether you would characterize Bruce Springsteen's "Streets of Philadelphia" (p. 32) as hard or soft.

POEMS FOR FURTHER STUDY

RUDYARD KIPLING (1865–1936)

If—

1910

If you can keep your head when all about you
    Are losing theirs and blaming it on you,
If you can trust yourself when all men doubt you,
    But make allowance for their doubting too;
If you can wait and not be tired by waiting, 5
    Or being lied about, don't deal in lies,
Or being hated, don't give way to hating,
    And yet don't look too good, nor talk too wise:

If you can dream — and not make dreams your master;
    If you can think — and not make thoughts your aim; 10
If you can meet with Triumph and Disaster
    And treat those two impostors just the same;
If you can bear to hear the truth you've spoken
    Twisted by knaves to make a trap for fools,
Or watch the things you gave your life to, broken, 15
    And stoop and build 'em up with worn-out tools:

If you can make one heap of all your winnings
    And risk it in one turn of pitch-and-toss,°   *pitching coins*
And lose, and start again at your beginnings
    And never breathe a word about your loss; 20
If you can force your heart and nerve and sinew
    To serve your turn long after they are gone,
And so hold on when there is nothing in you
    Except the Will which says to them: "Hold on!"

If you can talk with crowds and keep your virtue, 25
    Or walk with Kings — nor lose the common touch,
If neither foes nor loving friends can hurt you,
    If all men count with you, but none too much;
If you can fill the unforgiving minute
    With sixty seconds' worth of distance run, 30
Yours is the Earth and everything that's in it,
    And — which is more — you'll be a Man, my son!

CONSIDERATIONS FOR CRITICAL THINKING AND WRITING

1. FIRST RESPONSE. Though the poem is addressed to the speaker's son, could the speaker's advice apply to a daughter as well? Explain why or why not.

2. What does it mean that Kipling capitalized "Man" in the last line of the poem? Is this speaker defining masculinity or something else? Do these definitions seem dated to you? Why or why not?

3. Read the poem aloud and comment on the effects of the rhymes and rhythms of the lines.

CONNECTION TO ANOTHER SELECTION

1. Discuss Kipling's treatment of what a man is in contrast to Alice Walker's description of what a woman is not in "a woman is not a potted plant," the next poem. What significant differences do you find in their definitions?

ALICE WALKER (B. 1944)

a woman is not a potted plant   *1991*

A WOMAN IS NOT
A POTTED PLANT

her roots bound
to the confines
of her house   5

a woman is not
a potted plant
her leaves trimmed
to the contours
of her sex   10

a woman is not
a potted plant
her branches
espaliered
against the fences   15
of her race
her country
her mother
her man

her trained blossom   20
turning
this way
& that
to follow
the sun   25
of whoever feeds
and waters
her

a woman
is wilderness   30
unbounded

holding the future
between each breath
walking the earth
only because   35
she is free
and not creepervine
or tree.

Nor even honeysuckle
or bee.   40

CONSIDERATIONS FOR CRITICAL THINKING AND WRITING

1. FIRST RESPONSE. According to the speaker, how do the properties of a pot-
   ted plant inappropriately describe a woman? (Have you ever considered a
   woman to be *like* a potted plant?)
2. What *is* a woman, according to the speaker? What is the effect of defining
   her primarily by what she is not?
3. Describe the meaning and effect of the poem's final two lines.

CONNECTION TO ANOTHER SELECTION

1. Compare Walker's take on female identity in this poem with Piercy's in "The
   Secretary Chant" (p. 9). How are their conceptions similar? Different?

LISA PARKER (B. 1971)

Snapping Beans   1998

for Susan Squier

I snapped beans into the silver bowl
that sat on the splintering slats
of the porchswing between my grandma and me.
I was home for the weekend,
from school, from the North,   5
Grandma hummed "What A Friend We Have In Jesus"
as the sun rose, pushing its pink spikes
through the slant of cornstalks,
through the fly-eyed mesh of the screen.
We didn't speak until the sun overcame   10
the feathered tips of the cornfield
and Grandma stopped humming. I could feel
the soft gray of her stare
against the side of my face
when she asked, *How's school a-goin'?*   15
I wanted to tell her about my classes,
the revelations by book and lecture,
as real as any shout of faith
and potent as a swig of strychnine.
She reached the leather of her hand   20

over the bowl and cupped
my quivering chin; the slick smooth of her palm
held my face the way she held tomatoes
under the spigot, careful not to drop them,
and I wanted to tell her   25
about the nights I cried into the familiar
heartsick panels of the quilt she made me,
wishing myself home on the evening star.
I wanted to tell her
the evening star was a planet,   30
that my friends wore noserings and wrote poetry
about sex, about alcoholism, about Buddha.
I wanted to tell her how my stomach burned
acidic holes at the thought of speaking in class,
speaking in an accent, speaking out of turn,   35
how I was tearing, splitting myself apart
with the slow-simmering guilt of being happy
despite it all.
I said, *School's fine.*
We snapped beans into the silver bowl between us   40
and when a hickory leaf, still summer green,
skidded onto the porchfront,
Grandma said,
It's funny how things blow loose like that.

CONSIDERATIONS FOR CRITICAL THINKING AND WRITING

1. FIRST RESPONSE. Describe the speaker's feelings about starting a life at college. How do those feelings compare with your own experiences?

2. How does the grandmother's world differ from the speaker's at school? What details especially reveal those differences?

3. Given that the poem is about how "school['s] a-goin'," why do you think the title is "Snapping Beans"?

4. Discuss the significance of the grandmother's response to the hickory leaf in line 44. How do you read the last line?

CONNECTION TO ANOTHER SELECTION

1. Discuss the treatment of the grandmother in "Snapping Beans" and in "Behind Grandma's House" by Gary Soto (p. 167).

WYATT PRUNTY (B. 1947)

Elderly Lady Crossing on Green   1993

And give her no scouts doing their one good deed
Or sentimental cards to wish her well
During Christmas time or gallstone time —
Because there was a time, she'd like to tell,

She drove a loaded V8 powerglide   5
And would have run you flat as paint
To make the light before it turned on her,
Make it as she watched you faint

When looking up you saw her bearing down
Eyes locking you between the wheel and dash,   10
And you either scrambled back where you belonged
Or jaywalked to eternity, blown out like trash

Behind the grease spot where she braked on you. . . .
Never widow, wife, mother, or a bride,
And nothing up ahead she's looking for   15
But asphalt, the dotted line, the other side,

The way she's done a million times before,
With nothing in her brief to tell you more
Than she's a small tug on the tidal swell
Of her own sustaining notion that she's doing well.   20

CONSIDERATIONS FOR CRITICAL THINKING AND WRITING

1. FIRST RESPONSE. Does the description of the elderly lady in the poem un-
   dercut your expectations about her created by the title? Is this poem senti-
   mental, ironic, or something else?

2. In what ways is this elderly woman "doing well" (line 20)? Does the poem
   suggest any ways in which she's not?

3. Describe the effect produced by the first line's beginning with "And . . . ."
   Why is this a fitting introduction to this elderly lady?

CONNECTION TO ANOTHER SELECTION

1. Write an essay comparing the humor in this poem with that of Hathaway's
   "Oh, Oh" (p. 13).

ALBERTO RÍOS (B. 1952)

Seniors   *1985*

William cut a hole in his Levi's pocket
so he could flop himself out in class
behind the girls so the other guys
could see and shit what guts we all said.
All Konga wanted to do over and over   5
was the rubber band trick, but he showed
everyone how, so nobody wanted to see
anymore and one day he cried, just cried
until his parents took him away forever.
Maya had a Hotpoint refrigerator standing   10
in his living room, just for his family to show
anybody who came that they could afford it.

Me, I got a French kiss, finally, in the catholic
darkness, my tongue's farthest halt vacationing
loudly in another mouth like a man in Bermudas,   15
and my body jumped against a flagstone wall,
I could feel it through her thin, almost
nonexistent body: I had, at that moment, that moment,
a hot girl on a summer night, the best of all
the things we tried to do. Well, she   20
let me kiss her, anyway, all over.

Or it was just a flagstone wall
with a flaw in the stone, an understanding cavity
for burning young men with smooth dreams —
the true circumstance is gone, the true   25
circumstances about us all then
are gone. But when I kissed her, all water,
she would close her eyes, and they into somewhere
would disappear. Whether she was there
or not, I remember her, clearly, and she moves   30
around the room, sometimes, until I sleep.

I have lain on the desert in watch
low in the back of a pick-up truck
for nothing in particular, for stars, for
the things behind stars, and nothing comes   35
more than the moment: always now, here in a truck,
the moment again to dream of making love and sweat,
this time to a woman, or even to all of them
in some allowable way, to those boys, then,
who couldn't cry, to the girls before they were   40
women, to friends, me on my back, the sky over me
pressing its simple weight into her body
on me, into the bodies of them all, on me.

CONSIDERATIONS FOR CRITICAL THINKING AND WRITING

1. FIRST RESPONSE. Comment on the use of slang in the poem. Does it sur-
   prise you? How does it characterize the speaker?

2. How does the language of the final stanza differ from that of the first
   stanza? To what purpose?

3. Write an essay that discusses the speaker's attitudes toward sex and life.
   How are they related?

CONNECTION TO ANOTHER SELECTION

1. Compare the treatment of sex in this poem with that in Sharon Olds's "Sex
   without Love" (p. 76).

2. Think about "Seniors" as a kind of love poem and compare the speaker's
   voice here with the one in T. S. Eliot's "The Love Song of J. Alfred Prufrock"
   (p. 405). How are these two voices used to evoke different cultures? Of what
   value is love in these cultures?

JOHN DONNE (1572–1631)

The Sun Rising

c. 1633

Busy old fool, unruly sun,
    Why dost thou thus,
Through windows, and through curtains, call on us?
Must to thy motions lovers' seasons run?
    Saucy pedantic wretch, go chide   5
    Late schoolboys, and sour prentices,
  Go tell court-huntsmen that the king will ride,
  Call country ants° to harvest offices;   *farm workers*
Love, all alike, no season knows, nor clime,
Nor hours, days, months, which are the rags of time.   10

Thy beams, so reverend and strong
    Why shouldst thou think?
I could eclipse and cloud them with a wink,
But that I would not lose her sight so long:
    If her eyes have not blinded thine,   15
    Look, and tomorrow late, tell me
  Whether both the Indias° of spice and mine   *East and West Indies*
  Be where thou left'st them, or lie here with me.
Ask for those kings whom thou saw'st yesterday,
And thou shalt hear, all here in one bed lay.   20

She is all states, and all princes I,
    Nothing else is.
Princes do but play us; compared to this,
All honor's mimic, all wealth alchemy.
    Thou, sun, art half as happy as we,   25
    In that the world's contracted thus;
  Thine age asks ease, and since thy duties be
  To warm the world, that's done in warming us.
Shine here to us, and thou art every where;
This bed thy center° is, these walls thy sphere.   *of orbit* 30

CONSIDERATIONS FOR CRITICAL THINKING AND WRITING

1. FIRST RESPONSE. What is the situation in this poem? Why is the speaker angry with the sun? What does he urge the sun to do in the first stanza?

2. What claims does the speaker make about the power of love in stanzas 2 and 3? What does he mean when he says, "Shine here to us, and thou art every where"?

3. Are any of the speaker's exaggerations in any sense true? How?

CONNECTION TO ANOTHER SELECTION

1. Compare this lyric poem with Richard Wilbur's "A Late Aubade" (p. 68). What similarities do you find in the ideas and emotions expressed in each?

Li Ho (791–817)

A Beautiful Girl Combs Her Hair   *date unknown*

TRANSLATED BY DAVID YOUNG

Awake at dawn
she's dreaming
by cool silk curtains

fragrance of spilling hair
half sandalwood, half aloes   5

windlass creaking at the well
singing jade

the lotus blossom wakes, refreshed

her mirror
two phoenixes   10
a pool of autumn light

standing on the ivory bed
loosening her hair
watching the mirror

one long coil, aromatic silk   15
a cloud down to the floor

drop the jade comb — no sound

delicate fingers
pushing the coils into place
color of raven feathers   20

shining blue-black stuff
the jewelled comb will hardly hold it

spring wind makes me restless
her slovenly beauty upsets me

eighteen and her hair's so thick   25
she wears herself out fixing it!

she's finished now
the whole arrangement in place

in a cloud-patterned skirt
she walks with even steps   30
a wild goose on the sand

turns away without a word
where is she off to?

down the steps to break a spray of
        cherry blossoms   35

CONSIDERATIONS FOR CRITICAL THINKING AND WRITING

1. FIRST RESPONSE. Try to paraphrase the poem. What is lost by rewording?

2. How does the speaker use sensuous language to create a vivid picture of the girl?

3. What are the speaker's feelings toward the girl? Do they remain the same throughout the poem?

CONNECTIONS TO OTHER SELECTIONS

1. Compare the description of hair in this poem with that in Cathy Song's "The White Porch" (p. 111). What significant similarities do you find?

2. Write an essay that explores the differing portraits in this poem and in Sylvia Plath's "Mirror" (p. 126). Which portrait is more interesting to you? Explain why.

ROBERT HASS (B. 1941)

Happiness   *1996*

Because yesterday morning from the steamy window
we saw a pair of red foxes across the creek
eating the last windfall apples in the rain —
they looked up at us with their green eyes
long enough to symbolize the wakefulness of living things   5
and then went back to eating —

and because this morning
when she went into the gazebo with her black pen and yellow pad
to coax an inquisitive soul
from what she thinks of as the reluctance of matter,   10
I drove into town to drink tea in the cafe
and write notes in a journal — mist rose from the bay
like the luminous and indefinite aspect of intention,
and a small flock of tundra swans
for the second winter in a row were feeding on new grass   15
in the soaked fields; they symbolize mystery, I suppose,
they are also called whistling swans, are very white,
and their eyes are black —

and because the tea steamed in front of me,
and the notebook, turned to a new page,   20
was blank except for a faint blue idea of order,
I wrote: *happiness! it is December, very cold,*
we woke early this morning,
and lay in bed kissing,
our eyes squinched up like bats.   25

CONSIDERATIONS FOR CRITICAL THINKING AND WRITING

1. FIRST RESPONSE. What kinds of experiences contribute to the speaker's happiness? Describe the person speaking.

2. Try writing a paraphrase of "Happiness." What happens to the poem when it's changed to prose? What accounts for these changes?

3. As Hass has done, define happiness or a moment in which you felt that emotion, in poetry or prose.

CONNECTION TO ANOTHER SELECTION

1. Write an essay that compares and contrasts "Happiness" with Emily Dickinson's "I like a look of Agony" (p. 300). Do they both succeed in capturing an emotion? What message do you take away from each?

2

Writing about Poetry

FROM READING TO WRITING

Writing about poetry can be a rigorous means of testing the validity of your own reading of a poem. Anyone who has been asked to write several pages about a fourteen-line poem knows how intellectually challenging this exercise is, because it means paying close attention to language. Such scrutiny of words, however, not only sensitizes you to the poet's use of language, but to your own use of language as well. At first you may feel intimidated by having to compose a paper that is longer than the poem you're writing about, but a careful reading will reveal that there's plenty to write about what the poem says and how it says it. Keep in mind that your job is not to produce a definitive reading of the poem — even Carl Sandburg once confessed that "I've written some poetry I don't understand myself." It is enough to develop an interesting thesis and to present it clearly and persuasively.

An interesting thesis will come to you if you read and reread, take notes, annotate the text, and generate ideas (for a discussion of this process see Chapter 20, "Reading and Writing"). Although it requires energy to read closely and to write convincingly about the charged language found in poetry, there is nothing mysterious about such reading and writing. This chapter provides a set of questions designed to sharpen your reading and writing about poetry. Following these questions is a sample paper that offers a clear and well-developed thesis concerning Elizabeth Bishop's "Manners."

QUESTIONS FOR RESPONSIVE
READING AND WRITING

The following questions can help you respond to important elements that reveal a poem's effects and meanings. The questions are general, so not all of them will necessarily be relevant to a particular poem. Many, however, should prove useful for thinking, talking, and writing about each poem in this collection. If you are uncertain about the meaning of a term used in a question, consult the Glossary of Literary Terms beginning on page 687.

Before addressing these questions, read the poem you are studying in its entirety. Don't worry about interpretation on a first reading; allow yourself the pleasure of enjoying whatever makes itself apparent to you. Then on subsequent readings, use the questions to understand and appreciate how the poem works.

1. Who is the speaker? Is it possible to determine the speaker's age, sex, sensibilities, level of awareness, and values?
2. Is the speaker addressing anyone in particular?
3. How do you respond to the speaker? Favorably? Negatively? What is the situation? Are there any special circumstances that inform what the speaker says?
4. Is there a specific setting of time and place?
5. Does reading the poem aloud help you to understand it?
6. Does a paraphrase reveal the basic purpose of the poem?
7. What does the title emphasize?
8. Is the theme presented directly or indirectly?
9. Do any allusions enrich the poem's meaning?
10. How does the diction reveal meaning? Are any words repeated? Do any carry evocative connotative meanings? Are there any puns or other forms of verbal wit?
11. Are figures of speech used? How does the figurative language contribute to the poem's vividness and meaning?
12. Do any objects, persons, places, events, or actions have allegorical or symbolic meanings? What other details in the poem support your interpretation?
13. Is irony used? Are there any examples of situational irony, verbal irony, or dramatic irony? Is understatement or paradox used?
14. What is the tone of the poem? Is the tone consistent?
15. Does the poem use onomatopoeia, assonance, consonance, or alliteration? How do these sounds affect you?
16. What sounds are repeated? If there are rhymes, what is their effect? Do they seem forced or natural? Is there a rhyme scheme? Do the rhymes contribute to the poem's meaning?
17. Do the lines have a regular meter? What is the predominant meter? Are there significant variations? Does the rhythm seem appropriate for the tone of the poem?

18. Does the poem's form—its overall structure—follow an established pattern? Do you think the form is a suitable vehicle for the poem's meaning and effects?
19. Is the language of the poem intense and concentrated? Do you think it warrants more than one or two close readings?
20. Did you enjoy the poem? What, specifically, pleased or displeased you about what was expressed and how it was expressed?
21. Is there a particular critical approach that seems especially appropriate for this poem? (See the discussion of "Critical Strategies for Reading" beginning on p. 481.)
22. How might biographical information about the author help to determine the central concerns of the poem?
23. How might historical information about the poem provide a useful context for interpretation?
24. To what extent do your own experiences, values, beliefs, and assumptions inform your interpretation?
25. What kinds of evidence from the poem are you focusing on to support your interpretation? Does your interpretation leave out any important elements that might undercut or qualify your interpretation?
26. Given that there are a variety of ways to interpret the poem, which one seems the most useful to you?

A SAMPLE ANALYSIS

Memory in Elizabeth Bishop's "Manners"

The following sample paper on Elizabeth Bishop's "Manners" was written in response to an assignment that called for a 750-word discussion of the ways in which at least five of the following elements work to develop and reinforce the poem's themes:

diction and tone	irony	form
images	sound and rhyme	speaker
figures of speech	rhythm and meter	setting and situation
symbols		

In her paper, Debra Epstein discusses the ways in which a number of these elements contribute to what she sees as a central theme of "Manners": the loss of a way of life that Bishop associates with the end of World War I. Not all of the elements of poetry are covered equally in Epstein's paper because some, such as the speaker and setting, are more important to her argument than others. Notice how rather than merely listing each of the elements, Epstein mentions them in her discussion as she needs to in order to develop the thesis that she clearly and succinctly expresses in her opening paragraph.

ELIZABETH BISHOP (1911–1979)

Manners

1965

for a Child of 1918

My grandfather said to me
as we sat on the wagon seat,
"Be sure to remember to always
speak to everyone you meet."

We met a stranger on foot.   5
My grandfather's whip tapped his hat.
"Good day, sir. Good day. A fine day."
And I said it and bowed where I sat.

Then we overtook a boy we knew
with his big pet crow on his shoulder.   10
"Always offer everyone a ride;
don't forget that when you get older,"

my grandfather said. So Willy
climbed up with us, but the crow
gave a "Caw!" and flew off. I was worried.   15
How would he know where to go?

But he flew a little way at a time
from fence post to fence post, ahead;
and when Willy whistled he answered.
"A fine bird," my grandfather said,   20

"and he's well brought up. See, he answers
nicely when he's spoken to.
Man or beast, that's good manners.
Be sure that you both always do."

When automobiles went by,   25
the dust hid the people's faces,
but we shouted "Good day! Good day!
Fine day!" at the top of our voices.

When we came to Hustler Hill,
he said that the mare was tired,   30
so we all got down and walked,
as our good manners required.

Debra Epstein

Professor Brown

English 210

May 1, 20--

Memory in Elizabeth Bishop's "Manners"

The subject of Elizabeth Bishop's "Manners" has to do with behaving well, but the theme of the poem has more to do with a way of life than with etiquette. The poem suggests that modern society has lost something important-- a friendly openness, a generosity of spirit, a sense of decency and consideration--in its race toward progress. Although the narrative is simply told, Bishop enriches this poem about manners by developing an implicit theme through her subtle use of such elements of poetry as speaker, setting, rhyme, meter, symbol, and images.

The dedication suggests that the speaker is "a Child of 1918" who accompanies his or her grandfather on a wagon ride and who is urged to practice good manners by greeting people, offering everyone a ride, and speaking when spoken to by anyone. During the ride they say hello to a stranger, give a ride to a boy with a pet crow, shout greetings to a passing automobile, and get down from the wagon when they reach a hill because the horse is tired. They walk because "good manners required" (line 32) such consideration, even for a horse. This summary indicates what goes on in the poem but not its significance. That requires a closer look at some of the poem's elements.

Given the speaker's simple language (there are no metaphors or similes and only a few words out of thirty-two lines are more than two syllables), it seems likely that he or she is a fairly young child, rather than an adult reminiscing. (It is interesting to note that Bishop herself, though not identical with the speaker, would have

been seven in 1918.) Because the speaker is a young child
who uses simple diction, Bishop has to show us the ride's
significance indirectly rather than having the speaker
explicitly state it.

The setting for the speaker's narrative is important
because 1918 was the year World War I ended, and it marked
the beginning of a new era of technology that was the re-
sult of rapid industrialization during the war. Horses and
wagons would soon be put out to pasture. The grandfather's
manners emphasize a time gone by; the child must be told
to "remember" what the grandfather says because he or she
will take that advice into a new and very different world.

The grandfather's world of the horse and wagon is
uncomplicated, and this is reflected in both the simple
quatrains that move predictably along in an <u>abcb</u> rhyme
scheme and the frequent anapestic meter (ăs wĕ săt ŏn thĕ
wágŏn [2]) that pulls the lines rapidly and lightly. The
one moment Bishop breaks the set rhyme scheme is in the
seventh stanza when the automobile (the single four-
syllable word in the poem) rushes by in a cloud of dust so
that people cannot see or hear each other. The only off
rhymes in the poem—"faces" (26) and "voices" (28)—are
also in this stanza, which suggests that the automobile
and the people in it are somehow off or out of sync with
what goes on in the other stanzas. The automobile is a
symbol of a way of life in which people--their faces hid-
den--and manners take a back seat to speed and noise. The
people in the car don't wave, don't offer a ride, and
don't speak when spoken to.

Maybe the image of the crow's noisy cawing and flying
from post to post is a foreshadowing that should prepare
readers for the automobile. The speaker feels "worried"
about the crow's apparent directionlessness: "How would

he know where to go?" (16). However, neither the child
nor the grandfather (nor the reader on a first reading)
clearly sees the two worlds that Bishop contrasts in the
final stanza.

"Hustler Hill" is the perfect name for what finally
tires out the mare. There is no hurry for the grandfather
and child, but there is for those people in the car and
the postwar hustle and bustle they represent. The fast-
paced future overtakes the tired symbol of the past in
the poem. The pace slows as the wagon passengers get down
to walk, but the reader recognizes that the grandfather's
way has been lost to a world in which good manners are
not required.

3

Word Choice,
Word Order, and Tone

DICTION

Like all good writers, poets are keenly aware of *diction,* their choice of
words. Poets, however, choose words especially carefully because the words
in poems call attention to themselves. Characters, actions, settings, and
symbols may appear in a poem, but in the foreground, before all else, is the
poem's language. Also, poems are usually briefer than other forms of writ-
ing. A few inappropriate words in a 200-page novel (which would have
about 100,000 words) create fewer problems than they would in a 100-word
poem. Functioning in a compressed atmosphere, the words in a poem
must convey meanings gracefully and economically. Readers therefore have
to be alert to the ways in which those meanings are released.

Although poetic language is often more intensely charged than ordi-
nary speech, the words used in poetry are not necessarily different from
everyday speech. Inexperienced readers may sometimes assume that lan-
guage must be high-flown and out of date to be included in a poem: in-
stead of reading about a boy "enjoying a swim," they expect to read about a
boy "disporting with pliant arm o'er a glassy wave." During the eighteenth
century this kind of *poetic diction* — the use of elevated language over ordi-
nary language — was highly valued in English poetry, but since the nine-
teenth century poets have generally overridden the distinctions that were
once made between words used in everyday speech and those used in po-
etry. Today all levels of diction can be found in poetry.

A poet, like any writer, has several levels of diction from which to
choose; they range from formal to middle to informal. *Formal diction* con-
sists of a dignified, impersonal, and elevated use of language. Notice, for
example, the formality of Thomas Hardy's description of the sunken lux-
ury liner *Titanic* in this stanza from "The Convergence of the Twain" (the
entire poem appears on p. 73):

> In a solitude of the sea
> Deep from human vanity,
> And the Pride of Life that planned her, stilly couches she.

There is nothing casual or relaxed about these lines. Hardy's use of "stilly," meaning "quietly" or "calmly," is purely literary; the word rarely, if ever, turns up in everyday English.

The language used in Richard Wilbur's "A Late Aubade" (p. 68) represents a less formal level of diction; the speaker uses a *middle diction* spoken by most educated people. Consider how Wilbur's speaker tells his lover what she might be doing instead of being with him:

> You could be sitting now in a carrel
> Turning some liver-spotted page,
> Or rising in an elevator-cage
> Toward Ladies' Apparel.

The speaker elegantly enumerates his lover's unattractive alternatives to being with him — reading old books in a library or shopping in a department store — but the wit of his description lessens its formality.

Informal diction is evident in Larkin's "A Study of Reading Habits" (p. 22). The speaker's account of his early reading is presented *colloquially,* in a conversational manner that in this instance includes slang expressions not used by the culture at large:

> When getting my nose in a book
> Cured most things short of school,
> It was worth ruining my eyes
> To know I could still keep cool,
> And deal out the old right hook
> To dirty dogs twice my size.

This level of diction is clearly not that of Hardy's or Wilbur's speakers.

Poets may also draw on another form of informal diction, called *dialect.* Dialects are spoken by definable groups of people from a particular geographic region, economic group, or social class. New England dialects are often heard in Robert Frost's poems, for example. Gwendolyn Brooks employs a black dialect in "We Real Cool" (p. 81) to characterize a group of pool players. Another form of diction related to particular groups is *jargon,* a category of language defined by a trade or profession. Sociologists, photographers, carpenters, baseball players, and dentists, for example, all use words that are specific to their fields. E. E. Cummings manages to get quite a lot of mileage out of automobile jargon in "she being Brand" (p. 57).

Many levels of diction are available to poets. The variety of diction to be found in poetry is enormous, and that is how it should be. No language is foreign to poetry because it is possible to imagine any human voice as the speaker of a poem. When we say a poem is formal, informal, or somewhere in between, we are making a descriptive statement rather than an evaluative one. What matters in a poem is not only which words are used but how they are used.

DENOTATIONS AND CONNOTATIONS

One important way that the meaning of a word is communicated in a poem is through sound: snakes *hiss,* saws *buzz.* This and other matters related to sound are discussed in Chapter 7. Individual words also convey meanings through denotations and connotations. **Denotations** are the literal, dictionary meanings of a word. For example, *bird* denotes a feathered animal with wings (other denotations for the same word include a shuttlecock, an airplane, or an odd person), but in addition to its denotative meanings, *bird* also carries **connotations,** associations and implications that go beyond a word's literal meanings. Connotations derive from how the word has been used and the associations people make with it. Therefore, the connotations of *bird* might include fragility, vulnerability, altitude, the sky, or freedom, depending on the context in which the word is used. Consider also how different the connotations are for the following types of birds: hawk, dove, penguin, pigeon, chicken, peacock, duck, crow, turkey, gull, owl, goose, coot, and vulture. These words have long been used to refer to types of people as well as birds. They are rich in connotative meanings.

Connotations derive their resonance from a person's experiences with a word. Those experiences may not always be the same, especially when the people having them are in different times and places. *Theater,* for instance, was once associated with depravity, disease, and sin, whereas today the word usually evokes some sense of high culture and perhaps visions of elegant opulence. In several ethnic communities in the United States many people would find *squid* appetizing, but elsewhere the word is likely to produce negative connotations. Readers must recognize, then, that words written in other times and places may have unexpected connotations. Annotations usually help in these matters, which is why it makes sense to pay attention to them when they are available.

Ordinarily, though, the language of poetry is accessible, even when the circumstances of the reader and the poet are different. Although connotative language may be used subtly, it mostly draws on associations experienced by many people. Poets rely on widely shared associations rather than the idiosyncratic response that an individual might have to a word. Someone who has received a severe burn from a fireplace accident may associate the word *hearth* with intense pain instead of home and family life, but that reader must not allow a personal experience to undermine the response the poet intends to evoke. Connotative meanings are usually public meanings.

Perhaps this can be seen most clearly in advertising, where language is also used primarily to convey moods and feelings rather than information. For instance, nearly three decades of increasing interest in nutrition and general fitness have created a collective consciousness that advertisers have capitalized on successfully. Knowing that we want to be slender or lean or slim (not *spare* or *scrawny* and certainly not *gaunt*), advertisers have created a new word to describe beers, wines, sodas, cheeses, canned fruits, and other products that tend to overload what used to be called sweatclothes and sneakers. The word is *lite*. The assumed denotative meaning of *lite* is "low in calories," but as close readers of ingredient labels know, some *lites* are heavier than regularly prepared products. There can be no doubt about the connotative meaning of *lite*, however. Whatever is *lite* cannot hurt you; less is more. Even the word is lighter than *light*; there is no unnecessary droopy *g* or plump *h*. *Lite* is a brilliantly manufactured use of connotation.

Connotative meanings are valuable because they allow poets to be economical and suggestive simultaneously. In this way emotions and attitudes are carefully woven into the texture of the poem's language. Read the following poem and pay close attention to the connotative meanings of its words.

RANDALL JARRELL (1914–1965)

The Death of the Ball Turret Gunner   *1945*

From my mother's sleep I fell into the State
And I hunched in its belly till my wet fur froze.
Six miles from earth, loosed from its dream of life,
I woke to black flak and the nightmare fighters.
When I died they washed me out of the turret with a hose.

The title of this poem establishes the setting and the speaker's situation. Like the setting of a short story, the setting of a poem is important when the time and place influence what happens. "The Death of the Ball Turret Gunner" is set in the midst of a war and, more specifically, in a ball turret — a Plexiglas sphere housing machine guns on the underside of a bomber. The speaker's situation obviously places him in extreme danger; indeed, his fate is announced in the title.

Although the poem is written in the first-person singular, its speaker is clearly not the poet. Jarrell uses a **persona,** a speaker created by the poet. In this poem the persona is a disembodied voice that makes the gunner's story all the more powerful. What is his story? A paraphrase might read something like this:

> After I was born, I grew up to find myself at war, cramped into the turret of a bomber's belly some 31,000 feet above the ground. Below me were exploding shells from antiaircraft guns and attacking fighter planes. I was killed, but the bomber returned to base, where my remains were cleaned out of the turret so the next man could take my place.

This paraphrase is accurate, but its language is much less suggestive than the poem's. The first line of the poem has the speaker emerge from his "mother's sleep," the anesthetized sleep of her giving birth. The phrase also suggests the comfort, warmth, and security he knew as a child. This safety was left behind when he "fell," a verb that evokes the danger and involuntary movement associated with his subsequent "State" (*fell* also echoes, perhaps, the fall from innocence to experience related in the Bible).

Several dictionary definitions appear for the noun *state;* it can denote a territorial unit, the power and authority of a government, a person's social status, or a person's emotional or physical condition. The context provided by the rest of the poem makes clear that "State" has several denotative meanings here: because it is capitalized, it certainly refers to the violent world of a government at war, but it also refers to the gunner's vulnerable status as well as his physical and emotional condition. By having "State" carry more than one meaning, Jarrell has created an intentional ambiguity. *Ambiguity* allows for two or more simultaneous interpretations of a word, phrase, action, or situation, all of which can be supported by the context of a work. Through his ambiguous use of "State," Jarrell connects the horrors of war not just to bombers and gunners but to the governments that control them.

Related to this ambiguity is the connotative meaning of "State" in the poem. The context demands that the word be read with a negative charge. The word is not used with patriotic pride but to suggest an anonymous, impersonal "State" that kills rather than nurtures the life in its "belly." The state's "belly" is a bomber, and the gunner is "hunched" like a fetus in the cramped turret, where, in contrast to the warmth of his mother's womb, everything is frozen, even the "wet fur" of his flight jacket (newborn infants have wet fur too). The gunner is not just 31,000 feet from the ground but "Six miles from earth." *Six miles* has roughly the same denotative meaning as 31,000 feet, but Jarrell knew that the connotative meaning of *six miles* makes the speaker's position seem even more remote and frightening.

When the gunner is born into the violent world of war, he finds himself waking up to a "nightmare" that is all too real. The poem's final line is grimly understated, but it hits the reader with the force of an exploding shell: what the State-bomber-turret gives birth to is a gruesome death that is merely one of an endless series. It may be tempting to reduce the theme of this poem to the idea that "war is hell," but Jarrell's target is more specific. He implicates the "State," which routinely executes such violence, and he does so without preaching or hysterical denunciations. Instead, his use of language conveys his theme subtly and powerfully. Consider how this next poem uses connotative meanings to express its theme.

E. E. CUMMINGS (1894–1962)

she being Brand   *1926*

she being Brand

-new;and you
know consequently a
little stiff i was
careful of her and(having   5

thoroughly oiled the universal
joint tested my gas felt of
her radiator made sure her springs were O.

K.)i went right to it flooded-the-carburetor cranked her

up,slipped the   10
clutch(and then somehow got into reverse she
kicked what
the hell)next
minute i was back in neutral tried and

again slo-wly;bare,ly nudg. ing (my   15

lev-er Right-
oh and her gears being in
A 1 shape passed
from low through
second-in-to-high like   20
greasedlightning) just as we turned the corner of Divinity

avenue i touched the accelerator and give

her the juice,good

                    (it

was the first ride and believe i we was   25
happy to see how nice she acted right up to
the last minute coming back down by the Public
Gardens i slammed on

the
internalexpanding   30
&
externalcontracting
brakes Bothatonce and

brought allofher tremB
-ling   35
to a:dead.

stand-
;Still)

CONSIDERATIONS FOR CRITICAL THINKING AND WRITING

1. FIRST RESPONSE. How does Cummings's arrangement of the words on the page help you to read this poem aloud? What does the poem describe?

2. What ambiguities in language does the poem ride on? At what point were you first aware of these double meanings?

3. Explain why you think the poem is primarily serious or humorous.

4. Find some advertisements for convertibles or sports cars in magazines and read them closely. What similarities do you find in the use of connotative language in them and in Cummings's poem? Write a brief essay explaining how language is used to convey the theme of one of the advertisements and the poem.

WORD ORDER

Meanings in poems are conveyed not only by denotations and connotations but also by the poet's arrangement of words into phrases, clauses, and sentences to achieve particular effects. The ordering of words into meaningful verbal patterns is called *syntax.* A poet can manipulate the syntax of a line to place emphasis on a word; this is especially apparent when a poet varies normal word order. In Dickinson's "A narrow Fellow in the Grass" (p. 2), for example, the speaker says about the snake that "His notice sudden is." Ordinarily, that would be expressed as "his notice is sudden." By placing the verb *is* unexpectedly at the end of the line, Dickinson creates the sense of surprise we feel when we suddenly come upon a snake. Dickinson's inversion of the standard word order also makes the final sound of the line a hissing *is.*

Cummings uses one long sentence in "she being Brand" to take the reader on a ride that begins with a false start but accelerates quickly before coming to a halt. The jargon creates an exuberantly humorous mood that is helped along by the poem's syntax. How do Cummings's ordering of words and sentence structure reinforce the meaning of the lines?

TONE

Tone is the writer's attitude toward the subject, the mood created by all the elements in the poem. Writing, like speech, may be characterized as serious or light, sad or happy, private or public, angry or affectionate, bitter or nostalgic, or any other attitudes and feelings that human beings experience. In Jarrell's "The Death of the Ball Turret Gunner," the tone is clearly serious; the voice in the poem even sounds dead. Listen again to the persona's final words: "When I died they washed me out of the turret with a hose." The brutal, restrained matter-of-factness of this line is effective because the reader is called on to supply the appropriate anger and despair, a strategy that makes those emotions all the more convincing.

Consider how tone is used to convey meaning in the next poem, inspired by the poet's contemplation of mortality.

JUDITH ORTIZ COFER (B. 1952)
Common Ground   *1987*

Blood tells the story of your life
in heartbeats as you live it;
bones speak in the language
of death, and flesh thins
with age when up   5

through your pores rises
the stuff of your origin.

    These days,
when I look into the mirror I see
my grandmother's stern lips   10
speaking in parentheses at the corners
of my mouth of pain and deprivation
I have never known. I recognize
my father's brows arching in disdain
over the objects of my vanity, my mother's   15
nervous hands smoothing lines
just appearing on my skin,
like arrows pointing downward
to our common ground.

CONSIDERATIONS FOR CRITICAL THINKING AND WRITING

1. FIRST RESPONSE. How do you interpret the title? How did your idea of its meaning change as you read the poem?
2. What is the relationship between the first and second stanzas?
3. How does this poem make you feel? What is its tone? How do the diction and imagery create the tone?

ROBIN MORGAN (B. 1941)

Invocation   *1999*

for Isel Rivero

Gunmen attacked a school in northwestern Rwanda last Monday, killing seventeen girls. . . . The attack took place after the Hutu gunmen ordered the girls to separate into groups of ethnic Hutu and Tutsi, and the students refused to comply.
         —*from* The New York Times, *April 30, 1997*

Insane, sadistic gods to whom I offer
only my denial and disgust,
how do we bear witness to each other
when such defiance gleams beyond our trust?

They stupify us, these small, nameless girls   5
in whose name Love linked arms with her best friend.
Courage skulks shamed before these little skulls
rotting on the grassy school playground.

Let me be worthy of such children, slain
where they stand, who in the face of dying, cling.   10
Let me be equal to my small, sufficient pain
and in the broken teeth of horror, sing.

CONSIDERATIONS FOR CRITICAL THINKING AND WRITING

1. FIRST RESPONSE. How does your own response to the news report of the massacre compare with the poet's?
2. Look up *invocation* in the dictionary. In what sense is this poem an invocation?
3. Describe the tone of each stanza. How does the tone change from stanza to stanza?
4. What do lines 11 and 12 mean? What words and images affect you? How?

CONNECTION TO ANOTHER SELECTION

1. How is the strategy used in the final line of this poem similar to that of the final line in James Merrill's "Casual Wear" (p. 159)? Though the strategy is similar, how is the tone different at the end of each poem?

The next work is a **dramatic monologue,** a type of poem in which a character — the speaker — addresses a silent audience in such a way as to reveal unintentionally some aspect of his or her temperament or personality. What tone is created by Machan's use of a persona?

KATHARYN HOWD MACHAN (B. 1952)

Hazel Tells LaVerne   1976

```
last night
im cleanin out my
howard johnsons ladies room
when all of a sudden
up pops this frog                          5
musta come from the sewer
swimmin aroun an tryin ta
climb up the sida the bowl
so i goes ta flushin down
but sohelpmegod he starts talkin          10
bout a golden ball
an how i can be a princess
me a princess
well my mouth drops
all the way to the floor                   15
an he says
kiss me just kiss me
once on the nose
well i screams
ya little green pervert                     20
an i hitsm with my mop
an has ta flush
the toilet down three times
me
a princess                                 25
```

CONSIDERATIONS FOR CRITICAL THINKING AND WRITING

1. FIRST RESPONSE. What do you imagine the situation and setting are for this poem? Do you like this revision of the fairy tale "The Frog Prince"?

2. What creates the poem's humor? How does Hazel's use of language reveal her personality? Is her treatment of the frog consistent with her character?

3. Although it has no punctuation, this poem is easy to follow. How does the arrangement of the lines organize Hazel's speech for clarity and emphasis?

4. What is the theme? Is it conveyed through denotative or connotative language?

5. Write what you think might be LaVerne's reply to Hazel. First, write LaVerne's response as a series of ordinary sentences, and then try editing and organizing them into poetic lines.

CONNECTION TO ANOTHER SELECTION

1. Although Robert Browning's "My Last Duchess" (p. 164) is a more complex poem than Machan's, both use dramatic monologues to reveal character. How are the strategies in each poem similar?

MARTÍN ESPADA (B. 1957)

Latin Night at the Pawnshop   *1987*

Chelsea, Massachusetts
Christmas, 1987

The apparition of a salsa band
gleaming in the Liberty Loan
pawnshop window:

Golden trumpet,
silver trombone,
congas, maracas, tambourine,
all with price tags dangling
like the city morgue ticket
on a dead man's toe.

CONSIDERATIONS FOR CRITICAL THINKING AND WRITING

1. FIRST RESPONSE. What is "Latin" about this night at the pawnshop?

2. What kind of tone is created by the poet's word choice and by the rhythm of the poem?

3. Does it matter that this apparition occurs on Christmas night? Why or why not?

4. What do you think is the central point of this poem?

How do the speaker's attitude and tone change during the course of this next poem?

SARAH LINDSAY (B. 1958)

Aluminum Chlorohydrate   1997

Am I then to understand
that with every matins' sociable embalming of the armpit
molecular aluminum insinuates itself, through sheared follicles,
bright fleck by bright invisible fleck, into the tiny tender kinks
of capillaries? slides along their permeable wisps   5
into the jostling rivers of depleted scarlet doughnuts and white ghosts,
into a hectic Amazon, through endlessly wrung chambers,
out the roaring wide aorta, rising blandly through the neck
by ever subtler pulses toward the tingling gray curd
all flushed with its matted electrical storms? and lays   10
a glinting finger on one sparked synaptic mouth
that hushes. Whose voice may never be missed.
A number, a name, the Latin for *greed,*
clopping upstairs that March day in Florence with brand-new clogs,
the blister they raised. But supposing senility   15
takes the brain in its soft retriever's mouth
and carries it to be gutted, supposing all
the recent layers plucked away and memory's microscopic doors flung wide
for the oldest to come forth: Would third-grade Ruth be missing
and unmissed, or Mary or Brenda, with random trivial comrades,   20
or would the whole host stagger out, one missing legs, another clothes,
with synthetic pearls for eyes or carrot noses?
Or would each corridor dead-end on a scaly tinfoil mirror
showing nothing but the scowling smear
of some old unfamiliar woman's face?   25

CONSIDERATIONS FOR CRITICAL THINKING AND WRITING

1. FIRST RESPONSE. What do you make of this poem on the first reading?
   Carefully read the poem at least three times and record how your under-
   standing develops from reading to reading. How does your third reading
   differ from your initial response?

2. What is aluminum chlorohydrate? Why is it an appropriate title for this
   poem? How does it contribute to the poem's tone?

3. Explain how the tone shifts in the second half of the poem beginning with
   "But supposing . . ." (15)? Pay particular attention to the final image in
   lines 23 to 25.

4. What is the effect of the speaker asking a series of questions rather than
   making statements?

CONNECTION TO ANOTHER SELECTION

1. Discuss the ways in which diction helps create tone in "Aluminum Chloro-
   hydrate" and the "The Foot" by Alice Jones (p. 208). What does each poem
   have to say about what it means to be a human being?

DICTION AND TONE IN FOUR LOVE POEMS

The first three of these love poems share the same basic situation and theme: a male speaker addresses a female (in the first poem it is a type of female) urging that love should not be delayed because time is short. This theme is as familiar in poetry as it is in life. In Latin this tradition is known as **carpe diem,** "seize the day." Notice how the poets' diction helps create a distinctive tone in each poem, even though the subject matter and central ideas are similar (although not identical) in all three.

ROBERT HERRICK (1591–1674)

To the Virgins, to Make Much of Time   1648

Gather ye rose-buds while ye may,
  Old Time is still a-flying;
And this same flower that smiles today,
  Tomorrow will be dying.

The glorious lamp of heaven, the sun,   5
  The higher he's a-getting,
The sooner will his race be run,
  And nearer he's to setting.

That age is best which is the first,
  When youth and blood are warmer;   10
But being spent, the worse, and worst
  Times still succeed the former.

Then be not coy, but use your time,
  And while ye may, go marry;
For having lost but once your prime,   15
  You may for ever tarry.

CONSIDERATIONS FOR CRITICAL THINKING AND WRITING

1. FIRST RESPONSE. Would there be any change in meaning if the title of this poem were "To Young Women, to Make Much of Time"? Do you think the poem can apply to young men too?

2. What do the virgins have in common with the flowers (lines 1–4) and the course of the day (5–8)?

3. How does the speaker develop his argument? What will happen to the virgins if they don't "marry"? Paraphrase the poem.

4. What is the tone of the speaker's advice?

The next poem was also written in the seventeenth century, but it includes some words that have changed in usage and meaning over the past three hundred years. The title of Marvell's "To His Coy Mistress" requires some explanation. "Mistress" does not refer to a married man's illicit lover but to a woman who is loved and courted — a sweetheart. Marvell uses "coy" to describe a woman who is reserved and shy rather than coquettish or flirtatious. Often such shifts in meanings over time are explained in the notes that accompany reprintings of poems. You should keep in mind, however, that it is helpful to have a reasonably thick dictionary available when you are reading poetry. The most thorough is the *Oxford English Dictionary (OED)*, which provides histories of words. The *OED* is a multivolume leviathan, but there are other useful unabridged dictionaries and desk dictionaries.

Knowing its original meaning can also enrich your understanding of why a contemporary poet chooses a particular word. Elizabeth Bishop begins "The Fish" (p. 20) this way: "I caught a tremendous fish." We know immediately in this context that "tremendous" means very large. In addition, given that the speaker clearly admires the fish in the lines that follow, we might even understand "tremendous" in the colloquial sense of wonderful and extraordinary. But a dictionary gives us some further relevant insights. Because, by the end of the poem, we see the speaker thoroughly moved as a result of the encounter with the fish ("everything / was rainbow, rainbow, rainbow!"), the dictionary's additional information about the history of *tremendous* shows why it is the perfect adjective to introduce the fish. The word comes from the Latin *tremere* (to tremble) and therefore once meant "such as to make one tremble." That is precisely how the speaker is at the end of the poem: deeply affected and trembling. Knowing the origin of *tremendous* gives us the full heft of the poet's word choice.

Although some of the language in "To His Coy Mistress" requires annotations for the modern reader, this poem continues to serve as a powerful reminder that time is a formidable foe, even for lovers.

ANDREW MARVELL (1621–1678)

To His Coy Mistress   *1681*

Had we but world enough, and time,
This coyness, lady, were no crime.
We would sit down, and think which way
To walk, and pass our long love's day.
Thou by the Indian Ganges'° side   5
Shouldst rubies find; I by the tide
Of Humber° would complain.° I would   *write love songs*
Love you ten years before the Flood,
And you should, if you please, refuse
Till the conversion of the Jews.   10
My vegetable love should grow°
Vaster than empires, and more slow;

---

5 *Ganges:* A river in India sacred to the Hindus.   7 *Humber:* A river that flows through Marvell's native town, Hull.   11 *My vegetable love . . . grow:* A slow, unconscious growth.

An hundred years should go to praise
Thine eyes and on thy forehead gaze,
Two hundred to adore each breast,   15
But thirty thousand to the rest:
An age at least to every part,
And the last age should show your heart.
For, lady, you deserve this state,
Nor would I love at lower rate.   20
    But at my back I always hear
Time's wingèd chariot hurrying near;
And yonder all before us lie
Deserts of vast eternity.
Thy beauty shall no more be found,   25
Nor in thy marble vault shall sound
My echoing song; then worms shall try
That long preserved virginity,
And your quaint honor turn to dust,
And into ashes all my lust.   30
The grave's a fine and private place,
But none, I think, do there embrace.
    Now, therefore, while the youthful hue
Sits on thy skin like morning dew,
And while thy willing soul transpires°   *breathes forth* 35
At every pore with instant fires,
Now let us sport us while we may,
And now, like amorous birds of prey,
Rather at once our time devour
Than languish in his slow-chapped° power.   *slow-jawed* 40
Let us roll all our strength and all
Our sweetness up into one ball,
And tear our pleasures with rough strife
Thorough° the iron gates of life.   *through*
Thus, though we cannot make our sun   45
Stand still, yet we will make him run.

CONSIDERATIONS FOR CRITICAL THINKING AND WRITING

1. FIRST RESPONSE. Do you think this *carpe diem* poem is hopelessly dated or does it speak to our contemporary concerns?

2. This poem is divided into a three-part argument. Briefly summarize each section: if (lines 1–20), but (21–32), therefore (33–46).

3. What is the speaker's tone in lines 1–20? How much time would he spend adoring his mistress? Is he sincere? How does he expect his mistress to respond to these lines?

4. How does the speaker's tone change beginning with line 21? What is his view of time in lines 21–32? What does this description do to the lush and leisurely sense of time in lines 1–20? How do you think his mistress would react to lines 21–32?

5. In the final lines of Herrick's "To the Virgins, to Make Much of Time" (p. 64), the speaker urges the virgins to "go marry." What does Marvell's

speaker urge in lines 33–46? How is the pace of these lines (notice the verbs) different from that of the first twenty lines of the poem?

6. This poem is sometimes read as a vigorous but simple celebration of flesh. Is there more to the theme than that?

PERSPECTIVE

BERNARD DUYFHUIZEN (B. 1953)

"To His Coy Mistress": On How a Female Might Respond   1988

Clearly a female reader of "To His Coy Mistress" might have trouble identifying with the poem's speaker; therefore, her first response would be to identify with the listener-in-the-poem, the eternally silent Coy Mistress. In such a reading she is likely to recognize that she has heard this kind of line before although maybe not with the same intensity and insistence. Moreover, she is likely to (re)experience the unsettling emotions that such an egoistic assault on her virginal autonomy would provoke. She will also see differently, even by contemporary standards, the plot beyond closure, the possible consequences — both physical and social — that the Mistress will encounter. Lastly, she is likely to be angered by this poem, by her marginalization in an argument that seeks to overpower the core of her being.

From "Textual Harassment of Marvell's Coy Mistress:
The Institutionalization of Masculine Criticism,"
College English, April 1988

CONSIDERATIONS FOR CRITICAL THINKING AND WRITING

1. Explain whether you find convincing Duyfhuizen's description of a female's potential response to the poem. How does his description compare with your own response?

2. Characterize the silent mistress of the poem. How do you think the speaker treats her? What do his language and tone suggest about his relationship to her?

3. Does the fact that this description of a female response is written by a man make any difference in your assessment of it? Explain why or why not.

The third in this series of *carpe diem* poems is a twentieth century work. The language of Wilbur's "A Late Aubade" is more immediately accessible than that of Marvell's "To His Coy Mistress"; a dictionary will quickly identify any words unfamiliar to a reader, including the allusion to Arnold Schoenberg, the composer, in line 11. An *allusion* is a brief reference to a person, place, thing, event, or idea in history or literature. Allusive words, like connotative words, are both suggestive and economical; poets use allusions to conjure up biblical authority, scenes from Shakespeare's plays, historic figures, wars, great love stories, and anything else that might serve to deepen and enrich their own work. The speaker in "A Late Aubade" makes an allusion that an ordinary dictionary won't explain. He tells his lover: "I need not rehearse / The rosebuds-theme of centuries of verse." True to his word, he says no more about this for her or the reader. The lines refer, of course, to the *carpe diem* theme as found familiarly in Herrick's "To the Virgins, to Make Much of Time." Wilbur assumes that his reader will understand the allusion.

Allusions imply reading and cultural experiences shared by the poet and reader. Literate audiences once had more in common than they do today because more people had similar economic, social, and educational backgrounds. But a judicious use of specialized dictionaries, encyclopedias, and other reference tools can help you decipher allusions that grow out of this body of experience. (See page 559 for a list of useful reference works for students of literature.) As you read more, you'll be able to make connections based on your own experiences with literature. In a sense, allusions make available what other human beings have deemed worth remembering, and that is certainly an economical way of supplementing and enhancing your own experience.

Wilbur's version of the *carpe diem* theme follows. What strikes you as particularly modern about it?

Richard Wilbur (b. 1921)

A Late Aubade   *1968*

You could be sitting now in a carrel
Turning some liver-spotted page,
Or rising in an elevator-cage
Toward Ladies' Apparel.

You could be planting a raucous bed   5
Of salvia, in rubber gloves,
Or lunching through a screed of someone's loves
With pitying head,

Or making some unhappy setter
Heel, or listening to a bleak   10
Lecture on Schoenberg's serial technique.
Isn't this better?

Think of all the time you are not
Wasting, and would not care to waste,
Such things, thank God, not being to your taste.   15
Think what a lot

Of time, by woman's reckoning,
You've saved, and so may spend on this,

You who had rather lie in bed and kiss
Than anything.   20

It's almost noon, you say? If so,
Time flies, and I need not rehearse
The rosebuds-theme of centuries of verse.
If you *must* go,

Wait for a while, then slip downstairs   25
And bring us up some chilled white wine,
And some blue cheese, and crackers, and some fine
Ruddy-skinned pears.

CONSIDERATIONS FOR CRITICAL THINKING AND WRITING

1. FIRST RESPONSE. Explain whether or not you find the speaker appealing.

2. An *aubade* is a song about lovers parting at dawn, but in this "late aubade,"
   "It's almost noon." Is there another way of reading the adjective *late* in the
   title?

3. How does the speaker's diction characterize both him and his lover? What
   sort of lives do they live? What does the casual allusion to Herrick's poem
   (line 23) reveal about them?

4. What is the effect of using "liver-spotted page," "elevator-cage," "raucous
   bed," "screed," "unhappy setter," and "bleak / Lecture" to describe the
   woman's activities?

CONNECTIONS TO OTHER SELECTIONS

1. How does the man's argument in "A Late Aubade" differ from the speakers'
   in Herrick's and Marvell's poems? Which of the three arguments do you
   find most convincing?

2. Explain how the tone of each poem is suited to its theme.

This fourth love poem is by a woman. Listen to the speaker's voice. Does
it sound different from the way the men speak in the previous three poems?

DIANE ACKERMAN (B. 1948)

A Fine, a Private Place   *1983*

He took her one day
under the blue horizon
where long sea fingers
parted like beads
hitched in the doorway   5
of an opium den,
and canyons mazed the deep
reef with hollows,
cul-de-sacs, and narrow boudoirs,
and had to ask twice   10
before she understood

his stroking her arm
with a marine feather
slobbery as aloe pulp
was wooing, or saw the octopus   15
in his swimsuit
stretch one tentacle
and ripple its silky bag.

While bubbles rose
like globs of mercury,   20
they made love
mask to mask, floating
with oceans of air between them,
she his sea-geisha
in an orange kimono   25
of belts and vests,
her lacquered hair waving,
as Indigo Hamlets
tattooed the vista,
and sunlight   30
cut through the water,
twisting its knives
into corridors of light.

His sandy hair
and sea-blue eyes,   35
his kelp-thin waist
and chest ribbed wider
than a sandbar
where muscles domed
clear and taut as shells   40
(freckled cowries,
flat, brawny scallops
the color of dawn),
his sea-battered hands
gripping her thighs   45
like tawny starfish
and drawing her close
as a pirate vessel
to let her board:
who was this she loved?   50

Overhead, sponges
sweating raw color
jutted from a coral arch,
Clown Wrasses°   *brightly colored tropical fish*
hovered like fireworks,   55
and somewhere an abalone opened
its silver wings.
Part of a lusty dream
under aspic, her hips rolled
like a Spanish galleon,   60

her eyes swam
and chest began to heave.
Gasps melted on the tide.
Knowing she would soon be
breathless as her tank,   65
he pumped his brine
deep within her,
letting sea water drive it
through petals
delicate as anemone veils   70
to the dark purpose
of a conch-shaped womb.
An ear to her loins
would have heard the sea roar.

When panting ebbed,   75
and he signaled *Okay?*
as lovers have asked,
land or waterbound
since time heaved ho,
he led her to safety: 80
shallower realms,
heading back toward
the boat's even keel,
though ocean still petted her
cell by cell, murmuring   85
along her legs and neck,
caressing her
with pale, endless arms.

Later, she thought often
of that blue boudoir,   90
pillow-soft and filled
with cascading light,
where together
they'd made a bell
that dumbly clanged   95
beneath the waves
and minutes lurched
like mountain goats.
She could still see
the quilted mosaics   100
that were fish
twitching spangles overhead,
still feel the ocean
inside and out, turning her
evolution around.   105

She thought of it miles
and fathoms away, often,
at odd moments: watching
the minnow snowflakes

dip against the windowframe,   110
holding a sponge
idly under tap-gush,
sinking her teeth
into the cleft
of a voluptuous peach.   115

Considerations for Critical Thinking and Writing

1. FIRST RESPONSE. How is your response to this poem affected by the fact
that the speaker is female?

2. Read Marvell's "To His Coy Mistress" (p. 65). To what in Marvell's poem
does Ackerman's title allude? Explain how the allusion to Marvell is crucial
to understanding Ackerman's poem.

3. Comment on the descriptive passages of "A Fine, a Private Place." Which
images seem especially vivid to you? How do they contribute to the poem's
meanings?

4. What are the speaker's reflections on her experience in lines 106–115? What
echoes of Marvell do you hear in these lines?

Connections to Other Selections

1. Write an essay comparing the tone of Ackerman's poem with that of Mar-
vell's "To His Coy Mistress." To what extent are the central ideas in the
poems similar?

2. Compare the speaker's voice in Ackerman's poem with the voice you imag-
ine for the coy mistress in Marvell's poem.

POEMS FOR FURTHER STUDY

Margaret Atwood (b. 1939)

Bored   *1995*

All those times I was bored
out of my mind. Holding the log
while he sawed it. Holding
the string while he measured, boards,
distances between things, or pounded   5
stakes into the ground for rows and rows
of lettuces and beets, which I then (bored)
weeded. Or sat in the back
of the car, or sat still in boats,
sat, sat, while at the prow, stern, wheel   10
he drove, steered, paddled. It
wasn't even boredom, it was looking,
looking hard and up close at the small
details. Myopia. The worn gunwales,
the intricate twill of the seat   15
cover. The acid crumbs of loam, the granular
pink rock, its igneous veins, the sea-fans

of dry moss, the blackish and then the greying
bristles on the back of his neck.
Sometimes he would whistle, sometimes   20
I would. The boring rhythm of doing
things over and over, carrying
the wood, drying
the dishes. Such minutiae. It's what
the animals spend most of their time at,   25
ferrying the sand, grain by grain, from their tunnels,
shuffling the leaves in their burrows. He pointed
such things out, and I would look
at the whorled texture of his square finger, earth under
the nail. Why do I remember it as sunnier   30
all the time then, although it more often
rained, and more birdsong?
I could hardly wait to get
the hell out of there to
anywhere else. Perhaps though   35
boredom is happier. It is for dogs or
groundhogs. Now I wouldn't be bored.
Now I would know too much.
Now I would know.

CONSIDERATIONS FOR CRITICAL THINKING AND WRITING

1. FIRST RESPONSE. Atwood has described this poem as one of several about
   her father and his death. Is it possible to determine that "he" is the
   speaker's father from the details of the poem? Explain whether or not you
   think it matters who "he" is.

2. Play with the possible meanings of the word "bored" and its variations in
   the poem. What function does the repetition of the word serve?

3. What does the speaker "know" at the end of the poem that she didn't before?

CONNECTION TO ANOTHER SELECTION

1. Write an essay on the speaker's attitude toward the father in this poem and
   in Hayden's "Those Winter Sundays" (p. 10).

THOMAS HARDY (1840–1928)
The Convergence of the Twain   1912

Lines on the Loss of the "Titanic"°

I
      In a solitude of the sea
      Deep from human vanity,
And the Pride of Life that planned her, stilly couches she.

Titanic: A luxurious ocean liner, reputed to be unsinkable, which sank after hitting an ice-
berg on its maiden voyage in 1912. Only a third of the 2,200 passengers survived.

II
>   Steel chambers, late the pyres
>   Of her salamandrine fires,°   5
> Cold currents thrid,° and turn to rhythmic tidal lyres.   *thread*

III
>   Over the mirrors meant
>   To glass the opulent
> The sea-worm crawls — grotesque, slimed, dumb, indifferent.

IV
>   Jewels in joy designed   10
>   To ravish the sensuous mind
> Lie lightless, all their sparkles bleared and black and blind.

V
>   Dim moon-eyed fishes near
>   Gaze at the gilded gear
> And query: "What does this vaingloriousness down here?"   15

VI
>   Well: while was fashioning
>   This creature of cleaving wing,
> The Immanent Will that stirs and urges everything

VII
>   Prepared a sinister mate
>   For her — so gaily great —   20
> A Shape of Ice, for the time far and dissociate.

VIII
>   And as the smart ship grew
>   In stature, grace, and hue,
> In shadowy silent distance grew the Iceberg too.

IX
>   Alien they seemed to be: 25
>   No mortal eye could see
> The intimate welding of their later history,

X
>   Or sign that they were bent
>   By paths coincident
> On being anon twin halves of one august event,   30

XI
>   Till the Spinner of the Years
>   Said "Now!" And each one hears,
> And consummation comes, and jars two hemispheres.

---

5 *salamandrine fires:* Salamanders were, according to legend, able to survive fire; hence, the ship's fires burned even though under water.

CONSIDERATIONS FOR CRITICAL THINKING AND WRITING

1. FIRST RESPONSE. Describe a contemporary disaster comparable to the *Titanic*. How was your response to it similar to or different from the speaker's response to the *Titanic*?

2. How do the words used to describe the ship in this poem reveal the speaker's attitude toward the *Titanic*?

3. The diction of the poem suggests that the *Titanic* and the iceberg participate in something like an arranged marriage. What specific words imply this?

4. Who or what causes the disaster? Does the speaker assign responsibility?

DAVID R. SLAVITT (B. 1935)

Titanic   *1983*

Who does not love the *Titanic*?
If they sold passage tomorrow for that same crossing,
who would not buy?

To go down . . . We all go down, mostly
alone. But with crowds of people, friends, servants,   5
well fed, with music, with lights! Ah!

And the world, shocked, mourns, as it ought to do
and almost never does. There will be the books and movies
to remind our grandchildren who we were
and how we died, and give them a good cry.   10

Not so bad, after all. The cold
water is anesthetic and very quick.
The cries on all sides must be a comfort.

We all go: only a few, first-class.

CONSIDERATIONS FOR CRITICAL THINKING AND WRITING

1. FIRST RESPONSE. What, according to the speaker in this poem, is so compelling about the *Titanic*? Do you agree?

2. Discuss the speaker's tone. Why would it be inaccurate to describe it as solemn and mournful?

3. What is the effect of the poem's final line? What emotions does it produce in you?

CONNECTIONS TO OTHER SELECTIONS

1. How does "Titanic" differ in its attitude toward opulence from "The Convergence of the Twain" (p. 73)?

2. Which poem, "Titanic" or "The Convergence of the Twain," is more emotionally satisfying to you? Explain why.

3. Compare the speakers' tones in "Titanic" and "The Convergence of the Twain."

4. Hardy wrote his poem in 1912, the year the *Titanic* went down, but Slavitt wrote his more than seventy years later. How do you think Slavitt's poem would have been received if it had been published in 1912? Write an essay explaining why you think what you do.

LIONEL JOHNSON (1867–1902)

A Decadent's Lyric

1897

Sometimes, in very joy of shame,
Our flesh becomes one living flame:
And she and I
Are no more separate, but the same.

Ardour and agony unite;   5
Desire, delirium, delight:
And I and she
Faint in the fierce and fevered night.

Her body music is: and ah,
The accords of lute and viola!   10
When she and I
Play on live limbs love's opera!

CONSIDERATIONS FOR CRITICAL THINKING AND WRITING

1. FIRST RESPONSE. Comment on the title. To what extent do you think the title captures the tone of the poem?

2. What does the speaker mean by using the phrase "joy of shame" to characterize the couple's passion?

3. Read the poem aloud. How do the sounds of the lines contribute to its effects?

CONNECTION TO ANOTHER SELECTION

1. Discuss the views of sexuality presented in this poem and in the following poem, "Sex without Love," by Sharon Olds.

SHARON OLDS (B. 1942)

Sex without Love

1984

How do they do it, the ones who make love
without love? Beautiful as dancers,
gliding over each other like ice skaters
over the ice, fingers hooked
inside each other's bodies, faces   5
red as steak, wine, wet as the
children at birth whose mothers are going to

give them away. How do they come to the
come to the   come to the   God   come to the
still waters, and not love   10
the one who came there with them, light
rising slowly as steam off their joined
skin? These are the true religious,
the purists, the pros, the ones who will not
accept a false Messiah, love the   15
priest instead of the God. They do not
mistake the lover for their own pleasure,
they are like great runners: they know they are alone
with the road surface, the cold, the wind,
the fit of their shoes, their over-all cardio-   20
vascular health — just factors, like the partner
in the bed, and not the truth, which is the
single body alone in the universe
against its own best time.

CONSIDERATIONS FOR CRITICAL THINKING AND WRITING

1. FIRST RESPONSE. What is the nature of the question asked by the speaker in
   the poem's first two lines? What is being asked here?
2. What is the effect of describing the lovers as athletes? How do these de-
   scriptions and phrases reveal the speaker's tone toward the lovers?
3. To what extent does the title suggest the central meaning of this poem? Try
   to create some alternative titles that are equally descriptive.

CONNECTIONS TO OTHER SELECTIONS

1. How does the treatment of sex and love in Olds's poem compare with that
   in Cummings's "she being Brand" (p. 57)?
2. Just as Olds describes sex without love, she implies a definition of love in
   this poem. Consider whether the lovers in Wilbur's "A Late Aubade" (p. 68)
   fall within Olds's definition.

CATHY SONG (B. 1955)

The Youngest Daughter   *1983*

The sky has been dark
for many years.
My skin has become as damp
and pale as rice paper
and feels the way   5
mother's used to before the drying sun
parched it out there in the fields.

Lately, when I touch myself,
my hands react as if

I had just touched something 10
hot enough to burn.
My skin, aspirin-colored,
tingles with migraine. Mother
has been massaging the left side of my face
especially in the evenings 15
when it flares up.

This morning
her breathing was graveled,
her voice gruff with affection
when I took her into the bath. 20
She was in good humor,
making jokes about her great breasts,
floating in the milky water
like two walruses,
flaccid and whiskered around the nipples. 25
I scrubbed them with a sour taste
in my mouth, thinking:
six children and an old man
have sucked from these brown nipples.

I was almost tender 30
when I came to the blue bruises
that freckle her body,
places where she has been injecting insulin
for thirty years, ever since
I can remember. I soaped her slowly, 35
she sighed deeply, her eyes closed.

In the afternoons
when she has rested,
she prepares our ritual of tea and rice,
garnished with a shred of gingered fish, 40
a slice of pickled turnip
a token for my white body.
We eat in the familiar silence.
She knows I am not to be trusted,
even now planning my escape. 45
As I toast to her health
with the tea she has poured,
a thousand cranes curtain the window,
fly up in a sudden breeze.

CONSIDERATIONS FOR CRITICAL THINKING AND WRITING

1. FIRST RESPONSE. Though the speaker is the youngest daughter in the family, how old do you think she is based on the description of her in the poem? What, specifically, makes you think so?

2. How would you characterize the relationship between mother and daughter? How are lines 44–45 ("She knows I am not to be trusted, / even now planning my escape.") particularly revealing of the nature of the relationship?

3. Interpret the final four lines of the poem. Why do you think it ends with this image?

JOHN KEATS (1795–1821)

Ode on a Grecian Urn   *1819*

I

Thou still unravished bride of quietness,
   Thou foster-child of silence and slow time,
Sylvan° historian, who canst thus express
   A flowery tale more sweetly than our rhyme:
What leaf-fringed legend haunts about thy shape   5
    Of deities or mortals, or of both,
      In Tempe or the dales of Arcady?°
What men or gods are these? What maidens loath?
    What mad pursuit? What struggle to escape?
      What pipes and timbrels? What wild ecstasy?   10

II

Heard melodies are sweet, but those unheard
   Are sweeter; therefore, ye soft pipes, play on;
Not to the sensual ear, but, more endeared,
   Pipe to the spirit ditties of no tone:
Fair youth, beneath the trees, thou canst not leave   15
    Thy song, nor ever can those trees be bare;
      Bold Lover, never, never canst thou kiss,
Though winning near the goal — yet, do not grieve;
    She cannot fade, though thou hast not thy bliss,
      For ever wilt thou love, and she be fair!   20

III

Ah, happy, happy boughs! that cannot shed
   Your leaves, nor ever bid the Spring adieu;
And, happy melodist, unwearièd,
   For ever piping songs for ever new;
More happy love! more happy, happy love!   25
    For ever warm and still to be enjoyed,
      For ever panting, and for ever young;
All breathing human passion far above,
    That leaves a heart high-sorrowful and cloyed,
      A burning forehead, and a parching tongue.   30

IV

Who are these coming to the sacrifice?
   To what green altar, O mysterious priest,

---

3 *Sylvan:* Rustic. The urn is decorated with a forest scene.   7 *Tempe, Arcady:* Beautiful rural valleys in Greece.

Lead'st thou that heifer lowing at the skies,
  And all her silken flanks with garlands drest?
What little town by river or sea shore,   35
  Or mountain-built with peaceful citadel,
    Is emptied of this folk, this pious morn?
And, little town, thy streets for evermore
  Will silent be; and not a soul to tell
    Why thou art desolate, can e'er return.   40

  V
O Attic° shape! Fair attitude! with brede°
  Of marble men and maidens overwrought,
With forest branches and the trodden weed;
  Thou, silent form, dost tease us out of thought
As doth eternity: Cold Pastoral!   45
  When old age shall this generation waste,
    Thou shalt remain, in midst of other woe
Than ours, a friend to man, to whom thou say'st,
  Beauty is truth, truth beauty — that is all
    Ye know on earth, and all ye need to know.   50

41 *Attic:* Possessing classic Athenian simplicity; *brede:* Design.

Considerations for Critical Thinking and Writing

1. FIRST RESPONSE. What does the speaker's diction reveal about his attitude toward the urn in this ode? Does his view develop or change?

2. How is the happiness in stanza III related to the assertion in lines 11–12 that "Heard melodies are sweet, but those unheard / Are sweeter"?

3. What is the difference between the world depicted on the urn and the speaker's world?

4. What do lines 49 and 50 suggest about the relation of art to life? Why is the urn described as a "Cold Pastoral" (line 45)?

5. Which world does the speaker seem to prefer, the urn's or his own?

6. Describe the overall tone of the poem.

Connections to Other Selections

1. Write an essay comparing the view of time in this ode with that in Marvell's "To His Coy Mistress" (p. 65). Pay particular attention to the connotative language in each poem.

2. Discuss the treatment and meaning of love in this ode and in Richard Wilbur's "Love Calls Us to the Things of This World" (p. 643).

3. Compare the tone and attitude toward life in this ode with those in John Keats's "To Autumn" (p. 109).

GWENDOLYN BROOKS (1917–2000)

We Real Cool   *1960*

The Pool Players.
Seven at the Golden Shovel.

We real cool. We
Left school. We

Lurk late. We   5
Strike straight. We

Sing sin. We
Thin gin. We

Jazz June. We
Die soon.   10

CONSIDERATIONS FOR CRITICAL THINKING AND WRITING

1. FIRST RESPONSE. How does the speech of the pool players in this poem help
   to characterize them? What is the effect of the pronouns coming at the
   ends of the lines? How would the poem sound if the pronouns came at the
   beginnings of lines?

2. What is the author's attitude toward the players? Is there a change in tone
   in the last line?

3. How is the pool hall's name related to the rest of the poem and its theme?

ERIC ORMSBY (B. 1941)

Nose   *1997*

The nose is antithetical. It sniffs,
snuffles, wallows in sneezes, then recoils
in Roman nobility, profile-proud;
pampers its fleshy shadow in bas-
reliefs; or is serenely alcoved within   5
rotunda where the chiseled light
dapples its expansive flanges.
                          Nose
is tuberous, rootlike, with subsoil
affinities, has its own mossy   10
aromas, feels bulbous as corms or
crimped as rhizomes but, even so,
stands graced with little wings above
the harbored nostrils.
                  The nose   15
sunders the face in symmetry,
bisects us in hemispheres where selves

negotiate along the boundary lines
of smiles or scowls.
                              All night,   20
in the snug bed of the face,
the nose exults.

CONSIDERATIONS FOR CRITICAL THINKING AND WRITING

1. FIRST RESPONSE. What do you think is the speaker's attitude toward the nose?
2. In what ways is the nose "antithetical"?
3. Discuss the speaker's diction and its effect on your reading of the poem. What words or phrases are particularly effective? How?
4. Look up *exults* in the dictionary. Why is it just right in the final line?

CONNECTION TO ANOTHER SELECTION

1. Compare the central idea of the "Nose" with "The Larynx," the next poem by Alice Jones. Which poem do you prefer? Why?

ALICE JONES (B. 1949)

The Larynx   *1993*

        Under the epiglottic flap
      the long-ringed tube sinks
    its shaft down to the bronchial
          fork, divides from two
    to four then infinite branches,   5
    each ending finally in a clump
        of transparent sacs knit
    with small vessels into a mesh
    that sponge-like soaks up breath
        and gives it off with a push   10
from the diaphragm's muscular wall,
      forces wind out of the lungs'
    wide tree, up through this organ's
      single pipe, through the puzzle
      box of gristle, where resonant   15
        plates of cartilage fold
          into shield, horns, bows,
          bound by odd half-spirals
      of muscles that modulate air
as it rises through this empty place   20
        at our core, where lip-like
    folds stretch across the vestibule,
    small and tough, they flutter,
      bend like birds' wings finding
        just the right angle to stay   25

airborne; here the cords arch
in the hollow of this ancient instrument,
    curve and vibrate to make a song.

CONSIDERATIONS FOR CRITICAL THINKING AND WRITING

1. FIRST RESPONSE. What is the effect of having this poem written as one long
   sentence? How does the length of the sentence contribute to the poem's
   meaning?
2. Make a list of words and phrases from the poem that strike you as scientific,
   and compare those with a list of words that seem poetic. How do they com-
   pete or complement each other in terms of how they affect your reading?
3. Comment on the final three lines. How would your interpretation of this
   poem change if it ended before the semicolon in line 26?

CONNECTION TO ANOTHER SELECTION

1. Compare the diction and ending that Jones writes in "The Larynx" with
   those of "The Foot" (p. 208), another poem by Jones.

OLIVER RICE (B. 1921)

The Doll House   *1998*

Such authenticity may be more than cunning,
all this minuteness more than dear,
itsy highboy and ladderback,
bitsy tea set and banjo clock.
The figure in this teeny afghan,   5
the stick for this weeny candle
may be as credible as Ibsen's inkwell.°

    Stoop and enter this little milieu.
        An alertness hangs on the air.
        An anxiety rustles the light.   10
    Credulities nestle among the cushions.

In these rooms the very mores may lie in wait,
secret necessities and vulgar realities.

Here the rules may discover the game,

the self conceive a grace or splendor,   15

and love make its first mistake,

itty doilies on teensy upholstered arms,
bitty apples in weensy silver bowl.

---

7 *Ibsen's inkwell:* A reference to the Norwegian playwright Henrik Ibsen (1828–1906), who
wrote about the tensions of nineteenth-century middle-class marriage in *A Doll House* (1879).

CONSIDERATIONS FOR CRITICAL THINKING AND WRITING

1. FIRST RESPONSE. What do you think is the purpose of the childish diction in this poem?

2. Discuss the significance of the title and the reference to Ibsen. Why is an understanding of the allusion to Ibsen important for developing an interpretation of this poem? Is it possible to make sense of the poem without knowing anything about Ibsen? Explain.

3. Discuss what you take the meaning of line 14 to be: "Here the rules may discover the game."

LOUIS SIMPSON (B. 1923)

In the Suburbs

1963

There's no way out.
You were born to waste your life.
You were born to this middleclass life

As others before you
Were born to walk in procession
To the temple, singing.

CONSIDERATIONS FOR CRITICAL THINKING AND WRITING

1. FIRST RESPONSE. Is the title of this poem especially significant? What images does it conjure up for you?

2. What does the repetition in lines 2–3 suggest?

3. Discuss the possible connotative meanings of lines 5 and 6. Who are the "others before you"?

CONNECTION TO ANOTHER SELECTION

1. Write an essay on suburban life based on this poem and John Ciardi's "Suburban" (p. 161).

A NOTE ON READING TRANSLATIONS

Sometimes translation can inadvertently be a comic business. Consider, for example, the discovery made by John Steinbeck's wife, Elaine, when in a Yokohama bookstore she asked for a copy of her husband's famous novel *The Grapes of Wrath* and learned that it had been translated into Japanese as *Angry Raisins*. Close but no cigar (perhaps translated as: Nearby, yet no smoke). As amusing as that *Angry Raisins* title is, it teaches an important lesson about the significance of a poet's or a translator's choices when crafting a poem: a powerful piece moves us through diction and tone, both built word by careful word. Translations are frequently regarded as merely vehicular, a way to arrive at the original work. It is, of course, the original work — its spirit, style, and meaning — that most readers expect to find in a translation. Even so, it is important to understand that a translation is *by nature* different from the original — and that despite that difference, a fine translation can be an important part of the journey and become part of the literary landscape itself. Reading a translation of a poem is not the same as reading the original, but neither is watching two different performances of *Hamlet.* The translator provides a reading of the poem in much the same way that a director shapes the play. Each interprets the text from a unique perspective.

Basically, there are two distinct approaches to translation: literal translations and adaptations. A literal translation sets out to create a word-for-word equivalent that is absolutely faithful to the original. As simple and direct as this method may sound, literal translations are nearly impossible over extended passages because of the structural differences between languages. Moreover, the meaning of a single word in one language may not exist in another language, or it may require a phrase, clause, or entire sentence to capture its implications. Adaptations of works offer broader, more open-ended approaches to translation. Unlike a literal translation, an adaptation moves beyond denotative meanings in an attempt to capture the spirit of a work so that its idioms, dialects, slang, and other conventions are recreated in the language of the translation.

The question we ask of an adaptation should not be "Is this exactly how the original reads?" Instead, we ask "Is this an insightful, graceful rendering worth reading?" To translate poetry it is not enough to know the language of the original; it is also necessary that the translator be a poet. A translated poem is more than a collation of decisions based on dictionaries and grammars; it must also be poetry. However undefinable poetry may be, it is unmistakable in its intense use of language. Poems are not merely translated; they are savored.

Four Translations of a Poem by Sappho

Sappho, born about 630 B.C. and a native of the Greek island of Lesbos, is the author of a hymn to Aphrodite, the goddess of love and beauty in Greek myth. The four translations that follow suggest how widely translations can differ from one another. The first, by Henry T. Wharton, is intended to be a literal prose translation of the original Greek.

SAPPHO (C. 630 B.C.–C. 570 B.C.)

Immortal Aphrodite of the broidered throne   *date unknown*

TRANSLATED BY HENRY T. WHARTON (1885)

Immortal Aphrodite of the broidered throne, daughter of Zeus, weaver of wiles, I pray thee break not my spirit with anguish and distress, O Queen. But come hither, if ever before thou didst hear my voice afar, and listen, and leaving thy father's golden house camest with chariot yoked, and fair fleet sparrows drew thee, flapping fast their wings around the dark earth, from heaven through mid sky. Quickly arrived they; and thou, blessed one, smiling with immortal countenance, didst ask What now is befallen me, and Why now I call, and What I in my mad heart most desire to see. 'What Beauty now wouldst thou draw to love thee? Who wrongs thee, Sappho? For even if she flies she shall soon follow, and if she rejects gifts shall yet give, and if she loves not shall soon love, however loth.' Come, I pray thee, now too, and release me from cruel cares; and all that my heart desires to accomplish, accomplish thou, and be thyself my ally.

Beautiful-throned, immortal Aphrodite

TRANSLATED BY T. W. HIGGINSON (1871)

Beautiful-throned, immortal Aphrodite,
Daughter of Zeus, beguiler, I implore thee,
Weigh me not down with weariness and anguish
  O Thou most holy!

Come to me now, if ever thou in kindness   5
Hearkenedst my words, — and often hast thou
  hearkened —
Heeding, and coming from the mansions golden
  Of thy great Father,

Yoking thy chariot, borne by the most lovely   10
Consecrated birds, with dusky-tinted pinions,
Waving swift wings from utmost heights of
  heaven
   Through the mid-ether;

Swiftly they vanished, leaving thee, O goddess,   15
Smiling, with face immortal in its beauty,
Asking why I grieved, and why in utter longing
  I had dared call thee;

Asking what I sought, thus hopeless in desiring,
Wildered in brain, and spreading nets of   20
  passion —
Alas, for whom? and saidst thou, "Who has
  harmed thee?
   "O my poor Sappho!

"Though now he flies, ere long he shall pursue   25
  thee;
"Fearing thy gifts, he too in turn shall bring
  them;
"Loveless to-day, to-morrow he shall woo thee,
   "Though thou shouldst spurn him."   30

Thus seek me now, O holy Aphrodite!
Save me from anguish; give me all I ask for,
Gifts at thy hand; and thine shall be the glory,
    Sacred protector!

Invocation to Aphrodite

TRANSLATED BY RICHARD LATTIMORE (1955)

Throned in splendor, deathless, O Aphrodite,
child of Zeus, charm-fashioner, I entreat you
not with griefs and bitternesses to break my
    spirit, O goddess;

standing by me rather, if once before now   5
far away you heard, when I called upon you,
left your father's dwelling place and descended,
    yoking the golden

chariot to sparrows, who fairly drew you
down in speed aslant the black world, the bright   10
trembling at the heart to the pulse of countless
    fluttering wingbeats.

Swiftly then they came, and you, blessed lady,
smiling on me out of immortal beauty,
asked me what affliction was on me, why I   15
    called thus upon you,

what beyond all else I would have befall my
tortured heart: "Whom then would you have Per-
    suasion
force to serve desire in your heart? Who is it,   20
    Sappho, that hurt you?

Though she now escape you, she soon will follow;
though she take not gifts from you, she will give
    them:
though she love not, yet she will surely love you   25
    even unwilling."

In such guise come even again and set me
free from doubt and sorrow; accomplish all those
things my heart desires to be done; appear and
    stand at my shoulder.   30

Artfully adorned Aphrodite, deathless

TRANSLATED BY JIM POWELL (1993)

Artfully adorned Aphrodite, deathless
child of Zeus and weaver of wiles I beg you
please don't hurt me, don't overcome my spirit,
    goddess, with longing,

but come here, if ever at other moments   5
hearing these my words from afar you listened
and responded: leaving your father's house, all
    golden, you came then,

hitching up your chariot: lovely sparrows
drew you quickly over the dark earth, whirling   10
on fine beating wings from the heights of heaven
    down through the sky and

instantly arrived — and then O my blessed
goddess with a smile on your deathless face you
asked me what the matter was *this* time, what I   15
    called you for this time,

what I now most wanted to happen in my
raving heart: "Whom *this* time should I persuade to
lead you back again to her love? Who *now*, oh
    Sappho, who wrongs you?   20

If she flees you now, she will soon pursue you;
if she won't accept what you give, she'll give it;
if she doesn't love you, she'll love you soon now,
    even unwilling."

Come to me again, and release me from this   25
want past bearing. All that my heart desires to
happen — make it happen. And stand beside me,
    goddess, my ally.

CONSIDERATIONS FOR CRITICAL THINKING AND WRITING

1. FIRST RESPONSE. Try rewriting Wharton's prose version in contemporary language. How does your prose version differ in tone from Wharton's?
2. Explain which translation seems closest to Wharton's prose version.
3. Discuss the images and metaphors in Higginson's and Lattimore's versions. Which version is more appealing to you? Explain why.
4. How does Powell's use of language clearly make his version the most contemporary of the translations?

4

Images

POETRY'S APPEAL TO THE SENSES

A poet, to borrow a phrase from Henry James, is one of those on whom nothing is lost. Poets take in the world and give us impressions of what they experience through images. An **image** is language that addresses the senses. The most common images in poetry are visual; they provide verbal pictures of the poets' encounters — real or imagined — with the world. But poets also create images that appeal to our other senses. Richard Wilbur arouses several senses when he has the speaker in "A Late Aubade" (p. 68) gently urge his lover to linger in bed with him instead of getting on with her daily routines and obligations:

> Wait for a while, then slip downstairs
> And bring us up some chilled white wine,
> And some blue cheese, and crackers, and some fine
> Ruddy-skinned pears.

These images are simultaneously tempting and satisfying. We don't have to literally touch that cold, clear glass of wine (or will it come in a green bottle beaded with moisture?) or smell the cheese or taste the crackers to appreciate this vivid blend of colors, textures, tastes, and fragrances.

Images give us the physical world to experience in our imaginations. Some poems, like the following one, are written to do just that; they make no comment about what they describe.

WILLIAM CARLOS WILLIAMS (1883–1963)

Poem 1934

As the cat
climbed over
the top of

the jamcloset
first the right   5
forefoot

carefully
then the hind
stepped down

into the pit of   10
the empty
flowerpot

This poem defies paraphrase because it is all an image of agile move-
ment. No statement is made about the movement; the title, "Poem" —
really no title — signals Williams's refusal to comment on the movements.
To impose a meaning on the poem, we'd probably have to knock over the
flowerpot.

We experience the image in Williams's "Poem" more clearly because of
how the sentence is organized into lines and groups of lines, or stanzas.
Consider how differently the sentence is read if it is arranged as prose:

> As the cat climbed over the top of the jamcloset, first the right forefoot care-
> fully then the hind stepped down into the pit of the empty flowerpot.

The poem's line and stanza division transforms what is essentially an awk-
ward prose sentence into a rhythmic verbal picture. Especially when the poem
is read aloud, this line and stanza division allows us to feel the image we see.
Even the lack of a period at the end suggests that the cat is only pausing.

Images frequently do more than offer only sensory impressions, how-
ever. They also convey emotions and moods, as in the following poem.

JEANNETTE BARNES (B. 1956)

Battle-Piece 1999

Confederate monument, Ocean Pond, Olustee, Florida, 1864

Picknickers sojourn here an hour,
get their fill, get gone.
Seldom, they quickstep as far downhill
as this bivouac; they miss sting, snap,

grit in clenched teeth, carbine, cartridge,   5
cap, *hurrah boys*. Cannon-cracks
the peal, the clap of doom.

Into the billows, white, filthy,
choked by smoke, Clem, Eustace, Willy—
it would be useless to name names or call them all.   10

Anyway, that's done already. Every fall
sons of sons and reverent veterans' wives
lay wreaths, a prize of plastic daisies,

everlasting. Nobody calls this lazy.
It's August, and it's late, it's afternoon,   15
heat-mist glistens on slick granite, sun

fingers through sleek pines, their edges cropped
like the clipped elegant grass. It is a shock
to see a caisson blown

to flinders; a horse shrieks,   20
the mortar-shell zooms, spiral-
ripping tender belly. Oh, yes, here

are raked paths, cindered, sweet trees
and cool water. That whimper
you do not hear now was the doves,   25
spooning. Evening calls you all, eager

as spruce-gum-chewing, apple-filching boys
to pull one long last gulp of switchel
as if, now, somebody's sons had almost done

haying. Keen to victual, nearly home, feature the sharp   30
surprise when, smooth as oiled stone
stroking the clean edge of a scythe, these boys achieved
each his marble pillow, astonished by the sky.

Considerations for Critical Thinking and Writing

1. FIRST RESPONSE. Contrast the images used to describe the present moment at the battle site with the images used to describe the actual battle.
2. Describe the speaker's tone. What do the images reveal about the speaker's emotions?
3. Analyze the diction and images of the final stanza. What makes it so powerful?

What mood is established in this next poem's view of Civil War troops moving across a river?

WALT WHITMAN (1819–1892)

Cavalry Crossing a Ford 1865

A line in long array where they wind betwixt green islands,
They take a serpentine course, their arms flash in the sun — hark to the
     musical clank,
Behold the silvery river, in it the splashing horses loitering stop to drink,
Behold the brown-faced men, each group, each person, a picture, the
     negligent rest on the saddles,
Some emerge on the opposite bank, others are just entering the ford — while,
Scarlet and blue and snowy white,
The guidon flags flutter gaily in the wind.

CONSIDERATIONS FOR CRITICAL THINKING AND WRITING

1. FIRST RESPONSE. Do the colors and sounds establish the mood of this
   poem? What *is* the mood?
2. How would the poem's mood have been changed if Whitman had used
   "look" or "see" instead of "behold" (lines 3–4)?
3. Where is the speaker as he observes this troop movement?
4. Does "serpentine" in line 2 have an evil connotation in this poem? Explain
   your answer.

Whitman seems to capture momentarily all the troop's actions, and
through carefully chosen, suggestive details — really very few — he succeeds
in making "each group, each person, a picture." Specific details, even when
few are provided, give us the impression that we see the entire picture; it is as
if those are the details we would remember if we had viewed the scene our-
selves. Notice too that the movement of the "line in long array" is empha-
sized by the continuous winding syntax of the poem's lengthy lines.

    Movement is also central to the next poem, in which action and mo-
tion are created through carefully chosen verbs.

DAVID SOLWAY (B. 1941)

Windsurfing 1993

It rides upon the wrinkled hide
of water, like the upturned hull
of a small canoe or kayak
waiting to be righted — yet its law
is opposite to that of boats,   5
it floats upon its breastbone and
brings whatever spine there is to light.
A thin shaft is slotted into place.
Then a puffed right-angle of wind

pushes it forward, out into the bay,   10
where suddenly it glitters into speed,
tilts, knifes up, and for the moment's
nothing but a slim projectile
of cambered fiberglass,
peeling the crests.   15

           The man's
clamped to the mast, taut as a guywire.
Part of the sleek apparatus
he controls, immaculate nerve
of balance, plunge and curvet,   20
he clinches all component movements
into single motion.
It bucks, stalls, shudders, yaws, and dips
its hissing sides beneath the surface
that sustains it, tensing   25
into muscle that nude ellipse
of lunging appetite and power.

And now the mechanism's wholly
dolphin, springing toward its prey
of spume and beaded sunlight,   30
tossing spray, and hits the vertex
of the wide, salt glare of distance,
and reverses.

           Back it comes through
a screen of particles,   35
scalloped out of water, shimmer
and reflection, the wind snapping
and lashing it homeward,
shearing the curve of the wave,
breaking the spell of the caught breath   40
and articulate play of sinew, to enter
the haven of the breakwater
and settle in a rush of silence.

Now the crossing drifts
in the husk of its wake   45
and nothing's the same again
as, gliding elegantly on a film of water,
the man guides
his brash, obedient legend
into shore.   50

CONSIDERATIONS FOR CRITICAL THINKING AND WRITING

1. FIRST RESPONSE. Draw a circle around the verbs that seem especially effective in conveying a strong sense of motion, and explain why they are effective.

2. How is the man made to seem to be one with his board and sail?

3. How does the rhythm of the poem change beginning with line 45?

1. Consider the effects of the images in "Windsurfing" and Ho's "A Beautiful Girl Combs Her Hair" (p. 43). In an essay explain how these images produce emotional responses in you.

2. Compare the descriptions in "Windsurfing" and Bishop's "The Fish" (p. 20). How does each poet appeal to your senses to describe windsurfing and fishing?

"Windsurfing" is awash with images of speed, fluidity, and power. Even the calming aftermath of the breakwater is described as a "rush of silence," adding to the sense of motion that is detailed and expanded throughout the poem.

Poets choose details the way they choose the words to present those details: only telling ones will do. Consider the images Theodore Roethke uses in "Root Cellar."

THEODORE ROETHKE (1908–1963)

Root Cellar 1948

Nothing would sleep in that cellar, dank as a ditch,
Bulbs broke out of boxes hunting for chinks in the dark,
Shoots dangled and drooped,
Lolling obscenely from mildewed crates,
Hung down long yellow evil necks, like tropical snakes.   5
And what a congress of stinks!
Roots ripe as old bait,
Pulpy stems, rank, silo-rich,
Leaf-mold, manure, lime, piled against slippery planks.
Nothing would give up life: 10
Even the dirt kept breathing a small breath.

1. FIRST RESPONSE. Explain why you think this is a positive or negative rendition of a root cellar.

2. What senses are engaged by the images in this poem? Is the poem simply a series of sensations, or do the detailed images make some kind of point about the root cellar?

3. What controls the choice of details in the poem? Why isn't there, for example, a rusty shovel leaning against a dirt wall or a worn gardener's glove atop one of the crates?

4. Look up *congress* in a dictionary for its denotative meanings. Explain why "congress of stinks" is especially appropriate given the nature of the rest of the poem's imagery.

5. What single line in the poem suggests a theme?

The tone of the images and mood of the speaker are consistent in Roethke's "Root Cellar." In Matthew Arnold's "Dover Beach," however, they shift as the theme is developed.

MATTHEW ARNOLD (1822–1888)

Dover Beach   *1867*

The sea is calm tonight.
The tide is full, the moon lies fair
Upon the straits; — on the French coast the light
Gleams and is gone; the cliffs of England stand,
Glimmering and vast, out in the tranquil bay.   5
Come to the window, sweet is the night-air!
Only, from the long line of spray
Where the sea meets the moon-blanched land,
Listen! you hear the grating roar
Of pebbles which the waves draw back, and fling,   10
At their return, up the high strand,
Begin, and cease, and then again begin,
With tremulous cadence slow, and bring
The eternal note of sadness in.

Sophocles long ago   15
Heard it on the Aegean, and it brought
Into his mind the turbid ebb and flow
Of human misery;° we
Find also in the sound a thought,
Hearing it by this distant northern sea.   20

The Sea of Faith
Was once, too, at the full, and round earth's shore
Lay like the folds of a bright girdle furled.
But now I only hear
Its melancholy, long, withdrawing roar,   25
Retreating, to the breath
Of the night-wind, down the vast edges drear
And naked shingles° of the world.   *pebble beaches*

Ah, love, let us be true
To one another! for the world, which seems   30
To lie before us like a land of dreams,
So various, so beautiful, so new,
Hath really neither joy, nor love, nor light,
Nor certitude, nor peace, nor help for pain;

15–18 *Sophocles . . . misery:* In *Antigone* (lines 656–677), Sophocles likens the disasters that beset the house of Oedipus to a "mounting tide."

And we are here as on a darkling plain   35
Swept with confused alarms of struggle and flight,
Where ignorant armies clash by night.

CONSIDERATIONS FOR CRITICAL THINKING AND WRITING

1. FIRST RESPONSE. Discuss what you consider to be this poem's central point. How do the speaker's descriptions of the ocean work toward making that point?
2. Contrast the images in lines 4–8 and 9–13. How do they reveal the speaker's mood? To whom is he speaking?
3. What is the cause of the "sadness" in line 14? What is the speaker's response to the ebbing "Sea of Faith"? Is there anything to replace his sense of loss?
4. What details of the beach seem related to the ideas in the poem? How is the sea used differently in lines 1–14 and lines 21–28?
5. Describe the differences in tone between lines 1–8 and 35–37. What has caused the change?

CONNECTIONS TO OTHER SELECTIONS

1. Explain how the images in Wilfred Owen's "Dulce et Decorum Est" (p. 102) develop further the ideas and sentiments suggested by Arnold's final line concerning "ignorant armies clash[ing] by night."
2. Contrast Arnold's images with those of Anthony Hecht in his parody "The Dover Bitch" (p. 609). How do Hecht's images create a very different mood from that of "Dover Beach"?

Consider the poetic appetite for images displayed in the celebration of chile peppers in the following passionate poem.

JIMMY SANTIAGO BACA (B. 1952)

Green Chile   *1989*

I prefer red chile over my eggs
and potatoes for breakfast.
Red chile *ristras*° decorate my door,   *a braided string of peppers*
dry on my roof, and hang from eaves.
They lend open-air vegetable stands   5
historical grandeur, and gently swing
with an air of festive welcome.
I can hear them talking in the wind,
haggard, yellowing, crisp, rasping
tongues of old men, licking the breeze.   10

       But grandmother loves green chile.
When I visit her,
she holds the green chile pepper
in her wrinkled hands.

Ah, voluptuous, masculine,   15
an air of authority and youth simmers
from its swan-neck stem, tapering to a flowery
collar, fermenting resinous spice.
A well-dressed gentleman at the door
my grandmother takes sensuously in her hand,   20
rubbing its firm glossed sides,
caressing the oily rubbery serpent,
with mouth-watering fulfillment,
fondling its curves with gentle fingers.
Its bearing magnificent and taut   25
as flanks of a tiger in mid-leap,
she thrusts her blade into
and cuts it open, with lust
on her hot mouth, sweating over the stove,
bandanna round her forehead,   30
mysterious passion on her face
and she serves me green chile con carne
between soft warm leaves of corn tortillas,
with beans and rice — her sacrifice
to her little prince.   35
I slurp from my plate
with last bit of tortilla, my mouth burns
and I hiss and drink a tall glass of cold water.

All over New Mexico, sunburned men and women
drive rickety trucks stuffed with gunny-sacks   40
of green chile, from Belen, Veguita, Willard, Estancia,
San Antonio y Socorro, from fields
to roadside stands, you see them roasting green chile
in screen-sided homemade barrels, and for a dollar a bag,
we relive this old, beautiful ritual again and again.   45

CONSIDERATIONS FOR CRITICAL THINKING AND WRITING

1. FIRST RESPONSE. What's the difference between red and green chiles in this poem? Find the different images the speaker uses to draw a distinction between the two.

2. What kinds of images are used to describe the grandmother's preparation of green chile? What is the effect of those images?

3. Try writing a description — in poetry or prose — that uses vivid images to evoke a powerful response (either positive or negative) to a particular food.

POEMS FOR FURTHER STUDY

H. D. (HILDA DOOLITTLE/1886–1961)

Heat   *1916*

O wind, rend open the heat,
cut apart the heat,
rend it to tatters.

Fruit cannot drop
through this thick air —   5
fruit cannot fall into heat
that presses up and blunts
the points of pears
and rounds the grapes.

Cut the heat —   10
plough through it,
turning it on either side
of your path.

CONSIDERATIONS FOR CRITICAL THINKING AND WRITING

1. FIRST RESPONSE. Is this poem more about heat or fruit? Explain your answer.
2. What physical properties are associated with heat in this poem?
3. Explain the effect of the description of fruit in lines 4–9.
4. Why is the image of the cutting plow especially effective in lines 10–13?

MICHAEL COLLIER (B. 1953)

The Barber   *1995*

Even in death he roams the yard in his boxer shorts,
plowing the push-mower through bermuda grass,
bullying it against the fence and tree trunks,
chipping its twisted blades on the patio's edge.

The chalky flint and orange spark of struck concrete   5
floats in the air, tastes like metal, smells,
like the slow burn of hair on his electric clippers.
And smelling it, I feel the hot shoe of the shaver

as he guided it in a high arc around my ears,
then set the sharp toothy edge against my sideburns   10
to trim them square, and how he used his huge stomach
to butt the chair and his flat hand palming my head

to keep me still, pressing my chin down as he cleaned
the ragged wisps of hair along my neck.

A fat inconsolable man whose skill and pleasure   15
was to clip and shear, to make raw and stubble

all that grew in this world, expose the scalp,
the place of roots and nerves and make vulnerable,
there in the double mirrors of his shop, the long
stem-muscles of our necks. And so we hung below   20

his license in its cheap black frame, above the violet
light of the scissors shed with its glass jars
of germicide and the long tapered combs soaking
in its blue iridescence. Gruff when he wasn't silent,

he was a neighbor to fear, yet we trusted him   25
beyond his anger, beyond his privacy. He was like a father
we could hate, a foil for our unspent vengeance,
though vengeance was always his. He sent us back

into the world burning and itching, alive with the horror
of closing eyes in the pinkish darkness   30
of his shop and having felt the horse-hair brush, talc-filled,
cloying, too sweet for boyhood, whisked across the face.

CONSIDERATIONS FOR CRITICAL THINKING AND WRITING

1. FIRST RESPONSE. How does the speaker feel about the barber?

2. Which images do you think especially reveal the barber's character? How?
   How would *you* describe him?

3. How successful are the poem's images in evoking a sense of the barber-
   shop? What images in particular lend the poem a sense of the shop?

4. Comment on lines 26–27: "He was like a father / we could hate, a foil for our
   unspent vengeance." What is the speaker revealing about himself here?

CONNECTION TO ANOTHER SELECTION

1. Compare the treatment of the barber and barbershop in this poem with
   that of Stephen Perry's "Blue Spruce" (p. 135).

MARY ROBINSON (1758–1800)

London's Summer Morning   1806

Who has not wak'd to list° the busy sounds   *listen to*
Of summer's morning, in the sultry smoke
Of noisy London? On the pavement hot
The sooty chimney-boy, with dingy face
And tatter'd covering, shrilly bawls his trade,   5
Rousing the sleepy housemaid. At the door
The milk-pail rattles, and the tinkling bell
Proclaims the dustman's office; while the street

Is lost in clouds impervious. Now begins
The din of hackney-coaches, waggons, carts;   10
While tinmen's shops, and noisy trunk-makers,
Knife-grinders, coopers, squeaking cork-cutters,
Fruit-barrows, and the hunger-giving cries
Of vegetable venders, fill the air.
Now ev'ry shop displays its varied trade,   15
And the fresh-sprinkled pavement cools the feet
Of early walkers. At the private door
The ruddy housemaid twirls the busy mop,
Annoying the smart 'prentice, or neat girl,
Tripping with band-box° lightly. Now the sun   *hat box*   20
Darts burning splendour on the glitt'ring pane,
Save where the canvas awning throws a shade
On the gay merchandize. Now, spruce and trim,
In shops (where beauty smiles with industry,)
Sits the smart damsel; while the passenger   25
Peeps thro' the window, watching ev'ry charm.
Now pastry dainties catch the eye minute
Of humming insects, while the limy snare
Waits to enthral them. Now the lamp-lighter
Mounts the tall ladder, nimbly vent'rous,   30
To trim the half-fill'd lamp; while at his feet
The pot-boy° yells discordant! All along   *drink server*
The sultry pavement, the old-clothes-man cries
In tones monotonous, and side-long views
The area for his traffic: now the bag   35
Is slily open'd, and the half-worn suit
(Sometimes the pilfer'd treasure of the base
Domestic spoiler), for one half its worth,
Sinks in the green abyss. The porter now
Bears his huge load along the burning way;   40
And the poor poet wakes from busy dreams,
To paint the summer morning.

CONSIDERATIONS FOR CRITICAL THINKING AND WRITING

1. FIRST RESPONSE. How effective is this picture of a London summer morn-
   ing in 1806? Which images do you find particularly effective?
2. How does the end of the poem bring us full circle to its beginning? What
   effect does this structure have on your understanding of the poem?
3. Try writing about the start of your own day—in the dormitory, at home,
   the start of a class—using a series of images that provide a vivid sense of
   what happens and how you experience it.

CONNECTION TO ANOTHER SELECTION

1. How does Robinson's description of London differ from William Blake's
   "London," the next poem? What would you say is the essential difference in
   purpose between the two poems?

WILLIAM BLAKE (1757–1827)

London   1794

I wander through each chartered° street,   *defined by law*
Near where the chartered Thames does flow,
And mark in every face I meet
Marks of weakness, marks of woe.

In every cry of every man,   5
In every Infant's cry of fear,
In every voice, in every ban,
The mind-forged manacles I hear.

How the Chimney-sweeper's cry
Every black'ning Church appalls;   10
And the hapless Soldier's sigh
Runs in blood down Palace walls.

But most through midnight streets I hear
How the youthful Harlot's curse
Blasts the new-born Infant's tear,   15
And blights with plagues the Marriage hearse.

CONSIDERATIONS FOR CRITICAL THINKING AND WRITING

1. FIRST RESPONSE. What feelings do the visual images in this poem suggest to you?

2. What is the predominant sound heard in the poem?

3. What is the meaning of line 8? What is the cause of the problems that the speaker sees and hears in London? Does the speaker suggest additional causes?

4. The image in lines 11 and 12 cannot be read literally. Comment on its effectiveness.

5. How does Blake's use of denotative and connotative language enrich this poem's meaning?

6. An earlier version of Blake's last stanza appeared this way:

   > But most the midnight harlot's curse
   > From every dismal street I hear,
   > Weaves around the marriage hearse
   > And blasts the new-born infant's tear.

Examine carefully the differences between the two versions. How do Blake's revisions affect his picture of London life? Which version do you think is more effective? Why?

WILFRED OWEN (1893–1918)

Dulce et Decorum Est

1920

Bent double, like old beggars under sacks,
Knock-kneed, coughing like hags, we cursed through sludge,
Till on the haunting flares we turned our backs,
And towards our distant rest began to trudge.

Men marched asleep. Many had lost their boots,   5
But limped on, blood-shod. All went lame, all blind;
Drunk with fatigue; deaf even to the hoots
Of gas-shells dropping softly behind.

Gas! GAS! Quick, boys! — An ecstasy of fumbling,
Fitting the clumsy helmets just in time,   10
But someone still was yelling out and stumbling
And flound'ring like a man in fire or lime. —
Dim through the misty panes and thick green light,
As under a green sea, I saw him drowning.

In all my dreams before my helpless sight   15
He plunges at me, guttering, choking, drowning.

If in some smothering dreams, you too could pace
Behind the wagon that we flung him in,
And watch the white eyes writhing in his face,
His hanging face, like a devil's sick of sin,   20
If you could hear, at every jolt, the blood
Come gargling from the froth-corrupted lungs
Bitter as the cud
Obscene as cancer,
Of vile, incurable sores on innocent tongues, —   25
My friend, you would not tell with such high zest
To children ardent for some desperate glory,
The old lie: *Dulce et decorum est*
Pro patria mori.

CONSIDERATIONS FOR CRITICAL THINKING AND WRITING

1. FIRST RESPONSE. The Latin quotation in lines 27 and 28 is from Horace: "It is sweet and fitting to die for one's country." Owen served as a British soldier during World War I and was killed. Is this poem unpatriotic? What is its purpose?
2. Which images in the poem are most vivid? To which senses do they speak?
3. Describe the speaker's tone. What is his relationship to his audience?
4. How are the images of the soldiers in this poem different from the images that typically appear in recruiting posters?

SANDRA M. GILBERT (B. 1936)

Mafioso

1979

Frank Costello eating spaghetti in a cell at San Quentin,
Lucky Luciano mixing up a mess of bullets and
calling for parmesan cheese,
Al Capone baking a sawed-off shotgun into a
huge lasagna —   5
                    are you my uncles, my
only uncles?

          O Mafiosi,
bad uncles of the barren
cliffs of Sicily — was it only you   10
that they transported in barrels
like pure olive oil
across the Atlantic?

                    Was it only you
who got out at Ellis Island with   15
black scarves on your heads and cheap cigars
and no English and a dozen children?

No carts were waiting, gallant with paint,
no little donkeys plumed like the dreams of peacocks,
Only the evil eyes of a thousand buildings   20
stared across at the echoing debarcation center,
making it seem so much smaller than a piazza,

only a half dozen Puritan millionaires stood on the wharf,
in the wind colder than the impossible snows of the Abruzzi,
ready with country clubs and dynamos   25

to grind the organs out of you.

CONSIDERATIONS FOR CRITICAL THINKING AND WRITING

1. FIRST RESPONSE. In what sense are the gangsters Frank Costello, Lucky Lu-
   ciano, and Al Capone to be understood as "bad uncles"? How does the
   speaker, in particular, feel about the "uncles"?

2. Explain how nearly all the images in this poem are associated with Italian
   life. Does this poem reinforce stereotypes about Italians or invoke images
   about them for some other purpose? What other purpose?

3. What sort of people are the "Puritan millionaires"? What is their relation-
   ship to the "bad uncles"?

CONNECTION TO ANOTHER SELECTION

1. Discuss the ways in which ethnicity is used to create meaning in "Mafioso"
   and in Jimmy Santiago Baca's "Green Chile" (p. 96).

PATRICIA SMITH (B. 1955)

What It's Like to Be a Black Girl
(For Those of You Who Aren't)

1991

First of all, it's being 9 years old and
feeling like you're not finished, like your
edges are wild, like there's something,
everything, wrong. it's dropping food coloring
in your eyes to make them blue and suffering   5
their burn in silence. it's popping a bleached
white mophead over the kinks of your hair and
primping in front of the mirrors that deny your
reflection. it's finding a space between your
legs, a disturbance at your chest, and not knowing   10
what to do with the whistles. it's jumping
double dutch until your legs pop, it's sweat
and vaseline and bullets, it's growing tall and
wearing a lot of white, it's smelling blood in
your breakfast, it's learning to say fuck with   15
grace but learning to fuck without it, it's
flame and fists and life according to motown,
it's finally having a man reach out for you
then caving in
around his fingers.   20

CONSIDERATIONS FOR CRITICAL THINKING AND WRITING

1. FIRST RESPONSE. Describe the speaker's tone. What images in particular contribute to it? How do you account for it?
2. How does the speaker characterize her life? What elements of it does she focus on?
3. Discuss the poem's final image. What sort of emotions does it evoke in you?

JAMES DICKEY (1923–1997)

Deer Among Cattle

1981

Here and there in the searing beam
Of my hand going through the night meadow
They all are grazing

With pins of human light in their eyes.
A wild one also is eating   5
The human grass,

Slender, graceful, domesticated
By darkness, among the bred-
for-slaughter,

Having bounded their paralyzed fence   10
And inclined his branched forehead onto
Their green frosted table,

The only live thing in this flashlight
Who can leave whenever he wishes,
Turn grass into forest,   15

Foreclose inhuman brightness from his eyes
But stands here still, unperturbed,
In their wide-open country,

The sparks from my hand in his pupils
Unmatched anywhere among cattle,   20

Grazing with them the night of the hammer
As one of their own who shall rise.

CONSIDERATIONS FOR CRITICAL THINKING AND WRITING

1. FIRST RESPONSE. What images distinguish the deer from the cattle?
2. Do the words "domesticated" and "human" have positive or negative connotations in this poem? Explain your answer.
3. Discuss the possible implications of the last two lines. You may want to consider the speaker and his role in this tableau.

CONNECTION TO ANOTHER SELECTION

1. Discuss the idea of confinement in "Deer Among Cattle" and Rainer Maria Rilke's "The Panther" (below).

RAINER MARIA RILKE (1875–1926)

The Panther   1927

TRANSLATED BY STEPHEN MITCHELL

His vision, from the constantly passing bars,
has grown so weary that it cannot hold
anything else. It seems to him there are
a thousand bars; and behind the bars, no world.

As he paces in cramped circles, over and over,   5
the movement of his powerful soft strides
is like a ritual dance around a center
in which a mighty will stands paralyzed.

Only at times, the curtain of the pupils
lifts, quietly—. An image enters in,   10
rushes down through the tensed, arrested muscles,
plunges into the heart and is gone.

CONSIDERATIONS FOR CRITICAL THINKING AND WRITING

1. FIRST RESPONSE. Why do you think Rilke chooses a panther rather than, say, a lion as the subject of the poem's images?

2. What kind of "image enters in" the heart of the panther in the final stanza?

3. How are images of confinement achieved in the poem? Why doesn't Rilke describe the final image in lines 10–12?

CONNECTION TO ANOTHER SELECTION

1. Write an essay explaining how a sense of movement is achieved by the images and rhythms in this poem and in Dickinson's "A Bird came down the Walk—" (p. 173).

JANE KENYON (1947–1995)

The Blue Bowl   1990

Like primitives we buried the cat
with his bowl. Bare-handed
we scraped sand and gravel
back into the hole.
                    They fell with a hiss   5

and thud on his side,
on his long red fur, the white feathers
between his toes, and his
long, not to say aquiline, nose.

We stood and brushed each other off.   10
There are sorrows keener than these.

Silent the rest of the day, we worked,
ate, stared, and slept. It stormed
all night; now it clears, and a robin
burbles from a dripping bush   15
like the neighbor who means well
but always says the wrong thing.

CONSIDERATIONS FOR CRITICAL THINKING AND WRITING

1. FIRST RESPONSE. How do the descriptions of the cat—"the white feathers / between his toes"—affect your reading of the poem?

2. Why do you think Kenyon titles the poem "The Blue Bowl" rather than, perhaps, "The Cat's Bowl"?

3. What is the effect of being reminded that "There are sorrows keener than these"?

4. Why is the robin's song "the wrong thing"?

1. Write an essay comparing the death of this cat with the death of the dog in Updike's "Dog's Death" (p. 11). Which poem draws a more powerful response from you? Explain why.

SALLY CROFT (B. 1935)

Home-Baked Bread   *1981*

Nothing gives a household a greater sense of stability and common comfort than the aroma of cooling bread. Begin, if you like, with a loaf of whole wheat, which requires neither sifting nor kneading, and go on from there to more cunning triumphs.
       —*The Joy of Cooking*

What is it she is not saying?
Cunning triumphs. It rings
of insinuation. Step into my kitchen,
I have prepared a cunning triumph
for you. Spices and herbs   5
sealed in this porcelain jar,

a treasure of my great-aunt
who sat up past midnight
in her Massachusetts bedroom
when the moon was dark. Come,   10
rest your feet. I'll make
you tea with honey and slices

of warm bread spread with peach butter.
I picked the fruit this morning
still fresh with dew. The fragrance   15
is seductive? I hoped you would say that.
See how the heat rises
when the bread opens. Come,

we'll eat together, the small flakes
have scarcely any flavor. What cunning   20
triumphs we can discover in my upstairs room
where peach trees breathe their sweetness
beside the open window and
sun lies like honey on the floor.

CONSIDERATIONS FOR CRITICAL THINKING AND WRITING

1. FIRST RESPONSE. Why does the speaker in this poem seize on the phrase "cunning triumphs" from the *Joy of Cooking* excerpt?
2. Distinguish between the voice we hear in lines 1–3 and the second voice in lines 3–24. Who is the "you" in the poem?
3. Why is "insinuation" an especially appropriate word choice in line 3?

4. How do the images in lines 20–24 bring together all the senses evoked in the preceding lines?

5. Write a paragraph that describes the sensuous (and perhaps sensual) qualities of a food you enjoy.

ANN CHOI (B. 1969)

The Shower   *1991*

In the sixth grade
your hands were not much smaller
than they are now,
the reach between your thumb
and last finger not quite   5
an octave. You did not complain
and learned to choose
your music carefully.

Sharing noodles after school
in your house full of trophies,   10
we spoke of things expiring
without our knowledge. How time
quickens and wraps around us,
makes us women in bright clothes
caught by the permanence of the ring   15
around your finger.

I am your friend, accustomed
to your diligence.
Soon you will marry and fill
a house with sounds of dishes   20
and of children whose weight
you will gain and lose,
whose small fingers will separate
to play staccato,
one brief note after another.   25

CONSIDERATIONS FOR CRITICAL THINKING AND WRITING

1. FIRST RESPONSE. How does the speaker characterize her friend? Which images seem especially revealing?

2. Discuss the sense of time as it moves through the poem.

3. Do you think this is a sad or a celebratory poem? Explain why.

JOHN KEATS (1795–1821)

To Autumn

1819

I
Season of mists and mellow fruitfulness,
   Close bosom-friend of the maturing sun;
Conspiring with him how to load and bless
   With fruit the vines that round the thatch-eves run;
To bend with apples the mossed cottage-trees,   5
   And fill all fruit with ripeness to the core;
      To swell the gourd, and plump the hazel shells
   With a sweet kernel; to set budding more,
And still more, later flowers for the bees,
Until they think warm days will never cease,   10
      For summer has o'er-brimmed their clammy cells.

II
Who hath not seen thee oft amid thy store?
   Sometimes whoever seeks abroad may find
Thee sitting careless on a granary floor,
   Thy hair soft-lifted by the winnowing wind;   15
Or on a half-reaped furrow sound asleep,
   Drowsed with the fume of poppies, while thy hook°   *scythe*
      Spares the next swath and all its twinèd flowers:
And sometimes like a gleaner thou dost keep
   Steady thy laden head across a brook;   20
   Or by a cider-press, with patient look,
      Thou watchest the last oozings hours by hours.

III
Where are the songs of spring? Ay, where are they?
   Think not of them, thou hast thy music too,—
While barred clouds bloom the soft-dying day,   25
   And touch the stubble-plains with rosy hue;
Then in a wailful choir the small gnats mourn
   Among the river swallows,° borne aloft   *willows*
      Or sinking as the light wind lives or dies;
And full-grown lambs loud bleat from hilly bourn;°   *territory* 30
   Hedge-crickets sing; and now with treble soft
   The redbreast whistles from a garden-croft,
      And gathering swallows twitter in the skies.

CONSIDERATIONS FOR CRITICAL THINKING AND WRITING

1. FIRST RESPONSE. How is autumn made to seem like a person in each stanza of this ode?

2. Which senses are most emphasized in each stanza?

3. How is the progression of time expressed in the ode?

4. How does the imagery convey tone? Which words have particularly strong connotative values?

5. What is the speaker's view of death?

CONNECTIONS TO OTHER SELECTIONS

1. Compare this poem's tone and its perspective on death with those of Robert Frost's "After Apple-Picking" (p. 346).

2. Write an essay comparing the significance of the images of "mellow fruitfulness" (line 1) in "To Autumn" with that of the images of ripeness in Roethke's "Root Cellar" (p. 94). Explain how the images in each poem lead to very different feelings about the same phenomenon.

CHARLES SIMIC (B. 1938)

Filthy Landscape   *1999*

The season of lurid wildflowers
Strewn on the meadows
Drunk with kissing
The red-hot summer breezes.

A ditch opens its legs   5
In the half-undressed orchard
Teeming with foulmouthed birds
And smutty shadows.

Scandalous view of a hilltop
In pink clouds of debauchery.   10
The sun peeked between them
Now and then like a whoremaster.

CONSIDERATIONS FOR CRITICAL THINKING AND WRITING

1. FIRST RESPONSE. What do you think is the central point of this poem? Were you surprised by it? How does it differ from other poems about landscapes that you have read?

2. Describe the poem's images. How do they affect your response to this landscape?

3. How would you describe the tone of this description?

CONNECTION TO ANOTHER SELECTION

1. Discuss the use of images to evoke summer in "Filthy Landscape" and in "August" by Sophie Cabot Black (p. 125). How do the poems' images create very different perceptions of a summer landscape?

EZRA POUND (1885–1972)

In a Station of the Metro°   *1913*

The apparition of these faces in the crowd;
Petals on a wet, black bough.

Metro: Underground railroad in Paris.

CONSIDERATIONS FOR CRITICAL THINKING AND WRITING

1. FIRST RESPONSE. Why is the title essential for this poem?
2. What kind of mood does the image in the second line convey?
3. Why is "apparition" a better word choice than, say, "appearance" or "sight"?

CATHY SONG (B. 1955)

The White Porch   1983

I wrap the blue towel
after washing,
around the damp
weight of hair, bulky
as a sleeping cat,   5
and sit out on the porch.
Still dripping water,
it'll be dry by supper,
by the time the dust
settles off your shoes,   10
though it's only five
past noon. Think
of the luxury: how to use
the afternoon like the stretch
of lawn spread before me.   15
There's the laundry,
sun-warm clothes at twilight,
and the mountain of beans
in my lap. Each one,
I'll break and snap   20
thoughtfully in half.

But there is this slow arousal.
The small buttons
of my cotton blouse
are pulling away from my body.   25
I feel the strain of threads,
the swollen magnolias
heavy as a flock of birds
in the tree. Already,
the orange sponge cake   30
is rising in the oven.
I know you'll say it makes
your mouth dry
and I'll watch you
drench your slice of it   35
in canned peaches
and lick the plate clean.

So much hair, my mother
used to say, grabbing

the thick braided rope   40
in her hands while we washed
the breakfast dishes, discussing
dresses and pastries.
My mind often elsewhere
as we did the morning chores together.   45
Sometimes, a few strands
would catch in her gold ring.
I worked hard then,
anticipating the hour
when I would let the rope down   50
at night, strips of sheets,
knotted and tied,
while she slept in tight blankets.
My hair, freshly washed
like a measure of wealth,   55
like a bridal veil.
Crouching in the grass,
you would wait for the signal,
for the movement of curtains
before releasing yourself   60
from the shadow of moths.
Cloth, hair and hands,
smuggling you in.

CONSIDERATIONS FOR CRITICAL THINKING AND WRITING

1. FIRST RESPONSE. How is hair made erotic in this poem? Discuss the images that you deem especially effective.

2. Who is the "you" that the speaker refers to in each stanza?

3. What role does the mother play in this poem about desire?

4. Why do you think the poem is titled "The White Porch"?

CONNECTIONS TO OTHER SELECTIONS

1. Compare the images used to describe the speaker's "slow arousal" (line 22) in this poem with Croft's images in "Home-Baked Bread" (p. 107). What similarities do you see? What makes each description so effective?

2. Write an essay comparing the images of sensuality in this poem with those in Ho's "A Beautiful Girl Combs Her Hair" (p. 43). Which poem seems more erotic to you? Why?

PERSPECTIVE

T. E. HULME (1883–1917)

On the Differences between Poetry and Prose   1924

In prose as in algebra concrete things are embodied in signs or counters which are moved about according to rules, without being visualized at all in the process. There are in prose certain type situations and arrangements of words, which move as automatically into certain other arrangements as do functions in algebra. One only changes the X's and the Y's back into physical things at the end of the process. Poetry, in one aspect at any rate, may be considered as an effort to avoid this characteristic of prose. It is not a counter language, but a visual concrete one. It is a compromise for a language of intuition which would hand over sensations bodily. It always endeavors to arrest you, and to make you continuously see a physical thing, to prevent you gliding through an abstract process. It chooses fresh epithets and fresh metaphors, not so much because they are new, and we are tired of the old, but because the old cease to convey a physical thing and become abstract counters. A poet says a ship "coursed the seas" to get a physical image, instead of the counter word "sailed." Visual meanings can only be transferred by the new bowl of metaphor; prose is an old pot that lets them leak out. Images in verse are not mere decoration, but the very essence of an intuitive language. Verse is a pedestrian taking you over the ground, prose — a train which delivers you at a destination.

From "Romanticism and Classicism," in *Speculations*,
edited by Herbert Read

CONSIDERATIONS FOR CRITICAL THINKING AND WRITING

1. What distinctions does Hulme make between poetry and prose? Which seems to be the most important difference?

2. Write an essay that discusses Hulme's claim that poetry "is a compromise for a language of intuition which would hand over sensations bodily."

5

Figures of Speech

Figures of speech are broadly defined as a way of saying one thing in terms of something else. An overeager funeral director might, for example, be described as a vulture. Although figures of speech are indirect, they are designed to clarify, not obscure, our understanding of what they describe. Poets frequently use them because, as Emily Dickinson said, the poet's work is to "Tell all the Truth but tell it slant" to capture the reader's interest and imagination. But figures of speech are not limited to poetry. Hearing them, reading them, or using them is as natural as using language itself.

Suppose that in the middle of a class discussion concerning the economic causes of World War II your history instructor introduces a series of statistics by saying, "Let's get down to brass tacks." Would anyone be likely to expect a display of brass tacks for students to examine? Of course not. To interpret the statement literally would be to wholly misunderstand the instructor's point that the time has come for a close look at the economic circumstances leading to the war. A literal response transforms the statement into the sort of hilariously bizarre material often found in a sketch by Woody Allen.

The class does not look for brass tacks because, to put it in a nutshell, they understand that the instructor is speaking figuratively. They would understand, too, that in the preceding sentence "in a nutshell" refers to brevity and conciseness rather than to the covering of a kernel of a nut. Figurative language makes its way into our everyday speech and writing as well as into literature because it is a means of achieving color, vividness, and intensity.

Consider the difference, for example, between these two statements:

Literal: The diner strongly expressed anger at the waiter.
Figurative: The diner leaped from his table and roared at the waiter.

The second statement is more vivid because it creates a picture of ferocious anger by likening the diner to some kind of wild animal, such as a lion or tiger. By comparison, "strongly expressed anger" is neither especially strong nor especially expressive; it is flat. Not all figurative language avoids this kind of flatness, however. Figures of speech such as "getting down to brass tacks" and "in a nutshell" are clichés because they lack originality and freshness. Still, they suggest how these devices are commonly used to give language some color, even if that color is sometimes a bit faded.

There is nothing weak about William Shakespeare's use of figurative language in the following passage from *Macbeth*. Macbeth has just learned that his wife is dead, and he laments her loss as well as the course of his own life.

WILLIAM SHAKESPEARE (1564–1616)

From Macbeth *(Act V, Scene v)*   *1605–1606*

Tomorrow, and tomorrow, and tomorrow
Creeps in this petty pace from day to day
To the last syllable of recorded time;
And all our yesterdays have lighted fools
The way to dusty death. Out, out, brief candle!   5
Life's but a walking shadow, a poor player,
That struts and frets his hour upon the stage,
And then is heard no more. It is a tale
Told by an idiot, full of sound and fury,
Signifying nothing.   10

This passage might be summarized as "life has no meaning," but such a brief paraphrase does not take into account the figurative language that reveals the depth of Macbeth's despair and his view of the absolute meaninglessness of life. By comparing life to a "brief candle," Macbeth emphasizes the darkness and death that surround human beings. The light of life is too brief and unpredictable to be of any comfort. Indeed, life for Macbeth is a "walking shadow," futilely playing a role that is more farcical than dramatic, because life is, ultimately, a desperate story filled with pain and devoid of significance. What the figurative language provides, then, is the emotional force of Macbeth's assertion; his comparisons are disturbing because they are so apt.

The remainder of this chapter discusses some of the most important figures of speech used in poetry. A familiarity with them will help you to understand how poetry achieves its effects.

SIMILE AND METAPHOR

The two most common figures of speech are simile and metaphor. Both compare things that are ordinarily considered unlike each other. A *simile* makes an explicit comparison between two things by using words such as *like, as, than, appears,* or *seems:* "A sip of Mrs. Cook's coffee is like a punch in the stomach." The force of the simile is created by the differences between the two things compared. There would be no simile if the comparison were stated this way: "Mrs. Cook's coffee is as strong as the cafeteria's coffee." This is a literal comparison because Mrs. Cook's coffee is compared with something like it, another kind of coffee. Consider how simile is used in this poem.

MARGARET ATWOOD (B. 1939)

you fit into me   1971

you fit into me
like a hook into an eye

a fish hook
an open eye

If you blinked on a second reading, you got the point of this poem because you recognized that the simile "like a hook into an eye" gives way to a play on words in the final two lines. There the hook and eye, no longer a pleasant domestic image of fitting closely together, become a literal, sharp fishhook and a human eye. The wordplay qualifies the simile and drastically alters the tone of this poem by creating a strong and unpleasant surprise.

A **metaphor,** like a simile, makes a comparison between two unlike things, but it does so implicitly, without words such as *like* or *as:* "Mrs. Cook's coffee is a punch in the stomach." Metaphor asserts the identity of dissimilar things. Macbeth tells us that life *is* a "brief candle," life *is* "a walking shadow," life *is* "a poor player," life *is* "a tale / Told by an idiot." Metaphor transforms people, places, objects, and ideas into whatever the poet imagines them to be, and if metaphors are effective, the reader's experience, understanding, and appreciation of what is described are enhanced. Metaphors are frequently more demanding than similes because they are not signaled by particular words. They are both subtle and powerful.

Here is a poem about presentiment, a foreboding that something terrible is about to happen.

EMILY DICKINSON (1830–1886)

Presentiment — is that long Shadow —
on the lawn —   c. 1863

Presentiment — is that long Shadow — on the lawn —
Indicative that Suns go down —

The notice to the startled Grass
That Darkness — is about to pass —

The metaphors in this poem define the abstraction "Presentiment." The sense of foreboding that Dickinson expresses is identified with a particular moment, the moment when darkness is just about to envelop an otherwise tranquil ordinary scene. The speaker projects that fear onto the "startled Grass" so that it seems any life must be frightened by the approaching "Shadow" and "Darkness" — two richly connotative words associated with death. The metaphors obliquely tell us ("tell it slant" was Dickinson's motto, remember) that presentiment is related to a fear of death, and, more important, the metaphors convey the feelings that attend that idea.

Some metaphors are more subtle than others because their comparison of terms is less explicit. Notice the difference between the following two metaphors, both of which describe a shaggy derelict refusing to leave the warmth of a hotel lobby: "He was a mule standing his ground" is a quite explicit comparison. The man is a mule; X is Y. But this metaphor is much more covert: "He brayed his refusal to leave." This second version is an ***implied metaphor*** because it does not explicitly identify the man with a mule. Instead, it hints at or alludes to the mule. Braying is associated with mules and is especially appropriate in this context because of those animals' reputation for stubbornness. Implied metaphors can slip by readers, but they offer the alert reader the energy and resonance of carefully chosen, highly concentrated language.

Some poets write extended comparisons in which part or all of the poem consists of a series of related metaphors or similes. Extended metaphors are more common than extended similes. In "Catch" (p. 14), Francis creates an ***extended metaphor*** that compares poetry to a game of catch. The entire poem is organized around this comparison, just as all of the elements in Cummings's "she being Brand" (p. 57) are clustered around the extended comparison of a car and a woman. Because these comparisons are at work throughout the entire poem, they are called ***controlling metaphors.*** Extended comparisons can serve as a poem's organizing principle; they are also a reminder that in good poems metaphor and simile are not merely decorative but inseparable from what is expressed.

Notice the controlling metaphor in this poem, published posthumously by a woman whose contemporaries identified her more as a wife and mother than as a poet. Bradstreet's first volume of poetry, *The Tenth Muse,* was published by her brother-in-law in 1650 without her prior knowledge.

ANNE BRADSTREET   (c. 1612–1672)

The Author to Her Book   1678

Thou ill-formed offspring of my feeble brain,
Who after birth did'st by my side remain,
Till snatched from thence by friends, less wise than true,
Who thee abroad exposed to public view;

Made thee in rags, halting, to the press to trudge,   5
Where errors were not lessened, all may judge.
At thy return my blushing was not small,
My rambling brat (in print) should mother call;
I cast thee by as one unfit for light,
Thy visage was so irksome in my sight;   10
Yet being mine own, at length affection would
Thy blemishes amend, if so I could:
I washed thy face, but more defects I saw,
And rubbing off a spot, still made a flaw.
I stretched thy joints to make thee even feet,   15
Yet still thou run'st more hobbling than is meet;
In better dress to trim thee was my mind,
But nought save homespun cloth in the house I find.
In this array, 'mongst vulgars may'st thou roam;
In critics' hands beware thou dost not come;   20
And take thy way where yet thou are not known.
If for thy Father asked, say thou had'st none;
And for thy Mother, she alas is poor,
Which caused her thus to send thee out of door.

 The extended metaphor likening her book to a child came naturally to Bradstreet and allowed her to regard her work both critically and affectionately. Her conception of the book as her child creates just the right tone of amusement, self-deprecation, and concern.

 The controlling metaphor in the following poem is identified by the title. The game of chess these two players are engaged in is simultaneously literal and metaphoric.

Rosario Castellanos (1925–1974)

Chess   *1988*

TRANSLATED BY MAUREEN AHERN

Because we were friends and sometimes loved each other,
perhaps to add one more tie
to the many that already bound us,
we decided to play games of the mind.

We set up a board between us;   5
equally divided into pieces, values,
and possible moves.
We learned the rules, we swore to respect them,
and the match began.

We've been sitting here for centuries, meditating   10
ferociously
how to deal the one last blow that will finally
annihilate the other one forever.

CONSIDERATIONS FOR CRITICAL THINKING AND WRITING

1. FIRST RESPONSE. Why do the players decide to play chess? Are you surprised by the effect the game has on their relationship?

2. Why is chess a particularly resonant controlling metaphor? Explain why chess is more evocative than, say, cards or checkers.

3. How does the poem's diction suggest tensions between the two players that go beyond a literal game of chess? Which lines are especially suggestive to you?

4. Do you think the players are men, women, or a man and a woman? Explain your response. How does the sex of the players affect your reading of the poem?

OTHER FIGURES

Perhaps the humblest figure of speech — if not one of the most familiar — is the pun. A *pun* is a play on words that relies on a word having more than one meaning or sounding like another word. For example, "A fad is in one era and out the other" is the sort of pun that produces obligatory groans. But most of us find pleasant and interesting surprises in puns. Here's one that has a slight edge to its humor.

EDMUND CONTI (B. 1929)

Pragmatist   *1985*

Apocalypse soon
Coming our way
Ground zero at noon
Halve a nice day.

Grimly practical under the circumstances, the pragmatist divides the familiar cheerful cliché by half. As simple as this poem is, its tone is mixed because it makes us laugh and wince at the same time.

Puns can be used to achieve serious effects as well as humorous ones. Although we may have learned to underrate puns as figures of speech, it is a mistake to underestimate their power and the frequency with which they appear in poetry. A close examination, for example, of Henry Reed's "Naming of Parts" (p. 160), Robert Frost's "Design" (p. 356), or almost any lengthy passage from a Shakespeare play will confirm the value of puns.

Synecdoche is a figure of speech in which part of something is used to signify the whole: a neighbor is a "wagging tongue" (a gossip); a criminal is placed "behind bars" (in prison). Less typically, synecdoche refers to the whole used to signify the part: "Germany invaded Poland"; "Princeton won the fencing match." Clearly, certain individuals participated in these activities, not all of Germany or Princeton. Another related figure of speech is *metonymy,* in which something closely associated with a subject is substituted for it: "She preferred the silver screen [motion pictures] to reading." "At precisely ten o'clock the paper shufflers [office workers] stopped for coffee."

Synecdoche and metonymy may overlap and are therefore sometimes difficult to distinguish. Consider this description of a disapproving minister entering a noisy tavern: "As those pursed lips came through the swinging door, the atmosphere was suddenly soured." The pursed lips signal the presence of the minister and are therefore a synecdoche, but they additionally suggest an inhibiting sense of sin and guilt that makes the bar patrons feel uncomfortable. Hence, the pursed lips are also a metonymy, since they are in this context so closely connected with religion. Although the distinction between synecdoche and metonymy can be useful, when a figure of speech overlaps categories, it is usually labeled a metonymy.

Knowing the precise term for a figure of speech is, finally, less important than responding to its use in a poem. Consider how metonymy and synecdoche convey the tone and meaning of the following poem.

DYLAN THOMAS (1914–1953)

The Hand That Signed the Paper 1936

The hand that signed the paper felled a city;
Five sovereign fingers taxed the breath,
Doubled the globe of dead and halved a country;
These five kings did a king to death.

The mighty hand leads to a sloping shoulder, 5
The finger joints are cramped with chalk;
A goose's quill has put an end to murder
That put an end to talk.

The hand that signed the treaty bred a fever,
And famine grew, and locusts came; 10
Great is the hand that holds dominion over
Man by a scribbled name.

The five kings count the dead but do not soften
The crusted wound nor stroke the brow;
A hand rules pity as a hand rules heaven; 15
Hands have no tears to flow.

The "hand" in this poem is a synecdoche for a powerful ruler because it is a part of someone used to signify the entire person. The "goose's quill" is a metonymy that also refers to the power associated with the ruler's hand. By using these figures of speech, Thomas depersonalizes and ultimately dehumanizes the ruler. The final synecdoche tells us that "Hands have no tears to flow." It makes us see the political power behind the hand as remote and inhuman. How is the meaning of the poem enlarged when the speaker says, "A hand rules pity as a hand rules heaven"?

One of the ways writers energize the abstractions, ideas, objects, and animals that constitute their created worlds is through *personification,* the attribution of human characteristics to nonhuman things: temptation pursues the innocent; trees scream in the raging wind; mice conspire in the cupboard. We are not explicitly told that these things are people; instead, we are invited to see that they behave like people. Perhaps it is human vanity that makes personification a frequently used figure of speech. Whatever the reason, personification, a form of metaphor that connects the nonhuman with the human, makes the world understandable in human terms. Consider this concise example from William Blake's *The Marriage of Heaven and Hell,* a long poem that takes delight in attacking conventional morality: "Prudence is a rich ugly old maid courted by Incapacity." By personifying prudence, Blake transforms what is usually considered a virtue into a comic figure hardly worth emulating.

Often related to personification is another rhetorical figure called *apostrophe,* an address either to someone who is absent and therefore cannot hear the speaker or to something nonhuman that cannot comprehend. Apostrophe provides an opportunity for the speaker of a poem to think aloud, and often the thoughts expressed are in a formal tone. John Keats, for example, begins "Ode on a Grecian Urn" (p. 79) this way: "Thou still unravished bride of quietness." Apostrophe is frequently accompanied by intense emotion that is signaled by phrasing such as "O Life." In the right hands — such as Keats's — apostrophe can provide an intense and immediate voice in a poem, but when it is overdone or extravagant it can be ludicrous. Modern poets are more wary of apostrophe than their predecessors because apostrophizing strikes many self-conscious twentieth-century sensibilities as too theatrical. Thus modern poets tend to avoid exaggerated situations in favor of less charged though equally meditative moments, as in this next poem, with its amusing, half-serious cosmic twist.

JANICE TOWNLEY MOORE (B. 1939)

To a Wasp

1984

You must have chortled
finding that tiny hole
in the kitchen screen. Right
into my cheese cake batter
you dived,   5
no chance to swim ashore,
no saving spoon,
the mixer whirring

your legs, wings, stinger,
churning you into such   10
delicious death.
Never mind the bright April day.
Did you not see
rising out of cumulus clouds
That fist aimed at both of us?   15

Moore's apostrophe "To a Wasp" is based on the simplest of domestic cir-
cumstances; there is almost nothing theatrical or exaggerated in the poem's
tone until "That fist" in the last line, when exaggeration takes center stage. As
a figure of speech exaggeration is known as **overstatement** or **hyperbole** and
adds emphasis without intending to be literally true: "The teenage boy ate
everything in the house." Notice how the speaker of Marvell's "To His Coy
Mistress" (p. 65) exaggerates his devotion in the following overstatement:

> An hundred years should go to praise
> Thine eyes and on thy forehead gaze,
> Two hundred to adore each breast,
> But thirty thousand to the rest:

That comes to 30,500 years. What is expressed here is heightened emo-
tion, not deception.

The speaker also uses the opposite figure of speech, **understatement,**
which says less than is intended. In the next section he sums up why he
cannot take 30,500 years to express his love:

> The grave's a fine and private place,
> But none, I think, do there embrace.

The speaker is correct, of course, but by deliberately understating —
saying "I think" when he is actually certain — he makes his point, that
death will overtake their love, all the more emphatic. Another powerful ex-
ample of understatement appears in the final line of Randall Jarrell's "The
Death of the Ball Turret Gunner" (p. 56), when the disembodied voice of
the machine-gunner describes his death in a bomber: "When I died they
washed me out of the turret with a hose."

Paradox is a statement that initially appears to be self-contradictory
but that, on closer inspection, turns out to make sense: "The pen is might-
ier than the sword." In a fencing match, anyone would prefer the sword,
but if the goal is to win the hearts and minds of people, the art of persua-
sion can be more compelling than swordplay. To resolve the paradox, it is
necessary to discover the sense that underlies the statement. If we see that
"pen" and "sword" are used as metonymies for writing and violence, then
the paradox rings true. **Oxymoron** is a condensed form of paradox in
which two contradictory words are used together. Combinations such as
"sweet sorrow," "silent scream," "sad joy," and "cold fire" indicate the kinds
of startling effects that oxymorons can produce. Paradox is useful in po-
etry because it arrests a reader's attention by its seemingly stubborn refusal

to make sense, and once a reader has penetrated the paradox, it is difficult to resist a perception so well earned. Good paradoxes are knotty pleasures. Here is a simple but effective one.

J. PATRICK LEWIS (B. 1942)
The Unkindest Cut 1993

Knives can harm you, heaven forbid;
Axes may disarm you, kid;
Guillotines are painful, but
There's nothing like a paper cut!

This quatrain is a humorous version of "the pen is mightier than the sword." The wounds escalate to the paper cut, which paradoxically is more damaging than even the broad blade of a guillotine. "The unkindest cut" of all (an allusion to Shakespeare's *Julius Caesar*, III.ii.188) is produced by chilling words on a page rather than cold steel, but it is more painfully fatal nonetheless.

The following poems are rich in figurative language. As you read and study them, notice how their figures of speech vivify situations, clarify ideas, intensify emotions, and engage your imagination. Although the terms for the various figures discussed in this chapter are useful for labeling the particular devices used in poetry, they should not be allowed to get in the way of your response to a poem. Don't worry about rounding up examples of figurative language. First relax and let the figures work their effects on you. Use the terms as a means of taking you further into poetry, and they will serve your reading well.

POEMS FOR FURTHER STUDY

SUE OWEN (B. 1942)
Zero 1988

This is the story of zero,
born to live a life
of emptiness, only
child of plus and minus.

Its bones invisible   5
so it could be seen through
like an eye.
With that vision, you could

see the past and future
and how they mimic each other.   10
At first, it was thought
the zero was a mouth

and would say something
profound to the numbers.
But added to them, it never   15
amounted to much, and

subtracted, it never wanted
to take anything away.
Zero was a sad case,
only wanted to master emotion   20

and silence like chess.
Each winter, the approaching
degrees never could locate
its cold, missing heart.

CONSIDERATIONS FOR CRITICAL THINKING AND WRITING

1. FIRST RESPONSE. How does the poet's use of personification create a kind of life story of "zero"? What kind of story is it?

2. What is the poem's controlling metaphor?

3. How do the metaphors and similes in this poem enrich its meaning? Which ones seem particularly effective to you?

MARGARET ATWOOD (B. 1939)

February   1995

Winter. Time to eat fat
and watch hockey. In the pewter mornings, the cat,
a black fur sausage with yellow
Houdini eyes, jumps up on the bed and tries
to get onto my head. It's his   5
way of telling whether or not I'm dead.
If I'm not, he wants to be scratched; if I am
he'll think of something. He settles
on my chest, breathing his breath
of burped-up meat and musty sofas,   10
purring like a washboard. Some other tomcat,
not yet a capon, has been spraying our front door,
declaring war. It's all about sex and territory,
which are what will finish us off
in the long run. Some cat owners around here   15
should snip a few testicles. If we wise
hominids were sensible, we'd do that too,

or eat our young, like sharks.
But it's love that does us in. Over and over
again, *He shoots, he scores!* and famine   20
crouches in the bedsheets, ambushing the pulsing
eiderdown, and the windchill factor hits
thirty below, and pollution pours
out of our chimneys to keep us warm.
February, month of despair,   25
with a skewered heart in the centre.
I think dire thoughts, and lust for French fries
with a splash of vinegar.
Cat, enough of your greedy whining
and your small pink bumhole.   30
Off my face! You're the life principle,
more or less, so get going
on a little optimism around here.
Get rid of death. Celebrate increase. Make it be spring.

Considerations for Critical Thinking and Writing

1. FIRST RESPONSE. How do your own associations with February compare
   with the speaker's?
2. Explain how the poem is organized around an extended metaphor that de-
   fines winter as a "Time to eat fat / and watch hockey" (lines 1–2).
3. Explain the paradox in "it's love that does us in" (line 19).
4. What theme(s) do you find in the poem? How is the cat central to them?

Sophie Cabot Black (b. 1958)

August   *1994*

A doe puts her nose to sky: stark hub
Around which the second cut of hay spins
Into one direction. A man rests
Against the fence, waiting

For the last minute to turn home. By heart   5
He knows the tilt and decline of each field,
His own faulty predictions. The well
Hoards its shadow while a raw haze gluts

With harvest, with guessing rains, presses
At the temple and wrist. The pastures, tired   10
Of abiding, begin to burn. Gold takes over,
Loose, unguarded. Cows stay deep

In the chafe of underbush; reckless leaves shawl
The edges, unaware of the sap that will send them down.

CONSIDERATIONS FOR CRITICAL THINKING AND WRITING

1. FIRST RESPONSE. How does the final line affect your understanding of the poem?
2. What tone is created by the poem's images of August?
3. How does Black's use of personification contribute to the tone?
4. Discuss what you think is the poem's theme.

CONNECTION TO ANOTHER SELECTION

1. Discuss the moods created in "August" and Atwood's "February." To what extent do you think each poem is successful in capturing the essence of the title's subject?

ERNEST SLYMAN (B. 1946)

Lightning Bugs   1988

In my backyard,
They burn peepholes in the night
And take snapshots of my house.

CONSIDERATIONS FOR CRITICAL THINKING AND WRITING

1. FIRST RESPONSE. Explain why the title is essential to this poem.
2. What makes the description of the lightning bugs effective? How do the second and third lines complement each other?
3. As Slyman has done, take a simple, common fact of nature and make it vivid by using a figure of speech to describe it.

SYLVIA PLATH (1932–1963)

Mirror   1963

I am silver and exact. I have no preconceptions.
Whatever I see I swallow immediately
Just as it is, unmisted by love or dislike.
I am not cruel, only truthful—
The eye of a little god, four-cornered.   5
Most of the time I meditate on the opposite wall.
It is pink, with speckles. I have looked at it so long
I think it is a part of my heart. But it flickers.
Faces and darkness separate us over and over.

Now I am a lake. A woman bends over me,   10
Searching my reaches for what she really is.
Then she turns to those liars, the candles or the moon.
I see her back, and reflect it faithfully.

She rewards me with tears and an agitation of hands.
I am important to her. She comes and goes.   15
Each morning it is her face that replaces the darkness.
In me she has drowned a young girl, and in me an old woman
Rises toward her day after day, like a terrible fish.

CONSIDERATIONS FOR CRITICAL THINKING AND WRITING

1. FIRST RESPONSE. What is the effect of the personification in this poem?
   How would our view of the aging woman be different if she, rather than
   the mirror, told her story?

2. What is the mythical allusion in "Now I am a lake" (line 10)?

3. In what sense can "candles or the moon" be regarded as "liars"? Explain
   this metaphor.

4. Discuss the effectiveness of the simile in the final line of the poem.

SHARON OLDS (B. 1942)

Poem for the Breasts   *1999*

Like other identical twins, they can be
better told apart in adulthood.
One is fast to wrinkle her brow,
her brain, her quick intelligence. The other
dreams inside a constellation,   5
freckles of Orion. They were born when I was thirteen,
they rose up, half out of my chest,
now they're forty, wise, generous.
I am inside them — in a way, under them,
or I carry them, I was alive so long without them.   10
I can't say I am them, though their feelings are almost
        my feelings,
as with someone one deeply loves. They seem,
to me, like a gift that I have to give.
That boys were said to worship their category of   15
being, almost starve for it,
did not escape me, and some young men
loved them the way one would want, oneself, to be loved.
All year, they have been calling to my husband,
singing to him, like a pair of soaking   20
sirens on a scaled rock.
They cannot believe he could leave them, it isn't
vanity, they themselves
were made of promise and so they believed his word.
Sometimes, now, I hold them a moment,   25
one in each hand, twin widows.
heavy with grief. They were a gift to me,
and then they were ours, like little nurslings

of excitement and plenty. And now it is summer
again, late summer, the very week   30
he moved out. Didn't he whisper to them
wait here for me one year? No.
He said, God be with you, God
by with you, God
by, for the rest   35
of this life and for the long nothing. And they do not
know language, they are waiting for him, my
Christ they are dumb, they do not even
know they are mortal — sweet, I guess,
refreshing to live with, beings without   40
the knowledge of death, creatures of ignorant suffering.

CONSIDERATIONS FOR CRITICAL THINKING AND WRITING

1. FIRST RESPONSE. Personifying breasts and using them as extended meta-
   phors and similes may not seem like a promising premise for a poem. As
   you read the poem, did you find that the premise worked for you? Explain
   why or why not by considering the poem's personification, metaphors, and
   similes.

2. Describe the difference in tone between lines 1–18 and 19–41.

3. Read lines 31–36 aloud. How do you make sense of the fragmented nature
   of these lines?

4. What kinds of emotions does this poem create for you?

CONNECTIONS TO OTHER SELECTIONS

1. Compare and contrast the use of extended metaphor in "Poem for the
   Breasts" and in Anne Bradstreet's "The Author to Her Book" (p. 117).

2. Discuss Olds's strategies for using extended metaphors in "Poem for the
   Breasts" and in two other poems by her: "Sex without Love" (p. 76) and
   "Rite of Passage" (p. 265).

WILLIAM WORDSWORTH (1770–1850)

London, 1802   *1802*

Milton!° thou should'st be living at this hour:
England hath need of thee: she is a fen
Of stagnant waters: altar, sword, and pen,
Fireside, the heroic wealth of hall and bower,
Have forfeited their ancient English dower   5

---

1 *Milton:* John Milton (1608–1674), poet, famous especially for his religious epic *Paradise Lost*
and his defense of political freedom.

Of inward happiness. We are selfish men,
Oh! raise us up, return to us again;
And give us manners, virtue, freedom, power.
Thy soul was like a star, and dwelt apart:
Thou hadst a voice whose sound was like the sea: 10
Pure as the naked heavens, majestic, free,
So didst thou travel on life's common way,
In cheerful godliness; and yet thy heart
The lowliest duties on herself did lay.

CONSIDERATIONS FOR CRITICAL THINKING AND WRITING

1. FIRST RESPONSE. Describe the poem's tone. Is it nostalgic, angry, or something else?

2. Explain the metonymies in lines 3–6 of this poem. What is the speaker's assessment of England?

3. How would the effect of the poem be different if it were in the form of an address to Wordsworth's contemporaries rather than an apostrophe to Milton? What qualities does Wordsworth attribute to Milton by the use of figurative language?

JIM STEVENS (B. 1922)

Schizophrenia   *1992*

It was the house that suffered most.

It had begun with slamming doors, angry feet scuffing the carpets,
dishes slammed onto the table,
greasy stains spreading on the cloth.

Certain doors were locked at night,   5
feet stood for hours outside them,
dishes were left unwashed, the cloth
disappeared under a hardened crust.

The house came to miss the shouting voices,
the threats, the half-apologies, noisy   10
reconciliations, the sobbing that followed.

Then lines were drawn, borders established,
some rooms declared their loyalties,
keeping to themselves, keeping out the other.
The house divided against itself.   15

Seeing cracking paint, broken windows,
the front door banging in the wind,
the roof tiles flying off, one by one,
the neighbors said it was a madhouse.

It was the house that suffered most.   20

CONSIDERATIONS FOR CRITICAL THINKING AND WRITING

1. FIRST RESPONSE. What is the effect of personifying the house in this poem?

2. How are the people who live in the house characterized? What does their behavior reveal about them? How does the house respond to them?

3. Comment on the title. If the title were missing, what, if anything, would be missing from the poem? Explain your answer.

WALT WHITMAN (1819–1892)

A Noiseless Patient Spider

1868

A noiseless patient spider,
I mark'd where on a little promontory it stood isolated,
Mark'd how to explore the vacant vast surrounding,
It launch'd forth filament, filament, filament, out of itself,
Ever unreeling them, ever tirelessly speeding them.   5

And you O my soul where you stand,
Surrounded, detached, in measureless oceans of space,
Ceaselessly musing, venturing, throwing, seeking the spheres to connect
        them,
Till the bridge you will need be form'd, till the ductile anchor hold,
Till the gossamer thread you fling catch somewhere, O my soul.   10

CONSIDERATIONS FOR CRITICAL THINKING AND WRITING

1. FIRST RESPONSE. Spiders are not usually regarded as pleasant creatures. Why does the speaker in this poem liken his soul to one? What similarities are there in the poem between spider and soul? Are there any significant differences?

2. How do the images of space relate to the connections made between the speaker's soul and the spider?

JOHN DONNE (1572–1631)

A Valediction: Forbidding Mourning

1611

As virtuous men pass mildly away,
    And whisper to their souls to go,
While some of their sad friends do say,
    The breath goes now, and some say, no:

So let us melt, and make no noise,   5
    No tear-floods, nor sigh-tempests move;
'Twere profanation of our joys
    To tell the laity our love.

Moving of th' earth° brings harms and fears,   *earthquakes*
   Men reckon what it did and meant,   10
But trepidation of the spheres,°
   Though greater far, is innocent.

Dull sublunary° lovers' love
   (Whose soul is sense) cannot admit
Absence, because it doth remove   15
   Those things which elemented° it.   *composed*

But we by a love so much refined,
   That ourselves know not what it is,
Inter-assured of the mind,
   Care less, eyes, lips, and hands to miss.   20

Our two souls therefore, which are one,
   Though I must go, endure not yet
A breach, but an expansion,
   Like gold to airy thinness beat.

If they be two, they are two so   25
   As stiff twin compasses are two;
Thy soul the fixed foot, makes no show
   To move, but doth, if th' other do.

And though it in the center sit,
   Yet when the other far doth roam,   30
It leans, and hearkens after it,
   And grows erect, as that comes home.

Such wilt thou be to me, who must
   Like th' other foot, obliquely run;
Thy firmness makes my circle just,°   35
   And makes me end, where I begun.

11 *trepidation of the spheres:* According to Ptolemaic astronomy, the planets sometimes moved violently, like earthquakes, but these movements were not felt by people on earth.   13 *sublunary:* Under the moon; hence, mortal and subject to change.   35 *circle just:* The circle is a traditional symbol of perfection.

CONSIDERATIONS FOR CRITICAL THINKING AND WRITING

1. FIRST RESPONSE. A valediction is a farewell. Donne wrote this poem for his wife before leaving on a trip to France. What kind of "mourning" is the speaker forbidding?

2. Explain how the simile in lines 1–4 is related to the couple in lines 5–8. Who is described as dying?

3. How does the speaker contrast the couple's love to "sublunary lovers' love" (line 13)?

4. Explain the similes in lines 24 and 25–36.

LINDA PASTAN (B. 1932)

Marks

1978

My husband gives me an A
for last night's supper,
an incomplete for my ironing,
a B plus in bed.
My son says I am average,   5
an average mother, but if
I put my mind to it
I could improve.
My daughter believes
in Pass/Fail and tells me   10
I pass. Wait 'til they learn
I'm dropping out.

CONSIDERATIONS FOR CRITICAL THINKING AND WRITING

1. FIRST RESPONSE. Explain the appropriateness of the controlling metaphor
   in this poem. How does it reveal the woman's relationship to her family?
2. Discuss the meaning of the title.
3. How does the last line serve as both the climax of the woman's story and
   the controlling metaphor of the poem?

THOMAS LYNCH (B. 1948)

Liberty

1998

Some nights I go out and piss on the front lawn
as a form of freedom — liberty from
porcelain and plumbing and the Great Beyond
beyond the toilet and the sewage works.
Here is the statement I am trying to make: 5
to say I am from a fierce bloodline of men
who made their water in the old way, under stars
that overarched the North Atlantic where
the River Shannon empties into sea.
The ex-wife used to say, "Why can't you pee   10
in concert with the most of humankind
who do their business tidily indoors?"
It was gentility or envy, I suppose,
because I could do it anywhere, and do
whenever I begin to feel encumbered.   15
Still, there is nothing, here in the suburbs,
as dense as the darkness in West Clare
nor any equivalent to the nightlong wind
that rattles in the hedgerow of whitethorn there

on the east side of the cottage yard in Moveen.   20
It was market day in Kilrush, years ago:
my great-great-grandfather bargained with tinkers
who claimed it was whitethorn that Christ's crown was made from.
So he gave them two and six and brought them home —
mere saplings then — as a gift for the missus,   25
who planted them between the house and garden.
For years now, men have slipped out the back door
during wakes or wedding feasts or nights of song
to pay their homage to the holy trees
and, looking up into that vast firmament,   30
consider liberty in that last townland where
they have no crowns, no crappers and no ex-wives.

CONSIDERATIONS FOR CRITICAL THINKING AND WRITING

1. FIRST RESPONSE. Does "gentility or envy" (13) get in the way of your enjoy-
   ing and appreciating this poem? Explain why or why not.
2. Characterize the speaker and explain why you find him engaging or not.
3. How does the speaker metaphorically define *liberty*?
4. Discuss the tone of the speaker's definition of freedom. Explain why you
   find the purpose of this poem to be humorous or serious — or both.

CONNECTION TO ANOTHER SELECTION

1. Discuss Lynch's treatment of suburban life and compare it with John Ciar-
   di's in "Suburban" (p. 161). What similarities are there in the themes and
   metaphoric strategies of these two poems?

STEPHEN DUNN (B. 1939)

John & Mary   *1998*

John & Mary had never met. They were like two
   hummingbirds who also had never met.
      — from a freshman's short story

They were like gazelles who occupied different
grassy plains, running in opposite directions
from different lions. They were like postal clerks
in different zip codes, with different vacation time,
their bosses adamant and clock-driven.   5
How could they get together?
They were like two people who couldn't get together.
John was a Sufi with a love of the dervish,
Mary of course a Christian with a curfew.
They were like two dolphins in the immensity   10
of the Atlantic, one playful,

the other stuck in a tuna net—
two absolutely different childhoods!
There was simply no hope for them.
They would never speak in person.   15
When they ran across that windswept field
toward each other, they were like two freight trains,
one having left Seattle at 6:36 P.M.
at an unknown speed, the other delayed
in Topeka for repairs.   20
The math indicated that they'd embrace
in another world, if at all, like parallel lines.
Or merely appear kindred and close, like stars.

CONSIDERATIONS FOR CRITICAL THINKING AND WRITING

1. FIRST RESPONSE. Why is the epigraph "from a freshman's short story" crucial for an understanding of this poem?

2. What's the problem with the freshman's simile? How does it serve as an inspiration for the similes in the poem?

3. Discuss the speaker's tone. Did you find it amusing? Explain why you find it appealing or not. What does the tone contribute to your understanding of the poem?

4. How do the similes in lines 20–23 differ from those that precede it?

CONNECTION TO ANOTHER SELECTION

1. Compare the speaker's tone in "John & Mary" with that of Mark Halliday's "Graded Paper" (p. 445). What significant similarities and differences do you find in each speaker's attitude toward the student writer?

ELAINE MAGARRELL (B. 1928)

The Joy of Cooking   *1988*

I have prepared my sister's tongue,
scrubbed and skinned it,
trimmed the roots, small bones, and gristle.
Carved through the hump it slices thin and neat.
Best with horseradish   5
and economical—it probably will grow back.
Next time perhaps a creole sauce
or mold of aspic?

I will have my brother's heart,
which is firm and rather dry,   10
slow cooked. It resembles muscle
more than organ meat
and needs an apple-onion stuffing

to make it interesting at all
Although beef heart serves six   15
my brother's heart barely feeds two.
I could also have it braised
and served in sour sauce.

Considerations for Critical Thinking and Writing

1. FIRST RESPONSE. Describe the poem's tone. Do you find it amusing, bitter, or something else?
2. How are the tongue and heart used to characterize the sister and brother in this poem?
3. Describe the speaker's tone. What effect does the title have on your determining the tone?

Connection to Another Selection

1. Write an essay that explains how cooking becomes a way of talking about something else in this poem and in Croft's "Home-Baked Bread" (p. 107).

Stephen Perry (b. 1947)

Blue Spruce   1991

My grandfather worked in a barbershop
smelling of lotions he'd slap on your face,
hair and talc. The black razor strop

hung like the penis of an ox. He'd draw
the sharp blade in quick strokes over   5
the smooth-rough hide, and then carefully

over your face. The tiny hairs would gather
on the blade, a congregation singing
under blue spruce in winter,

a bandstand in the center of town   10
bright with instruments, alto sax, tenor
sax, tuba or sousaphone — the bright

oompah-pahs shaving the town somehow,
a bright cloth shaking the air
into flakes of silvering hair   15

floating down past the houses, the horses
pulling carriages past the town fountain,
which had frozen into a coiffure

of curly glass. My grandfather had an affair
with the girl who did their nails   20
bright pink, bright red, never blue,

perhaps as the horses clip-clopped on ice
outside his shop, his kisses
smelling of lather and new skin —

when she grew too big and round   25
with his child, with his oompah love,
with his bandstand love, with his brassy love,

and the town dropped its grace notes
of gossip and whispered hiss,
he bundled her out of town   30

with the savings which should have gone
to my mom. But how could you hate him?
My mother did, my father did,

and my grandmother, who bore his neglect.
When she was covered in sheets   35
at her last death,

he flirted with the nurses, bright
as winter birds in spruces
above a bandstand —

I'll always remember him in snow, a deep lather   40
of laughter, the picture
where he took me from my mother

and raised me high, a baby, into the bell
of his sousaphone, as if I were a note
he'd play into light —   45

CONSIDERATIONS FOR CRITICAL THINKING AND WRITING

1. FIRST RESPONSE. The grandfather is presented as an outrageous figure, "But how could you hate him?" (line 32). Do you think the speaker is successful in preventing the reader from hating his grandfather? Explain.

2. What are the controlling metaphors in "Blue Spruce"? How do they help to characterize the grandfather?

3. Write a paragraph detailing what you think the speaker means by his grandfather's "oompah love" (line 26).

PERSPECTIVE

JOHN R. SEARLE (B. 1932)

Figuring Out Metaphors   1979

If you hear somebody say, "Sally is a block of ice," or, "Sam is a pig," you are likely to assume that the speaker does not mean what he says literally, but that he is speaking metaphorically. Furthermore, you are not likely to have very much trouble figuring out what he means. If he says, "Sally is a prime number between 17 and 23," or "Bill is a barn door," you might still assume he is speaking metaphorically, but it is much harder to figure out what he means. The existence of such utterances — utterances in which the speaker means metaphorically something different from what the sentence means literally — poses a series of questions for any theory of language and communication: What is metaphor, and how does it differ from both literal and other forms of figurative utterances? Why do we use expressions metaphorically instead of saying exactly and literally what we mean? How do metaphorical utterances work, that is, how is it possible for speakers to communicate to hearers when speaking metaphorically inasmuch as they do not say what they mean? And why do some metaphors work and others do not?

From *Expression and Meaning*

CONSIDERATIONS FOR CRITICAL THINKING AND WRITING

1. Searle poses a series of important questions. Write an essay that explores one of these questions, basing your discussion on the poems in this chapter.

2. Try writing a brief poem that provides a context for the line "Sally is a prime number between 17 and 23" or the line "Bill is a barn door." Your task is to create a context so that either one of these metaphoric statements is as readily understandable as "Sally is a block of ice" or "Sam is a pig." Share your poem with your classmates and explain how the line generated the poem you built around it.

6

Symbol, Allegory, and Irony

SYMBOL

A *symbol* is something that represents something else. An object, person, place, event, or action can suggest more than its literal meaning. A handshake between two world leaders might be simply a greeting, but if it is done ceremoniously before cameras, it could be a symbolic gesture signifying unity, issues resolved, and joint policies that will be followed. We live surrounded by symbols. When an $80,000 Mercedes-Benz comes roaring by in the fast lane, we get a quick glimpse of not only an expensive car but an entire lifestyle that suggests opulence, broad lawns, executive offices, and power. One of the reasons some buyers are willing to spend roughly the cost of five Chevrolets for a single Mercedes-Benz is that they are aware of the car's symbolic value. A symbol is a vehicle for two things at once: it functions as itself, and it implies meanings beyond itself.

The meanings suggested by a symbol are determined by the context in which they appear. The Mercedes could symbolize very different things depending on where it was parked. Would an American political candidate be likely to appear in a Detroit blue-collar neighborhood with such a car? Probably not. Although a candidate might be able to afford the car, it would be an inappropriate symbol for someone seeking votes from all the people. As a symbol, the German-built Mercedes would backfire if voters perceived it as representing an entity partially responsible for layoffs of automobile workers or, worse, as a sign of decadence and corruption. Similarly, a huge portrait of Mao Tse-tung conveys different meanings to residents of Beijing than it would to farmers in Prairie Center, Illinois. Because symbols depend on contexts for their meaning, literary artists provide those contexts so that the reader has enough information to determine the probable range of meanings suggested by a symbol.

In the following poem the speaker describes walking at night. How is the night used symbolically?

ROBERT FROST (1874–1963)

Acquainted with the Night

1928

I have been one acquainted with the night.
I have walked out in rain—and back in rain.
I have outwalked the furthest city light.

I have looked down the saddest city lane.
I have passed by the watchman on his beat   5
And dropped my eyes, unwilling to explain.

I have stood still and stopped the sound of feet
When far away an interrupted cry
Came over houses from another street,

But not to call me back or say good-by;   10
And further still at an unearthly height
One luminary clock against the sky

Proclaimed the time was neither wrong nor right.
I have been one acquainted with the night

In approaching this or any poem, you should read for literal meanings first and then allow the elements of the poem to invite you to symbolic readings, if they are appropriate. Here the somber tone suggests that the lines have symbolic meaning too. The flat matter-of-factness created by the repetition of "I have" (lines 1–5, 7, 14) understates the symbolic subject matter of the poem, which is, finally, more about the "night" located in the speaker's mind or soul than it is about walking away from a city and back again. The speaker is "acquainted with the night." The importance of this phrase is emphasized by Frost's title and by the fact that he begins and ends the poem with it. Poets frequently use this kind of repetition to alert readers to details that carry more than literal meanings.

The speaker in this poem has personal knowledge of the night but does not indicate specifically what the night means. To arrive at the potential meanings of the night in this context, it is necessary to look closely at its connotations, along with the images provided in the poem. The connotative meanings of night suggest, for example, darkness, death, and grief. By drawing on these connotations, Frost uses a *conventional symbol,* something that is recognized by many people to represent certain ideas. Roses conventionally symbolize love or beauty; laurels, fame; spring, growth; the moon, romance. Poets often use conventional symbols to convey tone and meaning.

Frost uses the night as a conventional symbol, but he also develops it into a *literary* or *contextual symbol* that goes beyond traditional, public meanings. A literary symbol cannot be summarized in a word or two. It tends to be as elusive as experience itself. The night cannot be reduced to or equated with darkness or death or grief, but it evokes those associations and more. Frost took what perhaps initially appears to be an overworked, conventional symbol and prevented it from becoming a cliché by deepening and extending its meaning.

The images in "Acquainted with the Night" lead to the poem's symbolic meaning. Unwilling, and perhaps unable, to explain explicitly to the watchman (and to the reader) what the night means, the speaker nevertheless conveys feelings about it. The brief images of darkness, rain, sad city lanes, the necessity for guards, the eerie sound of a distressing cry coming over rooftops, and the "luminary clock against the sky" proclaiming "the time was neither wrong nor right" all help to create a sense of anxiety in this tight-lipped speaker. Although we cannot know what unnamed personal experiences have acquainted the speaker with the night, the images suggest that whatever the night means, it is somehow associated with insomnia, loneliness, isolation, coldness, darkness, death, fear, and a sense of alienation from humanity and even time. Daylight — ordinary daytime thoughts and life itself — seems remote and unavailable in this poem. The night is literally the period from sunset to sunrise, but, more important, it is an internal state of being felt by the speaker and revealed through the images.

Frost used symbols rather than an expository essay that would explain the conditions that cause these feelings because most readers can provide their own list of sorrows and terrors that evoke similar emotions. Through symbol, the speaker's experience is compressed and simultaneously expanded by the personal darkness that each reader brings to the poem. The suggestive nature of symbols makes them valuable for poets and evocative for readers.

ALLEGORY

Unlike expansive, suggestive symbols, *allegory* is a narration or description usually restricted to a single meaning because its events, actions, characters, settings, and objects represent specific abstractions or ideas. Although the elements in an allegory may be interesting in themselves, the emphasis tends to be on what they ultimately mean. Characters may be given names such as Hope, Pride, Youth, and Charity; they have few, if any, personal qualities beyond their abstract meanings. These personifications are a form of extended metaphor, but their meanings are severely restricted. They are not symbols because, for instance, the meaning of a character named Charity is precisely that virtue.

There is little or no room for broad speculation and exploration in allegories. If Frost had written "Acquainted with the Night" as an allegory, he might have named his speaker Loneliness and had him leave the City of Despair to walk the Streets of Emptiness, where Crime, Poverty, Fear, and other characters would define the nature of city life. The literal elements in an allegory tend to be de-emphasized in favor of the message. Symbols, however, function both literally and symbolically, so that "Acquainted with the Night" is about both a walk and a sense that something is terribly wrong.

Allegory especially lends itself to **didactic poetry,** which is designed to teach an ethical, moral, or religious lesson. Many stories, poems, and plays are concerned with values, but didactic literature is specifically created to convey a message. "Acquainted with the Night" does not impart advice or offer guidance. If the poem argued that city life is self-destructive or sinful, it would be didactic; instead, it is a lyric poem that expresses the emotions and thoughts of a single speaker.

Although allegory is often enlisted in didactic causes because it can so readily communicate abstract ideas through physical representations, not all allegories teach a lesson. Here is a poem describing a haunted palace while also establishing a consistent pattern that reveals another meaning.

EDGAR ALLAN POE (1809–1849)

The Haunted Palace   *1839*

I
In the greenest of our valleys,
    By good angels tenanted,
Once a fair and stately palace —
    Radiant palace — reared its head.
In the monarch Thought's dominion —   5
    It stood there!
Never seraph spread a pinion
    Over fabric half so fair.

II
Banners yellow, glorious, golden,
    On its roof did float and flow;   10
(This — all this — was in the olden
    Time long ago)
And every gentle air that dallied,
    In that sweet day,
Along the ramparts plumed and pallid,   15
    A wingèd odor went away.

III
Wanderers in that happy valley
    Through two luminous windows saw
Spirits moving musically
    To a lute's well-tunèd law,   20

Round about a throne, where sitting
    (Porphyrogene!)°   *born to purple, royal*
In state his glory well befitting,
    The ruler of the realm was seen.

IV
And all with pearl and ruby glowing   25
    Was the fair palace door,
Through which came flowing, flowing, flowing
    And sparkling evermore,
A troop of Echoes whose sweet duty
    Was but to sing,   30
In voices of surpassing beauty,
    The wit and wisdom of their king.

V
But evil things, in robes of sorrow,
    Assailed the monarch's high estate;
(Ah, let us mourn, for never morrow   35
    Shall dawn upon him, desolate!)
And, round about his home, the glory
    That blushed and bloomed
Is but a dim-remembered story
    Of the old time entombed.   40

VI
And travelers now within that valley,
    Through the red-litten windows see
Vast forms that move fantastically
    To a discordant melody;
While, like a rapid ghastly river,   45
    Through the pale door,
A hideous throng rush out forever,
    And laugh — but smile no more.

On one level this poem describes how a once happy palace is desolated by "evil things" (line 33). If the reader pays close attention to the diction, however, an allegorical meaning becomes apparent on a second reading. A systematic pattern develops in the choice of words used to describe the palace, so that it comes to stand for a human mind. The palace, banners, windows, door, echoes, and throng are equated with a person's head, hair, eyes, mouth, voice, and laughter. That mind, once harmoniously ordered, is overthrown by evil, haunting thoughts that lead to the mad laughter in the poem's final lines. Once the general pattern is seen, the rest of the details fall neatly into place to strengthen the parallels between the surface description of a palace and the allegorical representation of a disordered mind.

Modern writers generally prefer symbol over allegory because they tend to be more interested in opening up the potential meanings of an experience instead of transforming it into a closed pattern of meaning. Perhaps the major difference is that while allegory may delight a reader's imagination, symbol challenges and enriches it.

IRONY

Another important resource writers use to take readers beyond literal meanings is *irony,* a technique that reveals a discrepancy between what appears to be and what is actually true. Here is a classic example in which appearances give way to the underlying reality.

EDWIN ARLINGTON ROBINSON (1869–1935)

Richard Cory   1897

Whenever Richard Cory went down town,
We people on the pavement looked at him:
He was a gentleman from sole to crown,
Clean favored, and imperially slim.

And he was always quietly arrayed,   5
And he was always human when he talked;
But still he fluttered pulses when he said,
"Good-morning," and he glittered when he walked.

And he was rich — yes, richer than a king —
And admirably schooled in every grace: 10
In fine, we thought that he was everything
To make us wish that we were in his place.

So on we worked, and waited for the light,
And went without the meat, and cursed the bread;
And Richard Cory, one calm summer night,   15
Went home and put a bullet through his head.

Richard Cory seems to have it all. Those less fortunate, the "people on the pavement," regard him as well-bred, handsome, tasteful, and richly endowed with both money and grace. Until the final line of the poem, the reader, like the speaker, is charmed by Cory's good fortune, so quietly expressed in his decent, easy manner. That final, shocking line, however, shatters the appearances of Cory's life and reveals him to have been a desperately unhappy man. While everyone else assumes that Cory represented "everything" to which they aspire, the reality is that he could escape his miserable life only as a suicide. This discrepancy between what appears to be true and what actually exists is known as *situational irony:* what happens is entirely different from what is expected. We are not told why Cory shoots himself; instead, the irony in the poem shocks us into the recognition that appearances do not always reflect realities.

Words are also sometimes intended to be taken at other than face value. *Verbal irony* is saying something different from what is meant. After reading "Richard Cory," to say "That rich gentleman sure was happy" is ironic. The tone of voice would indicate that just the opposite was meant; hence, verbal irony is usually easy to detect in spoken language. In literature, however, a reader can sometimes take literally what a writer intends ironically. The remedy for this kind of misreading is to pay close attention to the poem's context. There is no formula that can detect verbal irony, but contradictory actions and statements as well as the use of understatement and overstatement can often be signals that verbal irony is present.

Consider how verbal irony is used in this poem.

KENNETH FEARING (1902–1961)

AD   *1938*

Wanted: Men;
Millions of men are *wanted at once* in a big new field;
New, tremendous, thrilling, great.
If you've ever been a figure in the chamber of horrors,
If you've ever escaped from a psychiatric ward,   5
If you thrill at the thought of throwing poison into wells, have heavenly
     visions of people, by the thousands, dying in flames —

You are the very man we want
We mean business and our business is *you*
Wanted: A race of brand-new men.   10

Apply: Middle Europe;
No skill needed;
No ambition required; no brains wanted and no character allowed;

Take a permanent job in the coming profession
Wages: *Death.*   15

This poem was written as Nazi troops stormed across Europe at the start of World War II. The advertisement suggests on the surface that killing is just an ordinary job, but the speaker indicates through understatement that there is nothing ordinary about the "business" of this "*coming profession.*" Fearing uses verbal irony to indicate how casually and mindlessly people are prepared to accept the horrors of war.

Consider how the next poem, by Janice Mirikitani, a third-generation Japanese American, uses a similar ironic strategy in a different context.

JANICE MIRIKITANI (B. 1942)

Recipe   *1987*

Round Eyes

Ingredients: scissors, Scotch magic transparent tape,
              eyeliner — water based, black.
              Optional: false eyelashes.

Cleanse face thoroughly.   5

For best results, powder entire face, including eyelids.
  (lighter shades suited to total effect desired)

With scissors, cut magic tape $\frac{1}{16}$" wide, $\frac{3}{4}$"–$\frac{1}{2}$" long —
depending on length of eyelid.

Stick firmly onto mid–upper eyelid area   10
  (looking down into handmirror facilitates finding
  adequate surface)

If using false eyelashes, affix first on lid, folding any
excess lid over the base of eyelash with glue.

Paint black eyeliner on tape and entire lid.   15

Do not cry.

CONSIDERATIONS FOR CRITICAL THINKING AND WRITING

1. FIRST RESPONSE. Discuss your response to the poem's final line.
2. What is the effect of the very specific details of this recipe?
3. Why is "false eyelashes" a particularly resonant phrase in the context of this poem?
4. Try writing your own "recipe" in poetic lines — one that makes a commentary concerning a social issue that you feel strongly about.

CONNECTION TO ANOTHER SELECTION

1. Why are the formulas for an advertisement and a recipe especially suited for Fearing's and Mirikitani's respective purposes? To what extent do the ironic strategies lead to a similar tone and theme?

Like "AD," "Recipe" is a *satire,* an example of the literary art of ridiculing a folly or vice in an effort to expose or correct it. The object of satire is usually some human frailty; people, institutions, ideas, and things are all fair game for satirists. Fearing satirizes the insanity of a world mobilizing itself for war: His irony reveals the speaker's knowledge that there is nothing *"New, tremendous, thrilling,* [or] *great"* about going off to kill and be killed. The implication of the poem is that no one should respond to advertisements for war. The poem serves as a satiric corrective to those who would troop off armed with unrealistic expectations; wage war and the wages consist of death.

Dramatic irony is used when a writer allows a reader to know more about a situation than a character does. This creates a discrepancy between what a character says or thinks and what the reader knows to be true. Dramatic irony is often used to reveal character. In the following poem the speaker delivers a public speech that ironically tells us more about him than it does about the patriotic holiday he is commemorating.

E. E. Cummings (1894–1962)

next to of course god america i 1926

"next to of course god america i
love you land of the pilgrims' and so forth oh
say can you see by the dawn's early my
country 'tis of centuries come and go
and are no more what of it we should worry 5
in every language even deafanddumb
thy sons acclaim your glorious name by gorry
by jingo by gee by gosh by gum
why talk of beauty what could be more beaut-
iful than these heroic happy dead 10
who rushed like lions to the roaring slaughter
they did not stop to think they died instead
then shall the voice of liberty be mute?"

He spoke. And drank rapidly a glass of water

This verbal debauch of chauvinistic clichés (notice the run-on phrases and lines) reveals that the speaker's relationship to God and country is not, as he claims, one of love. His public address suggests a hearty mindlessness that leads to "roaring slaughter" rather than to reverence or patriotism. Cummings allows the reader to see through the speaker's words to their dangerous emptiness. What the speaker means and what Cummings means are entirely different. Like Fearing's "AD," this poem is a satire that invites the reader's laughter and contempt in order to deflate the benighted attitudes expressed in it.

When a writer uses God, destiny, or fate to dash the hopes and expectations of a character or humankind in general, it is called **cosmic irony.** In "The Convergence of the Twain" (p. 73), for example, Hardy describes how "The Immanent Will" brought together the *Titanic* and a deadly iceberg. Technology and pride are no match for "the Spinner of the Years." Here's a painfully terse version of cosmic irony.

Stephen Crane (1871–1900)

A Man Said to the Universe 1899

A man said to the universe:
"Sir, I exist!"
"However," replied the universe,
"The fact has not created in me
A sense of obligation."

Unlike in "The Convergence of the Twain," there is the slightest bit of humor in Crane's poem, but the joke is on us.

Irony is an important technique that allows a writer to distinguish be-
tween appearances and realities. In situational irony a discrepancy exists
between what we expect to happen and what actually happens; in verbal
irony a discrepancy exists between what is said and what is meant; in dra-
matic irony a discrepancy exists between what a character believes and
what the reader knows to be true; and in cosmic irony a discrepancy exists
between what a character aspires to and what universal forces provide.
With each form of irony, we are invited to move beyond surface appear-
ances and sentimental assumptions to see the complexity of experience.
Irony is often used in literature to reveal a writer's perspective on matters
that previously seemed settled.

POEMS FOR FURTHER STUDY

JANE KENYON (1947–1995)

Surprise   *1996*

He suggests pancakes at the local diner,
followed by a walk in search of mayflowers,
while friends convene at the house
bearing casseroles and a cake, their cars
pulled close along the sandy shoulders   5
of the road, where tender ferns unfurl
in the ditches, and this year's budding leaves
push last year's spectral leaves from the tips
of the twigs of the ash trees. The gathering
itself is not what astounds her, but the casual   10
accomplishment with which he has lied.

CONSIDERATIONS FOR CRITICAL THINKING AND WRITING

1. FIRST RESPONSE. Does it matter that this poem is set in the spring?
2. Consider the connotative meaning of "ash trees." Why are they particularly
   appropriate?
3. Why do you suppose Kenyon uses "astounds" rather than "surprises" in
   line 10? Use a dictionary to help you determine the possible reasons for this
   choice.
4. Discuss the irony in the poem.

CONNECTIONS TO OTHER SELECTIONS

1. Write an essay on the nature of the surprises in Kenyon's poem and in
   Hathaway's "Oh, Oh" (p. 13). Include in your discussion a comparison of
   the tone and irony in each poem.
2. Compare and contrast in an essay the irony associated with the birthday
   parties in "Surprise" and Sharon Olds's "Rite of Passage" (p. 265).

Laure-Anne Bosselaar (b. 1943)

The Bumper-Sticker 1994

"Yield" says the sign, so you do. The bearded man
nods thank-you, pulls out. "It's never too late
to have a happy childhood" reads his bumper-sticker.
You want to stop him, ask him if he knows how. No one
waits for you at home, so you follow: it could be God 5
in that Buick, leading you to where you change
the past like tires with a bad grip, or get a quick lube,
the old stuff dripping out murky and dark.

You'd get a new mother first. You'd have the pick
of the lot: she'd be a bright color, green maybe, with safety 10
belts and such comfort you'd swear she was custom
made. A good, reliable car, never running on empty,
with enough room for the two of you. You'd leave
the garage smiling, head high, motor humming, gears
changing noiselessly, and never look back at the old jalopy 15
that nearly killed you and broke your back every day.

A new father next. He'd slide into the driver's seat,
teach you the right way to steer, check the rearview often,
stop holding your foot on the brake. He'd pull out
a technicolor map and with a finger like Michael Angelo's 20
"Adam" he'd show you where to go without getting lost.
No dead-ends, no potholes, a smooth ride my baby,
tell me where you're heading and I'll take you there,
no problem.
          The Buick signals left. You follow. You lose 25
him in a tunnel when a sixteen-wheeler reading "Safeway"
passes you and almost sends you to the wall.

Considerations for Critical Thinking and Writing

1. FIRST RESPONSE. Discuss the use of symbols in each stanza and explain what you think is the central theme of the poem. How do the symbols work together to contribute to the theme?
2. Why do you think the poet chooses a Buick rather than, say, a Honda for her narrator to follow?
3. Describe the speaker's sense of the present as well as of the past.
4. What is the effect of the speaker addressing the reader as "you"?

Connection to Another Selection

1. Discuss the use of irony in this poem and in Jane Kenyon's "Surprise" (p. 147). How does irony reveal the sensibilities of the speaker in each poem?

RENNIE MCQUILKIN (B. 1936)

The Lighters 1999

In her eighty-ninth year, she's reducing
her inventory — china to the children, mementos
to the trash — but in her boudoir
keeps half a dozen square-shouldered Zippos,

her husband's initials on one, 5
the best man's on a second, the rest anyone's guess.
Dry-chambered, their spark wheels rusted shut,
they are lined up gravely on a jewelry chest

full of antique gap-toothed keys,
elaborate scrollwork on their hilts, fit to open 10
high-backed steamer trunks, perhaps the secret entrance
to a sunken garden

where every night the dry-bones assemble
in mothballed flannels and handknit sweaters
to roll their own, light up 15
like fireflies and, *sotte voce*, remember her.

CONSIDERATIONS FOR CRITICAL THINKING AND WRITING

1. FIRST RESPONSE. How are the lighters more than simply mementos? What meanings are associated with them?
2. Discuss McQuilkin's use of diction. How does it contribute to the poem's mood?
3. How would you describe the physical appearance of this woman?

CONNECTION TO ANOTHER SELECTION

1. Compare the treatment of this elderly woman with that of Wyatt Prunty's "Elderly Lady Crossing on Green" (p. 39). How is aging depicted in each poem?

KATHY MANGAN (B. 1950)

An Arithmetic 1999

Because the world insists on still giving and giving at six,
mastering addition seemed its natural complement,
a kind of cataloguing the earth's surplus.
I loved the fat green pencil
shedding graphite as I pressed rounded 5
threes, looping eights into the speckled
yellow newsprint. Loved, too, the sturdy,
crossed bars of the plus sign, *carrying over*
in stacked columns of double,
triple digits: the plump sums I'd *arrive* at. 10

Subtraction proved another sort
of reckoning. First I had to learn
to *take away* (apples or pennies pictured
in the workbook), then settle
for the solace of a *remainder*.   15
I've never wanted less of anything—money, food
or love—but over time,
have come to understand the process:
like any human calculation,
the *difference* being   20
between what I have wanted
and what I got.

CONSIDERATIONS FOR CRITICAL THINKING AND WRITING

1. FIRST RESPONSE. How do addition and subtraction take on new meanings
   owing to Mangan's treatment of them?
2. Explain the difference in tone between stanzas one and two.
3. Try writing a stanza of your own that describes your take on multiplication
   or division, using Mangan's strategies for diction.

CONNECTION TO ANOTHER SELECTION

1. Compare the memory of childhood and school with that of Judy Page
   Heitzman's "The Schoolroom on the Second Floor of the Knitting Mill"
   (p. 446). What significant similarities do you find in the two poems?

ROBERT BLY (B. 1926)

Snowbanks North of the House   1975

Those great sweeps of snow that stop suddenly six feet
    from the house . . .
Thoughts that go so far.

The boy gets out of high school and reads no more books;
the son stops calling home.
The mother puts down her rolling pin and makes no more
    bread.   5
And the wife looks at her husband one night at a party
    and loves him no more.
The energy leaves the wine, and the minister falls leaving
    the church.
It will not come closer—
the one inside moves back, and the hands touch nothing,
    and are safe.

And the father grieves for his son, and will not leave the
    room where the coffin stands;   10
he turns away from his wife, and she sleeps alone.

And the sea lifts and falls all night; the moon goes on
   through the unattached heavens alone.
And the toe of the shoe pivots
in the dust. . . .
The man in the black coat turns, and goes back down the
   hill.   15
No one knows why he came, or why he turned away, and
   did not climb the hill.

CONSIDERATIONS FOR CRITICAL THINKING AND WRITING

1. FIRST RESPONSE. How can the varying images in the poem be related to one another? What do they have in common?

2. Describe the tone produced by the images. What emotions do you experience after carefully considering the images?

3. What symbolic meanings do you think are associated with the poem's images? Describe in a paragraph what you think the poem's themes are.

CONNECTIONS TO OTHER SELECTIONS

1. "Snowbanks North of the House" is the first poem in Bly's collection titled *The Man in the Black Coat Turns* (1981), a title drawn from line 15 of the poem. In *Selected Poems* (1986) Bly explains that

   > I wanted the poems in *The Man in the Black Coat Turns* to rise out of some darkness beneath us, as when the old Norse poets fished with an ox head as bait in the ocean. We know that the poem will break water only for a moment before it sinks again, but just seeing it rise beneath the boat is enough pleasure for one day; and to know that a large thing lives down there puts us in a calm mood, lets us endure our deprived lives with more grace.

   How does Bly's observation that such a poem "lets us endure our deprived lives with more grace" shed light on "Snowbanks North of the House" and Bly's "Snowfall in the Afternoon" (p. 593)? Write an essay that details your response.

2. Compare and contrast the symbolic images in "Snowbanks North of the House" and Robert Frost's "Stopping by Woods on a Snowy Evening" (p. 353).

PERSPECTIVE

ROBERT BLY (B. 1926)

On "Snowbanks North of the House"   1996

William Stafford has spoken so beautifully about what an assertion means in a poem, and how early you can make one. In one of his books, maybe *Writing the Australian Crawl*, he says if you make strong assertions too early in the poem, you can lose the reader. Readers need to receive a couple of assertions first that they can agree with, such as "It's summer," or "Animals own a fur world," or

"Those lines on your palm, they can be read," or "There was a river under First and Main." The reader needs to experience rather mild assertions so that he or she can begin to trust your mind; then when you make a wilder assertion later, the reader is more likely to climb up with you into that intense place from which the assertion came. My first assertion is

> Those great sweeps of snow that stop suddenly six feet from the house.

Some snow blows all the way down from Canada and then stops six feet from the house. For people who've never lived on the prairie and have experienced only gently falling snow or snow interrupted by woods, my first line may seem a risky assertion. So my second line is mild.

> Thoughts that go so far.

I want my poem to continue, but not to ascend, so I need an ordinary event, something we've all known a thousand times:

> The boy gets out of high school and reads no more books.

I can stay with that ordinariness for a little while:

> The son stops calling home.

I experienced that refusal to call home when I lived in New York during my late twenties. Certain ways of living come to an end:

> The mother puts down her rolling pin and makes no more bread.

I was thinking of my grandmother making Norwegian flat bread; readers correctly told me that ordinary bread these days is not made with rolling pins. But the child in me wrote that line. The adult in me wrote the next line:

> And the wife looks at her husband one night at a party and loves him no more.

I'm not conscious that that line happened to me, but it's possible. I do recall seeing both halves of the line at one instant in the wife's glance. It's another sadness. It's just an ordinary sadness. It doesn't happen only to special people.

> The energy leaves the wine, and the minister falls leaving the church.

My father always had a particular tenderness for the old Lutheran minister in our town, and made sure that he received game such as pheasants in the fall, and geese at Christmas; I had some sympathy for the way a minister has to hold himself up and perform his role no matter what is happening in his private life. He has to keep giving the Communion.

A month or two after I wrote the poem, I read it to a friend who was an Episcopal priest of great spirit; he told me that I had described exactly what had happened to him a month before. He couldn't say the Communion words whole-heartedly on that particular Sunday, and he fell on the steps outside. One could say that for many ordinary people — and I am one of those — a fine energy sometimes refuses to become friends with us, or perhaps we refuse to make the courtly gesture that would welcome that energy. When we fall, it's an ordinary sadness.

> It will not come closer —
> the one inside moves back, and the hands touch nothing, and are safe.

I think a lot of my childhood is alive in that last half-sentence. And I spent in my mid-twenties two years alone in New York, talking to people barely once a month. It was all right. I felt safe: "The hands touch nothing, and are safe."

I must have felt that grief during the poem. The poem is moving away from sadness now and toward grief. And I recalled a scene from Abraham Lincoln's life. He loved his son Tad so much, and when the boy was eight, he died of tuberculosis or some such thing. They put the coffin into a room by itself in that kind of home visitation that people did at that time. Lincoln went into the room and didn't come out. He stayed all afternoon, and then he stayed there all night, and then he stayed there the next day. Around noon people started pounding on the door and telling him to come out, but he paid no attention. There was something a little extraordinary in that, but the general situation is not unusual, it's something we've all noticed or heard about many times. Sometimes after the death of a child, the husband and wife never do come back to each other.

> The father grieves for his son, and will not leave the room where the coffin stands.
> He turns away from his wife, and she sleeps alone.

Now what to do? Now we've arrived at a really ordinary place, in which life and its motions go on, but the shocked man or woman doesn't pay much informed attention to those motions anymore. Donald Hall has written about this place in his poem called "Mr. Wakeville on Interstate 90":

> I will work forty hours a week clerking at the paintstore. . . .
> I will watch my neighbors' daughters grow up, marry,
> raise children. The joints of my fingers will stiffen.

The way such a life moves mechanically is a form of depression. At the beginning of *A Farewell to Arms*, Hemingway says, "That fall the war was still there, but we didn't go to it anymore."

> And the sea lifts and falls all night; the moon goes on through the unattached
> heavens alone.

I loved that word "unattached" when I saw it on the page. It brought together the son who stops calling home and the man who lives alone in New York for two years.

Then I saw the toe of a black shoe. It seemed like an ordinary shoe, not standing on marble or red carpet, but on ordinary dust. Some elegant movement as of a hinge suddenly arrived, breaking all these long forward motions:

> The toe of the shoe pivots
> in the dust . . .
> and the man in the black coat turns, and goes back down the hill.

The first time I read the poem to an audience, there was some silence afterwards, and a woman asked, "Who is the man in the black coat?" I said, "I don't know." She said, "That's outrageous; you wrote the poem." I didn't answer. It was only when I got back to the farm that I thought of the proper answer: "If I had known who the man in the black coat was, I could have written an essay." I don't mean to demean essays with such a sentence, but it's good to think clearly in an essay, which can be a series of really clear and interlocking thoughts that are luminous. But sometimes a poem amounts to the creation of some sort of nourishing mud pond in which partly developed tadpoles can live for a while, and certain images can receive enough sustenance from the darkness around them to keep breathing without being forced into some early adulthood or job or retirement. It's possible the man in the black coat is Lincoln. He did turn and go back down the hill, and his face got sadder every year that the war went on. I also noticed in a family album a photograph of my father about 25 years old, standing by the windmill holding a baby rather awkwardly couched in his right arm; it's possible the baby was myself. He was wearing a large black coat. I don't know exactly why the last line closes the poem. I didn't intend it. It just came along. Perhaps it's the most ordinary thing of all. Our mother, or our grandmother, or grandfather, or our father, goes through incredible labors, keeping despite turbulent winds and strong blows the chosen direction forward, following some route. But why? What was the aim of Lincoln's life? What was the aim of my father's life? Or my life? We know a little bit of the story — what's the rest of the story? Why don't we know that?

No one knows why he came, or why he turned away, and did not climb the hill.

From a typed manuscript sent to Michael Meyer, 1997

CONSIDERATIONS FOR CRITICAL THINKING AND WRITING

1. What do you think Bly means when he says he begins with "mild assertions" and "ordinariness" to help readers "climb up" to "wilder assertion[s]"? How does "Snowbanks North of the House" (p. 150) proceed this way?
2. Why do you think the woman in the audience thinks it "outrageous" that the poet doesn't know the identity of "the man in the black coat"? Explain why you agree or disagree with her response.
3. Discuss Bly's idea that "sometimes a poem amounts to the creation of some sort of nourishing mud pond in which partly developed tadpoles can live for a while." What does this description (and the rest of the sentence in which it appears) suggest about the nature of meaning in this poem?
4. How does Bly's reading and explanation of the poem compare with your own experience of it? Do you think his essay limits or expands your interpretation of the poem? Explain your response.

CARL SANDBURG (1878–1967)

Buttons   1905

I have been watching the war map slammed up for advertising in front of the
    newspaper office.
Buttons — red and yellow buttons — blue and black buttons — are shoved back
    and forth across the map.

A laughing young man, sunny with freckles,
Climbs a ladder, yells a joke to somebody in the crowd,
And then fixes a yellow button one inch west   5
And follows the yellow button with a black button one inch west.

(Ten thousand men and boys twist on their bodies in a red soak along a river
    edge,
Gasping of wounds, calling for water, some rattling death in their throats.)

Who would guess what it cost to move two buttons one inch on the war map
    here in front of the newspaper office where the freckle-faced young man
    is laughing to us?

Considerations for Critical Thinking and Writing

1. FIRST RESPONSE. Why is the date of this poem significant?

2. Discuss the symbolic meaning of the buttons and explain why you think
   the symbolism is too spelled out or not.

3. What purpose does the "laughing young man, sunny with freckles" serve in
   the poem?

Connection to Another Selection

1. Discuss the symbolic treatment of war in this poem, Kenneth Fearing's
   "AD" (p. 144), and Henry Reed's "Naming of Parts" (p. 160).

William Stafford (b. 1914)

Traveling through the Dark   1962

Traveling through the dark I found a deer
dead on the edge of the Wilson River road.
It is usually best to roll them into the canyon:
that road is narrow; to swerve might make more dead.

By glow of the tail-light I stumbled back of the car   5
and stood by the heap, a doe, a recent killing;
she had stiffened already, almost cold.
I dragged her off; she was large in the belly.

My fingers touching her side brought me the reason —
her side was warm; her fawn lay there waiting,   10
alive, still, never to be born.
Beside that mountain road I hesitated.

The car aimed ahead its lowered parking lights;
under the hood purred the steady engine.
I stood in the glare of the warm exhaust turning red;   15
around our group I could hear the wilderness listen.

I thought hard for us all — my only swerving —
then pushed her over the edge into the river.

Considerations for Critical Thinking and Writing

1. FIRST RESPONSE. Notice the description of the car in this poem: the "glow
   of the tail-light," the "lowered parking lights," and how the engine

"purred." How do these and other details suggest symbolic meanings for the car and the "recent killing"?

2. Discuss the speaker's tone. Does the speaker seem, for example, tough, callous, kind, sentimental, confused, or confident?

3. What is the effect of the last stanza's having only two lines rather than the established four lines of the previous stanzas?

4. Discuss the appropriateness of this poem's title. In what sense has the speaker "thought hard for us all"? What are those thoughts?

5. Is this a didactic poem?

ANDREW HUDGINS (B. 1951)

Seventeen   *1991*

Ahead of me, the dog reared on its rope,
and swayed. The pickup took a hard left turn,
and the dog tipped off the side. He scrambled, fell,
and scraped along the hot asphalt
before he tumbled back into the air.   5
I pounded on my horn and yelled. The rope
snapped and the brown dog hurtled into the weeds.
I braked, still pounding on my horn. The truck
stopped too.

            We met halfway, and stared   10
down at the shivering dog, which flinched
and moaned and tried to flick its tail.
Most of one haunch was scraped away
and both hind legs were twisted. *You stupid shit!*
I said. He squinted at me. "Well now, bud —   15
you best watch what you say to me."
I'd never cussed a grown-up man before.
I nodded. I figured on a beating. He grinned.
"You so damn worried about that ole dog,
he's yours." He strolled back to his truck,   20
gunned it, and slewed off, spraying gravel.
The dog whined harshly.

            By the road,
gnats rose waist-high as I waded through
the dry weeds, looking for a rock.   25
I knelt down by the dog — tail flick —
and slammed the rock down twice. The first
blow did the job, but I had planned for two.
My hands swept up and down again. I grabbed
the hind legs, swung twice, and heaved the dog   30
into a clump of butterfly weed and vetch.

But then I didn't know that they had names,
those roadside weeds. His truck was a blue Ford,
the dog a beagle. I was seventeen.
The gnats rose, gathered to one loose cloud,   35
then scattered through coarse orange and purple weeds.

CONSIDERATIONS FOR CRITICAL THINKING AND WRITING

1. FIRST RESPONSE. Hudgins has described "Seventeen" as a "rite of passage."
   How does the title focus this idea?

2. What kind of language does Hudgins use to describe the injured dog (lines
   1–14)? What is its effect?

3. Characterize the speaker and the driver of the pickup. What clues does the
   poem provide to the way each perceives the other?

4. Might killing the dog be understood as a symbolic action? Try to come up
   with more than one interpretation for the speaker's actions.

CONNECTIONS TO OTHER SELECTIONS

1. Write an essay that compares the speakers and themes of "Seventeen" and
   "Traveling through the Dark."

2. In an essay discuss the speakers' attitudes toward dogs in "Seventeen" and
   Ronald Wallace's "Dogs" (p. 685). What do these attitudes reveal about the
   speakers?

ALDEN NOWLAN (1933–1983)

The Bull Moose   *1962*

Down from the purple mist of trees on the mountain,
lurching through forests of white spruce and cedar,
stumbling through tamarack swamps,
came the bull moose
to be stopped at last by a pole-fenced pasture.   5

Too tired to turn or, perhaps, aware
there was no place left to go, he stood with the cattle.
They, scenting the musk of death, seeing his great head
like the ritual mask of a blood god, moved to the other end
of the field, and waited.   10

The neighbors heard of it, and by afternoon
cars lined the road. The children teased him
with alder switches and he gazed at them
like an old, tolerant collie. The women asked
if he could have escaped from a Fair.   15

The oldest man in the parish remembered seeing
a gelded moose yoked with an ox for plowing.

The young men snickered and tried to pour beer
down his throat, while their girl friends took their pictures.

The bull moose let them stroke his tick-ravaged flanks,   20
let them pry open his jaws with bottles, let a giggling girl
plant a little purple cap
of thistles on his head.

When the wardens came, everyone agreed it was a shame
to shoot anything so shaggy and cuddlesome.   25
He looked like the kind of pet
women put to bed with their sons.

So they held their fire. But just as the sun dropped in the river
the bull moose gathered his strength
like a scaffolded king, straightened and lifted his horns   30
so that even the wardens backed away as they raised their rifles.
When he roared, people ran to their cars. All the young men
leaned on their automobile horns as he toppled.

CONSIDERATIONS FOR CRITICAL THINKING AND WRITING

1. FIRST RESPONSE. How does the speaker present the moose and the towns-
   people? How are the moose and townspeople contrasted? Discuss specific
   lines to support your response.

2. Explain how the symbols in this poem point to a conflict between humanity
   and nature. What do you think the speaker's attitude toward this conflict is?

3. Read the section on mythological criticism in Chapter 19, "Critical Strate-
   gies for Reading," and write an essay on "The Bull Moose" that approaches
   the poem from a mythological perspective.

CONNECTION TO ANOTHER SELECTION

1. In an essay compare and contrast how the animals portrayed in "The Bull
   Moose" and in Stafford's "Traveling through the Dark" (p. 155) are used
   as symbols.

JULIO MARZÁN (B. 1946)

Ethnic Poetry   *1994*

The ethnic poet said: "The earth is maybe
a huge maraca / and the sun a trombone /
and life / is to move your ass / to slow beats."
The ethnic audience roasted a suckling pig.

The ethnic poet said: "Oh thank Goddy, Goddy /   5
I be me, my toenails curled downward /
deep, deep, deep into Mama earth."
The ethnic audience shook strands of sea shells.

The ethnic poet said: "The sun was created black /
so we should imagine light / and also dream /   10

a walrus emerging from the broken ice."
The ethnic audience beat on sealskin drums.

The ethnic poet said: "Reproductive organs /
Eagles nesting California redwoods /
Shut up and listen to my ancestors."   15
The ethnic audience ate fried bread and honey.

The ethnic poet said: "Something there is that
doesn't love a wall / That sends
the frozen-ground-swell under it."
The ethnic audience deeply understood humanity.   20

CONSIDERATIONS FOR CRITICAL THINKING AND WRITING

1. FIRST RESPONSE. What is the implicit definition of ethnic poetry in this poem?

2. The final stanza quotes lines from Robert Frost's "Mending Wall" (p. 342). Read the entire poem. Why do you think Marzán chooses these lines and this particular poem as one kind of ethnic poetry?

3. What is the poem's central irony? Pay particular attention to the final line. What is being satirized here?

CONNECTION TO ANOTHER SELECTION

1. Write an essay that discusses the speaker's ideas about what poetry should be in "Ethnic Poetry" and in Langston Hughes's "Formula" (p. 382).

JAMES MERRILL (1926–1995)

Casual Wear   *1984*

Your average tourist: Fifty. 2.3
Times married. Dressed, this year, in Ferdi Plinthbower
Originals. Odds 1 to 9
Against her strolling past the Embassy

Today at noon. Your average terrorist: 5
Twenty-five. Celibate. No use for trends,
At least in clothing. Mark, though, where it ends.
People have come forth made of colored mist

Unsmiling on one hundred million screens
To tell of his prompt phone call to the station,   10
"Claiming responsibility" — devastation
Signed with a flourish, like the dead wife's jeans.

CONSIDERATIONS FOR CRITICAL THINKING AND WRITING

1. FIRST RESPONSE. What is the effect of the statistics in this poem?

2. Describe the speaker's tone. Is it appropriate for the subject matter? Explain why or why not.

3. Comment on the ironies that emerge from the final two lines. How are the tourist and terrorist linked by the speaker's description? Explain why you think the speaker sympathizes more with the tourist or the terrorist — or with neither.

CONNECTION TO ANOTHER SELECTION

1. Compare the satire in this poem with that in Peter Meinke's "The ABC of Aerobics" (p. 270). What is satirized in each poem? Which satire is more pointed from your perspective?

HENRY REED (1914–1986)

Naming of Parts   *1946*

Today we have naming of parts. Yesterday,
We had daily cleaning. And tomorrow morning,
We shall have what to do after firing. But today,
Today we have naming of parts. Japonica
Glistens like coral in all of the neighboring gardens,   5
        And today we have naming of parts.

This is the lower sling swivel. And this
Is the upper sling swivel, whose use you will see,
When you are given your slings. And this is the piling swivel,
Which in your case you have not got. The branches   10
Hold in the gardens their silent, eloquent gestures,
        Which in our case we have not got.

This is the safety-catch, which is always released
With an easy flick of the thumb. And please do not let me
See anyone using his finger. You can do it quite easy   15
If you have any strength in your thumb. The blossoms
Are fragile and motionless, never letting anyone see
        Any of them using their finger.

And this you can see is the bolt. The purpose of this
Is to open the breech, as you see. We can slide it   20
Rapidly backwards and forwards: we call this
Easing the spring. And rapidly backwards and forwards
The early bees are assaulting and fumbling the flowers:
        They call it easing the Spring.

They call it easing the Spring: it is perfectly easy   25
If you have any strength in your thumb: like the bolt,
And the breech, and the cocking-piece, and the point of balance,
Which in our case we have not got; and the almond-blossom
Silent in all of the gardens and the bees going backwards and forwards,
        For today we have naming of parts.   30

CONSIDERATIONS FOR CRITICAL THINKING AND WRITING

1. FIRST RESPONSE. Characterize the two speakers in this poem. Identify the lines spoken by each. How do their respective lines differ in tone?

2. What is the effect of the last line of each stanza?

3. How do ambiguities and puns contribute to the poem's meaning?

4. What symbolic contrast is made between the rifle instruction and the gardens? How is this contrast ironic?

JOHN CIARDI (1916–1986)

Suburban

1978

Yesterday Mrs. Friar phoned. "Mr. Ciardi,
   how do you do?" she said. "I am sorry to say
this isn't exactly a social call. The fact is
   your dog has just deposited — forgive me —
a large repulsive object in my petunias."   5

I thought to ask, "Have you checked the rectal grooving
   for a positive I.D.?" My dog, as it happened,
was in Vermont with my son, who had gone fishing —
   if that's what one does with a girl, two cases of beer,
and a borrowed camper. I guessed I'd get no trout.   10

But why lose out on organic gold for a wise crack?
   "Yes, Mrs. Friar," I said, "I understand."
"Most kind of you," she said. "Not at all," I said.
   I went with a spade. She pointed, looking away.
"I always have loved dogs," she said, "but really!"   15

I scooped it up and bowed. "The animal of it.
   I hope this hasn't upset you, Mrs. Friar."
"Not really," she said, "but really!" I bore the turd
   across the line to my own petunias
and buried it till the glorious resurrection   20

when even these suburbs shall give up their dead.

CONSIDERATIONS FOR CRITICAL THINKING AND WRITING

1. FIRST RESPONSE. How does the speaker transform Mrs. Friar into a symbolic figure of the suburbs?

2. Why do you suppose Ciardi focuses on this particular incident to make a comment upon the suburbs? What is the speaker's attitude toward suburban life?

3. Write a one-paragraph physical description of Mrs. Friar that captures her character for you.

CONNECTION TO ANOTHER SELECTION

1. Compare the speakers' voices in "Suburban" and in Updike's "Dog's Death" (p. 11).

CHITRA BANERJEE DIVAKARUNI (B. 1956)

Indian Movie, New Jersey   *1990*

Not like the white filmstars, all rib
and gaunt cheekbone, the Indian sex-goddess
smiles plumply from behind a flowery
branch. Below her brief red skirt, her thighs
are satisfying-solid, redeeming   5
as tree trunks. She swings her hips
and the men-viewers whistle. The lover-hero
dances in to a song, his lip-sync
a little off, but no matter, we
know the words already and sing along.   10
It is safe here, the day
golden and cool so no one sweats,
roses on every bush and the Dal Lake
clean again.
      The sex-goddess switches   15
to thickened English to emphasize
a joke. We laugh and clap. Here
we need not be embarrassed by words
dropping like lead pellets into foreign ears.
The flickering movie-light   20
wipes from our faces years of America, sons
who want mohawks and refuse to run
the family store, daughters who date
on the sly.
      When at the end the hero   25
dies for his friend who also
loves the sex-goddess and now can marry her,
we weep, understanding. Even the men
clear their throats to say, "What *qurbani!*°   *sacrifice*
What *dosti!*"° After, we mill around   *friendship* 30
unwilling to leave, exchange greetings
and good news: a new gold chain, a trip
to India. We do not speak
of motel raids, canceled permits, stones
thrown through glass windows, daughters and sons   35
raped by Dotbusters.°
      In this dim foyer
we can pull around us the faint, comforting smell

36 *Dotbusters:* New Jersey gangs that attack Indians.

of incense and *pakoras,*° can arrange   *fried appetizers*
our children's marriages with hometown boys and girls,   40
open a franchise, win a million
in the mail. We can retire
in India, a yellow two-storied house
with wrought-iron gates, our own
Ambassador car. Or at least   45
move to a rich white suburb, Summerfield
or Fort Lee, with neighbors that will
talk to us. Here while the film-songs still echo
in the corridors and restrooms, we can trust
in movie truths: sacrifice, success, love and luck,   50
the America that was supposed to be.

CONSIDERATIONS FOR CRITICAL THINKING AND WRITING

1. FIRST RESPONSE. Why does the speaker feel comfortable at the movies? How is the world inside the theater different from life outside in New Jersey?

2. Explain the differences portrayed by the speaker between life in India and life in New Jersey. What connotative values are associated with each location in the poem?

3. Discuss the irony in the final two lines.

PAUL MULDOON (B. 1951)

Symposium   *1998*

You can lead a horse to water but you can't make it hold
its nose to the grindstone and hunt with the hounds.
Every dog has a stitch in time. Two heads? You've been sold
one good turn. One good turn deserves a bird in the hand.

A bird in the hand is better than no bread.   5
To have your cake is to pay Paul.
Make hay while you can still hit the nail on the head.
For want of a nail the sky might fall.

People in glass houses can't see the wood
for the new broom. Rome wasn't built between two stools.   10
Empty vessels wait for no man.

A hair of the dog is a friend indeed.
There's no fool like the fool
who's shot his bolt. There's no smoke after the horse is gone.

CONSIDERATIONS FOR CRITICAL THINKING AND WRITING

1. FIRST RESPONSE. What meanings can you draw from the poem on a first reading? Do the lines mean more to you after subsequent readings? Why or why not?

2. To what extent are these bits of clichés and aphorisms connected to each other? Explain why you find the poem coherent or not.

3. Look up the meaning and origin of *symposium* in a dictionary. Why is this an apt title for this poem?

CONNECTION TO ANOTHER SELECTION

1. Discuss the use of irony in this poem and in E. E. Cummings's "next to of course god america i" (p. 146).

ROBERT BROWNING (1812–1889)

My Last Duchess   *1842*

Ferrara°

That's my last Duchess painted on the wall,
Looking as if she were alive. I call
That piece a wonder, now: Frà Pandolf's° hands
Worked busily a day, and there she stands.
Will't please you sit and look at her? I said   5
"Frà Pandolf" by design, for never read
Strangers like you that pictured countenance,
The depth and passion of its earnest glance,
But to myself they turned (since none puts by
The curtain I have drawn for you, but I)   10
And seemed as they would ask me, if they durst,
How such a glance came there; so, not the first
Are you to turn and ask thus. Sir, 'twas not
Her husband's presence only, called that spot
Of joy into the Duchess' cheek: perhaps   15
Frà Pandolf chanced to say "Her mantle laps
Over my lady's wrist too much," or "Paint
Must never hope to reproduce the faint
Half-flush that dies along her throat": such stuff
Was courtesy, she thought, and cause enough   20
For calling up that spot of joy. She had
A heart — how shall I say? — too soon made glad,
Too easily impressed; she liked whate'er
She looked on, and her looks went everywhere.
Sir, 'twas all one! My favor at her breast,   25
The dropping of the daylight in the West,
The bough of cherries some officious fool
Broke in the orchard for her, the white mule

Ferrara: In the sixteenth century, the duke of this Italian city arranged to marry a second time after the mysterious death of his very young first wife.   3 *Frà Pandolf:* A fictitious artist.

She rode with round the terrace — all and each
Would draw from her alike the approving speech,   30
Or blush, at least. She thanked men, — good! but thanked
Somehow — I know not how — as if she ranked
My gift of a nine-hundred-years-old name
With anybody's gift. Who'd stoop to blame
This sort of trifling? Even had you skill   35
In speech — which I have not — to make your will
Quite clear to such an one, and say, "Just this
Or that in you disgusts me; here you miss,
Or there exceed the mark" — and if she let
Herself be lessoned so, nor plainly set   40
Her wits to yours, forsooth, and made excuse,
— E'en then would be some stooping; and I choose
Never to stoop. Oh sir, she smiled, no doubt,
Whene'er I passed her; but who passed without
Much the same smile? This grew; I gave commands;   45
Then all smiles stopped together. There she stands
As if alive. Will't please you rise? We'll meet
The company below, then. I repeat,
The Count your master's known munificence
Is ample warrant that no just pretense   50
Of mine for dowry will be disallowed;
Though his fair daughter's self, as I avowed
At starting, is my object. Nay, we'll go
Together down, sir. Notice Neptune, though,
Taming a sea-horse, thought a rarity,   55
Which Claus of Innsbruck° cast in bronze for me!

56 *Claus of Innsbruck:* Also a fictitious artist.

CONSIDERATIONS FOR CRITICAL THINKING AND WRITING

1. FIRST RESPONSE. What do you think happened to the duchess?

2. To whom is the duke addressing his remarks about the duchess in this poem? What is ironic about the situation?

3. Why was the duke unhappy with his first wife? What does this reveal about the duke? What does the poem's title suggest about his attitude toward women in general?

4. What seems to be the visitor's response (lines 53–54) to the duke's account of his first wife?

CONNECTION TO ANOTHER SELECTION

1. Write an essay describing the ways in which the speakers of "My Last Duchess" and "Hazel Tells LaVerne" (p. 61) by Katharyn Howd Machan inadvertently reveal themselves.

WILLIAM BLAKE (1757–1827)

The Chimney Sweeper

1789

When my mother died I was very young,
And my father sold me while yet my tongue
Could scarcely cry "'weep! 'weep! 'weep! 'weep!"
So your chimneys I sweep, and in soot I sleep.

There's little Tom Dacre, who cried when his head,   5
That curled like a lamb's back, was shaved: so I said
"Hush, Tom! never mind it, for when your head's bare
You know that the soot cannot spoil your white hair."

And so he was quiet, and that very night,
As Tom was a-sleeping, he had such a sight!   10
That thousands of sweepers, Dick, Joe, Ned, and Jack,
Were all of them locked up in coffins of black.

And by came an Angel who had a bright key,
And he opened the coffins and set them all free;
Then down a green plain leaping, laughing, they run,   15
And wash in a river, and shine in the sun.

Then naked and white, all their bags left behind,
They rise upon clouds and sport in the wind;
And the Angel told Tom, if he'd be a good boy,
He'd have God for his father, and never want joy.   20

And so Tom awoke; and we rose in the dark,
And got with our bags and our brushes to work.
Though the morning was cold, Tom was happy and warm;
So if all do their duty they need not fear harm.

CONSIDERATIONS FOR CRITICAL THINKING AND WRITING

1. FIRST RESPONSE. Discuss the validity of this statement: "'The Chimney Sweeper' is a sentimental poem about a shameful eighteenth-century social problem; such a treatment of child abuse cannot be taken seriously."
2. Characterize the speaker in this poem, and describe his tone. Is his tone the same as the poet's? Consider especially lines 7, 8, and 24.
3. What is the symbolic value of the dream in lines 11 to 20?
4. Why is irony central to the meaning of this poem?

DIANE THIEL (B. 1967)

The Minefield

2000

He was running with his friend from town to town.
They were somewhere between Prague and Dresden.

He was fourteen, His friend was faster
and knew a shortcut through the fields they could take.
He said there was lettuce growing in one of them,   5
and they hadn't eaten all day. His friend ran a few lengths ahead,
like a wild rabbit across the grass,
turned his head, looked back once,
and his body was scattered across the field.

My father told us this, one night,   10
and then continued eating dinner.

He brought them with him — the minefields.
He carried them underneath his good intentions.
He gave them to us — in the volume of his anger,
in the bruises we covered up with sleeves,   15
In the way he threw anything against the wall —
a radio, that wasn't even ours,
a melon, once, opened like a head.
In the way we still expect, years later and continents away,
that anything might explode at any time,   20
and we would have to run on alone
with a vision like that
only seconds behind.

CONSIDERATIONS FOR CRITICAL THINKING AND WRITING

1. FIRST RESPONSE. What are the effects of the minefields on the father — and
   on the speaker?
2. How does the speaker feel about the father? How does this poem make you
   feel about the father?
3. Discuss the significance of the title. How can it read symbolically in more
   than one way?

CONNECTION TO ANOTHER SELECTION

1. Discuss the treatment of fathers in "The Minefield" and in Regina Bar-
   reca's "Nighttime Fires" (p. 26). Compare how the memory of the father af-
   fects the speaker in each poem.

GARY SOTO (B. 1952)

Behind Grandma's House   1985

At ten I wanted fame. I had a comb
And two Coke bottles, a tube of Bryl-creem.
I borrowed a dog, one with
Mismatched eyes and a happy tongue,
And wanted to prove I was tough   5
In the alley, kicking over trash cans,

A dull chime of tuna cans falling.
I hurled light bulbs like grenades
And men teachers held their heads,
Fingers of blood lengthening   10
On the ground. I flicked rocks at cats,
Their goofy faces spurred with foxtails.
I kicked fences. I shooed pigeons.
I broke a branch from a flowering peach
And frightened ants with a stream of spit.   15
I said "*Chale*," "In your face," and "No way
Daddy-O" to an imaginary priest
Until grandma came into the alley,
Her apron flapping in a breeze,
Her hair mussed, and said, "Let me help you,"   20
And punched me between the eyes.

Considerations for Critical Thinking and Writing

1. FIRST RESPONSE. What is the central irony of this poem?

2. How does the speaker characterize himself at ten?

3. Though the "grandma" appears only briefly, she seems, in a sense, fully characterized. How would you describe her? Why do you think she says, "Let me help you"?

Connection to Another Selection

1. Write an essay comparing the themes of "Behind Grandma's House" and Sharon Olds's "Rite of Passage" (p. 265).

Robert Bly (b. 1927)

The Man Who Didn't Know What Was His   *1988*

There was a man who didn't know what was his.
He thought as a boy that some demon forced him
To wear "his" clothes and live in "his" room
And sit on "his" chair and be a child of "his" parents.

Each time he sat down to dinner, it happened again.   5
His own birthday party belonged to someone else.
And — was it sweet potatoes that he liked? —
He should resist them. Whose plate is this?

This man will be like a lean-to attached
To a house. It doesn't *have* a foundation.   10
This man is helpful and hostile in each moment.
This man leans toward you and leans away.

He's charming, this man who doesn't know what is his.

CONSIDERATIONS FOR CRITICAL THINKING AND WRITING

1. FIRST RESPONSE. Do you feel the speaker leaning toward you or away from you? Explain your response.

2. What kind of "demon" is described in line 2?

3. How do the boy's experiences serve to shape the man, according to the speaker?

4. Discuss the symbolic values associated with "dinner" in this poem.

CONNECTION TO ANOTHER SELECTION

1. In an essay consider how early childhood experiences affect adult identities in "The Man Who Didn't Know What Was His" and in Judy Page Heitzman's "The Schoolroom on the Second Floor of the Knitting Mill" (p. 446).

PERSPECTIVE

EZRA POUND (1885–1972)

On Symbols 1912

I believe that the proper and perfect symbol is the natural object, that if a man uses "symbols" he must so use them that their symbolic function does not obtrude; so that *a* sense, and the poetic quality of the passage, is not lost to those who do not understand the symbol as such, to whom, for instance, a hawk is a hawk.

From "Prolegomena," *Poetry Review*, February 1912

CONSIDERATIONS FOR CRITICAL THINKING AND WRITING

1. Discuss whether you agree with Pound that the "perfect symbol" is a "natural object" that does not insist on being read as a symbol.

2. Write an essay in which you discuss Alden Nowlan's "The Bull Moose" (p. 157) as an example of the "perfect symbol" Pound proposes.

7

Sounds

Poems yearn to be read aloud. Much of their energy, charm, and beauty comes to life only when they are heard. Poets choose and arrange words for their sounds as well as for their meanings. Most poetry is best read with your lips, teeth, and tongue because they serve to articulate the effects that sound may have in a poem. When a voice is breathed into a good poem, there is pleasure in the reading, the saying, and the hearing.

LISTENING TO POETRY

The earliest poetry—before writing and painting—was chanted or sung. The rhythmic quality of such oral performances served two purposes: it helped the chanting bard remember the lines, and it entertained audiences with patterned sounds of language, which were sometimes accompanied by musical instruments. Poetry has always been closely related to music. Indeed, as the word suggests, lyric poetry evolved from songs. "Western Wind" (p. 26), an anonymous Middle English lyric, survived as song long before it was written down. Had Robert Frost lived in a nonliterate society, he probably would have sung some version—a very different version to be sure—of "Acquainted with the Night" (p. 139) instead of writing it down. Even though Frost creates a speaking rather than a singing voice, the speaker's anxious tone is distinctly heard in any careful reading of the poem.

Like lyrics, early narrative poems were originally part of an anonymous oral folk tradition. A **ballad** such as "Bonny Barbara Allan" (p. 589) told a story that was sung from one generation to the next until it was finally transcribed. Since the eighteenth century, this narrative form has sometimes been imitated by poets who write **literary ballads.** John Keats's "La

Belle Dame sans Merci" (p. 618) is, for example, a more complex and sophisticated nineteenth-century reflection of the original ballad traditions that developed in the fifteenth century and earlier. In considering poetry as sound, we should not forget that poetry traces its beginnings to song.

These next lines exemplify poetry's continuing relation to song. What poetic elements can you find in this ballad, which was adapted by Simon and Garfunkel and became a popular antiwar song in the 1960s?

ANONYMOUS

Scarborough Fair   *date unknown*

Where are you going? To Scarborough Fair?
Parsley, sage, rosemary, and thyme,
Remember me to a bonny lass there,
For once she was a true lover of mine.

Tell her to make me a cambric shirt,   5
Parsley, sage, rosemary, and thyme,
Without any needle or thread work'd in it,
And she shall be a true lover of mine.

Tell her to wash it in yonder well,
Parsley, sage, rosemary, and thyme,   10
Where water ne'er sprung nor a drop of rain fell,
And she shall be a true lover of mine.

Tell her to plough me an acre of land,
Parsley, sage, rosemary, and thyme,
Between the sea and the salt sea strand,   15
And she shall be a true lover of mine.

Tell her to plough it with one ram's horn,
Parsley, sage, rosemary, and thyme,
And sow it all over with one peppercorn,
And she shall be a true lover of mine.   20

Tell her to reap it with a sickle of leather,
Parsley, sage, rosemary, and thyme,
And tie it all up with a tom tit's feather,
And she shall be a true lover of mine.

Tell her to gather it all in a sack,   25
Parsley, sage, rosemary, and thyme,
And carry it home on a butterfly's back,
And then she shall be a true lover of mine.

CONSIDERATIONS FOR CRITICAL THINKING AND WRITING

1. FIRST RESPONSE. What do you associate with "Parsley, sage, rosemary, and thyme"? What images does this poem evoke? How?

2. What kinds of demands does the speaker make on his former lover? What do these demands have in common?

3. What is the tone of this ballad?

4. Choose a contemporary song that you especially like and examine the lyrics. Write an essay explaining whether or not you consider the lyrics poetic.

Of course, reading "Scarborough Fair" is not the same as hearing it. Like the lyrics of a song, many poems must be heard — or at least read with listening eyes — before they can be fully understood and enjoyed. The sounds of words are a universal source of music for human beings. This has been so from ancient tribes to bards to the two-year-old child in a bakery gleefully chanting "Cuppitycake, cuppitycake!"

Listen to the sound of this poem as you read it aloud. How do the words provide, in a sense, their own musical accompaniment?

JOHN UPDIKE (B. 1932)

Player Piano   1958

My stick fingers click with a snicker
And, chuckling, they knuckle the keys;
Light-footed, my steel feelers flicker
And pluck from these keys melodies.

My paper can caper; abandon   5
Is broadcast by dint of my din,
And no man or band has a hand in
The tones I turn on from within.

At times I'm a jumble of rumbles,
At others I'm light like the moon,   10
But never my numb plunker fumbles,
Misstrums me, or tries a new tune.

The speaker in this poem is a piano that can play automatically by means of a mechanism that depresses keys in response to signals on a perforated roll. Notice how the speaker's voice approximates the sounds of a piano. In each stanza a predominant sound emerges from the carefully chosen words. How is the sound of each stanza tuned to its sense?

Like Updike's "Player Piano," this next poem is also primarily about sounds.

MAY SWENSON (B. 1919)

A Nosty Fright   1984

The roldengod and the soneyhuckle,
the sack eyed blusan and the wistle theed
are all tangled with the oison pivy,
the fallen nine peedles and the wumbleteed.

A mipchunk caught in a wobceb tried   5
to hip and skide in a dandy sune
but a stobler put up a EEP KOFF sign.
Then the unfucky lellow met a phytoon

and was sept out to swea. He difted for drays
till a hassgropper flying happened to spot   10
the boolish feast all debraggled and wet,
covered with snears and tot.

Loonmight shone through the winey poods
where rushmooms grew among risted twoots.
Back blats flew betreen the twees   15
and orned howls hounded their soots.

A kumkpin stood with tooked creeth
on the sindow will of a house
where a icked wold itch lived all alone
except for her stoombrick, a mitten and a kouse.   20

"Here we part," said hassgropper.
"Pere we hart," said mipchunk, too.
They purried away on opposite haths,
both scared of some "Bat!" or "Scoo!"

October was ending on a nosty fright   25
with scroans and greeches and chanking clains,
with oblins and gelfs, coaths and urses,
skinning grulls and stoodblains.

Will it ever be morning, Nofember virst,
skue bly and the sappy hun, our friend?   30
With light breaves of wall by the fayside?
I sope ho, so that this ocm can pend.

At just the right moments Swenson transposes letters to create amusing sound effects and wild wordplays. Although there is a story lurking in "A Nosty Fright," any serious attempt to interpret its meaning is confronted with "a EEP KOFF sign." Instead, we are invited to enjoy the delicious sounds the poet has cooked up.

Few poems revel in sound so completely. More typically, the sounds of a poem contribute to its meaning rather than become its meaning. Consider how sound is used in the next poem.

EMILY DICKINSON (1830–1886)

A Bird came down the Walk —   c. 1862

A Bird came down the Walk —
He did not know I saw —
He bit an Angleworm in halves
And ate the fellow, raw,

And then he drank a Dew 5
From a convenient Grass —
And then hopped sidewise to the Wall
To let a Beetle pass —

He glanced with rapid eyes
That hurried all around — 10
They looked like frightened Beads, I thought —
He stirred his Velvet Head

Like one in danger, Cautious,
I offered him a Crumb
And he unrolled his feathers 15
And rowed him softer home —

Than Oars divide the Ocean,
Too silver for a seam —
Or Butterflies, off Banks of Noon
Leap, plashless as they swim. 20

This description of a bird offers a close look at how differently a bird moves when it hops on the ground than when it flies in the air. On the ground the bird moves quickly, awkwardly, and irregularly as it plucks up a worm, washes it down with dew, and then hops aside to avoid a passing beetle. The speaker recounts the bird's rapid, abrupt actions from a some-what superior, amused perspective. By describing the bird in human terms (as if, for example, it chose to eat the worm "raw"), the speaker is almost condescending. But when the attempt to offer a crumb fails and the fright-ened bird flies off, the speaker is left looking up instead of down at the bird.

With that shift in perspective the tone shifts from amusement to awe in response to the bird's graceful flight. The jerky movements of lines 1 to 13 give way to the smooth motion of lines 15 to 20. The pace of the first three stanzas is fast and discontinuous. We tend to pause at the end of each line, and this reinforces a sense of disconnected movements. In con-trast, the final six lines are to be read as a single sentence in one flowing movement, lubricated by various sounds.

Read again the description of the bird flying away. Several *o*-sounds contribute to the image of the serene, expansive, confident flight, just as the *s*-sounds serve as smooth transitions from one line to the next. Notice how these sounds are grouped in the following vertical columns:

unrolled	softer	too	his	Ocean	Banks
rowed	Oars	Noon	feathers	silver	plashless
home	Or		softer	seam	as
Ocean	off		Oars	Butterflies	swim

This blending of sounds (notice how "Leap, plashless" brings together the *p*- and *l*-sounds without a ripple) helps convey the bird's smooth grace in the air. Like a feathered oar, the bird moves seamlessly in its element.

The repetition of sounds in poetry is similar to the function of the tones and melodies that are repeated, with variations, in music. Just as the patterned sounds in music unify a work, so do the words in poems, which have been carefully chosen for the combinations of sounds they create. These sounds are produced in a number of ways.

The most direct way in which the sound of a word suggests its meaning is through **onomatopoeia,** which is the use of a word that resembles the sound it denotes: *quack, buzz, rattle, bang, squeak, bowwow, burp, choo-choo, ding-a-ling, sizzle.* The sound and sense of these words are closely related, but they represent a very small percentage of the words available to us. Poets usually employ more subtle means for echoing meanings.

Onomatopoeia can consist of more than just single words. In its broadest meaning the term refers to lines or passages in which sounds help to convey meanings, as in these lines from Updike's "Player Piano":

> My stick fingers click with a snicker
> And, chuckling, they knuckle the keys.

The sharp, crisp sounds of these two lines approximate the sounds of a piano; the syllables seem to "click" against one another. Contrast Updike's rendition with the following lines:

> My long fingers play with abandon
> And, laughing, they cover the keys.

The original version is more interesting and alive because the sounds of the words are pleasurable and they reinforce the meaning through a careful blending of consonants and vowels.

Alliteration is the repetition of the same consonant sounds at the beginnings of nearby words: "*d*escending *d*ewdrops"; "*l*uscious *l*emons." Sometimes the term is also used to describe the consonant sounds within words: "tres*p*asser's re*p*roach"; "wed*d*ed la*d*y." Alliteration is based on sound rather than spelling. "*K*een" and "*c*ar" alliterate, but "*c*ar" does not alliterate with "*c*ite." Rarely is heavy-handed alliteration effective. Used too self-consciously, it can be distracting instead of strengthening meaning or emphasizing a relation between words. Consider the relentless *h*'s in this line: "Horrendous horrors haunted Helen's happiness." Those *h*'s certainly suggest that Helen is being pursued, but they have a more comic than serious effect because they are overdone.

Assonance is the repetition of the same vowel sound in nearby words: "asl*ee*p under a tr*ee*"; "t*i*me and t*i*de"; "h*au*nt" and "*aw*esome"; "*ea*ch *e*vening." Both alliteration and assonance help to establish relations among words in a line or a series of lines. Whether the effect is **euphony** (lines that are musically pleasant to the ear and smooth, like the final lines of Dickinson's "A Bird came down the Walk—") or the effect is **cacophony** (lines that are discordant and difficult to pronounce, like the claim that "never my numb plunker fumbles" in Updike's "Player Piano"), the sounds of words in poetry can be as significant as the words' denotative or connotative meanings.

This next poem provides a feast of sounds. Read the poem aloud and try to determine the effects of its sounds.

GALWAY KINNELL (B. 1927)

Blackberry Eating

1980

I love to go out in late September
among the fat, overripe, icy, black blackberries
to eat blackberries for breakfast,
the stalks very prickly, a penalty
they earn for knowing the black art   5
of blackberry-making; and as I stand among them
lifting the stalks to my mouth, the ripest berries
fall almost unbidden to my tongue,
as words sometimes do, certain peculiar words
like *strengths* or *squinched*,   10
many-lettered, one-syllabled lumps,
which I squeeze, squinch open, and splurge well
in the silent, startled, icy, black language
of blackberry-eating in late September.

CONSIDERATIONS FOR CRITICAL THINKING AND WRITING

1. FIRST RESPONSE. What types of sounds does Kinnell use throughout this poem? What categories can you place them in? What is the effect of these sounds?

2. How do lines 4–6 fit into the poem? What does this prickly image add to the poem?

3. Explain what you think the poem's theme is.

4. Write an essay that considers the speaker's love of blackberry eating along with the speaker's appetite for words. How are the two blended in the poem?

RHYME

Like alliteration and assonance, **rhyme** is a way of creating sound patterns. Rhyme, broadly defined, consists of two or more words or phrases that repeat the same sounds: *happy* and *snappy*. Rhyme words often have similar spellings, but that is not a requirement of rhyme; what matters is that the words sound alike: *vain* rhymes with *reign* as well as *rain*. Moreover, words may look alike but not rhyme at all. In **eye rhyme** the spellings are similar, but the pronunciations are not, as with *bough* and *cough*, or *brow* and *blow*.

Not all poems employ rhyme. Many great poems have no rhymes, and many weak verses use rhyme as a substitute for poetry. These are especially apparent in commercial messages and greeting-card lines. At its worst, rhyme is merely a distracting decoration that can lead to dullness and predictability. But used skillfully, rhyme creates lines that are memorable and musical.

Following is a poem using rhyme that you might remember the next time you are in a restaurant.

RICHARD ARMOUR (1906–1989)

Going to Extremes   *1954*

Shake and shake
  The catsup bottle
None'll come —
  And then a lot'll.

The experience recounted in Armour's poem is common enough, but the rhyme's humor is special. The final line clicks the poem shut, an effect that is often achieved by the use of rhyme. That click provides a sense of a satisfying and fulfilled form. Rhymes have a number of uses: they can emphasize words, direct a reader's attention to relations between words, and provide an overall structure for a poem.

Rhyme is used in the following poem to imitate the sound of cascading water.

ROBERT SOUTHEY (1774–1843)

From "The Cataract of Lodore"   *1820*

"How does the water

Come down at Lodore?"
. . . .
From its sources which well
  In the tarn on the fell;
    From its fountains   5
    In the mountains,
  Its rills and its gills;
Through moss and through brake,
    It runs and it creeps
    For awhile, till it sleeps   10
      In its own little lake.
    And thence at departing,
    Awakening and starting,
    It runs through the reeds
    And away it proceeds,   15

Through meadow and glade,
   In sun and in shade,
And through the wood-shelter,
    Among crags in its flurry,
     Helter-skelter, 20
     Hurry-scurry.
   Here it comes sparkling,
And there it lies darkling;
Now smoking and frothing
   Its tumult and wrath in, 25
    Till in this rapid race
     On which it is bent,
    It reaches the place
    Of its steep descent.

    The cataract strong 30
    Then plunges along,
   Striking and raging
    As if a war waging
Its caverns and rocks among:
    Rising and leaping, 35
   Sinking and creeping,
   Swelling and sweeping,
  Showering and springing,
     Flying and flinging,
    Writhing and ringing, 40
Eddying and whisking,
Spouting and frisking,
Turning and twisting,
    Around and around
   With endless rebound! 45
   Smiting and fighting,
    A sight to delight in;
   Confounding, astounding,
Dizzying and deafening the ear with its sound.
. . . .
Dividing and gliding and sliding, 50
And falling and brawling and spawling,
And driving and riving and striving,
And sprinkling and twinkling and wrinkling,
And sounding and bounding and rounding,
And bubbling and troubling and doubling, 55
And grumbling and rumbling and tumbling,
And clattering and battering and shattering;
Retreating and beating and meeting and sheeting,
Delaying and straying and playing and spraying,
Advancing and prancing and glancing and dancing, 60
Recoiling, turmoiling and toiling and boiling,
And gleaming and streaming and steaming and beaming,
And rushing and flushing and brushing and gushing,
And flapping and rapping and clapping and slapping,

And curling and whirling and purling and twirling,   65
And thumping and plumping and bumping and jumping,
And dashing and flashing and splashing and clashing;
And so never ending, but always descending,
Sounds and motions forever and ever are blending,
All at once and all o'er, with a mighty uproar;   70
And this way the water comes down at Lodore.

This deluge of rhymes consists of "Sounds and motions forever and ever . . . blending" (line 69). The pace quickens as the water creeps from its mountain source and then descends in rushing cataracts. As the speed of the water increases, so do the number of rhymes, until they run in fours: "dashing and flashing and splashing and clashing" (line 67). Most rhymes meander through poems instead of flooding them; nevertheless, Southey's use of rhyme suggests how sounds can flow with meanings. "The Cataract of Lodore" has been criticized, however, for overusing onomatopoeia. Some readers find the poem silly; others regard it as a brilliant example of sound effects. What do you think?

A variety of types of rhyme is available to poets. The most common form, ***end rhyme,*** comes at the ends of lines (lines 14–17).

> It runs through the reeds
>> And away it proceeds,
> Through meadow and glade,
>> In sun and in shade.

Internal rhyme places at least one of the rhymed words within the line, as in "Dividing and gliding and sliding" (line 50) or, more subtly, in the fourth and final words of "In mist or cloud, on mast or shroud."

The rhyming of single-syllable words such as *glade* and *shade* is known as ***masculine rhyme:***

> Loveliest of trees, the cherry now
> Is hung with bloom along the bough.
>> — A. E. Housman

Rhymes using words of more than one syllable are also called masculine when the same sound occurs in a final stressed syllable, as in *defend, contend; betray, away.* A ***feminine rhyme*** consists of a rhymed stressed syllable followed by one or more rhymed unstressed syllables, as in *butter, clutter; gratitude, attitude; quivering, shivering:*

> Lord confound this surly sister,
> Blight her brow and blotch and blister.
>> —John Millington Synge

All the examples so far have been ***exact rhymes*** because they share the same stressed vowel sounds as well as any sounds that follow the vowel. In ***near rhyme*** (also called ***off rhyme, slant rhyme,*** and ***approximate rhyme***), the sounds are almost but not exactly alike. There are several kinds of near rhyme. One of the most common is **consonance,** an identical consonant sound preceded by a different vowel sound: *home, same; worth, breath; trophy, daffy.* Near rhyme can also be achieved by using different vowel sounds with identical consonant sounds: *sound, sand; kind, conned; fellow, fallow.* The dissonance of *blade* and *blood* in the following lines helps to reinforce their grim tone:

> Let the boy try along this bayonet-blade
> How cold steel is, and keen with hunger of blood.
> — Wilfred Owen

Near rhymes greatly broaden the possibility for musical effects in English, a language that, compared with Spanish or Italian, contains few exact rhymes. Do not assume, however, that a near rhyme represents a failed attempt at exact rhyme. Near rhymes allow a musical subtlety and variety and can avoid the sometimes overpowering jingling effects that exact rhymes may create.

These basic terms hardly exhaust the ways in which the sounds in poems can be labeled and discussed, but the terms can help you to describe how poets manipulate sounds for effect. Read "God's Grandeur" (p. 181) aloud and try to determine how the sounds of the lines contribute to their sense.

PERSPECTIVE

DAVID LENSON (B. 1945)

On the Contemporary Use of Rhyme   *1988*

One impediment to a respectable return to rhyme is the popular survival of "functional" verse: greeting cards, pedagogical and mnemonic devices ("Thirty days hath September"), nursery rhymes, advertising jingles, and of course song lyrics. Pentameters, irregular rhymes, and free verse aren't much use in songwriting, where the meter has to be governed by the time signature of the music.

Far from universities, there has been a revival of rhymed couplets in rap music, in which, to the accompaniment of synthesizers, vocalists deliver lengthy first-person narratives in tetrameter. While most writing teachers would dismiss such lyrics as doggerel, the aim of the songs is really not so far from that of Alexander Pope: to use rhyme to sharpen social insight, in the hope that the world may be reordered.

From *The Chronicle of Higher Education,* February 24, 1988

CONSIDERATIONS FOR CRITICAL THINKING AND WRITING

1. Read some contemporary song lyrics from a wide range of groups or vocalists. Is Lenson correct in his assessment that irregular rhyme is not much use in songwriting?

2. Examine the rhymed couplets of some rap music. Discuss whether they are used "to sharpen social insight." What is the effect of using rhymes in rap music?

3. What is your own response to rhymed poetry? Do you like yours with or without? What do you think informs your preference?

SOUND AND MEANING

GERARD MANLEY HOPKINS (1844–1889)

God's Grandeur   1877

The world is charged with the grandeur of God
   It will flame out, like shining from shook foil;°   *shaken gold foil*
   It gathers to a greatness, like the ooze of oil
Crushed.° Why do men then now not reck his rod?°
Generations have trod, have trod, have trod;   5
   And all is seared with trade; bleared, smeared with toil;
   And wears man's smudge and shares man's smell: the soil
Is bare now, nor can foot feel, being shod.
And for all this, nature is never spent;
   There lives the dearest freshness deep down things;   10
And though the last lights off the black West went
   Oh, morning, at the brown brink eastward, springs —
Because the Holy Ghost over the bent
   World broods with warm breast and with ah! bright wings.

The subject of this poem is announced in the title and the first line: "The world is charged with the grandeur of God." The poem is a celebration of the power and greatness of God's presence in the world, but the speaker is also perplexed and dismayed by people who refuse to recognize God's authority and grandeur as they are manifested in the creation. Instead of glorifying God, "men" have degraded the earth through meaningless toil and cut themselves off from the spiritual renewal inherent in the beauty of nature. The relentless demands of commerce and industry have blinded people to the earth's natural and spiritual resources. In spite of this abuse and insensitivity to God's grandeur, however, "nature is never spent"; the morning light that "springs" in the east redeems the "black West" of the night and is a sign that the spirit of the Holy Ghost is ever present in the world. This summary of the poem sketches some of the thematic significance of the lines, but it does not do justice to how they are organized around the use of sound. Hopkins's poem, unlike Southey's "The Cataract of Lodore," employs sounds in a subtle and complex way.

---

4 *Crushed:* Olives crushed in their oil;   *reck his rod:* Obey God.

In the opening line Hopkins uses alliteration — a device apparent in almost every line of the poem — to connect "Go*d*" to the "worl*d*," which is "charge*d*" with his "gran*d*eur." These consonants unify the line as well. The alliteration in lines 2 and 3 suggests a harmony in the creation: the *f*'s in "*f*lame" and "*f*oil," the *sh*'s in "*sh*ining" and "*sh*ook," the *g*'s in "*g*athers" and "*g*reatness," and the visual (not alliterative) similarities of "*ooz*e of *oi*l" emphasize a world that is held together by God's will.

That harmony is abruptly interrupted by the speaker's angry question in line 4: "Why do men then now not reck his rod?" The question is as painful to the speaker as it is difficult to pronounce. The arrangement of the alliteration ("*n*ow," "*n*ot"; "*r*eck," "*r*od"), the assonance ("n*o*t," "r*o*d"; "m*e*n," "th*e*n," "r*e*ck"), and the internal rhyme ("m*en*," "th*en*") contribute to the difficulty in saying the line, a difficulty associated with human behavior. That behavior is introduced in line 5 by the repetition of "have trod" to emphasize the repeated mistakes — sins — committed by human beings. The tone is dirgelike because humanity persists in its mistaken path rather than progressing. The speaker's horror at humanity is evident in the cacophonous sounds of lines 6 to 8. Here the alliteration of "*sm*eared," "*sm*udge," and "*sm*ell" along with the internal rhymes of "s*eared*," "bl*eared*," and "sm*eared*" echo the disgust with which the speaker views humanity's "toil" with the "soil," an end rhyme that calls attention to our mistaken equation of nature with production rather than with spirituality.

In contrast to this cacophony, the final six lines build toward the joyful recognition of the new possibilities that accompany the rising sun. This recognition leads to the euphonic description of the "Holy Gh*o*st *o*ver" (notice the reassuring consistency of the assonance) the world. Traditionally represented as a dove, the Holy Ghost brings love and peace to the "*w*orld," and "*b*roods *w*ith *w*arm *b*reast and *w*ith ah! *b*right *w*ings." The effect of this alliteration is mellifluous: The sound bespeaks the harmony that prevails at the end of the poem resulting from the speaker's recognition that "nature is never spent" because God loves and protects the world.

The sounds of "God's Grandeur" enhance the poem's theme; more can be said about its sounds, but it is enough to point out here that for this poem the sound strongly echoes the theme in nearly every line. Here are some more poems in which sound plays a significant role.

POEMS FOR FURTHER STUDY

Edgar Allan Poe (1809–1849)

The Bells   1849

I

Hear the sledges with the bells —
    Silver bells!
What a world of merriment their melody foretells!

How they tinkle, tinkle, tinkle,
 In the icy air of night!   5
While the stars that oversprinkle
All the heavens, seem to twinkle
  With a crystalline delight;
   Keeping time, time, time,
  In a sort of Runic rhyme,   10
To the tintinnabulation that so musically wells
 From the bells, bells, bells, bells,
   Bells, bells, bells —
From the jingling and the tinkling of the bells

      II
Hear the mellow wedding bells —   15
   Golden bells!
What a world of happiness their harmony foretells!
 Through the balmy air of night
 How they ring out their delight! —
  From the molten-golden notes,   20
   And all in tune,
  What a liquid ditty floats
To the turtle-dove that listens, while she gloats
   On the moon!
  Oh, from out the sounding cells,   25
What a gush of euphony voluminously wells!
  How it swells!
  How it dwells
 On the Future! — how it tells
  Of the rapture that impels   30
  To the swinging and the ringing
  Of the bells, bells, bells —
Of the bells, bells, bells, bells,
  Bells, bells, bells —
To the rhyming and the chiming of the bells!   35

      III
Hear the loud alarum bells —
  Brazen bells!
What a tale of terror, now, their turbulency tells!
 In the startled ear of night
 How they scream out their affright!   40
  Too much horrified to speak,
  They can only shriek, shriek,
   Out of tune,
In a clamorous appealing to the mercy of the fire,
In a mad expostulation with the deaf and frantic fire,   45
  Leaping higher, higher, higher,
  With a desperate desire,
  And a resolute endeavor
  Now — now to sit, or never,
By the side of the pale-faced moon.   50
  Oh, the bells, bells, bells!

What a tale their terror tells
    Of Despair!
  How they clang, and clash, and roar!
  What a horror they outpour   55
On the bosom of the palpitating air!
    Yet the ear, it fully knows,
      By the twanging
      And the clanging,
    How the danger ebbs and flows;   60
  Yet the ear distinctly tells,
      In the jangling
      And the wrangling,
  How the danger sinks and swells,
By the sinking or the swelling in the anger of the bells —   65
    Of the bells, —
  Of the bells, bells, bells, bells,
    Bells, bells, bells —
In the clamor and the clangor of the bells!

             IV
Hear the tolling of the bells —   70
    Iron bells!
What a world of solemn thought their monody compels!
  In the silence of the night,
  How we shiver with affright
At the melancholy menace of their tone!   75
  For every sound that floats
  From the rust within their throats
    Is a groan.
    And the people — ah, the people —
    They that dwell up in the steeple,   80
      All alone,
  And who tolling, tolling, tolling,
    In that muffled monotone,
Feel a glory in so rolling
    On the human heart a stone —   85
  They are neither man nor woman —
  They are neither brute nor human —
    They are Ghouls: —
  And their king it is who tolls: —
  And he rolls, rolls, rolls,   90
    Rolls
    A pæan from the bells!
  And his merry bosom swells
    With the pæan of the bells!
  And he dances, and he yells;   95
Keeping time, time, time,
In a sort of Runic rhyme,
    To the pæan of the bells —
    Of the bells:
Keeping time, time, time,   100

In a sort of Runic rhyme,
     To the throbbing of the bells —
  Of the bells, bells, bells —
    To the sobbing of the bells;
  Keeping time, time, time,   105
    As he knells, knells, knells.
  In a happy Runic rhyme,
    To the rolling of the bells —
  Of the bells, bells, bells: —
    To the tolling of the bells —   110
  Of the bells, bells, bells, bells,
    Bells, bells, bells —
To the moaning and the groaning of the bells.

CONSIDERATIONS FOR CRITICAL THINKING AND WRITING

1. FIRST RESPONSE. How does Poe create the sounds of each kind of bell in each of the poem's four sections?
2. How is onomatopoeia used in each section to echo meanings?
3. What is the effect of the many repetitions of the word "bells"?
4. How do the length of the lines in the poem create musical rhythms?
5. What kinds of rhymes are used to achieve sound effects?
6. What do you think is the theme of "The Bells"?

CONNECTION TO ANOTHER SELECTION

1. Compare Poe's sound effects with Southey's in "The Cataract of Lodore" (p. 177). Which poem do you find more effective in its use of sound? Explain why.

PAULA GUNN ALLEN (B. 1939)

Hoop Dancer   *1982*

It's hard to enter
circling clockwise and counter
clockwise moving no
regard for time, metrics
irrelevant to this dance where pain   5
is the prime counter and soft
stepping feet praise water from the skies:
I have seen the face of triumph
the winding line stare down all moves to desecration
guts not cut from arms, fingers joined to minds,   10
together Sky and Water one dancing one
circle of a thousand turning lines beyond the march of years —
out of time, out of
time, out
of time.   15

CONSIDERATIONS FOR CRITICAL THINKING AND WRITING

1. FIRST RESPONSE. How does the sound of this Indian dance reflect its movement?

2. Discuss the images of circling in the poem. How are they related to the poem's theme?

LEWIS CARROLL (CHARLES LUTWIDGE DODGSON/1832–1898)

Jabberwocky 1871

'Twas brillig, and the slithy toves
   Did gyre and gimble in the wabe:
All mimsy were the borogoves,
   And the mome raths outgrabe.

"Beware the Jabberwock, my son! 5
   The jaws that bite, the claws that catch!
Beware the Jubjub bird, and shun
   The frumious Bandersnatch!"

He took his vorpal sword in hand;
   Long time the manxome foe he sought— 10
So rested he by the Tumtum tree,
   And stood awhile in thought.

And, as in uffish thought he stood,
   The Jabberwock, with eyes of flame,
Came whiffling through the tulgey wood, 15
   And burbled as it came!

One, two! One, two! And through and through
   The vorpal blade went snicker-snack!
He left it dead, and with its head
   He went galumphing back. 20

"And hast thou slain the Jabberwock?
   Come to my arms, my beamish boy!
O frabjous day! Callooh, Callay!"
   He chortled in his joy.

'Twas brillig, and the slithy toves 25
   Did gyre and gimble in the wabe:
All mimsy were the borogoves,
   And the mome raths outgrabe.

CONSIDERATIONS FOR CRITICAL THINKING AND WRITING

1. FIRST RESPONSE. What happens in this poem? Does it have any meaning?

2. Not all the words used in this poem appear in dictionaries. In *Through the Looking Glass,* Humpty Dumpty explains to Alice that "'slithy' means 'lithe and slimy.' 'Lithe' is the same as 'active.' You see it's like a portmanteau—

there are two meanings packed up into one word." Are there any other portmanteau words in the poem?

3. Which words in the poem sound especially meaningful, even if they are devoid of any denotative meanings?

CONNECTION TO ANOTHER SELECTION

1. Compare Carroll's strategies for creating sound and meaning with those used by Swenson in "A Nosty Fright" (p. 172).

SYLVIA PLATH (1932–1963)

Mushrooms 1960

Overnight, very
Whitely, discreetly,
Very quietly

Our toes, our noses
Take hold on the loam,   5
Acquire the air.

Nobody sees us,
Stops us, betrays us;
The small grains make room.

Soft fists insist on   10
Heaving the needles,
The leafy bedding,

Even the paving.
Our hammers, our rams,
Earless and eyeless,   15

Perfectly voiceless,
Widen the crannies,
Shoulder through holes. We

Diet on water,
On crumbs of shadow,   20
Bland-mannered, asking

Little or nothing.
So many of us!
So many of us!

We are shelves, we are   25
Tables, we are meek,
We are edible,

Nudgers and shovers
In spite of ourselves.
Our kind multiplies: 30

We shall by morning
Inherit the earth.
Our foot's in the door.

CONSIDERATIONS FOR CRITICAL THINKING AND WRITING

1. FIRST RESPONSE. Is the tone of this poem serious or comic? What effects do alliteration and assonance have on your reading of the tone?
2. How important is the title?
3. Discuss what you take to be the poem's theme.

WILLIAM HEYEN (B. 1940)

The Trains   *1984*

Signed by Franz Paul Stangl, Commandant,
there is in Berlin a document,
an order of transmittal from Treblinka:

248 freight cars of clothing,
400,000 gold watches,   5
25 freight cars of women's hair.

Some clothing was kept, some pulped for paper.
The finest watches were never melted down.
All the women's hair was used for mattresses, or dolls.

Would these words like to use some of that same paper?   10
One of those watches may pulse in your own wrist.
Does someone you know collect dolls, or sleep on human hair?

He is dead at last, Commandant Stangl of Treblinka,
but the camp's three syllables still sound like freight cars
straining around a curve, Treblinka,   15

Treblinka. Clothing, time in gold watches,
women's hair for mattresses and dolls' heads.
Treblinka. The trains from Treblinka.

CONSIDERATIONS FOR CRITICAL THINKING AND WRITING

1. FIRST RESPONSE. How does the sound of the word *Treblinka* inform your understanding of the poem?
2. Why does the place name of Treblinka continue to resonate over time? If you don't know why Treblinka is infamous, use the library to find out.
3. Why do you suppose Heyen uses the word *in* instead of *on* in line 11?
4. Why is sound so important for establishing the tone of this poem? In what sense do the "camp's three syllables still sound like freight cars"?
5. How does this poem make you feel? Why?

Virginia Hamilton Adair (b. 1913)
Dirty Old Man *1998*

A few beers make his mood pugnacious,
his jokes and stories more salacious,
his eye for nymphets more rapacious,
with older women most ungracious;
his appetite for fat, voracious, 5
swells his manly gut capacious.
With piety somewhat audacious
he calls upon his saint, Ignatius,
"Save me a bed in Heaven so spacious
that it will hold a hundred geishas." 10

Considerations for Critical Thinking and Writing

1. FIRST RESPONSE. What kind of tone does this series of rhymes create?

2. Is the poet cheating a bit with the final "geishas" rhyme, or can its two syllables be justified, given all the three syllable rhymes that precede it?

3. Try writing a brief poem that characterizes someone by using a series of rhymes.

John Donne (1572–1631)
Song *1633*

Go and catch a falling star
  Get with child a mandrake root,°
Tell me where all past years are,
  Or who cleft the Devil's foot,
Teach me to hear mermaids singing, 5
  Or to keep off envy's stinging,
      And find
      What wind
Serves to advance an honest mind.

If thou be'st borne to strange sights, 10
  Things invisible to see,
Ride ten thousand days and nights,
  Till age snow white hairs on thee,
Thou, when thou return'st, wilt tell me
  All strange wonders that befell thee, 15
      And swear
      Nowhere
Lives a woman true, and fair.

2 *mandrake root:* This V-shaped root resembles the lower half of the human body.

If thou findst one, let me know,
   Such a pilgrimage were sweet—   20
Yet do not, I would not go,
   Though at next door we might meet;
Though she were true, when you met her,
   And last, till you write your letter,
        Yet she   25
        Will be
False, ere I come, to two or three.

Considerations for Critical Thinking and Writing

1. FIRST RESPONSE. What is the speaker's tone in this poem? What is his view of a woman's love? What does the speaker's use of hyperbole reveal about his emotional state?

2. Do you think Donne wants the speaker's argument to be taken seriously? Is there any humor in the poem?

3. Most of these lines end with masculine rhymes. What other kinds of rhymes are used for end rhymes?

Mona van Duyn (b. 1921)

What the Motorcycle Said   *1973*

Br-r-r-am-m-m, rackety-am-m, OM, *Am:*
All— r-r-room, r-r-ram, ala-bas-ter—
Am, the world's my oyster.

I hate plastic, wear it black and slick,
hate hardhats, wear one on my head,   5
that's what the motorcycle said.

Passed phonies in Fords, knocked down billboards, landed
on the other side of The Gap, and Whee,
bypassed history.

When I was born (The Past), baby knew best.   10
They shook when I bawled, took Freud's path,
threw away their wrath.

R-r-rackety-am-m. *Am.* War, rhyme,
soap, meat, marriage, the Phantom Jet
are shit, and like that.   15

Hate pompousness, punishment, patience, am into Love,
hate middle-class moneymakers, live on Dad,
that's what the motorcycle said.

Br-r-r-am-m-m. It's Nowsville, man. Passed Oldies, Uglies,
Straighties, Honkies. I'll never be   20
mean, tired or unsexy.

Passed cigarette suckers, souses, mother-fuckers,
losers, went back to Nature and found
how to get VD, stoned.

Passed a cow, too fast to hear her moo, "*I rolled*   25
our leaves of grass into one ball.
I am the grassy All."

Br-r-r-am-m-m, rackety-am-m, OM, *Am.*
All—gr-r-rin, oooohgah, gl-l-lutton—
Am, the world's my smilebutton.   30

CONSIDERATIONS FOR CRITICAL THINKING AND WRITING

1. FIRST RESPONSE. Write a paraphrase of the poem, paying particular atten-
   tion to how you can paraphrase the *sounds* of the motorcycle.

2. What kind of personality emerges from the motorcycle? Explain which
   lines seem especially revealing to you.

CONNECTION TO ANOTHER SELECTION

1. Compare the theme and tone of "What the Motorcycle Said" with the ex-
   cerpt from Walt Whitman's "Song of the Open Road" (p. 202).

ALEXANDER POPE (1688–1774)

From An Essay on Criticism   *1711*

But most by numbers° judge a poet's song;   *versification*
And smooth or rough, with them, is right or wrong;
In the bright muse though thousand charms conspire,
Her voice is all these tuneful fools admire;
Who haunt Parnassus° but to please their ear,   5
Not mend their minds; as some to church repair,
Not for the doctrine, but the music there.
These equal syllables alone require,
Though oft the ear the open vowels tire;
While expletives° their feeble aid do join;   10
And ten low words oft creep in one dull line;
While they ring round the same unvaried chimes,
With sure returns of still expected rhymes;
Where'er you find "the cooling western breeze,"
In the next line, it "whispers through the trees":   15
If crystal streams "with pleasing murmurs creep,"
The reader's threatened (not in vain) with "sleep":
Then, at the last and only couplet fraught

5 *Parnassus:* A Greek mountain sacred to the Muses.   10 *expletives:* Unnecessary words
used to fill a line, as the *do* in this line.

With some unmeaning thing they call a thought,
A needless Alexandrine° ends the song,   20
That, like a wounded snake, drags its slow length along.
Leave such to tune their own dull rhymes, and know
What's roundly smooth, or languishingly slow;
And praise the easy vigor of a line,
Where Denham's strength, and Waller's° sweetness join.   25
True ease in writing comes from art, not chance,
As those move easiest who have learned to dance.
'Tis not enough no harshness gives offense,
The sound must seem an echo to the sense:
Soft is the strain when Zephyr° gently blows,   *the west wind* 30
And the smooth stream in smoother numbers flows;
But when loud surges lash the sounding shore,
The hoarse, rough verse should like the torrent roar:
When Ajax° strives some rock's vast weight to throw,
The line too labors, and the words move slow;   35
Not so, when swift Camilla° scours the plain,
Flies o'er th' unbending corn, and skims along the main.

20 *Alexandrine:* A twelve-syllable line, as line 21.   25 *Denham's . . . Waller's:* Sir John Denham (1615–1669) and Edmund Waller (1606–1687) were poets who used heroic couplets. 34 *Ajax:* A Greek warrior famous for his strength in the Trojan War.   36 *Camilla:* A goddess famous for her delicate speed.

CONSIDERATIONS FOR CRITICAL THINKING AND WRITING

1. FIRST RESPONSE. In these lines Pope describes some faults he finds in poems and illustrates those faults within the lines that describe them. How do the sounds in lines 4, 9, 10, 11, and 21 illustrate what they describe?

2. What is the objection to the "expected rhymes" in lines 12–17? How do they differ from Pope's end rhymes?

3. Some lines discuss how to write successful poetry. How do lines 23, 24, 32–33, 35, 36, and 37 illustrate what they describe?

4. Do you agree that in a good poem "The sound must seem an echo to the sense"?

GWENDOLYN BROOKS (1917–2000)

Sadie and Maud   *1945*

Maud went to college.
Sadie stayed at home.
Sadie scraped life
With a fine-tooth comb.

She didn't leave a tangle in.   5
Her comb found every strand.

Sadie was one of the livingest chits°   *pert girls*
In all the land.

Sadie bore two babies
Under her maiden name.   10
Maud and Ma and Papa
Nearly died of shame.

When Sadie said her last so-long
Her girls struck out from home.
(Sadie had left us heritage   15
Her fine-tooth comb.)

Maud, who went to college,
Is a thin brown mouse.
She is living all alone
In this old house.   20

CONSIDERATIONS FOR CRITICAL THINKING AND WRITING

1. FIRST RESPONSE. Read this poem aloud and describe the pattern and effect
   of the rhymes.

2. How does the speaker compare Sadie's and Maud's lives? With whom do
   you sympathize more?

3. How does this poem compare to any jump rope songs you remember from
   childhood?

MAXINE HONG KINGSTON (B. 1940)

Restaurant   *1981*

for Lilah Kan

The main cook lies sick on a banquette, and his assistant
has cut his thumb. So the quiche cook takes
their places at the eight-burner range, and you and I
get to roll out twenty-three rounds of pie
dough and break a hundred eggs, four at a crack,   5
and sift out shell with a China cap, pack
spinach in the steel sink, squish and squeeze
the water out, and grate a full moon of cheese.
Pam, the pastry chef, who is baking Choco-
late Globs (once called Mulattos) complains about the disco,   10
which Lewis, the salad man, turns up louder out of spite.
"Black so-called musician," "Broads. Whites."
The porters, who speak French, from the Ivory Coast,
sweep up droppings and wash the pans without soap.
We won't be out of here until three A.M. In this basement,   15
I lose my size. I am a bent-over
child, Gretel or Jill, and I can

lift a pot as big as a tub with both hands.
Using a pitchfork, you stoke the broccoli and bacon.
Then I find you in the freezer, taking   20
a nibble of a slab of chocolate as big as a table.
We put the quiches in the oven, then we are able
to stick our heads up out of the sidewalk into the night
and wonder at the clean diners behind glass in candlelight.

CONSIDERATIONS FOR CRITICAL THINKING AND WRITING

1. FIRST RESPONSE. How do the sounds of this poem contribute to the descriptions of what goes on in the restaurant kitchen? How do they contribute to the diners?

2. In what sense does the speaker "lose [her] size" in the kitchen? How would you describe her?

3. Examine the poem's rhymes. What effect do they have on your reading?

4. Describe the tone of the final line. How does it differ from the rest of the poem?

CONNECTION TO ANOTHER SELECTION

1. Write an essay analyzing how the kitchen activities described in "Restaurant," and Magarrell's "The Joy of Cooking" (p. 134) are used to convey the themes of these poems.

PAUL HUMPHREY (B. 1915)

Blow   *1983*

Her skirt was lofted by the gale;
When I, with gesture deft,
Essayed to stay her frisky sail
She luffed, and laughed, and left.

CONSIDERATIONS FOR CRITICAL THINKING AND WRITING

1. FIRST RESPONSE. How do alliteration and assonance contribute to the euphonic effects in this poem?

2. What is the poem's controlling metaphor? Why is it especially appropriate?

3. Explain the ambiguity of the title.

ROBERT FRANCIS (1901–1987)

The Pitcher   *1953*

His art is eccentricity, his aim
How not to hit the mark he seems to aim at,

His passion how to avoid the obvious,
His technique how to vary the avoidance.

The others throw to be comprehended. He   5
Throws to be a moment misunderstood.

Yet not too much. Not errant, arrant, wild,
But every seeming aberration willed.

Not to, yet still, still to communicate
Making the batter understand too late.   10

CONSIDERATIONS FOR CRITICAL THINKING AND WRITING

1. FIRST RESPONSE. Explain how each pair of lines in this poem works together to describe the pitcher's art.

2. Consider how the poem itself works the way a good pitcher does. Which lines illustrate what they describe?

3. Comment on the effects of the poem's rhymes. How are the final two lines different in their rhyme from the previous lines? How does sound echo sense in lines 9–10?

4. Write an essay that considers "The Pitcher" as an extended metaphor for talking about poetry. How well does the poem characterize strategies for writing poetry as well as pitching?

5. Write an essay that develops an extended comparison between writing or reading poetry and playing or watching another sport.

CONNECTIONS TO OTHER SELECTIONS

1. Compare this poem with Robert Wallace's "The Double-Play" (p. 641), another poem that explores the relation of baseball to poetry.

2. Write an essay comparing "The Pitcher" with Francis's "Catch" (p. 14). One poem defines poetry implicitly, the other defines it explicitly. Which poem do you prefer? Why?

HELEN CHASIN (B. 1938)

The Word Plum   *1968*

The word *plum* is delicious

pout and push, luxury of
self-love, and savoring murmur
full in the mouth and falling
like fruit   5

taut skin
pierced, bitten, provoked into
juice, and tart flesh

question
and reply, lip and tongue   10
of pleasure.

CONSIDERATIONS FOR CRITICAL THINKING AND WRITING

1. FIRST RESPONSE. What is the effect of the repetitions of the alliteration and assonance throughout the poem? How does it contribute to the poem's meaning?

2. Which sounds in the poem are like the sounds one makes while eating a plum?

3. Discuss the title. Explain whether you think this poem is more about the word *plum* or about the plum itself. Consider whether the two can be separated in the poem.

CONNECTION TO ANOTHER SELECTION

1. How is Kinnell's "Blackberry Eating" (p. 176) similar in technique to Chasin's poem? Try writing such a poem yourself: Choose a food to describe that allows you to evoke its sensuousness in sounds.

JOHN KEATS (1795–1821)

Ode to a Nightingale   *1819*

I
My heart aches, and a drowsy numbness pains
   My sense, as though of hemlock° I had drunk,   *a poison*
Or emptied some dull opiate to the drains
   One minute past, and Lethe-wards° had sunk:
'Tis not through envy of thy happy lot,   5
   But being too happy in thine happiness—
      That thou, light-wingèd Dryad° of the trees,   *wood nymph*
         In some melodious plot
   Of beechen green, and shadows numberless,
      Singest of summer in full-throated ease.   10

II
O, for a draught of vintage! that hath been
   Cooled a long age in the deep-delvèd earth,
Tasting of Flora° and the country green,   *goddess of flowers*
   Dance, and Provençal song,° and sunburnt mirth!
O for a beaker full of the warm South,   15
   Full of the true, the blushful Hippocrene,°
      With beaded bubbles winking at the brim,
         And purple-stainèd mouth;
   That I might drink, and leave the world unseen,
      And with thee fade away into the forest dim.   20

III
Fade far away, dissolve, and quite forget
   What thou among the leaves hast never known,

4 *Lethe-wards:* Toward Lethe, the river of forgetfulness in the Hades of Greek mythology.
14 *Provençal song:* The medieval troubadours of Provence, France, were known for their singing.   16 *Hippocrene:* The fountain of the Muses in Greek mythology.

The weariness, the fever, and the fret
  Here, where men sit and hear each other groan;
Where palsy shakes a few, sad, last gray hairs,   25
    Where youth grows pale, and specter-thin, and dies,
      Where but to think is to be full of sorrow
        And leaden-eyed despairs,
    Where Beauty cannot keep her lustrous eyes;
      Or new Love pine at them beyond tomorrow.   30

IV

Away! away! for I will fly to thee,
  Not charioted by Bacchus and his pards,°
But on the viewless wings of Poesy,
  Though the dull brain perplexes and retards:
Already with thee! tender is the night,   35
    And haply the Queen-Moon is on her throne,
      Clustered around by all her starry Fays;
        But here there is no light,
    Save what from heaven is with the breezes blown
      Through verdurous glooms and winding mossy ways.   40

V

I cannot see what flowers are at my feet,
  Nor what soft incense hangs upon the boughs,
But, in embalmèd° darkness, guess each sweet   *perfumed*
  Wherewith the seasonable month endows
The grass, the thicket, and the fruit-tree wild;   45
    What hawthorn, and the pastoral eglantine;
      Fast fading violets covered up in leaves;
        And mid-May's eldest child,
    The coming musk-rose, full of dewy wine,
      The murmurous haunt of flies on summer eves.   50

VI

Darkling° I listen; and for many a time   *in the dark*
  I have been half in love with easeful Death,
Called him soft names in many a musèd rhyme,
  To take into the air my quiet breath;
Now more than ever seems it rich to die,   55
    To cease upon the midnight with no pain,
      While thou art pouring forth thy soul abroad
        In such an ecstasy!
    Still wouldst thou sing, and I have ears in vain —
      To thy high requiem become a sod.   60

VII

Thou wast not born for death, immortal Bird!
  No hungry generations tread thee down;
The voice I hear this passing night was heard
  In ancient days by emperor and clown:

---

32 *Bacchus and his pards:* The Greek god of wine traveled in a chariot drawn by leopards.

Perhaps the selfsame song that found a path   65
   Through the sad heart of Ruth,° when, sick for home,
      She stood in tears amid the alien corn:
         The same that oft-times hath
   Charmed magic casements, opening on the foam
      Of perilous seas, in faery lands forlorn.   70

VIII

Forlorn! the very word is like a bell
   To toll me back from thee to my sole self!
Adieu! the fancy cannot cheat so well
   As she is famed to do, deceiving elf.
Adieu! adieu! thy plaintive anthem fades   75
   Past the near meadows, over the still stream,
      Up the hill side; and now 'tis buried deep
         In the next valley-glades:
   Was it a vision, or a waking dream?
      Fled is that music: — Do I wake or sleep?   80

66 *Ruth:* A young widow in the Bible (see the Book of Ruth).

CONSIDERATIONS FOR CRITICAL THINKING AND WRITING

1. FIRST RESPONSE. Why does the speaker in this ode want to leave his world for the nightingale's? What might the nightingale symbolize?

2. How does the speaker attempt to escape his world? Is he successful?

3. What changes the speaker's view of death at the end of stanza VI?

4. What does the allusion to Ruth (line 66) contribute to the ode's meaning?

5. In which lines is the imagery especially sensuous? How does this effect add to the conflict presented?

6. What calls the speaker back to himself at the end of stanza VII and the beginning of stanza VIII?

7. Choose a stanza and explain how sound is related to its meaning.

8. How regular is the stanza form of this ode?

PERSPECTIVE

DYLAN THOMAS (1914–1953)
On the Words in Poetry   1961

You want to know why and how I just began to write poetry. . . .

    To answer . . . this question, I should say I wanted to write poetry in the beginning because I had fallen in love with words. The first poems I knew were nursery rhymes, and before I could read them for myself I had come to love just the words of them, the words alone. What the words stood for, symbolized, or meant, was of very secondary importance. What mattered was the *sound* of them as I heard them for the first time on the lips of the remote and incomprehensible grown-ups who seemed, for some reason, to be living in my world. And these words were, to me, as the notes of bells, the sounds of musical instruments, the noises of wind, sea, and rain, the rattle of milkcarts, the clopping of hooves on cobbles, the lingering of branches on a window pane, might be to someone, deaf from birth, who has miraculously found his hearing. I did not care what the words said, overmuch, not what happened to Jack and Jill and the Mother Goose rest of them; I cared for the shapes of sound that their names, and the words describing their actions, made in my ears; I cared for the colors the words cast on my eyes. I realize that I may be, as I think back all that way, romanticizing my reactions to the simple and beautiful words of those pure poems; but that is all I can honestly remember, however much time might have falsified my memory. I fell in love — that is the only expression I can think of, at once, and am still at the mercy of words, though sometimes now, knowing a little of their behavior very well, I think I can influence them slightly and have even learned to beat them now and then, which they appear to enjoy. I tumbled for words at once. And, when I began to read the nursery rhymes for myself, and, later, to read other verses and ballads, I knew that I had discovered the most important things, to me, that could be ever. There they were, seemingly lifeless, made only of black and white, but out of them, out of their own being, came love and terror and pity and pain and wonder and all the other vague abstractions that make our ephemeral lives dangerous, great, and bearable. Out of them came the gusts and grunts and hiccups and heehaws of the common fun of the earth; and though what the words meant was, in its own way, often deliciously funny enough, so much funnier seemed to me, at that almost forgotten time, the shape and shade and size and noise of the words as they hummed, strummed, jugged, and galloped along. That was the time of innocence; words burst upon me, unencumbered by trivial or portentous association; words were their springlike selves, fresh with Eden's dew, as they flew out of the air. They made their own original associations as they sprang and shone. The words "Ride a cock-horse to Banbury Cross" were as haunting to me, who did not know then what a cock-horse was nor cared a damn where Banbury Cross might be, as, much later, were such lines as John Donne's "Go and catch a falling star, Get with child a mandrake root," which also I could not understand when I first read them. And as I read more and more, and it was not all verse, by any means, my love for the real life of words increased until I knew that I must live *with* them and *in* them always. I knew, in fact, that I must be a writer of words, and nothing else. The first thing was to feel and know their sound and substance; what I was going to do with those words, what use I was going to make of them, what I was going to *say* through them, would come later. I knew I had to know them most intimately in all their forms and moods, their ups and downs, their chops and changes, their needs and demands. (Here, I am afraid, I am beginning to talk too vaguely. I do not like writing *about* words, because then I often use bad and wrong and stale and wooly words. What I like to do is treat words as a craftsman does his wood or stone or what-have-you, to hew, carve, mold, coil, polish, and plane them into patterns, sequences, sculptures, fugues of sound expressing some lyrical impulse, some spiritual doubt or conviction, some dimly-realized truth I must try to reach and realize.)

From *Early Prose Writings*

CONSIDERATIONS FOR CRITICAL THINKING AND WRITING

1. Why does Thomas value nursery rhymes so highly? What nursery rhyme was your favorite as a child? Why were you enchanted by it?

2. Explain what you think Thomas would have to say about Carroll's "Jabberwocky" (p. 186) or Swenson's "A Nosty Fright" (p. 172).

3. Consider Thomas's comparison at the end of this passage, in which he likens a poet's work to a craftsman's. In what sense is making poetry similar to sculpting, painting, or composing music? What are some of the significant differences?

8

Patterns of Rhythm

The rhythms of everyday life surround us in regularly recurring movements and sounds. As you read these words, your heart pulsates while somewhere else a clock ticks, a cradle rocks, a drum beats, a dancer sways, a foghorn blasts, a wave recedes, or a child skips. We may tend to overlook rhythm since it is so tightly woven into the fabric of our experience, but it is there nonetheless, one of the conditions of life. Rhythm is also one of the conditions of speech because the voice alternately rises and falls as words are stressed or unstressed and as the pace quickens or slackens. In poetry *rhythm* refers to the recurrence of stressed and unstressed sounds. Depending on how the sounds are arranged, this can result in a pace that is fast or slow, choppy or smooth.

SOME PRINCIPLES OF METER

Poets use rhythm to create pleasurable sound patterns and to reinforce meanings. "Rhythm," Edith Sitwell once observed, "might be described as, to the world of sound, what light is to the world of sight. It shapes and gives new meaning." Prose can use rhythm effectively too, but prose that does so tends to be an exception. The following exceptional lines are from a speech by Winston Churchill to the House of Commons after Allied forces lost a great battle to German forces at Dunkirk during World War II:

> We shall not flag or fail. We shall go on to the end. We shall fight in France, we shall fight on the seas and oceans, we shall fight with growing confidence and growing strength in the air, we shall defend our island, whatever the cost may be, we shall fight on the beaches, we shall fight on the landing grounds, we

shall fight in the fields and in the streets, we shall fight in the hills; we shall never surrender.

The stressed repetition of "we shall" bespeaks the resolute singleness of purpose that Churchill had to convey to the British people if they were to win the war. Repetition is also one of the devices used in poetry to create rhythmic effects. In the following excerpt from "Song of the Open Road," Walt Whitman urges the pleasures of limitless freedom on his reader:

> Allons!° the road is before us!   *Let's go!*
> It is safe — I have tried it — my own feet have tried it well — be not detain'd!
> Let the paper remain on the desk unwritten, and the book on the
>   shelf unopen'd!
> Let the tools remain in the workshop! Let the money remain unearn'd!
> Let the school stand! mind not the cry of the teacher!   5
> Let the preacher preach in his pulpit! Let the lawyer plead in the
>   court, and the judge expound the law.
>
> Camerado,° I give you my hand!   *friend*
> I give you my love more precious than money,
> I give you myself before preaching or law;
> Will you give me yourself? will you come travel with me?   10
> Shall we stick by each other as long as we live?

These rhythmic lines quickly move away from conventional values to the open road of shared experiences. Their recurring sounds are not created by rhyme or alliteration and assonance (see Chapter 7) but by the repetition of words and phrases.

Although the repetition of words and phrases can be an effective means of creating rhythm in poetry, the more typical method consists of patterns of accented or unaccented syllables. Words contain syllables that are either stressed or unstressed. A **stress** (or **accent**) places more emphasis on one syllable than on another. We say "*syll*able" not "syll*a*ble," "*em*phasis" not "em*pha*sis." We routinely stress syllables when we speak: "*Is* she con*tent* with the *con*tents of the *yell*ow *pack*age?" To distinguish between two people we might say "Is *she* con*tent*. . . ?" In this way stress can be used to emphasize a particular word in a sentence. Poets often arrange words so that the desired meaning is suggested by the rhythm; hence, emphasis is controlled by the poet rather than left entirely to the reader.

When a rhythmic pattern of stresses recurs in a poem, the result is **meter.** Taken together, all the metrical elements in a poem make up what is called the poem's **prosody. Scansion** consists of measuring the stresses in a line to determine its metrical pattern. Several methods can be used to mark lines. One widely used system employs ´ for a stressed syllable and ˘ for an unstressed syllable. In a sense, the stress mark represents the equivalent of tapping one's foot to a beat:

> Híckŏrў, díckŏrў, dóck,
> The móuse răn úp the clóck.

The clock struck one,
And down he run,
Hickory, dickory, dock.

In the first two lines and the final line of this familiar nursery rhyme we hear three stressed syllables. In lines 3 and 4, where the meter changes for variety, we hear just two stressed syllables. The combination of stresses provides the pleasure of the rhythm we hear.

To hear the rhythms of "Hickory, dickory, dock" does not require a formal study of meter. Nevertheless, an awareness of the basic kinds of meter that appear in English poetry can enhance your understanding of how a poem achieves its effects. Understanding the sound effects of a poem and having a vocabulary with which to discuss those effects can intensify your pleasure in poetry. Although the study of meter can be extremely technical, the terms used to describe the basic meters of English poetry are relatively easy to comprehend.

The *foot* is the metrical unit by which a line of poetry is measured. A foot usually consists of one stressed and one or two unstressed syllables. A vertical line is used to separate the feet: "The clock | struck one" consists of two feet. A foot of poetry can be arranged in a variety of patterns; here are five of the chief ones:

Foot	Pattern	Example
iamb	˘ ´	away
trochee	´ ˘	Lovely
anapest	˘ ˘ ´	understand
dactyl	´ ˘ ˘	desperate
spondee	´ ´	dead set

The most common lines in English poetry contain meters based on iambic feet. However, even lines that are predominantly iambic will often include variations to create particular effects. Other important patterns include trochaic, anapestic, and dactylic feet. The spondee is not a sustained meter but occurs for variety or emphasis.

Iambic
    What kept | his eyes | from giv | ing back | the gaze
Trochaic
    He was | louder | than the | preacher
Anapestic
    I am called | to the front | of the room
Dactylic
    Sing it all | merrily

These meters have different rhythms and can create different effects. Iambic and anapestic are known as **rising meters** because they move from unstressed to stressed sounds, while trochaic and dactylic are known as *falling meters.* Anapests and dactyls tend to move more lightly and rapidly than iambs or trochees. Although no single kind of meter can be considered always better than another for a given subject, it is possible to determine whether the meter of a specific poem is appropriate for its subject. A serious poem about a tragic death would most likely not be well served by lilting rhythms. Keep in mind too that though one or another of these four basic meters might constitute the predominant rhythm of a poem, variations can occur within lines to change the pace or call attention to a particular word.

A *line* is measured by the number of feet it contains. Here, for example, is an iambic line with three feet: "If she | should write | a note." These are the names for line lengths:

monometer: one foot	pentameter: five feet
dimeter: two feet	hexameter: six feet
trimeter: three feet	heptameter: seven feet
tetrameter: four feet	octameter: eight feet

By combining the name of a line length with the name of a foot, we can describe the metrical qualities of a line concisely. Consider, for example, the pattern of feet and length of this line:

I didn't want the boy to hit the dog.

The iambic rhythm of this line falls into five feet; hence it is called *iambic pentameter.* Iambic is the most common pattern in English poetry because its rhythm appears so naturally in English speech and writing. Unrhymed iambic pentameter is called *blank verse;* Shakespeare's plays are built on such lines.

Less common than the iamb, trochee, anapest, or dactyl is the *spondee,* a two-syllable foot in which both syllables are stressed (´ ´). Note the effect of the spondaic foot at the beginning of this line:

Dead set | against | the plan | he went | away.

Spondees can slow a rhythm and provide variety and emphasis, particularly in iambic and trochaic lines. A line that ends with a stressed syllable is said to have a *masculine ending,* whereas a line that ends with an extra unstressed syllable is said to have a *feminine ending.* Consider, for example, these two lines from Timothy Steel's "Waiting for the Storm" (the entire poem appears on p. 206):

feminine: The sand | at my feet | grow cold | er,
masculine: The damp | air chill | and spread.

The effects of English meters are easily seen in the following lines by Samuel Taylor Coleridge, in which the rhythm of each line illustrates the meter described in it:

Trochee trips from long to short;
From long to long in solemn sort
Slow Spondee stalks; strong foot yet ill able
Ever to come up with Dactylic trisyllable.
Iambics march from short to long—
With a leap and a bound the swift Anapests throng.

The speed of a line is also affected by the number of pauses in it. A pause within a line is called a *caesura* and is indicated by a double vertical line (||). A caesura can occur anywhere within a line and need not be indicated by punctuation:

Camerado, || I give you my hand!
I give you my love || more precious than money.

A slight pause occurs within each of these lines and at its end. Both kinds of pauses contribute to the lines' rhythm.

When a line has a pause at its end, it is called an *end-stopped line.* Such pauses reflect normal speech patterns and are often marked by punctuation. A line that ends without a pause and continues into the next line for its meaning is called a *run-on line.* Running over from one line to another is also called *enjambment.* The first and eighth lines of the following poem are run-on lines; the rest are end-stopped.

WILLIAM WORDSWORTH (1770–1850)

My Heart Leaps Up   *1807*

My heart leaps up when I behold
    A rainbow in the sky:
So was it when my life began;
So is it now I am a man;
So be it when I shall grow old,
    Or let me die!
The child is father of the Man;
And I could wish my days to be
Bound each to each by natural piety.

Run-on lines have a different rhythm from end-stopped lines. Lines 3 and 4 and lines 8 and 9 are iambic, but the effect of their two rhythms is very different when we read these lines aloud. The enjambment of lines 8 and 9 reinforces their meaning; just as the "days" are bound together, so are the lines.

The rhythm of a poem can be affected by several devices: the kind and number of stresses within lines, the length of lines, and the kinds of pauses that appear within lines or at their ends. In addition, as we saw in Chapter 7, the sound of a poem is affected by alliteration, assonance, rhyme, and consonance. These sounds help to create rhythms by controlling our pronunciations, as in the following lines by Alexander Pope:

Soft is the strain when Zephyr gently blows,
And the smooth stream in smoother numbers flows;
But when loud surges lash the sounding shore,
The hoarse, rough verse should like the torrent roar.

These lines are effective because their rhythm and sound work with their meaning.

SUGGESTIONS FOR SCANNING A POEM

These suggestions should help you in talking about a poem's meter.

1. After reading the poem through, read it aloud and mark the stressed syllables in each line. Then mark the unstressed syllables.
2. From your markings, identify what kind of foot is dominant (iambic, trochaic, dactylic, or anapestic) and divide the lines into feet, keeping in mind that the vertical line marking a foot may come in the middle of a word as well as at its beginning or end.
3. Determine the number of feet in each line. Remember that there may be variations; some lines may be shorter or longer than the predominant meter. What is important is the overall pattern. Do not assume that variations represent the poet's inability to fulfill the overall pattern. Notice the effects of variations and whether they emphasize words and phrases or disrupt your expectation for some other purpose.
4. Listen for pauses within lines and mark the caesuras; many times there will be no punctuation to indicate them.
5. Recognize that scansion does not always yield a definitive measurement of a line. Even experienced readers may differ over the scansion of a given line. What is important is not a precise description of the line but an awareness of how a poem's rhythms contribute to its effects.

The following poem demonstrates how you can use an understanding of meter and rhythm to gain a greater appreciation for what a poem is saying.

TIMOTHY STEELE (B. 1948)

Waiting for the Storm   *1986*

Bréeze sént | ă wrínk | lĭng dárk | nĕss
Acróss | thĕ báy. ‖ Ĭ knélt
Bĕneáth | ăn úp | turnĕd bóat,
And, mó | mĕnt by mó | mĕnt, félt

Thĕ sánd | ăt my féet | grŏw cóld | ĕr,
Thĕ dămp | áir chíll | ănd spréad.

Then rhe | first rain | drops sound | ed
On rhe hull | above | my head.

The predominant meter of this poem is iambic trimeter, but there is plenty of variation as the storm rapidly approaches and finally begins to pelt the sheltered speaker. The emphatic spondee ("Breeze sent") pushes the darkness quickly across the bay while the caesura at the end of the sentence in line 2 creates a pause that sets up a feeling of suspense and expectation that is measured in the ticking rhythm of line 4, a run-on line that brings us into the chilly sand and air of the second stanza. Perhaps the most impressive sound effect used in the poem appears in the second syllable of "sounded" in line 7. That "ed" precedes the sound of the poem's final word "head" just as if it were the first drop of rain hitting the hull above the speaker. The visual, tactile, and auditory images make "Waiting for the Storm" an intense sensory experience.

This next poem also reinforces meanings through its use of meter and rhythm.

WILLIAM BUTLER YEATS (1865–1939)

That the Night Come   *1912*

She lived | in storm | and strife,
Her soul | had such | desire
For what | proud death | may bring
That it | could not | endure
The com | mon good | of life,   5
But lived | as 'twere | a king
That packed | his mar | riage day
With ban | neret | and pen | non,
Trumpet | and ket | tledrum,
And the | outrag | eous can | non,   10
To bun | dle time | away
That the | night come.

Scansion reveals that the predominant meter here is iambic trimeter. Each line contains three stressed and unstressed syllables that form a regular, predictable rhythm through line 7. That rhythm is disrupted, however, when the speaker compares the woman's longing for what death brings to a king's eager anticipation of his wedding night. The king packs the day with noisy fanfares and celebrations to fill up time and distract himself. Unable to accept "The common good of life," the woman fills her days with "storm and strife." In a determined effort "To bundle time away," she, like the king, impatiently awaits the night.

Lines 8–10 break the regular pattern established in the first seven lines. The extra unstressed syllable in lines 8 and 10 along with the trochaic feet in lines 9 ("trúmpet") and 10 ("Ánd the") interrupt the basic iambic trimeter and parallel the woman's and the king's frenetic activity. These lines thus echo the inability of the woman and king to "endure" regular or normal time. The last line is the most irregular in the poem. The final two accented syllables sound like the deep resonant beats of a kettledrum or a cannon firing. The words "night come" dramatically remind us that what the woman anticipates is not a lover but the mysterious finality of death. The meter serves, then, in both its regularity and variations to reinforce the poem's meaning and tone.

The following poems are especially rich in their rhythms and sounds. As you read and study them, notice how patterns of rhythm and the sounds of words reinforce meanings and contribute to the poems' effects. And, perhaps most important, read the poems aloud so that you can hear them.

POEMS FOR FURTHER STUDY

ALICE JONES (B. 1949)

The Foot   *1993*

Our improbable support, erected
on the osseous architecture
of the calcaneus, talus, cuboid,
navicular, cuneiforms, metatarsals,
phalanges, a plethora of hinges,   5

all strung together by gliding
tendons, covered by the pearly
plantar fascia, then fat-padded
to form the sole, humble surface
of our contact with earth.   10

Here the body's broadest tendon
anchors the heel's fleshy base,
the finely wrinkled skin stretches
forward across the capillaried arch,
to the ball, a balance point.   15

A wide web of flexor tendons
and branched veins maps the dorsum,
fades into the stub-laden bone
splay, the stuffed sausage sacks
of toes, each with a tuft   20

of proximal hairs to introduce
the distal nail, whose useless
curve remembers an ancestor,
the vanished creature's wild
and necessary claw.   25

CONSIDERATIONS FOR CRITICAL THINKING AND WRITING

1. FIRST RESPONSE. What is the effect of the diction? What sort of tone is established by the use of anatomical terms? How do the terms affect the rhythm?

2. Alice Jones has described the form of "The Foot" as "five stubby stanzas." Explain why the lines of this poem may or may not warrant this description of the stanzas.

3. Describe the effect of the final stanza. How would your reading be affected if the poem ended after the comma in the middle of line 22?

A. E. HOUSMAN (1859–1936)

When I was one-and-twenty   *1896*

When I was one-and-twenty
   I heard a wise man say,
"Give crowns and pounds and guineas
   But not your heart away;
Give pearls away and rubies   5
   But keep your fancy free."
But I was one-and-twenty,
   No use to talk to me.

When I was one-and-twenty
   I heard him say again,   10
"The heart out of the bosom
   Was never given in vain;
'Tis paid with sighs a plenty
   And sold for endless rue."
And I am two-and-twenty,   15
   And oh, 'tis true, 'tis true.

CONSIDERATIONS FOR CRITICAL THINKING AND WRITING

1. FIRST RESPONSE. How does the basic metrical pattern affect your understanding of the speaker?

2. How do lines 1–8 parallel lines 9–16 in their use of rhyme and metaphor? Are there any significant differences between the stanzas?

3. What do you think has happened to change the speaker's attitude toward love?

4. Explain why you agree or disagree with the advice given by the "wise man."

5. What is the effect of the repetition in line 16?

Nikki Giovanni (b. 1943)

Clouds

1999

I want to swim with hippos
jump with salmon
fly with geese
land with robins
walk with turtles   5
sleep with possum
dress with penguins
preen with peacocks
fish with grizzlies
hunt with lions   10
forage with pigs for truffles
eat nuts with the squirrels
plant seeds with the wind
and ride on off with the clouds
at the end   15

Considerations for Critical Thinking and Writing

1. FIRST RESPONSE. Explain how the rhythms of the lines render punctuation unnecessary in this poem.

2. Why do you suppose Giovanni begins to use longer lines with line 11?

3. What effect does the different metrical scheme have on your understanding of the poem? Comment on the appropriateness of the oxymoronic phrase "ride on off" in line 14.

Rachel Hadas (b. 1948)

The Red Hat

1995

It started before Christmas. Now our son
officially walks to school alone.
Semi-alone, it's accurate to say:
I or his father track him on the way.
He walks up on the east side of West End,   5
we on the west side. Glances can extend
(and do) across the street; not eye contact.
Already ties are feeling and not fact.
Straus Park is where these parallel paths part;
he goes alone from there. The watcher's heart   10
stretches, elastic in its love and fear,
toward him as we see him disappear,
striding briskly. Where two weeks ago,
holding a hand, he'd dawdle, dreamy, slow,
he now is hustled forward by the pull   15
of something far more powerful than school.

The mornings we turn back to are no more
than forty minutes longer than before,
but they feel vastly different — flimsy, strange,
wavering in the eddies of this change,   20
empty, unanchored, perilously light
since the red hat vanished from our sight.

CONSIDERATIONS FOR CRITICAL THINKING AND WRITING

1. FIRST RESPONSE. What emotions do the parents experience throughout the
   poem? How do you think the boy feels? Does the metrical pattern affect
   your understanding of the parents or the boy?

2. What prevents the rhymed couplets in this poem from sounding sing-
   songy? What is the predominant meter?

3. What is it that "pull[s]" the boy along in lines 15–16?

4. Why do you think Hadas titled the poem "The Red Hat" rather than, for ex-
   ample, "Paths Part" (line 9)?

CONNECTION TO ANOTHER SELECTION

1. In an essay discuss the themes of "The Red Hat" and Bly's "The Man Who
   Didn't Know What Was His" (p. 168). Pay particular attention to the way
   parents are presented in each poem.

ROBERT HERRICK (1591–1674)

Delight in Disorder   *1648*

A sweet disorder in the dress
Kindles in clothes a wantonness.
A lawn° about the shoulders thrown   *linen scarf*
Into a fine distraction;
An erring lace, which here and there   5
Enthralls the crimson stomacher,
A cuff neglectful, and thereby
Ribbons to flow confusedly;
A winning wave, deserving note,
In the tempestuous petticoat;   10
A careless shoestring, in whose tie
I see a wild civility;
Do more bewitch me than when art
Is too precise in every part.

CONSIDERATIONS FOR CRITICAL THINKING AND WRITING

1. FIRST RESPONSE. Why does the speaker in this poem value "disorder" so
   highly? How do the poem's organization and rhythmic order relate to its
   theme? Are they "precise in every part"?

2. Which words in the poem indicate disorder? Which words indicate the speaker's response to that disorder? What are the connotative meanings of each set of words? Why are they appropriate? What do they suggest about the woman and the speaker?

3. Write a short essay in which you agree or disagree with the speaker's views on dress.

Ben Jonson (1573–1637)

Still to Be Neat   *1609*

Still° to be neat, still to be dressed,   continually
As you were going to a feast;
Still to be powdered, still perfumed;
Lady, it is to be presumed,
Though art's hid causes are not found,   5
All is not sweet, all is not sound.

Give me a look, give me a face
That makes simplicity a grace;
Robes loosely flowing, hair as free;
Such sweet neglect more taketh me   10
Then all th' adulteries of art.
They strike mine eyes, but not my heart.

Considerations for Critical Thinking and Writing

1. FIRST RESPONSE. What are the speaker's reservations about the lady in the first stanza? What do you think "sweet" means in line 6?

2. What does the speaker want from the lady in the second stanza? How has the meaning of "sweet" shifted from line 6 to line 10? What other words in the poem are especially charged with connotative meanings?

3. How do the rhythms of Jonson's lines help to reinforce meanings? Pay particular attention to lines 6 and 12.

Connections to Other Selections

1. Write an essay comparing the themes of "Still to Be Neat" and Herrick's preceding poem, "Delight in Disorder." How do the speakers make similar points but from different perspectives?

2. How does the rhythm of "Still to Be Neat" compare with that of "Delight in Disorder"? Which do you find more effective? Explain why.

DIANE BURNS (B. 1950)

Sure You Can Ask Me a Personal Question   1981

How do you do?
   No, I am not Chinese.
No, not Spanish.
   No, I am American Indi — uh, Native American.
No, not from India.   5
   No, nor Apache.
No, not Navajo.
   No, not Sioux.
No, we are not extinct.
   Yes, Indin.   10
Oh?
   So that's where you got those high cheekbones.
Your great grandmother, huh?
   An Indian Princess, huh?
Hair down to there?   15
   Let me guess. Cherokee?
Oh, so you've had an Indian friend?
   That close?
Oh, so you've had an Indian lover?
   That tight?   20
Oh, so you've had an Indian servant?
   That much?
Yeah, it was awful what you guys did to us.
   It's real decent of you to apologize.
No. I don't know where you can get peyote.   25
   No, I don't know where you can get Navajo rugs real cheap.
No, I didn't make this. I bought it at Bloomingdales.
   Thank you. I like your hair too.
I don't know if anyone knows whether or not Cher is really Indian.
   No, I didn't make it rain tonight.   30
Yeah. Uh-huh. Spirituality.
   Uh-huh. Yeah. Spirituality. Uh-huh. Mother
Earth. Yeah. Uh-huh. Uh-huh. Spirituality.
   No. I didn't major in archery.
Yeah, a lot of us drink too much.   35
   Some of us can't drink enough.
This ain't no stoic look.
   This is my face.

CONSIDERATIONS FOR CRITICAL THINKING AND WRITING

1. FIRST RESPONSE. What sort of person do you imagine the speaker is addressing?

2. Discuss the poem's humor. Does it also have a serious theme? Explain.

3. What is the effect of the repeated phrases throughout the poem?

WILLIAM BLAKE (1757–1827)

The Lamb   *1789*

     Little Lamb, who made thee?
      Dost thou know who made thee?
Gave thee life, and bid thee feed
By the stream and o'er the mead;
Gave thee clothing of delight,   5
Softest clothing, wooly, bright;
Gave thee such a tender voice,
Making all the vales rejoice?
     Little Lamb, who made thee?
     Dost thou know who made thee?   10

     Little Lamb, I'll tell thee,
     Little Lamb, I'll tell thee:
He is callèd by thy name,
For he calls himself a Lamb.
He is meek, and he is mild;   15
He became a little child.
I a child, and thou a lamb,
We are callèd by his name.
     Little Lamb, God bless thee!
     Little Lamb, God bless thee!   20

CONSIDERATIONS FOR CRITICAL THINKING AND WRITING

1. FIRST RESPONSE. This poem is from Blake's *Songs of Innocence*. Describe its tone. How do the meter, rhyme, and repetition help to characterize the speaker's voice?

2. Why is it significant that the animal addressed by the speaker is a lamb? What symbolic value would be lost if the animal were, for example, a doe?

3. How does the second stanza answer the question raised in the first? What is the speaker's view of the creation?

WILLIAM BLAKE (1757–1827)

The Tyger   *1794*

Tyger! Tyger! burning bright
In the forests of the night,
What immortal hand or eye
Could frame thy fearful symmetry?

In what distant deeps or skies   5
Burnt the fire of thine eyes?
On what wings dare he aspire?
What the hand dare seize the fire?

And what shoulder, and what art,
Could twist the sinews of thy heart? 10
And when thy heart began to beat,
What dread hand? and what dread feet?

What the hammer? what the chain?
In what furnace was thy brain?
What the anvil? what dread grasp 15
Dare its deadly terrors clasp?

When the stars threw down their spears,
And watered heaven with their tears,
Did he smile his work to see?
Did he who made the Lamb make thee? 20

Tyger! Tyger! burning bright
In the forests of the night,
What immortal hand or eye
Dare frame thy fearful symmetry?

CONSIDERATIONS FOR CRITICAL THINKING AND WRITING

1. FIRST RESPONSE. This poem from Blake's *Songs of Experience* is often paired with "The Lamb." Describe the poem's tone. Is the speaker's voice the same here as in "The Lamb"? Which words are repeated, and how do they contribute to the tone?

2. What is revealed about the nature of the tiger by the words used to describe its creation? What do you think the tiger symbolizes?

3. Unlike in "The Lamb," more than one question is raised in "The Tyger." What are these questions? Are they answered?

4. Compare the rhythms in "The Lamb" and "The Tyger." Each basically uses a seven-syllable line, but the effects are very different. Why?

5. Using these two poems as the basis of your discussion, describe what distinguishes innocence from experience.

ANNA LAETITIA BARBAULD (1743–1825)

On a Lady's Writing 1773

Her even lines her steady temper show,
Neat as her dress, and polished as her brow;
Strong as her judgment, easy as her air;
Correct though free, and regular though fair:
And the same graces o'er her pen preside,
That form her manners and her footsteps guide.

CONSIDERATIONS FOR CRITICAL THINKING AND WRITING

1. FIRST RESPONSE. How does the date of this poem affect your reading of it? Would your response be any different if you had come across it in a magazine last week?

2. How is the style of this poem related to its meaning? More specifically, how do "Her even lines her steady temper show"?

3. Why is "On a Lady's Writing" a more appropriate title than, say, "On a Woman's Writing"?

CONNECTION TO ANOTHER SELECTION

1. Discuss the idea of order in "On a Lady's Writing" and in Robert Herrick's "Delight in Disorder" (p. 211). How does each poem implicitly — though co-incidentally — comment on the other?

ALFRED, LORD TENNYSON (1809–1892)

The Charge of the Light Brigade   *1855*

I

Half a league, half a league,
   Half a league onward,
All in the valley of Death
   Rode the six hundred.
"Forward, the Light Brigade!   5
Charge for the guns!" he said:
Into the valley of Death
   Rode the six hundred.

2

"Forward, the Light Brigade!"
Was there a man dismayed?   10
Not though the soldier knew
   Some one had blundered:
Their's not to make reply,
Their's not to reason why,
Their's but to do and die: 15
Into the valley of Death
   Rode the six hundred.

3

Cannon to right of them,
Cannon to left of them,
Cannon in front of them   20
   Volleyed and thundered;
Stormed at with shot and shell,
Boldly they rode and well,
Into the jaws of Death,
Into the mouth of Hell   25
   Rode the six hundred.

4

Flashed all their sabers bare,
Flashed as they turned in air
Sabring the gunners there,

Charging an army, while   30
  All the world wondered:
Plunged in the battery-smoke
Right through the line they broke;
Cossack and Russian
Reeled from the saber-stroke   35
  Shattered and sundered.
Then they rode back, but not
  Not the six hundred.

                    5
Cannon to right of them,
Cannon to left of them,   40
Cannon behind them
  Volleyed and thundered;
Stormed at with shot and shell,
While horse and hero fell,
They that had fought so well   45
Came through the jaws of Death,
Back from the mouth of Hell,
All that was left of them,
  Left of six hundred.

                    6
When can their glory fade?   50
O the wild charge they made!
  All the world wondered.
Honor the charge they made!
Honor the Light Brigade,
  Noble six hundred!   55

CONSIDERATIONS FOR CRITICAL THINKING AND WRITING

1. FIRST RESPONSE. How do the meter and rhyme contribute to the meaning of this poem's lines?

2. What is the speaker's attitude toward war?

3. Describe the tone, paying particular attention to stanza 2.

CONNECTION TO ANOTHER SELECTION

1. Compare the theme of "The Charge of the Light Brigade" with Owen's "Dulce et Decorum Est" (p. 102).

THEODORE ROETHKE (1908–1963)

My Papa's Waltz   *1948*

The whiskey on your breath
Could make a small boy dizzy;
But I hung on like death:
Such waltzing was not easy.

We romped until the pans   5
Slid from the kitchen shelf;
My mother's countenance
Could not unfrown itself.

The hand that held my wrist
Was battered on one knuckle;   10
At every step you missed
My right ear scraped a buckle.

You beat time on my head
With a palm caked hard by dirt,
Then waltzed me off to bed   15
Still clinging to your shirt.

CONSIDERATIONS FOR CRITICAL THINKING AND WRITING

1. FIRST RESPONSE. What details characterize the father in this poem? How does the speaker's choice of words reveal his feeling about his father? Is the remembering speaker still a boy?

2. Characterize the rhythm of the poem. Does it move "like death," or is it more like a waltz? Is the rhythm regular throughout the poem? What is its effect?

3. Comment on the appropriateness of the title. Why do you suppose Roethke didn't use "My Father's Waltz"?

ARON KEESBURY (B. 1971)

Song to a Waitress   1997

Yes. I want a big fat cup of coffee and
I want it hot. I want a big hot cup
of coffee in a big fat mug. And bring
it here and put it down and get the hell

away from me. And I want sugar in   5
a jar. A glass jar. Big, fat, glass jar with
a metal top and none of them pink, pansy
sugar packs in dainty little cups.

And come back every now and then and fill
my big fat mug and keep it hot and full.   10
And I don't want to hear your waitress talk
and I don't want to see you smile. So fill

my big fat mug and get the hell away.
I don't want to see your face today.

CONSIDERATIONS FOR CRITICAL THINKING AND WRITING

1. FIRST RESPONSE. What does this speaker want?

2. What is the predominant metrical pattern in the poem? Where does the poem deviate from that pattern? How do these deviations affect the speaker's tone?

3. In what ways does this poem resemble a sonnet? How does it differ? (See p. 226 for a description of a sonnet.) What do the similarities and differences to the form add to your understanding of the speaker's intent?

4. What is the effect of the repetition of "big," "fat," and "mug" throughout the poem? What other patterns of repetition can you find? Why does the speaker repeat those specific words when he does?

CONNECTION TO ANOTHER SELECTION

1. Write a reply to the speaker in "Song to a Waitress" from the point of view of the waitress. You might begin by writing a prose paragraph and then try organizing it into lines of poetry. Read Machan's "Hazel Tells LaVerne" (p. 61) for a source of inspiration.

EDWARD HIRSCH (B. 1950)

Fast Break   1985

(In Memory of Dennis Turner, 1946–1984)

A hook shot kisses the rim and
hangs there, helplessly, but doesn't drop

and for once our gangly starting center
boxes out his man and times his jump

perfectly, gathering the orange leather   5
from the air like a cherished possession

and spinning around to throw a strike
to the outlet who is already shoveling

an underhand pass toward the other guard
scissoring past a flat-footed defender   10

who looks stunned and nailed to the floor
in the wrong direction, turning to catch sight

of a high, gliding dribble and a man
letting the play develop in front of him

in slow motion, almost exactly   15
like a coach's drawing on the blackboard,

both forwards racing down the court
the way that forwards should, fanning out

and filling the lanes in tandem, moving
together as brothers passing the ball   20

between them without a dribble, without
a single bounce hitting the hardwood

until the guard finally lunges out
and commits to the wrong man

while the power-forward explodes past them   25
in a fury, taking the ball into the air

by himself now and laying it gently
against the glass for a layup,

but losing his balance in the process,
inexplicably falling, hitting the floor   30

with a wild, headlong motion
for the game he loved like a country

and swiveling back to see an orange blur
floating perfectly through the net.

CONSIDERATIONS FOR CRITICAL THINKING AND WRITING

1. FIRST RESPONSE. How might this poem — to borrow a phrase from Robert Frost — represent a "momentary stay against confusion"?

2. Why are run-on lines especially appropriate for this poem? How do they affect its sound and sense? Do the lines have a regular meter? What is the effect of the poem being one long sentence?

3. In addition to accurately describing a fast break, this poem is a tribute to a dead friend. How are the two purposes related in the poem?

DAVID BARBER (B. 1960)

A Colonial Epitaph Annotated   1999

Here lies as silent clay
Miss Arabella Young
Who on the 21st of May, 1771
Began to hold her tongue

Here rests as circumspect dust   5
A maid who spoke her mind
Without the ghost of a blush
Or a nod to her prim kind.

Here silt her tart remarks
And her spirited retorts,   10
Her mordant takes on politics
And the sermon's finer points.

Here chafes in stony hush
An erstwhile spitfire.
Finally they can rest in peace,   15
The fools she wouldn't suffer!

Here in her boneyard bower
Look sharp for the shards of a quip.
The lady was no flower.
She'd cut you to the quick.   20

Here beneath this slate
You can sense her mute dismay,
Who was the soul of wit
And revelled in repartee.

Here lies as silent clay   25
Miss Arabella Young.
Be that as it may,
Here's to the sting in her tongue.

CONSIDERATIONS FOR CRITICAL THINKING AND WRITING

1. FIRST RESPONSE. Based on just the first four lines, the original epitaph, what sort of person do you think Arabella Young was thought to be by her contemporaries?

2. How does the rest of the poem serve as a spirited toast to Arabella Young from the perspective of more than two hundred years later?

3. Comment on rhymes in stanzas three and four. How are they different from the other stanzas?

4. Try writing an additional stanza for the original epitaph as you think it would have been written in 1771.

CONNECTION TO ANOTHER SELECTION

1. Compare the rhythms and themes of this poem with those of "On a Lady's Writing" by Anna Laetitia Barbauld (p. 215).

PERSPECTIVE

LOUISE BOGAN (1897–1970)

On Formal Poetry   *1953*

What is formal poetry? It is poetry written in form. And what is *form*? The elements of form, so far as poetry is concerned, are meter and rhyme. Are these elements merely mold and ornaments that have been impressed upon poetry from without? Are they indeed restrictions which bind and fetter language and the thought and emotion behind, under, within language in a repressive way? Are they arbitrary rules which have lost all validity since they have been broken to good purpose by "experimental poets," ancient and modern? Does the breaking up of form, or its total elimination, always result in an increase of power and of effect; and is any return to form a sort of relinquishment of freedom, or retreat to old fogeyism?

From *A Poet's Alphabet*

CONSIDERATIONS FOR CRITICAL THINKING AND WRITING

1. Choose one of the questions Bogan raises and write an essay in response to it using two or three poems from this chapter to illustrate your answer.

2. Try writing a poem in meter and rhyme. Does the experience make your writing feel limited or not?

9

Poetic Forms

Poems come in a variety of shapes. Although the best poems always have their own unique qualities, many of them also conform to traditional patterns. Frequently the *form* of a poem — its overall structure or shape — follows an already established design. A poem that can be categorized by the patterns of its lines, meter, rhymes, and stanzas is considered a *fixed form* because it follows a prescribed model such as a sonnet. However, poems written in a fixed form do not always fit models precisely; writers sometimes work variations on traditional forms to create innovative effects.

Not all poets are content with variations on traditional forms. Some prefer to create their own structures and shapes. Poems that do not conform to established patterns of meter, rhyme, and stanza are called *free verse* or *open form* poetry. (See Chapter 10 for further discussion of open forms.) This kind of poetry creates its own ordering principles through the careful arrangement of words and phrases in line lengths that embody rhythms appropriate to the meaning. Modern and contemporary poets in particular have learned to use the blank space on the page as a significant functional element (for a striking example, see Cummings's "in Just-" p. 251). Good poetry of this kind is structured in ways that can be as demanding, interesting, and satisfying as fixed forms. Open and fixed forms represent different poetic styles, but they are identical in the sense that both use language in concentrated ways to convey meanings, experiences, emotions, and effects.

SOME COMMON POETIC FORMS

A familiarity with some of the most frequently used fixed forms of poetry is useful because it allows for a better understanding of how a poem works. Classifying patterns allows us to talk about the effects of established rhythm and rhyme and recognize how significant variations from them affect the pace and meaning of the lines. An awareness of form also allows us to anticipate how a poem is likely to proceed. As we shall see, a sonnet creates a different set of expectations in a reader from those of, say, a limerick. A reader isn't likely to find in limericks the kind of serious themes that often make their way into sonnets. The discussion that follows identifies some of the important poetic forms frequently encountered in English poetry.

The shape of a fixed form poem is often determined by the way in which the lines are organized into stanzas. A *stanza* consists of a grouping of lines, set off by a space, that usually has a set pattern of meter and rhyme. This pattern is ordinarily repeated in other stanzas throughout the poem. What is usual is not obligatory, however; some poems may use a different pattern for each stanza, somewhat like paragraphs in prose.

Traditionally, though, stanzas do share a common **rhyme scheme,** the pattern of end rhymes. We can map out rhyme schemes by noting patterns of rhyme with lowercase letters: the first rhyme sound is designated *a,* the second becomes *b,* the third *c,* and so on. Using this system, we can describe the rhyme scheme in the following poem this way: *aabb, ccdd, eeff.*

A. E. HOUSMAN (1859–1936)
Loveliest of trees, the cherry now   *1896*

Loveliest of trees, the cherry now	*a*
Is hung with bloom along the bough,	*a*
And stands about the woodland ride	*b*
Wearing white for Eastertide.	*b*
Now, of my threescore years and ten,	*c*
Twenty will not come again,	*c*
And take from seventy springs a score,	*d*
It only leaves me fifty more.	*d*
And since to look at things in bloom	*e*
Fifty springs are little room,	*e*
About the woodlands I will go	*f*
To see the cherry hung with snow.	*f*

5

10

CONSIDERATIONS FOR CRITICAL THINKING AND WRITING

1. FIRST RESPONSE. What is the speaker's attitude in this poem toward time and life?

2. Why is spring an appropriate season for the setting rather than, say, winter?

3. Paraphrase each stanza. How do the images in each reinforce the poem's themes?

4. Lines 1 and 12 are not intended to rhyme, but they are close. What is the effect of the near rhyme of "now" and "snow"? How does the rhyme enhance the theme?

Poets often create their own stanzaic patterns; hence there is an infinite number of kinds of stanzas. One way of talking about stanzaic forms is to describe a given stanza by how many lines it contains.

A *couplet* consists of two lines that usually rhyme and have the same meter; couplets are frequently not separated from each other by space on the page. A *heroic couplet* consists of rhymed iambic pentameter. Here is an example from Pope's "An Essay on Criticism":

One science only will one genius fit;	*a*
So vast is art, so narrow human wit:	*a*
Not only bounded to peculiar arts,	*b*
But oft in those confined to single parts.	*b*

A *tercet* is a three-line stanza. When all three lines rhyme they are called a *triplet.* Two triplets make up this captivating poem.

ROBERT HERRICK (1591–1674)

Upon Julia's Clothes   1648

Whenas in silks my Julia goes,	*a*
Then, then, methinks, how sweetly flows	*a*
That liquefaction of her clothes.	*a*
Next, when I cast mine eyes, and see	*b*
That brave vibration, each way free,	*b*
O, how that glittering taketh me!	*b*

CONSIDERATIONS FOR CRITICAL THINKING AND WRITING

1. FIRST RESPONSE. What purpose does alliteration serve in this poem?
2. Comment on the effect of the meter. How is it related to the speaker's description of Julia's clothes?
3. Look up the word *brave* in the *Oxford English Dictionary*. Which of its meanings is appropriate to describe Julia's movement? Some readers interpret lines 4–6 to mean that Julia has no clothes on. What do you think?

CONNECTION TO ANOTHER SELECTION

1. Compare the tone of this poem with that of Humphrey's "Blow" (p. 194). Are the situations and speakers similar? Is there any difference in tone between these two poems?

Terza rima consists of an interlocking three-line rhyme scheme: *aba, bcb, cdc, ded,* and so on. Dante's *The Divine Comedy* uses this pattern, as does Frost's "Acquainted with the Night" (p. 139) and Percy Bysshe Shelley's "Ode to the West Wind" (p. 243).

A *quatrain,* or four-line stanza, is the most common stanzaic form in the English language and can have various meters and rhyme schemes (if any). The most common rhyme schemes are *aabb, abba, aaba,* and *abcb.* This last pattern is especially characteristic of the popular **ballad stanza,** which consists of alternating eight- and six-syllable lines. Samuel Taylor Coleridge adopted this pattern in "The Rime of the Ancient Mariner"; here is one representative stanza:

> All in a hot and copper sky
> The bloody Sun, at noon,
> Right up above the mast did stand,
> No bigger than the Moon.

There are a number of longer stanzaic forms and the list of types of stanzas could be extended considerably, but knowing these three most basic patterns should prove helpful to you in talking about the form of a great many poems. In addition to stanzaic forms, there are fixed forms that characterize entire poems. Lyric poems can be, for example, sonnets, villanelles, sestinas, or epigrams.

Sonnet

The **sonnet** has been a popular literary form in English since the sixteenth century, when it was adopted from the Italian *sonnetto,* meaning "little song." A sonnet consists of fourteen lines, usually written in iambic pentameter. Because the sonnet has been such a favorite form, writers have experimented with many variations on its essential structure. Nevertheless, there are two basic types of sonnets: the Italian and the English.

The **Italian sonnet** (also known as the **Petrarchan sonnet,** from the fourteenth-century Italian poet Petrarch) divides into two parts. The first eight lines (the **octave**) typically rhyme *abbaabba.* The final six lines (the **sestet**) may vary; common patterns are *cdecde, cdcdcd,* and *cdccdc.* Very often the octave presents a situation, attitude, or problem that the sestet comments upon or resolves, as in John Keats's "On First Looking into Chapman's Homer."

JOHN KEATS (1795–1821)

On First Looking into Chapman's Homer°　　　　　　1816

Much have I traveled in the realms of gold,
　　And many goodly states and kingdoms seen;
　　Round many western islands have I been
Which bards in fealty to Apollo° hold.
Oft of one wide expanse had I been told　　　　　　　　　　　5

Chapman's Homer: Before reading George Chapman's (c. 1560–1634) poetic Elizabethan translations of Homer's *Iliad* and *Odyssey,* Keats had known only stilted and pedestrian eighteenth-century translations.　　4 *Apollo:* Greek god of poetry.

That deep-browed Homer ruled as his demesne;
Yet did I never breathe its pure serene°   *atmosphere*
Till I heard Chapman speak out loud and bold:
Then felt I like some watcher of the skies
    When a new planet swims into his ken;   10
Or like stout Cortez° when with eagle eyes
    He stared at the Pacific — and all his men
Looked at each other with a wild surmise —
    Silent, upon a peak in Darien.

11 *Cortez:* Vasco Núñez de Balboa, not Hernando Cortés, was the first European to sight the Pacific from Darien, a peak in Panama.

CONSIDERATIONS FOR CRITICAL THINKING AND WRITING

1. FIRST RESPONSE. How do the images shift from the octave to the sestet? How does the tone change? Does the meaning?
2. What is the controlling metaphor of this poem?
3. What is it that the speaker discovers?
4. How does the rhythm of the lines change between the octave and the sestet? How does that change reflect the tones of both the octave and the sestet?
5. Does Keats's mistake concerning Cortés and Balboa affect your reading of the poem? Explain why or why not.

The Italian sonnet pattern is also used in the next sonnet, but notice that the thematic break between octave and sestet comes within line 9 rather than between lines 8 and 9. This unconventional break helps to reinforce the speaker's impatience with the conventional attitudes he describes.

WILLIAM WORDSWORTH (1770–1850)

The World Is Too Much with Us   *1807*

The world is too much with us; late and soon,
Getting and spending, we lay waste our powers;
Little we see in Nature that is ours;
We have given our hearts away, a sordid boon!
This Sea that bares her bosom to the moon;   5
The winds that will be howling at all hours,
And are up-gathered now like sleeping flowers;
For this, for everything, we are out of tune;
It moves us not. — Great God! I'd rather be
A Pagan suckled in a creed outworn;   10
So might I, standing on this pleasant lea,
Have glimpses that would make me less forlorn;
Have sight of Proteus rising from the sea;
Or hear old Triton blow his wreathèd horn.

CONSIDERATIONS FOR CRITICAL THINKING AND WRITING

1. FIRST RESPONSE. What is the speaker's complaint in this sonnet? How do the conditions described affect him?
2. Look up "Proteus" and "Triton." What do these mythological allusions contribute to the sonnet's tone?
3. What is the effect of the personification of the sea and wind in the octave?

CONNECTION TO ANOTHER SELECTION

1. Compare the theme of this sonnet with that of Hopkins's "God's Grandeur" (p. 181).

The **English sonnet,** more commonly known as the **Shakespearean sonnet,** is organized into three quatrains and a couplet, which typically rhyme *abab cdcd efef gg.* This rhyme scheme is more suited to English poetry because English has fewer rhyming words than Italian. English sonnets, because of their four-part organization, also have more flexibility about where thematic breaks can occur. Frequently, however, the most pronounced break or turn comes with the concluding couplet.

In the following Shakespearean sonnet, the three quatrains compare the speaker's loved one to a summer's day and explain why the loved one is even more lovely. The couplet bestows eternal beauty and love upon both the loved one and the sonnet.

WILLIAM SHAKESPEARE (1564–1616)

Shall I compare thee to a summer's day?   *1609*

Shall I compare thee to a summer's day?
Thou art more lovely and more temperate:
Rough winds do shake the darling buds of May,
And summer's lease hath all too short a date.
Sometime too hot the eye of heaven shines,   5
And often is his gold complexion dimmed;
And every fair from fair sometime declines,
By chance, or nature's changing course, untrimmed.
But thy eternal summer shall not fade,
Nor lose possession of that fair thou ow'st°   *possess* 10
Nor shall death brag thou wand'rest in his shade,
When in eternal lines to time thou grow'st.
    So long as men can breathe or eyes can see,
    So long lives this, and this gives life to thee.

CONSIDERATIONS FOR CRITICAL THINKING AND WRITING

1. FIRST RESPONSE. Describe the shift in tone and subject matter that begins in line 9.
2. Why is the speaker's loved one more lovely than a summer's day? What qualities does he admire in the loved one?

3. What does the couplet say about the relation between art and love?

4. Which syllables are stressed in the final line? How do these syllables relate to the meaning of the line?

Sonnets have been the vehicles for all kinds of subjects, including love, death, politics, and cosmic questions. Although most sonnets tend to treat their subjects seriously, this fixed form does not mean a fixed expression; humor is also possible in it. Compare this next Shakespearean sonnet with "Shall I compare thee to a summer's day?" They are, finally, both love poems, but their tones are markedly different.

WILLIAM SHAKESPEARE (1564–1616)

My mistress' eyes are nothing like the sun   *1609*

My mistress' eyes are nothing like the sun;
Coral is far more red than her lips' red;
If snow be white, why then her breasts are dun;
If hairs be wires, black wires grow on her head.
I have seen roses damasked red and white,   5
But no such roses see I in her cheeks;
And in some perfumes is there more delight
Than in the breath that from my mistress reeks.
I love to hear her speak, yet well I know
That music hath a far more pleasing sound;   10
I grant I never saw a goddess go:
My mistress, when she walks, treads on the ground.
    And yet, by heaven, I think my love as rare
    As any she,° belied with false compare.   *lady*

CONSIDERATIONS FOR CRITICAL THINKING AND WRITING

1. FIRST RESPONSE. What does "mistress" mean in this sonnet? Write a description of this particular mistress based on the images used in the sonnet.

2. What sort of person is the speaker? Does he truly love the woman he describes?

3. In what sense are this sonnet and "Shall I compare thee to a summer's day" about poetry as well as love?

EDNA ST. VINCENT MILLAY (1892–1950)

I will put Chaos into fourteen lines   *1954*

I will put Chaos into fourteen lines
And keep him there; and let him thence escape
If he be lucky; let him twist, and ape
Flood, fire, and demon—his adroit designs
Will strain to nothing in the strict confines   5

Of this sweet Order, where, in pious rape,
I hold his essence and amorphous shape,
Till he with Order mingles and combines.
Past are the hours, the years, of our duress,
His arrogance, our awful servitude: 10
I have him. He is nothing more nor less
Than something simple not yet understood;
I shall not even force him to confess;
Or answer. I will only make him good.

CONSIDERATIONS FOR CRITICAL THINKING AND WRITING

1. FIRST RESPONSE. Does the poem contain "Chaos"? If so, how? If not, why not?
2. What properties of a sonnet does this poem possess?
3. What do you think is meant by the phrase "pious rape" in line 6?
4. What is the effect of the personification in the poem?

CONNECTION TO ANOTHER SELECTION

1. Compare the theme of this poem with that of Robert Frost's "Design" (p. 356).

MARK DOTY (B. 1953)

Golden Retrievals   1998

Fetch? Balls and sticks capture my attention
seconds at a time. Catch? I don't think so.
Bunny, tumbling leaf, a squirrel who's — oh
joy — actually scared. Sniff the wind, then

I'm off again: muck, pond, ditch, residue   5
of any thrillingly dead thing. And you?
Either you're sunk in the past, half our walk,
thinking of what you never can bring back,

or else you're off in some fog concerning
— tomorrow, is that what you call it? My work: 10
to unsnare time's warp (and woof!), retrieving,
my haze-headed friend, you. This shining bark,

a Zen master's bronzy gong, calls you here,
entirely, now: bow-wow, bow-wow, bow-wow.

CONSIDERATIONS FOR CRITICAL THINKING AND WRITING

1. FIRST RESPONSE. In what sense is the purpose (and voice) of this sonnet a golden retrieval?
2. How does the dog differ from the master? And what does the master need to learn from the dog?

3. As simple as the final line is, how and why does it work so well as the conclusion to this poem?

CONNECTION TO ANOTHER SELECTION

1. Compare the relationship between dog and master in this poem and horse and owner in Robert Frost's "Stopping by Woods on a Snowy Evening" (p. 353). Though these poems are quite different in tone, what similarities do you find in their themes?

MOLLY PEACOCK (B. 1947)

Desire   1984

It doesn't speak and it isn't schooled,
like a small foetal animal with wettened fur.
It is the blind instinct for life unruled,
visceral frankincense and animal myrrh.
It is what babies bring to kings,   5
an eyes-shut, ears-shut medicine of the heart
that smells and touches endings and beginnings
without the details of time's experienced *part*
fit-into-part-fit-into-part. Like a paw,
it is blunt; like a pet who knows you   10
and nudges your knee with its snout — but more raw
and blinder and younger and more divine, too,
than the tamed wild — it's the drive for what is real,
deeper than the brain's detail: the drive to feel.

CONSIDERATIONS FOR CRITICAL THINKING AND WRITING

1. FIRST RESPONSE. Taken together, what do all the metaphors that appear in this poem reveal about the speaker's conception of desire?
2. What is the "it" being described in lines 3–5? How do the allusions to the three wise men relate to the other metaphors used to define desire?
3. How is this English sonnet structured? What is the effect of its irregular meter?

CONNECTION TO ANOTHER SELECTION

1. Compare the treatment of desire in this poem with that of Ackerman's "A Fine, a Private Place" (p. 69). In an essay, identify the theme of each poem and compare their conceptions of desire. How alike are these two poems?

Mark Jarman (b. 1952)

Unholy Sonnet   *1993*

After the praying, after the hymn-singing,
After the sermon's trenchant commentary
On the world's ills, which make ours secondary,
After communion, after the hand-wringing,
And after peace descends upon us, bringing   5
Our eyes up to regard the sanctuary
And how the light swords through it, and how, scary
In their sheer numbers, motes of dust ride, clinging —
There is, as doctors say about some pain,
Discomfort knowing that despite your prayers,   10
Your listening and rejoicing, your small part
In this communal stab at coming clean,
There is one stubborn remnant of your cares
Intact. There is still murder in your heart.

Considerations for Critical Thinking and Writing

1. FIRST RESPONSE. Describe the rhyme scheme and structure of this sonnet. Explain why it is an English or Italian sonnet.

2. What are the effects of the use of "after" in lines 1, 2, 4, and 5 and "there" in lines 9, 13, and 14?

3. In what sense might this poem be summed up as a "communal stab" (line 12)? Discuss the accuracy of this assessment.

4. Try writing a reply to the theme of Jarman's poem using the same sonnet form that he uses.

Connections to Other Selections

1. Jarman has said that his "Unholy Sonnets" (there are about twenty of them) are modeled after John Donne's *Holy Sonnets* but that he does not share the same Christian assumptions about faith and mercy that inform Donne's sonnets. Instead, Jarman says, he "work[s] against any assumption or shared expression of faith, to write a devotional poetry against the grain." Keeping this statement in mind, write an essay comparing and contrasting the tone and theme of Jarman's sonnet with John Donne's "Batter My Heart" (p. 604) or "Death Be Not Proud" (p. 276).

Villanelle

The *villanelle* is a fixed form consisting of nineteen lines of any length divided into six stanzas: five tercets and a concluding quatrain. The first and third lines of the initial tercet rhyme; these rhymes are repeated in each subsequent tercet (*aba*) and in the final two lines of the quatrain (*abaa*). Moreover, line 1 appears in its entirety as lines 6, 12, and 18, while line 3 appears as lines 9, 15, and 19. This form may seem to risk monotony, but in competent hands a villanelle can create haunting echoes, as in Dylan Thomas's "Do not go gentle into that good night."

DYLAN THOMAS (1914–1953)

Do not go gentle into that good night 1952

Do not go gentle into that good night,
Old age should burn and rave at close of day;
Rage, rage against the dying of the light.

Though wise men at their end know dark is right,
Because their words had forked no lightning they 5
Do not go gentle into that good night.

Good men, the last wave by, crying how bright
Their frail deeds might have danced in a green bay,
Rage, rage against the dying of the light.

Wild men who caught and sang the sun in flight, 10
And learn, too late, they grieved it on its way,
Do not go gentle into that good night.

Grave men, near death, who see with blinding sight
Blind eyes could blaze like meteors and be gay,
Rage, rage against the dying of the light. 15

And you, my father, there on the sad height,
Curse, bless, me now with your fierce tears, I pray.
Do not go gentle into that good night.
Rage, rage against the dying of the light.

CONSIDERATIONS FOR CRITICAL THINKING AND WRITING

1. FIRST RESPONSE. How does Thomas vary the meanings of the poem's two refrains: "Do not go gentle into that good night," and "Rage, rage against the dying of the light"?
2. Thomas's father was close to death when this poem was written. How does the tone contribute to the poem's theme?
3. How is "good" used in line 1?
4. Characterize the men who are "wise" (line 4), "Good" (7), "Wild" (10), and "Grave" (13).
5. What do figures of speech contribute to this poem?
6. Discuss this villanelle's sound effects.

CONNECTION TO ANOTHER SELECTION

1. In Thomas's poem we experience "rage against the dying of the light." Contrast this with the rage you find in Sylvia Plath's "Daddy" (p. 630). What produces the emotion in Plath's poem?

ROBYN SARAH (B. 1949)

Villanelle for a Cool April

1998

I like a leafing-out by increments,
— not bolting bloom, in sudden heat begun.
Life's sweetest savoured in the present tense.

I like to watch the shadows pack their tents
before the creep of the advancing sun.   5
I like a leafing-out by increments:

to watch the tendrils inch along the fence,
to take my pleasures slow and one by one.
Life's sweetest savoured in the present tense.

Oh, leave tomorrow's fruit to providence   10
and dote upon the bud — from which is spun
a leafing-out to love in increments,

a greening in the cool of swooning sense,
a feathered touch, a button just undone.
Life's sweetest savoured in the present tense,   15

as love when it withholds and then relents,
as a cool April lets each moment stun.
I like a leafing-out by increments;
life's sweetest savoured in the present tense.

CONSIDERATIONS FOR CRITICAL THINKING AND WRITING

1. FIRST RESPONSE. How is "a cool April" compared to a love relationship?

2. Examine the poem carefully to determine if its structure is that of a conventional villanelle. Are there any significant variations?

3. Discuss how the images serve to reinforce the idea that life can be "savoured" best when it's "a leafing-out by increments."

CONNECTION TO ANOTHER SELECTION

1. Compare this description of April with Margaret Atwood's "February" (p. 124) and Sophie Cabot Black's "August" (p. 125). Which poem did you find to be the most effective description of a month? Explain why.

Sestina

Although the **sestina** usually does not rhyme, it is perhaps an even more demanding fixed form than the villanelle. A sestina consists of thirty-nine lines of any length divided into six, six-line stanzas and a three-line concluding stanza called an **envoy.** The difficulty is in repeating the six words at the ends of the first stanza's lines at the ends of the lines in the other

five, six-line stanzas as well. Those words must also appear in the final
three lines, where they often resonate important themes. The sestina origi-
nated in the Middle Ages, but contemporary poets continue to find it a fas-
cinating and challenging form.

ELIZABETH BISHOP (1911–1979)

Sestina   *1965*

September rain falls on the house.
In the failing light, the old grandmother
sits in the kitchen with the child
beside the Little Marvel Stove,
reading the jokes from the almanac,   5
laughing and talking to hide her tears.

She thinks that her equinoctial tears
and the rain that beats on the roof of the house
were both foretold by the almanac,
but only known to a grandmother.   10
The iron kettle sings on the stove.
She cuts some bread and says to the child,

It's time for tea now; but the child
is watching the teakettle's small hard tears
dance like mad on the hot black stove,   15
the way the rain must dance on the house.
Tidying up, the old grandmother
hangs up the clever almanac

on its string. Birdlike, the almanac
hovers half open above the child,   20
hovers above the old grandmother
and her teacup full of dark brown tears.
She shivers and says she thinks the house
feels chilly, and puts more wood in the stove.

It was to be, says the Marvel Stove.   25
I know what I know, says the almanac.
With crayons the child draws a rigid house
and a winding pathway. Then the child
puts in a man with buttons like tears
and shows it proudly to the grandmother.   30

But secretly, while the grandmother
busies herself about the stove,
the little moons fall down like tears
from between the pages of the almanac
into the flower bed the child   35
has carefully placed in the front of the house.

Time to plant tears, says the almanac.
The grandmother sings to the marvelous stove
and the child draws another inscrutable house.

CONSIDERATIONS FOR CRITICAL THINKING AND WRITING

1. FIRST RESPONSE. How are the six end words — "house," "grandmother," "child," "stove," "almanac," and "tears" — central to the sestina's meaning?
2. Number the end words of the first stanza 1, 2, 3, 4, 5, and 6, and then use those numbers for the corresponding end words in the remaining five stanzas to see how the pattern of the line-end words is worked out in this sestina. Also locate the six end words in the envoy.
3. What happens in this sestina? Why is the grandmother "laughing and talking to hide her tears" (line 6)?
4. Underline the images that seem especially vivid to you. What effects do they create? What is the tone of the sestina?
5. How is the almanac used symbolically? Does Bishop use any other symbols to convey meanings?
6. Write a brief essay explaining why you think a poet might derive pleasure from writing in a fixed form such as a villanelle or sestina. Can you think of similar activities outside the field of writing in which discipline and restraint give pleasure?

FLORENCE CASSEN MAYERS (B. 1940)

All-American Sestina   *1996*

One nation, indivisible
two-car garage
three strikes you're out
four-minute mile
five-cent cigar   5
six-string guitar

six-pack Bud
one-day sale
five-year warranty
two-way street   10
fourscore and seven years ago
three cheers

three-star restaurant
sixty-
four-dollar question   15
one-night stand
two-pound lobster
five-star general

five-course meal
three sheets to the wind   20
two bits
six-shooter

one-armed bandit
four-poster

four-wheel drive   25
five-and-dime
hole in one
three-alarm fire
sweet sixteen
two-wheeler   30

two-tone Chevy
four rms, hi flr, w/vu
six-footer
high five
three-ring circus   35
one-room schoolhouse

two thumbs up, five-karat diamond
Fourth of July, three-piece suit
six feet under, one-horse town

CONSIDERATIONS FOR CRITICAL THINKING AND WRITING

1. FIRST RESPONSE. Discuss the significance of the title; what is "All-American"? Why a sestina?

2. How is the structure of this poem different from a conventional sestina? (What structural requirement does Mayers add for this sestina?)

3. Do you think important themes are raised by this poem, as is traditional for a sestina? If so, what are they? If not, what is being played with by using this convention?

CONNECTION TO ANOTHER SELECTION

1. Describe and compare the strategy used to create meaning in "All-American Sestina" with that used by Cummings in "next to of course god america i" (p. 146).

Epigram

An *epigram* is a brief, pointed, and witty poem. Although most rhyme and often are written in couplets, epigrams take no prescribed form. Instead, they are typically polished bits of compressed irony, satire, or paradox. Here is an epigram that defines itself.

SAMUEL TAYLOR COLERIDGE (1772–1834)

What Is an Epigram?   *1802*

What is an epigram? A dwarfish whole;
Its body brevity, and wit its soul.

These additional examples by A. R. Ammons, David McCord, and Paul Laurence Dunbar satisfy Coleridge's definition.

A. R. AMMONS (B. 1926)
Coward   *1975*

Bravery runs in my family.

DAVID McCORD (1897–1997)
Epitaph on a Waiter   *1954*

By and by
God caught his eye.

PAUL LAURENCE DUNBAR (1872–1906)
Theology   *1896*

There is a heaven, for ever, day by day,
The upward longing of my soul doth tell me so.
There is a hell, I'm quite as sure; for pray,
If there were not, where would my neighbors go?

CONSIDERATIONS FOR CRITICAL THINKING AND WRITING

1. FIRST RESPONSE. In what sense is each of these epigrams, as Coleridge puts it, a "dwarfish whole"?
2. Explain which of these epigrams, in addition to being witty, makes a serious point.
3. Try writing a few epigrams that say something memorable about whatever you choose to focus upon.

Limerick

The *limerick* is always light and humorous. Its usual form consists of five predominantly anapestic lines rhyming *aabba;* lines 1, 2, and 5 contain three feet, while lines 3 and 4 contain two. Limericks have delighted everyone from schoolchildren to sophisticated adults, and they range in subject matter from the simply innocent and silly to the satiric or obscene. The sexual humor helps to explain why so many limericks are written anonymously. Here is one that is anonymous but more concerned with physics than physiology:

There was a young lady named Bright,
Who traveled much faster than light,
    She started one day
    In a relative way,
And returned on the previous night.

This next one is a particularly clever definition of a limerick.

Laurence Perrine (b. 1915)

The limerick's never averse

1982

The limerick's never averse
To expressing itself in a terse
    Economical style,
    And yet, all the while,
The limerick's *always* a verse.

Considerations for Critical Thinking and Writing

1. FIRST RESPONSE. How does this limerick differ from others you know? How is it similar?

2. Scan Perrine's limerick. How do the lines measure up to the traditional fixed metrical pattern?

3. Try writing a limerick. Use the following basic pattern.

```
  ˘ ˘ ˊ        ˘ ˘ ˊ        ˘ ˘ ˊ
  ˘ ˘ ˊ        ˘ ˘ ˊ        ˘ ˘ ˊ
               ˘ ˘ ˊ        ˘ ˘ ˊ
               ˘ ˘ ˊ        ˘ ˘ ˊ
  ˘ ˘ ˊ        ˘ ˘ ˊ        ˘ ˘ ˊ
```

You might begin with a friend's name or the name of your school or town. Your instructor is, of course, fair game, too, provided your tact matches your wit.

And here's a real tongue twister:

Keith Casto

She Don't Bop

1987

A nervous young woman named Trudy
Was at odds with a horn player, Rudy.
    His horn so annoyed her
    The neighbors would loiter
To watch Rudy toot Trudy fruity.

Haiku

Another brief fixed poetic form, borrowed from the Japanese, is the *haiku.*
A haiku is usually described as consisting of seventeen syllables organized
into three unrhymed lines of five, seven, and five syllables. Owing to lan-
guage difference, however, English translations of haiku are often only ap-
proximated, because a Japanese haiku exists in time (Japanese syllables
have duration). The number of syllables in our sense is not as significant as
the duration. These poems typically present an intense emotion or vivid
image of nature, which, in the Japanese, are also designed to lead to a spiri-
tual insight.

MATSUO BASHŌ (1644–1694)

Under cherry trees   *date unknown*

Under cherry trees
Soup, the salad, fish and all . . .
Seasoned with petals.

CAROLYN KIZER (B. 1925)

After Basho   *1984*

Tentatively, you
slip onstage this evening,
pallid, famous moon.

CONSIDERATIONS FOR CRITICAL THINKING AND WRITING

1. FIRST RESPONSE. What different emotions do these two haiku evoke?
2. What differences and similarities are there between the effects of a haiku
   and those of an epigram?
3. Compose a haiku. Try to make it as allusive and suggestive as possible.

Elegy

An elegy in classical Greek and Roman literature was written in alternat-
ing hexameter and pentameter lines. Since the seventeenth century, how-
ever, the term *elegy* has been used to describe a lyric poem written to
commemorate someone who is dead. The word is also used to refer to a
serious meditative poem produced to express the speaker's melancholy
thoughts. Elegies no longer conform to a fixed pattern of lines and stan-
zas, but their characteristic subject is related to death and their tone is
mournfully contemplative.

Seamus Heaney (b. 1939)

Mid-term Break   *1966*

I sat all morning in the college sick bay
Counting bells knelling classes to a close.
At two o'clock our neighbors drove me home.

In the porch I met my father crying —
He had always taken funerals in his stride —   5
And Big Jim Evans saying it was a hard blow.

The baby cooed and laughed and rocked the pram
When I came in, and I was embarrassed
By old men standing up to shake my hand

And tell me they were "sorry for my trouble,"   10
Whispers informed strangers I was the eldest,
Away at school, as my mother held my hand

In hers and coughed out angry tearless sighs.
At ten o'clock the ambulance arrived
With the corpse, stanched and bandaged by the nurses.   15

Next morning I went up into the room. Snowdrops
And candles soothed the bedside; I saw him
For the first time in six weeks. Paler now,

Wearing a poppy bruise on his left temple,
He lay in the four foot box as in his cot.   20
No gaudy scars, the bumper knocked him clear.

A four foot box, a foot for every year.

Considerations for Critical Thinking and Writing

1. FIRST RESPONSE. What effect does the title have on your understanding of the speaker? What else does the title imply?
2. How do simple details contribute to the effects of this elegy?
3. Does this elegy use any kind of formal pattern for its structure? What is the effect of the last line standing by itself?
4. Another spelling for *stanched* (line 15) is *staunched*. Usage is about evenly divided between the two in the United States. What is the effect of Heaney's choosing the former spelling rather than the latter?

Connections to Other Selections

1. Compare Heaney's elegy with A. E. Housman's "To an Athlete Dying Young" (p. 614). Which do you find more moving? Explain why.
2. Write an essay comparing this story of a boy's death with Updike's "Dog's Death" (p. 11). Do you think either of the poems is sentimental? Explain why or why not.

ANDREW HUDGINS (B. 1951)

Elegy for My Father, Who Is Not Dead   *1991*

One day I'll lift the telephone
and be told my father's dead. He's ready.
In the sureness of his faith, he talks
about the world beyond this world
as though his reservations have   5
been made. I think he wants to go,
a little bit — a new desire
to travel building up, an itch
to see fresh worlds. Or older ones.
He thinks that when I follow him   10
he'll wrap me in his arms and laugh,
the way he did when I arrived
on earth. I do not think he's right.
He's ready. I am not. I can't
just say good-bye as cheerfully   15
as if he were embarking on a trip
to make my later trip go well.
I see myself on deck, convinced
his ship's gone down, while he's convinced
I'll see him standing on the dock   20
and waving, shouting, Welcome back.

CONSIDERATIONS FOR CRITICAL THINKING AND WRITING

1. FIRST RESPONSE. Why does this speaker elegize his father if the father "is not dead"?

2. How does the speaker's view of immortality differ from his father's?

3. Explain why you think this is an optimistic or pessimistic poem — or explain why these two categories fail to describe the poem.

4. In what sense can this poem be regarded as an elegy?

CONNECTION TO ANOTHER SELECTION

1. Write an essay comparing attitudes toward death in this poem and in Thomas's "Do not go gentle into that good night" (p. 233). Both speakers invoke their fathers, nearer to death than they are; what impact does this have?

Ode

An *ode* is characterized by a serious topic and formal tone, but no prescribed formal pattern describes all odes. In some odes the pattern of each stanza is repeated throughout, while in others each stanza introduces a new pattern. Odes are lengthy lyrics that often include lofty emotions conveyed by a dignified style. Typical topics include truth, art, freedom, justice, and the meaning of life. Frequently such lyrics tend to be more public than private, and their speakers often employ apostrophe.

PERCY BYSSHE SHELLEY (1792–1822)

Ode to the West Wind   *1820*

I
O wild West Wind, thou breath of Autumn's being,
Thou, from whose unseen presence the leaves dead
Are driven, like ghosts from an enchanter fleeing,

Yellow, and black, and pale, and hectic red,
Pestilence-stricken multitudes: O thou,   5
Who chariotest to their dark wintry bed

The wingèd seeds, where they lie cold and low,
Each like a corpse within its grave, until
Thine azure sister of the Spring shall blow

Her clarion o'er the dreaming earth, and fill   10
(Driving sweet buds like flocks to feed in air)
With living hues and odors plain and hill:

Wild Spirit, which art moving everywhere;
Destroyer and preserver; hear, oh, hear!

II
Thou on whose stream, mid the steep sky's commotion,   15
Loose clouds like earth's decaying leaves are shed,
Shook from the tangled boughs of Heaven and Ocean,

Angels° of rain and lightning: there are spread   *messengers*
On the blue surface of thine airy surge,
Like the bright hair uplifted from the head   20

Of some fierce Maenad,° even from the dim verge
Of the horizon to the zenith's height,
The locks of the approaching storm. Thou dirge

Of the dying year, to which this closing night
Will be the dome of a vast sepulcher,   25
Vaulted with all thy congregated might

Of vapors, from whose solid atmosphere
Black rain, and fire, and hail will burst: oh, hear!

III
Thou who didst waken from his summer dreams
The blue Mediterranean, where he lay,   30
Lulled by the coil of his crystálline streams,

21 *Maenad:* In Greek mythology, a frenzied worshiper of Dionysus, god of wine and fertility.

Beside a pumice isle in Baiae's bay,°
And saw in sleep old palaces and towers
Quivering within the wave's intenser day,

All overgrown with azure moss and flowers   35
So sweet, the sense faints picturing them! Thou
For whose path the Atlantic's level powers

Cleave themselves into chasms, while far below
The sea-blooms and the oozy woods which wear
The sapless foliage of the ocean, know   40

Thy voice, and suddenly grow gray with fear,
And tremble and despoil themselves: oh, hear!

IV
If I were a dead leaf thou mightest bear;
If I were a swift cloud to fly with thee;
A wave to pant beneath thy power, and share   45

The impulse of thy strength, only less free
Than thou, O uncontrollable! If even
I were as in my boyhood, and could be

The comrade by thy wanderings over Heaven,
As then, when to outstrip thy skyey speed   50
Scarce seemed a vision; I would ne'er have striven

As thus with thee in prayer in my sore need.
Oh, lift me as a wave, a leaf, a cloud!
I fall upon the thorns of life! I bleed!

A heavy weight of hours has chained and bowed   55
One too like thee: tameless, and swift, and proud.

V
Make me thy lyre,° even as the forest is:
What if my leaves are falling like its own!
The tumult of thy mighty harmonies

Will take from both a deep, autumnal tone,   60
Sweet though in sadness. Be thou, Spirit fierce,
My spirit! Be thou me, impetuous one!

Drive my dead thoughts over the universe
Like withered leaves to quicken a new birth!
And, by the incantation of this verse,   65

Scatter, as from an unextinguished hearth
Ashes and sparks, my words among mankind!
Be through my lips to unawakened earth

The trumpet of a prophecy! O Wind,
If Winter comes, can Spring be far behind?   70

---

32 *Baiae's bay:* A bay in the Mediterranean Sea.   57 *Make me thy lyre:* Sound is produced
on an Aeolian lyre, or wind harp, by wind blowing across its strings.

CONSIDERATIONS FOR CRITICAL THINKING AND WRITING

1. FIRST RESPONSE. Write a summary of each of this ode's five sections.

2. What is the speaker's situation? What is his "sore need" (line 52)? What does the speaker ask of the wind in lines 57–70?

3. What does the wind signify in this ode? How is it used symbolically?

4. Determine the meter and rhyme of the first five stanzas. How do these elements contribute to the ode's movement? Is this pattern continued in the other four sections?

Picture Poem

By arranging lines into particular shapes, poets can sometimes organize typography into *picture poems* of what they describe. Words have been arranged into all kinds of shapes, from apples to light bulbs. Notice how the shape of this next poem embodies its meaning.

MICHAEL MCFEE (B. 1954)

In Medias Res°   1985

His waist
like the plot
thickens, wedding
pants now breathtaking,
belt no longer the cinch   5
it once was, belly's cambium
expanding to match each birthday,
his body a wad of anonymous tissue
swung in the same centrifuge of years
that separates a house from its foundation,   10
undermining sidewalks grim with joggers
and loose-filled graves and families
and stars collapsing on themselves,
no preservation society capable
of plugging entropy's dike,   15
under his zipper's sneer
a belly hibernation-
soft, ready for
the kill.

In Medias Res: A Latin term for a story that begins "in the middle of things."

CONSIDERATIONS FOR CRITICAL THINKING AND WRITING

1. FIRST RESPONSE. Explain how the title is related to this poem's shape. How is the meaning related?

2. Identify the puns. How do they work in the poem?

3. What is "cambium" (line 6)? Why is the phrase "belly's cambium" especially appropriate?

4. What is the tone of this poem? Is it consistent throughout?

Parody

A *parody* is a humorous imitation of another, usually serious, work. It can take any fixed or open form because parodists imitate the tone, language, and shape of the original. While a parody may be teasingly close to a work's style, it typically deflates the subject matter to make the original seem absurd. Parody can be used as a kind of literary criticism to expose the defects in a work, but it is also very often an affectionate acknowledgment that a well-known work has become both institutionalized in our culture and fair game for some fun. Read Marvell's "To His Coy Mistress" (p. 65) and then study this parody.

PETER DE VRIES (B. 1910)

To His Importunate Mistress   *1986*

Andrew Marvell Updated

Had we but world enough, and time,
My coyness, lady, were a crime,
But at my back I always hear
Time's wingèd chariot, striking fear
The hour is nigh when creditors   5
Will prove to be my predators.
As wages of our picaresque,
Bag lunches bolted at my desk
Must stand as fealty to you
For each expensive rendezvous.   10
Obeisance at your marble feet
Deserves the best-appointed suite,
And would have, lacked I not the pelf
To pleasure also thus myself;
But aptly sumptuous amorous scenes   15
Rule out the rake of modest means.

Since mistress presupposes wife,
It means a doubly costly life;
For fools by second passion fired
A second income is required,   20
The earning which consumes the hours
They'd hoped to spend in rented bowers.
To hostelries the worst of fates
That weekly raise their daily rates!
I gather, lady, from your scoffing   25

A bloke more solvent in the offing.
So revels thus to rivals go
For want of monetary flow.
How vexing that inconstant cash
The constant suitor must abash,   30
Who with excuses vainly pled
Must rue the undisheveled bed,
And that for paltry reasons given
His conscience may remain unriven.

CONSIDERATIONS FOR CRITICAL THINKING AND WRITING

1. FIRST RESPONSE. To what extent does this poem duplicate Marvell's style? How does it differ?

2. How is De Vries's use of "mistress" different from Marvell's (p. 65)? How does the speaker's complaint in this poem differ from that in "To His Coy Mistress"?

3. Explain how "picaresque" is used in line 7.

4. Choose a poet whose work you know reasonably well or would like to know better and determine what is characteristic about his or her style. Then choose a poem to parody. It's probably best to attempt a short poem or a section of a long work. If you have difficulty selecting an author, you might consider Herrick, Blake, Keats, Dickinson, Whitman, or Frost, since a number of their works are included in this book.

CONNECTION TO ANOTHER SELECTION

1. Read Anthony Hecht's "The Dover Bitch" (p. 609), a parody of Arnold's "Dover Beach" (p. 95). Write an essay comparing the effectiveness of Hecht's parody with that of De Vries's "To His Importunate Mistress." Which parody do you prefer? Explain why.

Here's a parody for all seasons — not just Christmas — that brings together two popular icons of our culture.

X. J. KENNEDY (B. 1929)

A Visit from St. Sigmund   *1993*

Freud is just an old Santa Claus.
  — Margaret Mead°

'Twas the night before Christmas, when all through each kid
Not an Ego was stirring, not even an Id.
The hangups were hung by the chimney with care
In hopes that St. Sigmund Freud soon would be there.
The children in scream class had knocked off their screams,   5

Margaret Mead (1901–1978): Noted American anthropologist.

Letting Jungian archetypes dance through their dreams,
And Mamma with her bra off and I on her lap
Had just snuggled down when a vast thunderclap
Boomed and from my unconscious arose such a chatter
As Baptist John's teeth made on Salome's platter.   10
Away from my darling I flew like a flash,
Tore straight to the bathroom and threw up, and — *smash!*
Through the windowpane hurtled and bounced on the floor
A big brick — holy smoke, it was hard to ignore.
As I heard further thunderclaps — lo and behold —   15
Came a little psychiatrist eighty years old.
He drove a wheeled couch pulled by five fat psychoses
And the gleam in his eye might induce a hypnosis.
Like subliminal meanings his coursers they came
And, consulting his notebook, he called them by name: 20
"Now Schizo, now Fetish, now Fear of Castration!
On Paranoia! on Penis-fixation!
Ach, yes, that big brick through your glass I should mention:
Just a simple device to compel your attention.
You need, boy, to be in an analyst's power: 25
You talk, I take notes — fifty schillings an hour."
A bag full of symbols he'd slung on his back;
He looked smug as a junk-peddler laden with smack
Or a shrewd politician soliciting votes
And his chinbeard was stiff as a starched billygoat's.   30
Then laying one finger aside of his nose,
He chortled, "What means this? Mein Gott, I suppose
There's a meaning in fingers, in candles und wicks,
In mouseholes und doughnut holes, steeples und sticks.
You see, it's the imminent prospect of sex   35
That makes all us humans run round till we're wrecks,
Und each innocent infant since people began
Wants to bed with his momma und kill his old man;
So never you fear that you're sick as a swine —
Your hangups are every sane person's und mine.   40
Even Hamlet was hot for his mom — there's the rub;
Even Oedipus Clubfoot was one of the club.
Hmmm, that's humor unconscious." He gave me rib-pokes
And for almost two hours explained phallic jokes.
Then he sprang to his couch, to his crew gave a nod,   45
And away they all flew like the concept of God.
In the worst of my dreams I can hear him shout still,
"Merry Christmas to all! In the mail comes my bill."

CONSIDERATIONS FOR CRITICAL THINKING AND WRITING

1. FIRST RESPONSE. What makes Freud a particularly appropriate substitute
   for Santa Claus? How does this substitute facilitate the poem's humor?

2. What is the tone of this parody? How does the quotation from Margaret
   Mead help to establish the poem's tone?

3. What do you think is the poet's attitude toward Freud? Cite specific lines to support your point.

4. Is the focus of this parody the Christmas story or Freud? Explain your response.

PERSPECTIVES

ROBERT MORGAN (B. 1944)

On the Shape of a Poem   1983

In the body of the poem, lineation is part flesh and part skeleton, as form is the towpath along which the burden of content, floating on the formless, is pulled. All language is both mental and sacramental, is not "real" but is the working of lip and tongue to subvert the "real." Poems empearl irritating facts until they become opalescent spheres of moment, not so much résumés of history as of human faculties working with pain. Every poem is necessarily a fragment empowered by its implicitness. We sing to charm the snake in our spines, to make it sway with the pulse of the world, balancing the weight of consciousness on the topmost vertebra.

From *Epoch,* Fall/Winter 1983

CONSIDERATIONS FOR CRITICAL THINKING AND WRITING

1. Explain Morgan's metaphors for describing lineation and form in a poem. Why are these metaphors useful?

2. Choose one of the poems in this chapter that makes use of a particular form and explain how it is "a fragment empowered by its implicitness."

ELAINE MITCHELL (B. 1924)

Form   1994

Is it a corset
or primal wave?
Don't try to force it.

Even endorse it
to shape and deceive.   5
Ouch, too tight a corset.

Take it off. No remorse. It
's an ace up your sleeve.
No need to force it.

Can you make a horse knit?   10
Who would believe?
Consider. Of course, it

might be a resource. Wit,
your grateful slave.
Form. Sometimes you force it,   15

sometimes divorce it
to make it behave.
So don't try to force it.
Respect a good corset.

CONSIDERATIONS FOR CRITICAL THINKING AND WRITING

1. FIRST RESPONSE. What is the speaker's attitude toward form?

2. Explain why you think the form of this poem does or does not conform to the advice of the speaker.

3. Why is the metaphor of a corset a particularly apt image for this poem?

10

Open Form

Many poems, especially those written in the twentieth century, are composed of lines that cannot be scanned for a fixed or predominant meter. Moreover, very often these poems do not rhyme. Known as *free verse* (from the French, *vers libre*), such lines can derive their rhythmic qualities from the repetition of words, phrases, or grammatical structures; the arrangement of words on the printed page; or some other means. In recent years the term **open form** has been used in place of *free verse* to avoid the erroneous suggestion that this kind of poetry lacks all discipline and shape.

Although the following two poems do not use measurable meters, they do have rhythm.

E. E. CUMMINGS (1894–1962)

in Just-   1923

in Just-
spring   when the world is mud-
luscious the little
lame balloonman

whistles   far   and wee   5

and eddieandbill come
running from marbles and
piracies and it's
spring

when the world is puddle-wonderful   10

the queer
old balloonman whistles
far   and   wee

and bettyandisbel come dancing
from hop-scotch and jump-rope and   15

it's
spring

and

   the

      goat-footed   20

balloonMan   whistles
far
and
wee

CONSIDERATIONS FOR CRITICAL THINKING AND WRITING

1. FIRST RESPONSE. What is the effect of this poem's arrangement of words and use of space on the page? How would the effect differ if it was written out in prose?

2. What is the effect of Cummings's combining the names "eddieandbill" and "bettyandisbel"?

3. The allusion in line 20 refers to Pan, a Greek god associated with nature. How does this allusion add to the meaning of the poem?

WALT WHITMAN (1819–1892)

From "I Sing the Body Electric"   1855

O my body! I dare not desert the likes of you in other men and women,
    nor the likes of the parts of you,
I believe the likes of you are to stand or fall with the likes of the soul, (and
    that they are the soul,)
I believe the likes of you shall stand or fall with my poems, and that they
    are my poems.
Man's, woman's, child's, youth's, wife's, husband's, mother's, father's,
    young man's, young woman's poems.
Head, neck, hair, ears, drop and tympan of the ears.   5
Eyes, eye-fringes, iris of the eye, eyebrows, and the waking or sleeping of
    the lids,
Mouth, tongue, lips, teeth, roof of the mouth, jaws, and the jaw-hinges,
Nose, nostrils of the nose, and the partition,
Cheeks, temples, forehead, chin, throat, back of the neck, neck-slue,
Strong shoulders, manly beard, scapula, hind-shoulders, and the ample
    side-round of the chest,   10
Upper-arm, armpit, elbow-socket, lower-arm, arm-sinews, arm-bones,
Wrist and wrist-joints, hand, palm, knuckles, thumb, forefinger, finger-
    joints, finger-nails,
Broad breast-front, curling hair of the breast, breast-bone, breast-side,

Ribs, belly, backbone, joints of the backbone,
Hips, hip-sockets, hip-strength, inward and outward round, man-balls,
    man-root,   15
Strong set of thighs, well carrying the trunk above,
Leg-fibers, knee, knee-pan, upper-leg, under-leg,
Ankles, instep, foot-ball, toes, toe-joints, the heel;
All attitudes, all the shapeliness, all the belongings of my or your body or
    of any one's body, male or female,
The lung-sponges, the stomach-sac, the bowels sweet and clean,   20
The brain in its folds inside the skull-frame,
Sympathies, heart-valves, palate-valves, sexuality, maternity,
Womanhood, and all that is a woman, and the man that comes from woman,
The womb, the teats, nipples, breast-milk, tears, laughter, weeping, love-
    looks, love-perturbations and risings,
The voice, articulation, language, whispering, shouting aloud,   25
Food, drink, pulse, digestion, sweat, sleep, walking, swimming,
Poise on the hips, leaping, reclining, embracing, arm-curving and tightening,
The continual changes of the flex of the mouth, and around the eyes,
The skin, the sunburnt shade, freckles, hair,
The curious sympathy one feels when feeling with the hand the naked
    meat of the body,   30
The circling rivers the breath, and breathing it in and out,
The beauty of the waist, and thence of the hips, and thence downward
    toward the knees,
The thin red jellies within you or within me, the bones and the marrow
    in the bones,
The exquisite realization of health;
O I say these are not the parts and poems of the body only, but of the soul,   35
O I say now these are the soul!

CONSIDERATIONS FOR CRITICAL THINKING AND WRITING

1. FIRST RESPONSE. What informs this speaker's attitude toward the human
   body?
2. Read the poem aloud. Is it simply a tedious enumeration of body parts, or
   do the lines achieve some kind of rhythmic cadence?

PERSPECTIVE

WALT WHITMAN (1819–1892)

On Rhyme and Meter   *1855*

The poetic quality is not marshaled in rhyme or uniformity or abstract ad-
dresses to things nor in melancholy complaints or good precepts, but is the life
of these and much else and is in the soul. The profit of rhyme is that it drops
seeds of a sweeter and more luxuriant rhyme, and of uniformity that it conveys

itself into its own roots in the ground out of sight. The rhyme and uniformity of perfect poems show the free growth of metrical laws and bud from them as unerringly and loosely as lilacs or roses on a bush, and take shapes as compact as the shapes of chestnuts and oranges and melons and pears, and shed the perfume impalpable to form. The fluency and ornaments of the finest poems or music or orations or recitations are not independent but dependent. All beauty comes from beautiful blood and a beautiful brain. If the greatnesses are in conjunction in a man or woman it is enough . . . the fact will prevail through the universe . . . but the gaggery and gilt of a million years will not prevail. Who troubles himself about his ornaments or fluency is lost.

From the preface to the 1855 edition of *Leaves of Grass*

CONSIDERATIONS FOR CRITICAL THINKING AND WRITING

1. According to Whitman, what determines the shape of a poem?
2. Why does Whitman prefer open forms over fixed forms such as the sonnet?
3. Is Whitman's poetry devoid of any structure or shape? Choose one of his poems (listed in the index) to illustrate your answer.

Open form poetry is sometimes regarded as formless because it is unlike the strict fixed forms of a sonnet, villanelle, or sestina. But even though open form poems may not employ traditional meters and rhymes, they still rely on an intense use of language to establish rhythms and relations between meaning and form. Open form poems use the arrangement of words and phrases on the printed page, pauses, line lengths, and other means to create unique forms that express their particular meaning and tone.

Cummings's "in Just-" and the excerpt from Whitman's "I Sing the Body Electric" demonstrate how the white space on a page and rhythmic cadences can be aligned with meaning, but there is one kind of open form poetry that doesn't even look like poetry on a page. A ***prose poem*** is printed as prose and represents, perhaps, the most clear opposite of fixed forms. Here is a brief example.

JAY MEEK (B. 1937)

Swimmers

1994

Coming out of the theater, in the light of the marquee, I can see there is something on my clothing and my hands. When I look back I can see it on the others too, the light off the screen on their faces during the film, or the grey illuminations made at night by summer lightning. It doesn't go away. We are covered with it, like grease, and when by accident we touch each other, we feel it on our bodies. It is not sensual, not exciting. It is slippery, this film over our lives, so that when we come up against one another and slide away, it is as if nothing has happened: we go on, as though swimming the channel at night, lights on the water, hundreds of us rising up on the beach on the far side.

CONSIDERATIONS FOR CRITICAL THINKING AND WRITING

1. FIRST RESPONSE. What is the effect of this prose poem? Does it have a theme?

2. What, if anything, is poetic in this work?

3. Arrange the lines so that they look like poetry on a page. What determines where you break the lines?

Much of the poetry published today is written in open form; however, many poets continue to take pleasure in the requirements imposed by fixed forms. Some write both fixed form and open form poetry. Each kind offers rewards to careful readers as well. Here are several more open form poems that establish their own unique patterns.

GALWAY KINNELL (B. 1927)

After Making Love We Hear Footsteps   1980

For I can snore like a bullhorn
or play loud music
or sit up talking with any reasonably sober Irishman
and Fergus will only sink deeper
into his dreamless sleep, which goes by all in one flash,   5
but let there be that heavy breathing
or a stifled come-cry anywhere in the house
and he will wrench himself awake
and make for it on the run — as now, we lie together,
after making love, quiet, touching along the length of our bodies,   10
familiar touch of the long-married,
and he appears — in his baseball pajamas, it happens,
the neck opening so small
he has to screw them on, which one day may make him wonder
about the mental capacity of baseball players —   15
and says, "Are you loving and snuggling? May I join?"
He flops down between us and hugs us and snuggles himself to sleep,
his face gleaming with satisfaction at being this very child.

In the half darkness we look at each other
and smile   20
and touch arms across his little, startlingly muscled body —
this one whom habit of memory propels to the ground of his making,
sleeper only the mortal sounds can sing awake,
this blessing love gives again into our arms.

CONSIDERATIONS FOR CRITICAL THINKING AND WRITING

1. FIRST RESPONSE. Explore Kinnell's line endings. Why does he break the lines where he does?

2. How does the speaker's language reveal his character?

3. Describe the shift in tone between lines 18 and 19 with the shift in focus from child to adult. How does the use of space here emphasize this shift?

4. Do you think this poem is sentimental? Explain why or why not.

CONNECTION TO ANOTHER SELECTION

1. Discuss how this poem helps to bring into focus the sense of loss Robert Frost evokes in "Home Burial" (p. 343).

KELLY CHERRY (B. 1940)

Alzheimer's   *1990*

He stands at the door, a crazy old man
Back from the hospital, his mind rattling
Like the suitcase, swinging from his hand,
That contains shaving cream, a piggy bank,
A book he sometimes pretends to read,   5
His clothes. On the brick wall beside him
Roses and columbine slug it out for space, claw the mortar.
The sun is shining, as it does late in the afternoon
In England, after rain.
Sun hardens the house, reifies it,   10
Strikes the iron grillwork like a smithy
And sparks fly off, burning in the bushes —
The rosebushes —
While the white wood trim defines solidity in space.
This is his house. He remembers it as his,   15
Remembers the walkway he built between the front room
And the garage, the rhododendron he planted in back,
The car he used to drive. He remembers himself,
A younger man, in a tweed hat, a man who loved
Music. There is no time for that now. No time for music,   20
The peculiar screeching of strings, the luxurious
Fiddling with emotion.
Other things have become more urgent.
Other matters are now of greater import, have more
Consequence, must be attended to. The first   25
Thing he must do, now that he is home, is decide who
This woman is, this old, white-haired woman
Standing here in the doorway,
Welcoming him in.

CONSIDERATIONS FOR CRITICAL THINKING AND WRITING

1. FIRST RESPONSE. Why is it impossible to dismiss the character in this poem as merely "a crazy old man"?

2. Discuss the effect of the line breaks in lines 1–6 of the first complete sentence of the poem. How do the line breaks contribute to the meaning of these lines?

3. What do the images in lines 6–20 indicate about the nature of the man's memory?

4. Why is the final image of the "white-haired woman" especially effective? How does the final line serve as the emotional climax of the poem?

CONNECTION TO ANOTHER SELECTION

1. Compare the treatment of remembering and forgetting in "Alzheimer's" and in Sarah Lindsay's "Aluminum Chlorohydrate" (p. 63). How does the final image of an old woman in each poem affect your understanding of the poem's thematics?

WILLIAM CARLOS WILLIAMS (1883–1963)

The Red Wheelbarrow   *1923*

so much depends
upon

a red wheel
barrow

glazed with rain
water

beside the white
chickens.

CONSIDERATIONS FOR CRITICAL THINKING AND WRITING

1. FIRST RESPONSE. What "depends upon" the things mentioned in the poem? What is the effect of these images? Do they have a particular meaning?

2. Do these lines have any kind of rhythm?

3. How does this poem resemble a haiku? How is it different?

KATE RUSHIN (B. 1951)

The Black Back-Ups   *1993*

This is dedicated to Merry Clayton, Fontella Bass, Vonetta
Washington, Carolyn Franklin, Yolanda McCullough,
Carolyn Willis, Gwen Guthrie, Helaine Harris, and Darlene
Love. This is for all of the Black women who sang back-up for
Elvis Presley, John Denver, James Taylor, Lou Reed.   5
Etc. Etc. Etc.

I said Hey Babe
Take a Walk on the Wild Side
I said Hey Babe
Take a Walk on the Wild Side   10

And the colored girls say
Do dodo do do dodododo
Do dodo do do dodododo
Do dodo do do dodododo ooooo

This is for my Great-Grandmother Esther, my Grandmother   15
Addie, my grandmother called Sister, my Great-Aunt
Rachel, my Aunt Hilda, my Aunt Tine, my Aunt Breda,
my Aunt Gladys, my Aunt Helen, my Aunt Ellie,
my Cousin Barbara, my Cousin Dottie and my Great-Great-
Aunt Vene.   20

This is dedicated to all the Black women riding on buses
and subways back and forth to the Main Line, Haddonfield,
Cherry Hill and Chevy Chase. This is for the women who
spend their summers in Rockport, Newport, Cape Cod and
Camden, Maine. This is for the women who open those   25
bundles of dirty laundry sent home from those ivy-covered
campuses.

My Great-Aunt Rachel worked for the Carters
Ever since I can remember
There was *The Boy*   30
Whose name I never knew
And there was *The Girl*
Whose name was Jane

Great-Aunt Rachel brought Jane's dresses for me to wear
Perfectly Good Clothes   35
And I should've been glad to get them
Perfectly Good Clothes
No matter they didn't fit quite right
Perfectly Good Clothes
Brought home in a brown paper bag   40
With an air of accomplishment and excitement
Perfectly Good Clothes
Which I hated

At school
In Ohio   45
I swear to Gawd
There was always somebody
Telling me that the only person
In their whole house
Who listened and understood them   50
Despite the money and the lessons
Was the housekeeper
And I knew it was true
But what was I supposed to say

I know it's true   55
I watch her getting off the train
Moving slowly toward the Country Squire
With her uniform in her shopping bag
And the closer she gets to the car

The more the two little kids jump and laugh   60
And even the dog is about to
Turn inside out
Because they just can't wait until she gets there
Edna Edna   Wonderful Edna

But Aunt Edna to me, or Gram, or Miz Johnson, or   65
Sister Johnson on Sundays

And the colored girls say
Do dodo do do dodododo
Do dodo do do dodododo
Do dodo do do dodododo ooooo   70

This is for Hattie McDaniels, Butterfly McQueen
Ethel Waters
Sapphire
Saphronia
Ruby Begonia   75
Aunt Jemima
Aunt Jemima on the Pancake Box
Aunt Jemima on the Pancake Box?
AuntJemimaonthepancakebox?
Ainchamamaonthepancakebox?   80
Ain't chure Mama on the pancake box?

Mama Mama
Get off that box
And come home to me
And my Mama leaps off that box   85
She swoops down in her nurse's cape
Which she wears on Sunday
And for Wednesday night prayer meeting
And she wipes my forehead
And she fans my face   90
And she makes me a cup of tea
And it don't do a thing for my real pain
Except she is my mama

Mama Mommy Mammy
Mam-mee Mam-mee   95
I'd Walk a Mill-yon Miles
For one of your smiles

This is for the Black Back-Ups
This is for my mama and your mama
My grandma and your grandma   100
This is for the thousand thousand Black Back-Ups

And the colored girls say
Do   dodo   do do   dodododo
do   dodo
  dodo   105
      do
        do

CONSIDERATIONS FOR CRITICAL THINKING AND WRITING

1. FIRST RESPONSE. What do you think is the point of the many dedications to various black women throughout the poem? In what sense are they all "Black Back-Ups"?

2. There are many allusions to popular culture that echo in the poem. Which can you identify, and how are they relevant to this tribute to black women?

3. What is the speaker's attitude toward the "Perfectly Good Clothes" in lines 34–45?

4. Explain the significance of lines 67–70. How do they reveal important class differences among whites and blacks?

5. Read lines 77–81 aloud, and explain how meaning evolves in these lines.

6. What is the effect of the use of repetition in the poem? Why would a paraphrase of this poem be particularly unsatisfying in capturing its meaning?

CONNECTION TO ANOTHER SELECTION

1. Compare Rushin's strategy for creating lists in this poem with Walt Whitman's in the excerpt from "I Sing the Body Electric" (p. 252). How do you respond to the lists in each poem?

JONATHAN HOLDEN (B. 1941)

Cutting Loose on an August Night   1985

Roll the windows all
the way down and keep it
floored until you can hear the doors
between the corn-rows bursting
open with the August hay   5
and the full force of the packed earth
being unpacked and shredded
up with speed as the center line
pours tracer bullets
at the bug-spattered windshield   10
and the night's rush outshouts
static on the radio
where New York trails Cincinnati
and Oklahoma City's
cutting in to say high   15
tomorrow in the mid to upper
90s, low, and a full slate
of night action out there
like dusty fairgrounds
fierce under arc light roars   20
no runs, no hits, no errors, one
man left, and the entire north
winces, takes the snap-
shot of a cloud

formed like a horse's head,   25
and you are fixed firmly
in the cool pressure of the night,
the glare of the Philadelphia
and Boston games as sure
as constellations,   30
you're weightless
in the thick of speed, going
nowhere in all directions
at once, nothing but the pennant
race at stake.   35

CONSIDERATIONS FOR CRITICAL THINKING AND WRITING

1. FIRST RESPONSE. Discuss how Holden punctuates this poem and describe
   how punctuation (or the lack of it) affects your reading.
2. Does the title adequately express the poem's central meaning, or is there
   more to be said about the theme?
3. How do the images produce a sensation of speed? How do the line breaks
   produce a sensation of speed? Explain which images and line breaks seem
   most effective to you.

CONNECTION TO ANOTHER SELECTION

1. Compare the sense of freedom expressed in this poem with that offered by
   Thomas Lynch in "Liberty" (p. 132). What significant similarities and differ-
   ences do you find in the poems' themes and the manner in which they are
   presented?

MARILYN NELSON WANIEK (B. 1946)

Emily Dickinson's Defunct   *1978*

She used to
pack poems
in her hip pocket.
Under all the
gray old lady   5
clothes she was
dressed for action.
She had hair,
imagine,
in certain places, and   10
believe me
she smelled human
on a hot summer day.
Stalking snakes
or counting   15
the thousand motes

in sunlight
she walked just
like an Indian.
She was New England's   20
favorite daughter,
she could pray
like the devil.
She was a
two-fisted woman,   25
this babe.
All the flies
just stood around
and buzzed
when she died.   30

CONSIDERATIONS FOR CRITICAL THINKING AND WRITING

1. FIRST RESPONSE. How does the speaker characterize Dickinson? Explain
   why this characterization is different from the popular view of Dickinson.
2. How does the diction of the poem serve to characterize the speaker?
3. Discuss the function of the poem's title.

CONNECTIONS TO ANOTHER SELECTION

1. Waniek alludes to at least two other poems in "Emily Dickinson's De-
   funct." The title refers to E. E. Cummings's "Buffalo Bill 's" (p. 602), and the
   final lines (27–30) refer to Dickinson's "I heard a Fly buzz—when I died—"
   (p. 320). Read those poems and write an essay discussing how they affect
   your reading of Waniek's poem.

JEFFREY HARRISON (B. 1957)

Horseshoe Contest   *1999*

East Woodstock, Connecticut
Fourth of July

After the parade
of tractors and fire trucks,
old cars and makeshift floats,
after speeches by
the minister and selectman,   5
after the cakewalk and hayrides
and children's games
are over and the cornet band
has packed up its instruments
and left the gazebo,   10
the crowd on the town
green begins to gather
around the horseshoe pit

where a tournament
has been going on all day   15
and is now down
to the four or five
best players — the same ones
every year, these old guys
who, beneath their feigned   20
insouciance, care about this
more than anything.
The stakes are high:
their names on a plaque,
their pride, their whole idea   25
of who they are,
held onto since high school
when they played football
or ran track — something
unchanging at their core,   30
small but of a certain heft.
Limber as gunslingers
preparing for a showdown,
they step up in pairs
to take their turns   35
pitching the iron shoes,
lofting these emblems
of luck with a skill
both deliberate and
offhand, landing ringer   40
after ringer, metal
clashing against metal,
while the others, those
who entered the contest
just for the hell of it   45
and who dropped out
hours ago, their throws
going wild or just
not good enough, stand
quietly at the sidelines,   50
watching with something close
to awe as their elders
stride with the casual
self-consciousness of heroes,
becoming young again   55
in the crowd's hush
and the flush of suspense,
elevated for these moments
like a horseshoe hanging
in the sunlit air   60
above them, above their lives
as dairymen and farmers,
their bodies moving
with a kind of knowledge

unknown to most of us   65
and too late for most of us
to learn — though I'd give
almost anything
to be able to do anything
that well.   70

CONSIDERATIONS FOR CRITICAL THINKING AND WRITING

1. FIRST RESPONSE. How does Harrison economically create a picture of a July 4th celebration in lines 1-10?

2. In what sense are the "stakes . . . high" for the horseshoe tournament players? Why is the tournament important to the speaker?

3. Type out this poem as a prose paragraph. How is the experience of reading the poem different from reading the paragraph? What do the line breaks of the poem contribute to your reading experience?

CONNECTION TO ANOTHER SELECTION

1. Consider the contest described by Harrison along with Edward Hirsch's "Fast Break" (p. 219). What similarities and differences are there in the theme?

ROBERT HASS (B. 1941)

A Story about the Body   1989

The young composer, working that summer at an artists' colony, had watched her for a week. She was Japanese, a painter, almost sixty, and he thought he was in love with her. He loved her work, and her work was like the way she moved her body, used her hands, looked at him directly when she made amused and considered answers to his questions. One night, walking back from a concert, they came to her door and she turned to him and said, "I think you would like to have me. I would like that too, but I must tell you that I have had a double mastectomy," and when he didn't understand, "I've lost both my breasts." The radiance that he had carried around in his belly and chest cavity — like music — withered very quickly, and he made himself look at her when he said, "I'm sorry. I don't think I could." He walked back to his own cabin through the pines, and in the morning he found a small blue bowl on the porch outside his door. It looked to be full of rose petals, but he found when he picked it up that the rose petals were on top; the rest of the bowl — she must have swept them from the corners of her studio — was full of dead bees.

CONSIDERATIONS FOR CRITICAL THINKING AND WRITING

1. FIRST RESPONSE. Why this title? What other potential titles can you come up with that evoke your reading of the poem?

2. What impression about the "young composer" do you derive from the poem?

3. Why are bees very appropriate in the final line rather than, for example, moths?

CONNECTIONS TO OTHER SELECTIONS

1. Discuss the treatments of love in "A Story about the Body" and Nims's "Love Poem" (p. 31).

2. Read Hulme's "On the Differences between Poetry and Prose" (p. 113) and write an essay on what you think Hulme would have to say about "A Story about the Body."

SHARON OLDS (B. 1942)

Rite of Passage   *1983*

As the guests arrive at my son's party
they gather in the living room —
short men, men in first grade
with smooth jaws and chins.
Hands in pockets, they stand around   5
jostling, jockeying for place, small fights
breaking out and calming. One says to another
How old are you? Six. I'm seven. So?
They eye each other, seeing themselves
tiny in the other's pupils. They clear their   10
throats a lot, a room of small bankers,
they fold their arms and frown. *I could beat you
up,* a seven says to a six,
the dark cake, round and heavy as a
turret, behind them on the table. My son,   15
freckles like specks of nutmeg on his cheeks,
chest narrow as the balsa keel of a
model boat, long hands
cool and thin as the day they guided him
out of me, speaks up as a host   20
for the sake of the group.
We could easily kill a two-year-old,
he says in his clear voice. The other
men agree, they clear their throats
like Generals, they relax and get down to   25
playing war, celebrating my son's life.

CONSIDERATIONS FOR CRITICAL THINKING AND WRITING

1. FIRST RESPONSE. In what sense is this birthday party a "Rite of Passage"?

2. How does the speaker transform these six- and seven-year-old boys into men? What is the point of doing so?

3. Comment on the appropriateness of the image of the cake in lines 14–15.

4. Why does the son's claim that "We could easily kill a two-year-old" (line 22) come as such a shock at that point in the poem?

CONNECTION TO ANOTHER SELECTION

1. Discuss the use of irony in "Rite of Passage" and Owen's "Dulce et Decorum Est" (p. 102). Which do you think is a more effective antiwar poem? Explain why.

JULIO MARZÁN (B. 1946)

The Translator at the Reception for Latin American Writers

1997

Air-conditioned introductions,
then breezy Spanish conversation
fan his curiosity to know
what country I come from.
"Puerto Rico and the Bronx."   5

Spectacled downward eyes
translate disappointment
like a poison mushroom
puffed in his thoughts as if,
after investing a sizable   10
intellectual budget, transporting
a huge cast and camera crew
to film on location
Mayan pyramid grandeur,
indigenes whose ancient gods   15
and comet-tail plumage
inspire a glorious epic
of revolution across a continent,
he received a lurid script
for a social documentary   20
rife with dreary streets
and pathetic human interest,
meager in the profits of high culture.

Understandably he turns,
catches up with the hostess,   25
praising the uncommon quality
of her offerings of cheese.

CONSIDERATIONS FOR CRITICAL THINKING AND WRITING

1. FIRST RESPONSE. What is the speaker's attitude toward the person he meets at the reception? What lines in particular lead you to that conclusion?
2. Why is that person so disappointed about "Puerto Rico and the Bronx"?
3. Explain lines 6–23. How do they reveal both the speaker and the person encountered at the reception?
4. Why is the setting of this poem significant?

CAROLYNN HOY (B. 1947)

In the Summer Kitchen   1993

We speared long wooden spoons
into steaming galvanized tubs
churning and scooping the checked cotton
to feed back and forth
through a wringer   5
from her hand to mine.

And there, on that Monday,
she mentioned Harry, her first born,
my uncle, who died at three months.
That was all,   10
a slip of the tongue
as she hastily turned away.

On the stoop by the clothesline
beyond the screen door,
she snapped our flattened   15
shirts to attention,
shoulders as straight and squared
as her chiselled headstone
I now visit.

That silence.   20

The dignity of it all.

CONSIDERATIONS FOR CRITICAL THINKING AND WRITING

1. FIRST RESPONSE. Explain how the details about doing the wash take on more than a literal significance.
2. How do the grouping of stanzas and the spacing of lines affect your reading?
3. How do you think the speaker feels about her grandmother?
4. How might the poem be regarded as a kind of elegy for the grandmother?

CONNECTION TO ANOTHER SELECTION

1. Compare the tone of this poem with that of Emily Dickinson's "The Bustle in a House" (p. 312?)

ALLEN GINSBERG (1926–1997)

First Party at Ken Kesey's with Hell's Angels   1965

Cool black night thru the redwoods
cars parked outside in shade
behind the gate, stars dim above

the ravine, a fire burning by the side
porch and a few tired souls hunched over 5
in black leather jackets. In the huge
wooden house, a yellow chandelier
at 3 A.M. the blast of loudspeakers
hi-fi Rolling Stones Ray Charles Beatles
Jumping Joe Jackson and twenty youths 10
dancing to the vibration thru the floor,
a little weed in the bathroom, girls in scarlet
tights, one muscular smooth skinned man
sweating dancing for hours, beer cans
bent littering the yard, a hanged man 15
sculpture dangling from a high creek branch,
children sleeping softly in their bedroom bunks.
And 4 police cars parked outside the painted
gate, red lights revolving in the leaves.

CONSIDERATIONS FOR CRITICAL THINKING AND WRITING

1. FIRST RESPONSE. How does the list of images help to set the poem's scene? What is the effect of the poem's last two lines (18–19) on the overall tone?

2. Who is Ken Kesey? Use the library to find out the kinds of books he writes. How does his name help to establish the poem's setting?

3. How does the absence of commas in lines 8–10 indicate how to read these lines aloud?

CONNECTION TO ANOTHER SELECTION

1. Write an essay that compares the impact of this poem's ending with that of Hathaway's "Oh, Oh" (p. 13).

ANONYMOUS

The Frog   *date unknown*

What a wonderful bird the frog are!
When he stand he sit almost;
When he hop he fly almost.
He ain't got no sense hardly;
He ain't got no tail hardly either.
When he sit, he sit on what he ain't got almost.

CONSIDERATIONS FOR CRITICAL THINKING AND WRITING

1. FIRST RESPONSE. How is the poem a description of the speaker as well as of a frog?

2. Though this poem is ungrammatical, it does have a patterned structure. How does the pattern of sentences create a formal structure?

Tato Laviera (b. 1951)

AmeRícan   1985

we gave birth to a new generation,
AmeRícan, broader than lost gold
never touched, hidden inside the
puerto rican mountains.

we gave birth to a new generation,   5
AmeRícan, it includes everything
imaginable you-name-it-we-got-it
society.

we gave birth to a new generation,
AmeRícan salutes all folklores,   10
european, indian, black, spanish,
and anything else compatible:

AmeRícan,   singing to composer pedro flores'° palm
            trees high up in the universal sky!

AmeRícan,   sweet soft spanish danzas gypsies   15
            moving lyrics la *española*° cascabelling   *Spanish*
            presence always singing at our side!

AmeRícan,   beating jíbaro° modern troubadours
            crying guitars romantic continental
            bolero love songs!   20

AmeRícan,   across forth and across back
            back across and forth back
            forth across and back and forth
            our trips are walking bridges!

            it all dissolved into itself, the attempt   25
            was truly made, the attempt was truly
            absorbed, digested, we spit out
            the poison, we spit out the malice,
            we stand, affirmative in action,
            to reproduce a broader answer to the   30
            marginality that gobbled us up abruptly!

AmeRícan,   walking plena- rhythms° in new york,
            strutting beautifully alert, alive,
            many turning eyes wondering,
            admiring!   35

AmeRícan,   defining myself my own way any way many
            ways Am e Rícan, with the big R and the
            accent on the í!

13 *Pedro Flores:* Puerto Rican composer of popular romantic songs.   18 *jíbaro:* A particular
style of music played by Puerto Rican mountain farmers.   32 *plena-rhythms:* African-Puerto
Rican folklore, music, and dance.

AméRícan,   like the soul gliding talk of gospel
            boogie music!   40

AméRícan,   speaking new words in spanglish tenements,
            fast tongue moving street corner *"que
            corta"*° talk being invented at the insistence   *that cuts*
            of a smile!

AméRícan,   abounding inside so many ethnic english   45
            people, and out of humanity, we blend
            and mix all that is good!

AméRícan,   integrating in new york and defining our
            own *destino,*° our own way of life,   *destiny*

AméRícan,   defining the new america, humane america,   50
            admired america, loved america, harmonious
            america, the world in peace, our energies
            collectively invested to find other civili-
            zations, to touch God, further and further,
            to dwell in the spirit of divinity!   55

AméRícan,   yes, for now, for i love this, my second
            land, and i dream to take the accent from
            the altercation, and be proud to call
            myself american, in the u.s. sense of the
            word, AméRícan, America!   60

CONSIDERATIONS FOR CRITICAL THINKING AND WRITING

1. FIRST RESPONSE. How does the arrangement of lines communicate a sense
   of energy and vitality?
2. How does the speaker portray Puerto Ricans living in the United States?
3. How does the poet describe the United States?

CONNECTION TO ANOTHER SELECTION

1. In an essay consider the themes, styles, and tones of "AméRícan" and Di-
   vakaruni's "Indian Movie, New Jersey" (p. 162).

PETER MEINKE (B. 1932)
The ABC of Aerobics   *1983*

Air seeps through alleys and our diaphragms
balloon blackly with this mix of
carbon monoxide and the thousand corrosives a city
doles out free to its constituents;
everyone's jogging through Edgemont Park,   5
frightened by death and fatty tissue,
gasping at the maximal heart rate,

hoping to outlive all the others streaming
in the lanes like lemmings lurching toward their last
jump. I join in despair   10
knowing my arteries jammed with
lint and tobacco, lard and bourbon — my
medical history a noxious marsh:
newts and moles slink through the sodden veins,
owls hoot in the lungs' dark branches;   15
probably I shall keel off the john like
queer Uncle George and lie on the bathroom floor
raging about Shirley Clark, my true love in
seventh grade, God bless her wherever she lives
tied to that turkey who hugely   20
undervalues the beauty of her tiny earlobes, one
view of which (either one: they are both perfect)
would add years to my life and I could skip these
x-rays, turn in my insurance card, and trade
yoga and treadmills and jogging and zen and   25
zucchini for drinking and dreaming of her, breathing hard.

CONSIDERATIONS FOR CRITICAL THINKING AND WRITING

1. FIRST RESPONSE. How does the title help to establish a pattern throughout
   the poem? How does the pattern contribute to the poem's meaning?

2. How does the speaker feel about exercise? How do his descriptions of his
   physical condition serve to characterize him?

3. A primer is a book that teaches children to read or introduces them, in an
   elementary way, to the basics of a subject. The title "The ABC of Aerobics"
   indicates that this poem is meant to be a primer. What is it trying to teach
   us? Is its final lesson serious or ironic?

4. Discuss Meinke's use of humor. Is it effective?

CONNECTIONS TO OTHER SELECTIONS

1. Write an essay comparing the way Olds connects sex and exercise in "Sex
   without Love" (p. 76) with Meinke's treatment here.

2. Compare the voice in this poem with that in Kinnell's "After Making Love
   We Hear Footsteps" (p. 255). Which do you find more appealing? Why?

GARY SOTO (B. 1952)

Mexicans Begin Jogging   *1995*

At the factory I worked
In the fleck of rubber, under the press
Of an oven yellow with flame,
Until the border patrol opened
Their vans and my boss waved for us to run.   5
"Over the fence, Soto," he shouted,

And I shouted that I was American.
"No time for lies," he said, and pressed
A dollar in my palm, hurrying me
Through the back door.   10

Since I was on his time, I ran
And became the wag to a short tail of Mexicans —
Ran past the amazed crowds that lined
The street and blurred like photographs, in rain.
I ran from that industrial road to the soft   15
Houses where people paled at the turn of an autumn sky.
What could I do but yell *vivas*
To baseball, milkshakes, and those sociologists
Who would clock me
As I jog into the next century   20
On the power of a great, silly grin.

Considerations for Critical Thinking and Writing

1. FIRST RESPONSE. What ironies are present in this poem?
2. Soto was born and raised in Fresno, California. How does this fact affect your reading of the first stanza?
3. In what different ways does the speaker become "the wag" (line 12) in this poem? (You may want to look up the word to consider all possible meanings.)
4. Explain lines 17–21. What serious point is being made in these humorous lines?

Connection to Another Selection

1. Compare the speakers' ironic attitudes toward exercise in this poem and in Meinke's "The ABC of Aerobics" (p. 270).

Found Poem

This next poem is a *found poem,* an unintentional poem discovered in a nonpoetic context, such as a conversation, news story, or an advertisement. Found poems are playful reminders that the words in poems are very often the language we use every day. Whether such found language should be regarded as a poem is an issue left for you to consider.

Donald Justice (b. 1925)
Order in the Streets   *1969*

(*From instructions printed on a child's toy, Christmas 1968, as reported in the* New York Times)

1. 2. 3.
Switch on.

Jeep rushes
to the scene
of riot   5

Jeep goes
in all directions
by mystery action.

Jeep stops periodically
to turn hood over   10

machine gun appears
with realistic
shooting noise.

After putting down riot,
jeep goes   15
back to the headquarters.

CONSIDERATIONS FOR CRITICAL THINKING AND WRITING

1. FIRST RESPONSE. What is the effect of arranging these instructions in lines? How are the language and meaning enhanced by this arrangement?

2. Look for phrases or sentences in ads, textbooks, labels, or directions — in anything that might inadvertently contain provocative material that would be revealed by arranging the words in lines. You may even discover some patterns of rhyme and rhythm. After arranging the lines, explain why you organized them as you did.

11

Combining the Elements
of Poetry

THE ELEMENTS TOGETHER

The elements of poetry that you have studied in the first ten chapters of this book offer a vocabulary and series of perspectives that open up avenues of inquiry into a poem. As you have learned, there are many potential routes that you can take. By asking questions, for example, about the speaker, diction, figurative language, sounds, rhythm, tone, or theme, you clarify your understanding while simultaneously sensitizing yourself to elements and issues especially relevant to the poem under consideration. This process of careful, informed reading allows you to see how the various elements of the poem reinforce its meanings.

A poem's elements do not exist in isolation, however. They work together to create a complete experience for the reader. Knowing how the elements combine helps you understand the poem's structure and to appreciate it as a whole. Robert Herrick's "Delight in Disorder," (p. 211), for example, is more easily understood (and the humor of the poem is better appreciated) when meter and rhyme are considered together with the poem's meaning. Musing about how he is more charmed by a naturally disheveled appearance than by those whose appearance seems contrived, the speaker lists several attributes of dishevelment and concludes that they

> Do more bewitch me than when art
> Is too precise in every part.

Noticing how the couplet's precise and sing-songy rhythm combines with the solid, obvious, and final rhyme of art / part helps in understanding what the speaker means by "too precise," since the lines are a little too precise themselves. Noticing this, you may even want to chart out how rhythm and rhyme work together throughout the early (more disheveled) lines of the poem. Finding a pattern in the ways the elements work together throughout the poem will help you understand how the poem works.

MAPPING THE POEM

When you write about a poem, you are, in some ways, providing a guide for a place that might otherwise seem unfamiliar and remote. Put simply, writing enables you to chart a work so that you can comfortably move around in it to discuss or write about what interests you. Your paper represents a record and a map of your intellectual journey through the poem, pointing out the things worth noting and your impressions about them. Your role as writer is to offer insights into the challenges, pleasures, and discoveries that the poem harbors. These insights are a kind of sightseeing, as you navigate the various elements of the poem to make some overall point about it.

This chapter shows you how one student, Rose Bostwick, moves through the stages of writing about how a poem's elements combine for a final effect. Included here are Rose's first response, her informal outline, and the final draft of an explication of a poem by John Donne, "Death Be Not Proud." A detailed explanation of what is implicit in a poem, an explication requires a line-by-line examination of the poem. (For more on explication, see page 537 in Chapter 20, "Reading and Writing.") After reviewing the elements of poetry covered in the preceding chapters, Rose read the poem (which follows) several times, paying careful attention to diction, figurative language, irony, symbol, rhythm, sound, and so on. Because her final paper is more concerned with the overall effect of the combination of elements than with a line-by-line breakdown, her early notes are not included here. As you read and reread "Death Be Not Proud," however, keep notes on how *you* think the elements of this poem work together and to what overall effect.

JOHN DONNE (1572–1631)

John Donne, now regarded as a major poet of the early seventeenth century, wrote love poems at the beginning of his career but shifted to religious themes after converting from Catholicism to Anglicanism in the early 1590s. Although trained in law, he was also ordained a priest and became dean of St. Paul's Cathedral in London in 1621. The following poem, from "Holy Sonnets," reflects both his religious faith and his ability to create elegant arguments in verse.

JOHN DONNE (1572–1631)

Death Be Not Proud   *1611*

Death be not proud, though some have callèd thee
Mighty and dreadful, for thou art not so;
For those whom thou think'st thou dost overthrow
Die not, poor Death, nor yet canst thou kill me.
From rest and sleep, which but thy pictures° be,   *images* 5
Much pleasure; then from thee much more must flow,
And soonest our best men with thee do go,
Rest of their bones, and soul's delivery.°   *deliverance*
Thou art slave to Fate, Chance, kings, and desperate men,
And dost with Poison, War, and Sickness dwell;   10
And poppy or charms can make us sleep as well,
And better than thy stroke; why swell'st° thou then?   *swell with pride*
One short sleep past, we wake eternally
And death shall be no more; Death, thou shalt die.

CONSIDERATIONS FOR CRITICAL THINKING AND WRITING

1. FIRST RESPONSE. Why doesn't the speaker fear death? Explain why you find the argument convincing or not.

2. How does the speaker compare death with rest and sleep in lines 5–8? What is the point of this comparison?

3. Discuss the poem's rhythm by examining the breaks and end-stopped lines. How does the poem's rhythm contribute to its meaning?

4. What are the signs that this poem is structured as a sonnet?

ASKING QUESTIONS ABOUT THE ELEMENTS

After reading a poem, use the "Questions for Responsive Reading and Writing" (pp. 47–48) to help you think, talk, and write about any poem. Before you do, though, be sure that you have read the poem several times without worrying actively about interpretation. With poetry, as with all literature, it's important to allow yourself the pleasure of enjoying whatever makes itself apparent to you. On subsequent readings, use the questions to understand and appreciate how the poem works; remember to keep in mind that not all questions will necessarily be relevant to a particular poem. A good starting point is to ask yourself what elements are exemplified in the parts of the poem that particularly interest you. Then ask the questions for responsive reading and writing that relate to those elements. Finally, as you begin to get a sense of what elements are important to the poem and how those elements fit together, it often helps to put your impressions on paper.

A SAMPLE FIRST RESPONSE

After Rose has carefully read "Death Be Not Proud" and has a sense of how the elements work, she takes the first step toward a formal explication by writing informally about the relevant elements and addressing the question *Why doesn't the speaker fear death? Explain why you find the argument convincing or not.* Note that at this point, she is not as concerned with textual evidence and detail as she will need to be in her final paper.

> I've read the poem "Death Be Not Proud" by John Donne a few times now, and I have a sense of how it works. The poem is a sonnet, and each of the three quatrains presents a piece of the argument that Death should not be proud, because it is not really all-powerful, and may even be a source of pleasure. As a reader, I resist this seeming paradox at first, but I know it must be a trick, a riddle of some sort that the poem will proceed to untangle. I think one of the reasons the poem comes off as such a powerful statement is that Donne at first seems to be playful and paradoxical in his characterizations of Death. He's almost teasing Death. But beneath the teasing tone you feel the strong foundation of the real reason Death should not be proud -- Donne's faith in the immortality of the soul. The poem begins to feel more solemn as it progresses, as the hints at the idea of immortality become more clearly articulated.
>
> Donne utilizes two literary conventions to increase the effect of this poem: he uses the convention of personifying death, so that he can address it directly, and he uses the metaphor of death as a kind of sleep. These two things determine the tone and the progression from playful to solemn in the poem.
>
> The last clause of the poem (line 14) plays with the paradoxical-seeming character of what he's been declaring. Ironically, it seems the only thing susceptible to death is death itself. Or, when death becomes powerless is when it only has power over itself.

ORGANIZING YOUR THOUGHTS

Showing in a paper how different elements of a particular poem work together is often quite challenging. While you may have a clear intuitive sense of what elements are important to the poem and how they complement each other, it is important to organize your thoughts in such a way as to make the relationships clear to your audience. The simplest way is to go line by line, but that can quickly become rote for writer and reader. Because you will want to organize your paper in the way that best serves your thesis, it may help to write an informal outline that charts how you think the argument moves. You may find, for example, that the argument is not persuasive if you start with the final lines and go back to the beginning of the poem or passage. However you decide to organize your argument, keep in mind that a single idea, or thesis, will have to run thoughout the entire paper.

A SAMPLE INFORMAL OUTLINE

In her informal outline (below), Rose discovers that her argument works best if she begins at the beginning. Note how, though her later paper concerns itself with how several elements of poetry contribute to the poem's theme and message, her informal outline concerns itself much more with what that message is and how it develops as the poem progresses. She will fill in the details later.

Thesis: *From the very first word, addressing "Death" directly, Donne uses the literary conventions of personifying death and comparing it to sleep to begin an argument that Death should not be proud of its might or dreadfulness. But these two elements of his argument come to be seen as the superficial points when the true reason for death's powerlessness becomes clear. The Christian belief in the immortality of the soul is the reason for death's powerlessness and likeness to sleep.*

Body of essay: *Show how argument proceeds by quatrains from playful address to Death, and statement that Death is much like sleep, its "picture," to statement that Death is "slave" to other forces (and so should not be proud of being the mightiest), to the couplet, which articulates clearly the idea of immortality and gives the final paradox, "Death, thou shalt die."*

Conclusion: *Donne's faith in the immortality of the soul enables him to "prove" in this argument that Death is truly like its metaphorical representation, sleep. Faith allows him to derive a source for this conventional trope, and it allows him to state his truth in paradoxes. He relies on the conventional idea that death is an end, and a conqueror, and the only all-powerful force, to make the paradoxes that lend his argument the force of mystery — the mystery of faith.*

THE ELEMENTS AND THEME

As you create an informal outline, your understanding of the poem will grow, change, and finally, solidify. You will develop a much clearer sense of what the poem's elements combine to create, and you will have chosen a scheme for organizing your argument. The next step before drafting is to determine the paper's thesis, which will not only keep your paper focused but will help you center your thoughts. For papers that discuss how the elements of poetry come together, the thesis is a single and concise statement of what the elements combine to create — the idea around which all the elements revolve. In the earlier discussion of Robert Herrick's "Delight in Disorder," for example, the two elements, rhythm and rhyme, work together to create the speaker's self-directed irony. To state this as a thesis, we might say that by making his own rhythm and rhyme "too precise," Herrick's speaker is making fun of himself while complimenting a certain type of woman. (You may ask yourself if he's doing a little flirting.)

Once you understand how all the elements of the poem fit together and have articulated your understanding in the thesis statement, the next step is to flesh out your argument. By including quotations from the poem to illustrate the points you will be making, you will better explain exactly how each element relates to the others and, more specifically, to your thesis, and you will have created a finished paper that helps readers navigate the poem's geography.

A SAMPLE EXPLICATION

In Rose's final draft, she focuses on the use of metaphor in "Death Be Not Proud." Her essay provides a coherent reading that relates each line of the poem to the speaker's intense awareness of death. Although the essay discusses each stanza in order, the introductory paragraph provides a brief overview explaining how the poem's metaphor and arguments contribute to its total meaning. In addition, Rose does not hesitate to discuss a line out of sequence when it can be usefully connected to another phrase. She also works quotations into her sentences to support her points. When she adds something to a quotation to clarify it, she encloses her words in brackets so that they will not be mistaken for the poet's, and she uses a slash to indicate line divisions: "soonest . . . with thee do go, / [for] Rest of their bones, and soul's delivery." Finally, because the essay focuses on a short poem, it is not necessary to include line numbers, though they would be required in a study of a longer work. As you read through her final draft, remember that the word *explication* comes from the Latin *explicare*, "to unfold." How successful do you think Rose is at unfolding this poem to reveal how its elements – here ranging from metaphor, structure, meter, personification, paradox, and irony to theme — contribute to its meaning?

Rose Bostwick

English 101

Prof. Hart

February 14, 20--

The Use of Conventional Metaphors for Death

in John Donne's "Death Be Not Proud"

In the sonnet which begins "Death be not proud . . ." John Donne argues that death is not "mighty and dreadful," but is more like its metaphorical representation, sleep, and is even a source of pleasure and rest. Donne builds this argument on two foundations. One is made up of the metaphors and literary conventions for death: death is compared with sleep and is often personified, so that it can be addressed directly. The poem is an address to death that at first seems paradoxical and somewhat playful, but which then rises in all the emotion of faith as it reveals the second foundation of the argument--the Christian belief in the immortality of the soul. Seen against the backdrop of this belief, death loses its powerful threat and comes to be seen as only a metaphorical sleep, or rest.

The poem is an ironic argument that proceeds according to the structure of the sonnet form. Each quatrain contains a new development or aspect of the argument, and the final couplet serves as a conclusion. The metrical scheme is mainly iambic pentameter, but in several places in the poem, the stress pattern is altered for emphasis. For example, the first foot of the poem is inverted, so that "Death," the first word, receives the stress. This announces to us right away that Death is being personified and addressed. This inversion also serves to begin the poem energetically and forcefully. The second line behaves in the same way. The first syllable of "Mighty" receives the stress, emphasizing the meaning of the word and its assumed relation to Death.

This first quatrain offers the first paradox and
sets up the argument that death has been conventionally
personified with the wrong attributes, might and dread-
fulness. The poet tells death not to be proud, "though
some have called thee / Mighty and dreadful," because,
he says, death is not so. Donne will turn this con-
ventional characterization of death on its head with
the paradox of the third and fourth lines: he says the
people overthrown by death (as if by a conqueror) "Die
not, poor death, nor yet canst thou kill me." These
lines establish the paradox of death not being able to
cause death.

The next quatrain will not begin to answer the
question of why this paradox is so, but will posit
another slight paradox -- the idea of death as pleasurable.
In lines 5-8, Donne uses the literary convention of
describing death as a metaphorical sleep, or rest, to
construct the argument that death must give pleasure:
"From rest and sleep, which but thy pictures be, / Much
pleasure, then from thee much more must flow." At this
point, the argument seems almost playful, but is care-
fully hinting at the solemnity of the deeper foundation
of the belief in immortality. The metaphor of sleep for
death includes the idea of waking; one doesn't sleep for-
ever. The next two lines put forth the idea that death
is pleasurable enough to be desired by "our best men"
who "soonest . . . with thee do go, / [for] Rest of their
bones, and soul's delivery." This last line comes closer
to announcing the true reason for death's powerlessness
and pleasure: it is the way to the "soul's delivery" from
the body and life on earth, and implicitly, into another,
better realm.

A new reason for death's powerlessness arises in the
next four lines. The poet says to death:

Thou art slave to Fate, Chance, kings, and
   desperate men,
And dost with Poison, War, and Sickness dwell;
And poppy or charms can make us sleep as well,
And better than thy stroke; why swell'st thou then?

Donne argues here that there are forces more powerful
than death that actually control it. Fate and chance
determine when death occurs, and to whom it comes. Kings,
with the powers of law and war, can summon death and
throw it on whom they wish. And desperate men, murderers
or suicides, can also summon death with the strength of
their emotions. In lines 11 and 12, Donne again uses the
metaphor of death as a kind of sleep, but says that drugs
or "charms" give one a better sleep than death. And he
asks playfully why death should be so proud, after all
these illustrations of its weakness have been given: "why
swell'st thou then?"

    Finally, with the last couplet, Donne reveals the
true, deeper reason behind his argument that death should
not be proud of its power. These lines also offer an
explanation of the metaphor for death of sleep, or rest:

One short sleep past, we wake eternally
And death shall be no more; Death, thou shalt die.

After death, the soul lives on, according to Christian
theology and belief. In the Christian heaven, where the
soul is immortal, death will no longer exist, and so this
last paradox, "Death, thou shalt die," becomes true.
Again in this line, a significant inversion of metrical
stress occurs. "Death," in the second clause, receives
the stress, recalling the first line, emphasizing that it
is an address and giving the clause a forceful sense of
finality. His belief in the immortality of the soul

Bostwick 4

enables Donne to "prove" in this argument that death is
in actuality like its metaphorical representation, sleep.
His faith allows him to derive a source for this conven-
tional metaphor and to "disprove" the metaphor of death
as an all-powerful conqueror. His Christian beliefs also
allow him to state his truth in paradoxes, the mysteries
which are justified by the mystery of faith.

Before you begin writing your own paper on poetry, review the Suggestions for Approaching Poetry (pp. 27–29) and Chapter 2, "Writing About Poetry," particularly the Questions for Responsive Reading and Writing (pp. 47–48). These suggestions and questions will help you to focus and sharpen your critical thinking and writing. You'll also find help in Chapter 20, "Reading and Writing," which offers a systematic overview of choosing a topic, developing a thesis, and organizing various types of assignments. If you use outside sources for the paper, be sure to acknowledge them adequately by using the conventional documentation procedures detailed in Chapter 21, "The Literary Research Paper."

Approaches
to Poetry

12

Emily Dickinson:
A Body of Work

This chapter includes a variety of poems by Emily Dickinson in order to provide an opportunity to study her work in some depth. While this collection is not wholly representative of her work, it does offer enough poems to suggest some of the techniques and concerns that characterize her writings. The poems speak not only to readers but also to one another. That's natural enough: the more familiar you are with a writer's work, the easier it is to perceive and enjoy the strategies and themes the poet employs. If you are asked to write about a number of poems by the same author, you may find useful the Questions for Writing about an Author in Depth (p. 325) and the sample paper on Emily Dickinson's attitudes toward religious faith in four of her poems (pp. 327–332).

A BRIEF BIOGRAPHY

Emily Dickinson (1830–1886) grew up in a prominent and prosperous household in Amherst, Massachusetts. Along with her younger sister Lavinia and older brother Austin, she experienced a quiet and reserved family life headed by her father, Edward Dickinson. In a letter to Austin at law school, she once described the atmosphere in her father's house as "pretty much all sobriety." Her mother, Emily Norcross Dickinson, was not as powerful a presence in her life; she seems not

PHOTO ABOVE: *Daguerreotype of Emily Dickinson at seventeen, the only authenticated likeness of the poet. Reprinted by permission of the Amherst College Library.*

to have been as emotionally accessible as Dickinson would have liked. Her daughter is said to have characterized her as not the sort of mother "to whom you hurry when you are troubled." Both parents raised Dickinson to be a cultured Christian woman who would one day be responsible for a family of her own. Her father attempted to protect her from reading books that might "joggle" her mind, particularly her religious faith, but Dickinson's individualistic instincts and irreverent sensibilities created conflicts that did not allow her to fall into step with the conventional piety, domesticity, and social duty prescribed by her father and the orthodox Congregationalism of Amherst.

The Dickinsons were well known in Massachusetts. Her father was a lawyer and served as the treasurer of Amherst College (a position Austin eventually took up as well), and her grandfather was one of the college's founders. Although nineteenth-century politics, economics, and social issues do not appear in the foreground of her poetry, Dickinson lived in a family environment that was steeped in them: her father was an active town official and served in the General Court of Massachusetts, the state senate, and the United States House of Representatives.

Dickinson, however, withdrew not only from her father's public world but also from almost all social life in Amherst. She refused to see most people, and aside from a single year at South Hadley Female Seminary (now Mount Holyoke College), one excursion to Philadelphia and Washington, and several brief trips to Boston to see a doctor about eye problems, she lived all her life in her father's house. She dressed only in white and developed a reputation as a reclusive eccentric. Dickinson selected her own society carefully and frugally. Like her poetry, her relationship to the world was intensely reticent. Indeed, during the last twenty years of her life she rarely left the house.

Though Dickinson never married, she had significant relationships with several men who were friends, confidantes, and mentors. She also enjoyed an intimate relationship with her friend Susan Huntington Gilbert, who became her sister-in-law by marrying Austin. Susan and her husband lived next door and were extremely close with Dickinson. Biographers have attempted to find in a number of her relationships the source for the passion of some of her love poems and letters. Several possibilities have been put forward as the person she addressed in three letters as "Dear Master": Benjamin Newton, a clerk in her father's office who talked about books with her; Samuel Bowles, editor of the *Springfield Republican* and friend of the family; the Reverend Charles Wadsworth, a Presbyterian preacher with a reputation for powerful sermons; and an old friend and widower, Judge Otis P. Lord. Despite these speculations, no biographer has been able to identify definitively the object of Dickinson's love. What matters, of course, is not with whom she was in love — if, in fact, there was any single person — but that she wrote about such passions so intensely and convincingly in her poetry.

Choosing to live life internally within the confines of her home, Dickinson brought her life into sharp focus. For she also chose to live within the limitless expanses of her imagination, a choice she was keenly aware of and which she described in one of her poems this way: "I dwell in Possibility—" (p. 304). Her small circle of domestic life did not impinge on her creative sensibilities. Like Henry David Thoreau, she simplified her life so that doing without was a means of being within. In a sense she redefined the meaning of deprivation because being denied something—whether it was faith, love, literary recognition, or some other desire—provided a sharper, more intense understanding than she would have experienced had she achieved what she wanted: "'Heaven,'" she wrote, "is what I cannot reach!" This poem (p. 299), along with many others, such as "Water, is taught by thirst" (p. 296) and "Success is counted sweetest / By those who ne'er succeed" (p. 294), suggests just how persistently she saw deprivation as a way of sensitizing herself to the value of what she was missing. For Dickinson hopeful expectation was always more satisfying than achieving a golden moment. Perhaps that's one reason she was so attracted to John Keats's poetry (see, for example, his "Ode on a Grecian Urn," p. 79).

Dickinson enjoyed reading Keats as well as Emily and Charlotte Brontë; Robert and Elizabeth Barrett Browning; Alfred, Lord Tennyson; and George Eliot. Even so, these writers had little or no effect on the style of her writing. In her own work she was original and innovative, but she did draw on her knowledge of the Bible, classical myths, and Shakespeare for allusions and references in her poetry. She also used contemporary popular church hymns, transforming their standard rhythms into free-form hymn meters. Among American writers she appreciated Ralph Waldo Emerson and Thoreau, but she apparently felt Walt Whitman was better left unread. She once mentioned to Thomas Wentworth Higginson, a leading critic with whom she corresponded about her poetry, that as for Whitman "I never read his Book—but was told that he was disgraceful" (for the kind of Whitman poetry she had been warned against, see his "I Sing the Body Electric," p. 252). Nathaniel Hawthorne, however, intrigued her with his faith in the imagination and his dark themes: "Hawthorne appals—entices," a remark that might be used to describe her own themes and techniques.

AN INTRODUCTION TO HER WORK

Today, Dickinson is regarded as one of America's greatest poets, but when she died at the age of fifty-six after devoting most of her life to writing poetry, her nearly two thousand poems—only a dozen of which were published, anonymously, during her lifetime—were unknown except to a small number of friends and relatives. Dickinson was not recognized as a major poet until the twentieth century, when modern readers ranked her as a major new voice whose literary innovations were unmatched by any other nineteenth-century poet in the United States.

Dickinson neither completed many poems nor prepared them for publication. She wrote her drafts on scraps of paper, grocery lists, and the backs of recipes and used envelopes. Early editors of her poems took the liberty of making them more accessible to nineteenth-century readers when several

Manuscript page for "What Soft—Cherubic Creatures—" (p. 302), taken from one of Dickinson's forty fascicles—small booklets hand-sewn with white string that contained her poetry as well as other miscellaneous writings. These fascicles are important for Dickinson scholars, as this manuscript page makes clear: her style to some extent resists translation into the conventions of print. Courtesy of the Amherst College Library.

volumes of selected poems were published in the 1890s. The poems were made to appear like traditional nineteenth-century verse by assigning them titles, rearranging their syntax, normalizing their grammar, and regularizing their capitalizations. Instead of dashes editors used standard punctuation;

instead of the highly elliptical telegraphic lines so characteristic of her poems editors added articles, conjunctions, and prepositions to make them more readable and in line with conventional expectations. In addition, the poems were made more predictable by organizing them into categories such as friendship, nature, love, and death. Not until 1955, when Thomas Johnson published Dickinson's complete works in a form that attempted to be true to her manuscript versions, did readers have the opportunity to see the full range of her style and themes.

Like that of Robert Frost, Dickinson's popular reputation has sometimes relegated her to the role of a New England regionalist who writes quaint uplifting verses that touch the heart. In 1971 that image was mailed first class all over the country by the United States Postal Service. In addition to issuing a commemorative stamp featuring a portrait of Dickinson, the Postal Service affixed the stamp to a first-day-of-issue envelope that included an engraved rose and one of her poems. Here's the poem chosen from among the nearly two thousand she wrote:

If I can stop one Heart from breaking   c. 1864

If I can stop one Heart from breaking
I shall not live in vain
If I can ease one Life the Aching
or cool one Pain

Or help one fainting Robin
Unto his Nest again
I shall not live in Vain.

This is typical not only of many nineteenth-century popular poems but of the kind of verse that can be found in contemporary greeting cards. The speaker tells us what we imagine we should think about and makes the point simply with a sentimental image of a "fainting Robin." To point out that robins don't faint or that altruism isn't necessarily the only rule of conduct by which one should live one's life is to make trouble for this poem. Moreover, its use of language is unexceptional, the metaphors used, like that robin, are a bit weary. If this poem were characteristic of Dickinson's poetry, the U.S. Postal Service probably would not have been urged to issue a stamp in her honor, nor would you be reading her poems in this anthology or many others. Here's a poem by Dickinson that is more typical of her writing:

If I shouldn't be alive   c. 1860

If I shouldn't be alive
When the Robins come,
Give the one in Red Cravat,
A Memorial crumb.

If I couldn't thank you,
Being fast asleep,
You will know I'm trying
With my Granite lip!

This poem is more representative of Dickinson's sensibilities and techniques. Although the first stanza sets up a rather mild concern that the speaker might not survive the winter (a not uncommon fear for those who fell prey to pneumonia, for example, during Dickinson's time), the concern can't be taken too seriously—a gentle humor lightens the poem when we realize that all robins have red cravats and are therefore the speaker's favorite. Furthermore, the euphemism that describes the speaker "Being fast asleep" in line 6 makes death seem not so threatening after all. But the sentimental expectations of the first six lines—lines that could have been written by any number of popular nineteenth-century writers—are dashed by the penultimate word of the last line. "Granite" is the perfect word here because it forces us to reread the poem and to recognize that it's not about feeding robins or offering a cosmetic treatment of death; rather, it's a bone-chilling description of a corpse's lip that evokes the cold, hard texture and grayish color of tombstones. These lips will never say "thank you" or anything else.

Instead of the predictable rhymes and sentiments of "If I can stop one Heart from breaking," this poem is unnervingly precise in its use of language and tidily points out how much emphasis Dickinson places on an individual word. Her use of near rhyme with "asleep" and "lip" brilliantly mocks a euphemistic approach to death by its jarring dissonance. This is a better poem, not because it's grim or about death, but because it demonstrates Dickinson's skillful use of language to produce a shocking irony.

Dickinson found irony, ambiguity, and paradox lurking in the simplest and commonest experiences. The materials and subject matter of her poetry are quite conventional. Her poems are filled with robins, bees, winter light, household items, and domestic duties. These materials represent the range of what she experienced in and around her father's house. She used them because they constituted so much of her life and, more important, because she found meanings latent in them. Though her world was simple, it was also complex in its beauties and its terrors. Her lyric poems capture impressions of particular moments, scenes, or moods, and she characteristically focuses on topics such as nature, love, immortality, death, faith, doubt, pain, and the self.

Though her materials were conventional, her treatment of them was innovative because she was willing to break whatever poetic conventions stood in the way of the intensity of her thought and images. Her conciseness, brevity, and wit are tightly packed. Typically she offers her observations via one or two images that reveal her thought in a powerful manner. She once characterized her literary art by writing "My business is circumference." Her method is to reveal the inadequacy of declarative statements by evoking qualifications and questions with images that complicate firm assertions and affirmations. In one of her poems she describes her strategies this way: "Tell all the Truth but tell it slant — / Success in Circuit lies." This might well stand as a working definition of Dickinson's aesthetics and is embodied in the following poem:

The Thought beneath so slight a film — c. 1860

The Thought beneath so slight a film —
Is more distinctly seen —
As laces just reveal the surge —
Or Mists — the Apennine° *Italian mountain range*

Paradoxically, "Thought" is more clearly understood precisely because a slight "film" — in this case language — covers it. Language, like lace, enhances what it covers and reveals it all the more — just as a mountain range is more engaging to the imagination if it is covered in mists rather than starkly presenting itself. Poetry for Dickinson intensifies, clarifies, and organizes experience.

Dickinson's poetry is challenging because it is radical and original in its rejection of most traditional nineteenth-century themes and techniques. Her poems require active engagement from the reader because she seems to leave out so much with her elliptical style and remarkable contracting metaphors. But these apparent gaps are filled with meaning if we are sensitive to her use of devices such as personification, allusion, symbolism, and startling syntax and grammar. Since her use of dashes is sometimes puzzling, it helps to read her poems aloud to hear how carefully the words are arranged. What might initially seem intimidating on a silent page can surprise the reader with meaning when heard. It's also worth keeping in mind that Dickinson was not always consistent in her views and that they can change from poem to poem, depending on how she felt at a given moment. For example, her definition of religious belief in "'Faith' is a fine invention" (p. 327) reflects an ironically detached wariness in contrast to the faith embraced in "I never saw a Moor—" (p. 328). Dickinson was less interested in absolute answers to questions than she was in examining and exploring their "circumference."

Because Dickinson's poems are all relatively brief (none is longer than fifty lines), they invite browsing and sampling, but perhaps a useful way into their highly metaphoric and witty world is this "how to" poem that reads almost like a recipe:

To make a prairie it takes a clover and one bee *date unknown*

To make a prairie it takes a clover and one bee,
One clover, and a bee,
And revery.
The revery alone will do,
If bees are few.

This quiet but infinite claim for a writer's imagination brings together the range of ingredients in Dickinson's world of domestic and ordinary natural details. Not surprisingly, she deletes rather than adds to the recipe, because the one essential ingredient is the writer's creative imagination. *Bon appétit.*

CHRONOLOGY

1830	Born December 10 in Amherst, Massachusetts.
1840	Starts her first year at Amherst Academy.
1847–48	Graduates from Amherst Academy and enters South Hadley Female Seminary (now Mount Holyoke College).
1855	Visits Philadelphia and Washington, D.C.
1857	Emerson lectures in Amherst.
1862	Starts corresponding with Thomas Wentworth Higginson, asking for advice about her poems.
1864	Visits Boston for eye treatments.
1870	Higginson visits her in Amherst.
1873	Higginson visits her for a second and final time.
1874	Her father dies in Boston.
1875	Her mother suffers from paralysis.
1882	Her mother dies.
1886	Dies on May 15 in Amherst, Massachusetts.
1890	First edition of her poetry, edited by Mabel Loomis Todd and Thomas Wentworth Higginson, is published.
1955	Thomas H. Johnson publishes *The Poems of Emily Dickinson* in three volumes, thereby making available her poetry known to that date.

Success is counted sweetest   *c. 1859*

Success is counted sweetest
By those who ne'er succeed.
To comprehend a nectar
Requires sorest need.

Not one of all the purple Host   5
Who took the Flag today
Can tell the definition
So clear of Victory

As he defeated — dying —
On whose forbidden ear   10

The distant strains of triumph
Burst agonized and clear!

CONSIDERATIONS FOR CRITICAL THINKING AND WRITING

1. FIRST RESPONSE. How is "success" defined in this poem? To what extent does that definition agree with your own understanding of the word?
2. What do you think is meant by the use of "comprehend" in line 3? How can a nectar be comprehended?
3. Why do the defeated understand victory better than the victorious?
4. Discuss the effect of the poem's final line.

CONNECTION TO ANOTHER SELECTION

1. In an essay compare the themes of this poem with those of John Keats's "Ode on a Grecian Urn" (p. 79).

These are the days when Birds come back —   *c. 1859*

These are the days when Birds come back —
A very few — a Bird or two —
To take a backward look.

These are the days when skies resume
The old — old sophistries   of June —   5
A blue and gold mistake.

Oh fraud that cannot cheat the Bee —
Almost thy plausibility
Induces my belief.

Till ranks of seeds their witness bear —   10
And softly thro' the altered air
Hurries a timid leaf.

Of Sacrament of summer days,
Oh Last Communion   in the Haze —
Permit a child to join.   15

The sacred emblems to partake —
Thy consecrated bread to take
And thine immortal wine!

CONSIDERATIONS FOR CRITICAL THINKING AND WRITING

1. FIRST RESPONSE. This poem was long known by the title "Indian Summer" (supplied by an unauthorized editor). How does an awareness of this bit of information affect your reading of the poem?
2. In what sense are "These . . . days" regarded as a "fraud" by the speaker?
3. Discuss the significance of the religious allusions in stanzas five and six. What, finally, do you think is the speaker's attitude toward Indian summer?

Water, is taught by thirst *c. 1859*

Water, is taught by thirst.
Land — by the Oceans passed.
Transport — by throe —
Peace — by its battles told —
Love, by Memorial Mold —
Birds, by the Snow.

CONSIDERATIONS FOR CRITICAL THINKING AND WRITING

1. FIRST RESPONSE. Which image do you find most powerful? Explain why.
2. How is the paradox of each line of the poem resolved? How is the first word of each line "taught" by the phrase that follows it?
3. Try your hand at writing similar lines in which something is "taught."

CONNECTIONS TO OTHER SELECTIONS

1. What does this poem have in common with "Success is counted sweetest" (p. 294) ? Which poem do you think is more effective? Explain why.
2. How is the crucial point of this poem related to "I like a look of Agony," (p. 300)?

Safe in their Alabaster Chambers — *1859 version*

Safe in their Alabaster Chambers —
Untouched by Morning
And untouched by Noon —
Sleep the meek members of the Resurrection —
Rafter of satin,   5
And Roof of stone.

Light laughs the breeze
In her Castle above them —
Babbles the Bee in a stolid Ear,
Pipe the Sweet Birds in ignorant cadence —   10
Ah, what sagacity perished here!

Safe in their Alabaster Chambers — *1861 version*

Safe in their Alabaster Chambers —
Untouched by Morning —
And untouched by Noon —
Lie the meek members of the Resurrection —
Rafter of Satin — and Roof of Stone!   5

Grand go the Years in the Crescent — above them —
Worlds scoop their arcs —
And Firmaments — row —
Diadems — drop — and Doges° — surrender —
Soundless as dots — on a Disc of Snow —   10

9 *Doges:* Chief magistrates of Venice from the twelfth to the sixteenth centuries.

CONSIDERATIONS FOR CRITICAL THINKING AND WRITING

1. FIRST RESPONSE. Dickinson permitted the 1859 version of this poem, en-
titled "The Sleeping," to be printed in the *Springfield Republican*. The second
version she sent privately to Thomas Wentworth Higginson. Why do you
suppose she would agree to publish the first but not the second version?

2. Are there any significant changes in the first stanzas of the two versions? If
you answered yes, explain the significance of the changes.

3. Describe the different kinds of images used in the two second stanzas. How
do those images affect the tones and meanings of those stanzas?

4. Discuss why you prefer one version of the poem to the other.

CONNECTIONS TO OTHER SELECTIONS

1. Compare the theme in the 1861 version with the theme of Robert Frost's
"Design" (p. 356).

2. In an essay discuss the attitude toward death in the 1859 version and in "Ap-
parently with no surprise" (p. 328).

How many times these low feet staggered —   *c. 1860*

How many times these low feet staggered —
Only the soldered mouth can tell —
Try — can you stir the awful rivet —
Try — can you lift the hasps of steel!

Stroke the cool forehead — hot so often —   5
Lift — if you care — the listless hair —
Handle the adamantine fingers
Never a thimble — more — shall wear —

Buzz the dull flies — on the chamber window —
Brave — shines the sun through the freckled pane —   10
Fearless — the cobweb swings from the ceiling —
Indolent Housewife — in Daisies — lain!

CONSIDERATIONS FOR CRITICAL THINKING AND WRITING

1. FIRST RESPONSE. List the images of death in this poem and discuss their
effects.

2. How is the housewife's life characterized? How is her death different from
her life?

3. Look up the definitions and origin of "indolent." Why is this an especially appropriate word for discussing the housewife?

CONNECTION TO ANOTHER SELECTION

1. Discuss Dickinson's treatment of the fly in this poem and in "I heard a Fly buzz — when I died —" (p. 307). How is the fly in each poem a significant element of the poems' themes?

Portraits are to daily faces   *c. 1860*

Portraits are to daily faces
As an Evening West,
To a fine, pedantic sunshine —
In a satin Vest!

CONSIDERATIONS FOR CRITICAL THINKING AND WRITING

1. FIRST RESPONSE. Dickinson once described her literary art this way: "My business is circumference." Does this poem fit her characterization of her poetry?
2. How is the basic strategy of this poem similar to the following statement: "Doorknob is to door as button is to sweater"?
3. Identify the four metonymies in the poem. Pay close attention to their connotative meanings.
4. If you don't know the meaning of "pedantic," look it up in a dictionary. How does its meaning affect your reading of "fine"?

CONNECTIONS TO OTHER SELECTIONS

1. Compare Dickinson's view of poetry in this poem with Francis's perspective in "Catch" (p. 14). What important similarities and differences do you find?
2. Write an essay describing Robert Frost's strategy in "Mending Wall" (p. 342) or "Birches" (p. 347) as the business of circumference.
3. How is the theme of this poem related to the central idea in "The Thought beneath so slight a film —" (p. 293)?
4. Compare the use of the word "fine" here with its use in "'Faith' is a fine invention" (p. 327).

Some keep the Sabbath going to Church —   *c. 1860*

Some keep the Sabbath going to Church —
I keep it, staying at Home —
With a Bobolink for a Chorister —
And an Orchard, for a Dome —

Some keep the Sabbath in Surplice°   *holy robes* 5
I just wear my Wings —
And instead of tolling the Bell, for Church,
Our little Sexton — sings.

God preaches, a noted Clergyman —
And the sermon is never long,   10
So instead of getting to Heaven, at last —
I'm going, all along.

CONSIDERATIONS FOR CRITICAL THINKING AND WRITING

1. FIRST RESPONSE. What is the effect of referring to "Some" people?
2. Characterize the speaker's tone.
3. How does the speaker distinguish himself or herself from those who go to church?
4. How might "Surplice" be read as a pun?
5. According to the speaker, how should the Sabbath be observed?

CONNECTION TO ANOTHER SELECTION

1. Write an essay that discusses nature in this poem and in Walt Whitman's "When I Heard the Learn'd Astronomer" (p. 642).

"Heaven"—is what I cannot reach!   *c. 1861*

"Heaven" — is what I cannot reach!
The Apple on the Tree —
Provided it do hopeless — hang —
That — "Heaven" is — to Me!

The Color, on the Cruising Cloud —   5
The interdicted Land —
Behind the Hill — the House behind —
There — Paradise — is found!

Her teasing Purples — Afternoons —
The credulous — decoy —   10
Enamored — of the Conjuror —
That spurned us — Yesterday!

CONSIDERATIONS FOR CRITICAL THINKING AND WRITING

1. FIRST RESPONSE. How does the speaker define heaven? How does that definition compare with conventional views of heaven?
2. Look up the myth of Tantalus and explain the allusion in line 3.
3. Given the speaker's definition of heaven, how do you think the speaker would describe hell?

CONNECTIONS TO OTHER SELECTIONS

1. Write an essay that discusses desire in this poem and in "Water, is taught by thirst" (p. 296).
2. Discuss the speakers' attitudes toward pleasure in this poem and in Ackerman's "A Fine, a Private Place" (p. 69).

I like a look of Agony,   c. 1861

I like a look of Agony,
Because I know it's true —
Men do not sham Convulsion,
Nor simulate, a Throe —

The Eyes glaze once — and that is Death —
Impossible to feign
The Beads upon the Forehead
By homely Anguish strung.

CONSIDERATIONS FOR CRITICAL THINKING AND WRITING

1. FIRST RESPONSE. Why does the speaker "like a look of Agony"? How do you respond to her appreciation of "Convulsion"?
2. Discuss the image of "The Eyes glaze once — ." Why is that a particularly effective metaphor for death?
3. Characterize the speaker. One critic once described the voice in this poem as "almost a hysterical shriek." Explain why you agree or disagree.

CONNECTION TO ANOTHER SELECTION

1. Write an essay on Dickinson's attitudes toward pain and deprivation, using this poem and " 'Heaven' — is what I cannot reach!" (p. 299).

Wild Nights — Wild Nights!   c. 1861

Wild Nights — Wild Nights!
Were I with thee
Wild Nights should be
Our luxury!

Futile — the Winds —   5
To a Heart in port —
Done with the Compass —
Done with the Chart!

Rowing in Eden —
Ah, the Sea!   10
Might I but moor — Tonight —
In Thee!

CONSIDERATIONS FOR CRITICAL THINKING AND WRITING

1. FIRST RESPONSE. Thomas Wentworth Higginson, Dickinson's mentor, once said he was afraid that some "malignant" readers might "read into [a poem like this] more than that virgin recluse ever dreamed of putting there." What do you think?

2. Look up the meaning of "luxury" in a dictionary. Why does this word work especially well here?

3. Given the imagery of the final stanza, do you think the speaker is a man or a woman? Explain why.

CONNECTION TO ANOTHER SELECTION

1. Write an essay that compares the voice, figures of speech, and theme of this poem with those of Atwood's "you fit into me" (p. 116).

Nature — sometimes sears a Sapling —   *c. 1862*

Nature — sometimes sears a Sapling —
Sometimes — scalps a Tree —
Her Green People recollect it
When they do not die —

Fainter Leaves — to Further Seasons —
Dumbly testify —
We — who have the Souls —
Die oftener — Not so vitally —

CONSIDERATIONS FOR CRITICAL THINKING AND WRITING

1. FIRST RESPONSE. How is nature presented in this poem? How is it compared with human nature?

2. Why do you suppose Dickinson uses "sometimes" twice? What does this repetition suggest about the nature of nature?

3. What sort of observation do you think Dickinson is making about what it means to be a human being in the final two lines?

CONNECTION TO ANOTHER SELECTION

1. Discuss the treatment of nature in this poem and in "Apparently with no surprise" (p. 328), paying particular attention to the verbs associated with nature in each poem.

I would not paint — a picture —   *c. 1862*

I would not paint — a picture —
I'd rather be the One
It's bright impossibility

To dwell — delicious — on —
And wonder how the fingers feel   5
Whose rare — celestial — stir —
Evokes so sweet a Torment —
Such sumptuous — Despair —

I would not talk, like Cornets —
I'd rather be the One   10
Raised softly to the Ceilings —
And out, and easy on —
Through Villages of Ether —
Myself endued Balloon
By but a lip of Metal —   15
The pier to my Pontoon —

Nor would I be a Poet —
It's finer — own the Ear —
Enamored — impotent — content —
The License to revere,   20
A privilege so awful
What would the Dower be,
Had I the Art to stun myself
With Bolts of Melody!

CONSIDERATIONS FOR CRITICAL THINKING AND WRITING

1. FIRST RESPONSE. Paraphrase each stanza and explain how they are themati-
   cally related to each other.
2. What is the speaker's attitude toward creativity and art?
3. What do the final two lines suggest about how the speaker thinks about the
   art of poetry?

CONNECTION TO ANOTHER SELECTION

1. Discuss Dickinson's attitude toward poetry in this poem, "I dwell in Possi-
   bility —" (p. 304), and "This was a Poet — It is That" (p. 305).

What Soft — Cherubic Creatures —   *1862*

What Soft — Cherubic Creatures —
These Gentlewomen are —
One would as soon assault a Plush —
Or violate a Star —

Such Dimity° Convictions —   *sheer cotton fabric* 5
A Horror so refined
Of freckled Human Nature —
Of Deity — ashamed —

It's such a common — Glory —
A Fisherman's — Degree —
Redemption — Brittle Lady —
Be so — ashamed of Thee —

10

CONSIDERATIONS FOR CRITICAL THINKING AND WRITING

1. FIRST RESPONSE. Characterize the "Gentlewomen" in this poem.

2. How do the sounds produced in the first line help to reinforce their meaning?

3. What are "Dimity Convictions," and what do they make "Of freckled Human Nature"?

4. Discuss the irony in the final stanza.

CONNECTION TO ANOTHER SELECTION

1. How are the "Gentlewomen" in this poem similar to the "Gentlemen" in "'Faith' is a fine invention" (p. 327)?

The Soul selects her own Society —

c. 1862

The Soul selects her own Society —
Then — shuts the Door —
To her divine Majority —
Present no more —

Unmoved — she notes the Chariots — pausing —   5
At her low Gate —
Unmoved — an Emperor be kneeling
Upon her Mat —

I've known her — from an ample nation —
Choose One —   10
Then — close the Valves of her attention —
Like Stone —

CONSIDERATIONS FOR CRITICAL THINKING AND WRITING

1. FIRST RESPONSE. Characterize the speaker. Is she self-reliant and self-sufficient? Cold? Angry?

2. Why do you suppose the "Soul" in this poem is female? Would it make any difference if it were male?

3. Discuss the effect of the images in the final two lines. Pay particular attention to the meanings of "Valves" in line 11.

Much Madness is divinest Sense —

c. 1862

Much Madness is divinest Sense —
To a discerning Eye —
Much Sense — the starkest Madness —
'Tis the Majority
In this, as All, prevail —
Assent — and you are sane —
Demur — you're straightway dangerous —
And handled with a Chain —

CONSIDERATIONS FOR CRITICAL THINKING AND WRITING

1. FIRST RESPONSE. Thomas Wentworth Higginson's wife once referred to Dickinson as the "partially cracked poetess of Amherst." Assuming that Dickinson had some idea of how she was regarded by the "Majority," how might this poem be seen as an insight into her life?

2. Discuss the conflict between the individual and society in this poem. Which images are used to describe each? How do these images affect your attitudes about them?

3. Comment on the effectiveness of the poem's final line.

CONNECTION TO ANOTHER SELECTION

1. Discuss the theme of self-reliance in this poem and in "The Soul selects her own Society —" (p. 303).

I dwell in Possibility —

c. 1862

I dwell in Possibility —
A fairer House than Prose —
More numerous of Windows —
Superior — for Doors —

Of Chambers as the Cedars —   5
Impregnable of Eye —
And for an Everlasting Roof
The Gambrels° of the Sky —   *angled roofs*

Of Visitors — the fairest —
For Occupation — This —   10
The spreading wide my narrow Hands
To gather Paradise —

CONSIDERATIONS FOR CRITICAL THINKING AND WRITING

1. FIRST RESPONSE. What distinction is made between poetry and prose in this poem? Explain why you agree or disagree with the speaker's distinctions.

2. What is the poem's central metaphor in the second and third stanzas?

3. How does the use of metaphor in this poem become a means for the speaker to envision and create a world beyond the circumstances of the speaker's actual life?

CONNECTIONS TO OTHER SELECTIONS

1. Compare what this poem says about poetry and prose with Hulme's comments in the perspective "On the Differences between Poetry and Prose" (p. 113).
2. How can the speaker's sense of expansiveness in this poem be reconciled with the speaker's insistence on contraction in "The Soul selects her own Society —" (p. 303)? Are these poems contradictory? Explain why or why not.

This was a Poet — It is That   *c. 1862*

This was a Poet — It is That
Distills amazing sense
From ordinary Meanings —
And Attar so immense

From the familiar species   5
That perished by the Door —
We wonder it was not Ourselves
Arrested it — before —

Of Pictures, the Discloser —
The Poet — it is He —   10
Entitles Us — by Contrast —
To ceaseless Poverty —

Of Portion — so unconscious —
The Robbing — could not harm —
Himself — to Him — a Fortune —   15
Exterior — to Time —

CONSIDERATIONS FOR CRITICAL THINKING AND WRITING

1. FIRST RESPONSE. According to the speaker, what powers does a poet have? Why are these powers important?
2. Explain the metaphors of "Poverty" (line 12) and "Fortune" (line 15) and how they contribute to the poem's theme.

CONNECTIONS TO OTHER SELECTIONS

1. Write an essay about a life lived in imagination as depicted in this poem and in "I dwell in Possibility —" (p. 304).
2. Discuss "A Bird came down the Walk —" (p. 173) as an example of a poem that "Distills amazing sense / From ordinary Meanings —" (lines 2-3).

I read my sentence — steadily —   *c. 1862*

I read my sentence — steadily —
Reviewed it with my eyes,
To see that I made no mistake
In its extremest clause —
The Date, and manner, of the shame —   5
And then the Pious Form
That "God have mercy" on the Soul
The Jury voted Him —
I made my soul familiar — with her extremity —
That at the last, it should not be a novel Agony —   10
But she, and Death, acquainted —
Meet tranquilly, as friends —
Salute, and pass, without a Hint —
And there, the Matter ends —

CONSIDERATIONS FOR CRITICAL THINKING AND WRITING

1. FIRST RESPONSE. What is the speaker's "sentence"? What do you think of the tone of the poem, considering its subject?

2. What is the central metaphor? Why is it appropriate for this poem's subject matter?

3. How does the speaker regard death in lines 9–14?

CONNECTIONS TO OTHER SELECTIONS

1. Compare the treatment of death in this poem and in "Because I could not stop for Death —" (p. 308).

2. In an essay discuss the "Agony" in this poem and in "I like a look of Agony," (p. 300).

After great pain, a formal feeling comes —   *c. 1862*

After great pain, a formal feeling comes —
The Nerves sit ceremonious, like Tombs —
The stiff Heart questions was it He, that bore,
And Yesterday, or Centuries before?

The Feet, mechanical, go round —   5
Of Ground, or Air, or Ought —
A Wooden way
Regardless grown,
A Quartz contentment, like a stone —

This is the Hour of Lead —   10
Remembered, if outlived,
As Freezing persons, recollect the Snow —
First — Chill — then Stupor — then the letting go —

1. FIRST RESPONSE. What do you think has caused the speaker's pain?

2. How does the rhythm of the lines create a slow, somber pace?

3. Discuss why "the Hour of Lead" (line 10) could serve as a useful title for this poem.

CONNECTIONS TO OTHER SELECTIONS

1. How might this poem be read as a kind of sequel to "The Bustle in a House" (p. 312).

2. Write an essay that discusses this poem in relation to Robert Frost's "Home Burial" (p. 343).

I heard a Fly buzz — when I died —
c. 1862

I heard a Fly buzz — when I died —
The Stillness in the Room
Was like the Stillness in the Air —
Between the Heaves of Storm —

The Eyes around — had wrung them dry —   5
And Breaths were gathering firm
For that last Onset — when the King
Be witnessed — in the Room —

I willed my Keepsakes — Signed away
What portion of me be   10
Assignable — and then it was
There interposed a Fly —

With Blue — uncertain stumbling Buzz —
Between the light — and me —
And then the Windows failed — and then   15
I could not see to see —

CONSIDERATIONS FOR CRITICAL THINKING AND WRITING

1. FIRST RESPONSE. What was expected to happen "when the King" was "witnessed"? What happened instead?

2. Why do you think Dickinson chooses a fly rather than perhaps a bee or gnat?

3. What is the effect of the last line? Why not end the poem with "I could not see" instead of the additional "to see"?

4. Discuss the sounds in the poem. Are there any instances of onomatopoeia?

CONNECTIONS TO OTHER SELECTIONS

1. Contrast the symbolic significance of the fly with the spider in Whitman's "A Noiseless Patient Spider" (p. 130).

2. Consider the meaning of "light" in this poem and in "There's a certain Slant of light" (p. 538).

One need not be a Chamber — to be Haunted —   *c. 1863*

One need not be a Chamber — to be Haunted —
One need not be a House —
The Brain has Corridors — surpassing
Material Place —

Far safer, of a Midnight Meeting   5
External Ghost
Than its interior Confronting —
That Cooler Host.

Far safer, through an Abbey gallop,
The Stones a'chase —   10
Than Unarmed, one's a'self encounter —
In lonesome Place —

Ourself behind ourself, concealed —
Should startle most —
Assassin hid in our Apartment   15
Be Horror's least.

The Body — borrows a Revolver —
He bolts the Door —
O'erlooking a superior spectre —
Or More —   20

CONSIDERATIONS FOR CRITICAL THINKING AND WRITING

1. FIRST RESPONSE. Paraphrase the poem. Which stanza is most difficult to paraphrase? Why?
2. What is the controlling metaphor? Explain why you think it is effective or not.
3. What is the "superior spectre" in line 19?

CONNECTIONS TO OTHER SELECTIONS

1. Compare and contrast this poem with Poe's "The Haunted Palace" (p. 141) and Stevens's "Schizophrenia" (p. 129). In an essay explain which poem you find the most frightening.

Because I could not stop for Death —   *c. 1863*

Because I could not stop for Death —
He kindly stopped for me —
The Carriage held but just Ourselves —
And Immortality.

We slowly drove — He knew no haste   5
And I had put away
My labor and my leisure too,
For His Civility —

We passed the School, where Children strove
At Recess — in the Ring —   10
We passed the Fields of Gazing Grain —
We passed the Setting Sun —

Or rather — He passed Us —
The Dews drew quivering and chill —
For only Gossamer, my Gown —   15
My Tippet° — only Tulle —   *shawl*

We paused before a House that seemed
A Swelling of the Ground —
The Roof was scarcely visible —
The Cornice — in the Ground —   20

Since then — 'tis Centuries — and yet
Feels shorter than the Day
I first surmised the Horses' Heads
Were toward Eternity —

CONSIDERATIONS FOR CRITICAL THINKING AND WRITING

1. FIRST RESPONSE. Why couldn't the speaker "stop for Death"?
2. How is death personified in this poem? How does the speaker respond to him? Why are they accompanied by immortality?
3. What is the significance of the things they "passed" in the third stanza?
4. What is the "House" in lines 17–20?
5. Discuss the rhythm of the lines. How, for example, is the rhythm of line 14 related to its meaning?

CONNECTIONS TO OTHER SELECTIONS

1. Compare the tone of this poem with that of Dickinson's "Apparently with no surprise" (p. 328).
2. Write an essay comparing Dickinson's view of death in this poem and in "If I shouldn't be alive" (p. 291). Which poem is more powerful for you? Explain why.

I felt a Cleaving in my Mind —   *c. 1864*

I felt a Cleaving in my Mind —
As if my Brain had split —
I tried to match it — Seam by Seam —
But could not make them fit.

The thought behind, I strove to join
Unto the thought before —
But Sequence ravelled out of Sound
Like Balls — upon a Floor.

CONSIDERATIONS FOR CRITICAL THINKING AND WRITING

1. FIRST RESPONSE. What is going on in the speaker's mind?

2. What is the poem's controlling metaphor? Describe the simile in lines 7 and 8. How does it clarify further the first stanza?

3. Discuss the rhymes. How do they reinforce meaning?

CONNECTION TO ANOTHER SELECTION

1. Compare the power of the speaker's mind described here with the power of imagination described in "To make a prairie it takes a clover and one bee" (p. 293).

The Wind begun to knead the Grass —   *c. 1864*

The Wind begun to knead the Grass —
As Women do a Dough —
He flung a Hand full at the Plain —
A Hand full at the Sky —
The Leaves unhooked themselves from Trees —   5
And started all abroad —
The Dust did scoop itself like Hands —
And throw away the Road —
The Wagons quickened on the Street —
The Thunders gossiped low —   10
The Lightning showed a Yellow Head —
And then a livid Toe —
The Birds put up the Bars to Nests —
The Cattle flung to Barns —
Then came one drop of Giant Rain —   15
And then, as if the Hands
That held the Dams — had parted hold —
The Waters Wrecked the Sky —
But overlooked my Father's House —
Just Quartering a Tree —   20

CONSIDERATIONS FOR CRITICAL THINKING AND WRITING

1. FIRST RESPONSE. How successfully do you think this poem captures the excitement of a violent storm?

2. What sort of tone is created by the use of personification to describe the storm?

3. How do you read the poem's last two lines? Explain why you think the tone is (or isn't) consistent with the rest of the poem.

CONNECTION TO ANOTHER SELECTION

1. Discuss the themes of this poem and "Nature — sometimes sears a sapling —" (p. 301).

A loss of something ever felt I—

c. 1864

A loss of something ever felt I—
The first that I could recollect
Bereft I was—of what I knew not
Too young that any should suspect

A Mourner walked among the children   5
I notwithstanding went about
As one bemoaning a Dominion
Itself the only Prince cast out—

Elder, Today, a session wiser
And fainter, too, as Wiseness is—   10
I find myself still softly searching
For my Delinquent Palaces—

And a Suspicion, like a Finger
Touches my Forehead now and then
That I am looking oppositely   15
For the site of the Kingdom of Heaven—

CONSIDERATIONS FOR CRITICAL THINKING AND WRITING

1. FIRST RESPONSE. How does the sense of loss affect the speaker's life?
2. Is it possible to know specifically what is mourned in this poem? Explain why or why not.
3. What distinction is made between the speaker's identity as a youth and the speaker's adult identity?
4. Discuss the final stanza. Do you think this is a hopeful or despairing poem? Explain.

CONNECTION TO ANOTHER SELECTION

1. To what extent are the "Delinquent Palaces" in this poem present in "I felt a Cleaving in my Mind—" (p. 309)? How are the themes in each poem related?

Oh Sumptuous moment

c. 1868

Oh Sumptuous moment
Slower go
That I may gloat on thee—
'Twill never be the same to starve
Now I abundance see—

Which was to famish, then or now—
The difference of Day
Ask him unto the Gallows led—
With morning in the sky

CONSIDERATIONS FOR CRITICAL THINKING AND WRITING

1. FIRST RESPONSE. How do the sounds of the first stanza contribute to its meaning?
2. What kind of moment do you imagine the speaker is describing?
3. How do the final three lines shed light on the meaning of lines 1–6?

CONNECTION TO ANOTHER SELECTION

1. Compare and contrast the themes of this poem, "Water, is taught by thirst" (p. 296) and "'Heaven' — is what I cannot reach!" (p. 299).

The Bustle in a House   c. 1866

The Bustle in a House
The Morning after Death
Is solemnest of industries
Enacted upon Earth —

The Sweeping up the Heart
And putting Love away
We shall not want to use again
Until Eternity.

CONSIDERATIONS FOR CRITICAL THINKING AND WRITING

1. FIRST RESPONSE. What is the relationship between love and death in this poem?
2. Why do you think mourning (notice the pun in line 2) is described as industry?
3. Discuss the tone of the ending of the poem. Consider whether you think it is hopeful, sad, resigned, or some other mood.

CONNECTIONS TO OTHER SELECTIONS

1. Compare this poem with "After great pain, a formal feeling comes —" (p. 306). Which poem is, for you, a more powerful treatment of mourning?
2. How does this poem qualify "I like a look of Agony," (p. 300)? Does it contradict the latter poem? Explain why or why not.

Tell all the Truth but tell it slant —   c. 1868

Tell all the Truth but tell it slant —
Success in Circuit lies
Too bright for our infirm Delight
The Truth's superb surprise

As Lightning to the Children eased
With explanation kind
The Truth must dazzle gradually
Or every man be blind—

CONSIDERATIONS FOR CRITICAL THINKING AND WRITING

1. FIRST RESPONSE. What do you think the first line means? Why should truth be told "slant" and circuitously?
2. How does the second stanza explain the first?
3. How is this poem an example of its own theme?

CONNECTIONS TO OTHER SELECTIONS

1. How does the first stanza of "I know that He exists" (p. 327) suggest an idea similar to this poem's? Why do you think the last eight lines of the former aren't similar in theme to this poem?
2. Write an essay on Dickinson's attitudes about the purpose and strategies of poetry by considering this poem as well as "The Thought beneath so slight a film—" (p. 293) and "Portraits are to daily faces" (p. 298).

PERSPECTIVES ON DICKINSON

Dickinson's Description of Herself 1862

Mr Higginson,
 Your kindness claimed earlier gratitude—but I was ill—and write today, from my pillow.
 Thank you for the surgery—it was not so painful as I supposed. I bring you others°—as you ask—though they might not differ—
 While my thought is undressed—I can make the distinction, but when I put them in the Gown—they look alike, and numb.
 You asked how old I was? I made no verse—but one or two°—until this winter—Sir—
 I had a terror since September—I could tell to none—and so I sing, as the Boy does by the Burying Ground—because I am afraid—You inquire my Books—For Poets—I have Keats—and Mr and Mrs Browning. For Prose—Mr Ruskin—Sir Thomas Browne—and the Revelations. I went to school—but in your manner of the phrase—had no education. When a little Girl, I had a friend, who taught me Immortality—but venturing too near, himself—he never returned—Soon after, my Tutor, died—and for several years, my Lexicon—was my only companion—Then I found one more—but he was not contented I be his scholar—so he left the Land.

others: Dickinson had sent poems to Higginson for his opinions and enclosed more with this letter. *one or two:* Actually she had written almost 300 poems.

You ask of my Companions Hills—Sir—and the Sundown—and a Dog—large as myself, that my Father bought me—They are better than Beings—because they know—but do not tell—and the noise in the Pool, at Noon—excels my Piano. I have a Brother and Sister—My Mother does not care for thought—and Father, too busy with his Briefs—to notice what we do—He buys me many Books—but begs me not to read them—because he fears they joggle the Mind. They are religious—except me—and address an Eclipse, every morning—whom they call their "Father." But I fear my story fatigues you—I would like to learn—Could you tell me how to grow—or is it unconveyed—like Melody—or Witchcraft?

From a letter to Thomas Wentworth Higginson, April 25, 1862

Considerations for Critical Thinking and Writing

1. What impression does this letter give you of Dickinson?
2. What kinds of thoughts are there in the foreground of her thinking?
3. To what extent is the style of her letter writing like that of her poetry?

Thomas Wentworth Higginson (1823–1911)

On Meeting Dickinson for the First Time   *1870*

A large county lawyer's house, brown brick, with great trees & a garden—I sent up my card. A parlor dark & cool & stiffish, a few books & engravings & an open piano. . . .

A step like a pattering child's in entry & in glided a little plain woman with two smooth bands of reddish hair & a face a little like Belle Dove's; not plainer—with no good feature—in a very plain & exquisitely clean white pique & a blue net worsted shawl. She came to me with two day lilies which she put in a sort of childlike way into my hand & said "These are my introduction" in a soft frightened breathless childlike voice—& added under her breath Forgive me if I am frightened; I never see strangers & hardly know what I say—but she talked soon & thenceforward continuously—& deferentially—sometimes stopping to ask me to talk instead of her—but readily recommencing . . . thoroughly ingenuous & simple . . . & saying many things which you would have thought foolish & I wise—& some things you wd. hv. liked. I add a few over the page. . . .

"Women talk; men are silent; that is why I dread women."

"My father only reads on Sunday—he reads *lonely* & *rigorous* books."

"If I read a book [and] it makes my whole body so cold no fire ever can warm me I know *that* is poetry. If I feel physically as if the top of my head were taken off, I know *that* is poetry. These are the only ways I know it. Is there any other way."

"How do most people live without any thoughts. There are many people in the world (you must have noticed them in the street) How do they live. How do they get strength to put on their clothes in the morning"

"When I lost the use of my Eyes it was a comfort to think there were so few real *books* that I could easily find some one to read me all of them"

"Truth is such a *rare* thing it is delightful to tell it."

"I find ecstasy in living — the mere sense of living is joy enough"

I asked if she never felt want of employment, never going off the place & never seeing any visitor "I never thought of conceiving that I could ever have the slightest approach to such a want in all future time" (& added) "I feel that I have not expressed myself strongly enough."

From a letter to his wife, August 16, 1870

CONSIDERATIONS FOR CRITICAL THINKING AND WRITING

1. How old is Dickinson when Higginson meets her? Does this description seem commensurate with her age? Explain why or why not.

2. Choose one of the quotations from Dickinson that Higginson includes and write an essay about what it reveals about her.

MABEL LOOMIS TODD (1856–1932)

The Character *of Amherst*   *1881*

I must tell you about the *character* of Amherst. It is a lady whom the people call the *Myth*. She is a sister of Mr. Dickinson, & seems to be the climax of all the family oddity. She has not been outside of her own house in fifteen years, except once to see a new church, when she crept out at night, & viewed it by moonlight. No one who calls upon her mother & sister ever see her, but she allows little children once in a great while, & one at a time, to come in, when she gives them cake or candy, or some nicety, for she is very fond of little ones. But more often she lets down the sweetmeat by a string, out of a window, to them. She dresses wholly in white, & her mind is said to be perfectly wonderful. She writes finely, but no one *ever* sees her. Her sister, who was at Mrs. Dickinson's party, invited me to come & sing to her mother sometime.... People tell me the *myth* will hear every note — she will be near, but unseen.... Isn't that like a book? So interesting.

From a letter to her parents, November 6, 1881

CONSIDERATIONS FOR CRITICAL THINKING AND WRITING

1. Todd, who in the 1890s would edit Dickinson's poems and letters, had known her for only two months when she wrote this letter. How does Todd characterize Dickinson?

2. Does this description seem positive or negative to you? Explain your answer.

3. A few of Dickinson's poems, such as "Much Madness is divinest Sense —" (p. 304) suggest that she was aware of this perception of her. Refer to her poems in discussing Dickinson's response to this perception.

RICHARD WILBUR (B. 1921)

On Dickinson's Sense of Privation   *1960*

What did Emily Dickinson do, as a poet, with her sense of privation? One thing she quite often did was to pose as the laureate and attorney of the empty-handed, and question God about the economy of His creation. Why, she asked, is a fatherly God so sparing of His presence? Why is there never a sign that prayers are heard? Why does Nature tell us no comforting news of its Maker? Why do some receive a whole loaf, while others must starve on a crumb? Where is the benevolence in shipwreck and earthquake? By asking such questions as these, she turned complaint into critique, and used her own sufferings as experiential evidence about the nature of the deity. The God who emerges from these poems is a God who does not answer, an unrevealed God whom one cannot confidently approach through Nature or through doctrine.

But there was another way in which Emily Dickinson dealt with her sentiment of lack — another emotional strategy which was both more frequent and more fruitful. I refer to her repeated assertion of the paradox that privation is more plentiful than plenty; that to renounce is to possess the more; that "The Banquet of abstemiousness / Defaces that of wine." We all know how the poet illustrated this ascetic paradox in her behavior — how in her latter years she chose to live in relative retirement, keeping the world, even in its dearest aspects, at a physical remove. She would write her friends, telling them how she missed them, then flee upstairs when they came to see her; afterward, she might send a note of apology, offering the odd explanation that "We shun because we prize." Any reader of Dickinson biographies can furnish other examples, dramatic or homely, of this prizing and shunning, this yearning and renouncing: in my own mind's eye is a picture of Emily Dickinson watching a gay circus caravan from the distance of her chamber window.

From "Sumptuous Destitution" in *Emily Dickinson: Three Views*,
by Richard Wilbur, Louise Bogan, and Archibald MacLeish

CONSIDERATIONS FOR CRITICAL THINKING AND WRITING

1. Which poems by Dickinson reprinted in this anthology suggest that she was "the laureate and attorney of the empty-handed"?
2. Which poems suggest that "privation is more plentiful"?
3. Of these two types of poems, which do you prefer? Write an essay that explains your preference.

SANDRA M. GILBERT (B. 1936) AND
SUSAN GUBAR (B. 1944)

On Dickinson's White Dress   *1979*

Today a dress that the Amherst Historical Society assures us is *the* white dress Dickinson wore — or at least one of her "Uniforms of Snow" — hangs in a drycleaner's plastic bag in the closet of the Dickinson homestead. Perfectly preserved, beautifully flounced and tucked, it is larger than most readers would have expected this self-consciously small poet's dress to be, and thus reminds visiting scholars of the enduring enigma of Dickinson's central metaphor, even while it draws gasps from more practical visitors, who reflect with awe upon the difficulties of maintaining such a costume. But what exactly did the literal and figurative whiteness of this costume represent? What rewards did it offer that would cause an intelligent woman to overlook those practical difficulties? Comparing Dickinson's obsession with whiteness to Melville's, William R. Sherwood suggests that "it reflected in her case the Christian mystery and not a Christian enigma . . . a decision to announce . . . the assumption of a worldly death that paradoxically involved regeneration." This, he adds, her gown — "a typically slant demonstration of truth" — should have revealed "to anyone with the wit to catch on."[1]

We might reasonably wonder, however, if Dickinson herself consciously intended her wardrobe to convey any one message. The range of associations her white poems imply suggests, on the contrary, that for her, as for Melville, white is the ultimate symbol of enigma, paradox, and irony, "not so much a color as the visible absence of color, and at the same time the concrete of all colors." Melville's question [in *Moby-Dick*] might, therefore, also be hers: "is it for these reasons that there is such a dumb blankness, full of meaning, in a wide landscape of snows — a colorless, all-color of atheism from which we shrink?" And his concluding speculation might be hers too, his remark "that the mystical cosmetic which produces every one of [Nature's] hues, the great principle of light, for ever remains white or colorless in itself, and if operating without medium upon matter, would touch all objects . . . with its own blank tinge." For white, in Dickinson's poetry, frequently represents both the energy (the white heat) of Romantic creativity, and the loneliness (the polar cold) of the renunciation or tribulation Romantic creativity may demand, both the white radiance of eternity — or Revelation — and the white terror of a shroud.

From *The Madwoman in the Attic: The Woman Writer and the Nineteenth-Century Literary Imagination*

[1] *Circumference and Circumstance: Stages in the Mind and Art of Emily Dickinson* (New York: Columbia UP, 1968) 152, 231.

CONSIDERATIONS FOR CRITICAL THINKING AND WRITING

1. What meanings do Gilbert and Gubar attribute to Dickinson's white dress?

2. Discuss the meaning of the implicit whiteness in "Safe in their Alabaster Chambers—" (p. 296) and "After great pain, a formal feeling comes—" (p. 306). To what extent do these poems incorporate the meanings of whiteness that Gilbert and Gubar suggest?

3. What other possible reasons can you think of that would account for Dickinson's wearing only white?

KARL KELLER (B. 1933)

Robert Frost on Dickinson   *1979*

Frost lived in Amherst for quite a number of years — 1917–20, 1923–25, 1926–38, and then intermittently in the late 1940s and throughout the 1950s when he taught regularly at Amherst College. He often recited her poems from memory, and he conversed with students, friends, and townspeople about her poetry; his concern was almost always over her ability to contain/limit an open-ended universe. He felt this was "what Emily Dickinson surely intends," as he put it, "when she contends: 'In insecurity to lie / Is Joy's insuring quality.'"

It appears that Frost had a one-track mind about Emily Dickinson — her doggedness. For him she was an example of the poet "whose 'state,'" as he put it himself, "never gets sidetracked."

> Since she wrote without thought of publication and was not under the necessity of revamping and polishing, it was easy for her to go right to the point and say precisely what she thought and felt. Her technical irregularities give her poems strength as if she were saying, "Look out, Rhyme and Meter, here I come."

Frost apparently liked this willfulness, the unmanageability of the thought by the poetic form, and yet he thought she arrived at it a little too easily and that it was therefore sometimes indistinguishable from carelessness. He felt she had given up the technical struggle too easily. For Frost, to use a general statement of his about poetic rhythm, she was a little too "easy in [her] harness."[1]

Emily Dickinson succeeded, Frost was forced to admit, by flouting poetic systems, by playing freely with the form.

> I try to make good sentences fit the meter. That is important. Good grammar. I don't like to twist the order around in order to fit a form. I try to keep to regular structure and good rhymes. Though I admit that Emily Dickinson, for one, didn't do this always. When she started a poem, it was "Here I come!" and she came plunging through. The meter and rhyme often had to take care of itself.[2]

Though envious of this carefree energy, Frost was also critical of her when she did not achieve regular forms.

> Emily Dickinson didn't study technique. But she should have been more careful. She was more interested in getting the poem down and writing a new one. I feel that she left some to be revised later, and she never revised them. And those two ladies at Amherst printed a lot of her slipshod work which she might not have liked to see printed. She has all kinds of off rhymes. Some that do not rhyme. Her meter does not always go together.[3]

She was therefore substantially different from him; her ability to be conscious of poetic conventions and yet to rise above them surprised him. He generously yielded her his highest admiration for the heresy.

> One of the great things in life is being true within the conventions. I deny in a good poem or a good life that there is compromise. When there is, it is an attempt to so flex the lines that no suspicion can be cast upon what the poet does. Emily Dickinson's poems are examples of this. When the rhyme begins to bother, she says, "Here I come with my truth. Let the rhyme take care of itself." This makes me feel her strength.[4]

For him the large strain of poetry was "a little shifted from the straight-out, a little curved from the straight." Emily Dickinson's poems were, for him, the best examples of this liberty, this flawing. "Can you imagine some people taking that? Can't you imagine some people not accepting that kind of play at all?"[5]

[1] Robert Francis, *Frost: A Time to Talk* (Amherst, 1972) 53–54.
[2] Daniel Smythe, *Robert Frost Speaks* (New York, np, 1964) 140.
[3] Smythe, 140.
[4] Reginald Lansing Cook, *The Dimensions of Robert Frost* (New York: Barnes and Noble, 1968) 57–58.
[5] Cook, 99.

It was this factor of play in Emily Dickinson's poetry that consistently at-tracted Frost. "Rime reminds you that poetry is play," he said on one occasion, after reciting a Dickinson poem ("The Mountains—grow unnoticed") and calling it "particularly fine," "and that is one of its chief importances. You shouldn't be too sincere to play or you'll be a fraud."[6] Her mischief with poetic form was an indication to him that she was serious about what she was saying and would bend conventions to get it said, and also that she was having a good time trying to say it, but more important than that, that with her poetry (and her ideas) she was *at play*. He appears to have marveled at that in her. "Poetry," Frost used to exclaim to his friends, "is fooling."[7]

From *The Only Kangaroo Among the Beauty: Emily Dickinson in America*

[6] Cook, 180.
[7] Cook, 181.

CONSIDERATIONS FOR CRITICAL THINKING AND WRITING

1. According to Keller, how did Frost respond to Dickinson's "poetic systems" of rhyme and meter?
2. Explain why you agree or disagree with Frost's assessment of Dickinson's poetry as being "slipshod."
3. Choose a poem from each poet and demonstrate how both are versions of "play."

CYNTHIA GRIFFIN WOLFF (B. 1935)

On the Many Voices in Dickinson's Poetry   1986

There were many "Voices." This fact has sometimes puzzled Dickinson's read-ers. One poem may be delivered in a child's Voice; another in the Voice of a young woman scrutinizing nature and the society in which she makes her place. Sometimes the Voice is that of a woman self-confidently addressing her lover in a language of passion and sexual desire. At still other times, the Voice of the verse seems so precariously balanced at the edge of hysteria that even its calmest observations grate like the shriek of dementia. There is the Voice of the housewife and the Voice that has recourse to the occasionally agonizing, occasionally regal language of the conversion experience of latter-day New En-gland Puritanism. In some poems the Voice is distinctive principally because it speaks in the aftermath of wounding and can comprehend extremities of pain. Moreover, these Voices are not always entirely distinct from one another: the child's Voice that opens a poem may yield to the Voice of a young woman speaking the idiom of ardent love; in a different poem, the speaker may fall into a mood of almost religious contemplation in an attempt to analyze or de-fine such abstract entities as loneliness or madness or eternity; the diction of the housewife may be conflated with the sovereign language of the New Jeru-salem, and taken together, they may render some aspect of the wordsmith's labor. No manageable set of discrete categories suffices to capture the diversity of discourse, and any attempt to simplify Dickinson's methods does violence to the verse.

Yet there is a paradox here. This is, by no stretch of the imagination, a body of poetry that might be construed as a series of lyrics spoken by many different people. Disparate as these many Voices are, somehow they all appear to issue from the same "self." . . . It is the enigmatic "Emily Dickinson" readers suppose themselves to have found in this poetry, even in the extreme case when Dickinson's supposed speaker is male. One explanation for this sense of intrinsic unity in the midst of diversity is the persistence with which Dickinson addresses the same set of problems, using a remarkably durable repertoire of linguistic modes. Evocations of injury and wounding — threats to the coherence of the self — appear in the earliest poems and continue until the end; ways of rendering face-to-face encounters change, but this preoccupation with "interview" is sustained by metaphors of "confrontation" that weave throughout. The summoning of one or another Voice in a given poem, then, is not an unselfconscious emotive reflection of Emily Dickinson's mood at the moment of creation. Rather, each different Voice is a calculated tactic, an attempt to touch her readers and engage them intimately with the poetry. Each Voice had its unique advantages; each its limitations. A poet self-conscious in her craft, she calculated this element as carefully as every other.

From Emily Dickinson

CONSIDERATIONS FOR CRITICAL THINKING AND WRITING

1. From the poems in this anthology, try adding to the list of voices Wolff cites.
2. Despite the many voices in Dickinson's poetry, why, according to Wolff, is there still a "sense of intrinsic unity" in her poetry?
3. Choose a Dickinson poem and describe how the choice of voice is a "calculated tactic."

PAULA BENNETT (B. 1936)

On "I heard a Fly buzz — when I died —" 1990

Dickinson's rage against death, a rage that led her at times to hate both life and death, might have been alleviated, had she been able to gather hard evidence about an afterlife. But, of course, she could not. "The *Bareheaded life* — under the grass —," she wrote to Samuel Bowles in c. 1860, "worries one like a Wasp." If death was the gate to a better life in "the childhood of the kingdom of Heaven," as the sentimentalists — and Christ — claimed, then, perhaps, there was compensation and healing for life's woes. . . . But how do we know? What can we know? In "I heard a Fly buzz — when I died," Dickinson concludes that we do not know much. . . .

Like many people in her period, Dickinson was fascinated by death-bed scenes. How, she asked various correspondents, did this or that person die? In particular, she wanted to know if their deaths revealed any information about the nature of the afterlife. In this poem, however, she imagines her own death-bed scene, and the answer she provides is grim, as grim (and, at the same time, as ironically mocking), as anything she ever wrote.

In the narrowing focus of death, the fly's insignificant buzz, magnified tenfold by the stillness in the room, is all that the speaker hears. This kind of distortion in scale is common. It is one of the "illusions" of perception. But here it is horrifying because it defeats every expectation we have. Death is supposed to be an experience of awe. It is the moment when the soul, departing the body, is taken up by God. Hence the watchers at the bedside wait for the moment when the "King" (whether God or death) "be witnessed" in the room. And hence the speaker assigns away everything but that which she expects God (her soul) or death (her body) to take.

What arrives instead, however, is neither God nor death but a fly, "[w]ith Blue — uncertain — stumbling Buzz," a fly, that is, no more secure, no more sure, than we are. Dickinson had associated flies with death once before in the exquisite lament, "How many times these low feet / staggered." In this poem, they buzz "on the / chamber window," and speckle it with dirt, reminding us that the housewife, who once protected us from such intrusions, will protect us no longer. Their presence is threatening but only in a minor way, "dull" like themselves. They are a background noise we do not have to deal with yet.

In "I heard a Fly buzz," on the other hand, there is only one fly and its buzz is not only foregrounded. Before the poem is over, the buzz takes up the entire field of perception, coming between the speaker and the "light" (of day, of life, of knowledge). It is then that the "Windows" (the eyes that are the windows of the soul as well as, metonymically, the light that passes through the panes of glass) "fail" and the speaker is left in darkness — in death, in ignorance. She cannot "see" to "see" (understand).

Given that the only sure thing we know about "life after death" is that flies — in their adult form and more particularly, as maggots — devour us, the poem is at the very least a grim joke. In projecting her death-bed scene, Dickinson confronts her ignorance and gives back the only answer human knowledge can with any certainty give. While we may hope for an afterlife, no one, not even the dying, can prove it exists.

From *Emily Dickinson: Woman Poet*

CONSIDERATIONS FOR CRITICAL THINKING AND WRITING

1. According to Bennett, what is the symbolic value of the fly?
2. Does Bennett leave out any significant elements of the poem in her analysis? Explain why you think she did or did not.
3. Choose a Dickinson poem and write a detailed analysis that attempts to account for all its major elements.

GALWAY KINNELL (B. 1927)

The Deconstruction of Emily Dickinson   1994

The lecture had ended when I came in,
and the professor was answering questions.
I do not know what he had been doing with her
poetry, but now he was speaking of her
as a victim of reluctant male publishers.   5
When the questions dwindled, I put up my hand.
I said the ignorant meddling of the Springfield *Daily Republican*

and the hidebound response of literary men,
and the gulf between the poetic wishfulness
then admired and her own harsh knowledge,   10
had let her see that her poems
would not be understood in her time;
and therefore, passionate to publish,
she vowed not to publish again. I said
I would recite a version of her vow,   15

      Publication — is the Auction
      Of the mind of Man —

But before I could, the professor broke in.
"Yes," he said, "'the Auction' — 'auction,' from *augere, auctum,* to augment,
      to author . . ."
"Let's hear the poem!" "The poem!" several women,   20
who at such a moment are more outspoken than men, shouted,
but I kept still and he kept going.
"In *auctum* the economy of the signifier is split, revealing an unconscious
      collusion in the bourgeois commodification of consciousness. While
      our author says 'no,' the unreified text says 'yes,' yes?"
He kissed his lips together and turned to me
saying, "Now, may we hear the poem?"   25
I waited a moment for full effect.
Without rising to my feet, I said,
"Professor, to understand Dickinson
it may not always be necessary to uproot her words.
Why not, first, try *listening* to her?   30
Loyalty forbids me to recite her poem now."
No, I didn't say that — I realized
she would want me to finish him off with one wallop.
So I said, "Professor, I thought you
would welcome the words of your author.   35
I see you prefer to hear yourself speak."
No, I held back — for I could hear her
urging me to put outrage into my voice
and substance into my argument.
I stood up so that everyone might see   40
the derision in my smile. "Professor," I said,
"you live in Amherst at the end of the twentieth century.
For you 'auction' means a quaint event
where somebody coaxes out the bids
on butter churns on a summer Saturday.   45
Forget etymology, this is history.
In Amherst in 1860 'auction' meant
the slave auction, you dope!"
Well, I didn't say that either,
although I have said them all,   50
many times, in the middle of the night.
In reality, I stood up and recited

like a schoolboy called upon in class.
My voice gradually weakened, and the women
who had called out for the poem   55
now looked as though they were thinking
of errands to be done on the way home.
When I finished, the professor smiled.
"Thank you. So, what at first some of us may have taken as
        a simple outcry, we all now see is an ambivalent,
        self-subversive text."
As people got up to go, I moved   60
into that sanctum within me where Emily
sometimes speaks a verse, and listened
for a sign of how she felt, such as,
"Thanks — Sweet — countryman —
for wanting — to Sing out — of Me —   65
after all that Humbug." But she was silent.

CONSIDERATIONS FOR CRITICAL THINKING AND WRITING

1. Describe the professor's critical approach to Dickinson's poetry (for information about deconstructionist criticism, see p. 501). How does it compare to the speaker's approach? What does he value in Dickinson's poetry?

2. Discuss the use of irony in the poem.

3. Do you think it inevitable that a poet's response to poetry will be different from a critic's? Explain your answer.

TWO COMPLEMENTARY CRITICAL READINGS

CHARLES R. ANDERSON (B. 1902)

Eroticism in "Wild Nights—Wild Nights!"   *1960*

The frank eroticism of this poem might puzzle the biographer of a spinster, but the critic can only be concerned with its effectiveness as a poem. Unless one insists on taking the "I" to mean Emily Dickinson, there is not even any reversal of the lovers' roles (which has been charged, curiously enough, as a fault in this poem). The opening declaration — "Wild Nights should be / Our luxury!" — sets the key of her song, for *luxuria* included the meaning of lust as well as lavishness of sensuous enjoyment, as she was Latinist enough to know. This is echoed at the end in "Eden," her recurring image, in letters and poems, for the paradise of earthly love. The theme here is that of sexual passion which is lawless, outside the rule of "Chart" and "Compass." But it lives by a law of its own, the law of Eden, which protects it from mundane wind and wave.

This is what gives the magic to her climactic vision, "Rowing in Eden," sheltered luxuriously in those paradisiac waters while the wild storms of this world break about them. Such love was only possible before the Fall. Since then the bower of bliss is frugal of her leases, limiting each occupant to "an instant" she says in another poem, for "Adam taught her Thrift / Bankrupt once through his excesses." In the present poem she limits her yearning to the mortal term, just "Tonight." But this echoes the surge of ecstasy that initiated her song and gives the reiterated "Wild Nights!" a double reference, to the passionate experience in Eden as well as to the tumult of the world shut out by it. So she avoids the chief pitfall of the love lyric, the tendency to exploit emotion for its own sake. Instead she generates out of the conflicting aspects of love, its ecstasy and its brevity, the symbol that contains the poem's meaning.

From *Emily Dickinson's Poetry: Stairway of Surprise*

CONSIDERATIONS FOR CRITICAL THINKING AND WRITING

1. According to Anderson what is the theme of "Wild Nights — Wild Nights!"?
2. How does Anderson discuss the "frank eroticism" of the poem? How detailed is his discussion?
3. If there is a "reversal of the lovers' roles" in this poem, do you think it represents, as some critics have charged, "a fault in this poem"? Explain why or why not.
4. Compare Anderson's treatment of this poem with David S. Reynolds's reading that follows. Discuss which one you find more useful and explain why.

DAVID S. REYNOLDS (B. 1949)
Popular Literature and "Wild Nights — Wild Nights!"   *1988*

It is not known whether Dickinson had read any of the erotic literature of the day or if she knew of the stereotype of the sensual woman. Given her fascination with sensational journalism and with popular literature in general, it is hard to believe she would not have had at least some exposure to erotic literature. At any rate, her treatment of the daring theme of woman's sexual fantasy in this deservedly famous poem bears comparison with erotic themes as they appeared in popular sensational writings. The first stanza of the poem provides an uplifting or purification of sexual fantasy not distant from the effect of Whitman's cleansing rhetoric, which, as we have seen, was consciously designed to counteract the prurience of the popular "love plot." Dickinson's repeated phrase "Wild Nights" is a simple but dazzling metaphor that communicates wild passion — even lust — but simultaneously lifts sexual desire out of the scabrous by fusing it with the natural image of the night. The second verse introduces a second nature image, the turbulent sea and the contrasting quiet port, which at once universalizes the passion and purifies it further by distancing it through a more abstract metaphor. Also, the second verse makes clear that this is not a poem of sexual consummation but rather of pure fantasy and sexual impossibility. Unlike popular erotic literature, the poem portrays neither a consummated seduction nor the heartless deception that it involves. There is instead a pure, fervent fantasy whose frustration is figured forth in the contrasting images of the ocean (the longed-for-but-never-achieved consummation) and the port (the reality of the poet's isolation). The third verse begins with an image, "Rowing in Eden," that further uplifts sexual passion by yoking it with a religious archetype. Here as elsewhere, Dickinson capitalizes nicely on the new religious style, which made possible such fusions of the divine and the earthly. The persona's concluding wish to "moor" in the sea expresses the sustained intense sexual longing and the simultaneous frustration of that longing. In the course of the poem, Dickinson has communicated great erotic passion, and yet, by effectively projecting this passion through unusual nature and religious images, has rid it of even the tiniest residue of sensationalism.

From *Beneath the American Renaissance: The Subversive Imagination in the Age of Emerson and Melville*

CONSIDERATIONS FOR CRITICAL THINKING AND WRITING

1. According to Reynolds, how do Dickinson's images provide a "cleansing" effect in the poem?

2. Explain whether you agree that the poem portrays a "pure, fervent fantasy" or something else.

3. Does Reynolds's reading of the poem compete with Anderson's or complement it? Explain your answer.

4. Given the types of critical strategies described in Chapter 19, how would you characterize Anderson's and Reynolds's approaches?

QUESTIONS FOR WRITING ABOUT AN AUTHOR IN DEPTH

This section includes four poems by Emily Dickinson as the subject of a sample in-depth study of her poetry. The following questions can help you to respond to multiple works by the same author. You're likely to be struck by the similarities and differences in works by the same author. Previous knowledge of a writer's work can set up useful expectations in a reader. By being familiar with a number of works by the same writer you can begin to discern particular kinds of concerns and techniques that characterize and help to shed light on a writer's work.

As you read multiple works by the same author you'll begin to recognize situations, events, characters, issues, perspectives, styles, and strategies — even recurring words or phrases — that provide a kind of signature, making the poem in some way identifiable with that particular writer. In the case of the four Dickinson poems included in this section, religion emerges as a central topic linked to a number of issues including faith, immortality, skepticism, and the nature of God. The student selected these poems because he noticed Dickinson's intense interest in religious faith owing to the many poems that explore a variety of religious attitudes in her work. He chose these four because they were closely related, but he also might have found equally useful clusters of poems about love, nature, domestic life, or writing as well as other topics. What especially intrigued him was some of the information he read about Dickinson's sternly religious father and the orthodox nature of the religious values of her hometown of Amherst, Massachusetts. Since this paper was not a research paper, he did not pursue these issues beyond the level of the general remarks provided in an introduction to her poetry (though he might have). He did, however, use this biographical and historical information as a means of framing his search for poems that were related to one another. In doing so he discovered consistent concerns along with contradictory themes that became the basis of his paper.

The questions provided below should help you to listen to how a writer's works can speak to each other and to you. Additional useful questions will be found in other chapters of this book. See Writing about Poetry (p. 46) and Arguing about Literature (p. 526).

1. What topics reappear in the writer's work? What seem to be the major concerns of the author?
2. Does the author have a definable world view that can be discerned from work to work? Is, for example, the writer liberal, conservative, apolitical, or religious?
3. What social values come through in the author's work? Does he or she seem to identify with a particular group or social class?
4. Is there a consistent voice or point of view from work to work? Is it a persona or the author's actual self?
5. How much of the author's own life experiences and historical moment make their way into the works?
6. Does the author experiment with style from work to work, or are the works mostly consistent with one another?
7. Can the author's work be identified with a literary tradition, such as *carpe diem* poetry, that aligns his or her work with that of other writers?
8. What is distinctive about the author's writing? Is the language innovative? Are the themes challenging? Are the voices conventional? Is the tone characteristic?
9. Could you identify another work by the same author without a name being attached to it? What are the distinctive features that allow you to do so?
10. Do any of the writer's works seem *not* to be by that writer? Why?
11. What other writers are most like this author in style and content? Why?
12. Has the writer's work evolved over time? Are there significant changes or developments? Are there new ideas and styles, or do the works remain largely the same?
13. How would you characterize the writing habits of the writer? Is it possible to anticipate what goes on in different works, or are you surprised by their content or style?

14. Can difficult or ambiguous passages in a work be resolved by referring to a similar passage in another work?
15. What does the writer say about his or her own work? Do you trust the teller or the tale? Which do you think is more reliable?

A SAMPLE IN-DEPTH STUDY

Religious Faith in Four Poems by Emily Dickinson

The following paper was written for an assignment that called for an analysis (about 750 words) on any topic that could be traced in three or four poems by Dickinson. The student chose "'Faith' is a fine invention," "I know that He exists," "I never saw a Moor —," and "Apparently with no surprise."

"Faith" is a fine invention   c. 1860

"Faith" is a fine invention
When Gentlemen can *see* —
But *Microscopes* are prudent
In an Emergency.

I know that He exists   c. 1862

I know that He exists.
Somewhere — in Silence —
He has hid his rare life
From our gross eyes.

'Tis an instant's play.   5
'Tis a fond Ambush
Just to make Bliss
Earn her own surprise!

But   should the play
Prove piercing earnest —   10
Should the glee-glaze —
In Death's — stiff — stare —

Would not the fun
Look too expensive!
Would not the jest —   15
Have crawled too far!

I never saw a Moor —

c. 1865

I never saw a Moor —
I never saw the Sea —
Yet know I how the Heather looks
And what a Billow be.

I never spoke with God
Nor visited in Heaven —
Yet certain am I of the spot
As if the Checks were given —

Apparently with no surprise

c. 1884

Apparently with no surprise
To any happy Flower
The Frost beheads it at its play —
In accidental power —
The blond Assassin passes on —
The Sun proceeds unmoved
To measure off another Day
For an Approving God.

Michael Weitz

Professor Pearl

English 270

May 5, 20--

Religious Faith in Four Poems by Emily Dickinson

Throughout much of her poetry, Emily Dickinson wrestles with complex notions of God, faith, and religious devotion. She adheres to no consistent view of religion; rather, her poetry reveals a vision of God and faith that is constantly evolving. Dickinson's gods range from the strict and powerful Old Testament father to a loving spiritual guide to an irrational and ridiculous imaginary figure. Through these varying images of God, Dickinson portrays contrasting images of the meaning and validity of religious faith. Her work reveals competing attitudes toward religious devotion as conventional religious piety struggles with a more cynical perception of God and religious worship.

Dickinson's "I never saw a Moor--" reveals a vision of traditional religious sensibilities. Although the speaker readily admits that "I never spoke with God / Nor visited in Heaven," her devout faith in a supreme being does not waver. The poem appears to be a straightforward profession of true faith stemming from the argument that the proof of God's existence is the universe's existence. Dickinson's imagery therefore evolves from the natural to the supernatural, first establishing her convictions that Moors and Seas exist, in spite of her lack of personal contact with either. This leads to the foundation of her religious faith, again based not on physical experience but on intellectual convictions. The speaker professes that she believes in the existence of Heaven even without conclusive evidence: "Yet certain am I of the spot / As if the

Checks were given--" But the appearance of such idealistic
views of God and faith in "I never saw a Moor--" are
transformed in Dickinson's other poems into a much more
skeptical vision of the validity of religious piety.

While faith is portrayed as an authentic and deeply
important quality in "I never saw a Moor--," Dickinson's
"'Faith' is a fine invention" portrays faith as much less
essential. Faith is defined in the poem as "a fine inven-
tion" suggesting that it is created by man for man and
therefore is not a crucial aspect of the natural universe.
Thus the strong idealistic faith of "I never saw a Moor--"
becomes discredited in the face of scientific rationalism.
The speaker compares religious faith with actual micro-
scopes, both of which are meant to enhance one's vision in
some way. But "Faith" is useful only "When Gentlemen can
see--" already; "In an Emergency," when one ostensibly
cannot see, "Microscopes are prudent." Dickinson pits re-
ligion against science, suggesting that science, with its
tangible evidence and rational attitude, is a more reli-
able lens through which to view the world. Faith is irrev-
erently reduced to a mere invention and one that is
ultimately less useful than microscopes or other scien-
tific instruments.

Rational, scientific observations are not the only
contributing factor to the portrayal of religious skepti-
cism in Dickinson's poems; nature itself is seen to be
incompatible in some ways with conventional religious ide-
ology. In "Apparently with no surprise," the speaker rec-
ognizes the inexorable cycle of natural life and death as
a morning frost kills a flower. But the tension in this
poem stems not from the "happy Flower" struck down by the
frost's "accidental power" but from the apparent indiffer-
ence of the "Approving God" who condones this seemingly

cruel and unnecessary death. God is seen as remote and uncompromising, and it is this perceived distance between the speaker and God that reveals the increasing absurdity of traditional religious faith. The speaker understands that praying to God or believing in religion cannot change the course of nature, and as a result feels so helplessly distanced from God that religious faith becomes virtually meaningless.

Dickinson's religious skepticism becomes even more explicit in "I know that He exists," in which the speaker attempts to understand the connection between seeing God and facing death. In this poem Dickinson characterizes God as a remote and mysterious figure; the speaker mockingly asserts, "I know that He exists," even though "He has hid his rare life / From our gross eyes." The skepticism toward religious faith revealed in this poem stems from the speaker's recognition of the paradoxical quest that people undertake to know and to see God. A successful attempt to see God, to win the game of hide-and-seek that He apparently is orchestrating, results inevitably in death. With this recognition the speaker comes to view religion as an absurd and reckless game in which the prize may be "Bliss" but more likely is "Death's--stiff--stare--" For to see God and to meet one's death as a result certainly suggests that the game of trying to see God (the so-called "fun") is much "too expensive" and that religion itself is a "jest" that, like the serpent in Genesis, has "crawled too far."

Ultimately, the vision of religious faith that Dickinson describes in her poems is one of suspicion and cynicism. She cannot reconcile the physical world to the spiritual existence that Christian doctrine teaches, and as a result the traditional perception of God becomes ludicrous. "I never saw a Moor--" does attempt to sustain a conventional vision of religious devotion, but Dickinson's poems overall are far more likely to suggest that God is elusive, indifferent, and often cruel, thus undermining the traditional vision of God as a loving father worthy of devout worship. Thus, not only religious faith but also those who are religiously faithful become targets for Dickinson's irreverent criticism of conventional belief.

13

Robert Frost: A Life and Work

Though all poets' works are undoubtedly affected by the facts of their biographies, Robert Frost's poems are especially known for their reflection of New England life. Although the poems included in this chapter evoke the landscapes of Frost's life and work, the depth and range of those landscapes are far more complicated than his popular reputation typically acknowledges. He was an enormously private man and a much more subtle poet than many of his readers have expected him to be. His poems warrant careful, close readings. As you explore his poetry, you may find useful the Questions for Writing about an Author in Depth (p. 325) as a means of stimulating your thinking about his life and work.

A BRIEF BIOGRAPHY

Few poets have enjoyed the popular success that Robert Frost (1874–1963) achieved during his lifetime, and no twentieth-century American poet has had his or her work as widely read and honored. Frost is as much associated with New England as the stone walls that help define its landscape; his reputation, however, transcends regional boundaries. Although he was named poet laureate of Vermont only two years before his death, he was for many years the nation's unofficial poet laureate. Frost collected honors the way some people pick up burrs on country walks. Among his awards were four Pulitzer Prizes, the Bollingen Prize, a Congressional Medal, and dozens of honorary degrees. Perhaps his most moving appearance was his recitation of "The Gift Outright" for millions of Americans at the inauguration of John F. Kennedy in 1961.

Frost's recognition as a poet is especially remarkable because his career as a writer did not attract any significant attention until he was nearly forty

Robert Frost at his writing desk in Franconia, New Hampshire, 1915. Courtesy of the Jones Library, Inc., Amherst, Mass. Reprinted by permission of the Robert Frost Estate.

years old. He taught himself to write while he labored at odd jobs, taught school, or farmed.

Frost's early identity seems very remote from the New England soil. Although his parents were descended from generations of New Englanders, he was born in San Francisco and was named Robert Lee Frost after the Confederate general. After his father died in 1885, his mother moved the family back to Massachusetts to live with relatives. Frost graduated from high school sharing valedictorian honors with the classmate who would become his wife three years later. Between high school and marriage, he attended Dartmouth College for a few months and then taught. His teaching prompted him to enroll in Harvard in 1897, but after less than two years he withdrew without a degree (though Harvard would eventually award him an honorary doctorate in 1937, four years after Dartmouth conferred its honorary degree on him). For the next decade, Frost read and wrote poems when he was not chicken farming or teaching. In 1912, he sold his farm and moved his family to England, where he hoped to find the audience that his poetry did not have in America.

Three years in England made it possible for Frost to return home as a poet. His first two volumes of poetry, *A Boy's Will* (1913) and *North of Boston* (1914), were published in England. During the next twenty years, honors and awards were conferred on collections such as *Mountain Interval* (1916), *New Hampshire* (1923), *West-Running Brook* (1928), and *A Further Range* (1936).

These are the volumes on which most of Frost's popular and critical reputation rests. Later collections include *A Witness Tree* (1942), *A Masque of Reason* (1945), *Steeple Bush* (1947), *A Masque of Mercy* (1947), *Complete Poems* (1949), and *In the Clearing* (1962). In addition to publishing his works, Frost endeared himself to audiences throughout the country by presenting his poetry almost as conversations. He also taught at a number of schools, including Amherst College, the University of Michigan, Harvard University, Dartmouth College, and Middlebury College.

Frost's countless poetry readings generated wide audiences eager to claim him as their poet. The image he cultivated resembled closely what the public likes to think a poet should be. Frost was seen as a lovable, wise old man; his simple wisdom and cracker-barrel sayings appeared comforting and homey. From this Yankee rustic, audiences learned that "There's a lot yet that isn't understood" or "We love the things we love for what they are" or "Good fences make good neighbors."

In a sense, Frost packaged himself for public consumption. "I am . . . my own salesman," he said. When asked direct questions about the meanings of his poems, he often winked or scratched his head to give the impression that the customer was always right. To be sure, there is a simplicity in Frost's language, but that simplicity does not fully reflect the depth of the man, the complexity of his themes, or the richness of his art.

The folksy optimist behind the public lectern did not reveal his private troubles to his audiences, although he did address those problems at his writing desk. Frost suffered from professional jealousies, anger, and depression. His family life was especially painful. Three of his four children died: a son at the age of four, a daughter in her late twenties from tuberculosis, and another son by suicide. His marriage was filled with tension. Although Frost's work is landscaped with sunlight, snow, birches, birds, blueberries, and squirrels, it is important to recognize that he was also intimately "acquainted with the night," a phrase that serves as the haunting title of one of his poems (see p. 139).

As a corrective to Frost's popular reputation, one critic, Lionel Trilling, described the world Frost creates in his poems as a "terrifying universe," characterized by loneliness, anguish, frustration, doubts, disappointment, and despair (see p. 362 for an excerpt from this essay). To point this out is not to annihilate the pleasantness and even good natured cheerfulness that can be enjoyed in Frost's poetry, but it is to say that Frost is not so one-dimensional as he is sometimes assumed to be. Frost's poetry requires readers who are alert and willing to penetrate the simplicity of its language to see the elusive and ambiguous meanings that lie below the surface.

AN INTRODUCTION TO HIS WORK

Frost's treatment of nature helps to explain the various levels of meaning in his poetry. The familiar natural world his poems evoke is sharply

> Neither Out Far nor In Deep
>
> The people along the sand
> All turn and look one way.
> They turn their backs on the land;
> They look at the sea all day.
>
> As long as it takes to pass
> A ship keeps raising its hull.
> The wetter ground like glass
> Reflects a standing gull.
>
> The land may vary more,
> But wherever the truth may be —
> The water comes ashore
> And the people look at the sea.
>
> They cannot look out far;
> They cannot look in deep;
> But when was that ever a bar
> To any watch they keep.
>
> Robert Frost
>
> With the permission of The Yale Review.

Manuscript page for Robert Frost's "Neither Out Far nor In Deep" (p. 356), which was first published in The Yale Review *in 1934 and later, with a few punctuation changes, in* A Further Range *in 1936. Courtesy of the Amherst College Library. Reprinted by permission of the Robert Frost Estate.*

detailed. We hear icy branches clicking against themselves, we see the snow-white trunks of birches, we feel the smarting pain of a twig lashing across a face. The aspects of the natural world Frost describes are designated to give pleasure, but they are also frequently calculated to provoke thought. His use of nature tends to be symbolic. Complex meanings are derived from simple facts, such as a spider killing a moth or the difference between fire and ice (see "Design," p. 356, and "Fire and Ice," p. 353). Although Frost's strategy is to talk about particular events and individual experiences, his poems evoke universal issues.

Frost's poetry has strong regional roots and is "versed in country things," but it flourishes in any receptive imagination because, in the final analysis, it is concerned with human beings. Frost's New England landscapes are the occasion rather than the ultimate focus of his poems. Like the rural voices he creates in his poems, Frost typically approaches his themes indirectly. He explained the reason for this in a talk titled "Education by Poetry":

> Poetry provides the one permissible way of saying one thing and meaning another. People say, "Why don't you say what you mean?" We never do that, do we, being all of us too much poets. We like to talk in parables and in hints and in indirections — whether from diffidence or some other instinct.

The result is that the settings, characters, and situations that make up the subject matter of Frost's poems are vehicles for his perceptions about life.

In "Stopping by Woods on a Snowy Evening" (p. 353), for example, Frost uses the kind of familiar New England details that constitute his poetry for more than descriptive purposes. He shapes them into a meditation on the tension we sometimes feel between life's responsibilities and the "lovely, dark, and deep" attraction that death offers. When the speaker's horse "gives his harness bells a shake," we are reminded that we are confronting a universal theme as well as a quiet moment of natural beauty.

Among the major concerns that appear in Frost's poetry are the fragility of life, the consequences of rejecting or accepting the conditions of one's life, the passion of inconsolable grief, the difficulty of sustaining intimacy, the fear of loneliness and isolation, the inevitability of change, the tensions between the individual and society, and the place of tradition and custom.

Whatever theme is encountered in a poem by Frost, a reader is likely to agree with him that "the initial delight is in the surprise of remembering something I didn't know." To achieve that fresh sense of discovery, Frost allowed himself to follow his instincts; his poetry

> inclines to the impulse, it assumes direction with the first line laid down, it runs a course of lucky events, and ends in a clarification of life — not necessarily a great clarification, such as sects and cults are founded on, but in a momentary stay against confusion.

This description from "The Figure a Poem Makes" (see p. 359 for the complete essay), Frost's brief introduction to *Complete Poems*, may sound as if his poetry is formless and merely "lucky," but his poems tend to be more conventional than experimental: "The artist in me," as he put the matter in one of his poems, "cries out for design."

From Frost's perspective, "free verse is like playing tennis with the net down." He exercised his own freedom in meeting the challenges of rhyme and meter. His use of fixed forms such as couplets, tercets, quatrains, blank verse, and sonnets was not slavish because he enjoyed working them into the natural English speech patterns — especially the rhythms, idioms, and tones of speakers living north of Boston — that give voice to his themes. Frost often liked to use "Stopping by Woods on a Snowy Evening" as an example of his graceful way of making conventions appear natural and inevitable. He explored "the old ways to be new."

Frost's eye for strong, telling details was matched by his ear for natural speech rhythms. His flexible use of what he called "iambic and loose iambic" enabled him to create moving lyric poems that reveal the personal thoughts of a speaker and dramatic poems that convincingly characterize people caught in intense emotional situations. The language in his poems appears to be little more than a transcription of casual and even rambling speech, but it is in actuality Frost's poetic creation, carefully crafted to reveal the joys and sorrows that are woven into people's daily lives. What is missing from Frost's poems is artificiality, not art. Consider this poem.

The Road Not Taken   *1916*

Two roads diverged in a yellow wood,
And sorry I could not travel both
And be one traveler, long I stood
And looked down one as far as I could
To where it bent in the undergrowth;   5

Then took the other, as just as fair,
And having perhaps the better claim,
Because it was grassy and wanted wear;
Though as for that the passing there
Had worn them really about the same,   10

And both that morning equally lay
In leaves no step had trodden black.
Oh, I kept the first for another day!
Yet knowing how way leads on to way,
I doubted if I should ever come back.   15

I shall be telling this with a sigh
Somewhere ages and ages hence:
Two roads diverged in a wood, and I —
I took the one less traveled by,
And that has made all the difference.   20

This poem intrigues readers because it is at once so simple and so deeply resonant. Recalling a walk in the woods, the speaker describes how he came to a fork in the road, which forced him to choose one path over another. Though "sorry" that he "could not travel both," he made a choice after carefully weighing his two options. This, essentially, is what happens in the poem; there is no other action. However, the incident is charged with symbolic significance by the speaker's reflections on the necessity and consequences of his decision.

The final stanza indicates that the choice concerns more than simply walking down a road, for the speaker says that choosing the "less traveled" path has affected his entire life — that "that has made all the difference." Frost draws on a familiar enough metaphor when he compares life to a journey, but he is also calling attention to a less commonly noted problem: despite our expectations, aspirations, appetites, hopes, and desires, we can't have it all. Making one choice precludes another. It is impossible to determine what particular decision the speaker refers to: perhaps he had to choose a college, a career, a spouse; perhaps he was confronted with mutually exclusive ideas, beliefs, or values. There is no way to know because Frost wisely creates a symbolic choice and implicitly invites us to supply our own circumstances.

The speaker's reflections about his choice are as central to an understanding of the poem as the choice itself; indeed, they may be more central. He describes the road taken as "having perhaps the better claim, / Because it was grassy and wanted wear"; he prefers the "less traveled" path. This seems to be an expression of individualism, which would account for "the difference" his choice made in his life. But Frost complicates matters by having the speaker also acknowledge that there was no significant difference between the two roads; one was "just as fair" as the other; each was "worn . . . really about the same"; and "both that morning equally lay / In leaves no step had trodden black."

The speaker imagines that in the future, "ages and ages hence," he will recount his choice with "a sigh" that will satisfactorily explain the course of his life, but Frost seems to be having a little fun here by showing us how the speaker will embellish his past decision to make it appear more dramatic. What we hear is someone trying to convince himself that the choice he made significantly changed his life. When he recalls what happened in the "yellow wood," a color that gives a glow to that irretrievable moment when his life seemed to be on verge of a momentous change, he appears more concerned with the path he did not choose than with the one he took. Frost shrewdly titles the poem to suggest the speaker's sense of loss at not being able to "travel both" roads. When the speaker's reflections about his choice are examined, the poem reveals his nostalgia instead of affirming his decision to travel a self-reliant path in life.

The rhymed stanzas of "The Road Not Taken" follow a pattern established in the first five lines (*abaab*). This rhyme scheme reflects, perhaps, the speaker's efforts to shape his life into a pleasing and coherent form. The natural speech rhythms Frost uses allow him to integrate the rhymes unobtrusively, but there is a slight shift in lines 19 and 20, when the speaker asserts self-consciously that the "less traveled" road — which we already know to be basically the same as the other road — "made all the difference." Unlike all the other rhymes in the poem, "difference" does not rhyme precisely with "hence." The emphasis that must be placed on "differ*ence*" to make it rhyme perfectly with "hence" may suggest that the speaker is trying just a little too hard to pattern his life on his earlier choice in the woods.

Perhaps the best way to begin reading Frost's poetry is to accept the invitation he placed at the beginning of many volumes of his poems. "The Pasture" means what it says of course; it is about taking care of some farm chores, but it is also a means of "saying one thing in terms of another."

The Pasture

1913

I'm going out to clean the pasture spring;
I'll only stop to rake the leaves away
(And wait to watch the water clear, I may):
I shan't be gone long. — You come too.

I'm going out to fetch the little calf
That's standing by the mother. It's so young
It totters when she licks it with her tongue.
I shan't be gone long. — You come too.

"The Pasture" is a simple but irresistible songlike invitation to the pleasure of looking at the world through the eyes of a poet.

CHRONOLOGY

1874	Born on March 26 in San Francisco, California.
1885	Father dies and family moves to Lawrence, Massachusetts.
1892	Graduates from Lawrence High School.
1893–94	Studies at Dartmouth College.
1895	Marries his high school sweetheart, Elinor White.
1897–99	Studies at Harvard College.
1900	Moves to a farm in West Derry, New Hampshire.
1912	Moves to England, where he farms and writes.
1913	*A Boy's Will* is published in London.
1914	*North of Boston* is published in London.
1915	Moves to a farm near Franconia, New Hampshire.
1916	Elected to National Institute of Letters.
1917–20	Teaches at Amherst College.

1919	Moves to South Shaftsbury, Vermont.
1921–23	Teaches at the University of Michigan.
1923	*Selected Poems* and *New Hampshire* are published; the latter is awarded a Pulitzer Prize.
1928	*West-Running Brook* is published.
1930	*Collected Poems* is published.
1936	*A Further Range* is published; teaches at Harvard.
1938	Wife dies.
1939–42	Teaches at Harvard.
1942	*A Witness Tree*, which is awarded a Pulitzer Prize, is published.
1943–49	Teaches at Dartmouth.
1945	*A Masque of Reason* is published.
1947	*Steeple Bush* and *A Masque of Mercy* are published.
1949	*Complete Poems* (enlarged) is published.
1961	Reads "The Gift Outright" at President John F. Kennedy's inauguration.
1963	Dies on January 29 in Boston.

Mowing *1913*

There was never a sound beside the wood but one,
And that was my long scythe whispering to the ground.
What was it it whispered? I knew not well myself;
Perhaps it was something about the heat of the sun,
Something, perhaps, about the lack of sound —   5
And that was why it whispered and did not speak.
It was no dream of the gift of idle hours,
Or easy gold at the hand of fay or elf:
Anything more than the truth would have seemed too weak
To the earnest love that laid the swale in rows,   10
Not without feeble-pointed spikes of flowers
(Pale orchises), and scared a bright green snake.
The fact is the sweetest dream that labour knows.
My long scythe whispered and left the hay to make.

CONSIDERATIONS FOR CRITICAL THINKING AND WRITING

1. FIRST RESPONSE. Describe the tone of "Mowing." How does reading it aloud affect your understanding of it?
2. Discuss the image of the scythe. Do you think it has any symbolic value? Explain why or why not.

3. Paraphrase the poem. What do you think its thematic significance is?

4. Describe the type of sonnet Frost uses in "Mowing."

Mending Wall   1914

Something there is that doesn't love a wall,
That sends the frozen-ground-swell under it,
And spills the upper boulders in the sun;
And makes gaps even two can pass abreast.
The work of hunters is another thing: 5
I have come after them and made repair
Where they have left not one stone on a stone,
But they would have the rabbit out of hiding,
To please the yelping dogs. The gaps I mean,
No one has seen them made or heard them made,   10
But at spring mending-time we find them there.
I let my neighbor know beyond the hill;
And on a day we meet to walk the line
And set the wall between us once again.
We keep the wall between us as we go.   15
To each the boulders that have fallen to each.
And some are loaves and some so nearly balls
We have to use a spell to make them balance:
"Stay where you are until our backs are turned!"
We wear our fingers rough with handling them.   20
Oh, just another kind of outdoor game,
One on a side. It comes to little more:
There where it is we do not need the wall:
He is all pine and I am apple orchard.
My apple trees will never get across   25
And eat the cones under his pines, I tell him.
He only says, "Good fences make good neighbors."
Spring is the mischief in me, and I wonder
If I could put a notion in his head:
"*Why* do they make good neighbors? Isn't it   30
Where there are cows? But here there are no cows.
Before I built a wall I'd ask to know
What I was walling in or walling out,
And to whom I was like to give offense.
Something there is that doesn't love a wall,   35
That wants it down." I could say "Elves" to him,
But it's not elves exactly, and I'd rather
He said it for himself. I see him there
Bringing a stone grasped firmly by the top
In each hand, like an old-stone savage armed.   40
He moves in darkness as it seems to me,
Not of woods only and the shade of trees.

He will not go behind his father's saying,
And he likes having thought of it so well
He says again, "Good fences make good neighbors." 45

CONSIDERATIONS FOR CRITICAL THINKING AND WRITING

1. FIRST RESPONSE. What might the "Something" be that "doesn't love a
   wall"? Why does the speaker remind his neighbor each spring that the wall
   needs to be repaired? Is it ironic that the *speaker* initiates the mending? Is
   there anything good about the wall?

2. How do the speaker and his neighbor in this poem differ in sensibilities?
   What is suggested about the neighbor in lines 41 and 42?

3. The neighbor likes the saying "Good fences make good neighbors" so well
   that he repeats it (lines 27, 45). Does the speaker also say something twice?
   What else suggests that the speaker's attitude toward the wall is not neces-
   sarily Frost's?

4. Although the speaker's language is colloquial, what is poetic about the
   sounds and rhythms he uses?

5. This poem was first published in 1914; Frost read it to an audience when he
   visited Russia in 1962. What do these facts suggest about the symbolic value
   of "Mending Wall"?

CONNECTIONS TO OTHER SELECTIONS

1. How do you think the neighbor in this poem would respond to Dickin-
   son's idea of imagination in "To make a prairie it takes a clover and one
   bee" (p. 293)?

2. What similarities and differences does the neighbor have with the people
   Frost describes in "Neither Out Far nor In Deep" (p. 356)?

Home Burial 1914

He saw her from the bottom of the stairs
Before she saw him. She was starting down,
Looking back over her shoulder at some fear.
She took a doubtful step and then undid it
To raise herself and look again. He spoke 5
Advancing toward her. "What is it you see
From up there always — for I want to know."
She turned and sank upon her skirts at that,
And her face changed from terrified to dull.
He said to gain time. "What is it you see," 10
Mounting until she cowered under him.
"I will find out now — you must tell me, dear."
She, in her place, refused him any help
With the least stiffening of her neck and silence.
She let him look, sure that he wouldn't see, 15

Blind creature; and awhile he didn't see.
But at last he murmured, "Oh," and again, "Oh."

"What is it — what?" she said.

        "Just that I see."

"You don't," she challenged. "Tell me what it is."   20

"The wonder is I didn't see at once.
I never noticed it from here before.
I must be wonted° to it — that's the reason.
The little graveyard where my people are!
So small the window frames the whole of it.   25
Not so much larger than a bedroom, is it?
There are three stones of slate and one of marble,
Broad-shouldered little slabs there in the sunlight
On the sidehill. We haven't to mind *those*.
But I understand: it is not the stones,   30
But the child's mound —"

        "Don't, don't, don't, don't," she cried.

She withdrew, shrinking from beneath his arm
That rested on the banister, and slid downstairs;
And turned on him with such a daunting look,   35
He said twice over before he knew himself:
"Can't a man speak of his own child he's lost?"

"Not you! — Oh, where's my hat? Oh, I don't need it!
I must get out of here. I must get air.
I don't know rightly whether any man can."   40

"Amy! Don't go to someone else this time.
Listen to me. I won't come down the stairs."
He sat and fixed his chin between his fists.
"There's something I should like to ask you, dear."

"You don't know how to ask it."   45

        "Help me, then."
Her fingers moved the latch for all reply.

"My words are nearly always an offense.
I don't know how to speak of anything
So as to please you. But I might be taught,   50
I should suppose. I can't say I see how.
A man must partly give up being a man
With women-folk. We could have some arrangement
By which I'd bind myself to keep hands off
Anything special you're a-mind to name.   55
Though I don't like such things 'twixt those that love.
Two that don't love can't live together without them.

23 *wonted:* Accustomed.

But two that do can't live together with them."
She moved the latch a little. "Don't — don't go.
Don't carry it to someone else this time.   60
Tell me about it if it's something human.
Let me into your grief. I'm not so much
Unlike other folks as your standing there
Apart would make me out. Give me my chance.
I do think, though, you overdo it a little.   65
What was it brought you up to think it the thing
To take your mother-loss of a first child
So inconsolably — in the face of love.
You'd think his memory might be satisfied —"

"There you go sneering now!"   70

             "I'm not, I'm not!

You make me angry. I'll come down to you.
God, what a woman! And it's come to this,
A man can't speak of his own child that's dead."

"You can't because you don't know how to speak.   75
If you had any feelings, you that dug
With your own hand — how could you? — his little grave;
I saw you from that very window there,
Making the gravel leap and leap in air,
Leap up, like that, like that, and land so lightly   80
And roll back down the mound beside the hole.
I thought, Who is that man? I didn't know you.
And I crept down the stairs and up the stairs
To look again, and still your spade kept lifting.
Then you came in. I heard your rumbling voice   85
Out in the kitchen, and I don't know why,
But I went near to see with my own eyes.
You could sit there with the stains on your shoes
Of the fresh earth from your own baby's grave
And talk about your everyday concerns.   90
You had stood the spade up against the wall
Outside there in the entry, for I saw it."

"I shall laugh the worst laugh I ever laughed.
I'm cursed. God, if I don't believe I'm cursed."

"I can repeat the very words you were saying.   95
'Three foggy mornings and one rainy day
Will rot the best birch fence a man can build.'
Think of it, talk like that at such a time!
What had how long it takes a birch to rot
To do with what was in the darkened parlor   100
You *couldn't* care! The nearest friends can go
With anyone to death, comes so far short
They might as well not try to go at all.
No, from the time when one is sick to death,

One is alone, and he dies more alone. 105
Friends make pretense of following to the grave.
But before one is in it, their minds are turned
And making the best of their way back to life
And living people, and things they understand.
But the world's evil. I won't have grief so 110
If I can change it. Oh, I won't, I won't!"

"There, you have said it all and you feel better.
You won't go now. You're crying. Close the door.
The heart's gone out of it: why keep it up.
Amy! There's someone coming down the road!" 115

"*You* — oh, you think the talk is all. I must go —
Somewhere out of this house. How can I make you —"

"If — you — do!" She was opening the door wider.
"Where do you mean to go? First tell me that.
I'll follow and bring you back by force. I *will!* —" 120

CONSIDERATIONS FOR CRITICAL THINKING AND WRITING

1. FIRST RESPONSE. This poem tells a story of a relationship. Is the husband insensitive and indifferent to his wife's grief? Characterize the wife. Has Frost invited us to sympathize with one character more than with the other?

2. How has the burial of the child within sight of the stairway window affected the relationship of the couple in this poem? Is the child's grave a symptom or a cause of the conflict between them?

3. What is the effect of splitting the iambic pentameter pattern in lines 18 and 19, 31 and 32, 45 and 46, and 70 and 71?

4. Is the conflict resolved at the conclusion of the poem? Do you think the husband and wife will overcome their differences?

After Apple-Picking 1914

My long two-pointed ladder's sticking through a tree
Toward heaven still,
And there's a barrel that I didn't fill
Beside it, and there may be two or three
Apples I didn't pick upon some bough. 5
But I am done with apple-picking now.
Essence of winter sleep is on the night,
The scent of apples: I am drowsing off.
I cannot rub the strangeness from my sight
I got from looking through a pane of glass 10
I skimmed this morning from the drinking trough
And held against the world of hoary grass.
It melted, and I let it fall and break.
But I was well

Upon my way to sleep before it fell,   15
And I could tell
What form my dreaming was about to take.
Magnified apples appear and disappear,
Stem end and blossom end,
And every fleck of russet showing clear.   20
My instep arch not only keeps the ache,
It keeps the pressure of a ladder-round.
I feel the ladder sway as the boughs bend.
And I keep hearing from the cellar bin
The rumbling sound   25
Of load on load of apples coming in.
For I have had too much
Of apple-picking: I am overtired
Of the great harvest I myself desired.
There were ten thousand thousand fruit to touch,   30
Cherish in hand, lift down, and not let fall.
For all
That struck the earth,
No matter if not bruised or spiked with stubble,
Went surely to the cider-apple heap   35
As of no worth.
One can see what will trouble
This sleep of mine, whatever sleep it is.
Were he not gone,
The woodchuck could say whether it's like his   40
Long sleep, as I describe its coming on,
Or just some human sleep.

CONSIDERATIONS FOR CRITICAL THINKING AND WRITING

1. FIRST RESPONSE. How does this poem illustrate Frost's view that "Poetry provides the one permissible way of saying one thing and meaning another"? When do you first sense that the detailed description of apple picking is being used that way?

2. What comes after apple picking? What does the speaker worry about in the dream beginning in line 18?

3. Why do you suppose Frost uses apples rather than, say, pears or squash?

Birches   1916

When I see birches bend to left and right
Across the lines of straighter darker trees,
I like to think some boy's been swinging them.
But swinging doesn't bend them down to stay
As ice-storms do. Often you must have seen them   5
Loaded with ice a sunny winter morning

After a rain. They click upon themselves
As the breeze rises, and turn many-colored
As the stir cracks and crazes their enamel.
Soon the sun's warmth makes them shed crystal shells   10
Shattering and avalanching on the snow-crust —
Such heaps of broken glass to sweep away
You'd think the inner dome of heaven had fallen.
They are dragged to the withered bracken by the load,
And they seem not to break; though once they are bowed   15
So low for long, they never right themselves:
You may see their trunks arching in the woods
Years afterwards, trailing their leaves on the ground
Like girls on hands and knees that throw their hair
Before them over their heads to dry in the sun.   20
But I was going to say when Truth broke in
With all her matter-of-fact about the ice-storm,
I should prefer to have some boy bend them
As he went out and in to fetch the cows —
Some boy too far from town to learn baseball,   25
Whose only play was what he found himself,
Summer or winter, and could play alone.
One by one he subdued his father's trees
By riding them down over and over again
Until he took the stiffness out of them,   30
And not one but hung limp, not one was left
For him to conquer. He learned all there was
To learn about not launching out too soon
And so not carrying the tree away
Clear to the ground. He always kept his poise   35
To the top branches, climbing carefully
With the same pains you use to fill a cup
Up to the brim, and even above the brim.
Then he flung outward, feet first, with a swish,
Kicking his way down through the air to the ground.   40
So was I once myself a swinger of birches.
And so I dream of going back to be.
It's when I'm weary of considerations,
And life is too much like a pathless wood
Where your face burns and tickles with the cobwebs   45
Broken across it, and one eye is weeping
From a twig's having lashed across it open.
I'd like to get away from earth awhile
And then come back to it and begin over.
May no fate willfully misunderstand me   50
And half grant what I wish and snatch me away
Not to return. Earth's the right place for love:
I don't know where it's likely to go better.
I'd like to go by climbing a birch tree,
And climb black branches up a snow-white trunk,   55
Toward heaven, till the tree could bear no more,
But dipped its top and set me down again.

That would be good both going and coming back.
One could do worse than be a swinger of birches.

CONSIDERATIONS FOR CRITICAL THINKING AND WRITING

1. FIRST RESPONSE. What do you think the swinging of birches symbolizes?

2. Why does the speaker in this poem prefer the birches to have been bent by boys instead of ice storms?

3. How is "earth" (line 52) described in the poem? Why does the speaker choose it over "heaven" (line 56)?

4. How might the effect of this poem be changed if it were written in heroic couplets instead of blank verse?

A Girl's Garden   *1916*

A neighbor of mine in the village
  Likes to tell how one spring
When she was a girl on the farm, she did
  A childlike thing.

One day she asked her father   5
  To give her a garden plot
To plant and tend and reap herself,
  And he said, "Why not?"

In casting about for a corner
  He thought of an idle bit   10
Of walled-off ground where a shop had stood,
  And he said, "Just it."

And he said, "That ought to make you
  An ideal one-girl farm,
And give you a chance to put some strength   15
  On your slim-jim arm."

It was not enough of a garden,
  Her father said, to plow;
So she had to work it all by hand,
  But she don't mind now.   20

She wheeled the dung in the wheelbarrow
  Along a stretch of road;
But she always ran away and left
  Her not-nice load,

And hid from anyone passing.   25
  And then she begged the seed.
She says she thinks she planted one
  Of all things but weed.

A hill each of potatoes,
  Radishes, lettuce, peas,   30

Tomatoes, beets, beans, pumpkins, corn
    And even fruit trees.

And yes, she has long mistrusted
    That a cider apple tree
In bearing there today is hers,   35
    Or at least may be.

Her crop was a miscellany
    When all was said and done,
A little bit of everything,
    A great deal of none.   40

Now when she sees in the village
    How village things go,
Just when it seems to come in right,
    She says, "*I* know!"

"It's as when I was a farmer—"   45
    Oh, never by way of advice!
And she never sins by telling the tale
    To the same person twice.

CONSIDERATIONS FOR CRITICAL THINKING AND WRITING

1. FIRST RESPONSE. Write a paraphrase of the poem. What do you think it is about?
2. Why do you suppose Frost uses a narrator to tell the story about the girl instead of having her tell the story herself?
3. What purpose does the father's character serve in the poem?
4. Discuss the distinction that is made between the "ideal one-girl farm" (line 14) and "How village things go" (42).

CONNECTIONS TO OTHER SELECTIONS

1. Compare the narrator in this poem to the narrator in "Stopping by Woods on a Snowy Evening" (p. 353). How, in each poem, do simple activities reveal something about the narrator?
2. Discuss the narrator's treatment of the neighbor in this poem and in "Mending Wall" (p. 342).

"Out, Out —"°   *1916*

The buzz-saw snarled and rattled in the yard
And made dust and dropped stove-length sticks of wood,
Sweet-scented stuff when the breeze drew across it.
And from there those that lifted eyes could count

"Out, Out —": From Act V, Scene v, of Shakespeare's *Macbeth*.

Five mountain ranges one behind the other   5
Under the sunset far into Vermont.
And the saw snarled and rattled, snarled and rattled,
As it ran light, or had to bear a load.
And nothing happened: day was all but done.
Call it a day, I wish they might have said   10
To please the boy by giving him the half hour
That a boy counts so much when saved from work.
His sister stood beside them in her apron
To tell them "Supper." At the word, the saw,
As if to prove saws knew what supper meant,   15
Leaped out at the boy's hand, or seemed to leap —
He must have given the hand. However it was,
Neither refused the meeting. But the hand!
The boy's first outcry was a rueful laugh,
As he swung toward them holding up the hand   20
Half in appeal, but half as if to keep
The life from spilling. Then the boy saw all —
Since he was old enough to know, big boy
Doing a man's work, though a child at heart —
He saw all spoiled. "Don't let him cut my hand off —   25
The doctor, when he comes. Don't let him, sister!"
So. But the hand was gone already.
The doctor put him in the dark of ether.
He lay and puffed his lips out with his breath.
And then — the watcher at his pulse took fright.   30
No one believed. They listened at his heart.
Little — less — nothing! — and that ended it.
No more to build on there. And they, since they
Were not the one dead, turned to their affairs.

CONSIDERATIONS FOR CRITICAL THINKING AND WRITING

1. FIRST RESPONSE. This narrative poem is about the accidental death of a Vermont boy. What is the purpose of the story? Some readers have argued that the final lines reveal the speaker's callousness and indifference. What do you think?

2. How does Frost's allusion to *Macbeth* contribute to the meaning of this poem? Does the speaker seem to agree with the view of life expressed in Macbeth's lines?

CONNECTIONS TO OTHER SELECTIONS

1. What are the similarities and differences in theme between this poem and Frost's "Nothing Gold Can Stay" (p. 354)?

2. Write an essay comparing how grief is handled by the boy's family in this poem and the couple in "Home Burial" (p. 343).

3. Compare the tone and theme of "'Out, Out—'" and those of Crane's "A Man Said to the Universe" (p. 146).

A Boundless Moment

1923

He halted in the wind, and — what was that
Far in the maples, pale, but not a ghost?
He stood there bringing March against his thought,
And yet too ready to believe the most.

"Oh, that's the Paradise-in-Bloom," I said;   5
And truly it was fair enough for flowers
Had we but in us to assume in March
Such white luxuriance of May for ours.

We stood a moment so, in a strange world,
Myself as one his own pretense deceives;   10
And then I said the truth (and we moved on).
A young beech clinging to its last year's leaves.

CONSIDERATIONS FOR CRITICAL THINKING AND WRITING

1. FIRST RESPONSE. Describe the speaker's temperament. How does his differ
   from his companion's?
2. How does the diction of the final line create a particular tone?
3. Discuss the significance of the title. How can the action in the poem be
   taken as boundless? What would be the effect of replacing the title with "A
   Mistaken Moment"? How would that change your reading of the poem?

CONNECTION TO ANOTHER SELECTION

1. Discuss the tone and theme of "A Boundless Moment" and "Nothing Gold
   Can Stay" (p. 354).

The Investment

1923

Over back where they speak of life as staying
(You couldn't call it living, for it ain't),
There was an old, old house renewed with paint,
And in it a piano loudly playing.

Out in the plowed ground in the cold a digger,   5
Among unearthed potatoes standing still,
Was counting winter dinners, one a hill,
With half an ear to the piano's vigor.

All that piano and new paint back there,
Was it some money suddenly come into?   10
Or some extravagance young love had been to?
Or old love on an impulse not to care —

Not to sink under being man and wife,
But get some color and music out of life?

CONSIDERATIONS FOR CRITICAL THINKING AND WRITING

1. FIRST RESPONSE. In what sense does the idea of "Over back where" or "back there" serve as more than a physical setting in the poem? What do these phrases imply about the poem's meaning?

2. Discuss the symbolic significance of the "piano and new paint" in contrast to the potato digger.

3. What kind of sonnet is this poem? Why is the concluding couplet an especially appropriate way to end the poem?

CONNECTION TO ANOTHER SELECTION

1. Compare the relationship of the man and wife in "The Investment" with that of "Home Burial" (p. 343).

Fire and Ice

1923

Some say the world will end in fire,
Some say in ice.
From what I've tasted of desire
I hold with those who favor fire.
But if it had to perish twice,
I think I know enough of hate
To say that for destruction ice
Is also great
And would suffice.

CONSIDERATIONS FOR CRITICAL THINKING AND WRITING

1. FIRST RESPONSE. What characteristics of human behavior does the speaker associate with fire and ice?

2. What theories about the end of the world are alluded to in lines 1 and 2?

3. How does the speaker's use of understatement and rhyme affect the tone of this poem?

Stopping by Woods on a Snowy Evening

1923

Whose woods these are I think I know.
His house is in the village, though;
He will not see me stopping here
To watch his woods fill up with snow.

My little horse must think it queer   5
To stop without a farmhouse near
Between the woods and frozen lake
The darkest evening of the year.

He gives his harness bells a shake
To ask if there is some mistake.   10
The only other sound's the sweep
Of easy wind and downy flake.

The woods are lovely, dark and deep,
But I have promises to keep,
And miles to go before I sleep,   15
And miles to go before I sleep.

CONSIDERATIONS FOR CRITICAL THINKING AND WRITING

1. FIRST RESPONSE. What is the significance of the setting in this poem? How is tone conveyed by the images?
2. What does the speaker find appealing about the woods? What is the purpose of the horse in the poem?
3. Although the last two lines are identical, they are not read at the same speed. Why the difference? What is achieved by the repetition?
4. What is the rhyme scheme of this poem? What is the effect of the rhyme in the final stanza?

Nothing Gold Can Stay   *1923*

Nature's first green is gold,
Her hardest hue to hold.
Her early leaf's a flower;
But only so an hour.
The leaf subsides to leaf.
So Eden sank to grief.
So dawn goes down to day.
Nothing gold can stay.

CONSIDERATIONS FOR CRITICAL THINKING AND WRITING

1. FIRST RESPONSE. What is meant by "gold" in the poem? Why can't it "stay"?
2. What do the leaf, humanity, and a day have in common?

CONNECTION TO ANOTHER SELECTION

1. Write an essay comparing the tone and theme of "Nothing Gold Can Stay" with Herrick's "To the Virgins, to Make Much of Time" (p. 64).

The Armful   *1928*

For every parcel I stoop down to seize
I lose some other off my arms and knees,
And the whole pile is slipping, bottles, buns—

Extremes too hard to comprehend at once,
Yet nothing I should care to leave behind.   5
With all I have to hold with, hand and mind
And heart, if need be, I will do my best
To keep their building balanced at my breast.
I crouch down to prevent them as they fall;
Then sit down in the middle of them all.   10
I had to drop the armful in the road,
And try to stack them in a better load.

CONSIDERATIONS FOR CRITICAL THINKING AND WRITING

1. FIRST RESPONSE. How does this poem add up to more than a simple vignette of dropping things? What words, in particular, suggest other interpretations?

2. Discuss the effects of the rhymes and meter. In what ways does the poem do with words what the speaker does with packages? How do you think this poem would read differently if it were written in free verse?

CONNECTION TO ANOTHER SELECTION

1. Compare the central metaphor and theme of "The Armful" with those of Emily Dickinson's "I felt a Cleaving in my Mind—" (p. 309).

Spring Pools   *1928*

These pools that, though in forests, still reflect
The total sky almost without defect,
And like the flowers beside them, chill and shiver,
Will like the flowers beside them soon be gone,
And yet not out by any brook or river,   5
But up by roots to bring dark foliage on.

The trees that have it in their pent-up buds
To darken nature and be summer woods—
Let them think twice before they use their powers
To blot out and drink up and sweep away   10
These flowery waters and these watery flowers
From snow that melted only yesterday.

CONSIDERATIONS FOR CRITICAL THINKING AND WRITING

1. FIRST RESPONSE. In what sense is this poem more than just a detailed picture of nature?

2. How does the speaker create tension between the pools, flowers, and trees? What do you see as the central conflict in the poem?

3. Comment on the rhythm and rhyme of lines 7 and 8. How do they differ from the other lines of the poem? How is their placement unique?

CONNECTION TO ANOTHER SELECTION

1. Compare the speaker's reaction to nature in this poem and in "Design," the next poem.

Design   1936

I found a dimpled spider, fat and white,
On a white heal-all,° holding up a moth
Like a white piece of rigid satin cloth —
Assorted characters of death and blight
Mixed ready to begin the morning right,   5
Like the ingredients of a witches' broth —
A snow-drop spider, a flower like a froth,
And dead wings carried like a paper kite.

What had the flower to do with being white,
The wayside blue and innocent heal-all?   10
What brought the kindred spider to that height,
Then steered the white moth thither in the night?
What but design of darkness to appall? —
If design govern in a thing so small.

2 *heal-all:* A common flower, usually blue, once used for medicinal purposes.

CONSIDERATIONS FOR CRITICAL THINKING AND WRITING

1. FIRST RESPONSE. What kinds of speculations are raised in the final two lines? Consider the meaning of the title. Is there more than one way to read it?

2. How does the division of the octave and sestet in this sonnet serve to organize the speaker's thoughts and feelings? What is the predominant rhyme? How does that rhyme relate to the poem's meaning?

3. Which words seem especially rich in connotative meanings? Explain how they function in the sonnet.

CONNECTIONS TO OTHER SELECTIONS

1. Compare the ironic tone of "Design" with the tone of Hathaway's "Oh, Oh" (p. 13). What would you have to change in Hathaway's poem to make it more like Frost's?

2. In an essay discuss Frost's view of God in this poem and Dickinson's perspective in "I know that He exists" (p. 327).

3. Compare "Design" with "In White," Frost's early version of it (p. 358).

Neither Out Far nor In Deep   1936

The people along the sand
All turn and look one way.

They turn their back on the land.
They look at the sea all day.

As long as it takes to pass   5
A ship keeps raising its hull;
The wetter ground like glass
Reflects a standing gull.

The land may vary more;
But wherever the truth may be —   10
The water comes ashore,
And the people look at the sea.

They cannot look out far.
They cannot look in deep.
But when was that ever a bar   15
To any watch they keep?

CONSIDERATIONS FOR CRITICAL THINKING AND WRITING

1. FIRST RESPONSE. Frost built this poem around a simple observation that raises some questions. Why do people at the beach almost always face the ocean? What feelings and thoughts are evoked by looking at the ocean?

2. Notice how the verb "look" takes on added meaning as the poem progresses. What are the people looking for?

3. How does the final stanza extend the poem's significance?

4. Does the speaker identify with the people described, or does he ironically distance himself from them?

The Silken Tent

1942

She is as in a field a silken tent
At midday when a sunny summer breeze
Has dried the dew and all its ropes relent,
So that in guys° it gently sways at ease,   *ropes that steady a tent*
And its supporting central cedar pole,   5
That is its pinnacle to heavenward
And signifies the sureness of the soul,
Seems to owe naught to any single cord,
But strictly held by none, is loosely bound
By countless silken ties of love and thought   10
To everything on earth the compass round,
And only by one's going slightly taut
In the capriciousness of summer air
Is of the slightest bondage made aware.

CONSIDERATIONS FOR CRITICAL THINKING AND WRITING

1. FIRST RESPONSE. What is being compared in this sonnet? How does the detail accurately describe both elements of the comparison?

2. How does the form of this one-sentence sonnet help to express its theme? Pay particular attention to the final three lines.

3. How do the sonnet's sounds contribute to its meaning?

PERSPECTIVES ON FROST

"In White": Frost's Early Version of "Design" 1912

A dented spider like a snow drop white
On a white Heal-all, holding up a moth
Like a white piece of lifeless satin cloth —
Saw ever curious eye so strange a sight? —
Portent in little, assorted death and blight   5
Like the ingredients of a witches' broth? —
The beady spider, the flower like a froth,
And the moth carried like a paper kite.

What had that flower to do with being white,
The blue prunella every child's delight.   10
What brought the kindred spider to that height?
(Make we no thesis of the miller's° plight.)   *miller moth*
What but design of darkness and of night?
Design, design! Do I use the word aright?

CONSIDERATIONS FOR CRITICAL THINKING AND WRITING

1. Read "In White" and "Design" (p. 356) aloud. Which version sounds better to you? Why?

2. Compare these versions line for line, paying particular attention to word choice. List the differences, and try to explain why you think Frost revised the lines.

3. How does the change in titles reflect a shift in emphasis in the poem?

Frost on the Living Part of a Poem 1914

The living part of a poem is the intonation entangled somehow in the syntax, idiom, and meaning of a sentence. It is only there for those who have heard it previously in conversation. . . . It is the most volatile and at the same time important part of poetry. It goes and the language becomes dead language, the poetry dead poetry. With it go the accents, the stresses, the delays that are not the property of vowels and syllables but that are shifted at will with the sense. Vowels have length there is no denying. But the accent of sense supersedes all other accent, overrides it and sweeps it away. I will find you the word *come* variously used in various passages, a whole, half, third, fourth, fifth, and sixth note. It is as long as the sense makes it. When men no longer know the intonations on which we string our words they will fall back on what I may call the absolute length of our syllables, which is the length we would give them in passages that meant nothing. . . . I say you can't read a single good sentence with the salt in it unless you have previously heard it spoken. Neither can you with the help of all the characters and diacritical marks pronounce a single word unless you have previously heard it actually pronounced. Words exist in the mouth not books.

From a letter to Sidney Cox in *A Swinger of Birches: A Portrait of Robert Frost*

CONSIDERATIONS FOR CRITICAL THINKING AND WRITING

1. Why does Frost place so much emphasis on hearing poetry spoken?

2. Choose a passage from "Home Burial" (p. 343) or "After Apple-Picking" (p. 346) and read it aloud. How does Frost's description of his emphasis on intonation help explain the effects he achieves in the passage you have selected?

3. Do you think it is true that all poetry must be heard? Do "Words exist in the mouth not books"?

AMY LOWELL (1874–1925)

On Frost's Realistic Technique   1915

I have said that Mr. Frost's work is almost photographic. The qualification was unnecessary, it is photographic. The pictures, the characters, are reproduced directly from life, they are burnt into his mind as though it were a sensitive plate. He gives out what has been put in unchanged by any personal mental process. His imagination is bounded by what he has seen, he is confined within the limits of his experience (or at least what might have been his experience) and bent all one way like the windblown trees of New England hillsides.

From a review of *North of Boston, The New Republic,* February 20, 1915

CONSIDERATIONS FOR CRITICAL THINKING AND WRITING

1. Consider the "photographic" qualities of Frost's poetry by discussing particular passages that strike you as having been "reproduced directly from life."

2. Write an essay that supports or refutes Lowell's assertion that "He gives out what has been put in unchanged by any personal mental process."

Frost on the Figure a Poem Makes   1939

Abstraction is an old story with the philosophers, but it has been like a new toy in the hands of the artists of our day. Why can't we have any one quality of poetry we choose by itself? We can have in thought. Then it will go hard if we can't in practice. Our lives for it.

Granted no one but a humanist much cares how sound a poem is if it is only *a* sound. The sound is the gold in the ore. Then we will have the sound out alone and dispense with the inessential. We do till we make the discovery that the object in writing poetry is to make all poems sound as different as possible from each other, and the resources for that of vowels, consonants, punctuation, syntax, words, sentences, meter are not enough. We need the help of context — meaning — subject matter. That is the greatest help towards variety. All that can be done with words is soon told. So also with meters — particularly in our language where there are virtually but two, strict iambic and loose iambic. The ancients with many were still poor if they depended on meters for all tune. It is painful to watch our sprung-rhythmists straining at the point of omitting one short from a foot for relief from monotony. The possibilities for tune from the dramatic tones of meaning struck across the rigidity of a limited meter are endless. And we are back in poetry as merely one more art of having something to say, sound or unsound. Probably better if sound, because deeper and from wider experience.

Then there is this wildness whereof it is spoken. Granted again that it has an equal claim with sound to being a poem's better half. If it is a wild tune, it is a poem. Our problem then is, as modern abstractionists, to have the wildness pure; to be wild with nothing to be wild about. We bring up as aberrationists, giving way to undirected associations and kicking ourselves from one chance suggestion to another in all directions as of a hot afternoon in the life of a grasshopper. Theme alone can steady us down. Just as the first mystery was how a poem could have a tune in such a straightness as meter, so the second mystery is how a poem can have wildness and at the same time a subject that shall be fulfilled.

It should be of the pleasure of a poem itself to tell how it can. The figure a poem makes. It begins in delight and ends in wisdom. The figure is the same as for love. No one can really hold that the ecstasy should be static and stand still in one place. It begins in delight, it inclines to the impulse, it assumes direction with the first line laid down, it runs a course of lucky events, and ends in a clarification of life — not necessarily a great clarification, such as sects and cults are founded on, but in a momentary stay against confusion. It has denouement. It has an outcome that though unforeseen was predestined from the first image of the original mood — and indeed from the very mood. It is but a trick poem and no poem at all if the best of it was thought of first and saved for the last. It finds its own name as it goes and discovers the best waiting for it in some final phrase at once wise and sad — the happy-sad blend of the drinking song.

No tears in the writer, no tears in the reader. No surprise for the writer, no surprise for the reader. For me the initial delight is in the surprise of remembering something I didn't know I knew. I am in a place, in a situation, as if I had materialized from cloud or risen out of the ground. There is a glad recognition of the long lost and the rest follows. Step by step the wonder of unexpected supply keeps going. The impressions most useful to my purpose seem always those I was unaware of and so made no note of at the time when taken, and the conclusion is come to that like giants we are always hurling experience ahead of us to pave the future with against the day when we may want to strike a line of purpose across it for somewhere. The line will have the more charm for not being mechanically straight. We enjoy the straight crookedness of a good walking stick. Modern instruments of precision are being used to make things crooked as if by eye and hand in the old days.

I tell how there may be a better wildness of logic than of inconsequence. But the logic is backward, in retrospect, after the act. It must be more felt than seen ahead like prophecy. It must be a revelation, or a series of revelations, as much for the poet as for the reader. For it to be that there must have been the greatest freedom of the material to move about in it and to establish relations in it regardless of time and space, previous relation, and everything but affinity. We prate of freedom. We call our schools free because we are not free to stay away from them till we are sixteen years of age. I have given up my democratic prejudices and now willingly set the lower classes free to be completely taken care of by the upper classes. Political freedom is nothing to me. I bestow it right and left. All I would keep for myself is the freedom of my material — the condition of body and mind now and then to summons aptly from the vast chaos of all I have lived through.

Scholars and artists thrown together are often annoyed at the puzzle of where they differ. Both work for knowledge; but I suspect they differ most importantly in the way their knowledge is come by. Scholars get theirs with conscientious thoroughness along projected lines of logic; poets theirs cavalierly and as it happens in and out of books. They stick to nothing deliberately, but let what will stick to them like burrs where they walk in the fields. No acquirement is on assignment, or even self-assignment. Knowledge of the second kind is much more available in the wild free ways of wit and art. A school boy may be defined as one who can tell you what he knows in the order in which he learned it. The artist must value himself as he snatches a thing from some previous order in time and space into a new order with not so much as a ligature clinging to it of the old place where it was organic.

More than once I should have lost my soul to radicalism if it had been the originality it was mistaken for by its young converts. Originality and initiative are what I ask for my country. For myself the originality need be no more than the freshness of a poem run in the way I have described: from delight to wisdom. The figure is the same as for love. Like a piece of ice on a hot stove the poem must ride on its own melting. A poem may be worked over once it is in being, but may not be worried into being. Its most precious quality will remain its having run itself and carried away the poet with it. Read it a hundred times: it will forever keep its freshness as a metal keeps its fragrance. It can never lose its sense of a meaning that once unfolded by surprise as it went.

From *Complete Poems of Robert Frost*

CONSIDERATIONS FOR CRITICAL THINKING AND WRITING

1. Frost places a high premium on sound in his poetry because it "is the gold in the ore." Choose one of Frost's poems in this book and explain the effects of its sounds and how they contribute to its meaning.

2. Discuss Frost's explanation of how his poems are written. In what sense is the process both spontaneous and "predestined"?

3. What do you think Frost means when he says he's given up his "democratic prejudices"? Why is "political freedom" nothing to him?

4. Write an essay that examines in more detail the ways scholars and artists "come by" knowledge.

5. Explain what you think Frost means when he writes that "Like a piece of ice on a hot stove the poem must ride on its own melting."

Frost on the Way to Read a Poem

1951

The way to read a poem in prose or verse is in the light of all the other poems ever written. We may begin anywhere. We *duff* into our first. We read that imperfectly (thoroughness with it would be fatal), but the better to read the second. We read the second the better to read the third, the third the better to read the fourth, the fourth better to read the fifth, the fifth better to read the first again, or the second if it so happens. For poems are not meant to be read in course any more than they are to be made a study of. I once made a resolve never to put any book to any use it wasn't intended for by its author. Improvement will not be a progression but a widening circulation. Our instinct is to settle down like a revolving dog and make ourselves at home among the poems, completely at our ease as to how they should be taken. The same people will be apt to take poems right as know how to take a hint when there is one and not to take a hint when none is intended. Theirs is the ultimate refinement.

From "Poetry and School," Atlantic Monthly, June 1951

CONSIDERATIONS FOR CRITICAL THINKING AND WRITING

1. Given your own experience, how good is Frost's advice about reading in general and his poems in particular?

2. In what sense is a good reader like a "revolving dog" and a person who knows "how to take a hint"?

3. Frost elsewhere in this piece writes, "One of the dangers of college to anyone who wants to stay a human reader (that is to say a humanist) is that he will become a specialist and lose his sensitive fear of landing on the lovely too hard. (With beak and talon.)" Write an essay in response to this concern. Do you agree with Frost's distinction between a "human reader" and a "specialist"?

LIONEL TRILLING (1905–1975)

On Frost as a Terrifying Poet

1959

I have to say that my Frost — *my Frost:* what airs we give ourselves when once we believe that we have come into possession of a poet! — I have to say that my Frost is not the Frost I seem to perceive existing in the minds of so many of his admirers. He is not the Frost who confounds the characteristically modern practice of poetry by his notable democratic simplicity of utterance: on the contrary. He is not the Frost who controverts the bitter modern astonishment at the nature of human life: the opposite is so. He is not the Frost who reassures us by his affirmation of old virtues, simplicities, pieties, and ways of feeling: anything but. I will not go so far as to say that my Frost is not essentially an American poet at all: I believe that he is quite as American as everyone thinks he is, but not in the way that everyone thinks he is.

In the matter of the Americanism of American literature one of my chief guides is that very remarkable critic, D. H. Lawrence. Here are the opening sentences of Lawrence's great outrageous book about classic American literature.

"We like to think of the old fashioned American classics as children's books. Just childishness on our part. The old American art speech contains an alien quality which belongs to the American continent and to nowhere else." And this unique alien quality, Lawrence goes on to say, the world has missed. "It is hard to hear a new voice," he says, "as hard as to listen to an unknown language. . . . Why? Out of fear. The world fears a new experience more than it fears anything. It can pigeonhole any idea. But it can't pigeonhole a real new experience. It can only dodge. The world is a great dodger, and the Americans the greatest. Because they dodge their own very selves." I should like to pick up a few more of Lawrence's sentences, feeling the freer to do so because they have an affinity to Mr. Frost's prose manner and substance: "An artist is usually a damned liar, but his art, if it be art, will tell you the truth of his day. And that is all that matters. Away with eternal truth. Truth lives from day to day. . . . The old American artists were hopeless liars. . . . Never trust the artist. Trust the tale. The proper function of the critic is to save the tale from the artist who created it. . . . Now listen to me, don't listen to him. He'll tell you the lie you expect, which is partly your fault for expecting it."

Now in point of fact Robert Frost is *not* a liar. I would not hesitate to say that he was if I thought he was. But no, he is not. In certain of his poems — I shall mention one or two in a moment — he makes it perfectly plain what he is doing; and if we are not aware of what he is doing in other of his poems, where he is not quite so plain, that is not his fault but our own. It is not from him that the tale needs to be saved.

I conceive that Robert Frost is doing in his poems what Lawrence says the great writers of the classic American tradition did. That enterprise of theirs was of an ultimate radicalism. It consisted, Lawrence says, of two things: a disintegration and sloughing off of the old consciousness, by which Lawrence means the old European consciousness, and the forming of a new consciousness underneath.

So radical a work, I need scarcely say, is not carried out by reassurance, nor by the affirmation of old virtues and pieties. It is carried out by the representation of the terrible actualities of life in a new way. I think of Robert Frost as a terrifying poet. Call him, if it makes things any easier, a tragic poet, but it might be useful every now and then to come out from under the shelter of that literary word. The universe that he conceives is a terrifying universe. Read the poem called "Design" and see if you sleep the better for it. Read "Neither Out Far nor In Deep," which often seems to me the most perfect poem of our time, and see if you are warmed by anything in it except the energy with which emptiness is perceived.

But the *people*, it will be objected, the *people* who inhabit this possibly terrifying universe! About them there is nothing that can terrify; surely the people in Mr. Frost's poems can only reassure us by their integrity and solidity. Perhaps so. But I cannot make the disjunction. It may well be that ultimately they reassure us in some sense, but first they terrify us, or should. We must not be misled about them by the curious tenderness with which they are represented, a tenderness which extends to a recognition of the tenderness which they themselves can often give. But when ever have people been so isolated, so lightning-blasted, so tied down and calcined by life, so reduced, each in his own way, to some last irreducible core of being. Talk of the disintegration and sloughing off of the old consciousness! The people of Robert Frost's poems have done that with a vengeance. Lawrence says that what the Americans refused to accept was "the post-Renaissance humanism of Europe," "the old European spontaneity," "the flowing easy humor of Europe" and that seems to me a good way to describe the people who inhabit Robert Frost's America. In the interests of what great other thing these people have made this rejection we cannot know for certain. But we can guess that it was in the interest of truth, of some truth of the self. This is what they all affirm by their humor (which is so *not* "the easy flowing humor of Europe"), by their irony, by their separateness and isolateness. They affirm *this* of themselves: that they are what they are, that this is their truth, and that if the truth be bare, as the truth often is, it is far better than a lie. For me the process by which they arrive at that truth is always terrifying. The manifest America of Mr. Frost's poems may be pastoral; the actual America is tragic.

From "A Speech on Robert Frost: A Cultural Episode,"
Partisan Review, Summer 1959

CONSIDERATIONS FOR CRITICAL THINKING AND WRITING

1. How does Trilling distinguish *"my Frost"* from other readers'?

2. Read the section on biographical criticism in Chapter 19 (p. 487) and familiarize yourself with Frost's life. How does a knowledge of Frost's biography influence your reading of his poems?

3. Write an essay indicating whether you agree or disagree with Trilling's assessment of Frost "as a Terrifying Poet." Use evidence from the poems to support your view.

HERBERT R. COURSEN JR. (B. 1932)

A Parodic Interpretation of "Stopping by Woods on a Snowy Evening" 1962

Much ink has spilled on many pages in exegesis of this little poem. Actually, critical jottings have only obscured what has lain beneath critical noses all these years. To say that the poem means merely that a man stops one night to observe a snowfall, or that the poem contrasts the mundane desire for creature comfort with the sweep of aesthetic appreciation, or that it renders worldly responsibilities paramount, or that it reveals the speaker's latent death-wish is to miss the point rather badly. Lacking has been that mind simple enough to see what is *really* there. . . .

The "darkest evening of the year" in New England is December 21st, a date near that on which the western world celebrates Christmas. It may be that December 21st *is* the date of the poem, or (and with poets this seems more likely) that this is the closest the poet can come to Christmas without giving it all away. Who has "promises to keep" at or near this date, and who must traverse much territory to fulfill these promises? Yes, and who but St. Nick would know the location of *each* home? Only he would know who had "just settled down for a long winter's nap" (the poem's third line — "He will not see me stopping here" — is clearly a veiled allusion) and would not be out inspecting his acreage this night. The unusual phrase "fill up with snow," in the poem's fourth line, is a transfer of Santa's occupational preoccupation to the countryside, he is mulling the filling of countless stockings hung above countless fire-places by countless careful children. "Harness bells," of course, allude to "Sleigh-ing Song," a popular Christmas tune of the time the poem was written in which the refrain "Jingle Bells! Jingle Bells!" appears; thus again are we put on the Christmas track. The "little horse," like the date, is another attempt at poetic ob-fuscation. Although the "rein-reindeer" ambiguity has been eliminated from the poem's final version,[1] probably because too obvious, we may speculate that the animal is really a reindeer disguised as a horse by the poet's desire for obscurity, a desire which we must concede has been fulfilled up to now.

The animal is clearly concerned, like the faithful Rudolph — another pos-sible allusion (post facto, hence unconscious) — lest his master fail to complete his mission. Seeing no farmhouse in the second quatrain, but pulling a load of presents, no wonder the little beast wonders! It takes him a full two quatrains to rouse his driver to remember all the empty stockings which hang ahead. And Santa does so reluctantly at that, poor soul, as he ponders the myriad farmhouses and villages which spread between him and his own "winter's nap." The modern St. Nick, lonely and overworked, tosses no "Happy Christ-mas to all and to all a good night!" into the precipitation. He merely shrugs his shoulders and resignedly plods away.

From "The Ghost of Christmas Past: 'Stopping by Woods
on a Snowy Evening,'" *College English*, December 1962

[1] The original draft contained the following line: "That bid me give the reins a shake" (Stageberg-Anderson, *Poetry as Experience* [New York, 1952], p. 457). [Coursen's note.]

CONSIDERATIONS FOR CRITICAL THINKING AND WRITING

1. Is this critical spoof at all credible? Does the interpretation hold any water? Is the evidence reasonable? Why or why not? Which of the poem's details are accounted for and which are ignored?

2. Choose a Frost poem and try writing a parodic interpretation of it.

3. What criteria do you use to distinguish between a sensible interpretation of a poem and an absurd one? In an essay compare and contrast your criteria with the criteria suggested by Peter Rabinowitz in his perspective "On Close Readings" (p. 512).

BLANCHE FARLEY (B. 1937)

The Lover Not Taken   1984

Committed to one, she wanted both
And, mulling it over, long she stood,
Alone on the road, loath
To leave, wanting to hide in the undergrowth.
This new guy, smooth as a yellow wood   5

Really turned her on. She liked his hair,
His smile. But the other, Jack, had a claim
On her already and she had to admit, he did wear

Well. In fact, to be perfectly fair,
He understood her. His long, lithe frame   10

Beside hers in the evening tenderly lay.
Still, if this blond guy dropped by someday,
Couldn't way just lead on to way?
No. For if way led on and Jack
Found out, she doubted if he would ever come back.   15

Oh, she turned with a sigh.
Somewhere ages and ages hence,
She might be telling this. "And I —"
She would say, "stood faithfully by."
But by then who would know the difference?   20

With that in mind, she took the fast way home,
The road by the pond, and phoned the blond.

CONSIDERATIONS FOR CRITICAL THINKING AND WRITING

1. Which Frost poem is the object of this parody?
2. Describe how the stylistic elements mirror Frost's poem.
3. Does this parody seem successful to you? Explain what makes a successful parody.
4. Choose a Frost poem — or a portion of one if it is long — and try writing a parody of it.

DEREK WALCOTT (B. 1930)

The Road Taken   *1996*

Robert Frost: the icon of Yankee values, the smell of wood smoke, the sparkle of dew, the reality of farmhouse dung, the jocular honesty of an uncle.

Why is the favorite figure of American patriotism not paternal but avuncular? Because uncles are wiser than fathers. They have humor, they keep their distance, they are bachelors, they can't be fooled by rhetoric. Frost loved playing the uncle, relishing the dry enchantment of his own voice, the homely gravel in the throat, the keep-your-distance pseudo-rusticity that suspected every stranger, meaning every reader. The voice is like its weather. It tells you to stay away until you are invited. Its first lines, in the epigraph to Frost's 1949 *Complete Poems,* are not so much invitations as warnings.

> I'm going out to clean the pasture spring;
> I'll only stop to rake the leaves away
> (And wait to watch the water clear, I may):
> I sha'n't be gone long. — You come too.

From the very epigraph, then, the surly ambiguities slide in. Why "I may"? Not for the rhyme, the desperation of doggerel, but because of this truth: that it would take too long to watch the agitated clouded water settle, that is, for as long as patience allows the poet to proceed to the next line. (Note that the parentheses function as a kind of container, or bank, or vessel, of the churned spring.) The refrain, "You come too." An invitation? An order? And how sincere is either? That is the point of Frost's tone, the authoritative but ambiguous distance of a master ironist.

Frost is an autocratic poet rather than a democratic poet. His invitations are close-lipped, wry, quiet; neither the voice nor the metrical line has the open-armed municipal mural expansion of the other democratic poet, Whitman. The people in Frost's dramas occupy a tight and taciturn locale. They are not part of Whitman's parade of blacksmiths, wheelwrights made communal by work. Besieged and threatened, their virtues are as cautious and measured as the scansion by which they are portrayed.

From Joseph Brodsky, Seamus Heaney, and Derek Walcott,
Homage to Robert Frost

Considerations for Critical Thinking and Writing

1. Why does Walcott characterize Frost as more an uncle than a father? Explain why you agree or disagree.

2. Choose one of Frost's poems in this anthology and use it to demonstrate that he is a "master ironist."

3. Write an essay that fleshes out Walcott's observation that the people in Frost's poems are "Besieged and threatened, their virtues . . . as cautious and measured as the scansion by which they are portrayed."

TWO COMPLEMENTARY CRITICAL READINGS

RICHARD POIRIER (B. 1925)

On Emotional Suffocation in "Home Burial" 1977

Frost's poetry recurrently dramatizes the discovery that the sharing of a "home" can produce imaginations of uncontrollable threat inside or outside. "Home" can become the source of those fears from which it is supposed to protect us; it can become the habitation of that death whose anguish it is supposed to ameliorate. And this brings us to one of Frost's greatest poetic dramatizations of the theme, "Home Burial." [T]he pressure is shared by a husband and wife, but . . . the role of the husband is ambiguous. Though he does his best to comprehend the wife's difficulties, he is only partly able to do so. The very title of the poem means something about the couple as well as about the dead child buried in back of the house. It is as if "home" were a burial plot for all of them.

The opening lines of Frost's dramatic narratives are usually wonderfully deft in suggesting the metaphoric nature of "home," the human opportunities or imperatives which certain details represent for a husband or a wife. . . . [I]n "Home Burial," the couple are trapped inside the house, which is described as a kind of prison, or perhaps more aptly, a mental hospital. Even the wife's glance out the window can suggest to the husband the desperation she feels within the confines of what has always been his family's "home"; it looks directly on the family graveyard which now holds the body of their recently dead child: [lines 1–30 of "Home Burial" are quoted here].

The remarkable achievement here is that the husband and wife have become so nearly inarticulate in their animosities that the feelings have been transferred to a vision of household arrangements and to their own bodily movements. They and the house conspire together to create an aura of suffocation. . . . Frost's special genius is in the placement of words. The first line poses the husband as a kind of spy; the opening of the second line suggests a habituated wariness on her part, but from that point to line 5 we are shifted back to his glimpse of her as she moves obsessively again, as yet unaware of being watched, to the window. Suggestions of alienation, secretiveness, male intimidation ("advancing toward her") within a situation of mutual distrust, a miasmic fear inside as well as outside the house — we are made to sense this before anyone speaks. Initially the fault seems to lie mostly with the husband. But as soon as she catches him watching her, and as soon as he begins to talk, it is the grim mutuality of their dilemma and the shared responsibilities for it that sustain the dramatic intelligence and power of the poem.

From *Robert Frost: The Work of Knowing*

CONSIDERATIONS FOR CRITICAL THINKING AND WRITING

1. According to Poirier, how can the couple's home be regarded as a kind of "mental hospital"? Compare Poirier's view with Kearns's description in the following perspective on the house as a "marital asylum."

2. Explain why you agree or disagree that the husband's behavior is a form of "male intimidation."

3. Write an essay that discusses the "grim mutuality" of the couple's "dilemma."

KATHERINE KEARNS (B. 1949)

On the Symbolic Setting of "Home Burial"   1987

"Home Burial" may be used to clarify Frost's intimate relationships between sex, death, and madness. The physical iconography is familiar — a stairwell, a window, a doorway, and a grave — elements which Frost reiterates throughout his poetry. The marriage in "Home Burial" has been destroyed by the death of a first and only son. The wife is in the process of leaving the house, crossing the threshold from marital asylum into freedom. The house is suffocating her. Her window view of the graveyard is not enough and is, in fact, a maddening reminder that she could not enter the earth with her son. With its transparent barrier, the window is a mockery of a widened vision throughout Frost's poetry and seems to incite escape rather than quelling it; in "Home Burial" the woman can "see" through the window and into the grave in a way her husband cannot, and the fear is driving her down the steps toward the door — "She was starting down — / Looking back over her shoulder at some fear" — even before she sees her husband. He threatens to follow his wife and bring her back by force, as if he is the cause of her leaving, but his gesture will be futile because it is based on the mistaken assumption that she is escaping him. Pathetically, he is merely an obstacle toward which she reacts at first dully and then with angry impatience. He is an inanimate part of the embattled household, her real impetus for movement comes from the grave.

The house itself, reduced symbolically and literally to a womblike passageway between the bedroom and the threshold, is a correlative for the sexual tension generated by the man's insistence on his marital rights. He offers to "give up being a man" by binding himself "to keep hands off," but their marriage is already sexually damaged and empty. The man and woman move in an intricate dance, she coming downward and then retracing a step, he "Mounting until she cower[s] under him," she "shrinking from beneath his arm" to slide downstairs. Randall Jarrell examines the image of the woman sinking into "a modest, compact, feminine bundle" upon her skirts;[1] it might be further observed that this childlike posture is also very much a gesture of sexual denial, body bent, knees drawn up protectively against the breasts, all encompassed by voluminous skirts. The two are in profound imbalance, and Frost makes the wife's speech and movements the poetic equivalent of stumbling and resistance; her lines are frequently eleven syllables, and often are punctuated by spondees whose forceful but awkward slowness embodies the woman's vacillations "from terrified to dull," and from frozen and silent immobility to anger. Her egress from the house will be symbolic verification of her husband's impotence, and if she leaves it and does not come back, the house will rot as the best birch fence will rot. Unfilled, without a woman with child, it will fall into itself, an image that recurs throughout Frost's poetry. Thus the child's grave predicts the dissolution of household, . . . almost a literal "home burial."

From " 'The Place Is the Asylum': Women and Nature in Robert Frost's Poetry," *American Literature*, May 1987

[1] "Robert Frost's 'Home Burial,'" in *The Moment of Poetry*, ed. Don Cameron Allen (Baltimore: Johns Hopkins UP, 1962), p. 104.

CONSIDERATIONS FOR CRITICAL THINKING AND WRITING

1. How does Kearns's discussion of the stairwell, window, doorway, and grave shed light on your reading of "Home Burial"?

2. Discuss whether Kearns sympathizes more with the wife or the husband. Which character do you feel more sympathetic toward? Do you think Frost sides with one or the other? Explain your response.

3. Write an essay in which you agree or disagree with Kearns's assessment that "The wife is in the process of crossing the threshold from marital asylum into freedom."

14

Langston Hughes: Culture and Work

The poetry of Langston Hughes represents a significant chapter in twentieth-century American literature. The poetry included here both chronicles and evokes African American life during the middle decades of the last century. Moreover, it celebrates the culture and heritage of what is called the "Harlem Renaissance" of the 1920s, which has continued to be a vital tradition and presence in American life. As you introduce yourself to Hughes's innovative techniques and the cultural life embedded in his poetry, keep in mind the Questions for Writing about an Author in Depth (p. 325), which can serve as a guide in your explorations.

A BRIEF BIOGRAPHY

Even as a child, Langston Hughes (1902–1967) was wrapped in an important African American legacy. He was raised by his maternal grandmother, who was the widow of Lewis Sheridan Leary, one of the band of men who participated in John Brown's raid on the federal arsenal at Harpers Ferry in 1859. The raid was a desperate attempt to

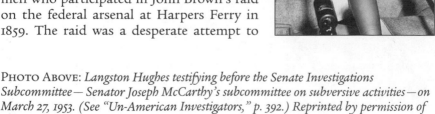

PHOTO ABOVE: *Langston Hughes testifying before the Senate Investigations Subcommittee — Senator Joseph McCarthy's subcommittee on subversive activities — on March 27, 1953. (See "Un-American Investigators," p. 392.) Reprinted by permission of UPI/Corbis-Bettmann.*

ignite an insurrection that would ultimately liberate slaves in the South. It was a failure. Leary was killed, but the shawl he wore, which was returned to his wife bloodstained and riddled with bullet holes, was proudly worn by Hughes's grandmother fifty years after the raid, and she used it to cover her grandson at night when he was a young boy.

Throughout his long career as a professional writer, Hughes remained true to the African American heritage he celebrated in his writings, which were frankly "racial in theme and treatment, derived from the life I know." In an influential essay published in *The Nation,* "The Negro Artist and the Racial Mountain" (1926), he insisted on the need for black artists to draw on their heritage rather than "to run away spiritually from . . . race":

> We younger Negro artists who create now intend to express our individual dark-skinned selves without fear or shame. If white people are pleased, we are glad. If they are not, it doesn't matter. We know we are beautiful. And ugly too. The tom-tom cries and the tom-tom laughs. If colored people are pleased we are glad. If they are not, their displeasure doesn't matter either. We build our temples for tomorrow, strong as we know how, and we stand on top of the mountain, free within ourselves.

That freedom was hard won for Hughes. His father, James Nathaniel Hughes, could not accommodate the racial prejudice and economic frustration that were the result of James's black and white racial ancestry. James abandoned his wife, Carrie Langston Hughes, only one year after their son was born in Joplin, Missouri, and went to find work in Mexico, where he hoped the color of his skin would be less of an issue than in the United States. During the periods when Hughes's mother shuttled from city to city in the Midwest looking for work, she sent her son to live with his grandmother.

Hughes's spotty relationship with his father—a connection he developed in his late teens and maintained only sporadically thereafter—consisted mostly of arguments about his becoming a writer rather than an engineer and businessman as his father wished. Hughes's father could not appreciate or even tolerate his son's ambition to write about the black experience, and Hughes (whose given name was also James but who refused to be identified by it) could not abide his father's contempt for blacks. Consequently, his determination, as he put it in "The Negro Artist," "to express our individual dark-skinned selves without fear or shame" was not only a profound response to African American culture but also an intensely personal commitment that made a relationship with his own father impossible. Though Hughes had been abandoned by his father, he nevertheless felt an early and deep connection to his ancestors, as he reveals in the following poem, written while crossing over the Mississippi River by train as he traveled to visit his father in Mexico, just a month after his high school graduation.

The Negro Speaks of Rivers

1921

I've known rivers:
I've known rivers ancient as the world and older than the
    flow of human blood in human veins.

My soul has grown deep like the rivers.

I bathed in Euphrates when dawns were young.   5
I built my hut near the Congo and it lulled me to sleep.
I looked upon the Nile and raised the pyramids above it.
I heard the singing of the Mississippi when Abe Lincoln
    went down to New Orleans, and I've seen its muddy
    bosom turn all golden in the sunset.   10

I've known rivers:
Ancient, dusky rivers.

My soul has grown deep like the rivers.

    This poem appeared in *The Crisis,* the official publication of the National Association for the Advancement of Colored People, which eventually published more of Hughes's poems than any other magazine or journal. This famous poem's simple and direct free verse makes clear that Africa's "dusky rivers" run concurrently with the poet's soul as he draws spiritual strength as well as individual identity from the collective experience of his ancestors. The themes of racial pride and personal dignity work their way through some forty books that Hughes wrote, edited, or compiled during his forty-five years of writing.

AN INTRODUCTION TO HIS WORK

His works include volumes of poetry, novels, short stories, essays, plays, opera librettos, histories, documentaries, autobiographies, biographies, anthologies, children's books, and translations, as well as radio and television scripts. This impressive body of work makes him an important literary artist and a leading African American voice of the twentieth century. First and foremost, he considered himself a poet. He set out to be a poet who could address himself to the concerns of his people in poems that could be read with no formal training or extensive literary background. He wanted his poetry to be "direct, comprehensible, and the epitome of simplicity."

    His poetry echoes the voices of ordinary African Americans and the rhythms of their music. Hughes drew on an oral tradition of working-class folk poetry that embraced black vernacular language at a time when some middle-class blacks of the 1920s felt that the use of the vernacular was an embarrassing handicap and an impediment to social progress. Hughes's response to such concerns was unequivocal; at his readings, some of which were accompanied by jazz musicians or singers, his innovative voice found

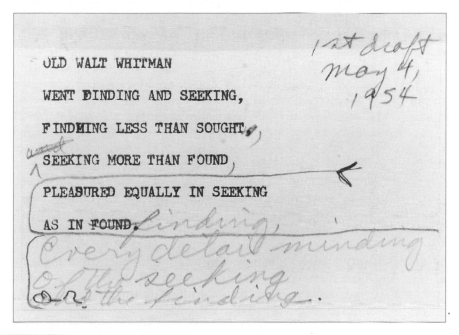

Manuscript page for "Old Walt" (1954) showing an earlier stage of the poem than the one published here (p. 393) and Hughes's revisions.

an appreciative audience. As Hughes very well knew, much of the pleasure associated with his poetry comes from reading it aloud; his many recorded readings give testimony to that pleasure.

The blues can be heard moving through Hughes's poetry as well as in the works of many of his contemporaries associated with the Harlem Renaissance, a movement of African American artists — writers, painters, sculptors, actors, and musicians — who were active in New York City's Harlem of the 1920s. Hughes's introduction to the "laughter and pain, hunger and heartache" of blues music began the year he spent at Columbia University. He dropped out after only two semesters because he preferred the night life and culture of Harlem to academic life. The sweet, sad blues songs captured for Hughes the intense pain and yearning that he saw around him and that he incorporated into poems such as "The Weary Blues" (p. 380). He also reveled in the jazz music of Harlem and discovered in its open forms and improvisations an energy and freedom that significantly influenced the style of his poetry.

Hughes's life, like the jazz music that influenced his work, was characterized by improvisation and openness. After leaving Columbia, he worked a series of odd jobs and then traveled as a merchant seaman to Africa and Europe from 1923 to 1924. He jumped ship to work for several months in the kitchen of a Paris nightclub. As he broadened his experience through travel, he continued to write poetry. After his return to the United States in

1925 he published poems in two black magazines, *The Crisis* and *Opportunity*, and met the critic Carl Van Vechten, who sent his poems to the publisher Alfred A. Knopf. He also — as a busboy in a Washington, D.C., hotel — met the poet Vachel Lindsay, who was instrumental in advancing Hughes's reputation as a poet. In 1926 Hughes published his first volume of poems, *The Weary Blues,* and enrolled in Lincoln University in Pennsylvania, his education funded by a generous patron. His second volume of verse, *Fine Clothes to the Jew,* appeared in 1927, and by the time he graduated from Lincoln in 1929 he was on a book tour of the South giving poetry readings. Hughes ended the decade as more than a promising poet; as Countee Cullen pronounced in a mixed review of *The Weary Blues* (mixed because Cullen believed that African American poets should embrace universal themes rather than racial themes), Hughes had "arrived."

Hughes wrote more prose than poetry during the 1930s, publishing his first novel, *Not Without Laughter* (1930), and a collection of stories, *The Ways of White Folks* (1934). In addition to writing a variety of magazine articles, he also worked on a number of plays and screenplays. Many of his poems from this period reflect proletarian issues. During this decade Hughes's travels took him to all points of the compass — Cuba, Haiti, the Soviet Union, China, Japan, Mexico, France, and Spain — but his general intellectual movement was decidedly toward the left. Hughes was attracted to the American Communist Party, owing to its insistence on equality for all working-class people regardless of race. Like many other Americans of the thirties, he turned his attention away from the exotic twenties and focused on the economic and political issues attending the Great Depression that challenged the freedom and dignity of common humanity.

During World War II, Hughes helped the war effort by writing jingles and catchy verses to sell war bonds and to bolster morale. His protest poems of the thirties were largely replaced by poems that returned to earlier themes centered on the everyday lives of African Americans. In 1942 Hughes described his new collection of poems, *Shakespeare in Harlem,* as "light verse. Afro-American in the blues mood . . . to be read aloud, crooned, shouted, recited, and sung. Some with gestures, some not — as you like." Soon after this collection appeared, the character of Jesse B. Simple emerged from Hughes's 1943 newspaper column for the Chicago *Defender.* Hughes developed this popular urban African American character in five humorous books published over a fifteen-year period: *Simple Speaks His Mind* (1950), *Simple Takes a Wife* (1953), *Simple Stakes a Claim* (1957), *The Best of Simple* (1961), and *Simple's Uncle Sam* (1965). Two more poetry collections appeared in the forties: *Fields of Wonder* (1947) and *One-Way Ticket* (1949).

In the 1950s and 1960s Hughes's poetry again revealed the strong influence of black music, especially in the rhythms of *Montage of a Dream Deferred* (1951) and *Ask Your Mama: 12 Moods for Jazz* (1961). From the poem "Harlem" (p. 391) in *Montage of a Dream Deferred,* Lorraine Hansberry derived the title of her 1959 play *A Raisin in the Sun.* This is only a small measure of Hughes's influence on his fellow African American writers, but it is suggestive nonetheless. For some in the 1950s, however, Hughes and his influence occasioned suspicion. He was watched closely by the FBI and the Special Committee on Un-American Activities of the House of Representatives because of his alleged communist activities in the 1930s. Hughes denied that he was ever a member of the Communist Party, but he and others, including Albert Einstein and Paul Robeson, were characterized as "dupes and fellow travelers" by *Life* magazine in 1949. Hughes was subpoenaed to appear before Senator Joseph McCarthy's subcommittee on subversive activities in 1953 and listed by the FBI as a security risk until 1959. His anger and indignation over these attacks from the right can be seen in his poem "Un-American Investigators" (p. 392), published posthumously in *The Panther and the Lash* (1967).

Despite the tremendous amount that Hughes published, including two autobiographies, *The Big Sea* (1940) and *I Wonder as I Wander* (1956), he remains somewhat elusive. He never married or had friends who can lay claim to truly knowing him beyond what he wanted them to know (even though there are several biographies). And yet Hughes is well known — not for his personal life but for his treatment of the possibilities of African American experiences and identities. Like Walt Whitman, one of his favorite writers, Hughes created a persona that spoke for more than himself. Consider Hughes's voice in the following poem.

I, Too   1925

I, too, sing America.

I am the darker brother.
They send me to eat in the kitchen
When company comes,
But I laugh,   5
And eat well,
And grow strong.

Tomorrow,
I'll be at the table
When company comes.   10
Nobody'll dare
Say to me,
"Eat in the kitchen,"
Then.

Besides,   15
They'll see how beautiful I am
And be ashamed —

I, too, am America.

The "darker brother" who celebrates America is certain of a better future when he will no longer be shunted aside by "company." The poem is characteristic of Hughes's faith in the racial consciousness of African Americans, a consciousness that reflects their integrity and beauty while simultaneously demanding respect and acceptance from others: "Nobody'll dare / Say to me, / 'Eat in the kitchen,' / Then."

Hughes's poetry reveals his hearty appetite for all humanity, his insistence on justice for all, and his faith in the transcendent possibilities of joy and hope that make room for everyone at America's table.

CHRONOLOGY

1902	Born on February 1, in Joplin, Missouri.
1903–14	Lives primarily with his grandmother in Lawrence, Kansas.
1920	Graduates from high school in Cleveland, Ohio.
1921–22	Attends Columbia University for one year but then drops out to work odd jobs and discover Harlem.
1923–24	Travels to Africa and Europe while working on a merchant ship.
1926	Publishes his first collection of poems, *The Weary Blues,* and enters Lincoln University in Pennsylvania.
1929	Graduates from Lincoln University.
1930	Publishes his first novel, *Not Without Laughter.*
1932	Travels to the Soviet Union.
1934	Publishes his first collection of short stories, *The Ways of White Folks.*
1935	His play *Mulatto* is produced on Broadway.
1937	Covers the Spanish Civil War for the Baltimore *Afro-American.*
1938–39	Founds African American theaters in Harlem and Los Angeles.
1940	Publishes his first autobiography, *The Big Sea.*
1943	Creates the character of Simple in columns for the Chicago *Defender.*
1947	Is poet-in-residence at Atlanta University.
1949	Teaches at University of Chicago's Laboratory School.
1950	Publishes his first volume of Simple sketches, *Simple Speaks His Mind.*
1951	Publishes a translation of Federico García Lorca's *Gypsy Ballads.*
1953	Is subpoenaed to appear before Senator Joseph McCarthy's subcommittee on subversive activities in Washington, D.C.
1954–55	Publishes a number of books for young readers including *The First Book of Jazz* and *Famous American Negroes.*
1956	Publishes his second autobiography, *I Wonder as I Wander.*
1958	Publishes *The Langston Hughes Reader.*

1960   Publishes *An African Treasury: Articles, Essays, Stories, Poems by Black Africans.*

1961   Is inducted into the National Institute of Arts and Letters.

1962   Publishes *Fight for Freedom: The Story of the NAACP.*

1963   Publishes *Five Plays by Langston Hughes.*

1964   Publishes *New Negro Poets: U.S.A.*

1965   Defends Martin Luther King Jr. from attacks by militant blacks.

1966   Is appointed by President Johnson to lead the American delegation to the First World Festival of Negro Arts in Dakar.

1967   Dies on May 22 in New York City; his last volume of poems, *The Panther and the Lash,* is published posthumously.

1994   *The Collected Poems of Langston Hughes,* edited by Arnold Rampersad and David Roessel, published posthumously.

Negro   1922

I am a Negro:
   Black as the night is black,
   Black like the depths of my Africa.

I've been a slave:
   Caesar told me to keep his door-steps clean.   5
   I brushed the boots of Washington.

I've been a worker:
   Under my hand the pyramids arose.
   I made mortar for the Woolworth Building.

I've been a singer: 10
   All the way from Africa to Georgia
   I carried my sorrow songs.
   I made ragtime.

I've been a victim:
   The Belgians cut off my hands in the Congo.   15
   They lynch me still in Mississippi.

I am a Negro:
   Black as the night is black,
   Black like the depths of my Africa.

CONSIDERATIONS FOR CRITICAL THINKING AND WRITING

1. FIRST RESPONSE. What sort of identity does the speaker claim for the "Negro"? What is the effect of the litany of roles?

2. What is the effect of the repetition of the first and last stanzas?

3. What kind of history of black people does the speaker describe?

CONNECTIONS TO OTHER SELECTIONS

1. How does Hughes's use of night and blackness in "Negro" help to explain their meaning in the poem "Dream Variations" (p. 380)?

2. Write an essay comparing the treatment of oppression in "Negro" with that in Blake's "The Chimney Sweeper" (p. 166).

Danse Africaine   *1922*

The low beating of the tom-toms,
The slow beating of the tom-toms,
    Low . . . slow
    Slow . . . low —
    Stirs your blood.   5
        Dance!
A night-veiled girl
    Whirls softly into a
    Circle of light.
    Whirls softly . . . slowly,   10
Like a wisp of smoke around the fire —
    And the tom-toms beat,
    And the tom-toms beat,
And the low beating of the tom-toms
    Stirs your blood.   15

CONSIDERATIONS FOR CRITICAL THINKING AND WRITING

1. FIRST RESPONSE. How do the sounds of this poem build its meaning? (What *is* its meaning?)

2. What effect do the repeated rhythms have? You may need to read the poem aloud to answer.

CONNECTION TO ANOTHER SELECTION

1. Try rewriting this poem based on the prescription for poetry in "Formula" (p. 382).

Mother to Son   *1922*

Well, son, I'll tell you:
Life for me ain't been no crystal stair.
It's had tacks in it,
And splinters,
And boards torn up,   5
And places with no carpet on the floor —
Bare.
But all the time

I'se been a-climbin' on,
And reachin' landin's,   10
And turnin' corners,
And sometimes goin' in the dark
Where there ain't been no light.
So boy, don't you turn back.
Don't you set down on the steps   15
'Cause you finds it's kinder hard.
Don't you fall now—
For I'se still goin', honey,
I'se still climbin',
And life for me ain't been no crystal stair.   20

CONSIDERATIONS FOR CRITICAL THINKING AND WRITING

1. FIRST RESPONSE. How is the central metaphor of climbing stairs a particularly appropriate idea for conveying this poem's theme?

2. Try rewriting the dialect of this poem in formal diction. How does this change your response to the poem?

3. What does it imply that the stairs are crystal rather than, say, carpeted?

Jazzonia   1923

Oh, silver tree!
Oh, shining rivers of the soul!

In a Harlem cabaret
Six long-headed jazzers play.
A dancing girl whose eyes are bold   5
Lifts high a dress of silken gold.

Oh, singing tree!
Oh, shining rivers of the soul!

Were Eve's eyes
In the first garden
Just a bit too bold?   10
Was Cleopatra gorgeous
In a gown of gold?

Oh, shining tree!
Oh, silver rivers of the soul!   15

In a whirling cabaret
Six long-headed jazzers play.

CONSIDERATIONS FOR CRITICAL THINKING AND WRITING

1. FIRST RESPONSE. Does "Jazzonia" capture what you imagine a Harlem cabaret to have been like? Discuss the importance of the setting.

2. What is the effect of the variations in lines 1–2, 7–8, and 14–15?

3. What do the allusions to Eve and Cleopatra add to the poem's meaning? Are the questions raised about them answered?

CONNECTION TO ANOTHER SELECTION

1. Compare in an essay the rhythms of "Jazzonia" and "Danse Africaine" (p. 378).

Dream Variations   1924

To fling my arms wide
In some place of the sun,
To whirl and to dance
Till the white day is done.
Then rest at cool evening   5
Beneath a tall tree
While night comes on gently,
    Dark like me —
That is my dream!

To fling my arms wide   10
In the face of the sun,
Dance! Whirl! Whirl!
Till the quick day is done.
Rest at pale evening . . .
A tall, slim tree . . .   15
Night coming tenderly
    Black like me.

CONSIDERATIONS FOR CRITICAL THINKING AND WRITING

1. FIRST RESPONSE. What distinctions are made in the poem between night and day? Which is the dream?
2. Describe the speaker's "Dream." How might the dream be understood metaphorically?
3. How do the rhythms of the lines contribute to the effects of the poem?

CONNECTIONS TO OTHER SELECTIONS

1. In an essay compare and contrast the meanings of darkness and the night in this poem and in Stafford's "Traveling through the Dark" (p. 155).
2. Discuss the significance of the dream in this poem and in "Dream Boogie" (p. 390).

The Weary Blues   1925

Droning a drowsy syncopated tune,
Rocking back and forth to a mellow croon,
    I heard a Negro play.

Down on Lenox Avenue° the other night   *street in Harlem*
By the pale dull pallor of an old gas light   5
      He did a lazy sway. . . .
      He did a lazy sway. . . .
To the tune o' those Weary Blues.
With his ebony hands on each ivory key
He made that poor piano moan with melody.   10
      O Blues!
Swaying to and fro on his rickety stool
He played that sad raggy tune like a musical fool.
      Sweet Blues!
Coming from a black man's soul.   15
      O Blues!
In a deep song voice with a melancholy tone
I heard that Negro sing, that old piano moan –
      "Ain't got nobody in all this world,
            Ain't got nobody but ma self.   20
            I's gwine to quit ma frownin'
            And put ma troubles on the shelf."

Thump, thump, thump, went his foot on the floor.
He played a few chords then he sang some more —
      "I got the Weary Blues   25
            And I can't be satisfied.
            Got the Weary Blues
            And can't be satisfied —
            I ain't happy no mo'
            And I wish that I had died."   30
And far into the night he crooned that tune.
The stars went out and so did the moon.
The singer stopped playing and went to bed
While the Weary Blues echoed through his head.
He slept like a rock or a man that's dead.   35

CONSIDERATIONS FOR CRITICAL THINKING AND WRITING

1. FIRST RESPONSE. Write a one-paragraph description of the blues based on how the poem presents blues music.

2. How does the rhythm of the lines reflect their meaning?

3. How does the speaker's voice compare with the singer's?

4. Comment on the effects of the rhymes.

CONNECTION TO ANOTHER SELECTION

1. Discuss "The Weary Blues" and "Lenox Avenue: Midnight" (p. 383) as vignettes of urban life in America. Do you think that, though written more than seventy years ago, they are still credible descriptions of city life? Explain why or why not.

Cross

My old man's a white old man
And my old mother's black.
If ever I cursed my white old man
I take my curses back.

If ever I cursed my black old mother   5
And wished she were in hell,
I'm sorry for that evil wish
And now I wish her well.

My old man died in a fine big house.
My ma died in a shack.   10
I wonder where I'm gonna die,
Being neither white nor black?

CONSIDERATIONS FOR CRITICAL THINKING AND WRITING

1. FIRST RESPONSE. What do you think has caused the speaker to retract his or her hard feelings about his or her parents?

2. Discuss the possible meaning of the title.

3. Why do you think the speaker regrets having "cursed" his or her father and mother? Is it possible to determine if the speaker is male or female? Why or why not?

4. What informs the speaker's attitude toward life?

CONNECTION TO ANOTHER SELECTION

1. Read the perspective by Francis, "On 'Hard' Poetry" (p. 35), and write an essay explaining why you would characterize "Cross" as "hard" or "soft" poetry.

Formula

Poetry should treat
    Of lofty things
Soaring thoughts
    And birds with wings.

The Muse of Poetry   5
    Should not know
That roses
    In manure grow.

The Muse of Poetry
    Should not care   10
That earthly pain
    Is everywhere.

Poetry!
    Treats of lofty things:
Soaring thoughts   15
    And birds with wings.

Considerations for Critical Thinking and Writing

1. FIRST RESPONSE. What makes this poem a parody? What assumptions about poetry are being made fun of in the poem?
2. How does "Formula" fit the prescriptions offered in the advice to greeting-card freelancers (p. 30)?

Connections to Other Selections

1. Choose any two poems by Hughes in this collection and explain why they do not fit the "Formula."
2. Write an essay that explains how Farries's "Magic of Love" (p. 30) conforms to the ideas about poetry presented in "Formula."

Lenox Avenue: Midnight   *1926*

The rhythm of life
Is a jazz rhythm,
Honey.
The gods are laughing at us.

The broken heart of love,   5
The weary, weary heart of pain,—
    Overtones,
    Undertones,
To the rumble of street cars,
To the swish of rain.   10

Lenox Avenue,
Honey.
Midnight,
And the gods are laughing at us.

Considerations for Critical Thinking and Writing

1. FIRST RESPONSE. What, in your own experience, is the equivalent of Lenox Avenue for the speaker?
2. For so brief a poem there are many sounds in these fourteen lines. What are they? How do they reinforce the poem's meanings?
3. What do you think is the poem's theme?

Connections to Other Selections

1. In an essay compare the theme of this poem with that of Emily Dickinson's "I know that He exists" (p. 327).

2. Compare and contrast the speaker's tone in this poem with the tone of the speaker in Thomas Hardy's "Hap" (p. 607).

Song for a Dark Girl 1927

Way Down South in Dixie
   (Break the heart of me)
They hung my black young lover
   To a cross roads tree.

Way Down South in Dixie 5
   (Bruised body high in air)
I asked the white Lord Jesus
   What was the use of prayer.

Way down South in Dixie
   (Break the heart of me) 10
Love is a naked shadow
   On a gnarled and naked tree.

CONSIDERATIONS FOR CRITICAL THINKING AND WRITING

1. FIRST RESPONSE. What allusion is made in the first line of each stanza? How is that allusion ironic?

2. What *is* "the use of prayer" in this poem? Is the question answered? What, in particular, leads you to your conclusion?

3. Discuss the relationship between love and hatred in the poem.

CONNECTION TO ANOTHER SELECTION

1. Compare the speaker's sensibilities in this poem and in Emily Dickinson's "If I can stop one Heart from breaking" (p. 291). What kinds of cultural assumptions are implicit in each speaker's voice?

Red Silk Stockings 1927

Put on yo' red silk stockings,
Black gal.
Go out an' let de white boys
Look at yo' legs.

Ain't nothin' to do for you, nohow, 5
Round this town, —
You's too pretty.

Put on yo' red silk stockings, gal,
An' tomorrow's chile'll
Be a high yaller. 10

Go out an' let de white boys
Look at yo' legs.

CONSIDERATIONS FOR CRITICAL THINKING AND WRITING

1. FIRST RESPONSE. Who do you think is speaking? Describe his or her tone.
2. Discuss the racial dimensions of this poem.
3. Write a response from the girl—does she put on the red silk stockings? Explain why you imagine her reacting in a certain way.

CONNECTION TO ANOTHER SELECTION

1. Write an essay that compares relations between whites and blacks in this poem and in "Dinner Guest: Me" (p. 394).

Bad Man

1927

I'm a bad, bad man
Cause everbody tells me so.
I'm a bad, bad man.
Everbody tells me so.
I takes ma meanness and ma licker   5
Everwhere I go.

I beats ma wife an'
I beats ma side gal too.
Beats ma wife an'
Beats ma side gal too.   10
Don't know why I do it but
It keeps me from feelin' blue.

I'm so bad I
Don't even want to be good.
So bad, bad I   15
Don't even want to be good.
I'm goin' to de devil an'
I wouldn't go to heaben if I could.

CONSIDERATIONS FOR CRITICAL THINKING AND WRITING

1. FIRST RESPONSE. What, if anything, do you find redeeming about this "bad, bad man"?
2. How would you describe the effects of the repetition in this poem? How does the repetition affect your understanding of the character and the meaning of the poem?

Rent-Party° Shout: For a Lady Dancer 1930

Whip it to a jelly!
Too bad Jim!
Mamie's got ma man —
An' I can't find him.
Shake that thing! O!   5
Shake it slow!
That man I love is
Mean an' low.
Pistol an' razor!
Razor an' gun!   10
If I sees ma man he'd
Better run —
For I'll shoot him in de shoulder,
Else I'll cut him down,
Cause I knows I can find him   15
When he's in de ground —
Then can't no other women
Have him layin' round.
So play it, Mr. Nappy!
Yo' music's fine!   20
I'm gonna kill that
Man o' mine!

Rent-Party: In Harlem during the 1920s, parties were given that charged admission to raise money for rent.

CONSIDERATIONS FOR CRITICAL THINKING AND WRITING

1. FIRST RESPONSE. Describe the type of music you think might be played at this party today.
2. In what sense is this poem a kind of "Shout"?
3. How is the speaker's personality characterized by her use of language?
4. How does Hughes's use of short lines affect your reading of the poem?

Drum 1931

Bear in mind
That death is a drum
Beating forever
Till the last worms come
To answer its call,   5
Till the last stars fall,
Until the last atom
Is no atom at all,
Until time is lost
And there is no air   10

And space itself
Is nothing nowhere,
Death is a drum,
A signal drum,
Calling life   15
To come!
Come!
Come!

CONSIDERATIONS FOR CRITICAL THINKING AND WRITING

1. FIRST RESPONSE. How would you read the poem differently if it had ended at line 14? Why are lines 15–18 so surprising?

2. Comment on the effects of the rhythm and rhymes.

3. Would the poem be better titled "Death" rather than "Drum"? Why or why not?

CONNECTION TO ANOTHER SELECTION

1. Discuss the definition of death in "Drum" and in Emily Dickinson's "If I shouldn't be alive" (p. 291).

Ballad of the Landlord   *1940*

Landlord, landlord,
My roof has sprung a leak.
Don't you 'member I told you about it
Way last week?

Landlord, landlord,   5
These steps is broken down.
When you come up yourself
It's a wonder you don't fall down.

Ten Bucks you say I owe you?
Ten Bucks you say is due?   10
Well, that's Ten Bucks more'n I'll pay you
Till you fix this house up new.

What? You gonna get eviction orders?
You gonna cut off my heat?
You gonna take my furniture and   15
Throw it in the street?

Um-huh! You talking high and mighty.
Talk on — till you get through.
You ain't gonna be able to say a word
If I land my fist on you.   20

Police! Police!
Come and get this man!

He's trying to ruin the government
And overturn the land!

Copper's whistle!   25
Patrol bell!
Arrest.

Precinct Station.
Iron cell.
Headlines in press: 30

MAN THREATENS LANDLORD
TENANT HELD NO BAIL
JUDGE GIVES NEGRO 90 DAYS IN COUNTY JAIL

CONSIDERATIONS FOR CRITICAL THINKING AND WRITING

1. FIRST RESPONSE. The poem incorporates both humor and serious social commentary. Which do you think is dominant? Explain.

2. Why is the literary ballad an especially appropriate form for the content of this poem?

3. How does the speaker's language simultaneously characterize him and the landlord?

CONNECTION TO ANOTHER SELECTION

1. Write an essay on landlords based on this poem and Soyinka's "Telephone Conversation" (p. 19).

Uncle Tom   *1944*

Within—
The beaten pride.
Without—
The grinning face,
The low, obsequious,   5
Double bow,
The sly and servile grace
Of one the white folks
Long ago
Taught well   10
To know his
Place.

CONSIDERATIONS FOR CRITICAL THINKING AND WRITING

1. FIRST RESPONSE. Explain whether or not you think the cultural evidence for this poem draws more on a stereotype or an archetype.

2. Why do you suppose Hughes devotes only one line to what is "Within" Uncle Tom compared to nine lines devoted to what is "Without"?

3. What is, finally, the speaker's attitude toward Uncle Tom?

CONNECTION TO ANOTHER SELECTION

1. Compare the treatment of Uncle Tom here with that of "Frederick Douglass: 1817–1895" (p. 395). How do these two figures represent polar opposites in the culture of African American manhood?

Madam and the Census Man   1949

The census man,
The day he came round,
Wanted my name
To put it down.

I said JOHNSON,   5
ALBERTA K.
But he hated to write
The K that way.

He said, What
Does K stand for?   10
I said K—
And nothing more.

He said, I'm gonna put it
K A-Y.
I said, If you do,   15
You lie.

My mother christened me
ALBERTA K.
You leave my name
Just that way!   20

He said, Mrs.,
(With a snort)
Just a K
Makes your name too short.

I said, I don't   25
Give a damn!
Leave me and my name
Just like I am!

Furthermore, rub out
that MRS., too—   30
I'll have you know
I'm *Madam* to you!

CONSIDERATIONS FOR CRITICAL THINKING AND WRITING

1. FIRST RESPONSE. How are Madam and the census man characterized in the poem? Try writing a physical description of each of them that captures their personalities for you.

2. Although an amusing conflict is presented in the poem, why is it also a serious issue?

CONNECTION TO ANOTHER SELECTION

1. Contrast Madam's demeanor with that of the subject of "Uncle Tom" (p. 388). How might the poems be read as companion pieces?

Dream Boogie   1951

Good morning, daddy!
Ain't you heard
The boogie-woogie rumble
Of a dream deferred?
Listen closely: 5
You'll hear their feet
Beating out and beating out a —

You think
It's a happy beat?

Listen to it closely: 10
Ain't you heard
something underneath
like a —

What did I say?

Sure,   15
I'm happy!
Take it away!

Hey, pop!
Re-bop!
Mop!   20

Y-e-a-h!

CONSIDERATIONS FOR CRITICAL THINKING AND WRITING

1. FIRST RESPONSE. Answer the question, *"You think / It's a happy beat?"*

2. Discuss the poem's musical qualities. Which lines are most musical?

3. Describe the competing tones in the poem. Which do you think is predominant?

CONNECTIONS TO OTHER SELECTIONS

1. In an essay compare and contrast the thematic tensions in this poem and in "Harlem," the next poem.

2. How are the "dreams" different in "Dream Boogie" and "Dream Variations" (p. 380)?

Harlem

1951

What happens to a dream deferred?

> Does it dry up
> like a raisin in the sun?
> Or fester like a sore —
> And then run?   5
> Does it stink like rotten meat?
> Or crust and sugar over —
> like a syrupy sweet?

> Maybe it just sags
> like a heavy load.   10

> *Or does it explode?*

CONSIDERATIONS FOR CRITICAL THINKING AND WRITING

1. How might the question asked in this poem be raised by any individual or group whose dreams and aspirations are thwarted?

2. In some editions of Hughes's poetry the title of this poem is "Dream Deferred." What would the effect of this change be on your reading of the poem's symbolic significance?

3. How might the final line be completed as a simile? What is the effect of the speaker not completing the simile? Why is this an especially useful strategy?

CONNECTION TO ANOTHER SELECTION

1. Write an essay on the themes of "Harlem" and Merrill's "Casual Wear" (p. 159).

Democracy

1949

Democracy will not come
Today, this year
   Nor ever
Through compromise and fear

I have as much right   5
As the other fellow has
   To stand
On my two feet
And own the land.

I tire so of hearing people say,   10
Let things take their course.
Tomorrow is another day.
I do not need my freedom when I'm dead.
I cannot live on tomorrow's bread.

Freedom 15
Is a strong seed
Planted
In a great need.

I live here, too.
I want freedom 20
Just as you.

CONSIDERATIONS FOR CRITICAL THINKING AND WRITING

1. FIRST RESPONSE. Comment on the way in which the lines are arranged. Explain what purpose the arrangement might serve. How?

2. Describe the speaker's tone. Is it too strong, too weak, or just right? Why?

3. "Tomorrow is another day" is a line spoken by Scarlett O'Hara at the end of Margaret Mitchell's novel *Gone with the Wind* (1936) about the Civil War (the line appears in the film version, too). Consider the appropriateness of this allusion.

Un-American Investigators 1953

The committee's fat,
Smug, almost secure
Co-religionists
Shiver with delight
In warm manure 5
As those investigated —
Too brave to name a name —
Have pseudonyms revealed
In Gentile game
    Of who, 10
    Born Jew,
    Is who?
Is not your name Lipshitz?
    Yes.
Did you not change it 15
For subversive purposes?
    No.
For nefarious gain?
    Not so.
Are you sure? 20
The committee shivers
With delight in
Its manure.

CONSIDERATIONS FOR CRITICAL THINKING AND WRITING

1. FIRST RESPONSE. What are the politics of the speaker, do you think? What in the poem suggests this?

2. Research in the library the hearings and investigations of the House of Representatives' Special Committee on Un-American Activities. How is this background information relevant to an understanding of this poem?

3. How does the speaker characterize the investigators?

4. Given the images in the poem, what might serve as a substitute for its ironic title?

CONNECTION TO ANOTHER SELECTION

1. Write an essay that connects the committee described in this poem with the speaker in E. E. Cummings's "next to of course god america i" (p. 146). What do they have in common?

Old Walt   *1954*

Old Walt Whitman
Went finding and seeking,
Finding less than sought
Seeking more than found,
Every detail minding   5
Of the seeking or the finding.

Pleasured equally
In seeking as in finding,
Each detail minding,
Old Walt went seeking   10
And finding.

CONSIDERATIONS FOR CRITICAL THINKING AND WRITING

1. FIRST RESPONSE. Read any poem by Whitman in this book. Do you agree with the speaker's take on Whitman's poetry?

2. Write an explication of "Old Walt." (For a discussion of how to explicate a poem, see the sample explication on p. 279.)

3. What is the effect of the poem's repeated sounds?

4. To what extent do you think lines 3 and 4 could be used to describe Hughes's poetry as well as Whitman's?

CONNECTION TO ANOTHER SELECTION

1. How does Hughes's tribute to Whitman compare with his tribute to Frederick Douglass (p. 395)?

doorknobs   *1961*

The simple silly terror
of a doorknob on a door
that turns to let in life

on two feet standing,
walking, talking,   5
wearing dress or trousers,
maybe drunk or maybe sober,
maybe smiling, laughing, happy,
maybe tangled in the terror
of a yesterday past grandpa   10
when the door from out there opened
into here where I, antenna,
recipient of your coming,
received the talking image
of the simple silly terror   15
of a door that opens
at the turning of a knob
to let in life
walking, talking, standing
wearing dress or trousers,   20
drunk or maybe sober,
smiling, laughing, happy,
or tangled in the terror
of a yesterday past grandpa
not of our own doing.   25

CONSIDERATIONS FOR CRITICAL THINKING AND WRITING

1. FIRST RESPONSE. Why is the doorknob associated with "terror"? Does it have any symbolic value or should it be read literally?

2. How do the style and content of this poem differ from those of the other poems by Hughes in this anthology?

3. The final eight lines repeat much of the first part of the poem. What is repeated and what is changed? What is the effect of this repetition?

CONNECTION TO ANOTHER SELECTION

1. Write an essay comparing the theme of this poem with that of Stevens's "Schizophrenia" (p. 129).

Dinner Guest: Me   *1965*

I know I am
The Negro Problem
Being wined and dined,
Answering the usual questions
That come to white mind   5
Which seeks demurely
To probe in polite way
The why and wherewithal
Of darkness U.S.A. —

Wondering how things got this way   10
In current democratic night,
Murmuring gently
Over *fraises du bois,*
"I'm so ashamed of being white."

The lobster is delicious,   15
The wine divine,
And center of attention
At the damask table, mine.
To be a Problem on
Park Avenue at eight   20
Is not so bad
Solutions to the Problem,
Of course, wait.

CONSIDERATIONS FOR CRITICAL THINKING AND WRITING

1. FIRST RESPONSE. What does the speaker satirize in this description of a dinner party? Do you think this "Problem" exists today?

2. Why is line 9, "Of darkness U.S.A. —," especially resonant?

3. What effects are created by the speaker's diction?

4. Discuss the effects of the rhymes in lines 15–23.

CONNECTION TO ANOTHER SELECTION

1. Write an essay on the speaker's treatment of the diners in this poem and in Kingston's "Restaurant" (p. 193).

Frederick Douglass: 1817–1895°   *1966*

Douglass was someone who,
Had he walked with wary foot
And frightened tread,
From very indecision
Might be dead,   5
Might have lost his soul,
But instead decided to be bold
And capture every street
On which he set his feet,
To route each path   10
Toward freedom's goal,
To make each highway
Choose *his* compass' choice,

1817–1895: Douglass was actually born in 1818; as a slave, he did not know his true birth date.

To all the world cried,
Hear my voice! . . .   15
Oh, to be a beast, a bird,
Anything but a slave! he said.

Who would be free
Themselves must strike
The first blow, he said.   20

    He died in 1895.
    He is not dead.

CONSIDERATIONS FOR CRITICAL THINKING AND WRITING

1. FIRST RESPONSE. This poem was published when the civil rights movement
   was very active in America. Does that information affect your reading of it?
2. What does Hughes celebrate about the life of Douglass, author of *Narrative*
   of the Life of Frederick Douglass, an American Slave, Written by Himself (1845)?

CONNECTION TO ANOTHER SELECTION

1. How is the speaker's attitude toward violence in this poem similar to that
   of the speaker in "Harlem" (p. 391)?

PERSPECTIVES ON HUGHES

Hughes on Racial Shame and Pride   *1926*

[J]azz to me is one of the inherent expressions of Negro life in America: the eternal tom-tom beating in the Negro soul — the tom-tom of revolt against weariness in a white world, a world of subway trains, and work, work, work; the tom-tom of joy and laughter, and pain swallowed in a smile. Yet the Philadelphia clubwoman is ashamed to say that her race created it and she does not like me to write about it. The old subconscious "white is best" runs through her mind. Years of study under white teachers, a lifetime of white books, pictures, and papers, and white manners, morals, and Puritan standards made her dislike the spirituals. And now she turns up her nose at jazz and all its manifestations — likewise almost everything else distinctly racial. She doesn't care for the Winold Reiss° portraits of Negroes because they are "too Negro." She does not want a true picture of herself from anybody. She wants the artist to flatter her, to make the white world believe that all Negroes are as smug and as near white in soul as she wants to be. But, to my mind, it is the duty of the younger Negro artist, if he accepts any duties at all from outsiders, to change through the force of his art that old whispering "I want to be white," hidden in the aspirations of his people, to "Why should I want to be white? I am a Negro — and beautiful!"

> From "The Negro Artist and the Racial Mountain,"
> *The Nation,* June 23, 1926

Winold Reiss (1887–1953): A white painter whose work emphasized the individuality of blacks.

CONSIDERATIONS FOR CRITICAL THINKING AND WRITING

1. Why does the Philadelphia clubwoman refuse to accept jazz as part of her heritage?
2. Compare and contrast Hughes's description of the Philadelphia clubwoman with M. Carl Holman's "Mr. Z" (p. 612). In what sense are these two characters made for each other?

Hughes on Harlem Rent Parties   *1940*

Then [in the late twenties and early thirties] it was that house-rent parties began to flourish — and not always to raise the rent either. But, as often as not, to have a get-together of one's own, where you could do the black-bottom with no stranger behind you trying to do it, too. Non-theatrical, non-intellectual Harlem was an unwilling victim of its own vogue. It didn't like to be stared at by white folks. But perhaps the downtowners never knew this — for the cabaret owners, the entertainers, and the speakeasy proprietors treated them fine — as long as they paid.

The Saturday night rent parties that I attended were often more amusing than any night club, in small apartments where God knows who lived — because the guests seldom did — but where the piano would often be augmented by a guitar, or an odd cornet, or somebody with a pair of drums walking in off the street. And where awful bootleg whiskey and good fried fish or steaming chitterling were sold at very low prices. And the dancing and singing and impromptu entertaining went on until dawn came in at the windows.

These parties, often termed whist parties or dances, were usually announced by brightly colored cards stuck in the grille of apartment house elevators. Some of the cards were highly entertaining in themselves:

> We got yellow girls, we've got black and tan
> Will you have a good time? - YEAH MAN !
>
> ## 𝔄 𝔖𝔬𝔠𝔦𝔞𝔩 𝔚𝔥𝔦𝔰𝔱 𝔓𝔞𝔯𝔱𝔶
> —GIVEN BY—
> **MARY WINSTON**
>
> 147 West 145th Street   Apt. 5
>
> **SATURDAY EVE., MARCH 19th, 1932**
>
> **GOOD MUSIC**   **REFRESHMENTS**

Almost every Saturday night when I was in Harlem I went to a house-rent party. I wrote lots of poems about house-rent parties, and ate thereat many a fried fish and pig's foot — with liquid refreshments on the side. I met ladies' maids and truck drivers, laundry workers and shoe shine boys, seamstresses and porters. I can still hear their laughter in my ears, hear the soft slow music, and feel the floor shaking as the dancers danced.

From "When the Negro Was in Vogue," in *The Big Sea*

CONSIDERATIONS FOR CRITICAL THINKING AND WRITING

1. What, according to Hughes, was the appeal of the rent parties in contrast to the nightclubs?
2. Describe the tone in which Hughes recounts his memory of these parties.

DONALD B. GIBSON (B. 1933)

The Essential Optimism of Hughes and Whitman   1971

As optimists generally do, Langston Hughes and Walt Whitman lacked a sense of evil. This (and all it implies) puts Hughes in a tradition with other American writers. He stands with Whitman, Emerson, Thoreau, and later Sandburg, Lindsay, and Steinbeck, as opposed to Hawthorne, Poe, Melville, James, Faulkner, and Eliot. This is not to say that he did not recognize the existence of evil, but, as Yeats says of Emerson and Whitman, he lacked the "Vision of Evil." He did not see evil as inherent in the character of nature and man, hence he felt that the evil (small *e*) about which he wrote so frequently in his poems (lynchings, segregation, discrimination of all kinds) would be eradicated with the passage of time. Of course the Hughes of *The Panther and the Lash* (1967) is not as easily optimistic as the poet was twenty or twenty-five years before. Hughes could not have written "I, Too," or even "The Negro Speaks of Rivers" in the sixties. But the evidence as I see it has it that though he does not speak so readily about the fulfillment of the American ideal for black people, and though something of the spirit of having waited too long prevails, still the optimism remains. . . .

Montage of a Dream Deferred (1951), included in *Selected Poems,* describes the dream as deferred, not dead nor incapable of fulfillment. There is a certain grimness in the poem, for example in its most famous section, "Harlem," which begins, "What happens to a dream deferred? / Does it dry up / like a raisin in the sun?" but the grimness is by no means unrelieved. There is, as a matter of fact, a lightness of tone throughout the poem which could not exist did the poet see the ravages of racial discrimination as manifestations of Evil. . . . The whole tone of *Montage of a Dream Deferred* is characterized by the well-known "Ballad of the Landlord." There the bitter-sweet quality of Hughes's attitude toward his subject is clear.

From "The Good Black Poet and the Good Grey Poet: The Poetry of Hughes and Whitman," in *Langston Hughes: Black Genius: A Critical Evaluation,* edited by Therman B. O'Daniel

CONSIDERATIONS FOR CRITICAL THINKING AND WRITING

1. What distinction does Gibson make between "Evil" and "evil"?
2. Discuss whether you agree or disagree that Hughes lacked a "Vision of Evil."

3. Why do you think Gibson writes that Hughes couldn't have written "The Negro Speaks of Rivers" (p. 372) or "I, Too" (p. 375) in the 1960s?

4. What aspects of Whitman does Hughes seem to admire in "Old Walt" (p. 393)?

James A. Emanuel (b. 1921)
Hughes's Attitudes toward Religion   1973

Religion, because of its historical importance during and after slavery, is an undeniably useful theme in the work of any major black writer. In a writer whose special province for almost forty-five years was more recent black experience, the theme is doubly vital. Hughes's personal religious orientation is pertinent. Asked about it by the Reverend Dana F. Kennedy of the "Viewpoint" radio and television show (on December 10, 1960), the poet responded:

> I grew up in a not very religious family, but I had a foster aunt who saw that I went to church and Sunday school . . . and I was very much moved, always, by the, shall I say, the rhythms of the Negro church . . . of the spirituals, . . . of those wonderful old-time sermons. . . . There's great beauty in the mysticism of much religious writing, and great help there — but I also think that we live in a world . . . of solid earth and vegetables and a need for jobs and a need for housing. . . .

Two years earlier, the poet had told John Kirkwood of British Columbia's *Vancouver Sun* (December 3, 1958): "I'm not anti-Christian. I'm not against anyone's religion. Religion is one of the innate needs of mankind. What I am against is the misuse of religion. But I won't ridicule it. . . . Whatever part of God is in anybody is not to be played with, and everybody has got a part of God in them."

These typical public protestations by Hughes boil down to his insistence that religion is naturally sacred and beautiful, and that its needed sustenance must not be exploited.

From "Christ in Alabama: Religion in the Poetry of Langston Hughes,"
in *Modern Black Poets,* edited by Donald B. Gibson

Considerations for Critical Thinking and Writing

1. Why do you think Emanuel asserts that, owing to slavery, religion "is an undeniably useful theme in the work of any major Black writer"?

2. How does Hughes's concern for the "solid earth and vegetables and a need for jobs and a need for housing" qualify his attitudes toward religion?

Richard K. Barksdale (b. 1915)
On Censoring "Ballad of the Landlord"   1977

In 1940, ["Ballad of the Landlord"] was a rather innocuous rendering of an imaginary dialogue between a disgruntled tenant and a tight-fisted landlord. In creating a poem about two such social archetypes, the poet was by no means taking any new steps in dramatic poetry. The literature of most capitalist and noncapitalist societies often pits the haves against the have-nots, and not infrequently the haves are wealthy men of property who "lord" it over improvident men who own nothing. So the confrontation between tenant and landlord was in 1940 just another instance of the social malevolence of a system that punished the powerless and excused the powerful. In fact, Hughes's tone of dry irony throughout the poem leads one to suspect that the poet deliberately overstated a situation and that some sardonic humor was supposed to be squeezed out of the incident. . . .

Ironically, this poem, which in 1940 depicted a highly probable incident in American urban life and was certainly not written to incite an economic revolt or promote social unrest, became, by the mid-1960s, a verboten assignment in a literature class in a Boston high school. In his Langston Hughes headnote in *Black Voices* (1967), Abraham Chapman reported that a Boston high school English teacher named Jonathan Kozol was fired for assigning it to his students. By the mid-sixties, Boston and many other American cities had become riot-torn, racial tinderboxes, and their ghettos seethed with tenant anger and discontent. So the poem gathered new meanings reflecting the times, and the word of its tenant persona bespoke the collective anger of thousands of black have-nots.

From *Langston Hughes: The Poet and His Critics*

CONSIDERATIONS FOR CRITICAL THINKING AND WRITING

1. Why do you think the Boston School Committee believed the "Ballad of the Landlord" (p. 387) should be censored?

2. Do you agree with Barksdale that the poem is a "rather innocuous rendering" of economic and social issues? Explain your answer.

3. How did the poem acquire "new meanings reflecting the times" between the 1940s and 1960s? What new meanings might it have for readers today?

DAVID CHINITZ (B. 1962)

The Romanticization of Africa in the 1920s 1997

In Europe black culture was an exotic import; in America it was domestic and increasingly mass-produced. If postwar [World War I] disillusionment judged the majority culture mannered, neurotic, and repressive, Americans had an easily accessible alternative. The need for such an Other produced a discourse in which black Americans figured as barely civilized exiles from the jungle, with — so the clichés ran — tom-toms beating in their blood and dark laughter in their souls. The African American became a model of "natural" human behavior to contrast with the falsified, constrained and impotent modes of the "civilized."

Far from being immune to the lure of this discourse, for the better part of the 1920s Hughes asserted an open pride in the supposed primitive qualities of his race, the atavistic legacy of the African motherland. Unlike most of those who romanticized Africa, Hughes had at least some firsthand experience of the continent; yet he processed what he saw there in images conditioned by European primitivism, rendering "[the land] wild and lovely, the people dark and beautiful, the palm trees tall, the sun bright, and the rivers deep."[1] His short story "Luani of the Jungle," in attempting to glorify aboriginal African vigor as against European anemia, shows how predictable and unextraordinary even Hughes's primitivism could be. To discover in the descendents of idealized Africans the same qualities of innate health, spontaneity, and naturalness requires no great leap; one has only to identify the African American as a displaced primitive, as Hughes does repeatedly in his first book, *The Weary Blues:*

> They drove me out of the forest.
> They took me away from the jungles.
> I lost my trees.
> I lost my silver moons.
>
> Now they've caged me
> In the circus of civilization.[2]

Hughes depicts black aravism vividly and often gracefully, yet in a way that is entirely consistent with the popular iconography of the time. His African Americans retain "among the skyscrapers" the primal fears and instincts of their ancestors "among the palms in Africa."[3] The scion of Africa is still more than half primitive: "All the tom-toms of the jungles beat in my blood, / And all the wild hot moons of the jungles shine in my soul."[4]

From "Rejuvenation through Joy: Langston Hughes, Primitivism and Jazz," in *American Literary History,* Spring 1997

---

[1] *The Big Sea.* 1940. N.Y.: Thunder's Mouth, 1986, 11.
[2] *The Weary Blues.* N.Y.: Knopf, 1926, 100.
[3] *Ibid.* 101.
[4] *Ibid.* 102.

CONSIDERATIONS FOR CRITICAL THINKING AND WRITING

1. According to Chinitz, why did Europeans and Americans romanticize African culture?

2. Consider the poems published by Hughes in the 1920s reprinted in this anthology. Explain whether you find any "primitivism" in these poems.

3. Later in this essay, Chinitz points out that Hughes eventually rejected the "reductive mischaracterizations of black culture, the commercialism, the sham sociology, and the downright silliness of the primitivist fad." Choose and discuss a poem from this anthology that you think reflects Hughes's later views of primitivism.

TWO COMPLEMENTARY CRITICAL READINGS

COUNTEE CULLEN (1903–1946)

On Racial Poetry

1926

Here is a poet with whom to reckon, to experience, and here and there, with that apologetic feeling of presumption that should companion all criticism, to quarrel.

What has always struck me most forcibly in reading Mr. Hughes' poems has been their utter spontaneity and expression of a unique personality. . . . This poet represents a transcendently emancipated spirit among a class of young writers whose particular battle-cry is freedom. With the enthusiasm of a zealot, he pursues his way, scornful, in subject matter, in photography, and rhythmical treatment, of whatever obstructions time and tradition have placed before him. To him it is essential that he be himself. Essential and commendable surely; yet the thought persists that some of these poems would have been better had Mr. Hughes held himself a bit in check. . . .

If I have the least powers of prediction, the first section of this book, *The Weary Blues,* will be most admired, even if less from intrinsic poetical worth than because of its dissociation from the traditionally poetic. Never having been one to think all subjects and forms proper for poetic consideration, I regard these jazz poems as interlopers in the company of the truly beautiful poems in other sections of the book. They move along with the frenzy and electric heat of a Methodist or Baptist revival meeting, and affect me in much the same manner. The revival meeting excites me, cooling and flushing me with alternate chills and fevers of emotion; so do these poems. But when the storm is over, I wonder if the quiet way of communing is not more spiritual for the God-seeking heart; and in the light of reflection I wonder if jazz poems really belong to that dignified company, that select and austere circle of high literary expression which we call poetry. . . .

Taken as a group the selections in this book seem one-sided to me. They tend to hurl this poet into the gaping pit that lies before all Negro writers, in the confines of which they become racial artists instead of artists pure and simple. There is too much emphasis here on strictly Negro themes; and this is probably an added reason for my coldness toward the jazz poems — they seem to set a too definite limit upon an already limited field.

From *Opportunity: A Journal of Negro Life*

CONSIDERATIONS FOR CRITICAL THINKING AND WRITING

1. In Cullen's review of *The Weary Blues,* what is his "quarrel" (para. 1) with Hughes?

2. Given the tenor of Hughes's comments on racial pride in the excerpt from "The Negro Artist and the Racial Mountain" (p. 396), what do you think his response to Cullen would be?

3. Explain why you agree or disagree with Cullen's view that Hughes's poems are "one-sided" (para. 4).

4. Do you think his argument is dated, or is it relevant to today's social climate?

ONWUCHEKWA JEMIE (B. 1940)

On Universal Poetry   1976

Hughes entertained no doubts as to the sufficiency and greatness of the molds provided by black music, nor of black life as subject matter. On the question of whether such black matter and manner could attain "universality," Hughes in his Spingarn Speech issued a definitive answer:

There is so much richness in Negro humor, so much beauty in black dreams, so much dignity in our struggle, and so much universality in our problems, in us—in each living human being of color—that I do not understand the tendency today that some American Negro artists have of seeking to run away from themselves, of running away from us, of being afraid to sing our own songs, paint our own pictures, write about ourselves—when it is our music that has given America its greatest music, our humor that has enriched its entertainment media, our rhythm that has guided its dancing feet from plantation days to the Charleston, the Lindy Hop, and currently the Madison. . . .

Could you possibly be afraid that the rest of the world will not accept it? Our spirituals are sung and loved in the great concert halls of the whole world. Our blues are played from Topeka to Tokyo. Harlem's jive talk delights Hong Kong. Those of our writers who have concerned themselves with our very special problems are translated and read around the world. The local, the regional can—and does—become universal. Sean O'Casey's Irishmen are an example. So I would say to young Negro writers, do not be afraid of yourselves. You are the world.[1]

Hughes's confidence in blackness is a major part of his legacy, for the questions he had to answer have had to be answered over again by subsequent generations of black artists. Black culture is still embattled; and Hughes provides a model for answering the questions and making the choices. Whether they say so or not, those who, like Cullen, . . . plead the need to be "universal" as an excuse for avoiding racial material, or for treating such material from perspectives rooted in alien sensibilities, invariably equate "white" or "Western" with "universal," and "black" or "non-Western" with its opposite, forgetting that the truly universal—that is, the foundation elements of human experience, the circumstances attending birth, growth, decline, and death, the emotions of joy and grief, love and hate, fear and guilt, anger and pain—are common to all humanity. The multiplicity of nations and cultures in the world makes it inevitable that the details and particulars of human experience will vary according to time, place, and circumstance, and it follows that the majority of writers will dramatize and interpret human life according to the usages of their particular nation and epoch. Indeed, the question whether a writer's work is universal or not rarely arises when that writer is European or white American. It arises so frequently in discussions of black writers for no other reason than that the long-standing myth of white superiority and black inferiority has led so many to believe that in literature, and in other areas of life as well, the black particular of universal human experience is less appropriate than the white particular.

From *Langston Hughes: An Introduction to Poetry*

[1] See Hughes, Letter to the Editor, *The Crisis,* 35:9 (September 1928), 302.

CONSIDERATIONS FOR CRITICAL THINKING AND WRITING

1. How does Jemie go beyond Hughes's own argument to make a case for the universality of poetry about black experience?

2. How might Jemie's argument be extended to other minority groups or to women?

3. Do you think that Jemie's or Cullen's argument is more persuasive? Explain.

15

Critical Case Study: T. S. Eliot's "The Love Song of J. Alfred Prufrock"

This chapter provides several critical approaches to a challenging but highly rewarding poem by T. S. Eliot. After studying this poem, you're likely to find yourself quoting bits of its striking imagery. At the very least, you'll recognize the lines when you hear other people fold them into their own conversations. There have been numerous critical approaches to this poem because it raises so many issues relating to matters such as history and biography as well as imagery, symbolism, irony, and myth. The following critical excerpts offer a small and partial sample of the possible formalist, biographical, historical, mythological, psychological, sociological, and other perspectives that have attempted to shed light on the poem (see Chapter 19, "Critical Strategies for Reading," for a discussion of a variety of critical methods). They should help you to enjoy the poem more by raising questions, providing insights, and inviting you further into the text.

T. S. ELIOT (1888–1965)

Born into a prominent New England family that had moved to St. Louis, Missouri, Thomas Stearns Eliot was a major in English literature between the two world wars. He studied literature and philosophy at Harvard and on the Continent, subsequently choosing to live in England for most of his life and becoming a citizen of that country in 1927. His allusive and challenging poetry had a powerful influence on other writers, particularly his treatment of postwar life in *The Waste Land* (1922) and his exploration of religious questions in *The Four Quartets* (1943). In addition, he wrote plays, including *Mur-*

T. S. Eliot (November 10, 1959), in a pose that suggests the Prufrock persona, holding a book containing some of his earlier work during a press conference at the University of Chicago. Reprinted by permission of Corbis-Bettmann.

der in the Cathedral (1935) and The Cocktail Party (1950). He was awarded the Nobel Prize for literature in 1948. In "The Love Song of J. Alfred Prufrock," Eliot presents a comic but serious figure who expresses through a series of fragmented images the futility, boredom, and meaninglessness associated with much of modern life.

The Love Song of J. Alfred Prufrock   1917

*S'io credesse che mia risposta fosse
A persona che mai tornasse al mondo,
Questa fiamma staria senza più scosse.
Ma perciocchè giammai di questo fondo*

Non tornò vivo alcun, s'i'odo il vero,
Senza tema d'infamia ti rispondo. °

 Let us go then, you and I,
When the evening is spread out against the sky
Like a patient etherized upon a table;
Let us go, through certain half-deserted streets,
The muttering retreats   5
Of restless nights in one-night cheap hotels
And sawdust restaurants with oyster-shells:
Streets that follow like a tedious argument
Of insidious intent
To lead you to an overwhelming question . . .   10

Oh, do not ask, "What is it?"
Let us go and make our visit.

In the room the women come and go
Talking of Michelangelo.

 The yellow fog that rubs its back upon the window panes, 15
The yellow smoke that rubs its muzzle on the window panes
Licked its tongue into the corners of the evening,
Lingered upon the pools that stand in drains,
Let fall upon its back the soot that falls from chimneys,
Slipped by the terrace, made a sudden leap,   20
And seeing that it was a soft October night,
Curled once about the house, and fell asleep.

 And indeed there will be time°
For the yellow smoke that slides along the street,
Rubbing its back upon the window panes;   25
There will be time, there will be time
To prepare a face to meet the faces that you meet;
There will be time to murder and create,
And time for all the works and days° of hands
That lift and drop a question on your plate: 30
Time for you and time for me,
And time yet for a hundred indecisions,
And for a hundred visions and revisions,
Before the taking of a toast and tea.

Epigraph: *S'io credesse . . . rispondo:* Dante's *Inferno*, XXVII, 58–63. In the Eighth Chasm of the Inferno, Dante and Virgil meet Guido da Montefeltro, one of the False Counselors, who is punished by being enveloped in an eternal flame. When Dante asks Guido to tell his life story, the spirit replies: "If I thought that my answer were to one who might ever return to the world, this flame would shake no more; but since from this depth none ever returned alive, if what I hear is true, I answer you without fear of infamy."

23 *there will be time:* An allusion to Ecclesiastes 3:1–8: "To everything there is a season, and a time to every purpose under heaven. . . ."

29 *works and days:* Hesiod's eighth-century B.C. poem *Works and Days* gave practical advice on how to conduct one's life in accordance with the seasons.

In the room the women come and go   35
Talking of Michelangelo.

    And indeed there will be time
To wonder, "Do I dare?" and, "Do I dare?" —
Time to turn back and descend the stair,
With a bald spot in the middle of my hair —   40
(They will say: "How his hair is growing thin!")
My morning coat, my collar mounting firmly to the chin,
My necktie rich and modest, but asserted by a simple pin —
(They will say: "But how his arms and legs are thin!")
Do I dare   45
Disturb the universe?
In a minute there is time
For decisions and revisions which a minute will reverse.

    For I have known them all already, known them all:
Have known the evenings, mornings, afternoons,   50
I have measured out my life with coffee spoons;
I know the voices dying with a dying fall
Beneath the music from a farther room.
    So how should I presume?

    And I have known the eyes already, known them all —   55
The eyes that fix you in a formulated phrase.
And when I am formulated, sprawling on a pin,
When I am pinned and wriggling on the wall,
Then how should I begin
To spit out all the butt-ends of my days and ways?   60
    And how should I presume?

    And I have known the arms already, known them all —
Arms that are braceleted and white and bare
(But in the lamplight, downed with light brown hair!)
    Is it perfume from a dress   65
    That makes me so digress?
Arms that lie along a table, or wrap about a shawl.
    And should I then presume?
    And how should I begin?

    Shall I say, I have gone at dusk through narrow streets,   70
And watched the smoke that rises from the pipes
Of lonely men in shirtsleeves, leaning out of windows? . . .

I should have been a pair of ragged claws
Scuttling across the floors of silent seas.

    And the afternoon, the evening, sleeps so peacefully!   75
Smoothed by long fingers,
Asleep . . . tired . . . or it malingers,
Stretched on the floor, here beside you and me.
Should I, after tea and cakes and ices,
Have the strength to force the moment to its crisis?   80

But though I have wept and fasted, wept and prayed,
Though I have seen my head (grown slightly bald) brought in upon a platter,°
I am no prophet — and here's no great matter;
I have seen the moment of my greatness flicker,
And I have seen the eternal Footman hold my coat, and snicker,   85
    And in short, I was afraid.

    And would it have been worth it, after all,
After the cups, the marmalade, the tea,
Among the porcelain, among some talk of you and me,
Would it have been worth while   90
To have bitten off the matter with a smile,
To have squeezed the universe into a ball°
To roll it toward some overwhelming question,
To say: "I am Lazarus,° come from the dead,
Come back to tell you all, I shall tell you all" —   95
If one, settling a pillow by her head,
    Should say: "That is not what I meant at all;
        That is not it, at all."

    And would it have been worth it, after all,
Would it have been worth while,   100
After the sunsets and the dooryards and the sprinkled streets,
After the novels, after the teacups, after the skirts that trail along the floor —
And this, and so much more? —
It is impossible to say just what I mean!
But as if a magic lantern threw the nerves in patterns on a screen: 105
Would it have been worth while
If one, settling a pillow or throwing off a shawl,
And turning toward the window, should say:
    "That is not it at all,
    That is not what I meant, at all."   110

No! I am not Prince Hamlet, nor was meant to be;
Am an attendant lord,° one that will do
To swell a progress,° start a scene or two   *state procession*
Advise the prince: withal, an easy tool,
Deferential, glad to be of use,   115
Politic, cautious, and meticulous;
Full of high sentence, but a bit obtuse;
At times, indeed, almost ridiculous —
Almost, at times, the Fool.

82 *head . . . upon a platter:* At Salome's request, Herod had John the Baptist decapitated and had the severed head delivered to her on a platter (see Matt. 14:1–12 and Mark 6:17–29).

92 *squeezed the universe into a ball:* See Marvell's "To His Coy Mistress" (p. 65), lines 41–42: "Let us roll all our strength and all / Our sweetness up into one ball."

94 *Lazarus:* The brother of Mary and Martha who was raised from the dead by Jesus (John 11:1–44). In Luke 16:19–31, a rich man asks that another Lazarus return from the dead to warn the living about their treatment of the poor.

112 *attendant lord:* Like Polonius in Shakespeare's *Hamlet.*

I grow old . . . I grow old . . .   120
I shall wear the bottoms of my trowsers rolled.

   Shall I part my hair behind? Do I dare to eat a peach?
I shall wear white flannel trowsers, and walk upon the beach.
I have heard the mermaids singing, each to each.

I do not think that they will sing to me.   125

I have seen them riding seaward on the waves,
Combing the white hair of the waves blown back
When the wind blows the water white and black.

We have lingered in the chambers of the sea
By seagirls wreathed with seaweed red and brown,   130
Till human voices wake us, and we drown.

Considerations for Critical Thinking and Writing

1. What does J. Alfred Prufrock's name connote? How would you characterize
   him?
2. What do you think is the purpose of the epigraph from Dante's *Inferno*?
3. What is it that Prufrock wants to do? How does he behave? What does he
   think of himself? Which parts of the poem answer these questions?
4. Who is the "you" of line 1 and the "we" in the final lines?
5. Discuss the imagery in the poem. How does the imagery reveal Prufrock's
   character? Which images seem especially striking to you?

Connections to Other Selections

1. Write an essay comparing Prufrock's sense of himself as an individual with
   that of Walt Whitman's speaker in "One's-Self I Sing" (p. 642).
2. Discuss in an essay the tone of "The Love Song of J. Alfred Prufrock" and
   Frost's "Acquainted with the Night" (p. 139).

PERSPECTIVES ON ELIOT

Elisabeth Schneider (1897–1984)

Schneider uses a biographical approach to the poem to suggest that part
of what went into the characterization of Prufrock were some of Eliot's
own sensibilities.

Hints of Eliot in Prufrock   *1952*

Perhaps never again did Eliot find an epigraph quite so happily suited to his
use as the passage from the *Inferno* which sets the underlying serious tone for
Prufrock and conveys more than one level of its meaning: "S'io credesse che mia
risposta . . . ," lines in which Guido da Montefeltro consents to tell his story to

Dante only because he believes that none ever returns to the world of the living from his depth. One in Hell can bear to expose his shame only to another of the damned; Prufrock speaks to, will be understood only by, other Prufrocks (the "you and I" of the opening, perhaps), and, I imagine the epigraph also hints, Eliot himself is speaking to those who know this kind of hell. The poem, I need hardly say, is not in a literal sense autobiographical: for one thing, though it is clear that Prufrock will never marry, the poem was published in the year of Eliot's own first marriage. Nevertheless, friends who knew the young Eliot almost all describe him, retrospectively but convincingly, in Prufrockian terms; and Eliot himself once said of dramatic monologue in general that what we normally hear in it "is the voice of the poet, who has put on the costume and make-up either of some historical character, or of one out of fiction." . . . I suppose it to be one of the many indirect clues to his own poetry planted with evident deliberation throughout his prose. "What every poet starts from," he also once said, "is his own emotions," and, writing of Dante, he asserted that the *Vita nuova* "could only have been written around a personal experience," a statement that, under the circumstances, must be equally applicable to Prufrock; Prufrock was Eliot, though Eliot was much more than Prufrock. We miss the whole tone of the poem, however, if we read it as social satire only. Eliot was not either the dedicated apostle in theory, or the great exemplar in practice, of complete "depersonalization" in poetry that one influential early essay of his for a time led readers to suppose.

From "Prufrock and After: The Theme of Change," *PMLA*, October 1952

CONSIDERATIONS FOR CRITICAL THINKING AND WRITING

1. Though Schneider concedes that the poem is not literally autobiographical, she does assert that "Prufrock was Eliot." How does she argue this point? Explain why you find her argument convincing or unconvincing.

2. Find information in the library about Eliot's early career when he was writing this poem. To what extent does the poem reveal his circumstances and concerns at that point in his life?

BARBARA EVERETT

Everett's discussion of tone is used to make a distinction between Eliot and his characterization of Prufrock.

The Problem of Tone in Prufrock   1974

Eliot's poetry presents a peculiar problem as far as tone is concerned. *Tone* really means the way the attitude of a speaker is manifested by the inflections of his speaking voice. Many critics have already recognized that for a mixture of reasons it is difficult, sometimes almost impossible, to ascertain Eliot's tone in this way. It is not that the poetry lacks "voice," for in fact Eliot has an extraordinarily recognizable poetic voice, often imitated and justifying his own comment in the . . . *Paris Review* that "in a poem you're writing for your own voice, which is very important. You're thinking in terms of your own voice." It is this authoritative, idiosyncratic, and exact voice that holds our complete attention in poem after poem, however uninterested we are in what opinions it may seem or happen to be expressing. But Eliot too seems uninterested in what opinions it may happen to be expressing, for he invariably dissociates himself from his poems before they are even finished — before they are hardly begun — by balancing a derisory name or title against an "I," by reminding us that there is always going to be a moment at which detachment will take place or has taken place, a retrospective angle from which, far in the future, critical judgment alters the scene, and the speaking voice of the past has fallen silent. "I have known them all already, known them all." Thus whatever started to take place in the beginning of a poem by Eliot cannot truly be said to be Eliot's opinion because at some extremely early stage he began that process of dissociation to be loosely called "dramatization," a process reflected in the peculiar distances of the tone, as though everything spoken was in inverted commas.

From "In Search of Prufrock," *Critical Quarterly*, Summer 1974

CONSIDERATIONS FOR CRITICAL THINKING AND WRITING

1. According to Everett, why is it difficult to describe Eliot's tone in his poetry?
2. How does Eliot's tone make it difficult to make an autobiographical connection between Prufrock and Eliot?
3. How does Everett's reading of the relationship between Prufrock and Eliot differ from Schneider's in the preceding perspective?

MICHAEL L. BAUMANN (B. 1926)

Baumann takes a close look at the poem's images in his formalist efforts to make a point about Prufrock's character.

The "Overwhelming Question" for Prufrock   1981

Most critics . . . have seen the overwhelming question related to sex. . . . They have implicitly assumed — and given their readers to understand — that Prufrock's is the male's basic question: Can I?

Delmore Schwartz once said that "J. Alfred Prufrock is unable to make love to women of his own class and kind because of shyness, self-consciousness, and fear of rejection."[1] This is undoubtedly true, but Prufrock's inability to *feel* love has something to do with his inability to *make* love, too. . . . A simple desire, lust, is more than honest Prufrock can cope with as he mounts the stairs.

But Prufrock is coping with another, less simple desire as well. . . . If birth, copulation, and death is all there is, then, once we are born, once we have

[1] "T. S. Eliot as the International Hero," *Partisan Review*, 12 (1945), 202; rpt in *T. S. Eliot: A Selected Critique*, ed. Leonard Unger (New York: Rinehart & Company, Inc., 1948), 46.

copulated, only death remains (for the male of the species, at least). Prufrock, having "known them all already, known them all," having "known the evenings, mornings, afternoons," having "measured out" his life "with coffee spoons," desires death. The "overwhelming question" that assails him would no longer be the romantic rhetorical "Is life worth living?" (to which the answer is obviously No), but the more immediate shocker: "Should one commit suicide?" which is to say: "Should I?" . . .

. . . The poem makes clear that Prufrock wants more than the "entire destruction of consciousness as we understand it," a notion Prufrock expresses by wishing he were "a pair of ragged claws, / Scuttling across the floors of silent seas." Prufrock wants death itself, physical death, and the poem, I believe, is explicit about this desire.

Not only does Prufrock seem to be tired of time — "time yet for a hundred indecisions" — a tiredness that goes far beyond the acedia Prufrock is generally credited with feeling, if only because "there will be time to murder and create," time, in other words (in one sense at least) to copulate, but Prufrock is also tired of his own endless vanities, from feeling he must "prepare a face to meet the faces that you meet," to having to summon up those ironies with which to contemplate his own thin arms and legs, and, indeed, to asking if, in the rather tedious enterprise of preparing for copulation, the moment is worth "forcing to its crisis." No wonder Prufrock compares himself to John the Baptist and, in conjuring up this first concrete image of his own death, sees his head brought in upon a platter. That would be the easy way out. He had, after all, "wept and fasted, wept and prayed," but he realizes he is no prophet — and no Salome will burst into passion, will ignite for him. When the eternal Footman, Death, who holds his coat, snickers, he does so because Prufrock has let "the moment" of his "greatness" flicker, because Prufrock was unable to comply with the one imperative greatness would have thrust upon him: to kill himself. Prufrock explains: "I was afraid." Yet the achievement of his vision at the end of the poem, his being able to linger "in the chambers of the sea / By seagirls wreathed with seaweed red and brown," is an act of the imagination that only physical death can complete, unless Prufrock wants human voices to wake him, and drown him. His romantic vision demands the voluntary act: suicide. It is to be expected that he will fail in this too, as he has failed in everything else.

From "Let Us Ask 'What Is It,'" *Arizona Quarterly*, Spring 1981

CONSIDERATIONS FOR CRITICAL THINKING AND WRITING

1. Describe the evidence used by Baumann to argue that Prufrock contemplates suicide.

2. Explain in an essay why you do or do not find Baumann's argument convincing.

3. Later in his essay Baumann connects Prufrock's insistence that "No, I am not Prince Hamlet" with Hamlet's "To be or not to be" speech. How do you think this reference might be used to support Baumann's argument?

FREDERIK L. RUSCH (B. 1938)

Rusch makes use of the insights developed by Erich Fromm, a social psychologist who believed "psychic forces [are] a process of constant interaction between man's needs and the social and historical reality in which he participates."

Society and Character in "The Love Song of J. Alfred Prufrock"   1984

In looking at fiction, drama, and poetry from the Frommian point of view, the critic understands literature to be social portrayal as well as character portrayal or personal statement. Society and character are inextricably joined. The Frommian approach opens up the study of literary work, giving a social context to its characters, which suggests why those characters behave as they do. The Frommian approach recognizes human beings for what they are — basically gregarious individuals who are interdependent upon each other, in need of each other, and thus, to a certain degree, products of their social environments, although those environments may be inimical to their mental well-being. That is, as stated earlier, the individual's needs and drives have a social component and are not purely biological. The Frommian approach to literature assumes that a writer is — at least by implication — analyzing society and its setting as well as character. . . .

In T. S. Eliot's "The Love Song of J. Alfred Prufrock," Prufrock is talking to himself, expressing a fantasy or daydream. In his monologue, Prufrock, as noted by Grover Smith, "is addressing, as if looking into a mirror, his whole public personality."[1] Throughout the poem, Prufrock is extremely self-conscious, believing that the people in his imaginary drawing room will examine him as a specimen insect, "sprawling on a pin, / . . . pinned and wriggling on the wall. . . ." Of course, self-consciousness — being conscious of one's self — is not necessarily neurotic. Indeed, it is part of being a human being. It is only when self-consciousness, which has always led man to feel a separation from nature, becomes obsessive that we have a problem. Prufrock is certainly obsessed with his self-consciousness, convinced that everyone notices his balding head, his clothes (his prudent frocks), his thin arms and legs.

On one level, however, Prufrock is merely expressing the pain that all human beings must feel. Although his problem is extreme, he is quite representative of the human race:

> Self-awareness, reason, and imagination have disrupted the "harmony" that characterizes animal existence. Their emergence has made man into an anomaly, the freak of the universe. He is part of nature, subject to her physical laws and unable to change them, yet he transcends nature. He is set apart while being a part; he is homeless, yet chained to the home he shares with all creatures. . . . Being aware of himself, he realizes his powerlessness and the limitations of his existence. He is never free from the dichotomy of his existence: he cannot rid himself of his mind, even if he would want to; he cannot rid himself of his body as long as he is alive — and his body makes him want to be alive.[2]

---

[1] Grover Smith, *T. S. Eliot's Poetry and Plays: A Study in Sources and Meaning* (Chicago: U of Chicago P, 1962), 16.
[2] Erich Fromm, *The Anatomy of Human Destructiveness* (New York: Holt, Rinehart & Winston, 1973), 225.

This is the predicament of the human being. His self-awareness has made him feel separate from nature. This causes pain and sorrow. What, then, is the solution to the predicament? Fromm believed that mankind filled the void of alienation from nature with the creation of a culture, a society: "Man's existential, and hence unavoidable disequilibrium can be relatively stable when he has found, with the support of his culture, a more or less adequate way of coping with his existential problems" (*Destructiveness* 225). But, unfortunately for Prufrock, his culture and society do not allow him to overcome his existential predicament. The fact is, he is bored by his modern, urban society.

In image after image, Prufrock's mind projects boredom:

> For I have known them all already, known them all:
> Have known the evenings, mornings, afternoons,
> I have measured out my life with coffee spoons. . . .
> . . . .
>
> And I have known the eyes already, known them all —
> . . . .
>
> Then how should I begin
> To spit out all the butt-ends of my days and ways?
> . . . .
>
> And I have known the arms already, known them all — . . . .

Prufrock is completely unstimulated by his social environment, to the point of near death. The evening in which he proposes to himself to make a social visit is "etherized upon a table." The fog, as a cat, falls asleep; it is "tired . . . or it malingers, / Stretched on the floor. . . ."

Prufrock, living in a city of "half-deserted streets, / . . . one-night cheap hotels/ And sawdust restaurants with oyster-shells," gets no comfort, no nurturing from his environment. He is, in the words of Erich Fromm, a "modern mass man . . . isolated and lonely" (*Destructiveness* 107). He lives in a destructive environment. Instead of providing communion with fellow human beings, it alienates him through boredom. Such boredom leads to "a state of chronic depression" that can cause the pathology of "insufficient inner productivity" in the individual (*Destructiveness* 243). Such a lack of productivity is voiced by Prufrock when he confesses that he is neither Hamlet nor John the Baptist.

An interesting tension in "The Love Song of J. Alfred Prufrock" is caused by the reader's knowledge that Prufrock understands his own predicament quite well. Although he calls himself a fool, he has wisdom about himself and his predicament. This, however, only reinforces his depression and frustration. In his daydream, he is able to reveal truths about himself that, while they lead to self-understanding, apparently cannot alleviate his problems in his waking life. The poem suggests no positive movement out of the predicament. Prufrock is like a patient cited by Fromm, who under hypnosis envisioned "a black barren place with many masks," and when asked what the vision meant said "that everything was dull, dull, dull; that the masks represent the different roles he takes to fool people into thinking he is feeling well" (*Destructiveness* 246). Likewise, Prufrock understands that "There will be time, there will be time / To prepare a face to meet the faces that you meet. . . ." But despite his understanding of the nature of his existence, he cannot attain a more productive life.

It was Fromm's belief that with boredom "the decisive conditions are to be found in the overall environmental situation. . . . It is highly probable that even cases of severe depression-boredom would be less frequent and less intense . . . in a society where a mood of hope and love of life predominated. But in recent decades the opposite is increasingly the case, and thus a fertile soil for the development of individual depressive states is provided" (*Destructiveness* 251). There is no "mood of hope and love of life" in Prufrock's society. Prufrock is a lonely man, as lonely as "the lonely men in shirt-sleeves, leaning out of windows" of his fantasy. His only solution is to return to the animal state that his race was in before evolving into human beings.

Animals are one with nature, not alienated from their environments. They *are* nature, unselfconscious. Prufrock would return to a preconscious existence in the extreme: "I should have been a pair of ragged claws / Scuttling across the floors of silent seas." Claws *without a head* surely would not be alienated, bored, or depressed. They would seek and would need no psychological nurturing from their environment. And in the end Prufrock's fantasy of becoming claws is definitely more positive for him than his life as a human being. He completes his monologue with depressing irony, to say the least: it is with human voices waking us, bringing us back to human society, that we drown.

From "Approaching Literature through the Social Psychology of Erich Fromm," in *Psychological Perspectives on Literature: Freudian Dissidents and Non-Freudians,* edited by Joseph Natoli

CONSIDERATIONS FOR CRITICAL THINKING AND WRITING

1. According to Rusch, why is Fromm's approach useful for understanding Prufrock's character as well as his social context?

2. In what ways is Prufrock "representative of the human race" (para. 3)? Is he like any other characters you have read about in this anthology? Explain your response.

3. In an essay consider how Rusch's analysis of Prufrock might be used to support Baumann's argument that Prufrock's "overwhelming question" is whether or not he should kill himself (p. 411).

ROBERT SWARD (B. 1933)

Sward, a poet, provides a detailed explication, framed by his own personal experiences during the war in Korea.

A Personal Analysis of "The Love Song of J. Alfred Prufrock."   1996

In 1952, sailing to Korea as a U.S. Navy librarian for Landing Ship Tank 914, I read T. S. Eliot's "The Love Song of J. Alfred Prufrock." Ill-educated, a product of Chicago's public-school system, I was nineteen-years-old and, awakened by Whitman, Eliot, and Williams, had just begun writing poetry. I was also reading all the books I could get my hands on.

Eliot had won the Nobel Prize in 1948 and, curious, I was trying to make sense of poems like "Prufrock" and "The Waste Land."

"What do you know about T. S. Eliot?" I asked a young officer who'd been to college and studied English literature. I knew from earlier conversations that we shared an interest in what he called "modern poetry." A yeoman third class, two weeks at sea and bored, I longed for someone to talk to. "T. S. Eliot was born in St. Louis, Missouri, but he lives now in England and is studying to become an Englishman," the officer said, tapping tobacco into his pipe. "The 'T. S.' stands for 'tough shit.' You read Eliot's 'Love Song of J. Alfred Prufrock,' what one English prof called 'the first poem of the modern movement,' and if you don't understand it, 'tough shit.' All I can say is that's some love song."

An anthology of poetry open before us, we were sitting in the ship's all-metal, eight by eight-foot library eating bologna sandwiches and drinking coffee. Fortunately, the captain kept out of sight and life on the slow-moving (eight to ten knots), flat-bottomed amphibious ship was unhurried and anything but formal.

"Then why does Eliot bother calling it a love song?" I asked, as the ship rolled and the coffee sloshed onto a steel table. The tight metal room smelled like a cross between a diesel engine and a New York deli.

"Eliot's being ironic, sailor. 'Prufrock' is the love song of a sexually repressed and horny man who has no one but himself to sing to." Drawing on his pipe, the officer scratched his head. "Like you and I, Mr. Prufrock is a lonely man on his way to a war zone. We're sailing to Korea and we know the truth, don't we? We may never make it back. Prufrock marches like a brave soldier to a British drawing room that, he tells us, may be the death of him. He's a mock heroic figure who sings of mermaids and peaches and drowning."

Pointing to lines 129–31, the officer read aloud:

> We have lingered in the chambers of the sea
> By sea-girls wreathed with seaweed red and brown
> Till human voices wake us and we drown.

"Prufrock is also singing because he's a poet. Prufrock *is* T. S. Eliot and, the truth is, Eliot is so much like Prufrock that he has to distance himself from his creation. That's why he gives the man that pompous name. Did you know 'Tough Shit,' as a young man, sometimes signed himself 'T. Stearns Eliot'? You have to see the humor—the irony—in 'Prufrock' to understand the poem."

"I read it, I hear it in my head, but I still don't get it," I confessed. "What is 'Prufrock' about?"

"'Birth, death and copulation, that's all there is.' That's what Eliot himself says. Of course the poem also touches on aging, social status, and fashion."

"Aging and fashion?" I asked.

The officer threw back his head and recited:

> (They will say: "How his hair is growing thin!")
> My morning coat, my collar mounting firmly to the chin,
> My necktie rich and modest, but asserted by a simple pin.

He paused, then went on:

> I grow old . . . I grow old . . .
> I shall wear the bottoms of my trousers rolled.

"At the time the poem was written it was fashionable for young men to roll their trousers. In lines 120–21, Thomas Stearns Prufrock is laughing at himself for being middle-aged and vain.

"Anyway, 'The Love Song of J. Alfred Prufrock' is an interior monologue," said the officer, finishing his bologna sandwich and washing it down with dark rum. Wiping mustard from his mouth, he continued. "The whole thing takes place in J. Alfred Prufrock's head. That's clear, isn't it?"

I had read Browning's "My Last Duchess" and understood about interior monologues.

"Listen, sailor: Prufrock thinks about drawing rooms, but he never actually sets foot in one. Am I right?"

"Yeah," I said after rereading the first ten lines. "I think so."

"The poem is about what goes through Prufrock's mind on his way to some upper-class drawing room. It's a foggy evening in October, and what Mr. Prufrock really needs is a drink. He's a tightass Victorian, a lonely teetotaling intellectual. Anyone else would forget the toast and marmalade and step into a pub and ask for a pint of beer."

Setting down his pipe, the naval officer opened the flask and refilled our coffee mugs.

"Every time I think I know what 'Prufrock' means it turns out to mean something else," I said. "Eliot uses too many symbols. Why doesn't he just say what he means?"

"The city—'the lonely men in shirt-sleeves' and the 'one-night cheap hotels'—are masculine," said the officer. "That's what cities are like, aren't they: ugly and oppressive. What's symbolic—or should I say, what's obscure—about that?"

"Nothing," I said. "That's the easy part—Prufrock walking along like that."

"Okay," said the officer. "And in contrast to city streets, you've got the oppressive drawing room that, in Prufrock's mind, is feminine—'Arms that are braceleted and white and bare' and 'the marmalade, the tea, / Among the porcelain, among some talk of you and me.'" Using a pencil, the officer underlined those images in the paperback anthology.

"You ever been to a tea party, Sward?"

"No, sir, I haven't. Not like Prufrock's."

"Well," said the officer, "I have and I have a theory about that 'overwhelming question' Prufrock wants to ask in line 10—and again in line 93. Twice in the poem we hear about an 'overwhelming question.' What do you think he's getting at with that 'overwhelming question,' sailor?"

"Prufrock wants to ask the women what they're doing with their lives, but he's afraid they'll laugh at him," I said.

"Guess again, Sward," he said leaning back in his chair, stretching his arms.

"What's your theory, sir?"

"Sex," said the officer. "On the one hand, it's true, he wants to fit in and play the game because, after all, he's privileged. He belongs in the drawing room with the clever Englishwomen. At the same time he fantasizes. If he could, I think he'd like to shock them. Prufrock longs to put down his dainty porcelain teacup and shout, 'I am Lazarus, come from the dead, / Come back to tell you all, I shall tell you all.'"

"Why doesn't he do it?" I asked.

"Because Prufrock is convinced no matter what he says he won't reach them. He feels the English gentlewomen he's dealing with are unreachable. He believes his situation is as hopeless as theirs. He's dead and they're dead, too. That's why the poem begins with an image of sickness, 'a patient etherized upon a table,' and ends with people drowning. Prufrock is tough shit, man."

"You said you think there's a connection between Eliot the poet and J. Alfred Prufrock," I said.

"Of course there's a connection. Tommy Eliot from St. Louis, Missouri," said the officer. "Try as he will, he doesn't fit in. His English friends call him 'The American' and laugh. Tom Eliot the outsider with his rolled umbrella. T. S. Eliot is a self-conscious, make-believe Englishman and you have to understand that to understand 'Prufrock.'

"The poem is dark and funny at the same time. It's filled with humor and Prufrock is capable of laughing at himself. Just read those lines, 'Is it perfume from a dress / That makes me so digress?'"

"You were talking about Prufrock being sexually attracted to the women. How could that be if he is, as you say, 'dead.'" I asked.

"By 'dead' I mean desolate, inwardly barren, godforsaken. Inwardly, spiritually, Prufrock is a desolate creature. He's a moral man, he's a civilized man, but he's also hollow. But there's hope for him. In spite of himself, Prufrock is drawn to women.

"Look at line 64. He's attracted and repelled. Prufrock attends these teas, notices the women's arms 'downed with light brown hair!' and it scares the hell out of him because what he longs to do is to get them onto a drawing-room floor or a beach somewhere and bury his face in that same wonderfully tantalizing 'light brown hair.' What do you think of that, sailor?"

"I think you're right, sir."

"Then tell me this, Mr. Sward. Why doesn't he ask the overwhelming question? Hell, man, maybe it's not sexual. Maybe I'm wrong. Maybe what he wants to do is to ask some question like what you yourself suggested: 'What's the point in going on living when, in some sense, we're all already dead?'"

"I think he doesn't ask the question because he's so repressed, sir. He longs for physical contact, like you say, but he also wants another kind of intimacy, and he's afraid to ask for it and it's making him crazy."

"That's right, sailor. He's afraid. Eliot wrote the poem in 1911 when women were beginning to break free."

"Break free of what?" I asked.

"Of the prim and proper Victorian ideal. Suffragettes, feminists they called themselves. At the time Eliot wrote 'Prufrock,' women in England and America were catching on to the fact that they were disfranchised and had begun fighting for the right to vote, among other things, and for liberation, equality with men.

"Of course Prufrock is more prim and proper than the bored, overcivilized women in the poem. And it's ironic, isn't it, that he doesn't understand that the women are one step ahead of him. What you have in Prufrock is a man who tries to reconcile the image of real women with 'light brown hair' on their arms with some ideal, women who are a cross between the goddess Juno and a sweet Victorian maiden."

"Prufrock seems to know pretty well what he's feeling," I said. "He's not a liar and he's not a coward. To be honest, sir, I identify with Prufrock. He may try on one mask or another, but he ends up removing the mask and exposing himself."

"Now, about interior monologues: to understand 'Prufrock' you have to understand that most poems have one or more speakers and an audience, implied or otherwise. Let's go back to line 1. Who is this 'you and I' Eliot writes about?"

"Prufrock is talking to both his inner self and the reader," I said.

"How do you interpret the first ten lines?" the officer asked, pointing with his pencil.

" 'Let us go then, you and I,' he's saying, let us stroll, somnolent and numb as a sedated patient, through these seedy 'half-deserted streets, / The muttering retreats / Of restless nights in one-night cheap hotels.' "

"That's it, sailor. And while one might argue that Prufrock 'wakes' at the end of the poem, he is for the most part a ghostly inhabitant of a world that is, for him, a sort of hell. He is like the speaker in the Italian epigraph from Dante's *Inferno*, who says, essentially, 'Like you, reader, I'm in purgatory and there is no way out. Nobody ever escapes from this pit and, for that reason, I can speak the truth without fear of ill fame.'

"Despairing and sick of heart, Prufrock is a prisoner. Trapped in himself and trapped in society, he attends another and another in an endless series of effete, decorous teas.

> In the room the women come and go
> Talking of Michelangelo.

"Do you get it now? Do you see what I mean when I say 'tough shit'?" said the officer.

"Yeah, I'm beginning to," I said.

"T. S. Eliot's 'Prufrock' has become so much a part of the English language that people who have never read the poem are familiar with phrases like 'I have measured out my life with coffee spoons' and 'I grow old . . . I grow old . . . / I shall wear the bottoms of my trousers rolled' and 'Do I dare to eat a peach?' and 'In the room the women come and go.'

"Do you get it now? Eliot's irregularly rhymed, 131-line interior monologue has become part of the monologue all of us carry on in our heads. We are all of us, whether we know it or not, love-hungry, sex-crazed soldiers and sailors, brave, bored and lonely. At some level in our hearts, we are all J. Alfred Prufrock, every one of us, and we are all sailing into a war zone from which, as the last line of the poem implies, we may never return."

From "T. S. Eliot's 'Love Song of J. Alfred Prufrock' " in *Touchstones: American Poets on a Favorite Poem*, edited by Robert Pack and Jay Parini

CONSIDERATIONS FOR CRITICAL THINKING AND WRITING

1. How satisfactory is this reading of the poem? Are any significant portions of the poem left out of this reading?

2. Compare the tone of this critical approach to any other in this chapter. Explain why you prefer one over another.

3. Using Sward's personal approach, write an analysis of a poem of your choice in this anthology.

16

Cultural Case Study:
Julia Alvarez's "Queens, 1963"

Close readings allow us to appreciate and understand the literary art of a text. These formalist approaches to literature study the intrinsic elements of a work to determine how it is constructed, emphasizing how various elements such as diction, image, figures of speech, tone, symbol, irony, sound, rhythm, and other literary techniques provide patterns related to the work's meaning. Instead of examining extrinsic matters such as social, political, and economic contexts related to a poem, formalist critics focus on the intrinsic qualities of the text itself. A formalist might, for example, approach Thomas Hardy's 1912 poem "The Convergence of the Twain" (p. 73) by placing significant emphasis on the form of this poem — its rhyming three-line stanzas — rather than the historical contexts around the sinking of the *Titanic*. A formalist would be more concerned with the effects produced by these triplets rather than the identities of some of the enormously wealthy people who went down with the ship. In more recent literary criticism, however, there has been a renewed interest in the historical and cultural contexts of works that go beyond close readings of the text.

Cultural critics pay close attention to the historical contexts of a work, but unlike literary historians, they do not limit themselves to major historical events or famous people. A cultural critic might, for example, approach "The Convergence of the Twain" not only as an opportunity to examine the "vaingloriousness" of the rich who put their faith in the technology that produced the *Titanic*, but also as an occasion to investigate how poor people made jokes about the sinking to deflate the pretensions of the rich. The ironies that go unsuspected by "human vanity" can be seen to go even deeper in the nervous jokes that infiltrate popular culture when such a catastrophe occurs. Hardy's dignified, if pessimistic, poetic response can be illuminated in radically different ways such as by advertising before the voyage or the jokes and sentimental poetic eulogies published after the disaster.

Cultural critics study material drawn from a broad spectrum that includes "high" culture and popular culture. A cultural critic's approach to Hardy's treatment of the *Titanic*'s fate — captained by what Hardy calls the "Spinner of the Years" — might include discussions of everything from the actual construction plans of the ship, to passenger cabin accommodations, to manuals for lifeboat drills, as well as connections to Hardy's contemporaries, who also wrote about the *Titanic*.

The documents that follow Alvarez's "Queens, 1963" are provided to suggest how cultural criticism can be used to contextualize a literary work historically. The documents include an excerpt from an interview with Alvarez on growing up as an immigrant in New York City; an advertisement showing typical row houses; a newspaper article that summarizes the Chamber of Commerce's perspective of Queens in 1963; an excerpt from a television script for *All in the Family* (set in Queens); and a photograph of a civil rights demonstration at a Queens construction site. These documents offer some possible approaches to understanding the culture contemporary to "Queens, 1963." A variety of such approaches can create a wider and more informed understanding of the poem while deepening one's appreciation of Alvarez's achievement in writing it.

JULIA ALVAREZ (B. 1950)

Although Julia Alvarez was born in New York City, she lived in the Dominican Republic until she was ten years old. She returned to New York after her father, a physician, was connected to a plot to overthrow the dictatorship of Rafael Trujillo, and the family had to flee. Growing up in Queens was radically different from the Latino Caribbean world she experienced during her early childhood. A new culture and new language sensitized Alvarez to her surroundings and her use of language so that emigration from the Dominican Republic to Queens was the beginning of her movement toward becoming a writer. Alvarez quotes the Polish poet Czeslow Milosz's assertion that "Language is the only homeland" to explain her own sense that what she really settled into was not so much the United States as the English language.

Her fascination with English continued into high school and took shape in college as she became a serious writer — first at Connecticut College from 1967 to 1969 and then at Middlebury College, where she earned her B.A. in 1971. At Syracuse University she was awarded the American Academy of Poetry Prize and, in 1975, earned an M.A. in creative writing.

Since then she has worked as a writer-in-residence for the Kentucky Arts Commission, the Delaware Arts Council, and the Arts Council of Fayetteville, North Carolina, working in schools and community organizations. She has taught at California State College, College of Sequoias, Phillips Andover Academy, the University of Vermont, George Washington University, the University of Illinois, and, since 1988, at Middlebury College where she is a professor of literature and creative writing.

Alvarez's poetry has been widely published in journals and magazines ranging from *The New Yorker* to *Mirabella* to *The Kenyon Review*. Her book of poems, *Homecoming* (1984; second edition, 1986), uses simple — yet incisive — language to explore issues related to love, domestic life, and work. Her second book of poetry, *The Other Side/El Otro Lado* (1995), is a bilingual collection of meditations on her childhood memories of immigrant life that served to shape her adult identity and sensibilities.

In addition to her two volumes of poetry, Alvarez has also published three novels. The first, *How the García Girls Lost Their Accents* (1991), is a collection of fifteen separate but interrelated stories that cover thirty years of the lives of the García sisters from the late 1950s to the late 1980s. Drawing upon her own experiences, Alvarez describes the sisters fleeing the Dominican Republic and growing up as Latinas in the United States as well as their relationship to the country they left behind. Alvarez's second novel, *In the Time of the Butterflies* (1994), is a fictional account of a true story concerning four sisters who opposed Trujillo's dictatorship. Three of the sisters were murdered in 1960 by the government, and the fourth surviving sister recounts the events of their personal and political lives that led up to her sisters' deaths. Shaped by the history of Dominican freedom and tyranny, the novel also explores the sisters' relationships to each other and their country.

In *¡Yo!* (1997), her third novel, Alvarez focuses on Yolanda, one of the García sisters from her first novel, who is now a writer. Written in the different voices of Yo's friends and family members, this fractured narrative constructs a complete picture of a woman who uses her relationships as fodder for fiction; a woman who is selfish, aggravating, and finally lovable — and who is deeply embedded in American culture while remaining aware of her Dominican roots. Alvarez's book, *Something to Declare* (1998), is a collection of essays that describes her abiding concerns about how to respond to competing cultures. Her most recent books include the novel, *In the Name of Salome,* and the illustrated poetry collection, *The Secret Footprints.*

In "Queens, 1963" Alvarez remembers the neighborhood she lived in when she was thirteen-years-old and how "Everyone seemed more American / than we, newly arrived." The tensions that arose when new immigrants and ethnic groups moved onto the block were mirrored in many American neighborhoods in 1963. Indeed, the entire nation was made keenly aware of such issues as antisegregation when demonstrations were organized across the South and a massive march on Washington in support of civil rights for African Americans drew hundreds of thousands of demonstrators who listened to Martin Luther King deliver his electrifying "I have a dream" speech.

But the issues were hardly resolved, as evidenced by 1963's two best-selling books: *Happiness Is a Warm Puppy* and *Security Is a Thumb and a Blanket,* by Charles M. Schulz of "Peanuts" cartoon fame. The popularity of these books is, perhaps, understandable given the tensions that moved across the country and which seemed to culminate on November 22, 1963, when President Kennedy was assassinated in Dallas, Texas. These events are not mentioned in "Queens, 1963," but they are certainly part of the context that helps us to understand Alvarez's particular neighborhood.

CHRONOLOGY

1950	Born on March 27 in New York City.
1950–60	Raised in the Dominican Republic.
1960	Alvarez family flees the Dominican Republic for New York City after her father joins efforts to overthrow the dictatorship of Rafael Trujillo.
1961	Rafael Trujillo is assassinated.
1967–69	Attends Connecticut College.
1971	Graduates from Middlebury College with a B.A.
1975	Graduates from Syracuse University with an M.A.
1979–80	Attends Bread Loaf School of English.
1979–81	Instructor at Phillips Andover Academy.
1981–83	Visiting assistant professor at University of Vermont.
1984	Publishes *Homecoming,* a volume of poems.
1984–85	Visiting writer-in-residence at George Washington University.
1985–88	Assistant professor of English at University of Illinois.
1987–88	Awarded a National Endowment for the Arts fellowship.
1988–Present	Professor of English at Middlebury College.
1991	Publishes *How the García Girls Lost Their Accents,* a novel.
1994	Publishes *In the Time of the Butterflies,* a novel.
1995	Publishes *The Other Side/El Otro Lado,* a volume of poems.
1997	Publishes *¡Yo!,* a novel.
1998	Publishes *Something to Declare,* essays.

Queens, 1963   *1995*

Everyone seemed more American
than we, newly arrived,
foreign dirt still on our soles.
By year's end, a sprinkler waving

like a flag on our mowed lawn,   5
we were melted into the block,
owned our own mock Tudor house.
Then the house across the street
sold to a black family.
Cop cars patrolled our block   10
from the Castellucci's at one end
to the Balakian's on the other.
We heard rumors of bomb threats,
a burning cross on their lawn.
(It turned out to be a sprinkler.)   15
Still the neighborhood buzzed.
The barber's family, Haralambides,
our left side neighbors, didn't want trouble.
They'd come a long way to be free!
Mr. Scott, the retired plumber,   20
and his plump midwestern wife,
considered moving back home
where white and black got along
by staying where they belonged.
They had cultivated our street   25
like the garden she'd given up
on account of her ailing back,
bad knees, poor eyes, arthritic hands.
She went through her litany daily.
Politely, my mother listened —   30
¡Ay, Mrs. Scott, qué pena!°
— her Dominican good manners
still running on automatic.
The Jewish counselor next door,
had a practice in her house;   35
clients hurried up her walk
ashamed to be seen needing.
(I watched from my upstairs window,
gloomy with adolescence,
and guessed how they too must have   40
hypocritical old world parents.)
Mrs. Bernstein said it was time
the neighborhood opened up.
As the first Jew on the block,
she remembered the snubbing she got   45
a few years back from Mrs. Scott.
But real estate worried her,
our houses' plummeting value.
She shook her head as she might
at a client's grim disclosures.   50
Too bad the world works this way.
The German girl playing the piano

31 *qué pena:* What a shame!

down the street abruptly stopped
in the middle of a note.
I completed the tune in my head   55
as I watched *their* front door open.
A dark man in a suit
with a girl about my age
walked quickly into a car.
My hand lifted but fell   60
before I made a welcoming gesture.
On her face I had seen a look
from the days before we had melted
into the United States of America.
It was hardness mixed with hurt.   65
It was knowing she never could be
the right kind of American.
A police car followed their car.
Down the street, curtains fell back.
Mrs. Scott swept her walk   70
as if it had just been dirtied.
Then the German piano commenced
downward scales as if tracking
the plummeting real estate.
One by one I imagined the houses   75
sinking into their lawns,
the grass grown wild and tall
in the past tense of this continent
before the first foreigners owned
any of this free country.   80

CONSIDERATIONS FOR CRITICAL THINKING AND WRITING

1. FIRST RESPONSE. What nationalities live in this neighborhood in the New York City Borough of Queens? Are they neighborly to each other?

2. In line 3, why do you suppose Alvarez writes "foreign dirt still on our soles" rather than "foreign soil still on our shoes"? What does Alvarez's particular word choice suggest about her feelings for her native country?

3. Characterize the speaker. How old is she? How does she feel about having come from the Dominican Republic? About living in the United States?

4. Do you think this poem is optimistic or pessimistic about racial relations in the United States? Explain your answer by referring to specific details in the poem.

CONNECTIONS TO OTHER SELECTIONS

1. Compare the use of irony in "Queens, 1963" with that in John Ciardi's "Suburban" (p. 161). How does irony contribute to each poem?

2. Discuss the problems immigrants encounter in this poem and in Chitra Banerjee Divakaruni's "Indian Movie, New Jersey" (p. 162).

3. Write an essay comparing and contrasting the tone and theme in "Queens, 1963" and in Tato Laviera's "AmeRícan" (p. 269).

DOCUMENTS

MARNY REQUA (B. 1971)

From an Interview with Julia Alvarez 1997

M.R. What was it like when you came to the United States?

J.A. When we got to Queens, it was really a shock to go from a totally Latino, *familia* Caribbean world into this very cold and kind of forbidding one in which we didn't speak the language. I didn't grow up with a tradition of writing or reading books at all. People were always telling stories but it wasn't a tradition of literary ... reading a book or doing something solitary like that. Coming to this country I discovered books, I discovered that it was a way to enter into a portable homeland that you could carry around in your head. You didn't have to suffer what was going on around you. I found in books a place to go. I became interested in language because I was learning a language intentionally at the age of ten. I was wondering, "Why is it that word and not another?" which any writer has to do with their language. I always say I came to English late but to the profession early. By high school I was pretty set: that's what I want to do, be a writer.

M.R. Did you have culture shock returning to the Dominican Republic as you were growing up?

J.A. The culture here had an effect on me — at the time this country was coming undone with protests and flower children and drugs. Here I was back in the Dominican Republic and I wouldn't keep my mouth shut. I had my own ideas and I had my own politics, and it, I just didn't gel anymore with the family. I didn't quite feel I ever belonged in this North American culture and I always had this nostalgia that when I went back I'd belong, and then I found out I didn't belong there either.

M.R. Was it a source of inspiration to have a foot in both cultures?

J.A. I only came to that later. [Then], it was a burden because I felt torn. I wanted to be part of one culture and then part of the other. It was a time when the model for the immigrant was that you came and you became an American and you cut off your ties and that was that. My parents had that frame of mind, because they were so afraid, and they were "Learn your English" and "Become one of them," and that left out so much. Now I see the richness. Part of what I want to do with my work is that complexity, that richness. I don't want it to be simplistic and either/or.

From "The Politics of Fiction," *Frontera* magazine 5 (1997)

CONSIDERATIONS FOR CRITICAL THINKING AND WRITING

1. What do you think Alvarez means when she describes books as "a portable homeland that you could carry around in your head"?

2. Why is it difficult for Alvarez to feel that she belongs in either the Dominican or the North American culture?

3. Alvarez says that in the 1960s "the model for the immigrant was that you came and you became an American and you cut off your ties and that was

that." Do you think this model has changed in the United States since then? Explain your response.

4. How might this interview alter your understanding of "Queens, 1963"? What light is shed, for example, on the speaker's feeling that her family "melted into the block" in line 6?

An Advertisement for Tudor Row Houses   1920

From *Queen's Borough New York City, 1910–1920*

1. This advertisement from a publication of the Queens Chamber of Commerce shows row houses as the "Ideal Home Place." Write a paragraph describing how the details in the photograph make you feel about living there.

2. Compare the neighborhood in this picture with the neighborhood Alvarez describes in "Queens, 1963." How might the physical characteristics of such a neighborhood have changed between 1920 and 1963? What factors might have influenced such a change?

3. How does this advertisement shed light on "Queens, 1963"?

Queens: "The 'Fair' Borough"   1963

This newspaper account anticipates the opening of the 1964 World's Fair in Queens.

Cariello Glorifies Queens as Example of Gracious Living

The borough of Queens "truly represents the full flowering of advanced urban living," Borough President Mario J. Cariello says.

His encomium is in a brightly colored eight-page brochure entitled "The 'Fair' Borough." Mr. Cariello's foreword says the brochure was prepared "to reacquaint our residents" with the borough's history and present stature when they play host to "millions of visitors to the World's Fair."

Twenty-five thousand copies have been printed by photo-offset at a competitive bid cost of $1,600. The money came from the Borough President's special expense fund for proclamations, certificates and the like, a spokesman said yesterday.

A section on current "Data about Queens," compiled by the Queens Chamber of Commerce, says the borough has "such beautiful rural home communities as Forest Hills, Jamaica Estates, Kew Gardens, Jackson Heights, Flushing and Douglaston."

The booklet includes a map of 44 communities, a list of bus routes, a description of the Borough President's functions, the text of the 1657 Flushing Remonstrance as "the first declaration of religious freedom by a group of free citizens in America," a picture of the borough flag, and a brief history.

From the *New York Times*, July 18, 1963

1. Based on the newspaper article, how would you describe the probable tone of the eight-page brochure about Queens?

2. After reading Alvarez's poem about Queens, do you see any irony in the title of the brochure, "The 'Fair' Borough"? Explain why or why not.

3. What is left out of Borough President Cariello's account of Queens? Why do you suppose its focus is very different from that of "Queens, 1963"?

4. Try writing a dialogue between the Borough President and Alvarez on the subject of Queens as a representation of "the full flowering of advanced urban living." If you prefer, write an essay on this topic instead.

"Talkin' about Prejudice" in Queens

All in the Family, created by Norman Lear, was produced for nine seasons from 1971 to 1979, and at the height of its popularity, an estimated one-third of all Americans regularly viewed the program. Although this famous series has ceased production, reruns have preserved its popularity. The show's main character, Archie Bunker—a resident of a row house in a working-class Queens neighborhood—is so well known that his name has been used to describe anyone who is loud, stubborn, and blindly prejudiced. The basic conflict of the series centers on the verbal skirmishes that occur when Archie's middle-aged, working-class biases are challenged by his son-in-law Mike's liberal views. One reason for the show's popularity during its original run was that it mirrored so many issues of its time, such as racism, sexism, politics, religion, and alternative lifestyles. The following excerpt is from the first episode of *All in the Family.*

NORMAN LEAR (B. 1922)
Meet the Bunkers   *1971*

CHARACTERS

Archie Bunker
Edith Bunker, Archie's wife
Michael Stivic, the Bunkers' son-in-law
Gloria Stivic, the Bunkers' daughter
Lionel, a neighbor

In this scene, Lionel, a black neighbor of the Bunkers, appears at the door on the heels of a dinner conversation in which Archie has fervently denied but amply demonstrated his prejudices. Earlier we learn from Lionel that Archie likes to ask him what he wants to study when he goes to college so that Lionel will say, "Ahm gwana be a 'lectical ingineer." Lionel obliges Archie because he believes that by giving "people what they want," he indeed can become an electrical engineer. He also enjoys watching Archie fall for his put-ons.

Mike: Hey, Lionel. How you doin'? Come on in. You know, in a way we were just talking about you.
Gloria: Michael!
Archie: Talkin' about prejudice, I'm glad you're here Lionel. (*Gets up and goes to living room.*)
Lionel: Yes, sir. Mr. Bunker, sir. (*Hands flowers to Edith.*) These are for you, Mrs. Bunker. A present from an admirer.
Edith (overwhelmed): For me? Oh my goodness, I ain't had a present for ten years.
Gloria: I wonder who it's from.
Archie (coming back to table): There's something I want to ask you, Lionel
Gloria: Wait a minute, Daddy. Let her open her gift first.

Archie: She waited ten years; another minute ain't gonna kill her! (*Puts gift on table, takes Lionel to living room.*) Come here, Lionel. Let me ask your opinion of somethin' there, Lionel. When you started doin' odd jobs in the neighborhood, wasn't I one of the first guys to throw a little work your way — by the way, didya fix the TV up in the bedroom?

Lionel: Sure did, Mr. Bunker. (*Lionel nods. Archie slips him some change.*)

Archie: Swell. Good boy . . . Here, put this in your pocket.

Edith: Cheaper than a repairman, believe me.

Archie: Is anybody talkin' to you . . . Now, Lionel you could say by throwin' you these little jobs, in a way I was helpin' you get some money so you can get through college so's you can become . . .

Lionel: A 'lectical ingineer.

Archie (loves it): Yeah. Ya hear that?

Mike (impatient): Archie, ask your question already!

Archie: Will you keep your drawers on? Hey, by the way, that's a pretty nice looking suit you got on there. I mean it's classy, it's quiet. Where'd you get it?

Lionel: Up in Harlem.

Archie (looks): Nah.

Lionel: Now I got two more, but one's in yellow with stripes, the other one's in purple with checks. You know, for when I'm with *my* people.

Archie: Well, anyway Lionel, I'd say you know me pretty good, wouldn't you?

Lionel: Oh, yes, sir. I got a bead on you, all right. I know you real good.

Archie: Good, good.

Mike (crossing to living room): Alright, alright, let's get to the point. Lionel, what he wants to know, is if you think he's prejudiced.

Lionel (feigning innocence): Prejudiced?

Archie: Yeah.

Lionel: Prejudiced against who?

Mike: Against Black People.

Lionel: Against Black People! Mr. Bunker! That's the most ridiculous thing I ever heard!

Archie turns proudly to the others.

Archie: There, you see that, wise guy. (*Turns to Mike.*) You thought you knew him. You thought you knew me. Oh these liberals — they're supposed to be so sensitive, ya know. I'll tell you where this guy's sensitive, Lionel — right in his tochas. (*Archie goes to dining room table.*)

Lionel (surprise): Where?

Mike: It's a Yiddish word. It means — (*points to buttocks*).

Lionel: Oh, I know where it's at. I was just wonderin', Mr. Bunker — what's with the Jewish word?

Archie: I hear them. We got a couple of Hebes working down the building.

Lionel: Does he use words like that very often?

Mike: Now and then.

Archie: I told ya, I work with a couple of Jews.

Lionel: Beggin' your pardon, Mr. Bunker, but you wouldn't happen to be one of them, would you?

Archie (no humor about this): What??

Lionel: I mean people don't use Jewish words just like that, do they, Mike?

Mike (crossing to table, sits): No, not in my experience.

Archie: Maybe people don't but *I* do! And I ain't no Yid!

Mike. Come to think of it... when your father was visiting last year... wasn't his name Davie, or somethin'?

Archie: David, my father's name is David.

Mike: Yeah, David. And your mother's name... uh... Sarah, wasn't it?

Archie (to Lionel): Sarah, my mother's name is Sarah — So what?

Lionel: David and Sarah, two Jewish names.

Archie: David and Sarah. Two names right out of the Bible — which is got nothin' to do with the Jews.

Lionel: You don't wanna get up tight about it, Mr. Bunker. There's nothing to be ashamed of being Jewish.

Archie: But I ain't Jewish!

Mike: Look at that — see the way he uses his hands when he argues. A very Semitic gesture.

Archie: What do you know about it, you dumb Polack.

Mike: All right, I'm a Polack.

Archie: You sure are! You're a Polack Joke!

Mike: Okay, I don't mind, so I'm Polish. I don't mind. I'm proud of it!

Lionel: There you are, Mr. Bunker. Now you oughta be proud that you're Jewish.

Archie (whining): But I ain't Jewish.

Edith: I didn't know you was Jewish.

Archie: What the hell are you talking about? You, of all people, should *know* that I ain't Jewish.

Edith: You *are* talking with your hands.

Lionel: See, the Jews tend to be emotional.

Archie (blowing): Now listen to me, Lionel. I'm going to give it to you just once more and that's all. I am not Jewish.

Lionel: Yes, Sir, Mr. Bunker. But even if you are, it doesn't change things between you and me. I mean I'm not gonna throw away nine years of friendship over a little thing like that. So long, everybody. (*He exits.*)

All: Bye, Lionel!

Archie watches him go and turns to others. They resume eating quickly.

Archie: Well, I hate a smart aleck kid, and I don't care what color he is!

Applause. Fade to black.

CONSIDERATIONS FOR CRITICAL THINKING AND WRITING

1. What kinds of assumptions does Archie make about Lionel because he is black? How does Lionel use Archie's prejudices to satirize him?

2. Some critics have insisted that *All in the Family* negatively affected society because the series presents a bigot who is likable, thereby characterizing his racial prejudices as funny and acceptable rather than harmful and repugnant. Do you think Archie is a dangerous character because his prejudices are presented humorously? Explain why or why not.

3. Compare and contrast how racial prejudice is treated in this script and in "Queens, 1963." Which treatment do you find more effective? Explain why.

4. How do the script and the poem suggest what it was like to be Jewish in Queens in the 1960s? Write an essay that explores how each work treats Jewishness. Consider whether these treatments are simplistic and reductive or complex and subtle.

A Civil Rights Demonstration   1963

In this photograph police remove a Congress of Racial Equality (CORE) demonstrator from a Queens construction site. Demonstrators blocked the delivery entrance to the site because they wanted more African Americans and Puerto Ricans hired in the building-trade industry. Reprinted by permission of AP/Wide World Photos.

Considerations for Critical Thinking and Writing

1. Discuss the role played by the police in this photograph and in "Queens, 1963." What attitudes toward the police do the photograph and the poem display?

2. How do you think the Scotts and Mrs. Bernstein would have responded to this photograph in 1963?

3. Compare the tensions in "Queens, 1963" to those depicted in this picture. How do the speaker's private reflections relate to this public protest?

17

Two Thematic Case Studies

Behind all the elements that make up a poem, and even behind its cultural contexts and critical reception, lies its theme. Its idea and the point around which the entire poem revolves, the theme is ultimately what we respond to — or fail to respond to. All the other elements, in fact, are typically there to contribute to the theme, whether or not that theme is explicitly stated. Reading thematically means extending what you have learned about the analysis of individual elements at work in the poem to make connections between the text and the world we inhabit.

This chapter focuses on single themes as they reappear throughout various parts of poetic history. The poems here are organized into two case studies. The first consists of love poems and the second consists of poems about teaching and learning. These poems have much to say about human experience – experience that is contradictory, confusing, complicated, and fascinating. You'll find diverse perspectives in each case study from different historical, cultural, generational, or political moments in time. You'll also discover writers who aim to entertain, to describe, to convince, to teach, and to complain. After reading these poems in the context of one another, you're likely to come away with a richer understanding of how the themes of love and of learning and teaching play out in your own life.

POEMS ABOUT LOVE

Poems about love have probably enchanted and intrigued their hearers since people began making poetry. Like poetry itself, love is, after all, about intensity, acute impressions, and powerful responsibilities. The emotional dimensions of love do not lend themselves to analytic expository essays.

Although such writing can be satisfying intellectually, it is most inadequate for evoking and capturing the thick excitement and swooning reveries that love engenders. The poems in this section include spiritual as well as physical explorations of love that range over four centuries. As you'll see, poetic responses to love by men and women can be quite similar as well as different from one another, just as poems from different periods can reflect a variety of values and attitudes toward love. It is indeed an engaging theme — but as you read, don't forget to pay attention to the formal elements of each of these selections and how they work together to create the particular points about love each poem makes. Also, remember to read not only for the presence of love; many other themes can be found in these works, and many other connections can be made to the literature elsewhere in this anthology.

The oldest love poem in this case study, Christopher Marlowe's "The Passionate Shepherd to His Love," opens with the line, "Come live with me and be my love." This famous pastoral lyric set a tone for love poetry that has been replicated since its publication. Before concluding with "Then live with me and be my love," Marlowe embraces the kinds of generous pleasure that readers have traditionally and happily received for centuries. The feelings, if not the particular images, are likely to be quite familiar to you.

CHRISTOPHER MARLOWE (1564–1593)

The Passionate Shepherd to His Love   *1599?*

Come live with me and be my love,
And we will all the pleasure prove
That valleys, groves, hills, and fields,
Woods, or steepy mountain yields.

And we will sit upon the rocks,   5
Seeing the shepherds feed their flocks,
By shallow rivers to whose falls
Melodious birds sing madrigals.

And I will make thee beds of roses
And a thousand fragrant posies,   10
A cap of flowers, and a kirtle°   11 *kirtle:* Dress or skirt.
Embroidered all with leaves of myrtle;

A gown made of the finest wool
Which from our pretty lambs we pull;
Fair lined slippers for the cold,   15
With buckles of the purest gold;

A belt of straw and ivy buds,
With coral clasps and amber studs:

And if these pleasures may thee move,
Come live with me, and be my love.   20

The shepherd swains shall dance and sing
For thy delight each May morning:
If these delights thy mind may move,
Then live with me and be my love.

CONSIDERATIONS FOR CRITICAL THINKING AND WRITING

1. FIRST RESPONSE. How persuasive do you find the shepherd's arguments to his potential lover?

2. What do you think might be the equivalent of the shepherd's arguments in the twenty-first century? What kinds of appeals and images of love would be made by a contemporary lover?

3. Try writing a response to the shepherd from the female's point of view using the rhythms, rhyme scheme, and quatrains employed by Marlowe.

CONNECTION TO ANOTHER SELECTION

1. Read Sir Walter Raleigh's "The Nymph's Reply to the Shepherd" (p. 632). How does the nymph's response compare with your imagined reply?

While Marlow's shepherd focuses his energies on convincing his potential love to join him (in the delights associated with love), the speaker in the following sonnet by William Shakespeare demonstrates his love for poetry as well and focuses on the beauty of the object of the poem. In doing so, he introduces a theme that has become a perennial challenge to love — the corrosive, destructive nature of what Shakespeare shockingly calls "sluttish time." His resolution of this issue is intriguing: see if you agree with it.

WILLIAM SHAKESPEARE (1564–1616)

Not marble, nor the gilded monuments   *1609*

Not marble, nor the gilded monuments
Of princes, shall outlive this powerful rhyme;
But you shall shine more bright in these conténts
Than unswept stone, besmeared with sluttish time.
When wasteful war shall statues overturn,   5
And broils root out the work of masonry,
Nor Mars his° swords nor war's quick fire shall burn   *possessive of Mars*
The living record of your memory.
'Gainst death and all-oblivious enmity
Shall you pace forth; your praise shall still find room   10
Even in the eyes of all posterity
That wear this world out to the ending doom.
   So, till the judgment that yourself arise,
   You live in this, and dwell in lovers' eyes.

CONSIDERATIONS FOR CRITICAL THINKING AND WRITING

1. FIRST RESPONSE. What do you think is the central point of this poem? Explain whether you agree or disagree with its theme.

2. How does "sluttish time" represent the poem's major conflict?

3. Consider whether this poem is more about the poet's loved one or the poet's love of his own poetry.

CONNECTIONS TO OTHER SELECTIONS

1. Compare the theme of this poem with that of Marvell's "To His Coy Mistress" (p. 65), paying particular attention to the speaker's beliefs about how time affects love.

2. Discuss whether you find this love poem more or less appealing than Marlowe's "The Passionate Shepherd to His Love" (p. 434). As you make this comparison, consider what the criteria for an appealing love poem should be.

As Shakespeare's speaker presents a love that will withstand the destruction of time, Anne Bradstreet's "To My Dear and Loving Husband" evokes a marital love that confirms a connection that transcends space and matter as well as time. Although Bradstreet wrote more than three centuries ago, such devotion remains undated for many (but, of course, not all) readers of love poetry. She begins, naturally enough, with the pleasure and paradox of how two people can be one.

ANNE BRADSTREET (c. 1612–1672)

To My Dear and Loving Husband   *1678*

If ever two were one, then surely we.
If ever man were loved by wife, then thee;
If ever wife was happy in a man,
Compare with me, ye women, if you can.
I prize thy love more than whole mines of gold   5
Or all the riches that the East doth hold.
My love is such that rivers cannot quench,
Nor ought but love from thee, give recompense.
Thy love is such I can no way repay,
The heavens reward thee manifold, I pray.   10
Then while we live, in love let's so persevere
That when we live no more, we may live ever.

CONSIDERATIONS FOR CRITICAL THINKING AND WRITING

1. FIRST RESPONSE. Describe the poem's tone. Is it what you'd expect from a seventeenth-century Puritan? Why or why not?

2. Consider whether Bradstreet's devotion is directed more toward her husband here on earth or toward the eternal rewards of heaven.

3. What is the paradox of the final line? How is it resolved?

CONNECTIONS TO OTHER SELECTIONS

1. How does the theme of this poem compare with that of Bradstreet's "Before the Birth of One of Her Children" (p. 595)? Explain why you find the poems consistent or contradictory.

2. Discuss the relation between love and the contemplation of death in this poem and the relation between love and the reality of death in Donald Hall's "Letter with No Address" (p. 673).

The remaining poems in this case study are modern and contemporary pieces that both maintain and revise the perspectives on love provided by Marlowe, Shakespeare, and Bradstreet. As you read them, consider what each adds to your understanding of the others and of love in general.

ELIZABETH BARRETT BROWNING (1806–1861)

How Do I Love Thee?
Let Me Count the Ways   *1850*

How do I love thee? Let me count the ways.
I love thee to the depth and breadth and height
My soul can reach, when feeling out of sight
For the ends of being and ideal grace.
I love thee to the level of every day's   5
Most quiet need, by sun and candle-light.
I love thee freely, as men strive for right.
I love thee purely, as they turn from praise.
I love thee with the passion put to use
In my old griefs, and with my childhood's faith.   10
I love thee with a love I seemed to lose
With my lost saints. I love thee with the breath,
Smiles, tears, of all my life; and, if God choose,
I shall but love thee better after death.

CONSIDERATIONS FOR CRITICAL THINKING AND WRITING

1. FIRST RESPONSE. This poem has remained extraordinarily popular for more than 150 years. Why do you think it has been so often included in collections of love poems? What is its appeal? Does it speak to a contemporary reader? To you?

2. Comment on the effect of the diction. What kind of tone does it create?

3. Would you characterize this poem as having a religious theme — or is it a substitute for religion?

CONNECTION TO ANOTHER SELECTION

1. Compare and contrast the images, tone, and theme of this poem with those of Christina Rossetti's "Promises Like Pie-Crust" (p. 634). Explain why you find one poem more promising than the other.

E. E. Cummings (1894–1962)

since feeling is first 1926

since feeling is first
who pays any attention
to the syntax of things
will never wholly kiss you;

wholly to be a fool   5
while Spring is in the world

my blood approves,
and kisses are a better fate
than wisdom
lady i swear by all flowers. Don't cry   10
— the best gesture of my brain is less than
your eyelids' flutter which says

we are for each other: then
laugh, leaning back in my arms
for life's not a paragraph   15
And death i think is no parenthesis

Considerations for Critical Thinking and Writing

1. FIRST RESPONSE. What is the speaker's initial premise? Why is it crucial to his argument? What is his argument?

2. Does this poem fit into the *carpe diem* tradition? How?

3. How are nature and society presented in the conflict? Why is this relevant to the speaker's argument?

4. List and describe the grammatical metaphors in the poem. How do they further the speaker's argument?

Connections to Other Selections

1. Contrast the theme of this poem with that of Marlowe's "The Passionate Shepherd to His Love" (p. 434). How do you account for the differences, in both style and content, between the two love poems?

2. Discuss attitudes toward "feeling" in this poem and in Molly Peacock's "Desire" (p. 231).

Jane Kenyon (1947–1995)

The Shirt 1978

The shirt touches his neck
and smooths over his back.
It slides down his sides.
It even goes down below his belt —

down into his pants.
Lucky shirt.

CONSIDERATIONS FOR CRITICAL THINKING AND WRITING

1. FIRST RESPONSE. Chart your emotions as you experienced this poem. Were you surprised? Explain why you were delighted or offended by this poem.

2. Discuss whether you consider this to be a love poem or something else.

3. Why is the title, "The Shirt," a much better title than, for example, "Below His Belt"?

CONNECTIONS TO OTHER SELECTIONS

1. What does a comparison of "The Shirt" with Bradstreet's "To My Dear and Loving Husband" (p. 436) and Browning's "How Do I Love Thee? Let Me Count the Ways" (p. 437) suggest to you about the history of women writing love poems?

TIMOTHY STEELE (B. 1948)

An Aubade   *1986*

As she is showering, I wake to see
A shine of earrings on the bedside stand,
A single yellow sheet which, over me,
Has folds as intricate as drapery
In paintings from some fine old master's hand.   5

The pillow which, in dozing, I embraced
Retains the salty sweetness of her skin;
I sense her smooth back, buttocks, belly, waist,
The leggy warmth which spread and gently laced
Around my legs and loins, and drew me in.   10

I stretch and curl about a bit and hear her
Singing among the water's hiss and race.
Gradually the early light makes clearer
The perfume bottles by the dresser's mirror,
The silver flashlight, standing on its face,   15

Which shares the corner of the dresser with
An ivy spilling tendrils from a cup.
And so content am I, I can forgive
Pleasure for being brief and fugitive.
I'll stretch some more, but postpone getting up   20

Until she finishes her shower and dries
(Now this and now that foot placed on a chair)
Her fineboned ankles, and her calves and thighs,
The pink full nipples of her breasts, and ties
Her towel up, turban-style, about her hair.   25

CONSIDERATIONS FOR CRITICAL THINKING AND WRITING

1. FIRST RESPONSE. Characterize the poem's speaker. What does his language reveal about him?
2. How does this poem fit the definition of an aubade?
3. What do you think is the central point of this poem?
4. Is this a *carpe diem* poem? Explain why or why not.

CONNECTIONS TO OTHER SELECTIONS

1. How does the tone of Steele's poem compare with Wilbur's "A Late Aubade" (p. 68)? Explain why you prefer one over the other.
2. Write an essay that compares and contrasts the speaker/observer in "An Aubade" with that of Joan Murray's in "Play-By-Play" (p. 683), or Jane Kenyon's "The Shirt" (p. 438).

RON KOERTGE (B. 1940)

1989   *1999*

Because AIDS was slaughtering people left and right,
    I went to a lot of memorial services that year.
There were so many, I'd pencil them in between
    a movie or a sale at Macy's. The other thing that
made them tolerable was the funny stories people   5
    got up and told about the deceased: the time he
hurled a mushroom frittata across a crowded room,
    those green huaraches he refused to throw away,
the joke about the flight attendant and the banana
    that cracked him up every time.   10

But this funeral was for a blind friend of my wife's
    who'd merely died. And the interesting thing
about it was the guide dogs; with all the harness
    and the sniffing around, the vestibule of the church
looked like the starting line of the Iditarod. But   15
    nobody got up to talk. We just sat there
and the pastor read the King James version. Then he
    said someday we would see Robert and he us.

Throughout the service, the dogs slumped beside their
    masters. But when the soloist stood and launched   20
into a screechy rendition of "Abide with Me," they sank
    into the carpet. A few put their paws over their ears.
Someone whispered to one of the blind guys; he told
    another, and the laughter started to spread. People
in the back looked around, startled and embarrassed,   25
    until they spotted all those chunky Labradors
flattened out like animals in a cartoon about
    steamrollers. Then they started, too.

That was more like it. That was what I was used to —
   a roomful of people laughing and crying, taking off   30
their sunglasses to blot their inconsolable eyes.

CONSIDERATIONS FOR CRITICAL THINKING AND WRITING

1. FIRST RESPONSE. In what sense can "1989" be read as a love poem? Explain why it does or doesn't fit your definition of a love poem.
2. Describe the tone of each of the stanzas and trace your emotional response to them as you move through the poem. What is your emotional reaction to the entire poem?
3. Describe the relation between death and love in the poem. How is that relation central to the theme?

CONNECTION TO ANOTHER SELECTION

1. Discuss the connection between love and death in "1989" and in "Thinking about Bill, Dead of AIDS" (p. 644), by Miller Williams.

POEMS ABOUT TEACHING AND LEARNING

You've spent a significant portion of your life in school learning and being taught, and as you well know, the lessons come in many forms and sometimes at unexpected moments. The poems included in this section all depict a lesson of sorts — even if what has been taught and what has been learned are not always clear (and they are not always the same thing). With the exception of Emily Dickinson's "From all the Jails the Boys and Girls," all the poetry included here was written within the last fifty years or so, and most of it is quite recent. The contemporary nature of these poems should allow you to make some vivid and striking connections to your own experience — and it may make you grind your teeth a bit, too. As you read, think about who is learning what, how you might link each reading with another, and how you personally respond to the work in question. The lessons discovered in this poetry will undoubtedly add to your understanding that learning is a complicated matter that goes well beyond anyone's lesson plans.

    In the first poem here, Emily Dickinson's description of the "Jails" inhabited by children is a metaphor that nearly every child has learned the truth of first-hand. The sense of relief and escape expressed in this poem is, however, as complicated as it is welcomed.

EMILY DICKINSON (1830–1886)

From all the Jails the Boys and Girls

c. 1881

From all the Jails the Boys and Girls
Ecstatically leap —
Beloved only Afternoon
That Prison doesn't keep

They storm the Earth and stun the Air,
A Mob of solid Bliss —
Alas — that Frowns should lie in wait
For such a Foe as this —

CONSIDERATIONS FOR CRITICAL THINKING AND WRITING

1. FIRST RESPONSE. What are the "Jails"? How are children characterized in this poem?
2. Comment on the effectiveness of the description in lines 5 and 6.
3. How might "Frowns" be read symbolically?

CONNECTION TO ANOTHER SELECTION

1. In an essay discuss the treatment of childhood in this poem and in Robert Frost's "Out, Out —" (p. 350).

As Emily Dickinson's idea of school is complicated in her poem, the writing assignment in Langston Hughes's "Theme for English B" is more problematic than it seems — especially for the African American student who must complete it for a white teacher. There are themes within themes in this poem.

LANGSTON HUGHES (1902–1967)

Theme for English B

1949

The instructor said,

> *Go home and write*
> *a page tonight.*
> *And let that page come out of you —*
> *Then, it will be true.*   5

I wonder if it's that simple?
I am twenty-two, colored, born in Winston-Salem.
I went to school there, then Durham, then here
to this college on the hill above Harlem.
I am the only colored student in my class.   10

The steps from the hill lead down into Harlem,
through a park, then I cross St. Nicholas,
Eighth Avenue, Seventh, and I come to the Y,
the Harlem Branch Y, where I take the elevator
up to my room, sit down, and write this page: 15

It's not easy to know what is true for you or me
at twenty-two, my age. But I guess I'm what
I feel and see and hear, Harlem, I hear you:
hear you, hear me — we two — you, me, talk on this page.
(I hear New York, too.) Me — who?   20
Well, I like to eat, sleep, drink, and be in love
I like to work, read, learn, and understand life.
I like a pipe for a Christmas present,
or records — Bessie,° bop, or Bach.
I guess being colored doesn't make me *not* like   25
the same things other folks like who are other races.
So will my page be colored that I write?
Being me, it will not be white.
But it will be
a part of you, instructor.   30
You are white —
yet a part of me, as I am part of you.
That's American.
Sometimes perhaps you don't want to be a part of me.
Nor do I often want to be a part of you.   35
But we are, that's true!
As I learn from you,
I guess you learn from me —
although you're older — and white —
and somewhat more free.   40

This is my page for English B.

24 *Bessie:* Bessie Smith (1898?–1937), a famous blues singer.

Considerations for Critical Thinking and Writing

1. FIRST RESPONSE. Try to write "a page" in response to the instructor that, like the speaker's, captures who you are.

2. What complicates the writing assignment for the speaker? Does he fulfill the assignment? Explain why or why not.

3. What are the circumstances of the speaker's life? How does the speaker respond to the question "So will my page be colored that I write?" (line 27). Discuss the tone of lines 27–40.

4. Write a one-paragraph response to this poem as you think the speaker's instructor would in grading it.

Connection to Another Selection

1. Use your imagination and write about an encounter between the student-speaker in this poem and the instructor-speaker of Mark Halliday's "Graded

Paper" (p. 445). Choose a form (such as an essay, a dialogue, or a short story) that will allow you to explore their responses to one another.

While the speaker in "Theme for English B" wrote a poem as a student in a composition class, the next poem features a speaker from the other side of the assignments in a poetry class. If you've ever been in a creative writing class or simply been asked to write a poem in an English course, you may have experienced some version of what's going on in this classroom. The picture may not be pretty, but it is brilliantly drawn in Marilyn Hacker's "Groves of Academe."

MARILYN HACKER (B. 1942)

Groves of Academe 1984

The hour dragged on, and I was badly needing
coffee; that encouraged my perversity.
I asked the students of Poetry Writing,
"Tell me about the poetry you're reading."
There was some hair chewing and some nail biting. 5
Snowdrifts piled up around the university.
"I've really gotten into science fiction."
"I don't read much — it breaks my concentration.
I wouldn't want to influence my style."
"We taped some Sound Poems for the college station." 10
"When *I* give readings, should I work on diction?"
"Is it true that no really worthwhile
contemporary poets write in rhyme?"
"Do you think it would be a waste of time
to send my poems to *Vanity Fair*? 15
I mean — could they relate to my work there?"

CONSIDERATIONS FOR CRITICAL THINKING AND WRITING

1. FIRST RESPONSE. Characterize the speaker. How do the students compare?
2. What do the students' comments and questions in response to their teacher's request (line 4) reveal about themselves?
3. How does the speaker implicitly answer the question about poetic rhyme in lines 12 and 13?

CONNECTION TO ANOTHER SELECTION

1. Write an essay that compares the teachers in "Groves of Academe" and in Mark Halliday's "Graded Paper" (p. 445). Which teacher would you rather have teach you? Explain why.

The next four poems in this case study depict various teaching and learning situations as well as various teaching and learning personalities. As

you read them, consider how much diversity of perspective and approach
can be represented, all within the context of a single subject.

MARK HALLIDAY (B. 1949)

Graded Paper   1991

On the whole this is quite successful work:
your main argument about the poet's ambivalence —
how he loves the very things he attacks —
is mostly persuasive and always engaging.

At the same time,   5
                    there are spots
where your thinking becomes, for me,
alarmingly opaque, and your syntax seems to jump
backwards through unnecessary hoops,
as on p. 2 where you speak of "precognitive awareness   10
not yet disestablished by the shell that encrusts
each thing that a person actually says"
or at the top of p. 5 where your discussion of
"subverbal undertow miming the subversion of self-belief
woven counter to desire's outreach"   15
leaves me groping for firmer footholds.
(I'd have said it differently,
or rather, said something else.)
And when you say that women "could not fulfill themselves" (p. 6)
"in that era" (only forty years ago, after all!)   20
are you so sure that the situation is so different today?
Also, how does Whitman bluff his way into
your penultimate paragraph? He is the *last* poet
I would have quoted in this context!
What plausible way of behaving   25
does the passage you quote represent? Don't you think
literature should ultimately reveal possibilities for *action*?

Please notice how I've repaired your use of semicolons.

And yet, despite what may seem my cranky response,
I do admire the freshness of   30
your thinking and your style; there is
a vitality here; your sentences thrust themselves forward
with a confidence as impressive as it is cheeky. . . .
You are not
            me, finally,   35
and though this is an awkward problem, involving
the inescapable fact that you are so young, so young
it is also a delightful provocation.

(A—)

CONSIDERATIONS FOR CRITICAL THINKING AND WRITING

1. FIRST RESPONSE. How do you characterize the grader of this paper based on the comments of the paper?

2. Is the speaker a man or a woman? What makes you think so? Does the sex of the speaker affect your reading of the poem? How?

3. Explain whether or not you think the teacher's comments on the paper are consistent with the grade awarded it. How do you account for the grade?

CONNECTION TO ANOTHER SELECTION

1. Compare the ways in which Halliday reveals the speaker's character in this poem with the strategies used by Browning in "My Last Duchess" (p. 164).

JUDY PAGE HEITZMAN (B. 1952)

The Schoolroom on the Second Floor of the Knitting Mill

1991

While most of us copied letters out of books,
Mrs. Lawrence carved and cleaned her nails.
Now the red and buff cardinals at my back-room window
make me miss her, her room, her hallway,
even the chimney outside   5
that broke up the sky.

In my memory it is afternoon.
Sun streams in through the door
next to the fire escape where we are lined up
getting our coats on to go out to the playground,   10
the tether ball, its towering height, the swings.
She tells me to make sure the line
does not move up over the threshold.
That would be dangerous.
So I stand guard at the door.   15
Somehow it happens
the way things seem to happen when we're not really looking,
or we are looking, just not the right way.
Kids crush up like cattle, pushing me over the line.

Judy is not a good leader is all Mrs. Lawrence says.   20
She says it quietly. Still, everybody hears.
Her arms hang down like sausages.
I hear her every time I fail.

CONSIDERATIONS FOR CRITICAL THINKING AND WRITING

1. FIRST RESPONSE. Does your impression of Mrs. Lawrence change from the beginning to the end of the poem? How?

2. How can line 2 be read as an implied metaphor?

3. Discuss the use of similes in the poem. How do they contribute to the poem's meaning?

CONNECTIONS TO OTHER SELECTIONS

1. Compare the representations and meanings of being a schoolchild in this poem with those in Dickinson's "From all the Jails the Boys and Girls" (p. 442).

2. Discuss how the past impinges on the present in Heitzman's poem and in Larkin's "This Be the Verse" (p. 621).

R. S. GWYNN (B. 1948)

The Classroom at the Mall   1993

Our Dean of Something thought it would be good
For Learning (even better for P.R.)
To make the school "accessible to all"
And leased the bankrupt bookstore at the Mall
A few steps from Poquito's Mexican Food   5
And Chocolate Chips Aweigh. So here we are —

Four housewives, several solemn student nurses,
Ms. Light — serious, heavy, and very dark —
Pete Fontenot, who teaches high-school shop
And is besides a part-time private cop   10
Who leaves his .38 among the purses,
And I, not quite as thin as Chaucer's Clerk —

Met for our final class while Season's Greetings
Echo subliminally with calls to buy
Whatever this year's ads deem necessary   15
For Happiness and Joy. The Virgin Mary,
Set up outside to audit our last meetings,
Adores her infant with a glassy eye.

Descend, O Musak! Hail to thee, World Lit!
Hail, Epic ("most of which was wrote in Greek")   20
And hail three hours deep in Dante's Hell
(The occupants of which no one could spell) —
As much as our tight schedule might admit
Of the Great Thoughts of Man — one thought per week.

I've lectured facing towards "The Esplanade"   25
Through plate-glass windows. Ah, what do I see?
Is that the face "that launched a thousand ships"
Awash with pimples? Oh, those chocolate chips!
Ms. Light breaks in: "Will this be for a grade?"
It's a good thing the students all face me.   30

One night near Halloween I filled the board
With notes on FAUST. A Pentacostal hair-
Do with a woman underneath looked in,
Copying down my scrawl with a tight grin
That threatened she'd be back with flaming sword   35
To corner me and Satan in our lair.

Tonight, though, all is calm. They take their quiz
While I sit calculating if I've made
Enough to shop for presents. From my chair
I watch the Christmas window-shoppers stare   40
At what must seem a novelty, and is,
The Church of Reason in the Stalls of Trade —

Like the blond twins who press against the door,
Accompanied by footsore, pregnant Mummy,
Who tiredly spells out for them the reason   45
I am not price-tagged as befits the season,
Explaining what is sold in such a store
With nothing but this animated dummy

Who rises, takes the papers one by one
With warm assurances that all shall pass   50
Because "requirements have been met," because
I am an academic Santa Claus,
Because mild-mannered Pete's strapped on his gun.
Ms. Light declares she has enjoyed the class:

"They sure had thoughts, those old guys," she begins,   55
Then falters for the rest. And I agree
Because, for once, I've nothing left to say
And couldn't put it better anyway.
I pack the tests, gather my grading pens,
And fumble in my jacket for the key,   60

With time to spend and promises to keep
And not one "hidden meaning" to the tale,
Among these drifting schools of moon-eyed teens,
License and credit pulsing in their jeans,
Who circle, hungry for the choice and cheap —   65
Something of value, soon to go on sale.

CONSIDERATIONS FOR CRITICAL THINKING AND WRITING

1. FIRST RESPONSE. What expectations does the title of the poem set up for
   you? What values are juxtaposed between the classroom and the mall?
2. How does the first stanza characterize both the speaker and the school?
3. Discuss the poem's humor. Locate and analyze specific lines that strike you
   as especially amusing. What is the point of this humor?
4. What is the theme? Can you find the theme summed up or alluded to in a
   specific passage, or is the theme implicit? Explain.

CONNECTION TO ANOTHER SELECTION

1. How do the students in this poem compare with those in Marilyn Hacker's "Groves of Academe" (p. 444)? Where would you rather be a student? Why?

RICHARD WAKEFIELD (B. 1952)

In a Poetry Workshop   1999

Let us begin with the basics of modern verse.
Meter, of course, is forbidden, and lines must be,
like life, broken arbitrarily
lest anyone mistake us for budding Wordsworths
(don't be alarmed if you've never heard of him).   5
Rhyme is allowed, but only in moderation
and preferably very slant. Alliteration
and assonance must only be used at whim
so the reader doesn't think we're playing God
by sneaking in a pattern of sounds and echoes.   10
As for subjects, the modern poet knows
that modern readers prefer the decidedly odd,
so flowers, except for weeds, are out, and love,
except the very weed-like, is also out.
So thistles and incest are fine to write about   15
but roses and happy marriage get the shove
into the editor's outbox with hardly a glance.
Now note that language matters, so "I" must be
in lower case, thus "i," to show that we
don't put on airs despite our government grants.   20
This also shows we've read our Marx and know
the self is a bourgeois fiction. We understand
the common speech, and so the ampersand,
pronounced "uhn," replaces "and," although
judicious use of allusions to classical thought   25
will keep the great unwashed from getting our drift,
while those outside of Plato's cave will lift
a knowing eyebrow, declaring our work "well-wrought."
And speaking of work, this is not a "class":
We modern poets roll up our sleeves and write   30
our verse in "workshops," no place for sissies, we fight
to find "a voice," and only the fittest pass.
I've summarized these rules in a convenient list,
it's wallet-sized, laminated, so keep
it handy, use it, recite it in your sleep.   35
First poems are due tomorrow. You're dismissed.

CONSIDERATIONS FOR CRITICAL THINKING AND WRITING

1. FIRST RESPONSE. What are the speaker's attitudes toward modern poetry? How does this parallel the speaker's attitudes toward students?

2. How accurate do you think the speaker's assessment of modern poetry is? Explain why you agree or disagree.

3. What about that list of rules on the "wallet-sized, laminated" card? How does this reveal the speaker to you?

4. Write a character sketch of a teacher who reminds you of this kind of instructor. No names, please.

CONNECTION TO ANOTHER SELECTION

1. How does the speaker's use of language in this poem suggest a very different sort of teacher than Mark Halliday's in "Graded Paper" (p. 445)?

18

Biographies of
Selected Poets

The following biographical notes for selected poets represented in this book briefly describe their writings and lives in order to provide contexts that will enhance your readings of their poems. Poets who are in some way connected to one another and referred to in a biographical note are cross-referenced to their own entry by way of small capital letters. For example, in the entry for Gwendolyn Brooks, cross-references appear for Langston Hughes, T. S. Eliot, Ezra Pound, E. E. Cummings, and Carl Sandburg. In addition, at the end of many of the entries, you'll also find a revealing or provocative quotation from the poet to stimulate your reading and thinking about the poetry.

A. R. Ammons (American, b. 1926). Born on a farm outside Whiteville, North Carolina, Archie Randolph Ammons was educated at Wake Forest College, where he earned his bachelor of science degree in 1949. He wrote his first poetry aboard a U.S. Navy destroyer escort in the South Pacific. After a two-year period at the University of California, Berkeley, Ammons became an executive of a New Jersey glass-making firm. In 1964, he took a teaching position at Cornell University and has remained there since; he is currently Goldwin Smith Professor of Poetry. His first book of poetry, *Ommateum with Doxology*, appeared in 1955; a second vol-

ume, *Expressions of Sea Level* (1964), established him as a major American poetic voice. His work combines the minute particulars and detailed observation of science (as the title of his first book suggests: *ommateum* is the compound eye of an insect) with an at times sweeping lyricism; many of his poems conduct journeys through symbolic landscapes, arriving at some measure of clarity or light. His works have been gathered in several editions, among them *Collected Poems: 1951–1971* (1972), *The Selected Poems: 1951–1977* (1977), and *Selected Longer Poems* (1980). His poetry has received many awards, including the Lannan Poetry Award (1992), the National Book Critics Circle Award (1981), the Bollingen Prize (1975), and the National Book Award (1973). One of the first recipients of a MacArthur Fellowship, he has received other fellowships from the Guggenheim Foundation and the American Academy of Arts and Letters. He currently lives in Ithaca, New York.

Matthew Arnold (English, 1822–1888). Matthew Arnold was born in Middlesex and educated at Winchester, Rugby, and Balliol College, Oxford. While at Oxford, he won the Newdigate Prize for poetry with his poem "Cromwell." He traveled abroad in the late 1840s, and by 1851 he was working as an inspector of schools, a position that brought him financial security enough to marry Frances Lucy Wightman. He held this post until 1886, working tirelessly to improve English education. What Arnold's poetic career lacked in longevity, it compensated for in variety. There are lyrics—the "Marguerite" poems (based on a Swiss girl he met in the 1840s) and "Dover Beach"—as well as poetic drama, narrative poems, and elegies. After the 1867 volume *New Poems,* he wrote prose for the rest of his life, becoming one of the most influential literary and cultural critics of his age. Like many Victorian thinkers, he was absorbed with the theological controversies of the time, the rise of Darwinism, and the loss of faith, and he writes movingly of intellectuals "wandering between two worlds, / One dead, the other powerless to be born." His prose volumes *Essays in Criticism* and *Culture and Anarchy* are valuable for their pioneering and synthetic approach to a kind of total culture, "the pursuit of total perfection by means of getting to know, on all the matters which most concern us, the best which has been thought and said in the world."

Quotable: "Poetry is simply the most beautiful, impressive and wisely effective mode of saying things, and hence its importance." —*Essays in Criticism*

MARGARET ATWOOD (CANADIAN, b. 1939). As does much of her work, Margaret Atwood's retelling of how she became a poet blurs the line between the poetic and prosaic, the mundane and the marvelous: "The day I became a poet was a sunny day of no particular ominousness. I was walking across the football field . . . scuttling along in my usual furtive way, suspecting no ill, when a large invisible thumb descended from the sky and pressed down on the top of my head. A poem formed." This "gift from an anonymous donor," she recalls, was "both exciting and sinister at the same time." Born in 1939 in Ottawa, Ontario, Atwood has become one of the preeminent writers of her time, as well known for her fiction as for her poetry. She was educated at Victoria College, the University of Toronto, and Harvard University. Her first collection of poems, *The Circle Game,* appeared in 1964; since that time she has produced a steady line of work in many genres—poetry, short stories, novels, chil-

dren's books, nonfiction, and scripts for television. Her 1985 novel, *The Handmaid's Tale,* was adapted for the screen and released as a film in 1990. Her poetry collections include *Selected Poems* (1976), *Selected Poems II* (1986), and *Eating Fire: Selected Poems 1965–1995.* She has been the recipient of numerous literary awards; from 1981 to 1982 she served as president of the Writers' Union of Canada and from 1984 to 1986 as president of International P.E.N., Canadian Centre. She lives in Toronto.

W. H. AUDEN (ENGLISH, 1907–1973). The most influential English poet of the generation immediately following that of YEATS and ELIOT, Wystan Hugh Auden was born in 1907 in York. He was educated at St. Edmund's preparatory school (where his future collaborator Christopher Isherwood was a pupil) and later at Christ Church, Oxford. While at Oxford, he met Stephen Spender, C. Day-Lewis, and Louis MacNeice, all of whom would, with Auden, soon announce a new voice in English letters. After graduation, Auden took a post as a schoolmaster and worked on film documentaries for the English Postal Service. His early books, beginning with *Poems* (1930), and especially *Look Stranger!* (1936), quickly established him as a leading poet. He wrote plays with Isherwood during the 1930s and spent time in Spain as an ambulance driver for the Republicans in the Spanish Civil War. He emigrated to the United States in 1939 and became an American citizen in 1946. Before this time, Auden's work showed strong left-wing and materialistic sympathies. His early poems are influenced by his reading of Marx and reveal a deep interest in Freudian psychology. Following his move to America, Auden converted to the Anglican Church. While his interest in Freud continued, many of his earlier political sympathies fell away; Anglicanism informs a large part of his later poetry. He became professor of poetry at Oxford in 1956 and returned to live there in 1972. Much of his later life was spent in Austria; he died there, at Kirchstetten, in 1973.

Quotable: "Speaking for myself, the questions which interest me most when reading a poem are two. The first is technical: 'Here is a verbal contraption. How does it work?' The second is, in the broadest sense, moral: 'What kind of guy inhabits this poem? What is his notion of the good life or the good place? His notion of the Evil One? What does he conceal from the reader? What does he conceal even from himself?'" — *The Dyer's Hand*

ELIZABETH BISHOP (AMERICAN, 1911–1979). Elizabeth Bishop was born in Worcester, Massachusetts in 1911. Following the death of her father and her mother's mental illness, Bishop was raised by her grandparents in Nova Scotia and in Worcester. She was educated at Vassar and lived after that in New York, France, Mexico, Key West, and, for sixteen years, Brazil. These varied landscapes and experiences inform her 1965 volume of poems, *Questions of Travel*, and much of her later work. Her *Poems: North and South a Cold Spring* (1955) won the Pulitzer Prize; *Complete Poems* (1969) won the National Book Award. Her poetry, like that of her longtime friend MARIANNE MOORE, is admired for its fastidious attention to the natural world, as well as for its muted irony and humor. ROBERT LOWELL and RANDALL JARRELL thought her work exquisite; Lowell modeled his "Skunk Hour" after Bishop, to whom the poem is dedicated. *Collected Prose*, published in 1984, includes autobiographical sketches, travel accounts, a memoir of Marianne Moore, and short stories. She lived in Cambridge, Massachusetts, during the last years of her life, teaching at Harvard.

WILLIAM BLAKE (ENGLISH, 1757–1827). Poet, mystic, engraver, painter — William Blake remains one of the most enigmatic, and popular, figures of English literature. He was born in London in 1757 and never went to school. Educated at home, he read widely in Milton, Shakespeare, and the Bible, and somehow picked up a knowledge of French, Italian, Latin, Greek, and Hebrew. At fourteen, Blake was apprenticed to an engraver. His talent for art flourished, and he was eventually made a member of London's Royal Academy. In 1782 he married Catherine Boucher, and the two would work together for the rest of their lives developing colored engravings of Blake's poems. His first book, *Poetical Sketches* (1783), was printed by friends. In 1789 he published *Songs of Innocence*, followed in

1794 by *Songs of Experience*. At times deceptively simple, at others most profound, these lyrics express Blake's ardent belief in the freedom of the imagination and his scorn of rationalism and materialism. Also issued during this time were his mystical and prophetic works, *The Book of Thel* (1789) and his principle prose work, *The Marriage of Heaven and Hell* (1791). In 1793 the Blakes moved to Lambeth, south of London, and here Blake began work on *The Book of Job*, arguably his finest illustrations, completed when he was nearly seventy. Largely dismissed in his time as eccentric, even mad, his books attracted no more than a circle of readers. At his death in 1827 he was buried in an unmarked grave.

Quotable: "If the doors of perception were cleansed every thing would appear to man as it is: infinite."
— *The Marriage of Heaven and Hell*

ROBERT BLY (AMERICAN, b. 1926). Of Norwegian descent, Robert Bly was born in Madison, Minnesota, in 1926. Following naval service in World War II, he attended St. Olaf College before transferring to Harvard, where he earned his degree in 1950. While at Harvard, and during several years' residence in New York, he wrote the poems that form his first book, *The Lute of Three Loudnesses*. Of them he has said, "The early poems I wrote were musical, but the 'I' in them had no weight. I lived for several years in various parts of New York City, longing for 'the depths,' by which I meant the fruitful depths. I was already underground, but in a solitary dry well, not a depth." In his later poems, especially in their exploration of the unconscious, of myth, and of psychological landscapes, he was to discover a fruitful depth that has informed most of his work since. His poems, along with those of JAMES WRIGHT and W. S. MERWIN, have been called poems of "the deep image," full of quiet archetypal resonance culled from the natural world. His work also has a political dimension; during the Vietnam War he founded American Writers against the Vietnam War and was an ardent supporter of that cause. He has also been responsible for translating into English many previously unknown European and South American poets, Eugene Montale and PABLO NERUDA among them. He lives on a farm in Minnesota.

Quotable: "All poems are journeys. They go from somewhere to somewhere else. The best poems take long journeys. I like poetry best that journeys — while remaining in the human scale — to the other world, which may be a place as easily overlooked as a bee's wing. . . . The old people say that each object in the universe — seashell, bat's wing, pine cone, patch of lichen — contains some fragment of our missing soul, and so our soul is thin. Making journeys of this sort could be called thickening the soul."

— *Selected Poems*

ANNE BRADSTREET (AMERICAN, 1612–1672). The first American poet to be published in America, Anne Bradstreet was born in England in 1612, the daughter of Thomas Dudley, former steward to the earl of London. At sixteen she married Simon Bradstreet and sailed two years later for America with her husband and father, both of whom eventually became governors of Massachusetts. She lived in Ipswich, then in Andover, and had eight children. Her first collection of poems, *The Tenth Muse,* was published without her knowledge in 1650 by her brother-in-law in London. The book concerns itself with historical, cosmological, and metaphysical matters; it is conventional in style, and shows the influence of Spenser, SIDNEY, and Raleigh. Along with the familiar preoccupations of the age — time and mutability — it contains elegies on Sidney and on Queen Elizabeth. A second edition, with corrections and additions, appeared in Boston six years after the poet's death. In this group, Bradstreet turns more frequently towards the personal, often addressing domestic topics from a religious point of view. This latter group contains elegies on her children and the poems to her beloved husband.

GWENDOLYN BROOKS (AMERICAN, 1917–2000). Though born in Topeka, Kansas, Gwendolyn Brooks is most closely associated with Chicago, particularly with the city's South Side, where her family moved shortly after her birth and where she lived until her death. She was educated at Wilson Junior College and taught at Columbia College (Chicago), Northeastern Illinois University, Columbia University, and the University of Wisconsin, to name a few. Early in her writing career, she met LANGSTON HUGHES, who encouraged her to read the poetry of T. S. ELIOT, EZRA POUND, and E. E. CUMMINGS — all of whom had some impact on her development. In the 1960s her work took a turning point, influenced by the politically and socially radical Black Arts Movement. Her poetry has been distinguished by its variety of voices and styles — traditional and experimental — and Brooks herself by her consummate command of technique. She authored more than twenty books of poetry, beginning with *A Street in Bronzeville* (1945), followed by *Annie Allen* (1949), for which she received the Pulitzer Prize (the first time that honor had been conveyed to a black poet). Her *Selected Poems* appeared in 1982. In 1986 she was named poetry consultant to the Library of Congress, and she succeeded CARL SANDBURG in 1968 as poet laureate of Illinois. She was also the author of a novel, an autobiography, and critical prose.

ELIZABETH BARRETT BROWNING (ENGLISH, 1806–1861). The eldest of twelve children, Elizabeth Barrett Browning was born at Coxhoe Hall, near Durham, in 1806. She spent most of her childhood and youth at the family estate of Hope End, near Malvern. She was an avid learner and began to write verse at an early age. Her first volume, *The Battle of Marathon,* was privately printed in 1820, and a second book followed in 1826. In 1832 the family moved to London, where Elizabeth began to associate with literary circles. Her volume *The Seraphim and Other Poems* (1838) was well received, and *Poems* (1844) attracted considerable acclaim. One of its admirers, ROBERT BROWNING, initiated a correspondence; the two met in 1843 and fell in love. Seeking to avoid her father's suspected prohibitions, they eloped in 1846 and left for Italy. There, in Florence, their son Robert was born in 1849. In 1850, Elizabeth published a further volume of poems, among them the *Sonnets from the Portuguese,* which had been composed during her and Robert's courtship ("Portuguese" being his pet name for her). Her fame continued to grow; she was the foremost woman poet of her time, and at WORDSWORTH's death there was talk of making her poet laureate. She died in Florence in 1861. Her husband prepared her posthumous *Last Poems* for publication later that year.

ROBERT BROWNING (ENGLISH, 1812–1889). One of the most famous poets of the Victorian age, Robert Browning was the son of a bank clerk. He received little formal education, though he read voraciously from his father's library. He wrote poems from an early age, taking as his model SHELLEY, under whose influence he briefly became a vegetarian and touted atheistic principles. Until the publication of *Paracelsus* (1835) and *Bells and Pomegranates* (1841–1846), his poetry attracted little attention. His first volume, *Pauline: A Fragment of a Confession,* published anonymously in 1833, prompted a strong reaction from John Stuart Mill. in these poems the philosopher noted "a more intense and morbid self-consciousness than I ever knew in any sane human being." Such censure may have been responsible for Browning's subsequent turning to the creation of dramatic characters and his development of the dramatic monologue, a form now associated almost exclusively with him. In 1846 he married Elizabeth Barrett and the two moved to Florence, where he composed *Men and Women* (1855) and *Dramatis Personae* (1864). After the death of his wife, he returned to London, where he wrote his masterpiece, *The Ring and the Book* (1869). He died in 1889 while visiting his son in Venice. His request for burial in Florence being impossible to fulfill, his body was returned to England and buried in Westminster Abbey. His work, especially the dramatic monologues, had great influence on writers in the early twentieth century, notably EZRA POUND.

GEORGE GORDON, LORD BYRON (ENGLISH, 1788–1824). Lord Byron — poet, celebrity, and father of the "Byronic hero" — was born in London. Descended from James I, his mother was a Scottish heiress. His father, "Mad Jack" Byron, was a captain notorious for squandering the family's money. Wishing to avoid creditors, his father fled to France, where he died when his son was three. Byron's mother returned to Scotland, and the boy was educated at home and at Aberdeen Grammar School. He went on to study at Cambridge, where he published a small volume of verse, *Fugitive Pieces*

(1807), followed by *Hours of Idleness* in the same year. The second volume was attacked for its pretension in the *Edinburgh Review;* Byron responded with his satirical *English Bards and Scotch Reviewers* (1809). Soon after taking his seat in the House of Lords, Byron left on a tour of the Mediterranean, an experience that informed the first two cantos of *Childe Harold's Pilgrimage* (1812), completed after his return. Of its publication and immediate success, Byron later wrote, "I awoke one morning and found myself famous." Following his brief marriage to Annabella Milbanke and the ensuing scandal over their separation, Byron left England for Switzerland and never returned. He met the poet SHELLEY and lived for two years in Venice, where he completed the first cantos of *Don Juan* (1819–1824) and other important works. Ever a man of action, he was an ardent supporter of the Italian revolutionaries. He died in 1824 assisting the Greek war for independence.

LEWIS CARROLL (ENGLISH, 1832–1898). Charles Lutwidge Dodgson was born in Cheshire, the son of a scholarly country parson. He was educated at Yorkshire Grammar School, at Rugby, and at Christ Church, Oxford, where he studied mathematics. Following graduation, he took a university teaching post and was ordained to the ministry in 1861. He taught and preached only rarely, however, due to his shyness and a bad stammer. He published mathematical textbooks and occasional comic writing, but it was in 1865, with the publication of *Alice's Adventures under Ground* (now generally known as *Alice in Wonderland*), that he became immediately established as a children's writer of the first order. Indeed, the book was revolutionary in its time for its absence of educational or religious pieties, seeking instead to amuse for amusement's sake. His later successes include *Through the Looking-Glass and What Alice Found There* (1871) and nonsense poems such as *The Hunting of the Snark* (1876) and "Jabberwocky."

JOHN CIARDI (AMERICAN, 1916–1986). John Ciardi — poet, critic, translator, and editor — was born in Boston and grew up in the nearby suburb of Medford. He studied at Tufts University and at the University of

Michigan before serving as an aerial gunner aboard B-29 bombers in World War II. Among his nearly forty volumes of poetry are *Homeward to America* (1940); *Other Skies* (1947), a collection of war poems; *In the Stoneworks* (1961); and *Manner of Speaking* (1972). His *Selected Poems* was published in 1984. He is widely known for his translation of Dante's *Divine Comedy* (1954–1970) into colloquial American verse. His works of criticism include *How Does a Poem Mean?* (1950) and *Dialogue with an Audience* (1963). From 1956 to 1972 he was poetry editor of *Saturday Review/World;* he taught at the University of Kansas City and at Harvard and Rutgers Universities and lectured at the annual Bread Loaf Writers' Conference at Middlebury College in Vermont. From 1980 on, Ciardi broadcast a popular weekly program on etymology titled "A Word in Your Ear."

Quotable: "What has any poet to trust more than the feel of the thing? Theory concerns him only until he picks up his pen, and it begins to concern him again as soon as he lays it down."

— *New York Times*

SAMUEL TAYLOR COLERIDGE (ENGLISH, 1772–1834). The poet, philosopher, and critic Samuel Taylor Coleridge was born at Ottery St. Mary, Devon, where his father was vicar. He entered Jesus College, Cambridge, in 1791, intending a profession in the church, but abandoned his studies in 1793 to enlist in the Light Dragoons. His first poems were published in 1794, but it was in 1798, in *Lyrical Ballads,* that his mature writing appeared. The book was a collaborative venture between Coleridge and **WILLIAM WORDSWORTH**. In that work, and in their later poems, the two not only laid the foundations of English Romanticism but also expanded the contours of poetic form. One of Coleridge's most important developments was the conversation poem, which was influential on later forms such as the dramatic monologue and the confessional poem. He also experimented with preexisting forms, ranging from the ballad (*Lyrical Ballads* included his *Rime of the Ancient Mariner*) to the ode. His visionary fragment, "Kubla Khan," was written in 1797. Despite his break with Wordsworth after 1810 and the decline of his poetic powers (due in part to a long-term opium addiction), Coleridge continued to write philosophical and social tracts, as well as sermons and literary criticism. His magnum opus, *Biographia Literaria,* belongs to this later period. Revolutionary in thought, catholic in work and taste, Coleridge has continued to inspire generations of writers since his death in 1834.

Quotable: "The poet, described in *ideal* perfection, brings the whole soul of man into activity, with the subordination of its faculties to each other, according to their relative worth and dignity. He diffuses a tone and spirit of unity, that blends, and (as it were) *fuses,* each into each, by that synthetic and magical power . . . imagination."

— *Biographia Literaria,* Chapter 14

COUNTEE CULLEN (AMERICAN, 1903–1946). A leading poet of the Harlem Renaissance, Countee Cullen was born in New York and was brought up by foster parents there. He attended New York University and Harvard. His first book, *Color* (1925), showed a poet highly adept at traditional forms. Later volumes include *Copper Sun* (1927) and *The Ballad of the Brown Girl: An Old Ballad Retold* (1927). Cullen received a Guggenheim fellowship and went to France; while there, he wrote *The Black Christ and Other Poems* (1929). He authored one novel, *One Way to Heaven* (1932), and collaborated with Arna Bontemps on the play *St. Louis Woman* (1946). His 1935 collection, *The Medea and Some Poems,* combines sonnets and other lyrics with a translation of Euripides' tragedy. He edited the magazine *Opportunity* and an anthology of black poetry, *Caroling Dusk* (1927).

E. E. CUMMINGS (AMERICAN, 1894–1962). One of the more eccentric poets of the twentieth century, Edward Estlin Cummings was born in 1894 in Cambridge, Massachusetts. His father was a Unitarian minister who also taught sociology at Harvard. Cummings attended Harvard, taking his B.A. in 1915 and his M.A. in 1916. Following graduation, he volunteered to go to France and serve in the ambulance corps. After the war he lived in Paris, where he took up painting as well as writing. His first book of poems, *Tulips and Chimneys,* was published in 1923, followed by *XLI Poems* in 1925. But it is in *&* and *is 5* (both published 1925) that his innovative style begins to appear. Influenced by jazz rhythms and slang, and marked by idiosyncratic use of syntax, punctuation, and typography, Cummings's poetry is antiestablishment. It bridles at rules, regulations, and restrictions, which he thought corroded the fluid life of the soul. Against science, mechanism, and the collective tyranny of "manunkind" he holds the spontaneous, childlike "is"-ness of the individual. His heroes are typically the poor, the misfits, the lovers, those who dare to be themselves. He is best known for his satires and love poems. He died in Conway, New Hampshire, in 1962 and is buried in the Forest Hills Cemetery in Boston.

JAMES DICKEY (AMERICAN, 1923–1997). "Gothic," "surreal," "morbid," "grotesque" — such are the terms some critics use to describe the poetry of James Dickey. Born in Atlanta, Georgia, as a boy Dickey was inspired by the poetry of LORD BYRON. He also loved athletics and was a high school football star. These interests combine in his ideal of the poet as a man of action, as one who walks "the razor's edge between sublimity and absurdity." Dickey entered Clemson College in 1942, but left after a year to serve in the air force in World War II. He completed his undergraduate education at Vanderbilt University following the war, and went on for graduate study there and later at Rice University. His first book of poems, *Into the Stone and Other Poems,* was published in 1960, but his reputation was secured by *Drowning with Others* (1962) and *Helmets* (1964), both drawing on his experiences as a pilot. Most of his work has been gathered in *Whole Motion: Collected Poems 1948–1992* (1992). Dickey traveled widely and taught at a variety of universities besides working for a number of years as a writer of advertisements. Between 1966 and 1968 he was poetry consultant to the Library of Congress. In addition to his poems, he is best known for his novel *Deliverance* (1970), for which he also wrote the screenplay.

JOHN DONNE (ENGLISH, 1572–1631). John Donne was born in London. Though educated at Oxford and Cambridge, he left without taking any degrees. During the 1590s he traveled widely, read voraciously, and lived the mayfly life of a courtier in Queen Elizabeth's court. In 1601 he married Ann Moore, still a minor, an offense for which he was briefly imprisoned and left unemployed. Ann died in 1617, leaving him with seven children. In 1621, however, Donne's prospects turned: King James, convinced of his promise as a preacher, made Donne the dean of St. Paul's Cathedral, a position he held until his death in 1631. Donne's metaphysical poetry is characterized by passionate thought and intellectual play; it delights in puns, paradox, poses, and conceits. In love poems such as "The Good Morrow" and "Go and Catch a Falling Star," Donne injected life into the tired Petrarchan conventions of the 1590s. Similarly, in his *Holy Sonnets* he infused English religious verse with sinewy toughness. Though his poetry fell out of favor in the seventeenth and eighteenth centuries, it has since been reclaimed as one of the treasures of English Renaissance literature.

HILDA DOOLITTLE (AMERICAN, 1886–1961). Also known by her pseudonym, H. D., Hilda Doolittle was born in Bethlehem, Pennsylvania, in 1886. In 1911 she went to London, where she married the poet Richard Aldingham in 1913. She became associated with EZRA POUND (to whom she had been briefly engaged) and with him developed the literary form Imagism, which seeks among other things concrete expression of a particular experience. Pound arranged for her early work to be published in *Poetry* magazine and in the anthology *Des Imagistes* (1914). Her first collection of poems, *Sea Garden,* appeared in 1916, followed by *Hymen* (1921), *Heliodora and Other Poems* (1924), and *Red Roses for Bronze* (1929). Her work is heavily informed by the classical Greek tradition; indeed she produced numerous translations of Sappho, Meleager, Euripides, and others. Her fiction includes *Palimpsest* and *Hedylus* (both published 1928); three additional works, *Pilate's Wife, Asphodel,* and *Her,* were published posthumously as *Hermione* in 1981. After her divorce in 1937, she settled near Lake Geneva and continued a stream of literary output: *Trilogy* (1944–1946), a description of London during the blitz of

World War II; *By Avon River* (1949), a tribute to SHAKESPEARE and other Elizabethans; *Bid Me to Live* (1960), which treats London during World War I; and *Helen in Egypt* (1961), a long poem about Helen of Troy. A final set of poetic sequences was published in 1972.

PAUL LAURENCE DUNBAR (AMERICAN, 1872–1906). Paul Laurence Dunbar was born in Dayton, Ohio, the son of former slaves. His first collection of poems, *Oak and Ivy*, was printed privately in 1893. A second collection, *Majors and Minors*, appeared in 1895. William Dean Howells, influential novelist and journalist, took an interest in Dunbar's work and wrote the preface to his third volume, *Lyrics of Lowly Life* (1896). His later collections of poetry include *Lyrics of the Hearthside* (1899), *Lyrics of Love and Laughter* (1903), and *Lyrics of Sunshine and Shadow* (1905). Dunbar achieved national recognition in his time, conducted numerous lecture tours, and was known primarily as a writer of dialect verse. Since then, his poems have fallen under criticism for their alleged sentimental treatment of black life in the South. In addition to poetry, he wrote four novels: *The Uncalled* (1898), *The Love of Landry* (1900), *The Fanatics* (1901), and *The Sport of the Gods* (1902).

MARTÍN ESPADA (AMERICAN, b. 1957). Hailed as "well on his way to becoming the Latino poet of his generation," Martín Espada writes a primarily political poetry that seeks to combine politics with art, to find what he calls the "political imagination [which] goes beyond protest to articulate an artistry of dissent." Claiming WALT WHITMAN and PABLO NERUDA as precursors, Espada has allied himself with poets who, against the suffering and injustice of the world, sing "defiant, extravagant hope." Born in Brooklyn in 1957, Espada was early immersed in the climate of political activism by his father, a leader in the Puerto Rican community. "Long Island was tough when you were the only Puerto Rican in town. I needed a way to respond. I think writing poetry is a great way to assert your humanity. So I started to do that, and I never looked back." His 1996 collection *Imagine the Angels of Bread* won the Ameri-

can Book Award. Other books of poetry include *Rebellion Is the Circle of a Lover's Hand* (1990) and *City of Coughing and Dead Radiators* (1993); a collection of essays, *Zapata's Disciple,* appeared in 1998. The recipient of a Massachusetts Artists' Fellowship, a PEN/Revson Fellowship, and the Paterson Poetry Prize, he teaches at the University of Massachusetts in Amherst.

Quotable: "Poetry of the political imagination is a matter of both vision and language. Any progressive social change must be imagined first, and that vision must find its most eloquent possible expression to move from vision to reality."

—*Zapata's Disciple*

ALLEN GINSBERG (AMERICAN, 1926–1997). Leading Beat poet Allen Ginsberg was born in Newark, New Jersey. His father was a high school teacher, his mother a Communist who may have encouraged her son's radical views. Ginsberg grew up in Paterson, New Jersey, where he fell under the tutelage of WILLIAM CARLOS WILLIAMS. He attended Columbia, where he met fellow writers Jack Kerouac and William Burroughs. He completed his B.A. in 1948, after a temporary suspension, and in 1953 left for San Francisco, where he joined Kerouac, Burroughs, Lawrence Ferlinghetti, and others associated with the newly emerging Beat movement. In 1956 his first collection, *Howl and Other Poems,* appeared. Numerous collections followed, significantly *Kaddish and Other Poems* (1961), *Reality Sandwiches* (1963), and *Poems All Over the Place: Mostly Seventies* (1978). His *Collected Poems* appeared in 1984. In addition to poems, he wrote two plays and several volumes of prose. Ginsberg's style is, like that of his predecessor WALT WHITMAN, open, expansive, at times journalistic, always improvisatory. Apart from Whitman, he claimed WILLIAM BLAKE as an influence, and he shares with both the vision of poet as prophet. Over the course of his career, his work continued to open American poetry to a new range of styles and subjects.

Quotable: "[I see myself] as someone in the tradition of the oldtime American transcendentalist individualism . . . Thoreau, Emerson . . . Whitman . . . just carrying it on into the 20th century."   —*Interview*

THOMAS HARDY (ENGLISH, 1840–1928). Thomas Hardy was born in Higher Brockhampton near Dorchester, a town that would become the center of his fictional Wessex. He attended a village school in Dorchester, where he studied to be an architect. At twenty-two he moved to London and began to write his first verses. Unable to publish his poetry, however, Hardy turned to fiction. His first successful novel, *Far from the Madding Crowd*, appeared in 1874 and allowed him to marry Emma Gifford. Hardy took up writing as a profession and produced a stream of remarkable novels, notably *The Return of the Native* (1878), *The Mayor of Casterbridge* (1886), *Tess of the D'Urbervilles* (1891), and *Jude the Obscure* (1896). Following the cold reception of *Jude*, Hardy turned again to poetry, of which he published a vast amount during the remaining thirty years of his life. Collections such as *Wessex Poems and Other Verses* (1898), *Poems of the Past and Present* (1902), and *Satires of Circumstance, Lyrics and Reveries* (1914) contain sardonic lyrics (Hardy had long been known as a pessimist) as well as moving elegies to his wife, who died in 1912. In addition to poems and novels, he wrote two plays, *The Dynasts* (1903–1908) and *The Famous Tragedy of the Queen of Cornwall* (1923). Technically and metrically adroit, Hardy's work strongly influenced later poets such as W. H. AUDEN, PHILIP LARKIN, and DYLAN THOMAS.

ROBERT HASS (AMERICAN, b. 1941). Born in San Francisco of German and Irish parents, Robert Hass was educated at St. Mary's College and at Stanford University. His first book of poems, *Field Guide* (1973), was selected by the poet Stanley Kunitz as a winner of the prestigious Yale Series of Younger Poets Award. Other collections include *Praise* (1979), *Human Wishes* (1989), *Sun under Wood: New Poems* (1996), and a volume of criticism, *Twentieth Century Pleasures: Prose on Poetry* (1984); the latter two won National Book Critics Circle Awards. Hass has also published translations from the Japanese of Bashō, Buson, and Issa (*The Essential Haiku*, 1994) and has collaborated with the Polish poet Czeslaw Milosz on *Unattainable Earth* (1986), *Provinces* (1993), and *Facing the River* (1995); with Robert Pinsky he has

translated Milosz's *The Separate Notebooks* (1983). From 1995 to 1997 he served as poet laureate of the United States. He has taught at the State University of New York, Buffalo, and at St. Mary's College, California; since 1987 he has been a professor of English at the University of California, Berkeley.

ROBERT HAYDEN (AMERICAN, 1913–1980). Robert Hayden once described himself as "a romantic forced to be realistic." Hayden was raised by a foster family in the Detroit ghetto sardonically nicknamed "Paradise Valley." After a traumatic childhood in a house fraught with "chronic angers," Hayden attended Detroit City College (later Wayne State University) and worked for the Federal Writers' Project, where he was chief researcher on negro history and folklore. His first book, *Heart-Shape in the Dust* (1940), showed Hayden's awareness of Harlem Renaissance writers such as LANGSTON HUGHES and COUNTEE CULLEN. Later collections would continue to explore the complexities of African American life. In 1941 Hayden enrolled in the graduate program at the University of Michigan. There he studied under W. H. AUDEN, who turned his attention to matters of poetic technique and form. He won the Jule and Avery Hopwood Prize for Poetry in 1942 and in 1944. After graduation, he taught for several years at Michigan, then took a post at Fisk University. In 1969 he returned to Michigan to complete his teaching career. During the 1960s Hayden's poetry received international attention; his book *The Ballad of Remembrance* (1966) won the grand prize at the First World Festival of Negro Arts in Dakar, Senegal. In 1976 he became the first black American to be appointed poetry consultant to the Library of Congress.

Quotable: "There is no such thing as Black literature. There's good literature and bad. That's all."

— *Dictionary of Literary Biography*

SEAMUS HEANEY (IRISH, b. 1939). Of Seamus Heaney's poetry, fellow poet and former classmate Seamus Deane has said, "At the root of every word there is a tentacular handshake between the speaker and the thing spoken of." Indeed, it is this tactile correspondence between things and their representations that has attracted readers to Heaney's work since his first volume of poetry appeared in 1966. He was born in Mossbawn, County Derry, into a Roman Catholic farming family. The landscape of rural Mossbawn figures prominently in his early poetry, particularly in his first two books, *Death of a Naturalist* (1966) and *Door into the Dark* (1969), as do the memories of childhood. In later works, particularly in his acclaimed collection *North* (1975), he turns to confront the greater political and historical matters of Ireland. He was educated at St. Columb's College and at Queen's University, Belfast. After a stint as a lecturer at the University of California, Berkeley, he left Northern Ireland, moving first to County Wicklow and then to Dublin. In 1984 he was appointed Boylston Professor of Rhetoric at Harvard and in 1989 professor of poetry at Oxford. He won the Nobel Prize for Literature in 1995, the third Irish writer after YEATS to achieve that honor. Recently, his poetry has lightened in tone, though not in expressive vigor: his latest books, *Seeing Things* (1991) and *The Spirit Level* (1996), aim "to credit marvels." Apart from poetry, he has published three volumes of criticism and one play. He divides his time between Dublin and Cambridge, Massachusetts.

Quotable: "I have always listened for poems, they come sometimes like bodies come out of a bog, almost complete, seeming to have been laid down a long time ago, surfacing with a touch of mystery. They certainly involve craft and determination, but chance and instinct have a role in the thing too."   — *Preoccupations*

GEORGE HERBERT (ENGLISH, 1593–1633). A member of the noble family that included the earldoms of Pembroke and Montgomery, George Herbert was born in 1593 in Montgomery Castle, Powys. He studied at Westminster and at Trinity College, Cambridge; upon graduation he became a fellow and was public orator to the university from 1619 to 1627. Though he seems to have entertained aspirations for public advancement, Herbert became a deacon in 1626, a position that barred him from civil office. His mother, who was a patron of JOHN

DONNE, died in 1627, and Herbert married Jane Danvers in 1629. During this period, Herbert was working on the poems that would form his collection *The Temple* (published after his death). He became a priest in 1630, but soon after his health began to decline; he died in 1633. By 1680 his poems had gone through thirteen editions. Celebrated for their craft as well as their quiet yet passionate devotion, Herbert's poems rank among the finest of English religious verse. The ingenuity of their imagery, tight logic, and meticulous attention to shape situate them in the metaphysical tradition of poets like Donne. COLERIDGE greatly admired them; they have been influential on poets as different as T. S. ELIOT and DYLAN THOMAS.

ROBERT HERRICK (ENGLISH, 1591–1674). Extremely prolific (throughout his life he was responsible for 2,000 compositions), Robert Herrick was born in London. On taking his M.A. from Cambridge in 1620, he returned to London, where he began to mix with literary circles. There he met BEN JONSON, the poet with whom he is now most closely associated. In 1623, he took holy orders and in 1629 was appointed by Charles I to the living of Dean Prior in Exeter. Herrick enjoyed the quiet country life that the parish afforded but was ejected under the Commonwealth for his royalist sympathies. (He was reinstated in 1662 after the Restoration.) Just before leaving, he had published his major collection of verse, *Hesperides* (1648), which contains epigrams, epigraphs, elegies, hymns, songs, as well as imitations of the Roman writers Horace and Catullus. He is best known, however, for his love lyrics, of which the *carpe diem* poem "To the Virgins, to Make Much of Time" is a classic example. He died a bachelor, in his own parish, in 1674 at the age of eighty-three. The nineteenth-century poet Charles Swinburne would praise him as "the greatest songwriter ever born of English race."

GERARD MANLY HOPKINS (ENGLISH, 1844–1889). Of the expansive verbal range and variety of Gerard Manley Hopkins's work, the poet and critic Donald Davie has said, "One feels [he] could have found a place for every word in the language if only he could have written enough poems. One feels the same about Shakespeare." Born in Stratford, Essex, in 1844, Hopkins was educated at Highgate School, where he won the poetry prize, and at Balliol College, Oxford. In 1866 he shocked his family by converting to Roman Catholicism, and in 1868 he became a Jesuit priest. Doubting his ability to combine poetry with his vocation, he burned most of his early work and vowed to write "no more . . . unless by the wish of my superiors." He remained silent until 1875. In that year, encouraged by a rector to compose some verses on the sinking of the *Deutschland,* in which five Franciscan nuns had been drowned, he wrote *The Wreck of the Deutschland,* a splendid ode in thirty-five stanzas. The editor of the Jesuit paper, however, refused to print it. Hopkins continued to write, composing "God's Grandeur," "The Windhover," and "Pied Beauty" before his ordination; his poetic career ended in his last post, in Dublin, where he wrote his "terrible sonnets" before his death from typhoid fever in 1889. None of his poems were published in his lifetime. Despite the brevity of his career and his small literary output, his poems, and particularly his metrical innovations, had—and continue to have—enormous influence on later writers.

Quotable: "The poetical language of an age should be the current language heightened, to any degree heightened and unlike itself, but not . . . an obsolete one."

— *Letters*

A. E. HOUSMAN (ENGLISH, 1859-1936). The poet and classics scholar Alfred Edward Housman was born in 1859 and attended St. John's College, Oxford. After graduation he worked as a clerk in the London Patent Office, publishing his work on Propertius, Ovid, and Juvenal in his spare time. The quality of his scholarship earned him the post of professor of Latin at London University in 1892. He later became professor of Latin at Cambridge and was made a fellow of Trinity College, Oxford, in 1911. Chiefly known for his collection *A Shropshire Lad,* which he published in 1896 at his own expense, Housman was an accomplished lyricist who celebrated the English countryside and the "golden" lads and lasses who inhabited it. A healthy dose of pessimism keeps many of his poems free of sentimentality, and lyrics like "To an Ath-

lete Dying Young," and "Is My Team Ploughing," continue to delight readers. His "Loveliest of Trees, the Cherry now" is a fine example of the *carpe diem* poem in English. Despite the success of his first book, Housman wrote little poetry after it, though in 1922 he issued his collection *Last Poems.* A further collection, *More Poems,* was published by his brother Laurence after his death in 1936.

Quotable: "Good literature continually read for pleasure must, let us hope, do some good to the reader: must quicken his perception though dull, and sharpen his discrimination though blunt, and mellow the rawness of his personal opinions."

— *The Name and Nature of Poetry*

ANDREW HUDGINS (AMERICAN, b. 1951). Called "the most readable poet of his generation," Andrew Hudgins is the author of five books of poems. He was born in Killeen, Texas, into a military family and raised in Alabama, an experience vividly, humorously, and poignantly described in his collection *The Glass Hammer: A Southern Childhood* (1994). Other books of poetry are *Saints and Sinners* (1985), runner-up for the Pulitzer Prize; *After the Lost War* (1988), a narrative based on the life of the early American poet Sidney Lanier; *The Never Ending: New Poems* (1991), finalist for the National Book Award; and most recently *Babylon in a Jar* (1998). Largely autobiographical, ironically yet sensitively attuned to history and religion, Hudgins's work is at home inside contemporary American life. In "Compost: An Ode," he celebrates its indiscriminate variety and improbable regeneration: "The compost heap is both—life, death—a slow / simmer, / a leisurely collapsing of / the thing / into its possibilities . . . the opulence / of everything that rots." Winner of the Poet's Prize and numerous fellowships, he has taught at Princeton and at the University of Cincinnati, where he is currently professor of English. His collection of essays, *The Glass Anvil,* was published in 1997.

RANDALL JARRELL (AMERICAN, 1914-1965). A poet as well as an influential critic of poetry, Randall Jarrell was born in Nashville, Tennessee. Following his education at Vanderbilt, he joined the army and served in the air corps from 1942 to 1946. Two volumes of poetry, *Blood for a Stranger* (1942) and *Little Friend, Little Friend* (1945), were issued during this time. The poet Robert Fitzgerald has described Jarrell as "practically the only American poet able to cope with the Second Great War"; the experience of war and its grotesque realities form an important feature of much of his work. His *Selected Poems* was issued in 1955 (again in 1964), and in 1961 he won the National Book Award. His *Complete Poems* was published posthumously in 1969. Jarrell worked in various editorial positions at *The Nation, Partisan Review,* the *Yale Review,* and *American Scholar.* He taught English literature and creative writing at Kenyon College (where he was friends with ROBERT LOWELL and John Crowe Ransom), Sarah Lawrence College, and, from 1947 until his death in 1965, at the Women's College of the University of North Carolina, Greensboro.

Quotable: "Poetry does not need to be defended, any more than air or food needs to be defended."   — *Poetry and the Age*

ALICE JONES (AMERICAN, b. 1949). Born in 1949, Alice Jones is a graduate of Goddard College and New York Medical College. After several years of practice in internal medicine, she completed a second residency in psychiatry, which she now practices in California. Her work, then, uniquely combines the vocations of the poet and the psychoanalyst. Jones's first collection of poetry, *The Knot* (1992), won the 1992 Beatrice Hawley Award from Alice James Books and was praised as an "extraordinary combination of lyricism, mythmaking, and an informed use of the language of medicine." She is the author of two chapbooks of poems, *Anatomy,* published in letter edition by Bullnettle Press, San Francisco, and *Isthmus,* from Alice James Books and winner of the Jane Kenyon Award. Jones has been awarded fellowships in poetry from the Bread Loaf Writers' Conference and from the National Endowment for the Arts; her poems have appeared in *Ploughshares, Poetry, Kenyon Review,* and *The Best American Poetry: 1994.* She lives in Oakland, California, and is a member of the San Francisco Psychoanalytic Institute.

BEN JONSON (ENGLISH, 1572–1637). Born in Westminster and educated at Westminster School, Ben Jonson is probably the best-known Elizabethan playwright next to SHAKESPEARE. Though an accomplished lyric poet and scholar, it is on the strength of his comedies that his reputation primarily rests: *Every Man in His Humour* (1598) made Jonson a celebrity; it was followed by the great comedies *Volpone* (1605), *The Alchemist* (1610), and *Bartholomew Fair* (1614). He was rewarded with a royal pension and was made England's first poet laureate. Heavily influenced by classical Roman literature, particularly Horace, whose *Ars Poetica* (*The Art of Poetry*) he translated, Jonson embodies the urbanity and broad learning that are characteristic of the Renaissance. In 1678 he was appointed city chronologer of London; in that same year he suffered a debilitating stroke. His friends remained loyal to him in his final years, and he was honored with a collection of memorial elegies, *Jonsonus virbius,* at his death in 1637. He is buried in Westminster Abbey; his stone in Poet's Corner reads simply, "O rare Ben Jonson."

JOHN KEATS (ENGLISH, 1795–1821). John Keats was born in London, the eldest of four children. After his father's death in 1804, Keats's mother moved the family to Edmonton; she died of tuberculosis in 1810. Keats studied medicine at Guy's Hospital, intending to become a surgeon, but gave up that field in 1816 for a life of writing. His first poems were composed in 1814. In 1816 *The Examiner* printed his sonnet "On First Looking into Chapman's Homer" and hailed Keats, alongside SHELLEY, as one of the most promising writers of his generation. His *Poems* (1817), however, appeared to little applause. Keats began work on his long poem *Endymion,* published in 1818, but by then his brother Tom had become ill with tuberculosis, and Keats devoted much time to nursing him. In 1818, after Tom's death, he moved to Hampstead, where he fell in love with Fanny Brawne, the subject of some of his poems. He finished *Hyperion,* wrote lyrics such as "La Belle Dame sans Merci," and completed the great odes of 1819, for which he is chiefly remembered. In the winter of 1820 he fell seriously ill with tuberculosis and sailed for Italy. He died in Rome that summer, aged twenty-five. Despite doubts over the permanence of his achievement, Keats exerted enormous influence on later poets, notably TENNYSON and ARNOLD, and remains one of the best-loved poets of the later Romantic period.

Quotable: "Poetry should surprise by a fine excess, and not by singularity. It should strike the reader as a wording of his own highest thoughts, and appear almost as a remembrance."   — *Letters*

JANE KENYON (AMERICAN, 1947–1995). Born in Ann Arbor, Michigan, Jane Kenyon received her M.A. in English language and literature from the University of Michigan. Her first book, *From Room to Room,* was published in 1978; of it one critic was to remark, "Rarely does one encounter a first book which gives so much, so economically, and it is also rare that a first book leaves the reader with so rich a sense of reward, for the poet's careful labors are in the interest of the Mystery lying beneath everyday circumstances." Indeed, it was Kenyon's gift to see, as WORDSWORTH said, "into the mystery of things." She published four other volumes: *The Boat of Quiet Hours* (1986), *Let Evening Come* (1990), *Constance* (1993), and *Otherwise: New and Selected Poems* (published posthumously in 1996). Apart from her poetry she translated *Twenty Poems of Anna Akhmatova.* The recipient of a Guggenheim fellowship, the PEN/Voelcker Award, and a Creative Writing Fellowship from the National Endowment for the Arts, she lived with her husband, the poet DONALD HALL, on Eagle Pond Farm in New Hampshire. She died there of leukemia in 1995.

MAXINE HONG KINGSTON (AMERICAN, b. 1940). Born in Stockton, California, to Chinese emigrants, Maxine Hong Kingston attended both American and Chinese schools while working with her parents in the family laundry. She has described her childhood as rich in story, with her mother the dominant storyteller. Her first book, *The Woman Warrior: Memoir of a Girlhood Among Ghosts* (1976), a partly fictionalized memoir of her childhood with her Chinese ancestors, explores bicultural identity, myth, and memory and was an immediate critical success. It won the 1976 National Book Critics Circle Award for nonfiction and was named one of the top ten nonfiction works of the decade by *Time* magazine. Following her graduation from the University of California, Berkeley, Kingston taught

high school English in Hayward, California, then moved to Hawaii, where she worked as a schoolteacher. She currently lives in Oakland, California, and teaches at her alma mater. Apart from her novels and nonfiction, Kingston has published poems, short stories, and articles. Her collection of twelve prose sketches, *Hawaii One Summer,* was published in a limited edition with original woodblock print and calligraphy. She is currently working on what she calls "The Global Novel."

Quotable: "I learned to make my mind large, as the universe is large, so that there is room for paradoxes."
    — *The Woman Warrior*

GALWAY KINNELL (AMERICAN, b. 1927). Galway Kinnell was born in Providence, Rhode Island, and attended Princeton and the University of Rochester. He served in the navy in World War II. His first three books, *What a Kingdom It Was* (1960), *Flower Herding on Mount Monadnock* (1964), and *Body Rags* (1968), established him as an accomplished writer of free verse. His ten-part poem, *The Book of Nightmares* (1971), is a sustained exploration of human finitude and loss, leading the reader to the point where "one / and zero / walk off together, / walk off the end of these pages together, / one creature / walking away side by side with the emptiness." His *Selected Poems* won the Pulitzer Prize and the American Book Award in 1982. Later collections include *When One Has Lived a Long Time Alone* (1990) and *Imperfect Thirst* (1994). Apart from his own poems, he has published translations of François Villon and RAINER MARIA RILKE, among others. His prose includes one novel, *Black Light* (1966), and a collection of interviews, *Walking Down the Stairs* (1978). A former MacArthur fellow and state poet of Vermont, he teaches creative writing at New York University. He lives in New York and Vermont.

Quotable: "The death of the self I seek, in poetry and out of poetry, is not a drying up or withering. It is a death, yes, but a death out of which one might hope to be reborn more giving, more alive, more open, more related to the natural life."
    — *Walking Down the Stairs*

PHILIP LARKIN (ENGLISH, 1922–1985). Philip Larkin was born in Coventry, Warwickshire.

After graduation from St. John's College, Oxford, he moved to Shropshire to take a library position. He remained a librarian throughout his life, working at universities in Leicester and Belfast before settling at the University of Hull in 1955. As an undergraduate at Oxford, Larkin belonged to a group of poets that came to be known as the Movement. The Movement Poets (of whom Donald Davie and Thom Gunn were two) sought an evenness of expression, a conversational, plain idiom opposed to the rhetorical excess and apocalyptic urgency of poets such as DYLAN THOMAS and George Barker. Peter Levi has said of the poems in Larkin's last two books that Larkin's reputation rests on "85 perfect poems" in which he treats, with characteristic wryness, compassionate generosity, and consummate craftsmanship, the England of his time. In 1973 he edited *The Oxford Book of Twentieth-Century English Verse*, and he was a strong candidate for the post of poet laureate of England in 1984. His death in December of 1985 intervened.

Quotable: "The poetry I've enjoyed has been the kind of poetry you'd associate with me [. . .] on the whole, people to whom technique seems to matter less than content, people who accept the forms they have inherited but use them to express their own content." — *Four Conversations*

HENRY WADSWORTH LONGFELLOW (AMERICAN, 1807–1882). Henry Wadsworth Longfellow was born in Portland, Maine, and attended Bowdoin College, where he was later a professor of languages. Following a tour of Europe from 1826 to 1829 he married Mary Potter who then died during a second journey abroad in 1835. In 1836 he took a post as professor at Harvard and moved to Cambridge, Massachusetts, where he became a prominent figure in literary circles. His first collection of poems, *Voices in the Night* (1839), was followed by *Ballads and Other Poems* (1842). He was married again, to Frances Appleton, but she died in 1861. His remaining years were overshadowed by her death. Longfellow remained until recent years one of the most popular of American poets. His work, at times sentimental or didactic, was well suited to the tastes of its time. Such poems as "A Psalm of Life," "The Village Blacksmith," and "Paul Revere's Ride" have been cherished as much for their narrative delight as for their moral edification and expression of communally accepted values. In later works such as *The Song of Hiawatha* (1855) and *The Courtship of Miles Standish* (1858) he attempted the creation of an American mythology drawn from native lore. Apart from his poetry, he published a prose romance, *Hyperion* (1839), and a translation of Dante's *Divine Comedy* in 1867. He died in 1882.

ROBERT LOWELL (AMERICAN, 1917–1977). A descendant of the Fireside Poet James Russell Lowell and distant cousin of the modern experimental poet AMY LOWELL, Robert Lowell was born in Boston in 1917. He attended Harvard before transferring to Kenyon College to study under John Crowe Ransom. Following graduation, Lowell married the novelist Jean Stafford and the two moved to Louisiana, were Lowell attended Louisiana State University. In 1948 the couple divorced, and in 1949 Lowell married Elizabeth Hardwick. At LSU, under the tutelage of Robert Penn Warren and Allen Tate, Lowell composed much of his early work; its style, formally rigorous, dense in imagery and symbolism, was informed as well by his conversion to Catholicism. His first book, *Land of Unlikeness,* appeared in 1944, followed by the Pulitzer Prize-winning *Lord Weary's Castle* in 1946. In 1959 he published *Life Studies;* its looser style and personal subject matter had a great effect on the emerging confessional verse. During World War II, Lowell was arrested for his role as a conscientious objector and was held six months. During the Vietnam War, which he also opposed, his work exhibited a political dimension. Later collections, *Notebooks* (1970), *History* (1973), and *Day by Day* (1977), continued to explore the nexus of private life and public events. In 1970 Lowell withdrew from the political scene and moved to England, where he married Caroline Blackwood. He was on his way back to his second wife in 1977 when he died in a New York City taxicab.

ARCHIBALD MACLEISH (AMERICAN, 1892–1982). The poet and playwright Archibald MacLeish was born in Glencoe, Illinois. Following his graduation from Yale University in 1915, he served as an ambulance driver and captain of field artillery in World War I. His first collection of poems, *Tower of Ivory*, appeared in 1917. After the war he attended Harvard Law School and practiced briefly in Boston before moving to Paris, where he published four books of poetry. On returning to America, he wrote *New Found Land* (1930) and *Conquistador* (1932), winner of the Pulitzer Prize. A second Pulitzer was awarded him in 1953 for his *Collected Poems* (1952). Aside from poetry, he wrote verse-plays and radio plays; his best-known work for the stage is *J. B.* (1958), a modern retelling of the story of Job that won him yet another Pulitzer in 1959. MacLeish played an active role in politics and the academy as well as being a distinguished man of letters. He was librarian of Congress from 1939 to 1944, assistant secretary of state from 1944 to 1945, and a U.S. representative at the first UNESCO conference in Paris in 1946. From 1949 to 1962 he was Boylston Professor of Rhetoric and Oratory at Harvard University; his lectures on poetry were published as *Poetry and Experience* (1961). He died in 1982.

Quotable: "A book of poems is not a bouquet from which to pick a choice of posies. A book of poems is an attempt to come to terms with the experiences of a mortal life and it is almost always a whole thing—as whole in its way as a well-made novel."
— Foreword to *Selected Poems 1926–1972*

CHRISTOPHER MARLOWE (ENGLISH, 1564–1593). Little is known about the short life and violent death of Christopher Marlowe. He was born two months before SHAKESPEARE in 1564, the son of a Canterbury shoemaker. He attended King's School in Canterbury and then Corpus Christi College, Cambridge, taking his B.A. in 1583. By the time he received his M.A. from Cambridge in 1587 he had certainly written his first successful work for the London stage, the first part of *Tamburlaine the Great* (1587). The second part of *Tamburlaine* soon followed, rivaling the first in popularity; English theatergoers thrilled as much to the hero's energy and overreaching ambition as to his language, "Threatening the world in high astounding terms." Other dramatic successes followed in the six short years left to him: *The Jew of Malta* (1590), *Edward II* (c. 1592), and his best-known work, *The Tragical*

History of Doctor Faustus (1604, 1616). In these plays Marlowe laid the foundations for the English chronicle play and the new English tragedy. In the last few months of his life he worked in plague-ridden London completing his long narrative poem, *Hero and Leander* (1598), which, with "The Passionate Shepherd to His Love," stands as his poetic achievement. He was stabbed in a Deptford tavern in 1593 and, as a contemporary wrote, "dyed swearing."

ANDREW MARVELL (ENGLISH, 1621–1678). Into the century that included writers as disparate as DONNE, SHAKESPEARE, and MILTON, Andrew Marvell was born in 1621 in Yorkshire, the son of a vicar. He was educated at Trinity College, Cambridge, where he read Juvenal and Horace, Roman satirists who were to influence his own poetry. From 1642 to 1647 Marvell traveled widely in Europe. He was greatly influenced by John Donne, whose metaphysical conceit became more supple in Marvell's hands. He was a friend of John Milton, by whom he was recommended in 1653 for the post of assistant Latin secretary to the Council of State, a position he finally secured in 1657. Throughout the 1660s and 1670s he was embroiled in political matters and wrote many of his best satires. But Marvell is perhaps best remembered for his lyrics, especially "To His Coy Mistress" and "The Garden." In these and like poems, Marvell's chief ability lies in his minute attention to the physical world and human perception of that world. He also wrote political verse—"An Horatian Ode upon Cromwell's Return from Ireland" being his best-known poem of this kind—and highly wrought, elaborately sustained pastoral poems such as "Upon Appleton House." Little of his poetry appeared before 1681, when *Miscellaneous Poems* was published. His work was rediscovered in the nineteenth century, and was highly influential on TENNYSON.

JULIO MARZÁN (AMERICAN, b. 1946). The poet and fiction writer Julio Marzán has published a variety of works in English and in Spanish. His poetry, deeply immersed in Latino culture, has appeared in *Parnassus: Poetry in Review* and *Harper's* magazine. His most recent books of nonfiction are

The Spanish American Roots of William Carlos Williams (1994) and *The Numinous Site: The Poetry of Luis Palés Matos* (1995); he has also edited *Luna, Luna: Creative Writing Ideas from Spanish & Latino Literature* (1997). He has been an artist-in-residence at the Millay Colony and has taught at William Paterson University. He is presently a professor at Nassau Community College. A book of poetry in Spanish, *Puerta de Tierra,* is forthcoming.

JAMES MERRILL (AMERICAN, 1926–1995). Born in New York City, James Merrill was educated at Amherst College, where he received his B.A. in 1947 following brief service in World War II. His earliest volume, *Jim's Book: A Collection of Poems and Short Stories* (1942), appeared when he was still in his teens, but it was his second, *First Poems* (1951), that gained him the attention of poetry readers. His reputation as an exquisite craftsman and elegant lyric poet was established in succeeding volumes such as *The Country of a Thousand Years of Peace and Other Poems* (1959, revised in 1970), *Selected Poems* (1961), and *Water Street* (1962). Later works such as *The Divine Comedies* (1976), *Metamorphosis of 741* (1977), and *Mirabell: Books of Numbers* (1978) turned toward the esoteric and the metaphysical, culminating in his epic *The Changing Light at Sandhover* (1982), which uses a Ouija board and a host of personages (many of them dead) to assemble a poetic galaxy in the tradition of WILLLAM BLAKE's prophetic books. His most recent volumes include *Marbled Paper* (1982), *Santorini: Stopping the Leak* (1982), *Souvenirs* (1984), *Bronze* (1984), *Late Settings* (1985), and *The Inner Room* (1988). His *New Selected Poems* appeared in 1993. A winner of the National Book Award, the Bollingen Prize, and a Pulitzer, he also authored two novels, *The Seraglio* (1957) and *The (Diblos) Notebook* (1965), and a collection of essays, *Recitative* (1986). He was elected to the American Academy of Poets in 1971 and served there until his death in 1995.

EDNA ST. VINCENT MILLAY (AMERICAN, 1892–1950). Edna St. Vincent Millay was born in Rockport, Maine. With her mother's encouragement, she developed her literary interests and wrote her first poem at the age of five. She attended Vassar College, and her first collection, *Renascence and Other Poems* (1917), contained much she had written as an undergraduate. It was followed by *A Few Figs from Thistles* (1920), which established her as one of the more popular poets of her time. She moved to Greenwich Village and immersed herself in the Bohemian lifestyle, developing the literary personality of one hungry for experience, at odds with conventional morality, haunted by the brevity of life. Her third volume, *The Harp-Weaver and Other Poems* (1923), won the Pulitzer Prize in 1923. A member of the Provincetown Players, she was the author of *Three Plays* (1926); a libretto, *The King's Henchman* (1927); and a sonnet sequence, *Fatal Interview* (1928). Though her literary output slowed with the years, she still continued to publish poetry collections; later volumes include *Wine from These Grapes* (1934), *Conversation at Midnight* (1937), *Huntsman, What Quarry?* (1939), and *Make Bright the Arrows* (1940), a book dealing with the experience of World War II. Her reputation dimmed considerably during her life, but she is still admired for her graceful work within traditional lyric forms, particularly the sonnet.

JOHN MILTON (ENGLISH, 1608–1674). John Milton was born in London's Cheapside district, the son of a businessman. He was educated at St. Paul's, where he showed great aptitude with languages. Following his graduation from Christ's College, Cambridge, where he earned his B.A. in 1629 and his M.A. in 1632, Milton returned to his father's house in Buckinghamshire and continued his education, reading day and night for six years. In 1634 he wrote his masque, *Comus,* and in 1637 the great elegy *Lycidas* for a college classmate who had been drowned. From 1640 to 1660, he was embroiled in the political-religious controversies of the time, publishing tract after tract in what are known as the pamphlet wars. In 1663, following marriage to his third wife, blind and impoverished, Milton began work on his masterpiece, a long poem aimed at "justifying the ways of God to men." *Paradise Lost* was published in 1667 and was at once recognized as a supreme epic achievement. It was followed by *Paradise Regained* in 1671 and *Samson Agonistes,* a tragedy, in 1674. He died that year from complications arising from gout. Combining Renaissance learning and Latinate style with a staunchly Reformation temperament, Milton's work continues to inspire and challenge readers three centuries after his death.

Quotable: "By labor and intent study (which I take to be my portion in this life), joined with the strong propensity of nature, I might perhaps leave something so written to aftertimes, as they should not willingly let it die."

— *The Reason of Church Government*

MARIANNE MOORE (AMERICAN, 1887–1972). Marianne Moore was born in St. Louis, Missouri. Her father left the family when she was an infant, and Moore grew up with her mother in the home of her grandfather, a Presbyterian minister. In 1894, the family moved to Carlisle, Pennsylvania, where Moore attended the Metzger Institute before going to Bryn Mawr. In 1918 she moved to New York City where she attended literary functions at which she met other young poets, WALLACE STEVENS and WILLIAM CARLOS WILLIAMS among them. In 1921 her first book, *Poems,* was published by friends without her knowledge. A second volume, *Marriage,* appeared in 1923. Her *Observations* (1924) won *Dial* magazine's award for "distinguished service to American letters." *Selected Poems* appeared in 1935; of it T. S. ELIOT remarked, "Miss Moore's poems form part of the small body of durable poetry written in our time." In 1947 Moore became a member of the National Institute of Arts and Letters. In 1951 her *Collected Poems* received Bollingen and Pulitzer Prizes as well as the National Book Award. In 1955 she was elected to the American Academy. Her poems reveal the quiet, restrained passion of the details of this world. Writers as diverse as ROBERT LOWELL, ELIZABETH BISHOP, and DONALD HALL have paid tribute to her unerring vision in their works.

SHARON OLDS (AMERICAN, b. 1942). With the publication of her first book, *Satan Says* (1980), Sharon Olds established herself as a breaker of restrictive social norms. In ensuing collections, she has explored domestic and political violence, sexuality, and the body. Though her concentration on pain and suffering has been called a "dark witness-bearing," she is also seen as a poet of purification and redemption. Her confessional style situates her in a line of American poetry descending from Anne Sexton and SYLVIA PLATH; one critic allies her with WALT WHITMAN: "Like Whitman, Ms. Olds sings the body in celebration of a power stronger than political oppression." A native of San Francisco, Olds was educated at Stanford and then at Columbia, where she received her Ph.D. Her first collection appeared when she was thirty-seven. Her second book, *The Dead and the Living* (1984), won the Lamont Poetry Prize and the National Book Critics Circle Award. *The Gold Cell* (1987) and *The Father* (1992) were followed by *The Wellspring* (1996) and, most recently, *Blood, Tin, Straw* (1999). A popular reader of her work and a leader of workshops across the country, she currently teaches at the Writing Program at Goldwater Hospital for the severely physically disabled and chairs the creative writing program at New York University.

Quotable: "There are some things that have to do with art that we can't control. This creature of the poem may assemble itself into a being with its own centrifugal force. That's what I'm thinking about when I'm trying to get out of art's way. Not trying to look good, if a poem's about me. Not trying to look bad. Not asking a poem to carry a lot of rocks in its pockets. But just being an ordinary observer and liver and feeler and letting the experience get through you onto the notebook with the pen, through the arm, out of the body, onto the page, without distortion."

— *Interview*

WILFRED OWEN (ENGLISH, 1893–1918). "My subject is War, and the pity of War," wrote Wilfred Owen in a draft preface to his poems. "The Poetry is in the pity." And in works such as "Dulce et Decorum Est" he records with slant rhyme and steady eye the horror and the pity of his subject. Born in Plas Wilmot, Oswestry, in 1893, Owen graduated from Shrewsbury Technical College in 1911, though without the honors necessary to enter university. He left England in 1913 for France, where he taught at the

Berlitz School of Languages at Bordeaux. At the outbreak of World War I, Owen returned to England to enlist. On the Western Front in January 1917, he endured the worst winter of the war. In May, 1917, he was diagnosed with shell-shock and sent to Craiglockhart Hospital in Edinburgh, where he met the poet Siegfried Sassoon, whose poems Owen admired. Sassoon encouraged Owen in his writing. Discharged in late October, Owen returned to the front and was killed on November 4, 1918, one week before the armistice. Only four of his poems were published during his lifetime. Enlarged editions began to appear, first in 1920 (edited by Sassoon), and then in 1931 and 1963. *The Complete Poems and Fragments* was published in 1983, edited by John Stallworthy.

SYLVIA PLATH (AMERICAN, 1932–1963). Born in Boston, Sylvia Plath was educated at Smith College. Her father, Otto Plath, was a German emigrant who taught biology and German at Boston University. In 1957, while on a Fulbright Fellowship at Cambridge, Plath met the poet Ted Hughes, whom she married that year. She returned to Boston to study at Boston University with ROBERT LOWELL; the painful personal element in her work aligns her with confessional poets like him and Anne Sexton. Her work is laced with archetypal resonance, fired by what Ted Hughes called a "crackling verbal energy." It is also laced with terror. While at Smith she had suffered a breakdown, and over the years, despite congenial outward appearances, she made numerous attempts at suicide. She spent the last part of her life living in London with her two children. Her collection, *The Colossus and Other Poems* (1960), was the only one of her books of poetry to be published in her lifetime. Posthumous collections include *Ariel* (1965), *Crossing the Water* (1971), and *Winter Trees* (1971). She wrote one autobiographical novel, *The Bell Jar* (1963); *The Journals of Sylvia Plath* appeared in 1982. Her posthumous *Collected Poems* was awarded the Pulitzer Prize in 1982. She took her own life in 1963.

Quotable: "What I fear most, I think, is the death of the imagination. When the sky outside is merely pink, and the rooftops merely black: that photographic mind which paradoxically tells the truth, but the worthless truth, about the world. It is that

synthesizing spirit, that 'shaping' force, which prolifically sprouts and makes up its own worlds with more inventiveness than God which I desire."   *—Journals*

EDGAR ALLAN POE (AMERICAN, 1809–1849). Edgar Allan Poe, author of "The Tell-Tale Heart," was born in Boston in 1809. Following his parents' early death, he was adopted by a merchant, John Allan, and spent most of his childhood in England. In 1826, he entered the University of Virginia, but left soon after to pursue a literary career. His first book, *Tamerlane and Other Poems* (1827), was published anonymously and at his own expense; another volume of poems, *Al Araaf,* followed in 1829. In 1830, he entered West Point, but was dismissed for neglect of duty the next year. Having settled briefly in New York, where he published his third volume, *Poems* (1831), Poe moved to Baltimore and began to write stories for magazines. In 1836, he married his thirteen-year-old cousin, Virginia Clemm. The two moved to Richmond, Virginia. The next few years were marked by more moves—New York, Philadelphia—until, at his wife's death in 1847, he returned to Richmond. He died in Baltimore in 1849, in poverty and under mysterious circumstances. Despite his itinerant and brief career, Poe produced a varied and admirable body of work, ranging from reviews and literary criticism to poems, short stories, and one novel. The title piece of *The Raven and Other Poems* (1845) is perhaps his best-known work and provided him with considerable popular success. His obsession with darkness, with psychological terror and the macabre, influenced later French Symbolist poets, notably Charles Baudelaire.

Quotable: "With me poetry has been not a purpose, but a passion; and the passions should be held in reverence: they must not—they cannot at will be excited, with an eye to the paltry compensations, or the more paltry commendations, of mankind."
— The Raven and Other Poems, Preface.

ALEXANDER POPE (ENGLISH, 1688–1744). A brilliant satirist in an age of satire, Alexander Pope was born in London to a Roman Catholic family in 1688, the year of the Protestant Revolution. Debarred from university education because of his religion,

Pope was largely self-taught. As a child he suffered from tuberculosis and asthma. He also had a curvature of the spine, resulting in his diminutive stature (four feet, six inches), a condition that later became a target for critics in the literary vendettas of the time. In 1711 he moved to London and wrote his *Essay on Criticism*. In this and other works, notably *The Rape of the Lock* (1712–1720), he showed himself a master of the heroic couplet; its concision and balance made it a fit form for the play of wit, for logical or philosophical meditation, and of course for the whip and sting of satire. The success of his translation of Homer's *Iliad* (1715–1720) allowed him to set up a home in Twickenham after he had been forced to leave London following the Jacobite rebellion of 1715. There he wrote his major poem, *The Dunciad* (1728, continued in 1742), the *Epistle to Doctor Arbuthnot* (1734), and the philosophical *Essay on Man* (1733–1734). Though his reputation suffered later due to vast changes in taste, he was influential among many mid-twentieth-century poets, notably Allen Tate and ROBERT LOWELL.

EZRA POUND (AMERICAN, 1885–1972). There is virtually no modern poet whose work Ezra Pound's influence has not touched. His dictum, "Make it New!," along with his tireless promotion of others, left an indelible mark on English letters. Born in Hailey, Idaho, in 1885, he was educated at the University of Pennsylvania and Hamilton College. In 1908 he sailed for Venice, where he published his first book of poems, *A Lume Spento* (1908). Later volumes, especially *Personae* (1910), showed the influence of ROBERT BROWNING's dramatic monologues. In 1908 Pound moved to London, where he began to promote the work of new writers like T. S. ELIOT, HILDA DOOLITTLE, WILLIAM CARLOS WILLIAMS, and ROBERT FROST. During World War I, he continued to write. His *Hugh Selwyn Mauberly* (1920) records his disillusionment with modern civilization. In 1924 Pound returned to Italy and began work on his major poem, an epic conceived in his school days. *A Draft of XVI Cantos* was published in 1925; he continued to work on *The Cantos* for the rest of his life. During World War II, Pound remained in Italy, making pro-Axis broadcasts in Rome. Following the war, he was turned over to American authorities and imprisoned near Pisa. On return to the United States, he was charged with treason but declared insane and unfit to stand trial. He was confined at St. Elizabeth's Hospital, where he spent the next thirteen years. On his release in 1958 (which was partially negotiated by Robert Frost), he returned to Italy, where he lived until his death in 1972.

Quotable: "Poetry must be *as well written as prose*[. . . .] There must be no book words, no periphrases, no inversions[. . . .] no hindside-beforeness, no straddled adjectives (as 'addled mosses dank), no Tennysonianness of speech; nothing—nothing that you couldn't, in some circumstance, in the stress of some emotion, actually say."

— *Letters*

RAINER MARIA RILKE (GERMAN, 1875–1926). Rainer Maria Rilke was born in Prague, the son of an army officer. After attending military school, he studied philosophy, history, literature, and art in Prague, Munich, and Berlin. He wrote verses from a very early age. In 1899 he traveled to Russia (one of his two visits there) and, returning, married Clara Westhoff in 1901. Following the birth of their daughter, Ruth, the two moved to Paris, where Clara worked for the sculptor Rodin (Rilke was writing a monograph on the artist). During the next twelve years, Rilke traveled widely, using Paris as his base. He composed much of his major work during this time: *Stundenbuch* (*The Book of Objects*), *Neue Gedichte* (*New Poems*), and his autobiographical prose work, *The Notebooks of Malte Laurids Brigge*. The Book of Objects was particularly influential in its invention of a new form of lyric poetry, the object poem, which attempts to capture the essence of a physical thing. After the outbreak of World War I he lived mostly in Munich, and in 1919 moved to Switzerland. There he was to write his masterworks, the *Duineser Elegien* (*Duino Elegies*) and *Sonette an Orpheus* (*Sonnets to Orpheus*). The former stands as his supreme testament of spiritual experience. He died at Valmont near Glion in 1926.

Quotable: "Works of art are indeed always products of having been in danger, of having gone to the very end in an experience, to where man can go no further."

— *Letters*

EDWIN ARLINGTON ROBINSON (AMERICAN, 1869–1935). Born in Head Tide, Maine, Edwin Arlington Robinson was educated at Harvard University from 1891 to 1893. His early poetry was deeply influenced by such Romantic and Victorian giants as WILLIAM WORDSWORTH and Rudyard Kipling. Despite his denial of ROBERT BROWNING's influence, many have felt a likeness in Robinson's creation of character sketches and particularly in his use of dramatic monologues. His treatment of the New England landscape also invites comparison with Robert Frost, five years his junior. In 1896 he published his first collection, *The Torrent and the Night Before,* expanded and reissued in 1897 as *The Children of the Night.* His mature style dates from 1916 with *The Man against the Sky* and *Collected Poems* (1921). Though his predilection for formal poetry and traditional forms situated him against the rising tide of modernism, he enjoyed popularity throughout his career and was three times awarded the Pulitzer Prize. His many later volumes include a trilogy based on Arthurian romance, *Merlin* (1917), *Lancelot* (1920), and *Tristam* (1927), and *The Man Who Died Twice* (1924). He is best known, however, for his shorter lyrics, particularly his Tilbury poems, which include such wry, ironic works as "Richard Cory."

THEODORE ROETHKE (AMERICAN, 1908–1963). Theodore Roethke was born in Saginaw, Michigan, and educated at the University of Michigan and at Harvard. He taught at several universities, his last and longest appointment at the University of Washington. In his first book, *Open House* (1941), he treats the themes of childhood and nature; "I have a genuine love of nature," he was later to say. Later collections include *The Lost Son and Other Poems* (1948), *Praise to the Endi* (1951), and the posthumously published *The Far Field* (1964). In 1953 he received the Pulitzer Prize for his collection *The Waking: Poems, 1933–1953.* His *Words for the Wind: The Collected Verse of Theodore Roethke* (1957) won the 1958 Bollingen Prize and the 1959 National Book Award. A tormented man, a victim of breakdowns and alcoholism, he nonetheless achieved a kind of transcendence in his work; he traced his lineage along the line of visionaries that in-

cludes Emerson, Thoreau, WHITMAN, BLAKE, WORDSWORTH, and YEATS. A new edition of *Collected Poems* was issued in 1975.

CHRISTINA GEORGINA ROSSETTI (ENGLISH, 1830–1894). The daughter of a Neapolitan political exile and sister of Dante Gabriel Rossetti, Christina Rossetti was born in London in 1830. She was educated at home by her mother. While still a youth she showed so much poetic promise that her grandfather had small collections of her poems published when she was twelve and fifteen. Her first mature volume of verse, *Goblin Market and Other Poems,* was published in 1862. Before that, lyrics such as "An End" and "Dream Lane" had found publication in magazines under her pseudonym, Ellen Alleyne. *Goblin Market* was followed by *The Prince's Progress and Other Poems* (1866) and *Sing Song: A Nursery Rhyme Book* (1872). By the 1880s, ill health had made her an invalid, but she continued to write poetry. *A Pageant and Other Poems* was published in 1881; it contains her sonnet sequence "Monna Innominata." It was followed by *Time Flies: A Reading Diary* (1885) and *The Face of the Deep: A Devotional Commentary on the Apocalypse* (1892), her last published work. Highly accomplished in its verbal precision and metrical invention, her verse bears the influence of the pre-Raphaelite movement, which her brother Dante Gabriel helped to found. Her brother William edited her complete works (1904) after her death in 1894.

CARL SANDBURG (AMERICAN, 1878–1967). Born in Galesburg, Illinois, to Swedish immigrant parents, Carl Sandburg left school at the age of thirteen. He worked as an itinerant laborer and served in the Spanish-American War before becoming a journalist and advertising copywriter. In 1904 he published his first book of poems, *Reckless Ecstasy.* In 1916, with the publication of *Chicago Poems,* he was firmly established as a major poet of the American Midwest. His poetry, like WALT WHITMAN's, takes America as its subject matter; it champions the underdog and extols the enduring qualities of ordinary, working-class Americans. Though labeled "artless" by some of his contemporaries (ROBERT FROST called him a fraud), he was widely read and admired during his lifetime. His *Complete Poems* (1950) won the Pulitzer Prize. The governor of Illinois proclaimed his seventy-fifth birthday "Carl Sandburg Day," he was decorated by the king of Sweden, and in 1964, he received the Presidential Medal of Freedom from Lyndon B. Johnson. In addition to his poetry, he is known for his four-volume biography of Abraham Lincoln.

WILLIAM SHAKESPEARE (ENGLISH, 1564–1616). The Bard of Avon was born in 1564 in Stratford-upon-Avon, the eldest son of a glover and wool dealer. The young Shakespeare probably went to Stratford Grammar School, where he established his wide knowledge of classical literature, on which he would draw continually in his plays. In 1582, he married Anne Hathaway, with whom he fathered three children. Not much is known of Shakespeare's life after he came to London, but by 1594 he was a presence on the English stage. In that decade he composed at least some of his sonnets, published together in folio edition in 1609. Throughout the 1590s Shakespeare continued to write plays, averaging about two a year. In 1603 the new monarch, James, honored his troupe with royal patronage; now a member of The King's Men, Shakespeare launched into his great period, following his earlier *Julius Caesar* and *Hamlet* with such masterpieces as *Macbeth, King Lear,* and *Antony and Cleopatra.* After 1613 Shakespeare returned to Stratford, where he lived the rest of his life. After his death appeared the folio edition (1623), containing high tributes from fellow writers, among them Ben Jonson's "He was not of an age, but for all time!"

PERCY BYSSHE SHELLEY (ENGLISH, 1792–1822). Belonging to the generation of later Romantic poets including BYRON and KEATS, Percy Bysshe Shelley was born at Field Place, near Horsham, West Sussex, in 1792. He attended Oxford but was expelled after he published his pamphlet *The Necessity of Atheism* (1811). He eloped to Scotland with Harriet Westbrook, a move that, combined with his refusal to retract his pamphlet, caused a permanent break with his family. While in Scotland, Shelley corresponded with the radical thinker William Godwin, published a series of political works, and composed his poem *Queen Mab* (1813). Having moved to London, Shelley joined Godwin and fell in love with his sixteen-year old daughter, Mary (later the author of *Frankenstein*). The two eloped to the Continent in 1814, despite the birth of a daughter by Harriet. Harriet drowned herself that autumn, and Shelley immediately married Mary. In 1818, they left England permanently and settled in Italy. Shelley completed his long poem *Prometheus Unbound* in 1819; that year and the next comprised his most productive period. *The Cenci* and *Ode to the West Wind,* as well as many important lyrics, belong to this time. At twenty-nine he was drowned when his boat went down in a tempest in the Gulf of Spezia. Grudgingly admired in his own day, his poetry was a dominant influence on later nineteenth-century poets, such as TENNYSON and BROWNING. Mary Shelley collected his *Poetical Works* in 1839.

Quotable: "All high poetry is infinite; it is as the first acorn, which contained all oaks potentially. Veil after veil may be undrawn, and the inmost naked beauty of the meaning never exposed. A great poem is a fountain for ever overflowing with the waters of wisdom and delight; and after one person and one age has exhausted all its divine effluence which their peculiar relations enable them to share, another and yet another succeeds, and new relations are ever developed, the source of an unforeseen and an unconceived delight."

— *A Defence of Poetry*

CHARLES SIMIC (AMERICAN, b. 1938). Charles Simic was born in Belgrade, Yugoslavia. He emigrated to the United States with his family in 1949, settled in Chicago, and began attending the University of Chicago. He served briefly in the army before completing his B.A. at New York University. Since 1974 he has taught at the University of New Hampshire. His first book of poems, *What the Grass Says,* was published in 1967; *Selected Poems: Nineteen Sixty-Three to Nineteen Eighty-Five* appeared in 1985. In the many books written between those dates, and in the poems since published, Simic is continually drawn to the surreal and the strange, the dream image, the archetypal form. He places his readers in a world where, as he says, "magic is possible, where chance reigns, where metaphors have their supreme logic." Besides work on his own poetry, he has devoted much time to translations of other Yugoslav poets, contained in *Four Modern Yugoslav Poets* (1970) and *Horse Has Six Legs: Contemporary Serbian Poetry* (1992). He has translated and co-edited with Mark Strand *Another Republic: 17 European and South American Writers* (1976). The recipient of numerous awards, including a MacArthur Foundation Fellowship and a Pulitzer Prize (1990), he currently resides in New Hampshire.

CATHY SONG (AMERICAN, b. 1955). Cathy Song's work explores the world of family and ancestry, the complications of one's moving through life, sensing all that lies behind. Of Chinese and Korean descent, she was born in Honolulu. Her first book, *Picture Bride* (1983), takes its title from the "mail order" brides that were sent from Asia to Hawaii, in the hope of being accepted on the strength of the photograph. (Song's grandmother was one of these.) The book won the Yale Series of Younger Poets Award in 1983. Her later collections, *Frameless Windows, Squares of Light* (1988), and *School Figures* (1994), have continued to probe the knowns and unknowns of bloodline and descent. Song received her B.A. from Wellesley College before pursuing an M.A. in creative writing at Boston University. The recipient of a number of grants and awards, including the Shelley Memorial Award from the Poetry Society of America and the Hawaii Award for Literature, she has taught creative writing at various universities. She currently serves as consulting editor for Bamboo Ridge Press in Honolulu, where she resides.

GARY SOTO (AMERICAN, b. 1952). Chicano life and the world of the San Joaquin Valley worker comprise much of the work of Gary Soto. He was born in Fresno, California, in 1952 to a family of field and factory workers. When Soto was five, his father died in an industrial accident. Soto took up writing poetry at an early age. In 1974 he earned his B.A. from California State University and

his M.F.A. at the University of California, Irvine, in 1976. His first collections of poems, *The Element of San Joaquin* (1977) and *The Tale of Sunlight* (1978), document a journey from his own beginnings to the town of Taxco, in central Mexico, where, as his narrator says, "we all begin." Along the way, Soto treats the experience of the migrant worker in the San Joaquin Valley (work that Soto himself has done), where, as a custom, "The skin of my belly will tighten like a belt / And there will be no reason for pockets." Since then he has authored eight other books of poetry and three short story collections; his *New and Selected Poems* appeared in 1995 and was a finalist for both the Los Angeles Times Book Prize and the National Book Award. He has taught Chicano studies and English at the University of California, Berkeley; recently he was appointed distinguished professor of creative writing at the University of California, Riverside.

WOLE SOYINKA (NIGERIAN, b. 1934). Wole Soyinka, the popular name of Akinwande Oluwole Soyinka, was born in Nigeria, near Abeokuta. He studied at Ibadan and Leeds. While in England he was a play reader for the Royal Court Theatre. His first play, *The Invention,* was performed there in 1955. In 1959 he returned to Ibaban, where he founded two theaters for the establishment of a Nigerian drama. During the Nigerian Civil War he was imprisoned (1967–1969), an experience he has written about in *Poems from Prison* (1969) and *A Shuttle in the Crypt* (1972). His first novel, *The Interpreters* (1965), has been called the first modern African novel. He became professor of comparative literature at Obafemi Awolowo University (formerly the University of Ife) and was professor of African studies and theater at Cornell University in 1988. Deeply engaged with the politics of his country, especially in the tensions between an old Africa and a new one, Soyinka has been praised for his work's verbal inventiveness and imaginative power. His plays draw on traditional African myths; these include *The Swamp Dwellers* and *The Strong Breed* (both in *Three Plays*, 1963), *The Road* (1965), and *Death and the King's Horseman* (1975). He has adapted Euripides in *The Bacchae* (1973), Gay and Brecht in *Opera*

Wonyosi (1981). He has edited *Poems from Black Africa* (1975); many of his essays have been collected in *Art, Dialogue and Outrage: Essays on Literature and Culture* (1988). In 1986 he was awarded the Nobel Prize for Literature.

WILLIAM STAFFORD (AMERICAN, 1914–1993). William Stafford was born in Hutchinson, Kansas. He was educated at the University of Kansas and at the University of Iowa, where he earned his Ph.D. An extremely prolific writer—he published thirty-four volumes of poetry alone—he early began his lifelong habit of writing before dawn each day. His first book, *Poems,* was not published until he was forty-five; it was followed by *West of the City* (1960) and *Traveling through the Dark* (1962), winner of the National Book Award. *The Way It Is: New and Selected Poems* was published in 1998. Stafford's work is distinguished by its evenness of tone and its conversational idiom: he likes his poetry, as he has said, "much like talk, with some enhancement." His favored landscapes, mental and physical, are planes: "In scenery I like flat country. / In life I don't like much to happen," he wrote in "Passing Remark." Apart from poems, he has published critical prose, including *Writing the Australian Crawl: Views on the Writer's Vocation* (1978), *You Must Revise Your Life* (1986), and the posthumous *Crossing Unmarked Snow.* For thirty years he taught at Lewis and Clarke College in Portland, Oregon, and in 1970 he served as poetry consultant to the Library of Congress. He was named Oregon's poet laureate in 1975 and was honored in 1992 with a Western States Book Award for lifetime achievement in poetry. He died in his home in Oregon in 1993.

WALLACE STEVENS (AMERICAN, 1879–1955). The facts of Wallace Stevens's professional life are perhaps different from what one would expect of a poet one critic has named the twentieth century's "third great imaginative force" along with YEATS and ELIOT. Born in Reading, Pennsylvania, in 1879 and educated at Harvard, Stevens worked first as a journalist with the *New York Herald Tribune.* He was, however, unhappy, and at his father's suggestion entered New York Law School and was admitted to the New York Bar in 1904. In 1916 he joined the legal staff of Hartford Accident and Indemnity Company and remained with the firm all his life, becoming vice president in 1934. Stevens's early verse had been published in *Poetry* magazine. His first collection, *Harmonium,* appeared in 1923 and, though it sold little, was well received by reviewers such as MARIANNE MOORE. His second volume, *Ideas of Order,* appeared in 1935. In these and other collections—*The Man with the Blue Guitar and Other Poems* (1937), *Parts of a World,* and *Notes toward a Supreme Fiction* (both published 1942)—Stevens puts forth his views on reality, art, and the imagination. He combines his Romantic heritage with a distinctly modern sensibility, aiming to capture a "physical poetry" of the world while placing poetry against religion as "the supreme fiction." He was awarded the Bollingen Prize in 1950, and his *Collected Poems* (1954) won the Pulitzer Prize. *Opus Posthumous* (1957) contains poems, essays, and plays, many previously unpublished.

Quotable: "There is, in fact, a world of poetry indistinguishable from the world in which we live, or, I ought to say, no doubt, from the world in which we shall come to live, since what makes the poet the potent figure that he is, or was, or ought to be, is that he creates the world to which we turn incessantly and without knowing it and that he gives to life the supreme fictions without which we are unable to conceive it."
— *The Necessary Angel*

MAY SWENSON (AMERICAN, 1919–1989). May Swenson was born in Logan, Utah, and earned her bachelor's degree from Utah State University in 1939. Her first book of poems, *Another Animal,* appeared in 1954, followed by *A Cage of Spines* (1958) and *To Mix with Time: New and Selected Poems* (1963). From 1959 to 1966, she served as editor at New Directions publishers; she taught poetry at Bryn Mawr, the University of North Carolina, the University of California, Riverside, Purdue University, and Utah State University. Though much of her later poetry is devoted to children, she also published translations of contemporary Swedish poets, including the collection *Iconographs* (1970) and the selected poems of Tomas Tranströmer (*Windows and Stones,* 1972). A recipient of numerous grants and fellowships — among them a Guggenheim, a Ford Foundation Poet-Playwright Grant, an Amy Lowell Poetry Traveling Scholarship, and a Robert Frost Fellowship — she was a member of the National Institute of Arts and Letters and served as chancellor of The Academy of American Poets from 1980 until her death in 1989. Experimental yet formally sound, her work delights in artistic arrangement and visual placement, in the shape of a poem on the page. According to the critic Harold Bloom, she ranks with MARIANNE MOORE and ELIZABETH BISHOP as one of the three best women poets of the twentieth century.

ALFRED, LORD TENNYSON (ENGLISH, 1809–1892). Born in Somersby, Lincolnshire, Alfred, Lord Tennyson was educated at Trinity College, Cambridge but left without taking a degree. His early collection, *Poems, Chiefly Lyrical,* was published in 1830 but was not well received. Following ten years' silence, during which his friend from Cambridge, Arthur Henry Hallam, died, Tennyson published a revised edition of *Poems* (1842), including such major works as "The Lady of Shallott," "Ulysses," and "The Lotos-Eaters." He had begun his long elegy for Hallam as early as 1834, published in 1850 as *In Memoriam.* In that year he succeeded WORDSWORTH as poet laureate. In 1855 he published *Maud and Other Poems,* including the monodrama of the title and "The Charge of the Light Brigade," and from 1859 to 1885 he issued his series of Arthurian poems, *The Idylls of the King.* He continued to write poems and plays until his death in 1892. A meticulous craftsman with an exquisite ear for the music of verse and the fluctuations of thought, Tennyson stands with ROBERT BROWNING as creator of the Victorian dramatic monologue. His variety of verse forms extended the range of metrical poetry in English. Though his reputation has wavered somewhat since his death, his work has deeply influenced poets of the twentieth century, particularly on T. S. ELIOT. Of Tennyson's technical accomplishment in *In Memoriam,* Eliot wrote: "I do not think any poet in English has ever had a finer ear for vowel sound, as well as a subtler feeling for some moods of anguish."

DYLAN THOMAS (WELSH, 1914–1953). Dylan Marlais Thomas was born in what he later remembered as the "ugly lovely town" of Swansea, Wales. His father taught English at Swansea Grammar School, and Thomas was educated there. He left school in 1931 and worked for a time as a reporter. In 1934 he moved to London and published his first book, *18 Poems.* A second collection, *Twenty-five Poems* (1936), attracted the attention of distinguished literary figures, among them Dame Edith Sitwell. During World War I, Thomas worked as a scriptwriter and broadcaster for the BBC. His volumes of stories, *The Map of Love* (1939) and *Portrait of the Artist as a Young Dog* (1940), as well as his *New Poems* (1943), established his reputation. Following the publication of *Collected Poems* (1953), Thomas embarked on a number of reading tours in the United States, where his charismatic and ebullient personality and rich intoning of his work drew large audiences. His play for voices, *Under Milk Wood,* was written in 1952. In 1953, while in New York, he died of alcohol poisoning. His poems revel in rhetorical exuberance and formal limitation: they seem, like his speaker in "Fern Hill," to "[sing] in [their] chains like the sea." Their linguistic richness and clotted texture at times recall the poetry of GERARD MANLEY HOPKINS, while their networks of religious, archetypal, and biological imagery and wealth of paradox resemble the poetry of the metaphysical and symbolist traditions.

Quotable: "Poetry is the rhythmic, inevitably narrative, movement from an over-clothed blindness to a naked vision that depends in its intensity on the strength of the labour put into the creation of the poetry. My poetry is, or should be, useful to me for one reason: it is the record of my individual struggle from darkness towards some measure of light."

— Reply to a Questionnaire

JOHN UPDIKE (AMERICAN, b. 1932). Born in Shillington, Pennsylvania, John Updike has authored numerous works of prose fiction, poetry, and literary criticism. His mother was a writer, his father a high school mathematics teacher. He graduated *summa cum laude* from Harvard in 1954 and left for England, where he spent a year on fellowship at the Ruskin School of Drawing and Fine Art in Oxford. Following his return to the United States, Updike took a position on the staff of *The New Yorker*, to which he has contributed short stories, poems, humor, and book reviews since 1960. In 1958 he published his first collection of verse, *The Carpentered Hen* (issued in Britain as *Hoping for a Hoopoe*). His novels, beginning with *The Poorhouse Fair* (1959), established him as a keen observer of American life; his tetralogy *Rabbit, Run* (1960), *Rabbit Redux* (1971), *Rabbit Is Rich* (1981), and *Rabbit at Rest* (1990), won two Pulitzer Prizes and secured his reputation. *The Centaur* won the National Book Award; other novels, notably *The Witches of Eastwick* (1982) and *Roger's Version* (1986), have turned to metaphysical matters. His prose has been collected in *Forty Stories* (1987) and the autobiographical *Self-Consciousness* (1989), while his book reviews and essays for *The New Yorker* and *The New York Review of Books* may be found in *Assorted Prose* (1965), *Picked-Up Pieces* (1978), *Hugging the Shore* (1983), and *Odd Jobs* (1991). Of his life in letters he has written, "We walk through volumes of the unexpressed and like snails leave behind a faint thread excreted out of ourselves."

ALICE WALKER (AMERICAN, b. 1944). The eighth child of Southern sharecroppers, Alice Walker was born in Eatonton, Georgia. A gunshot accident at the age of eight left her permanently blind in one eye. Of that time she has written, "I no longer felt like the little girl I was . . . I retreated into solitude, and read stories and began to write poems." In 1961, Walker received a scholarship to attend Spelman College in Atlanta; she was dismissed for her involvement in civil rights demonstrations. She transferred to Sarah Lawrence College in 1963 and received her B.A. in 1965. She was awarded a writing fellowship after graduation, with which she planned to return to Africa, where she had been an exchange student. She decided, however, to spend the time as a volunteer in the voter registration drive in Mississippi in the summer of 1966, later claiming that she "could never live happily in Africa — or anywhere else — until [she] could live freely in Mississippi." Her first book of poetry, *Once*, appeared in 1968, followed by *Revolutionary Petunias and Other Poems* in 1973. In 1982, her novel *The Color Purple* was published; it won the Pulitzer Prize and was adapted into a film in 1985. Since that time, she has continued to write poetry and fiction, as well as critical essays. In all of her work, she treats with insight and clarity the experience of African Americans in the twentieth century.

Quotable: "No one could wish for a more advantageous heritage than that bequeathed to the black writer in the South: a compassion for the earth, a trust in humanity beyond our knowledge of evil, and abiding love of justice. We inherit a great responsibility . . . for we must give voice to centuries not only of silent bitterness and hate but also of neighborly kindness and sustaining love." — *Everyday Use*

WALT WHITMAN (AMERICAN, 1819–1892). Born on Long Island, Walt Whitman left school in 1830 to become a printer's apprentice. Through the mid-1840s he worked as an editor for newspapers in Brooklyn and Long Island. During this time he also began to write poetry and short stories. In 1855, he published his first book of poems, *Leaves of Grass*. The book made little impression, though Whitman did receive a letter of praise from Ralph Waldo Emerson, which was printed in the second edition (1856). *Leaves of Grass*, Whitman's chief work, contains such major poems as *Song of Myself*, *Crossing Brooklyn Ferry*, and *When Lilacs Last in the Dooryard Bloom'd* — Whitman's elegy for Abraham Lincoln. *Drum Taps*, the sequence inspired by his experience in the Civil War (he served as a nurse), was included in the 1867 edition. Whitman's verse represents a turning point in American poetry. In form, in subject matter, it was revolutionary; its scope seemed determined to include everything. Nothing human was to be alien, and if such inclusiveness disturbed the reader, it did not bother Whitman: "Do I contradict myself?" he asks famously in *Song of Myself*. "Very well then I contradict myself. / (I am large, I contain multitudes.)" Barbaric, profane, crude — all charges to which Whitman was subjected in his career (and which he welcomed) — he has continued to influence American poets.

Quotable: "Every really new person (poet or other,) *makes* his style — sometimes a little removed from the previous models — sometimes very far removed." — *Letters*

RICHARD WILBUR (AMERICAN, b. 1921). Of the distinguished generation of American poets that included A. R. AMMONS, ROBERT BLY, JAMES DICKEY, GALWAY KINNELL, Adrienne Rich, and W. D. Snodgrass, Richard Wilbur was born in New York City in 1921, the son of a portrait painter. He attended Amherst College and served in World War II. Following the war, he completed his education at Harvard and then taught, first there, then at Wellesley College, Wesleyan University, and Smith College. He has since retired to write. His first volume of poems, *The Beautiful Changes* (1947), established him as an already adroit practitioner in traditional verse forms; it was followed by *Ceremony and Other Poems* (1950). His *Things of This World* (1956), achieved the rare distinction of winning both the Pulitzer Prize and the National Book Award for poetry. Numerous collections have followed; his *New and Collected Poems* was issued in 1988, earning him another Pulitzer. Apart from his own poetry he has shown himself an accomplished translator of the plays of Racine and Molière (for which he won the Bollingen Prize in 1963) and the poetry of Jorge Luis Borges. In 1987 he was named poet laureate of the United States. Witty, urbane, yet passionately attached to the world, his poems at their best clarify and sharpen consciousness, record "The Beautiful Changes" subtly, gracefully, "as a forest is changed / By a chameleon's tuning his skin to it."

Quotable: "In general, I would say that [poetic] limitation makes for power: the strength of the genie comes of his being confined in a bottle."
— *Mid-Century American Poets*

WILLIAM CARLOS WILLIAMS (AMERICAN, 1883-1963). William Carlos Williams was born in Rutherford, New Jersey, the son of an English father and a Puerto Rican mother. He attended French and Swiss schools before entering the University of Pennsylvania, where he studied medicine. While there, he became acquainted with EZRA POUND and HILDA DOOLITTLE, figures who perhaps inspired his conviction that poetry must occupy itself with the objective and concrete treatment of things ("No

ideas but in things," he was later to write). Following further medical study in New York and Leipzig, Williams returned to Rutherford in 1909 and began to practice medicine there. His first volume, *Poems,* had appeared in 1900; it was followed by *The Tempers* (1913), *Al Que Quiere!* (1917), *Kora in Hell: Improvisations* (1920), *Sour Grapes* (1921), and *Spring and All* (1923). In these and later works Williams established himself as one of the more innovative and original poets of his day. His poetry was extremely influential in its casting off of traditional verse structures and in its forging of a colloquial language for poetry "in the American grain." For Williams, the ordinary provided world enough for poems; the treatment was all. His *Pictures from Brueghel and Other Poems* (1962) was awarded the Pulitzer Prize in 1963. His *Collected Poems* appeared posthumously in two volumes from 1986 to 1988.

Quotable: "I propose sweeping changes from top to bottom of the poetic structure . . . . I say we are *through* with the iambic pentameter as presently conceived, at least for dramatic verse; through with the measured quatrain, the staid concatenations of sounds in the usual stanza, the sonnet."
— *Selected Essays*

WILLIAM WORDSWORTH (ENGLISH, 1770–1850). William Wordsworth was born in Cockermouth, Cumberland. He was educated at Hawkshead in the Lake District and at St. John's College, Cambridge. In 1790 he embarked on a walking tour through France and Switzerland, commemorated in his early collection, *Descriptive Sketches* (1793). While in France, Wordsworth became devoted to the ideals of the French Revolution. On returning to England, Wordsworth lived with his sister, Dorothy, who was to have a profound effect on his early poetry. Settling at Somerset, he developed a friendship with SAMUEL TAYLOR COLERIDGE, and the two began to compose the poems that would appear in *Lyrical Ballads* (1798), issued with a preface by Wordsworth that was effectively a manifesto for early English Romanticism. Following a year in Germany with Coleridge and Dorothy, Wordsworth married Mary Hutchinson in 1802 and began work on *The Prelude,* in which he traces the growth of a poet's mind. The first thirteen books were published in 1805; a revised edition appeared posthumously in 1850. In 1843 he was made poet laureate. In later life Wordsworth became a kind of institution, receiving visits from admirers and political sympathizers at his home in Rydal Mount. Though his poetic powers waned in old age, and though his conservatism fell under criticism by the younger generation of Romantic poets, his revolutionary early work, his experiment with new verse forms, and his opening of new territory for poetry remained a deep and enduring legacy.

Quotable: "I have said that poetry is the spontaneous overflow of powerful feelings; it takes its origin from emotion recollected in tranquillity: the emotion is contemplated till, by a species of reaction, the tranquillity gradually disappears, and an emotion, kindred to that which was before the subject of contemplation, is gradually produced, and does itself exist in the mind. In this mood successful composition generally begins, and in a mood similar to this it is carried on."

— *Preface to Lyrical Ballads*

WILLIAM BUTLER YEATS (IRISH, 1865–1939). Born near Dublin, William Butler Yeats remains one of the most influential and widely studied poets of the twentieth century. His early work is immersed in the mythology and folktales of his native Ire-

land, combined with an interest in mysticism and the occult. His childhood was divided between London and Sligo, in the west of Ireland, where his mother's family lived. He was involved in Ireland's struggle for independence, concentrating his energies in the creation of a national literature and culture rather than in the political insurgence of many nationalists of the time. One of these, the beautiful Maud Gonne, remained his love throughout his life, and he composed a number of love poems to and about her. Yeats was also an accomplished playwright, and he helped to found the Abbey, Ireland's national theater, in 1904. In 1922 he became senator of the Irish Free State and in 1923 was awarded the Nobel Prize for Literature. His poems, plays, essays, memoirs, and correspondence have appeared in numerous editions; they include *The Collected Poems of W. B. Yeats* (1989), *Collected Plays* (1953), *Essays and Introductions* (1961), *Explorations* (1962), *Autobiographies* (1955), and *Collected Letters* (1986). He died in France in 1939; his coffin was disinterred in 1948 and taken to Sligo to be buried, as one of his last poems dictates, "Under Ben Bulben."

Quotable: "We make out of the quarrel with others, rhetoric, but of the quarrel with ourselves, poetry."

— *Mythologies*

Critical Thinking
and Writing

19

Critical Strategies
for Reading

CRITICAL THINKING

Maybe this has happened to you: the assignment is to write an analysis of some aspect of a work, let's say Nathaniel Hawthorne's *The Scarlet Letter*, that interests you, taking into account critical sources that comment on and interpret the work. You cheerfully begin research in the library but quickly find yourself bewildered by several seemingly unrelated articles. The first traces the thematic significance of images of light and darkness in the novel; the second makes a case for Hester Prynne as a liberated woman; the third argues that Arthur Dimmesdale's guilt is a projection of Hawthorne's own emotions; and the fourth analyzes the introduction, "The Custom House," as an attack on bourgeois values. These disparate treatments may seem random and capricious — a confirmation of your worst suspicions that interpretations of literature are hit-or-miss excursions into areas that you know little about or didn't know even existed. But if you understand that the articles are written from different perspectives — formalist, feminist, psychological, and Marxist — and that the purpose of each is to enhance your understanding of the work by discussing a particular element of it, then you can see that their varying strategies represent potentially interesting ways of opening up the text that might otherwise never have occurred to you. There are many ways to approach a text, and a useful first step is to develop a sense of direction, an understanding of how a perspective — your own or a critic's — shapes a discussion of a text.

This chapter offers an introduction to critical approaches to literature by outlining a variety of strategies for reading poetry, fiction, or drama. The emphasis is of course on poetry and to that end the approaches focus on Robert Frost's "Mending Wall" (p. 342); a rereading of that well-known poem will equip you for the discussions that follow. In addition to the emphasis on this poem to illustrate critical approaches, some fiction and drama examples are also included along the way to demonstrate how these critical approaches can be applied to any genre. These strategies include approaches that have long been practiced by readers who have used, for example, the insights gleaned from biography and history to illuminate literary works as well as more recent approaches, such as those used by feminist, reader-response, and deconstructionist critics. Each of these perspectives is sensitive to image, symbol, tone, irony, and other literary elements that you have been studying, but each also casts those elements in a special light. The formalist approach emphasizes how the elements within a work achieve their effects, whereas biographical and psychological approaches lead outward from the work to consider the author's life and other writings. Even broader approaches, such as historical and sociological perspectives, connect the work to historic, social, and economic forces. Mythological readings represent the broadest approach, because they discuss the cultural and universal responses readers have to a work.

Any given strategy raises its own types of questions and issues while seeking particular kinds of evidence to support itself. An awareness of the assumptions and methods that inform an approach can help you to understand better the validity and value of a given critic's strategy for making sense of a work. More important, such an understanding can widen and deepen the responses of your own reading.

The critical thinking that goes into understanding a professional critic's approach to a work is not foreign to you because you have already used essentially the same kind of thinking to understand the work itself. The skills you have developed to produce a literary *analysis* that, for example, describes how a character, symbol, or rhyme scheme supports a theme are also useful for reading literary criticism, because such skills allow you to keep track of how the parts of a critical approach create a particular reading of a literary work. When you analyze a poem, story, or play by closely examining how its various elements relate to the whole, your *interpretation* — your articulation of what the work means to you as supported by an analysis of its elements — necessarily involves choosing what you focus upon in the work. The same is true of professional critics.

Critical readings presuppose choices in the kinds of material that are discussed. An analysis of the setting of Robert Frost's "Home Burial" (p. 343) would probably bring into focus the oppressive environment of the couple's domestic life rather than, say, the economic history of New England farming. The economic history of New England farming might be useful to a Marxist critic concerned with how class is revealed in "Home Burial," but for a formalist critic interested in identifying the unifying structures of the poem such information would be irrelevant.

The Perspectives, Complementary Readings, and Critical Case Studies in this anthology offer opportunities to read critics using a wide variety of approaches to analyze and interpret texts. In the Critical Case Study on T. S. Eliot's "The Love Song of J. Alfred Prufrock" (Chapter 15), for instance, Elisabeth Schneider offers a biographical interpretation of Prufrock by suggesting that Eliot shared some of his character's sensibilities. In contrast, Michael L. Baumann argues that Prufrock's character can be understood through a close examination of the poem's images. Each of these critics raises different questions, examines different evidence, and employs different assumptions to interpret Prufrock's character. Being aware of those differences — teasing them out so that you can see how they lead to competing conclusions — is a useful way to analyze the analysis itself. What is left out of an interpretation is sometimes as significant as what is included. As you read the critics, it's worth reminding yourself that your own critical thinking skills can help you to determine the usefulness of a particular approach.

The following overview is neither exhaustive in the types of critical approaches covered nor complete in its presentation of the complexities inherent in them, but it should help you to develop an appreciation of the intriguing possibilities that attend literary interpretation. The emphasis in this chapter is on ways of thinking about literature rather than on daunting lists of terms, names, and movements. Although a working knowledge of critical schools may be valuable and necessary for a fully informed use of a given critical approach, the aim here is more modest and practical. This chapter is no substitute for the shelves of literary criticism that can be found in your library, but it does suggest how readers using different perspectives organize their responses to texts.

The summaries of critical approaches that follow are descriptive, not evaluative. Each approach has its advantages and limitations, but those matters are best left to further study. Like literary artists, critics have their personal values, tastes, and styles. The appropriateness of a specific critical approach will depend, at least in part, on the nature of the literary work under discussion as well as on your own sensibilities and experience. However, any approach, if it is to enhance understanding, requires sensitivity, tact, and an awareness of the various literary elements of the text, including, of course, its use of language.

Successful critical approaches avoid eccentric decodings that reveal so-called hidden meanings, which are not only hidden but totally absent from the text. For a parody of this sort of critical excess, see "A Parodic Interpretation of 'Stopping by Woods on a Snowy Evening'" (p. 364), in which Herbert R. Coursen, Jr., has some fun with a Robert Frost poem and Santa Claus while making a serious point about the dangers of overly ingenious readings. Literary criticism attempts, like any valid hypothesis, to account for phenomena — the text — without distorting or misrepresenting what it describes.

THE LITERARY CANON: DIVERSITY AND CONTROVERSY

Before looking at the various critical approaches discussed in this chapter, it makes sense to consider first which literature has been traditionally considered worthy of such analysis. The discussion in the Introduction called

The Changing Literary Canon (p. 5) may have already alerted you to the fact that in recent years many more works by women, minorities, and writers from around the world have been considered by scholars, critics, and teachers to merit serious study and inclusion in what is known as the literary canon. This increasing diversity has been celebrated by those who believe that multiculturalism taps new sources for the discovery of great literature while raising significant questions about language, culture, and society. At the same time, others have perceived this diversity as a threat to the established, traditional canon of Western culture.

The debates concerning whose work should be read, taught, and written about have sometimes been acrimonious as well as lively and challenging. Bitter arguments have been waged recently on campuses and in the press over what has come to be called "political correctness." Two camps — roughly — have formed around these debates: liberals and conservatives (the appropriateness of these terms is debatable but the oppositional positioning is unmistakable). The liberals are said to insist upon politically correct views from colleagues and students opening up the curriculum to multicultural texts from Asia, Africa, Latin America, and elsewhere, and to encourage more tolerant attitudes about race, class, gender, and sexual orientation. These revisionists, seeking a change in traditional attitudes, are sometimes accused of intimidating the opposition into silence and substituting ideological dogma for reason and truth. The conservatives are also portrayed as ideologues; in their efforts to preserve what they regard as the best from the past, they refuse to admit that Western classics, mostly written by white male Europeans, represent only a portion of human experience. These traditionalists are seen as advocating values that are neither universal nor eternal but merely privileged and entrenched. Conservatives are charged with refusing to acknowledge that their values also represent a political agenda, which is implicit in their preference for the works of canonical authors such as Homer, Virgil, Shakespeare, Milton, Tolstoy, and Faulkner. The reductive and contradictory nature of this national debate between liberals and conservatives has been neatly summed up by Katha Pollitt: "Read the conservatives' list and produce a nation of sexists and racists — or a nation of philosopher kings. Read the liberals' list and produce a nation of spiritual relativists — or a nation of open-minded world citizens" ("Canon to the Right of Me . . . ," *The Nation*, Sept. 23, 1991, p. 330).

These troubling and extreme alternatives can be avoided, of course, if the issues are not approached from such absolutist positions. Solutions to these issues cannot be suggested in this limited space, and, no doubt, solutions will evolve over time, but we can at least provide a perspective. Books — regardless of what list they are on — are not likely to unite a fragmented nation or to disunite a unified one. It is perhaps more useful and accurate to see issues of canonicity as reflecting political changes rather than being the primary causes of them. This is not to say that books don't have an impact on readers — that *Uncle Tom's Cabin*, for instance, did not galvanize antislavery sentiments in nineteenth-century America — but that book lists do not by themselves preserve or destroy the status quo.

It's worth noting that the curricula of American universities have always undergone significant and, some would say, wrenching changes. Only a little more than one hundred years ago there was strong opposition to teaching English, as well as other modern languages, alongside programs dominated by Greek and Latin. Only since the 1920s has American literature been made a part of the curriculum, and just five decades ago writers such as Emily Dickinson, Robert Frost, W. H. Auden, and Marianne Moore were regarded with the same raised eyebrows that today might be raised about contemporary writers such as Sharon Olds, Galway Kinnell, Linda Hogan, or Robert Bly. New voices do not drown out the past; they build on it, and eventually become part of the past as newer writers take their place alongside them. Neither resistance to change nor a denial of the past will have its way with the canon. Though both impulses are widespread, neither is likely to dominate the other, because there are too many reasonable, practical readers and teachers who instead of replacing Shakespeare, Frost, and other canonical writers have supplemented them with neglected writers from Western and other cultures. These readers experience the current debates about the canon not as a binary opposition but as an opportunity to explore important questions about continuity and change in our literature, culture, and society.

FORMALIST STRATEGIES

Formalist critics focus on the formal elements of a work — its language, structure, and tone. A formalist reads literature as an independent work of art rather than as a reflection of the author's state of mind or as a representation of a moment in history. Historic influences on a work, an author's intentions, or anything else outside the work are generally not treated by formalists (this is particularly true of the most famous modern formalists, known as the **New Critics,** who dominated American criticism from the 1940s through the 1960s). Instead, formalists offer intense examinations of the relationship between form and meaning within a work, emphasizing the subtle complexity of how a work is arranged. This kind of close reading pays special attention to what are often described as *intrinsic* matters in a literary work, such as diction, irony, paradox, metaphor, and symbol, as well as larger elements, such as plot, characterization, and narrative technique. Formalists examine how these elements work together to give a coherent shape to a work while contributing to its meaning. The answers to the questions formalists raise about how the shape and effect of a work are related come from the work itself. Other kinds of information that go beyond the text — biography, history, politics, economics, and so on — are typically regarded by formalists as *extrinsic* matters, which are considerably less important than what goes on within the autonomous text.

Poetry especially lends itself to close readings, because a poem's relative brevity allows for detailed analyses of nearly all its words and how they achieve their effects. For a sample formalist reading of how a pervasive sense of death is worked into a poem, see "A Reading of Dickinson's 'There's a certain Slant of light'" (p. 538).

Formalist strategies are also useful for analyzing drama and fiction. In his well-known essay "The World of *Hamlet*," Maynard Mack explores Hamlet's character and predicament by paying close attention to the words and images that Shakespeare uses to build a world in which appearances mask reality and mystery is embedded in scene after scene. Mack points to recurring terms, such as *apparition, seems, assume,* and *put on,* as well as repeated images of acting, clothing, disease, and painting, to indicate the treacherous surface world Hamlet must penetrate to get to the truth. This pattern of deception provides an organizing principle around which Mack offers a reading of the entire play:

> Hamlet's problem, in its crudest form, is simply the problem of the avenger: he must carry out the injunction of the ghost and kill the king. But this problem . . . is presented in terms of a certain kind of world. The ghost's injunction to act becomes so inextricably bound up for Hamlet with the character of the world in which the action must be taken — its mysteriousness, its baffling appearances, its deep consciousness of infection, frailty, and loss — that he cannot come to terms with either without coming to terms with both.

Although Mack places *Hamlet* in the tradition of revenge tragedy, his reading of the play emphasizes Shakespeare's arrangement of language rather than literary history as a means of providing an interpretation that accounts for various elements of the play. Mack's formalist strategy explores how diction reveals meaning and how repeated words and images evoke and reinforce important thematic significances.

A formalist reading of Robert Frost's "Mending Wall" leads to an examination of the tensions produced by the poem's diction, repetitions, and images that take us beyond a merely literal reading. The speaker describes how every spring he and his neighbor walk beside the stone wall bordering their respective farms to replace the stones that have fallen during winter. As they repair the wall, the speaker wonders what purpose the wall serves, given that "My apple trees will never get across / And eat the cones under his pines"; his neighbor, however, "only says, 'Good fences make good neighbors.'" The moment described in the poem is characteristic of the rural New England life that constitutes so much of Frost's poetry, but it is also typical of how he uses poetry as a means of "saying one thing in terms of another," as he once put it in an essay titled "Education by Poetry."

Just as the speaker teases his neighbor with the idea that the apple trees won't disturb the pines, so too does Frost tease the reader into looking at what it is "that doesn't love a wall." Frost's use of language in the poem does not simply consist of homespun casual phrases enlisted to characterize rural neighbors. From the opening lines, the "Something . . . that doesn't love a wall" and "That sends the frozen-ground swell under it" is, on the literal level, a frost heave that causes the stones to tumble from the wall. But after several close readings of the poem, we can see the implicit pun in these lines which suggest that it is *Frost* who objects to the wall, thus aligning the poet's perspective with the speaker's. A careful examination of some of the other formal elements in the poem supports this reading.

In contrast to the imaginative wit of the speaker who raises fundamental questions about the purpose of any wall, the images associated with his neighbor indicate that he is a traditionalist who "will not go behind his father's saying." Moreover, the neighbor moves "like an old-stone savage" in "darkness" that is attributed to his rigid, tradition-bound, walled-in sensibilities rather than to "the shade of trees." Whereas the speaker's wit and intelligence are manifested by his willingness to question the necessity or desirability of "walling in or walling out" anything, his benighted neighbor can only repeat again that "good fences make good neighbors." The stone-heavy darkness of the neighbor's mind is emphasized by the contrasting light wit and agility of the speaker, who speculates: "Before I built a wall I'd ask to know . . . to whom I was like to give offense." The pun on the final word of this line makes a subtle but important connection between giving "offense" and creating "a fence." Frost's careful use of diction, repetition, and images deftly reveals and reenforces thematic significances suggesting that the stone wall serves as a symbol of isolation, confinement, fear, and even savagery. The neighbor's conservative tradition-bound mindless support of the wall is a foil to the speaker's — read Frost's — poetic, liberal response, which imagines and encourages the possibilities of greater freedom and brotherhood.

Although this brief discussion of some of the formal elements of Frost's poem does not describe all there is to say about how they produce an effect and create meaning, it does suggest the kinds of questions, issues, and evidence that a formalist strategy might raise in providing a close reading of the text itself.

BIOGRAPHICAL STRATEGIES

A knowledge of an author's life can help readers understand his or her work more fully. Events in a work might follow actual events in a writer's life just as characters might be based on people known by the author. Ernest Hemingway's "Soldier's Home" is a story about the difficulties of a World War I veteran named Krebs returning to his small hometown in Oklahoma, where he cannot adjust to the pious assumptions of his family and neighbors. He refuses to accept their innocent blindness to the horrors he has witnessed during the war. They have no sense of the brutality of modern life; instead they insist he resume his life as if nothing has happened. There is plenty of biographical evidence to indicate that Krebs's unwillingness to lie about his war experiences reflects Hemingway's own responses upon his return to Oak Park, Illinois, in 1919. Krebs, like Hemingway, finds he has to leave the sentimentality, repressiveness, and smug complacency that threaten to render his experiences unreal: "the world they were in was not the world he was in."

An awareness of Hemingway's own war experiences and subsequent disillusionment with his hometown can be readily developed through available biographies, letters, and other works he wrote. Consider, for example, this passage from *By Force of Will: The Life and Art of Ernest Hemingway,* in which Scott Donaldson describes Hemingway's response to World War I:

> In poems, as in [*A Farewell to Arms*], Hemingway expressed his distaste for the first war. The men who had to fight the war did not die well:
>
> Soldiers pitch and cough and twitch —
>   All the world roars red and black;
> Soldiers smother in a ditch,
>   Choking through the whole attack.
>
> And what did they die for? They were "sucked in" by empty words and phrases —
>
> King and country,
> Christ Almighty,
> And the rest,
> Patriotism,
> Democracy,
> Honor —
>
> which spelled death. The bitterness of these outbursts derived from the distinction Hemingway drew between the men on the line and those who started the wars that others had to fight.

This kind of information can help to deepen our understanding of just how empathetically Krebs is presented in the story. Relevant facts about Hemingway's life will not make "Soldier's Home" a better written story than it is, but such information can make clearer the source of Hemingway's convictions and how his own experiences inform his major concerns as a storyteller.

Some formalist critics — some New Critics, for example — argue that interpretation should be based exclusively on internal evidence rather than on any biographical information outside the work. They argue that it is not possible to determine an author's intention and that the work must stand by itself. Although this is a useful caveat for keeping the work in focus, a reader who finds biography relevant would argue that biography can at the very least serve as a control on interpretation. A reader who, for example, finds Krebs at fault for not subscribing to the values of his hometown would be misreading the story, given both its tone and the biographical information available about the author. Although the narrator never *tells* the reader that Krebs is right or wrong for leaving town, the story's tone sides with his view of things. If, however, someone were to argue otherwise, insisting that the tone is not decisive and that Krebs's position is problematic, a reader familiar with Hemingway's own reactions could refute that argument with a powerful confirmation of Krebs's instincts to withdraw. Hence, many readers find biography useful for interpretation.

However, it is also worth noting that biographical information can complicate a work. For example, readers who interpret "Mending Wall" as a celebration of an iconoclastic sensibility that seeks to break down the psychological barriers and physical walls that separate human beings may be surprised to learn that very few of Frost's other writings support this view. His life was filled with emotional turmoil, a life described by a number of biographers as egocentric and vindictive rather than generous and open to others. He once commented that "I always hold that we get forward as much by hating as by loving." Indeed, many facts about Frost's life—as well as many of the speakers in his poems—are typified by depression, alienation, tension, suspicion, jealous competitiveness, and suicidal tendencies. Instead of challenging wall-builders, Frost more characteristically built walls of distrust around himself among his family, friends, and colleagues. In this biographical context, it is especially worth noting that it is the speaker of "Mending Wall" who alone repairs the damage done to the walls by hunters, and it is he who initiates each spring the rebuilding of the wall. However much he may question its value, the speaker does, after all, rebuild the wall between himself and his neighbor. This biographical approach raises provocative questions about the text. Does the poem suggest that boundaries and walls are, in fact, necessary? Are walls a desirable foundation for relationships between people? Although these and other questions raised by a biographical approach cannot be answered here, this kind of biographical perspective certainly adds to the possibilities of interpretation.

Sometimes biographical information does not change our understanding so much as it enriches our appreciation of a work. It matters, for instance, that much of John Milton's poetry, so rich in visual imagery, was written after he became blind; and it is just as significant—to shift to a musical example—that a number of Ludwig van Beethoven's greatest works, including the Ninth Symphony, were composed after he succumbed to total deafness.

PSYCHOLOGICAL STRATEGIES

Given the enormous influence that Sigmund Freud's psychoanalytic theories have had on twentieth-century interpretations of human behavior, it is nearly inevitable that most people have some familiarity with his ideas concerning dreams, unconscious desires, and sexual repression, as well as his terms for different aspects of the psyche—the id, ego, and superego. Psychological approaches to literature draw upon Freud's theories and other psychoanalytic theories to understand more fully the text, the writer, and the reader. Critics use such approaches to explore the motivations of characters and the symbolic meanings of events, while biographers speculate about a writer's own motivations — conscious or unconscious — in a literary work. Psychological approaches are also used to describe and analyze the reader's personal responses to a text.

Although it is not feasible to explain psychoanalytic terms and concepts in so brief a space as this, it is possible to suggest the nature of a psychological approach. It is a strategy based heavily on the idea of the existence of a human unconscious — those impulses, desires, and feelings about which a person is unaware but which influence emotions and behavior.

Central to a number of psychoanalytic critical readings is Freud's concept of what he called the **Oedipus complex,** a term derived from Sophocles' tragedy *Oedipus the King.* This complex is predicated on a boy's unconscious rivalry with his father for his mother's love and his desire to eliminate his father in order to take his father's place with his mother. The female version of the psychological conflict is known as the **Electra complex,** a term used to describe a daughter's unconscious rivalry for her father. The name comes from a Greek legend about Electra, who avenged the death of her father, Agamemnon, by killing her mother. In *The Interpretation of Dreams,* Freud explains why *Oedipus the King* "moves a modern audience no less than it did the contemporary Greek one." What unites their powerful attraction to the play is an unconscious response:

> There must be something which makes a voice within us ready to recognize the compelling force of destiny in the *Oedipus.* . . . His destiny moves us only because it might have been ours — because the oracle laid the same curse upon us before our birth as upon him. It is the fate of all of us, perhaps, to direct our first sexual impulse towards our mother and our first hatred and our first murderous wish against our father. Our dreams convince us that this is so. King Oedipus, who slew his father Laius and married his mother Jocasta, merely shows us the fulfillment of our own childhood wishes . . . and we shrink back from him with the whole force of the repression by which those wishes have since that time been held down within us.

In this passage Freud interprets the unconscious motives of Sophocles in writing the play, Oedipus in acting within it, and the audience in responding to it.

A further application of the Oedipus complex can be observed in a classic interpretation of *Hamlet* by Ernest Jones, who used this concept to explain why Hamlet delays in avenging his father's death. This reading has been tightly summarized by Norman Holland, a recent psychoanalytic critic, in *The Shakespearean Imagination.* Holland shapes the issues into four major components:

> One, people over the centuries have been unable to say why Hamlet delays in killing the man who murdered his father and married his mother. Two, psychoanalytic experience shows that every child wants to do just exactly that. Three, Hamlet delays because he cannot punish Claudius for doing what he

himself wished to do as a child and, unconsciously, still wishes to do: he would be punishing himself. Four, the fact that this wish is unconscious explains why people could not explain Hamlet's delay.

Although the Oedipus complex is, of course, not relevant to all psychological interpretations of literature, interpretations involving this complex do offer a useful example of how psychoanalytic critics tend to approach a text.

The situation in Frost's "Mending Wall" is not directly related to an Oedipus complex, but the poem has been read as a conflict in which the "father's saying" represents the repressiveness of a patriarchal order that challenges the speaker's individual poetic consciousness. "Mending Wall" has also been read as another kind of struggle with repression. In "Up against the 'Mending Wall': The Psychoanalysis of a Poem by Frost" Edward Jayne offers a detailed reading of the poem as "the overriding struggle to suppress latent homosexual attraction between two men separated by a wall" (*College English* 1973). Jayne reads the poem as the working out of "unconscious homosexual inclinations largely repugnant to Frost and his need to divert and sublimate them." Regardless of whether or not a reader finds these arguments convincing, it is clear that the poem does have something to do with powerful forms of repression. And what about the reader's response? How might a psychological approach account for different responses from readers who argue that the poem calls for either a world that includes walls or one that dismantles them? One needn't be versed in psychoanalytic terms to entertain this question.

HISTORICAL STRATEGIES

Historians sometimes use literature as a window onto the past, because literature frequently provides the nuances of an historic period that cannot be readily perceived through other sources. The characters in Harriet Beecher Stowe's novel *Uncle Tom's Cabin* (1852) display, for example, a complex set of white attitudes toward blacks in mid-nineteenth-century America that is absent from more traditional historic documents such as census statistics or state laws. Another way of approaching the relationship between literature and history, however, is to use history as a means of understanding a literary work more clearly. The plot pattern of pursuit, escape, and capture in nineteenth century slave narratives had a significant influence on Stowe's plotting of action in *Uncle Tom's Cabin*. This relationship demonstrates that the writing contemporary to an author is an important element of the history that helps to shape a work. There are many ways to talk about the historical and cultural dimensions of a work. Such readings treat a literary text as a document reflecting, producing, or being produced by the social conditions of its time, giving equal focus to the social milieu and the work itself. Four historical strategies that have been especially influential are literary history criticism, Marxist criticism, new historicist criticism, and cultural criticism.

Literary History Criticism

Literary historians shift the emphasis from the period to the work. Hence a literary historian might also examine mid-nineteenth-century abolitionist attitudes toward blacks to determine whether Stowe's novel is representative of those views or significantly to the right or left of them. Such a study might even indicate how closely the book reflects racial attitudes of twentieth-century readers. A work of literature may transcend time to the extent that it addresses the concerns of readers over a span of decades or centuries, but it remains for the literary historian a part of the past in which it was composed, a past that can reveal more fully a work's language, ideas, and purposes.

Literary historians move beyond both the facts of an author's personal life and the text itself to the social and intellectual currents in which the author composed the work. They place the work in the context of its time (as do many critical biographers who write "life and times" studies), and sometimes they make connections with other literary works that may have influenced the author. The basic strategy of literary historians is to illuminate the historic background in order to shed light on some aspect of the work itself.

In Hemingway's "Soldier's Home" we learn that Krebs had been at Belleau Wood, Soissons, the Champagne, St. Mihiel, and the Argonne. Although nothing is said of these battles in the story, they were among the most bloody battles of the war; the wholesale butchery and staggering casualties incurred by both sides make credible the way Krebs's unstated but lingering memories have turned him into a psychological prisoner of war. Knowing something about the ferocity of those battles helps us account for Krebs's response in the story. Moreover, we can more fully appreciate Hemingway's refusal to have Krebs lie about the realities of war for the folks back home if we are aware of the numerous poems, stories, and plays published during World War I that presented war as a glorious, manly, transcendent sacrifice for God and country. Juxtaposing those works with "Soldier's Home" brings the differences into sharp focus.

Similarly, a reading of Blake's poem "London" (p. 101) is less complete if we do not know of the horrific social conditions — the poverty, disease, exploitation, and hypocrisy — that characterized the city Blake laments in the late eighteenth century.

One last example: The potential historical meaning of the wall that is the subject of Frost's "Mending Wall" might be more distinctly seen if it is placed in the context of its publication date, 1914, when the world was on the verge of collapsing into the violent political landscape of World War I. The insistence that "Good fences make good neighbors" suggests a grim ironic tone in the context of European nationalist hostilities that seemed to be moving inexorably toward war. The larger historical context for the poem would have been more apparent to its readers contemporary with World War I, but a historical reconstruction of the horrific tensions produced by shifting national borders and shattered walls during the war can shed some light on the larger issues that may be at stake in the poem. Moreover, an examination of Frost's attitudes toward the war and America's potential involvement in it could help to produce a reading of the meaning and value of a world with or without walls.

Marxist Criticism

Marxist readings developed from the heightened interest in radical reform during the 1930s, when many critics looked to literature as a means of furthering proletarian social and economic goals, based largely on the writings of Karl Marx. *Marxist critics* focus on the ideological content of a work — its explicit and implicit assumptions and values about matters such as culture, race, class, and power. Marxist studies typically aim at not only revealing and clarifying ideological issues but also correcting social injustices. Some Marxist critics have used literature to describe the competing socioeconomic interests that too often advance capitalist money and power rather than socialist morality and justice. They argue that criticism, like literature, is essentially political because it either challenges or supports economic oppression. Even if criticism attempts to ignore class conflicts, it is politicized, according to Marxists, because it supports the status quo.

It is not surprising that Marxist critics pay more attention to the content and themes of literature than to its form. A Marxist critic would more likely be concerned with the exploitive economic forces that cause Willy Loman to feel trapped in Miller's *Death of a Salesman* than with the playwright's use of nonrealistic dramatic techniques to reveal Loman's inner thoughts. Similarly, a Marxist reading of Frost's "Mending Wall" might draw upon the poet's well-known conservative criticisms of President Franklin Delano Roosevelt's New Deal during the 1930s as a means of reading conservative ideology into the poem. Frost's deep suspicions of collective enterprise might suggest to a Marxist that the wall represents the status quo, that is, a capitalist construction that unnaturally divides individuals (in this case, the poem's speaker from his neighbor) and artificially defies nature. Complicit in their own oppression, both farmers, to a lesser and greater degree, accept the idea that "good fences make good neighbors," thereby maintaining and perpetuating an unnatural divisive order that oppresses and is mistakenly perceived as necessary and beneficial. A Marxist reading would see the speaker's and neighbor's conflicts as not only an individual issue but part of a larger class struggle.

New Historicist Criticism

Since the 1960s a development in historical approaches to literature known as *new historicism* has emphasized the interaction between the historic context of a work and a modern reader's understanding and interpretation of the work. In contrast to many traditional literary historians, however, new historicists attempt to describe the culture of a period by reading many different kinds of texts that traditional historians might have previously left for sociologists and anthropologists. New historicists attempt to read a period in all its dimensions, including political, economic, social, and aesthetic concerns. These considerations could be used to explain something about the nature of rural New England life early in the twentieth century. The process of mending the stone wall authentically suggests how this tedious job simultaneously draws the two men together and keeps them apart. Pamphlets and other contemporary writings about farming and maintaining property lines could offer insight into either the necessity or the uselessness of the spring wall-mending rituals. A new historicist might find useful how advice offered in texts about running a farm reflect or refute the speaker's or neighbor's competing points of view in the poem.

New historicist criticism acknowledges more fully than traditional historical approaches the competing nature of readings of the past and thereby tends to offer new emphases and perspectives. New historicism reminds us that there is not only one historic context for "Mending Wall." The year before Frost died, he visited Moscow as a cultural ambassador from the United States. During this 1962 visit — only one year after the Soviet Union's construction of the Berlin Wall — he read "Mending Wall" to his Russian audience. Like the speaker in that poem, Frost clearly enjoyed the "mischief" of that moment, and a new historicist would clearly find intriguing the way the poem was both intended and received in so volatile a context. By emphasizing that historical perceptions are governed, at least in part, by our own concerns and preoccupations, new historicists sensitize us to the fact that the history on which we choose to focus is colored by being reconstructed from our own present moment. This reconstructed history affects our reading of texts.

Cultural Criticism

Cultural critics, like new historicists, focus on the historical contexts of a literary work, but they pay particular attention to popular manifestations of social, political, and economic contexts. Popular culture — mass-produced and consumed cultural artifacts, today ranging from advertising to popular fiction to television to rock music — and "high" culture are given equal emphasis. A cultural critic might be interested in looking at how Baz Luhrmann's movie version of *Romeo and Juliet* (1996) was influenced by the fragmentary nature of MTV videos. Adding the "low" art of everyday life to "high" art opens up previously unexpected and unexplored areas of criticism. Cultural critics use widely eclectic strategies drawn from new historicism, psychology, gender studies, and deconstructionism (to name only a handful of approaches) to analyze not only literary texts but radio talk shows, comic strips, calendar art, commercials, travel guides, and baseball cards. Because all human activity falls within the ken of cultural criticism, nothing is too minor or major, obscure or pervasive, to escape the range of its analytic vision.

Cultural criticism also includes ***postcolonial criticism,*** the study of cultural behavior and expression in relationship to the formerly colonized world. Postcolonial criticism refers to the analysis of literary works written by writers from countries and cultures that at one time were controlled by colonizing powers — such as Indian writers during or after British colonial rule. The term also refers to the analysis of literary works written about colonial cultures by writers from the colonizing country. Many of these kinds of analyses point out how writers from colonial powers sometimes misrepresent colonized cultures by reflecting more of their own values: Joseph Conrad's *Heart of Darkness* (published in 1899) represents African culture differently than Chinua Achebe's *Things Falling Apart* does, for example. Cultural criticism and postcolonial criticism represent a broad range of approaches to examining race, gender, and class in historical contexts in a variety of cultures.

A cultural critic's approach to Frost's "Mending Wall" might emphasize how the poem reflects New England farmers' attitudes toward hunters, or it might examine how popular poems about stone walls contemporary to "Mending Wall" endorse such wall building instead of making problematic the building of walls between neighbors as Frost does. Each of these perspectives can serve to create a wider and more informed understanding of the poem. For a deeper sense of the range of documents used by cultural critics to shed light on literary works and the historical contexts in which they are written and read, see the Cultural Case Study on Julia Alvarez's poem "Queens, 1963" (p. 423).

GENDER STRATEGIES

Gender critics explore how ideas about men and women — what is masculine and feminine — can be regarded as socially constructed by particular cultures. According to some critics, sex is determined by simple biological and anatomical categories of male or female, and gender is determined by a culture's values. Thus, ideas about gender and what constitutes masculine and feminine behavior are created by cultural institutions and conditioning. A gender critic might, for example, focus on Frost's characterization of the narrator's neighbor as an emotionally frozen son of a father who overshadowed his psychological and social development. The narrator's rigid masculinity would then be seen as a manifestation of socially constructed gender identity in the 1910s. Gender criticism expands categories and definitions of what is masculine or feminine and tends to regard sexuality as more complex than merely masculine or feminine, heterosexual or homosexual. Gender criticism, therefore, has come to include gay and lesbian criticism as well as feminist criticism. Although there are complex and sometimes problematic relationships among these approaches because some critics argue that heterosexuals and homosexuals are profoundly biologically different, gay and lesbian criticism, like feminist criticism, can be usefully regarded as a subset of gender criticism.

Feminist Criticism

Like Marxist critics, *feminist critics* would also be interested in examining the status quo in "Mending Wall," because they seek to correct or supplement what they regard as a predominantly male-dominated critical perspective with a feminist consciousness. Like other forms of sociological criticism, feminist criticism places literature in a social context, and, like those of Marxist criticism, its analyses often have sociopolitical purposes, purposes that might explain, for example, how images of women in literature reflect the patriarchal social forces that have impeded women's efforts to achieve full equality with men.

Feminists have analyzed literature by both men and women in an effort to understand literary representations of women as well as the writers and cultures that create them. Related to concerns about how gender affects the way men and women write about each other is an interest in whether women use language differently from the way men do. Consequently, feminist critics' approach to literature is characterized by the use of a broad range of disciplines, including history, sociology, psychology, and linguistics, to provide a perspective sensitive to feminist issues.

A feminist approach to Frost's "Mending Wall" might initially appear to offer few possibilities given that no women appear in the poem and that no mention or allusion is made about women. And that is precisely the point: the landscape presented in the poem is devoid of women. Traditional gender roles are evident in the poem because it is men, not women, who work outdoors building walls and who discuss the significance of their work. For a feminist critic, the wall might be read as a symbol of patriarchal boundaries that are defined exclusively by men. If the wall can be seen as a manifestation of the status quo built upon the "father's saying[s]," then mending the wall each year and keeping everything essentially the same — with women securely out of the picture — essentially benefits the established patriarchy. The boundaries are reconstructed and rationalized in the absence of any woman's potential efforts to offer an alternative to the boundaries imposed by the men's rebuilding of the wall. Perhaps one way of considering the value of a feminist perspective on this work can be discerned if a reader imagines the speaker or the neighbor as a woman and how that change might extend the parameters of their conversation about the value of the wall.

Gay and Lesbian Criticism

Gay and lesbian critics focus on a variety of issues, including how homosexuals are represented in literature, how they read literature, and whether sexuality and gender are culturally constructed or innate. Gay critics have produced new readings and discovered homosexual concerns in writers such as Herman Melville and Henry James, while lesbian critics have done the same with writers such as Emily Dickinson and Sylvia Plath. Some readers have found in "Mending Wall," for example, homosexual tensions between the narrator and his neighbor that are suppressed by both men as they build their wall to fence in forbidden and unbidden desires. Although gay and lesbian readings often raise significant interpretative controversies among critics, they have opened up provocative discussions of seemingly familiar texts.

MYTHOLOGICAL STRATEGIES

Mythological approaches to literature attempt to identify what in a work creates deep universal responses in readers. Whereas psychological critics interpret the symbolic meanings of characters and actions in order to understand more fully the unconscious dimensions of an author's mind, a character's motivation, or a reader's response, mythological critics (also frequently referred to as archetypal critics) interpret the hopes, fears, and expectations of entire cultures.

In this context myth is not to be understood simply as referring to stories about imaginary gods who perform astonishing feats in the causes of love, jealousy, or hatred. Nor are myths to be judged as merely erroneous, primitive accounts of how nature runs its course and humanity its affairs. Instead, literary critics use myths as a strategy for understanding how human beings try to account for their lives symbolically. Myths can be a window onto a culture's deepest perceptions about itself, because myths attempt to explain what otherwise seems unexplainable: a people's origin, purpose, and destiny.

All human beings have a need to make sense of their lives, whether they are concerned about their natural surroundings, the seasons, sexuality, birth, death, or the very meaning of existence. Myths help people organize their experiences; these systems of belief (less formally held than religious or political tenets but no less important) embody a culture's assumptions and values. What is important to the mythological critic is not the validity or truth of those assumptions and values; what matters is that they reveal common human concerns.

It is not surprising that although the details of mythic stories vary enormously, the essential patterns are often similar, because these myths attempt to explain universal experiences. There are, for example, numerous myths that redeem humanity from permanent death through a hero's resurrection and rebirth. For Christians the resurrection of Jesus symbolizes the ultimate defeat of death and coincides with the rebirth of nature's fertility in spring. Features of this rebirth parallel the Greek myths of Adonis

and Hyacinth, who die but are subsequently transformed into living flow-
ers; there are also similarities that connect these stories to the reincarna-
tion of the Indian Buddha or the rebirth of the Egyptian Osiris. To be sure,
important differences exist among these stories, but each reflects a basic
human need to limit the power of death and to hope for eternal life.

   Mythological critics look for underlying, recurrent patterns in literature
that reveal universal meanings and basic human experiences for readers re-
gardless of when or where they live. The characters, images, and themes
that symbolically embody these meanings and experiences are called **arche-
types.** This term designates universal symbols, which evoke deep and per-
haps unconscious responses in a reader because archetypes bring with
them the heft of our hopes and fears since the beginning of human time.
Surely one of the most powerfully compelling archetypes is the death/re-
birth theme that relates the human life cycle to the cycle of the seasons.
Many others could be cited and would be exhausted only after all human
concerns were catalogued, but a few examples can suggest some of the
range of plots, images, and characters addressed.

   Among the most common literary archetypes are stories of quests, ini-
tiations, scapegoats, meditative withdrawals, descents to the underworld,
and heavenly ascents. These stories are often filled with archetypal images:
bodies of water that may symbolize the unconscious or eternity or bap-
tismal rebirth; rising suns, suggesting reawakening and enlightenment;
setting suns, pointing toward death; colors such as green, evocative of
growth and fertility, or black, indicating chaos, evil, and death. Along the
way are earth mothers, fatal women, wise old men, desert places, and para-
disal gardens. No doubt your own reading has introduced you to any num-
ber of archetypal plots, images, and characters.

   Mythological critics attempt to explain how archetypes are embodied
in literary works. Employing various disciplines, these critics articulate the
power a literary work has over us. Some critics are deeply grounded in clas-
sical literature, whereas others are more conversant with philology, anthro-
pology, psychology, or cultural history. Whatever their emphases, however,
mythological critics examine the elements of a work in order to make
larger connections that explain the work's lasting appeal.

   A mythological reading of Sophocles' *Oedipus the King,* for example,
might focus on the relationship between Oedipus's role as a scapegoat and
the plague and drought that threaten to destroy Thebes. The city is saved
and the fertility of its fields restored only after the corruption is located in
Oedipus. His subsequent atonement symbolically provides a kind of re-
birth for the city. Thus, the plot recapitulates ancient rites in which the
well-being of a king was directly linked to the welfare of his people. If a
leader were sick or corrupt, he had to be replaced in order to guarantee the
health of the community.

   A similar pattern can be seen in the rottenness that Shakespeare ex-
poses in Hamlet's Denmark. *Hamlet* reveals an archetypal pattern similar
to that of *Oedipus the King:* not until the hero sorts out the corruption in

his world and in himself can vitality and health be restored in his world. Hamlet avenges his father's death and becomes a scapegoat in the process. When he fully accepts his responsibility to set things right, he is swept away along with the tide of intrigue and corruption that has polluted life in Denmark. The new order — established by Fortinbras at the play's end — is achieved precisely because Hamlet is willing and finally able to sacrifice himself in a necessary purgation of the diseased state.

These kinds of archetypal patterns exist potentially in any literary period. Frost's "Mending Wall," for example, is set in spring, an evocative season that marks the end of winter and earth's renewal. The action in the poem, however, does not lead to a celebration of new life and human community; instead there is for the poem's speaker and his neighbor an annual ritual to "set the wall between us as we go" that separates and divides human experience rather than unifying it. We can see that the rebuilding of the wall runs counter to nature itself because the stones are so round that "We have to use a spell to make them balance." The speaker also resists the wall and sets out to subvert it by toying with the idea of challenging his neighbor's assumption that "good fences make good neighbors," a seemingly ancient belief passed down through one "father's saying" to the next. The speaker, however, does not heroically overcome the neighbor's ritual; he merely points out that the wall is not needed where it is. The speaker's acquiescence results in the continuation of a ritual that confirms the old order rather than overthrowing the "old-stone savage," who demands the dark isolation and separateness associated with the "gaps" produced by winter's frost. The neighbor's old order prevails in spite of nature's and the speaker's protestations. From a mythological critic's perspective, the wall might itself be seen as a "gap," an unnatural disruption of nature and the human community.

READER-RESPONSE STRATEGIES

Reader-response criticism, as its name implies, focuses its attention on the reader rather than the work itself. This approach to literature describes what goes on in the reader's mind during the process of reading a text. In a sense, all critical approaches (especially psychological and mythological criticism) concern themselves with a reader's response to literature, but there is a stronger emphasis in reader-response criticism on the reader's active construction of the text. Although many critical theories inform reader-response criticism, all **reader-response critics** aim to describe the reader's experience of a work: in effect we get a reading of the reader, who comes to the work with certain expectations and assumptions, which are either met or not met. Hence the consciousness of the reader — produced by reading the work — is the subject matter of reader-response critics. Just as writing is a creative act, reading is, since it also produces a text.

Reader-response critics do not assume that a literary work is a finished product with fixed formal properties, as, for example, formalist critics do. Instead, the literary work is seen as an evolving creation of the reader's as he or she processes characters, plots, images, and other elements while reading. Some reader-response critics argue that this act of creative reading is, to a degree, controlled by the text, but it can produce many interpretations of the same text by different readers. There is no single definitive reading of a work, because the crucial assumption is that readers create rather than discover meanings in texts. Readers who have gone back to works they had read earlier in their lives often find that a later reading draws very different responses from them. What earlier seemed unimportant is now crucial; what at first seemed central is now barely worth noting. The reason, put simply, is that two different people have read the same text. Reader-response critics are not after the "correct" reading of the text or what the author presumably intended; instead they are interested in the reader's experience with the text.

These experiences change with readers; although the text remains the same, the readers do not. Social and cultural values influence readings, so that, for example, an avowed Marxist would be likely to come away from Miller's *Death of a Salesman* with a very different view of American capitalism than that of, say, a successful sales representative, who might attribute Willy Loman's fall more to his character than to the American economic system. Moreover, readers from different time periods respond differently to texts. An Elizabethan — concerned perhaps with the stability of monarchical rule — might respond differently to Hamlet's problems than would a twentieth-century reader well versed in psychology and concepts of what Freud called the Oedipus complex. This is not to say that anything goes, that Miller's play can be read as an amoral defense of cheating and rapacious business practices or that *Hamlet* is about the dangers of living away from home. The text does, after all, establish some limits that allow us to reject certain readings as erroneous. But reader-response critics do reject formalist approaches that describe a literary work as a self-contained object, the meaning of which can be determined without reference to any extrinsic matters, such as the social and cultural values assumed by either the author or the reader.

Reader-response criticism calls attention to how we read and what influences our readings. It does not attempt to define what a literary work means on the page but rather what it does to an informed reader, a reader who understands the language and conventions used in a given work. Reader-response criticism is not a rationale for mistaken or bizarre readings of works but an exploration of the possibilities for a plurality of readings shaped by the readers' experience with the text. This kind of strategy can help us understand how our responses are shaped by both the text and ourselves.

Frost's "Mending Wall" illustrates how reader-response critical strategies read the reader. Among the first readers of the poem in 1914, those who were eager to see the United States enter World War I might have been inclined to see the speaker as an imaginative thinker standing up for freedom rather than antiquated boundaries and sensibilities that don't know what they are "walling in or walling out." But for someone whose son could be sent to the trenches of France to fight the Germans, the phrase "Good fences make good neighbors" might sound less like an unthinking tradition and more like solid, prudent common sense. In each instance the reader's circumstances could have an effect upon his or her assessment of the value of walls and fences. Certainly the Russians who listened to Frost's reading of "Mending Wall" in 1962, only one year after the construction of the Berlin Wall, had a very different response from the Americans who heard about Frost's reading and who relished the discomfort they thought the reading had caused the Russians.

By imagining different readers we can imagine a variety of responses to the poem that are influenced by the readers' own impressions, memories, or experiences. Such imagining suggests the ways in which reader-response criticism opens up texts to a number of interpretations. As one final example, consider how readers' responses to "Mending Wall" would be affected if it were printed in two different magazines, read in the context of either the *Farmer's Almanac* or *The New Yorker*. What assumptions and beliefs would each magazine's readership be likely to bring to the poem? How do you think the respective experiences and values of each magazine's readers would influence their readings?

DECONSTRUCTIONIST STRATEGIES

Deconstructionist critics insist that literary works do not yield fixed, single meanings. They argue that there can be no absolute knowledge about anything because language can never say what we intend it to mean. Anything we write conveys meanings we did not intend, so the deconstructionist argument goes. Language is not a precise instrument but a power whose meanings are caught in an endless web of possibilities that cannot be untangled. Accordingly, any idea or statement that insists on being understood separately can ultimately be "deconstructed" to reveal its relations and connections to contradictory and opposite meanings.

Unlike other forms of criticism, deconstructionism seeks to destabilize meanings instead of establishing them. In contrast to formalists such as the New Critics, who closely examine a work in order to call attention to how its various components interact to establish a unified whole, deconstructionists try to show how a close examination of the language in a text inevitably reveals conflicting, contradictory impulses that "deconstruct" or break down its apparent unity.

Although deconstructionists and New Critics both examine the language of a text closely, deconstructionists focus on the gaps and ambiguities that reveal a text's instability and indeterminacy, whereas New Critics look for patterns that explain how the text's fixed meaning is structured. Deconstructionists painstakingly examine the competing meanings within the text rather than attempting to resolve them into a unified whole.

The questions deconstructionists ask are aimed at discovering and describing how a variety of possible readings are generated by the elements of a text. In contrast to a New Critic's concerns about the ultimate meaning of a work, a deconstructionist's primary interest is in how the use of language — diction, tone, metaphor, symbol, and so on — yields only provisional, not definitive, meanings. Consider, for example, the following excerpt from an American Puritan poet, Anne Bradstreet. The excerpt is from "The Flesh and the Spirit" (1678), which consists of an allegorical debate between two sisters, the body and the soul. During the course of the debate, Flesh, a consummate materialist, insists that Spirit values ideas that do not exist and that her faith in idealism is both unwarranted and insubstantial in the face of the material values that earth has to offer — riches, fame, and physical pleasure. Spirit, however, rejects the materialistic worldly argument that the only ultimate reality is physical reality and pledges her faith in God:

> Mine eye doth pierce the heavens and see
> What is invisible to thee.
> My garments are not silk nor gold,
> Nor such like trash which earth doth hold,
> But royal robes I shall have on,
> More glorious than the glist'ring sun;
> My crown not diamonds, pearls, and gold,
> But such as angels' heads enfold
> The city where I hope to dwell,
> There's none on earth can parallel;
> The stately walls both high and strong,
> Are made of precious jasper stone;
> The gates of pearl, both rich and clear,
> And angels are for porters there;
> The streets thereof transparent gold,
> Such as no eye did e'er behold;
> A crystal river there doth run,
> Which doth proceed from the Lamb's throne.

A deconstructionist would point out that Spirit's language — her use of material images such as jasper stone, pearl, gold, and crystal — cancels the explicit meaning of the passage by offering a supermaterialistic reward to the spiritually faithful. Her language, in short, deconstructs her intended meaning by employing the same images that Flesh would use to describe the rewards of the physical world. A deconstructionist reading, then, reveals the impossibility of talking about the invisible and spiritual worlds without using materialistic (that is, metaphoric) language. Thus Spirit's very language demonstrates a contradiction and conflict in her conviction that the world of here and now must be rejected for the hereafter. Her language deconstructs her meaning.

Deconstructionists look for ways to question and extend the meanings of a text. In Frost's "Mending Wall," for example, the speaker presents himself as being on the side of the imaginative rather than hidebound, rigid responses to life. He seems to value freedom and openness rather than restrictions and narrowly defined limits. Yet his treatment of his Yankee farmer neighbor can be read as condescending and even smug in its superior attitude toward his neighbor's repeating his "father's saying," as if he were "an old-stone savage armed." The condescending attitude hardly suggests a robust sense of community and shared humanity. Moreover, for all the talk about unnecessary conventions and traditions, a deconstructionist would likely be quick to point out that Frost writes the poem in blank verse — unrhymed iambic pentameter — rather than free verse; hence the very regular rhythms of the narrator's speech may be seen to deconstruct its liberationist meaning.

As difficult as it is controversial, deconstructionism is not easily summarized or paraphrased. For an example of deconstructionism in practice and how it differs from New Criticism, see Andrew P. Debicki's "New Criticism and Deconstructionism: Two Attitudes in Teaching Poetry" in *Perspectives* (p. 509).

SELECTED BIBLIOGRAPHY

Given the enormous number of articles and books written about literary theory and criticism in recent years, the following bibliography is necessarily highly selective. Even so, it should prove useful as an introduction to many of the issues associated with the critical strategies discussed in this chapter. For a general encyclopedic reference book that describes important figures, schools, and movements, see *The Johns Hopkins Guide to Literary Theory and Criticism,* edited by Michael Grodin and Martin Kreiswirth (Baltimore: Johns Hopkins UP, 1994); and for its concise discussions, see Ross Murfin and Supryia M. Ray, *The Bedford Glossary of Critical and Literary Terms* (Boston: Bedford/St. Martin's, 1998).

Canonical Issues

"The Changing Culture of the University." Special Issue. *Partisan Review* 58 (Spring 1991): 185–410.

Gates, Henry Louis, Jr. *The Signifying Monkey.* New York: Oxford UP, 1988.

Greenblatt, Stephen, and Giles Gunn. *Redrawing the Boundaries: The Transformation of English and American Literary Studies.* New York: MLA, 1992.

Lauter, Paul. *Canons and Contexts.* New York: Oxford UP, 1991.

"The Politics of Liberal Education." Special Issue. *South Atlantic Quarterly* 89 (Winter 1990): 1–234.

Sykes, Charles J. *The Hollow Men: Politics and Corruption in Higher Education.* Washington, DC: Regnery Gateway, 1990.

Formalist Strategies

Brooks, Cleanth. *The Well Wrought Urn: Studies in the Structure of Poetry.* New York: Reynal and Hitchcock, 1947.

Crane, Ronald Salmon. *The Languages of Criticism and the Structure of Poetry.* Toronto: U of Toronto P, 1953.

Eliot, Thomas Stearns. *The Sacred Wood: Essays in Poetry and Criticism.* London: Methuen, 1920.

Fekete, John. *The Critical Twilight: Explorations in the Ideology of Anglo-American Literary Theory from Eliot to McLuhan.* London: Routledge, 1977.

Lemon, Lee T., and Marion J. Reis, eds. *Russian Formalist Criticism: Four Essays.* Lincoln: U of Nebraska P, 1965.

Ransom, John Crowe. *The New Criticism.* Norfolk, CT: New Directions, 1941.

Wellek, René, and Austin Warren. *Theory of Literature.* New York: Harcourt, Brace and World, 1949.

Biographical and Psychological Strategies

Bleich, David. *Subjective Criticism.* Baltimore: Johns Hopkins UP, 1978.

Bloom, Harold. *The Anxiety of Influence.* New York: Oxford UP, 1975.

Brennan, Teresa. *The Interpretation of the Flesh: Freud and Femininity.* New York: Routledge, 1994.

Crews, Frederick. *Out of My System: Psychoanalysis, Ideology, and Critical Method.* New York: Oxford UP, 1975.

——. *The Sins of the Fathers: Hawthorne's Psychological Themes.* New York: Oxford UP, 1966.

Felman, Shoshana. *Writing and Madness (Literature/Philosophy/Psychoanalysis).* Ithaca: Cornell UP, 1985.

——, ed. *Literature and Psychoanalysis: The Question of Reading: Otherwise.* Baltimore: Johns Hopkins UP, 1981.

Freud, Sigmund. *The Standard Edition of the Complete Psychological Works.* 24 vols. 1940–1968. London: Hogarth Press and the Institute of Psychoanalysis, 1953.

Holland, Norman. *The Dynamics of Literary Response.* New York: Oxford UP, 1968.

Jones, Ernest. *Hamlet and Oedipus.* New York: Doubleday, 1949.

Lacan, Jacques. *Écrits: A Selection.* Trans. Alan Sheridan. New York: Norton, 1977.

——. *The Four Fundamental Concepts of Psychoanalysis.* Trans. Alan Sheridan. London: Penguin, 1980.

Lesser, Simon O. *Fiction and the Unconscious.* Chicago: U of Chicago P, 1957.

Skura, Meredith Anne. *The Literary Use of the Psychoanalytic Process.* New Haven: Yale UP, 1981.

Zizek, Slavoj. *Looking Awry: An Introduction to Jacques Lacan through Popular Culture.* Cambridge: MIT P, 1991.

Historical Strategies, Including Marxist, New Historicist, and Cultural Strategies

Ang, Ien. *Watching Television*. New York: Routledge, 1991.

Armstrong, Nancy. *Desire and Domestic Fiction*. New York: Oxford UP, 1987.

Ashcroft, Bill, Ga Breth Griffiths, and Helen Tiffin, eds. *The Post-Colonial Studies Reader*. New York: Routledge, 1995.

Bhabha, Homi K. *The Location of Culture*. New York: Routledge, 1994.

Dollimore, Jonathan. *Radical Tragedy: Religion, Ideology and Power in the Drama of Shakespeare and His Contemporaries*. Brighton, Eng.: Harvester, 1984.

Frow, John. *Marxist and Literary History*. Cambridge: Harvard UP, 1986.

Geertz, Clifford. *The Interpretation of Cultures: Selected Essays*. New York: Basic, 1973.

Greenblatt, Stephen. *Renaissance Self-Fashioning: From More to Shakespeare*. Chicago: U of Chicago P, 1980.

——. *Shakespearean Negotiations: The Circulation of Social Energy in Renaissance England*. Berkeley: U of California P, 1985.

Lindenberger, Herbert. *Historical Drama: The Relation of Literature and Reality*. Chicago: U of Chicago P, 1975.

McGann, Jerome. *The Beauty of Inflections: Literary Investigations in Historical Method and Theory*. Oxford: Clarendon, 1985.

Storey, John, ed. *What Is Cultural Studies?* New York: St. Martin's, 1996.

White, Hayden. *Tropics of Discourse: Essays in Cultural Criticism*. Baltimore: Johns Hopkins UP, 1978.

Williams, Raymond. *Marxism and Literature*. Oxford: Oxford UP, 1977.

Gender Strategies, Including Feminist and Gay and Lesbian Strategies

Ablelove, Henry, Michèle Aina Barale, and David M. Halperin, eds. *The Lesbian and Gay Studies Reader*. New York: Routledge, 1993.

Baym, Nina. *Feminism and American Literary History*. New Brunswick: Rutgers UP, 1992.

Beauvoir, Simone de. *The Second Sex*. Trans. H. M. Parshley. New York: Knopf, 1972. Trans. of *Le deuxième sexe*. Paris: Gallimard, 1949.

Benstock, Shari, ed. *Feminist Issues and Literary Scholarship*. Bloomington: Indiana UP, 1987.

Cixous, Hélène, and Catherine Clément. *The Newly Born Woman*. Trans. Betsy Wing. Minneapolis: U of Minnesota P, 1986.

Edelman, Lee. *Homographesis: Essays in Gay Literary and Cultural Theory*. New York: Routledge, 1994.

Fetterley, Judith. *The Resisting Reader: A Feminist Approach to American Fiction*. Bloomington: Indiana UP, 1978.

Flynn, Elizabeth A., and Patrocino P. Schweickert. *Gender and Reading: Essays on Readers, Texts, and Contexts*. Baltimore: Johns Hopkins UP, 1986.

Gilbert, Sandra M., and Susan Gubar. *The Madwoman in the Attic: The Woman Writer and the Nineteenth-Century Literary Imagination*. New Haven: Yale UP, 1979.

Irigaray, Luce. *This Sex Which Is Not One*. Ithaca: Cornell UP, 1985. Trans. of *Ce sexe qui n'en est pas un*. Paris: Éditions de Minuit, 1977.

Jagose, Annamarie. *Queer Theory*. Victoria: Melbourne UP, 1996.

Kolodny, Annette. "Some Notes on Defining a 'Feminist Literary Criticism.'" *Critical Inquiry* 2 (1975): 75–92.

Millett, Kate. *Sexual Politics*. New York: Avon, 1970.

Sedgwick, Eve Kosofsky. *Epistemology of the Closet*. Berkeley: U of California P, 1990.

Showalter, Elaine. *A Literature of Their Own: British Women Novelists from Brontë to Lessing*. Princeton: Princeton UP, 1977.

Smith, Barbara. *Toward a Black Feminist Criticism*. New York: Out and Out, 1977.

Mythological Strategies

Bodkin, Maud. *Archetypal Patterns in Poetry*. London: Oxford UP, 1934.

Frye, Northrop. *Anatomy of Criticism: Four Essays*. Princeton: Princeton UP, 1957.

Jung, Carl Gustav. *Complete Works*. Ed. Herbert Read, Michael Fordham, and Gerhard Adler. 17 vols. New York: Pantheon, 1953–.

Reader-Response Strategies

Booth, Wayne C. *The Rhetoric of Fiction*. 2nd ed. Chicago: U of Chicago P, 1983.

Eco, Umberto. *The Role of the Reader: Explorations in the Semiotics of Texts*. Bloomington: Indiana UP, 1979.

Escarpit, Robert. *Sociology of Literature*. Painesville, OH: Lake Erie College P, 1965.

Fish, Stanley. *Is There a Text in This Class? The Authority of Interpretive Communities*. Cambridge: Harvard UP, 1980.

Freund, Elizabeth. *The Return of the Reader: Reader-Response Criticism*. London: Methuen, 1987.

Holland, Norman N. *The Critical I*. New York: Columbia UP, 1992.

———. *Five Readers Reading*. New Haven: Yale UP, 1975.

Iser, Wolfgang. *The Implied Reader: Patterns of Communication in Prose Fiction from Bunyan to Beckett*. Baltimore: Johns Hopkins UP, 1974.

Jauss, Hans Robert. "Literary History as a Challenge to Literary Theory." *Toward an Aesthetics of Reception*. Trans. Timothy Bahti. Minneapolis: U of Minnesota P, 1982. 3–46.

Rosenblatt, Louise. *Literature as Exploration*. 1938. New York: MLA, 1983.

Suleiman, Susan, and Inge Crosman, eds. *The Reader in the Text: Essays on Audience and Interpretation*. Princeton: Princeton UP, 1980.

Tompkins, Jane P., ed. *Reader-Response Criticism: From Formalism to Post Structuralism.* Baltimore: Johns Hopkins UP, 1980.

Deconstructionist and Other Poststructuralist Strategies

Barthes, Roland. *The Rustle of Language.* New York: Hill and Wang, 1986.
Culler, Jonathan. *On Deconstruction: Theory and Criticism after Structuralism.* Ithaca: Cornell UP, 1982.
de Man, Paul. *Blindness and Insight.* New York: Oxford UP, 1971.
Derrida, Jacques. *Of Grammatology.* 1967. Baltimore: Johns Hopkins UP, 1976.
———. *Writing and Difference.* 1967. Chicago: U of Chicago P, 1978.
Foucault, Michel. *Language, Counter-Memory, Practice.* Ithaca: Cornell UP, 1977.
———. *The Order of Things: An Archaeology of the Human Sciences.* 1966. London: Tavistock, 1970.
Gasche, Rodolphe. "Deconstruction as Criticism." *Glyph* 6 (1979): 177–216.
Hartman, Geoffrey H. *Criticism in the Wilderness.* New Haven: Yale UP, 1980.
Johnson, Barbara. *The Critical Difference: Essays in the Contemporary Rhetoric of Reading.* Baltimore: Johns Hopkins UP, 1980.
Martin, Bill. *Humanism and Its Aftermath: The Shared Fate of Deconstructionism and Politics.* Atlantic Highlands, NJ: Humanities, 1995.
Melville, Stephen W. *Philosophy Beside Itself: On Deconstruction and Modernism. Theory and History of Literature* 27. Minneapolis: U of Minnesota P, 1986.
Royle, Nicholas. *After Derrida.* Manchester: Manchester UP, 1995.
Said, Edward W. *The World, the Text, and the Critic.* Cambridge: Harvard UP, 1983.
Smith, Barbara Herrnstein. *On the Margins of Discourse: The Relation of Literature to Language.* Chicago: U of Chicago P, 1979.

PERSPECTIVES ON CRITICAL READING

SUSAN SONTAG (B. 1933)

Against Interpretation 1964

Like the fumes of the automobile and of heavy industry which befoul the urban atmosphere, the effusion of interpretations of art today poisons our sensibilities. In a culture whose already classical dilemma is the hypertrophy of the intellect at the expense of energy and sensual capability, interpretation is the revenge of the intellect upon art.

Even more. It is the revenge of the intellect upon the world. To interpret is to impoverish, to deplete the world — in order to set up a shadow world of "meanings." It is to turn *the* world into *this* world. ("This world"! As if there were any other.)

The world, our world, is depleted, impoverished enough. Away with all duplicates of it, until we again experience more immediately what we have. . . .

In most modern instances, interpretation amounts to the philistine refusal to leave the work of art alone. Real art has the capacity to make us nervous. By reducing the work of art to its content and then interpreting *that,* one tames the work of art. Interpretation makes art manageable, conformable.

This philistinism of interpretation is more rife in literature than in any other art. For decades now, literary critics have understood it to be their task to translate the elements of the poem or play or novel or story into something else.

From *Against Interpretation*

CONSIDERATIONS FOR CRITICAL THINKING AND WRITING

1. What are Sontag's objections to interpretation? Explain whether you agree or disagree with them.

2. In what sense does interpretation make art "manageable" and "conformable"?

3. In an essay explore what you take to be both the dangers of interpretation and its contributions to your understanding of literature.

ANNETTE KOLODNY (B. 1941)

On the Commitments of Feminist Criticism   *1980*

If feminist criticism calls anything into question, it must be that dog-eared myth of intellectual neutrality. For what I take to be the underlying spirit or message of any consciously ideologically premised criticism — that is, that ideas are important *because* they determine the ways we live, or want to live, in the world — is vitiated by confining those ideas to the study, the classroom, or the pages of our books. To write chapters decrying the sexual stereotyping of women in our literature, while closing our eyes to the sexual harassment of our women students and colleagues; to display Katharine Hepburn and Rosalind Russell in our courses on "The Image of the Independent Career Women in Film," while managing not to notice the paucity of female administrators on our own campus; to study the women who helped make universal enfranchisement a political reality, while keeping silent about our activist colleagues who are denied promotion or tenure; to include segments on "Women in the Labor Movement" in our American studies or women's studies courses, while remaining willfully ignorant of the department secretary fired for efforts to organize a clerical workers' union; to glory in the delusions of "merit," "privilege," and "status" which accompany campus life in order to insulate ourselves from the millions of women who labor in poverty — all this is not merely hypocritical; it destroys both the spirit and the meaning of what we are about.

From "Dancing through the Minefield: Some Observations on the
Theory, Practice, and Politics of a Feminist Literary
Criticism," *Feminist Studies,* 6, 1980

CONSIDERATIONS FOR CRITICAL THINKING AND WRITING

1. Why does Kolodny reject "intellectual neutrality" as a "myth"? Explain whether you agree or disagree with her point of view.

2. Kolodny argues that feminist criticism can be used as an instrument for so-
cial reform. Discuss the possibility and desirability of her position. Do you
think other kinds of criticism can and should be used to create social
change?

ANDREW P. DEBICKI (B. 1934)

New Criticism and Deconstructionism:
Two Attitudes in Teaching Poetry   *1985*

[Let's] look at the ways in which a New Critic and a deconstructivist might
handle a poem. My first example, untitled, is a work by Pedro Salinas, which I
first analyzed many years ago and which I have recently taught to a group of
students influenced by deconstruction:

> Sand: sleeping on the beach today
> and tomorrow caressed
> in the bosom of the sea:
> the sun's today, water's prize tomorrow.
> Softly you yield
> to the hand that presses you
> and go away with the first
> courting wind that appears.
> Pure and fickle sand,
> changing and clear beloved,
> I wanted you for my own,
> and held you against my chest and soul.
> But you escaped with the waves, the wind, the sun,
> and I remained without a beloved,
> my face turned to the wind which robbed her,
> and my eyes to the far-off sea in which she had
> green loves in a green shelter.

My original study of this poem, written very much in the New Critical tra-
dition, focused on the unusual personification of sand as beloved and on the
metaphorical pattern that it engendered. In the first part of the work, the
physical elusiveness of sand (which slips through one's hand, flies with
the wind, moves from shore to sea) evokes a coquettish woman, yielding to her
lover and then escaping, running off with a personified wind, moving from
one being to another. Watching these images, the reader gradually forgets that
the poem is metaphorically describing sand and becomes taken up by the un
usual correspondences with the figure of a flirting woman. When in the last
part of the poem the speaker laments his loss, the reader is drawn into his
lament for a fickle lover who has abandoned him.

Continuing a traditional analysis of this poem, we would conclude that
its unusual personification/metaphor takes us beyond a literal level and leads
us to a wider vision. The true subject of this poem is not sand, nor is it a flirt
who tricks a man. The comparison between sand and woman, however, has
made us feel the elusiveness of both, as well as the effect that this elusiveness
has had on the speaker, who is left sadly contemplating it at the end of the
poem. The poem has used its main image to embody a general vision of fleet-
ingness and its effects.

My analysis, as developed thus far, is representative of a New Critical study. It focuses on the text and its central image, it describes a tension produced within the text, and it suggests a way in which this tension is resolved so as to move the poem beyond its literal level. In keeping with the tenets of traditional analytic criticism, it shows how the poem conveys a meaning that is far richer than its plot or any possible conceptual message. But while it is careful not to reduce the poem to a simple idea or to an equivalent of its prose summary, it does attempt to work all of its elements into a single interpretation which would satisfy every reader . . . : it makes all of the poem's meanings reside in its verbal structures, and it suggests that those meanings can be discovered and combined into a single cohesive vision as we systematically analyze those structures.

By attempting to find a pattern that will incorporate and resolve the poem's tensions, however, this reading leaves some loose ends, which I noticed even in my New Critical perspective — and which I found difficult to explain. To see the poem as the discovery of the theme of fleetingness by an insightful speaker, we have to ignore the fanciful nature of the comparison, the whimsical attitude to reality that it suggests, and the excessively serious lament of the speaker, which is difficult to take at face value — he laments the loss of *sand* with the excessive emotion of a romantic lover! The last lines, with their evocation of the beloved/sand in an archetypal kingdom of the sea, ring a bit hollow. Once we notice all of this, we see the speaker as being somehow unreliable in his strong response to the situation. He tries too hard to equate the loss of sand with the loss of love, he paints himself as too much of a romantic, and he loses our assent when we realize that his rather cliché declarations are not very fitting. Once we become aware of the speaker's limitations, our perspective about the poem changes: we come to see its "meaning" as centered, not on the theme of fleetingness as such, but on a portrayal of the speaker's exaggerated efforts to embody this theme in the image of sand.

For the traditional New Critic, this would pose a dilemma. The reading of the poem as a serious embodiment of the theme of evanescence is undercut by an awareness of the speaker's unreliability. One can account for the conflict between readings, to some extent, by speaking of the poem's use of irony and by seeing a tension between the theme of evanescence and the speaker's excessive concern with an imaginary beloved (which blinds him to the larger issues presented by the poem). That still leaves unresolved, however, the poem's final meaning and effect. In class discussions, in fact, a debate between those students who asserted that the importance of the poem lay in its engendering the theme of fleetingness and those who noted the absurdity of the speaker often ended in an agreement that this was a "problem poem" which never resolved or integrated its "stresses" and its double vision. . . .

The deconstructive critic, however, would not be disturbed by a lack of resolution in the meanings of the poem and would use the conflict between interpretations as the starting point for further study. Noting that the view of evanescence produced by the poem's central metaphor is undercut by the speaker's unreliability, the deconstructive critic would explore the play of signification that the undercutting engenders. Calling into question the attempt to neatly define evanescence, on the one hand, and the speaker's excessive romanticism on the other, the poem would represent, for this critic, a creative confrontation of irresoluble visions. The image of the sand as woman, as well as the portrayal of the speaker, would represent a sort of "seam" in the text, an area of indeterminacy that would open the way to further readings. This image lets us see the speaker as a sentimental poet, attempting unsuccessfully to define evanescence by means of a novel metaphor but getting trapped in the theme of lost love, which he himself has engendered; it makes us think of the inadequacy of language, of the ways in which metaphorical expression and the clichés of a love lament can undercut each other.

Once we adopt such a deconstructivist perspective, we will find in the text details that will carry forward our reading. The speaker's statement that he held "her" against his "chest and his soul" underlines the conflict in his perspective: it juggles a literal perspective (he rubs sand against himself) and a metaphorical one (he reaches for his beloved), but it cannot fully combine them — "soul" is ludicrously inappropriate in reference to the former. The reader, noting the inappropriateness, has to pay attention to the inadequacy of language as used here. All in all, by engendering a conflict between various levels and perspectives, the poem makes us feel the incompleteness of any one reading, the way in which each one is a "misreading" (not because it is wrong, but because it is incomplete), and the creative lack of closure in the poem. By not being subject to closure, in fact, this text becomes all the more exciting: its view of the possibilities and limitations of metaphor, language, and perspective seems more valuable than any static portrayal of "evanescence."

The analyses I have offered of this poem exemplify the different classroom approaches that would be taken by a stereotypical New Critic, on the one hand, and a deconstructive critic on the other. Imbued with the desire to come to an overview of the literary work, the former will attempt to resolve its tensions (and probably remain unsatisfied with the poem). Skeptical of such a possibility and of the very existence of a definable "work," the latter will focus on the tensions that can be found in the text as vehicles for multiple readings. Given his or her attitude to the text, the deconstructive critic will not worry about going beyond its "limits" (which really do not exist). This will allow, of course, for more speculative readings; it will also lead to a discussion of ways in which the text can be extended and "cured" in successive readings, to the fact that it reflects on the process of its own creation, and to ways in which it will relate to other texts.

From *Writing and Reading DIFFERENTLY: Deconstruction
and the Teaching of Composition and Literature,*
edited by G. Douglas Atkins and Michael L. Johnson

CONSIDERATIONS FOR CRITICAL THINKING AND WRITING

1. Explain how the New Critical and deconstructionist approaches to the Salinas poem differ. What kinds of questions are raised by each? What elements of the poem are focused on in each approach?

2. Write an essay explaining which reading of the poem you find more interesting. In your opening paragraph define what you mean by "interesting."

3. Choose one of the critical strategies for reading discussed in this chapter and discuss Salinas's poem from that perspective.

PETER RABINOWITZ (B. 1944)

On Close Readings

1988

Belief in close reading may be the nearest thing literary scholars have to a shared critical principle. Academics who teach literature tend to accept as a matter of course that good reading is slow, attentive to linguistic nuance (especially figurative language), and suspicious of surface meanings.

Close reading is a fundamental link between the New Critics and the Yale deconstructionists. Indeed, deconstructionist J. Hillis Miller has gone so far as to characterize what he saw as an attack on close reading by Gerald Graff as "a major treason against our profession." Similarly, what Naomi Schor calls "clitoral" feminist criticism, and its "hermeneutics focused on the detail," is a variant of close reading. So is much reader-response criticism.

Despite its broad acceptance by scholars, however, close reading is not the natural, the only, or always the best way to approach a text. I'm not suggesting that it should never be taught or used. But I do want to argue that close reading rests on faulty assumptions about how literature is read, which can lead, especially in the classroom, to faulty prescriptions about how it *ought* to be read.

The fact is that there are a variety of ways to read, all of which engage the reader in substantially different kinds of activity. Which kind depends in part on the reader and his or her immediate purpose. Teasing out the implicit homo-erotic tendencies in Turgenev's *Asya,* for instance, is a different activity from trying to determine its contribution to the development of first-person narrative techniques. In part, the way one reads also varies from text to text. Different authors, different genres, different periods, different cultures expect readers to approach texts in different ways.

The bias in academe toward close reading reduces that multiplicity. While all close readers obviously don't read in exactly the same way, the variations have a strong family resemblance. Their dominance in the aristocracy of critical activity—virtually undiminished by the critical revolutions of the last twenty years—can skew evaluation, distort interpretation, discourage breadth of vision, and separate scholars from students and other ordinary readers.

David Daiches was not being eccentric when he argued that literary value depends on the "degree to which the work lends itself" to the kind of reading demanded by New Critical theory. The schools in vogue may change, but we still assign value to what fits our prior conceptions of reading, and the academically sanctioned canon consequently consists largely of texts that respond well to close reading.

Once you give priority to close reading, you implicitly favor figurative writing over realistic writing, indirect expression over direct expression, deep meaning over surface meaning, form over content, and the elite over the popular. In the realm of poetry, that means giving preference to lyric over narrative poems, and in the realm of fiction, to symbolism and psychology over plot. Such preferences, in turn, devalue certain voices. A writer directly confronting brute oppression, for instance, is apt to be ranked below another who has the luxury minutely to explore the details of subtle middle-class crises. Thus, for a close reader, the unresonant prose of Harriet Wilson's *Our Nig* will automatically make the novel seem less "good" than Henry James's more intricate *What Maisie Knew,* although the racist brutality endured by Ms. Wilson's heroine is arguably more important for our culture — and thus more deserving of our consideration — than the affluent sexual merry-go-round that dizzies Maisie.

It would be bad enough if the preference for close reading simply meant that texts that didn't measure up were chucked onto a noncanonical pile — then, at least, the rebellious could rummage through the rejects. But close reading also has an insidious effect on interpretation. Not only do we reject many works that don't fit; more damaging, we also twist many others until they *do* fit.

Yet we fail to recognize the magnitude of this distortion. One of the major problems with much current critical practice is the tendency to underestimate the extent to which texts can serve as mirrors — not of the external world but of the reader, who is apt to find in a text not what is really there but what he expects or wants to find. . . .

When reading for class, many students read closely, but few continue the practice once they've left college. In fact, most people — including teachers — who really enjoy literature recognize that close reading is a special kind of interpretive practice. Literary scholars are apt to make a distinction between "real reading" and "reading for fun"; most nonacademic readers are likely to divide "real reading" from "reading for class." In either case, an artificial split is created between academe and "real life," which leads to theories that devalue the kinds of reading (and therefore the kinds of books) that engage most readers most of the time.

If I'm against close reading, then what am I for? The obvious alternative is pluralism.

We can legitimately show our students that different writers in different social, historical, and economic contexts write for different purposes and with different expectations. Likewise, we can teach our students that different readers (or the same reader under different circumstances) read for different reasons.

We must also give our students actual practice in various kinds of reading. For example, an introductory literature course should include many different sorts of texts: long novels as well as lyric poems; realistic (even didactic) works as well as symbolic ones; writing aimed at a broad audience as well as at a literate elite. The course should also include different kinds of tasks. Students should learn to approach a given text in several different ways, at least some of which arise out of their personal and cultural situations. Most important, we must help our students to be self-conscious about what they are doing, and to realize that every decision about how to read opens certain doors only by closing others.

It is not simply that learning new, less rigid ways of reading increases the number of works we can enjoy and learn from. More important, learning to read in different ways allows us to enjoy a wider range of texts and gain new perspectives on our cultural assumptions. Only such flexible reading leads to intellectual growth, for it is only that kind of reading that can enable us to be conscious of — and therefore able to deal effectively with — the narrowness of "standard" interpretive techniques.

From "Our Evaluation of Literature Has Been Distorted
by Academe's Bias toward Close Readings of Texts,"
Chronicle of Higher Education, April 6, 1988

CONSIDERATIONS FOR CRITICAL THINKING AND WRITING

1. Why does Rabinowitz object to the bias toward close reading as the primary way to approach a literary work? Explain why you agree or disagree.

2. According to Rabinowitz, how does a critical emphasis on close reading affect the formation of the canon?

3. In an essay discuss Rabinowitz's observation that an emphasis on close reading "devalue[s] the kinds of reading (and therefore the kinds of books) that engage most readers most of the time."

HARRIET HAWKINS (B. 1939)

Should We Study King Kong *or* King Lear?   *1988*

There is nothing either good or bad, but thinking makes it so.
                                        —Hamlet

Troilus: *What's aught but as 'tis valued?*
Hector: *But value dwells not in particular will:*
  It holds its estimate and dignity
  As well wherein 'tis precious of itself
  As in the prizer.
                          —Troilus and Cressida

To what degree is great literature—or bad literature—an artificial category? Are there any good—or bad—reasons why most societies have given high status to certain works of art and not to others? Could Hamlet be right in concluding that there is *nothing* either good or bad but thinking—or critical or ideological discourse—makes it so? Or are certain works of art so precious, so magnificent—or so trashy—that they obviously ought to be included in the canon or expelled from the classroom? So far as I know, there is not now any sign of a critical consensus on the correct answer to these questions either in England or in the United States.

In England there are, on the one hand, eloquent cases for the defense of the value of traditional literary studies, like Dame Helen Gardner's last book, *In Defence of the Imagination.* On the other hand, there are critical arguments insisting that what really counts is not what you read, but the way that you read it. You might as well study *King Kong* as *King Lear,* because what matters is not the script involved, but the critical or ideological virtues manifested in your own "reading" of whatever it is that you are reading. Reviewing a controversial book entitled *Re-Reading English,* the poet Tom Paulin gives the following account of the issues involved in the debate:

> The contributors are collectively of the opinion that English literature is a dying subject and they argue that it can be revived by adopting a "socialist pedagogy" and introducing into the syllabus "other forms of writing and cultural production than the canon of literature" . . . it is now time to challenge "hierarchical" and "elitist" conceptions of literature and to demolish the

bourgeois ideology which has been "naturalised" as literary value. . . . They wish to develop "a politics of reading" and to redefine the term "text" in order to admit newspaper reports, songs, and even mass demonstrations as subjects for tutorial discussion. Texts no longer have to be books: indeed, "it may be more democratic to study *Coronation Street* [England's most popular soap opera] than *Middlemarch*."

However one looks at these arguments, it seems indisputably true that the issues involved are of paramount critical, pedagogical, and social importance. There are, however, any number of different ways to look at the various arguments. So far as I am, professionally, concerned, they raise the central question, "Why should any of us still study, or teach, Shakespeare's plays (or *Paradise Lost* or *The Canterbury Tales*)?" After all, there are quite enough films, plays, novels, and poems being produced today (to say nothing of all those "other forms of writing," including literary criticism, that are clamoring for our attention) to satisfy anyone interested in high literature, or popular genres, or any form of "cultural production" whatsoever. They also raise the obviously reflexive question: "Assuming that all traditionally 'canonized' works were eliminated, overnight, from the syllabus of every English department in the world, would not comparable problems of priority, value, elitism, ideological pressure, authoritarianism, and arbitrariness almost(?) immediately arise with reference to *whatever* works — of whatsoever kind and nature — were substituted for them?"

If, say, the place on the syllabus currently assigned to *King Lear* were reassigned to *King Kong*, those of us currently debating the relative merits of the Quarto, the Folio, or a conflated version of *King Lear* would, *mutatis mutandis,*° have to decide whether to concentrate classroom attention on the "classic" version of *King Kong*, originally produced in 1933, or to focus on the 1974 remake (which by now has many ardent admirers of its own). Although classroom time might not allow the inclusion of both, a decision to exclude either version might well seem arbitrary or authoritarian and so give rise to grumbles about the "canon." Moreover, comparable questions of "canonization" might well arise with reference to other films excluded from a syllabus that included either version (or both versions) of *King Kong*. For example: why assign class time to *King Kong* and not to (say) *Slave Girls of the White Rhinoceros*? Who, if any, of us has the right to decide whether *King Lear* or *King Kong* or the *Slave Girls* should, or should not, be included on, or excluded from, the syllabus? And can the decision to include, or exclude, any one of them be made, by any one of us, on any grounds whatsoever that do *not* have to do with comparative merit, or comparative value judgments, or with special interests — that is, with the aesthetic or ideological priorities, preferences, and prejudices of the assigners of positions on whatever syllabus there is? And insofar as most, if not all, of our judgments and preferences are comparative, are they not, inevitably, hierarchical?

Is there, in fact, any form of endeavor or accomplishment known to the human race — from sport to ballet to jazz to cooking — wherein comparative standards of excellence comparable to certain "hierarchical" and "elitist" conceptions of literature are nonexistent? Even bad-film buffs find certain bad films more gloriously bad than others. And, perhaps significantly given its comparatively short lifetime, the avant-garde cinema has, by now, produced

mutatis mutandis: Substituting different terms (Latin).

snobs to rival the most elitist literary critic who ever lived, such as the one who thus puts down a friend who likes ordinary Hollywood films:

> Ah that's all right for you, I know the sort you are, but give me a private job that's shot on faded sepia sixteen millimetre stock with non-professional actors . . . no story and dialogue in French *any day of the week.*

What is striking about this snob's assumption is how characteristic it is of a long tradition of critical elitism that has consistently sneered at popular genres (e.g., romance fiction, soap operas, horror films, westerns, etc.) that are tainted by the profit motive and so tend to "give the public what it wants" in the way of sentimentality, sensationalism, sex, violence, romanticism, and the like.

From *"King Lear* to *King Kong* and Back: Shakespeare and Popular Modern Genres" in *"Bad" Shakespeare: Revaluations of the Shakespeare Canon,* edited by Maurice Charney

CONSIDERATIONS FOR CRITICAL THINKING AND WRITING

1. Do you agree or disagree that "great literature — or bad literature — [is] an artificial category"? Explain why.

2. Why would problems of "priority, value, elitism, ideological pressure, authoritarianism, and arbitrariness" probably become issues for evaluating any new works that replaced canonized works?

3. Write an essay in which you argue for (or against) studying popular arts (for example, popular song lyrics) alongside the works of classic writers such as Shakespeare.

MORRIS DICKSTEIN (B. 1940)

On the Social Responsibility of the Critic 1993

. . . Many critics today, as if in violent reaction to the reading habits of the ordinary citizen, are haunted by the fear of becoming the passive consumer of ideological subtexts or messages. As the country grew more conservative in the eighties, many academic critics turned more radical, and this led to an onslaught by national magazines and media pundits on political correctness, the supposed left-wing and multicultural orthodoxy in American universities.

Here we encounter a number of puzzling paradoxes about "reading" in America today. As reading diminishes — not in absolute terms but in relation to other ways of receiving information — as reading loses its hold on people, the metaphor of reading constantly expands. Molecular biologists like Robert Pollack talk about "reading DNA," the structure of genetic transmission in each living cell. Students of urban life discuss "the city as text" and how to read it, as they did at a conference I attended in 1989. Film scholars publish books about "how to read a film" reflecting on our constantly expanding (and increasingly undifferentiated) notion of what constitutes a text. And literary critics over the past sixty years have developed ever more subtle and complex ways of reading those texts, often using obscure, specialized language that itself resists being read.

As educators worry about the role of video and electronic media in displacing the written word, as the skills of ordinary readers seem to languish, the sophistication and territorial ambition of academic readers continue to grow, widening a split that has been one of the hallmarks of the modern period. The common reader still exists, but many professional readers dissociate themselves on principle from the habits of the tribe: they deliberately read against the grain of the text, against common sense, against most people's way of reading — indeed, against their own way of reading in their ordinary lives. If the reader of *Scarlett* or *Gone with the Wind* reads passively, wanting to be possessed and carried away by a book, as by an old-fashioned movie or piece of music, the critical reader, influenced by theory and by the new historicism, has developed an active, aggressive, even adversarial approach to writing. What Paul Ricoeur in his book on Freud calls the "hermeneutics of suspicion" has become a primary feature of academic criticism, which aims above all to disclose the institutional pressures and ideological formations that speak through texts and influence us as we read.° . . .

Our advanced criticism is especially marked by the suspicion and the hostility with which it performs such operations: its failure to distinguish art from propaganda, literature from advertising; its fierce resistance to the mental framework of the works it examines. "All right, what's wrong with this book?" asks one programmatically suspicious instructor of the students in her humanities class, to make sure they don't get taken in by those "great" books. Some of our recent ideological criticism turns the social understanding of literature, which can be intrinsically valuable, into an all too predictable exercise in debunking and demystification. . . .

The role of the critic is not to read notionally and cleverly, and certainly not to castigate writers for their politics, but to raise ordinary reading to its highest power — to make it more insightful, more acute, without losing touch with our deepest personal responses. It is ironic to speak for the social responsibility of the writer while betraying the public sphere of reading. Criticism, even academic criticism, is neither a sect nor a priesthood but ultimately a public trust, mediating between artists or writers and their often puzzled audience. . . .

A naive reading, anchored in wonder, must remain an indispensable moment of a more self-conscious reading, not just a piece of scaffolding to be kicked away as our suspicion and professionalism take over. We need a better balance between the naive and suspicious readers in ourselves: between the willing suspension of disbelief and our ability to withhold ourselves and read skeptically; between our appreciation of art and our wary knowledge of its persuasive power; between a sympathy for the author as an individual like ourselves — working out creative problems, making contingent choices — and our critical sense of a literary work as the discursive formation of a cultural moment.

From "Damaged Literacy: The Decay of Reading," *Profession 93*

What . . . read: Paul Ricoeur (b. 1913), a French philosopher and critic, author of *Freud and Philosophy: An Essay on Interpretation* (1970). Hermeneutics refers to the theory and method of perceiving and interpreting texts.

Considerations for Critical Thinking and Writing

1. Do you think video and electronic media are "displacing the written word"? What evidence can you point to in your own experience that refutes or supports this claim?

2. What do you think Dickstein means when he refers to academic criticism as "a public trust"? What should the function of criticism be, according to Dickstein? In what sense is the role of the critic "to raise ordinary reading to its highest power"?

3. What criticism does Dickstein level against contemporary literary criticism? Explain why you agree or disagree with his perspective.

20

Reading and Writing

THE PURPOSE AND VALUE
OF WRITING ABOUT LITERATURE

Introductory literature courses typically include three components: reading, discussion, and writing. Students usually find the readings a pleasure, the class discussions a revelation, and the writing assignments — at least initially — a little intimidating. Writing an analysis of the symbolic use of a wall in Robert Frost's "Mending Wall" (p. 342) or in Herman Melville's "Bartleby, the Scrivener," for example, may seem considerably more daunting than making a case for animal rights or analyzing a campus newspaper editorial that calls for grade reforms. Like Bartleby, you might want to respond with "I would prefer not to." Literary topics are not, however, all that different from the kinds of papers assigned in English composition courses; many of the same skills are required for both. Regardless of the type of paper, you must develop a thesis and support it with evidence in language that is clear and persuasive.

Whether the subject matter is a marketing survey, a political issue, or a literary work, writing is a method of communicating information and perceptions. Writing teaches. But before writing becomes an instrument for informing the reader, it serves as a means of learning for the writer. An essay is a process of discovery as well as a record of what has been discovered. One of the chief benefits of writing is that we frequently realize what we want to say only after trying out ideas on a page and seeing our thoughts take shape in language.

More specifically, writing about a literary work encourages us to be better readers, because it requires a close examination of the elements of a short story, poem, or play. To determine how plot, character, setting, point of view, style, tone, irony, or any number of other literary elements function in a work, we must study them in relation to one another as well as separately. Speed-reading won't do. To read a text accurately and validly—neither ignoring nor distorting significant details—we must return to the work repeatedly to test our responses and interpretations. By paying attention to details and being sensitive to the author's use of language, we develop a clearer understanding of how the work conveys its effects and meanings.

Nevertheless, students sometimes ask why it is necessary or desirable to write about a literary work. Why not allow stories, poems, and plays to speak for themselves? Isn't it presumptuous to interpret Hemingway, Dickinson, or Shakespeare? These writers do, of course, speak for themselves, but they do so indirectly. Literary criticism does not seek to replace the text by explaining it but to enhance our readings of works by calling attention to elements that we might have overlooked or only vaguely sensed.

Another misunderstanding about the purpose of literary criticism is that it crankily restricts itself to finding faults in a work. Critical essays are sometimes mistakenly equated with newspaper and magazine reviews of recently published works. Reviews typically include summaries and evaluations to inform readers about a work's nature and quality, but critical essays assume that readers are already familiar with a work. Although a critical essay may point out limitations and flaws, most criticism — and certainly the kind of essay usually written in an introductory literature course — is designed to explain, analyze, and reveal the complexities of a work. Such sensitive consideration increases our appreciation of the writer's achievement and significantly adds to our enjoyment of a short story, poem, or play. In short, the purpose and value of writing about literature are that doing so leads to greater understanding and pleasure.

READING THE WORK CLOSELY

Know the piece of literature you are writing about before you begin your essay. Think about how the work makes you feel and how it is put together. The more familiar you are with how the various elements of the text convey effects and meanings, the more confident you will be explaining whatever perspective on it you ultimately choose. Do not insist that everything make sense on a first reading. Relax and enjoy yourself; you can be attentive and still allow the author's words to work their magic on you. With subsequent readings, however, go more slowly and analytically as you try to establish relations between characters, actions, images, or whatever else seems important. Ask yourself why you respond as you do. Think as you read, and notice how the parts of a work contribute to its overall nature. Whether the work is a short story, poem, or play, you will read relevant portions of it over and over, and you will very likely find more to discuss in each review if the work is rich.

It's best to avoid reading other critical discussions of a work before you are thoroughly familiar with it. There are several good reasons for following this advice. By reading interpretations before you know a work, you deny yourself the pleasure of discovery. That is a bit like starting with the last chapter in a mystery novel. But perhaps even more important than protecting the surprise and delight that a work might offer is that a premature reading of a critical discussion will probably short-circuit your own responses. You will see the work through the critic's eyes and have to struggle with someone else's perceptions and ideas before you can develop your own.

Reading criticism can be useful, but not until you have thought through your own impressions of the text. A guide should not be permitted to become a tyrant. This does not mean, however, that you should avoid background information about a work, for example, that the title of Diane Ackerman's "A Fine, a Private Place" (p. 69) alludes to Andrew Marvell's earlier *carpe diem* poem, "To His Coy Mistress" (p. 65). Knowing something about the author as well as historic and literary contexts can help to create expectations that enhance your reading.

ANNOTATING THE TEXT
AND JOURNAL NOTE TAKING

As you read, get in the habit of making marginal notations in your textbook. If you are working with a library book, use notecards and write down page or line numbers so that you can easily return to annotated passages. Use these cards to record reactions, raise questions, and make comments. They will freshen your memory and allow you to keep track of what goes on in the text.

Whatever method you use to annotate your texts — whether by writing marginal notes, highlighting, underlining, or drawing boxes and circles around important words and phrases — you'll eventually develop a system that allows you to retrieve significant ideas and elements from the text. Another way to record your impressions of a work — as with any other experience — is to keep a journal. By writing down your reactions to characters, images, language, actions, and other matters in a reading journal, you can often determine why you like or dislike a work or feel sympathetic or antagonistic to an author or discover paths into a work that might have eluded you if you hadn't preserved your impressions. Your journal notes and annotations may take whatever form you find useful; full sentences and grammatical correctness are not essential (unless they are to be handed in and your instructor requires that), though they might allow you to make better sense of your own reflections days later. The point is simply to put in writing thoughts that you can retrieve when you need them for class discussion or a writing assignment. Consider the following student annotation of the first twenty-four lines of Andrew Marvell's "To His Coy Mistress" and the journal entry that follows it:

Annotated Text

If we
had
time...

(Had we but world enough, and time,
This coyness, lady, were no (crime) ————— Waste life and you
We would sit down, and think which way   steal from yourself.
To walk, and pass our long love's day.
Thou by the Indian (Ganges) side   5
Shouldst rubies find; I by the tide
Of (Humber) would complain.° I would
Love you ten years before the Flood,   write love songs
And you should, if you please, refuse   Measurements
Till the conversion of the Jews.   of time   10
My vegetable love should grow,°   slow, unconscious growth
Vaster than empires, and more slow;
An hundred years should go to praise
Thine eyes and on thy forehead gaze,
Two hundred to adore each breast,   15
But thirty thousand to the rest:
An age at least to every part,
And the last age should show your heart.
For, lady, you deserve this state,
Nor would I love at lower rate.   20
But at my back I always hear
Time's wingèd chariot hurrying near;   Lines move faster here —
And yonder all before us lie   tone changes.
(Deserts) of vast (eternity.) —— This eternity rushes in.

Contrast
river
and
desert
images

Journal Note

> He'd be patient and wait for his "mistress" if they had
> the time--sing songs, praise her, adore her, etc. But they
> don't have that much time according to him. He <u>seems</u> to be
> patient but he actually begins by calling patience--her coy-
> ness--a "crime." Looks to me like he's got his mind made up
> from the beginning of the poem. Where's her response? I'm
> not sure about him.

This journal note responds to some of the effects noted in the annotations of the poem; it's an excellent beginning for making sense of the speaker's argument in the poem.

Taking notes will preserve your initial reactions to the work. Many times first impressions are the best. Your response to a peculiar character, a striking phrase, or a subtle pun might lead to larger perceptions. The student paper on "The Love Song of J. Alfred Prufrock" (p. 545), for example, began with the student making notes in the margins of the text about the disembodied images of eyes and arms that appear in the poem. This, along with the fragmentary thoughts and style of the speaker eventually led her to examine the significance of the images and how they served to characterize Prufrock.

You should take detailed notes only after you've read through the work. If you write too many notes during the first reading, you're likely to disrupt your response. Moreover, until you have a sense of the entire work, it will be difficult to determine how connections can be made among its various elements. In addition to recording your first impressions and noting significant passages, images, diction, and so on, you should consult the Questions for Responsive Reading and Writing on page 47. These questions can assist you in getting inside a work as well as organizing your notes.

Inevitably, you will take more notes than you finally use in the paper. Note taking is a form of thinking aloud, but because your ideas are on paper you don't have to worry about forgetting them. As you develop a better sense of a potential topic, your notes will become more focused and detailed.

CHOOSING A TOPIC

If your instructor assigns a topic or offers a choice from among an approved list of topics, some of your work is already completed. Instead of being asked to come up with a topic about Emily Dickinson's poems in this anthology, you may be assigned a three-page essay that specifically discusses "Dickinson's Treatment of Grief in 'The Bustle in a House.'" You also have the assurance that a specified topic will be manageable within the suggested number of pages. Unless you ask your instructor for permission to write on a different or related topic, be certain to address yourself to the assignment. An essay that does not discuss grief but instead describes Dickinson's relationship with her father would be missing the point. Notice too that there is room even in an assigned topic to develop your own approach. One question that immediately comes to mind is whether grief defeats or helps the speaker in the poem. Assigned topics do not relieve you of thinking about an aspect of a work, but they do focus your thinking.

At some point during the course, you may have to begin an essay from scratch. You might, for example, be asked to write about a poem that somehow impressed you or that seemed particularly well written or filled with insights. Before you start considering a topic, you should have a sense of how long the paper will be, because the assigned length can help to determine the extent to which you should develop your topic. Ideally, the paper's length should be based on how much space you deem necessary to present your discussion clearly and convincingly, but if you have any doubts and no specific guidelines have been indicated, ask. The question is important; a topic that might be appropriate for a three-page paper could be too narrow for ten pages. Three pages would probably be adequate for a discussion of the speaker's view of death in John Keats's "To Autumn." Conversely, it would be futile to try to summarize Keats's use of sensuality in his poetry in even ten pages; the topic would have to be narrowed to something like "Images of Sensuality in 'La Belle Dame sans Merci.'" Be sure that the topic you choose can be adequately covered in the assigned number of pages.

Once you have a firm sense of how much you are expected to write, you can begin to decide on your topic. If you are to choose what work to write about, select one that genuinely interests you. Too often students pick a poem, because it is mercifully short or seems simple. Such works can certainly be the subjects of fine essays, but simplicity should not be the major reason for selecting them. Choose a work that has moved you so that you have something to say about it. The student who wrote about "The Love Song of J. Alfred Prufrock" was initially attracted to the poem's imagery because she had heard a friend (no doubt an English major) jokingly quote Prufrock's famous lament that "I should have a pair of ragged claws / Scuttling across the floors of silent seas." Her paper then grew out of her curiosity about the meaning of the images. When a writer is engaged in a topic, the paper has a better chance of being interesting to a reader.

After you have settled on a particular work, your notes and annotations of the text should prove useful for generating a topic. The student paper on Prufrock developed naturally from the notes (p. 543) that the student jotted down about the images. If you think with a pen in your hand, you are likely to find when you review your notes that your thoughts have clustered into one or more topics. Perhaps there are patterns of imagery that seem to make a point about life. There may be symbols that are ironically paired or levels of diction that reveal certain qualities about the speaker. Your notes and annotations on such aspects can lead you to a particular effect or impression. Having chuckled your way through Meinke's "The ABC of Aerobics" (p. 270), you may discover that your notations about the poem's humor point to a serious satire of society's values.

DEVELOPING A THESIS

When you are satisfied that you have something interesting to say about a work and that your notes have led you to a focused topic, you can formulate a ***thesis,*** the central idea of the paper. Whereas the topic indicates what the paper focuses on (the disembodied images in "Prufrock," for example), the thesis explains what you have to say about the topic (the frightening images of eyes, arms, and claws reflect Prufrock's disjointed, fragmentary response to life). The thesis should be a complete sentence (though sometimes it may require more than one sentence) that establishes your topic in clear, unambiguous language. The thesis may be revised as you get further into the topic and discover what you want to say about it, but once the thesis is firmly established it will serve as a guide for you and your reader, because all the information and observations in your essay should be related to the thesis.

One student on an initial reading of Andrew Marvell's "To His Coy Mistress" (p. 65) saw that the male speaker of the poem urges a woman to love now before time runs out for them. This reading gave him the impression that the poem is a simple celebration of the pleasures of the flesh, but on subsequent readings he underlined or noted these images: "Time's wingèd chariot hurrying near"; "Deserts of vast eternity"; "marble vault"; "worms"; "dust"; "ashes"; and these two lines: "The grave's a fine and private place, / But none, I think, do there embrace."

By listing these images associated with time and death, he established an inventory that could be separated from the rest of his notes on point of view, character, sounds, and other subjects. Inventorying notes allows patterns to emerge that you might have only vaguely perceived otherwise. Once these images are grouped, they call attention to something darker and more complex in Marvell's poem than a first impression might suggest.

These images may create a different feeling about the poem, but they still don't explain very much. One simple way to generate a thesis about a literary work is to ask the question "why?" Why do these images appear in the poem? Why does the speaker in William Stafford's "Traveling through the Dark" (p. 115) push the dead deer into the river? Why does disorder appeal so much to the speaker in Robert Herrick's "Delight in Disorder" (p. 211)? Your responses to these kinds of questions can lead to a thesis.

Writers sometimes use free writing to help themselves explore possible answers to such questions. It can be an effective way of generating ideas. Free writing is exactly that: the technique calls for nonstop writing without concern for mechanics or editing of any kind. Free writing for ten minutes or so on a question will result in fragments and repetitions, but it can also produce some ideas. Here's an example of a student's response to the question about the images in "To His Coy Mistress":

He wants her to make love. Love poem. There's little time. Her crime. He exaggerates. Sincere? Sly? What's he want? She says nothing--he says it all. What about deserts, ashes, graves, and worms? Some love poem. Sounds like an old Vincent Price movie. Full of sweetness but death creeps in. Death--hurry hurry! Tear pleasures. What passion! Where's death in this? How can a love poem be so ghoulish? She does nothing. Maybe frightened? Convinced? Why death? Love and death--time--death.

This free writing contains several ideas; it begins by alluding to the poem's plot and speaker, but the central idea seems to be death. This emphasis led the student to five potential thesis statements for his essay about the poem:

1. "To His Coy Mistress" is a difficult poem.

2. Death in "To His Coy Mistress."

3. There are many images of death in "To His Coy Mistress."

4. "To His Coy Mistress" celebrates the pleasures of the flesh but it also recognizes the power of death to end that pleasure.

5. On the surface, "To His Coy Mistress" is a celebration of the pleasures of the flesh, but this witty seduction is tempered by a chilling recognition of the reality of death.

The first statement is too vague to be useful. In what sense is the poem difficult? A more precise phrasing, indicating the nature of the difficulty, is needed. The second statement is a topic rather than a thesis. Because it is not a sentence, it does not express a complete idea about how the poem treats death. Although this could be an appropriate title, it is inadequate as a thesis statement. The third statement, like the first one, identifies the topic, but even though it is a sentence, it is not a complete idea that tells us anything significant beyond the fact it states. After these preliminary attempts to develop a thesis, the student remembered his first impression of the poem and incorporated it into his thesis statement. The fourth thesis is a useful approach to the poem because it limits the topic and indicates how it will be treated in the paper: the writer will begin with an initial impression of the poem and then go on to qualify it. However, the fifth thesis is better than the fourth because it indicates a shift in tone produced by the ironic relationship between death and flesh. An effective thesis, like this one, makes a clear statement about a manageable topic and provides a firm sense of direction for the paper.

Most writing assignments in a literature course require you to persuade readers that your thesis is reasonable and supported with evidence. Papers that report information without comment or evaluation are simply summaries. Similarly, a paper that merely pointed out the death images in "To His Coy Mistress" would not contain a thesis, but a paper that attempted to make a case for the death imagery as a grim reminder of how vulnerable flesh is would involve persuasion. In developing a thesis, remember that you are expected not merely to present information but to argue a point.

ARGUING ABOUT LITERATURE

An argumentative essay is designed to make persuasive your interpretation of a work. Arguing about literature doesn't mean that you're engaged in an angry, antagonistic dispute (though controversial topics do sometimes engender heated debates). Instead, argumentation requires that you present your interpretation of a work (or a portion of it) by supporting your discussion with clearly defined terms, ample evidence, and a detailed analysis of relevant portions of the text.

If you have a choice, it's generally best to write about a topic that you feel strongly about. Even if you don't like cats you might find Jane Kenyon's "The Blue Bowl" (p. 106) just the sort of treatment that helps explain why you don't want one. On the other hand, if you're a cat fan, the poem may suggest something essential about cats that you've experienced but have never quite put your finger on. If your essay is to be interesting and convincing, what is important is that it be written from a strong point of view that persuasively argues your evaluation, analysis, and interpretation of a work. It is not enough to say that you like or dislike a work; instead you must give your reader some ideas and evidence that can be accepted or rejected based on the quality of the answers to the questions you raise.

One way to come up with persuasive answers is to generate good questions that will lead you further into the text and to critical issues related to it. Notice how the Perspectives, Complementary Readings, and Critical Case Study in this anthology raise significant questions and issues about texts from a variety of points of view. Moreover, the critical strategies for reading summarized in Chapter 19 can be a resource for raising questions that can be shaped into an argument. The following lists of questions for the critical approaches covered in Chapter 19 should be useful for discovering arguments you might make about a short story, poem, or play. The page number that follows each heading refers to the discussion in the anthology for that particular approach.

Formalist Questions (p. 485)

1. How do various elements of the work — plot, character, point of view, setting, tone, diction, images, symbol, and so on — reinforce its meanings?
2. How are the elements related to the whole?
3. What is the work's major organizing principle? How is its structure unified?
4. What issues does the work raise? How does the work's structure resolve those issues?

Biographical Questions (p. 487)

1. Are facts about the writer's life relevant to your understanding of the work?
2. Are characters and incidents in the work versions of the writer's own experiences? Are they treated factually or imaginatively?
3. How do you think the writer's values are reflected in the work?

Psychological Questions (p. 489)

1. How does the work reflect the author's personal psychology?
2. What do the characters' emotions and behavior reveal about their psychological states? What types of personalities are they?

3. Are psychological matters such as repression, dreams, and desire presented consciously or unconsciously by the author?

Historical Questions (p. 491)

1. How does the work reflect the period in which it is written?
2. What literary or historical influences helped to shape the form and content of the work?
3. How important is the historical context to interpreting the work?

Marxist Questions (p. 493)

1. How are class differences presented in the work? Are characters aware or unaware of the economic and social forces that affect their lives?
2. How do economic conditions determine the characters' lives?
3. What ideological values are explicit or implicit?
4. Does the work challenge or affirm the social order it describes?

New Historicist Questions (p. 493)

1. What kinds of documents outside the work seem especially relevant for shedding light on the work?
2. How are social values contemporary to the work reflected or refuted in the work?
3. How does your own historical moment affect your reading of the work and its historical reconstruction?

Cultural Studies Questions (p. 494)

1. What does the work reveal about the cultural behavior contemporary to it?
2. How does popular culture contemporary to the work reflect or challenge the values implicit or explicit in the work?
3. What kinds of cultural documents contemporary to the work add to your reading of it?
4. How do your own cultural assumptions affect your reading of the work and the culture contemporary to it?

Gender Studies Questions (p. 495)

1. How are the lives of men and women portrayed in the work? Do the men and women in the work accept or reject these roles?
2. Is the form and content of the work influenced by the author's gender?
3. What attitudes are explicit or implicit concerning heterosexual, homosexual, or lesbian relationships? Are these relationships sources of conflict? Do they provide resolutions to conflicts?

4. Does the work challenge or affirm traditional ideas about men and women and same-sex relationships?

Mythological Questions (p. 497)

1. How does the story resemble other stories in plot, character, setting, or use of symbols?
2. Are archetypes presented, such as quests, initiations, scapegoats, or withdrawals and returns?
3. Does the protagonist undergo any kind of transformation such as a movement from innocence to experience that seems archetypal?
4. Do any specific allusions to myths shed light on the text?

Reader-Response Questions (p. 499)

1. How do you respond to the work?
2. How do your own experiences and expectations affect your reading and interpretation?
3. What is the work's original or intended audience? To what extent are you similar to or different from that audience?
4. Do you respond in the same way to the work after more than one reading?

Deconstructionist Questions (p. 501)

1. How are contradictory and opposing meanings expressed in the work?
2. How does meaning break down or deconstruct itself in the language of the text?
3. Would you say that ultimate definitive meanings are impossible to determine and establish in the text? Why? How does that affect your interpretation?
4. How are implicit ideological values revealed in the work?

These questions will not apply to all texts; and they are not mutually exclusive. They can be combined to explore a text from several critical perspectives simultaneously. A feminist approach to Anne Bradstreet's "The Author to Her Book" (p. 117) could also use Marxist concerns about class to make observations about the oppression of women's lives in the historical context of the seventeenth century. Your use of these questions should allow you to discover significant issues from which you can develop an argumentative essay that is organized around clearly defined terms, relevant evidence, and a persuasive analysis.

ORGANIZING A PAPER

After you have chosen a manageable topic and developed a thesis, a central idea about it, you can begin to organize your paper. Your thesis, even if it is still somewhat tentative, should help you decide what information will need to be included and provide you with a sense of direction.

Consider again the sample thesis in the section on developing a thesis:

```
On the surface, "To His Coy Mistress" is a celebration of
the pleasures of the flesh, but this witty seduction is tem-
pered by a chilling recognition of the reality of death.
```

This thesis indicates that the paper can be divided into two parts: the pleasures of the flesh and the reality of death. It also indicates an order: Because the central point is to show that the poem is more than a simple celebration, the pleasures of the flesh should be discussed first so that another, more complex, reading of the poem can follow. If the paper began with the reality of death, its point would be anticlimactic.

Having established such a broad and informal outline, you can draw upon your underlinings, margin notations, and notecards for the subheadings and evidence required to explain the major sections of your paper. This next level of detail would look like the following:

```
1. Pleasures of the flesh
     Part of the traditional tone of love poetry
2. Recognition of death
   Ironic treatment of love
     Diction
     Images
     Figures of speech
     Symbols
     Tone
```

This list was initially a jumble of terms, but the student arranged the items so that each of the two major sections leads to a discussion of tone. (The student also found it necessary to drop some biographical information from his notes because it was irrelevant to the thesis.) The list indicates that the first part of the paper will establish the traditional tone of love poetry that celebrates the pleasures of the flesh, while the second part will present a more detailed discussion about the ironic recognition of death. The emphasis is on the latter because that is the point to be argued in the paper. Hence, the thesis has helped to organize the parts of the paper, establish an order, and indicate the paper's proper proportions.

The next step is to fill in the subheadings with information from your notes. Many experienced writers find that making lists of information to be included under each subheading is an efficient way to develop paragraphs. For a longer paper (perhaps a research paper), you should be able to develop a paragraph or more on each subheading. On the other hand, a shorter paper may require that you combine several subheadings in a paragraph. You may also discover that while an informal list is adequate for a brief paper, a ten-page assignment could require a more detailed outline. Use the method that is most productive for you. Whatever the length of the essay, your presentation must be in a coherent and logical order that allows your reader to follow the argument and evaluate the evidence. The quality of your reading can be demonstrated only by the quality of your writing.

WRITING A DRAFT

The time for sharpening pencils, arranging your desk, and doing almost anything else instead of writing has ended. The first draft will appear on the page only if you stop avoiding the inevitable and sit, stand up, or lie down to write. It makes no difference how you write, just so you do. Now that you have developed a topic into a tentative thesis, you can assemble your notes and begin to flesh out whatever outline you have made.

Be flexible. Your outline should smoothly conduct you from one point to the next, but do not permit it to railroad you. If a relevant and important idea occurs to you now, work it into the draft. By using the first draft as a means of thinking about what you want to say, you will very likely discover more than your notes originally suggested. Plenty of good writers don't use outlines at all but discover ordering principles as they write. Do not attempt to compose a perfectly correct draft the first time around. Grammar, punctuation, and spelling can wait until you revise. Concentrate on what you are saying. Good writing most often occurs when you are in hot pursuit of an idea rather than in a nervous search for errors.

To make revising easier, leave wide margins and extra space between lines so that you can easily add words, sentences, and corrections. Write on only one side of the paper. Your pages will be easier to keep track of that way, and, if you have to clip a paragraph to place it elsewhere, you will not lose any writing on the other side.

If you are working on a word processor, you can take advantage of its capacity to make additions and deletions as well as move entire paragraphs by making just a few simple keyboard commands. Some software programs can also check spelling and certain grammatical elements in your writing. It's worth remembering, however, that though a clean copy fresh off a printer may look terrific, it will read only as well as the thinking and writing that have gone into it. Many writers prudently store their data on disks and print their pages each time they finish a draft to avoid losing any material because of power failures or other problems. These printouts are also easier to read than the screen when you work on revisions.

Once you have a first draft on paper, you can delete material that is unrelated to your thesis and add material necessary to illustrate your points and make your paper convincing. The student who wrote "Disembodied Images in 'The Love Song of J. Alfred Prufrock'" (p. 545) wisely dropped a paragraph that questioned whether Prufrock displays chauvinistic attitudes toward women. Although this could be an interesting issue, it has nothing to do with the thesis, which explains how the images reflect Prufrock's inability to make a meaningful connection to his world.

Remember that your initial draft is only that. You should go through the paper many times—and then again—working to substantiate and clarify your ideas. You may even end up with several entire versions of the paper. Rewrite. The sentences within each paragraph should be related to a single topic. Transitions should connect one paragraph to the next so that there are no abrupt or confusing shifts. Awkward or wordy phrasing or unclear sentences and paragraphs should be mercilessly poked and prodded into shape.

Writing the Introduction and Conclusion

After you have clearly and adequately developed the body of your paper, pay particular attention to the introductory and concluding paragraphs. It's probably best to write the introduction—at least the final version of it—last, after you know precisely what you are introducing. Because this paragraph is crucial for generating interest in the topic, it should engage the reader and provide a sense of what the paper is about. There is no formula for writing effective introductory paragraphs, because each writing situation is different—depending on the audience, topic, and approach—but if you pay attention to the introductions of the essays you read, you will notice a variety of possibilities. The introductory paragraph to the Prufrock paper, for example, is a straightforward explanation of why the disembodied images are important for understanding Prufrock's character. The rest of the paper then offers evidence to support this point.

Concluding paragraphs demand equal attention because they leave the reader with a final impression. The conclusion should provide a sense of closure instead of starting a new topic or ending abruptly. In the final paragraph about the disembodied images in "Prufrock" the student explains their significance in characterizing Prufrock's inability to think of himself or others as complete and whole human beings. We now see that the images of eyes, arms, and claws are reflections of the fragmentary nature of Prufrock and his world. Of course, the body of your paper is the most important part of your presentation, but do remember that first and last impressions have a powerful impact on readers.

Using Quotations

Quotations can be a valuable means of marshaling evidence to illustrate and support your ideas. A judicious use of quoted material will make your points clearer and more convincing. Here are some guidelines that should help you use quotations effectively.

1. Brief quotations (four lines or fewer of prose or three lines or fewer of poetry) should be carefully introduced and integrated into the text of your paper with quotation marks around them.

> According to the narrator, Bertha "had a reputation for
> strictness." He tells us that she always "wore dark clothes,
> dressed her hair simply, and expected contrition and obedi-
> ence from her pupils."

For brief poetry quotations, use a slash to indicate a division between lines.

> The concluding lines of Blake's "The Tyger" pose a disturb-
> ing question: "What immortal hand or eye / Dare frame thy
> fearful symmetry?"

Lengthy quotations should be separated from the text of your paper. More than three lines of poetry should be double spaced and centered on the page. More than four lines of prose should be double spaced and indented ten spaces from the left margin, with the right margin the same as for the text. Do *not* use quotation marks for the passage; the indentation indicates that the passage is a quotation. Lengthy quotations should not be used in place of your own writing. Use them only if they are absolutely necessary.

2. If any words are added to a quotation, use brackets to distinguish your addition from the original source.

> "He [Young Goodman Brown] is portrayed as self-righteous and
> disillusioned."

Any words inside quotation marks and not in brackets must be precisely those of the author. Brackets can also be used to change the grammatical structure of a quotation so that it fits into your sentence.

> Smith argues that Chekhov "present[s] the narrator in an
> ambivalent light."

If you drop any words from the source, use an ellipsis (three spaced periods within brackets) to indicate that the omission is yours.

```
"Early to bed [ . . . ] makes a man healthy, wealthy,
and wise."
```

Use an ellipsis preceding a period to indicate an omission at the end of a sentence.

```
"Early to bed and early to rise makes a man healthy [. . .]."
```

Use a single line of spaced periods to indicate the omission of a line or more of poetry or more than one paragraph of prose.

```
Nothing would sleep in that cellar, dank as a ditch,
Bulbs broke out of boxes hunting for chinks in the dark,
. . . . . . . . . . . . . . . . . . . . . . . . . .
Nothing would give up life:
Even the dirt kept breathing a small breath.
```

3. You will be able to punctuate quoted material accurately and confidently if you observe these conventions.
Place commas and periods inside quotation marks.

```
"Even the dirt," Roethke insists, "kept breathing a small
breath."
```

Even though a comma does not appear after "dirt" in the original quotation, it is placed inside the quotation mark. The exception to this rule occurs when a parenthetical reference to a source follows the quotation.

```
"Even the dirt," Roethke insists, "kept breathing a small
breath" (11).
```

Punctuation marks other than commas or periods go outside the quotation marks unless they are part of the material quoted.

```
What does Roethke mean when he writes that "the dirt kept
breathing a small breath"?

Yeats asked, "How can we know the dancer from the dance?"
```

REVISING AND EDITING

Put some distance—a day or so if you can—between yourself and each draft of your paper. The phrase that seemed just right on Wednesday may be revealed as all wrong on Friday. You'll have a better chance of detecting lumbering sentences and thin paragraphs if you plan ahead and give yourself the time to read your paper from a fresh perspective. Through the process of revision, you can transform a competent paper into an excellent one.

Begin by asking yourself if your approach to the topic requires any rethinking. Is the argument carefully thought out and logically presented? Are there any gaps in the presentation? How well is the paper organized? Do the paragraphs lead into one another? Does the body of the paper deliver what the thesis promises? Is the interpretation sound? Are any relevant and important elements of the work ignored or distorted to advance the thesis? Are the points supported with evidence? These large questions should be addressed before you focus on more detailed matters. If you uncover serious problems as a result of considering these questions, you'll probably have quite a lot of rewriting to do, but at least you will have the opportunity to correct the problems — even if doing so takes several drafts.

A useful technique for spotting awkward or unclear moments in the paper is to read it aloud. You might also try having a friend read it aloud to you. If your handwriting is legible, your friend's reading — perhaps accompanied by hesitations and puzzled expressions — could alert you to passages that need reworking. Having identified problems, you can readily correct them on a word processor or on the draft provided you've skipped lines and used wide margins. The final draft you hand in should be neat and carefully proofread for any inadvertent errors.

The following checklist offers questions to ask about your paper as you revise and edit it. Most of these questions will be familiar to you; however, if you need help with any of them, ask your instructor or review the appropriate section in a composition handbook.

Revision Checklist

1. Is the topic manageable? Is it too narrow or too broad?
2. Is the thesis clear? Is it based on a careful reading of the work?
3. Is the paper logically organized? Does it have a firm sense of direction?
4. Is your argument persuasive? Do you use evidence from the text to support your main points?
5. Should any material be deleted? Do any important points require further illustration or evidence?
6. Does the opening paragraph introduce the topic in an interesting manner?
7. Are the paragraphs developed, unified, and coherent? Are any too short or long?
8. Are there transitions linking the paragraphs?
9. Does the concluding paragraph provide a sense of closure?
10. Is the tone appropriate? Is it unduly flippant or pretentious?
11. Is the title engaging and suggestive?
12. Are the sentences clear, concise, and complete?
13. Are simple, complex, and compound sentences used for variety?
14. Have technical terms been used correctly? Are you certain of the meanings of all the words in the paper? Are they spelled correctly?

15. Have you documented any information borrowed from books, articles, or other sources? Have you quoted too much instead of summarizing or paraphrasing secondary material?
16. Have you used a standard format for citing sources (see p. 565)?
17. Have you followed your instructor's guidelines for the manuscript format of the final draft?
18. Have you carefully proofread the final draft?

When you proofread your final draft, you may find a few typographical errors that must be corrected but do not warrant printing an entire page again. Provided there are not more than a handful of such errors throughout the page, they can be corrected as shown in the following passage. This example condenses a short paper's worth of errors; no single passage should be this shabby in your essay.

```
To add a letter or word, use a caret on the line where the
                 is
addition needed. To delete a word draw a single line
          ^
through  through  it. Run-on words are separated by a verti-
cal line, and inadvertent spaces are closed like this.
Transposed letters are indicated this way. New paragraphs
are noted with the sign ¶ in front of where the next
paragraph is to begin. ¶ Unless you . . .
```

These sorts of errors can be minimized by proofreading on the screen, and simply entering corrections as you go along.

MANUSCRIPT FORM

The novelist and poet Peter De Vries once observed in his characteristically humorous way that he very much enjoyed writing but that he couldn't bear the "paper work." Behind this playful pun is a half-serious impatience with the mechanics of it all. You may feel some of that too, but this is not the time to allow a thoughtful, carefully revised paper to trip over minor details that can be easily accommodated. The final draft you hand in to your instructor should not only read well but look neat. If your instructor does not provide specific instructions concerning the format for the paper, follow these guidelines.

1. Papers (particularly long ones) should be typed on 8½ × 11–inch paper in double space. Avoid transparent paper such as onionskin; it is difficult to read and write comments on. The ribbon should be dark and the letters on the machine clear. If you compose on a word processor with a

dot-matrix printer, be certain that the dots are close enough together to be legible. And don't forget to separate your pages and remove the strips of holes on each side of the pages if your printer uses a continuous paper feed. If your instructor accepts handwritten papers, write legibly in ink on only one side of a wide-lined page.

2. Use a one inch margin at the top, bottom, and sides of each page. Unless you are instructed to include a separate title page, type your name, instructor's name, course number and section, and date on separate lines one inch below the upper-left corner of the first page. Double space between these lines and then center the title below the date. Do not underline or put quotation marks around your paper's title, but do use quotation marks around the titles of poems, short stories, or other brief works, and underline the titles of books and plays (a sample paper title: "Mending Wall" and Other Boundaries in Frost's *North of Boston*). Begin the text of your paper two spaces below the title. If you have used secondary sources, center the heading "Notes" or "Works Cited" one inch from the top of a separate page and then double space between it and the entries.

3. Number each page consecutively, beginning with page 2, a half inch from the top of the page in the upper-right corner.

4. Gather the pages with a paper clip rather than staples, folders, or some other device. That will make it easier for your instructor to handle the paper.

TYPES OF WRITING ASSIGNMENTS

The types of papers most frequently assigned in literature classes are explication, analysis, and comparison and contrast. Most writing about literature involves some combination of these skills. This section includes a sample explication, an analysis, and a comparison and contrast paper. For a sample research paper that demonstrates a variety of strategies for documenting outside sources, see page 575. For other examples of student papers, see pages 540, 545, and 552.

Explication

The purpose of this approach to a literary work is to make the implicit explicit. *Explication* is a detailed explanation of a passage of poetry or prose. Because explication is an intensive examination of a text line by line, it is mostly used to interpret a short poem in its entirety or a brief passage from a long poem, short story, or play. Explication can be used in any kind of paper when you want to be specific about how a writer achieves a certain effect. An explication pays careful attention to language: the connotations of words, allusions, figurative language, irony, symbol, rhythm, sound, and so on. These elements are examined in relation to one another and to the overall effect and meaning of the work.

The simplest way to organize an explication is to move through the passage line by line, explaining whatever seems significant. It is wise to avoid, however, an assembly-line approach that begins each sentence with "In line one. . . ." Instead, organize your paper in whatever way best serves your thesis. You might find that the right place to start is with the final lines, working your way back to the beginning of the poem or passage. The following sample explication on Emily Dickinson's "There's a certain Slant of light" does just that. The student's opening paragraph refers to the final line of the poem in order to present her thesis. She explains that though the poem begins with an image of light, it is not a bright or cheery poem but one concerned with "the look of Death." Since the last line prompted her thesis, that is where she begins the explication.

You might also find it useful to structure a paper by discussing various elements of literature, so that you have a paragraph on connotative words followed by one on figurative language and so on. However your paper is organized, keep in mind that the aim of an explication is not simply to summarize the passage but to comment on the effects and meanings produced by the author's use of language in it. An effective explication (the Latin word *explicare* means "to unfold") displays a text to reveal how it works and what it signifies. Although writing an explication requires some patience and sensitivity, it is an excellent method for coming to understand and appreciate the elements and qualities that constitute literary art.

A SAMPLE EXPLICATION

A Reading of Dickinson's "There's a certain Slant of light"

The sample paper by Bonnie Katz is the result of an assignment calling for an explication of about 750 words on any poem by Emily Dickinson. Katz selected "There's a certain Slant of light."

EMILY DICKINSON (1830–1886)

There's a certain Slant of light

c. 1861

There's a certain Slant of light,
Winter Afternoons —
That oppresses, like the Heft
Of Cathedral Tunes —

Heavenly Hurt, it gives us —   5
We can find no scar,

But Internal difference,
Where the Meanings, are —

None may teach it — Any —
'Tis the Seal Despair —   10
An imperial affliction
Sent us of the Air —

When it comes, the Landscape listens —
Shadows — hold their breath —
When it goes, 'tis like the Distance   15
On the look of Death —

This essay comments on every line of the poem and provides a coherent reading that relates each line to the speaker's intense awareness of death. Although the essay discusses each stanza in the order that it appears, the introductory paragraph provides a brief overview explaining how the poem's images contribute to its total meaning. In addition, the student does not hesitate to discuss a line out of sequence when it can be usefully connected to another phrase. This is especially apparent in the third paragraph, in her discussion of stanzas 2 and 3. The final paragraph describes some of the formal elements of the poem. It might be argued that this discussion could have been integrated into the previous paragraphs rather than placed at the end, but the student does make a connection in her concluding sentence between the pattern of language and its meaning.

Several other matters are worth noticing. The student works quotations into her own sentences to support her points. She quotes exactly as the words appear in the poem, even Dickinson's irregular use of capital letters. When something is added to a quotation to clarify it, it is enclosed in brackets so that the essayist's words will not be mistaken for the poet's: "Seal [of] Despair." A slash is used to separate line divisions as in "imperial affliction / Sent us of the Air." And, finally, because the essay focuses on a short poem, it is not necessary to include line numbers, though they would be required in a study of a longer work.

Bonnie Katz

Professor Quiello

English 109-2

October 26, 20--

A Reading of Dickinson's

"There's a certain Slant of light"

Because Emily Dickinson did not provide titles for
her poetry, editors follow the customary practice of
using the first line of a poem as its title. However, a
more appropriate title for "There's a certain Slant of
light," one that suggests what the speaker in the poem is
most concerned about, can be drawn from the poem's last
line, which ends with "the look of Death." Although the
first line begins with an image of light, nothing bright,
carefree, or cheerful appears in the poem. Instead, the
predominant mood and images are darkened by a sense of
despair resulting from the speaker's awareness of death.

In the first stanza, the "certain Slant of light" is
associated with "Winter Afternoons," a phrase that con-
notes the end of a day, a season, and even life itself.
Such light is hardly warm or comforting. Not a ray or
beam, this slanting light suggests something unusual or
distorted and creates in the speaker a certain slant on
life that is consistent with the cold, dark mood that
winter afternoons can produce. Like the speaker, most of
us have seen and felt this sort of light: it "oppresses"
and pervades our sense of things when we encounter it.
Dickinson uses the senses of hearing and touch as well as
sight to describe the overwhelming oppressiveness that
the speaker experiences. The light is transformed into
sound by a simile that tells us it is "like the Heft / Of
Cathedral Tunes." Moreover, the "Heft" of that sound--the
slow, solemn measures of tolling church bells and organ

music--weighs heavily on our spirits. Through the use of
shifting imagery, Dickinson evokes a kind of spiritual
numbness that we keenly feel and perceive through our
senses.

By associating the winter light with "Cathedral
Tunes," Dickinson lets us know that the speaker is con-
cerned about more than the weather. Whatever it is that
"oppresses" is related by connotation to faith, mortal-
ity, and God. The second and third stanzas offer several
suggestions about this connection. The pain caused by the
light is a "Heavenly Hurt." This "imperial affliction /
Sent us of the Air" apparently comes from God above, and
yet it seems to be part of the very nature of life. The
oppressiveness we feel is in the air, and it can neither
be specifically identified at this point in the poem nor
be eliminated, for "None may teach it--Any." All we can
know is that existence itself seems depressing under the
weight of this "Seal [of] Despair." The impression left
by this "Seal" is stamped within the mind or soul rather
than externally. "We can find no scar," but once experi-
enced this oppressiveness challenges our faith in life
and its "Meanings."

The final stanza does not explain what those "Mean-
ings" are, but it does make clear that the speaker is
acutely aware of death. As the winter daylight fades,
Dickinson projects the speaker's anxiety onto the sur-
rounding landscape and shadows, which will soon be en-
gulfed by the darkness that follows this light: "The
Landscape listens-- / Shadows--hold their breath." This
image firmly aligns the winter light in the first stanza
with darkness. Paradoxically, the light in this poem il-
luminates the nature of darkness. Tension is released
when the light is completely gone, but what remains is

the despair that the "imperial affliction" has imprinted on the speaker's sensibilities, for it is "like the Distance / On the look of Death." There can be no relief from what that "certain Slant of light" has revealed, because what has been experienced is permanent--like the fixed stare in the eyes of someone who is dead.

The speaker's awareness of death is conveyed in a thoughtful, hushed tone. The lines are filled with fluid l and smooth s sounds that are appropriate for the quiet, meditative voice in the poem. The voice sounds tentative and uncertain--perhaps a little frightened. This seems to be reflected in the slightly irregular meter of the lines. The stanzas are trochaic with the second and fourth lines of each stanza having five syllables, but no stanza is identical because each works a slight variation on the first stanza's seven syllables in the first and third lines. The rhymes also combine exact patterns with variations. The first and third lines of each stanza are not exact rhymes, but the second and fourth lines are exact so that the paired words are more closely related: Afternoons, Tunes; scar, are; Despair, Air; and breath, Death. There is a pattern to the poem, but it is unobtrusively woven into the speaker's voice in much the same way that "the look of Death" is subtly present in the images and language of the poem.

Analysis

The preceding sample essay shows how an explication examines in detail the important elements in a work and relates them to the whole. An analysis, however, usually examines only a single element — such as diction, character, point of view, symbol, tone, or irony — and relates it to the entire work. An analytic topic separates the work into parts and focuses on a specific one; you might consider "Point of View in 'The Love Song of J. Alfred Prufrock,'" "Patterns of Rhythm in Robert Browning's 'My Last Duchess,'" or "Irony in 'The Road Not Taken.'" The specific element must be related to the work as a whole or it will appear irrelevant. It is not enough to point out that there are many death images in Andrew Marvell's "To His Coy Mistress"; the images must somehow be connected to the poem's overall effect.

Whether an analytic paper is just a few pages or many, it cannot attempt to discuss everything about the work it is considering. Only those elements that are relevant to the topic can be treated. This kind of focusing makes the topic manageable; this is why most papers that you write will probably be some form of analysis. Explications are useful for a short passage, but a line-by-line commentary on a story, play, or long poem simply isn't practical. Because analysis allows you to consider the central effect or meaning of an entire work by studying a single important element, it is a useful and common approach to longer works.

A SAMPLE ANALYSIS

Disembodied Images in
"The Love Song of J. Alfred Prufrock"

Beth Hart's paper analyzes some of the images in T. S. Eliot's "The Love Song of J. Alfred Prufrock" (the poem appears on p. 405). The assignment simply called for an essay of approximately 750 words on a poem written in the twentieth century. The approach was left to the student.

The idea for this essay began with Hart asking herself why there are so many fragmentary, disjointed images in the poem. The initial answer to this question was that "The disjointed images are important for understanding Prufrock's character." This answer was the rough beginning of a tentative thesis. What still had to be explained, though, was how the images are important. To determine the significance of the disjointed images, Hart jotted down some notes based on her underlinings and marginal notations.

Prufrock	Images
odd name--nervous, timid?	fog
"indecisions," "revisions"	lost, wandering
confessional tone, self- conscious	watching eyes
	ladies' arms

"bald spot"	polite talk, meaningless talk
"afraid"	"ragged claws" that scuttle
questioning, tentative	oppressive
"I am not Prince Hamlet"	distorted
"I grow old"	weary longing
wake--to drown	entrapped--staircase

From these notes Hart saw that the images—mostly fragmented and dis-jointed—suggested something about Prufrock's way of describing himself and his world. This insight led eventually to the final version of her thesis statement: "Eliot's use of frightening disembodied images such as eyes, arms, and claws reflects Prufrock's terror at having to face a world to which he feels no meaningful connection." Her introductory paragraph con-cludes with this sentence so that her reader can fully comprehend why she then discusses the images of eyes, arms, and claws that follow.

The remaining paragraphs present details that explain the significance of the images of eyes in the second paragraph, the arms in the third, the claws in the fourth, and in the final paragraph all three images are the basis for concluding that Prufrock's vision of the world is disconnected and dis-jointed.

Hart's notes certainly do not constitute a formal outline, but they were useful to her in establishing a thesis and recognizing what elements of the poem she needed to cover in her discussion. Her essay is sharply focused, well organized, and generally well written (though some readers might wish for a more engaging introductory paragraph that captures a glint of Prufrock's "bald spot" or some other small detail in order to generate some immediate interest in his character).

Beth Hart

Professor Lucas

English 110-3

March 30, 20--

Disembodied Images in

"The Love Song of J. Alfred Prufrock"

T. S. Eliot's poem "The Love Song of J. Alfred Prufrock," addresses the dilemma of a man who finds himself trapped on the margins of the social world, unable to make any meaningful interpersonal contact because of his deep-seated fear of rejection and misunderstanding. Prufrock feels acutely disconnected from society, which makes him so self-conscious that he is frightened into a state of social paralysis. His overwhelming self-consciousness, disillusionment with social circles, and lack of connection with those around him are revealed through Eliot's use of fragmented imagery. Many of the predominant images are disembodied pieces of a whole, revealing that Prufrock sees the world not as fully whole or complete, but as disjointed, fragmented parts of the whole. Eliot's use of frightening disembodied images such as eyes, arms, and claws reflects Prufrock's terror at having to face a world to which he feels no meaningful connection.

Eliot suggests Prufrock's acute self-consciousness through the fragmentary image of "eyes." Literally, these eyes merely represent the people who surround Prufrock, but this disembodied image reveals his obsessive fear of being watched and judged by others. His confession that "I have known the eyes already, known them all-- / The eyes that fix you in a formulated phrase" (lines 55-56) suggests how deeply he resists being watched, and how uncomfortable he is with himself, both externally--

referring in part to his sensitivity to the "bald spot in the middle of my hair" (40)--and internally--his relentless self-questioning "'Do I dare?' and, 'Do I dare?'" (38). The disembodied eyes force the reader to recognize the oppression of being closely watched, and so to share in Prufrock's painful self-awareness. Prufrock's belief that the eyes have the terrifying and violent power to trap him like a specimen insect "pinned and wriggling on the wall" (58), to be scrutinized in its agony, further reveals the terror of the floating, accusatory image of the eyes.

The disembodied image of "arms" also reflects Prufrock's distorted vision of both himself and others around him. His acknowledgment that he has "known the arms already, known them all-- / Arms that are braceleted and white and bare" (62-63) relates to the image of the eyes, yet focuses on a very different aspect of the people surrounding Prufrock. Clearly, the braceleted arms belong to women, and that these arms are attached to a perfumed dress (65) suggests that these arms belong to upper-class, privileged women. This is partially what makes the disembodied image of the arms so frightening for Prufrock: he is incapable of connecting with a woman the way he, as a man, is expected to. The image of the arms, close enough to Prufrock to reveal their down of "light brown hair" (64), suggests the potential for reaching out and possibly touching Prufrock. The terrified self-consciousness that the image elicits in him leads Prufrock to wish that he could leave his own body and take on the characteristics of yet another disembodied image.

Prufrock's despairing declaration, "I should have been a pair of ragged claws / Scuttling across the floors of silent seas" (73-74), offers yet another example of his vision of the world as fragmented and incomplete. The "pair of claws" that he longs to be not only connotes a complete separation from the earthly life that he finds so threatening, so painful, and so meaningless, but also suggests an isolation from others that would allow Prufrock some freedom and relief from social pressures. However, this image of the claws as a form of salvation for Prufrock in fact offers little suggestion of actual progress from his present circumstances; crabs can only "scuttle" from side to side and are incapable of moving directly forward or backward. Similarly, Prufrock is trapped in a situation in which he feels incapable of moving either up or down the staircase (39). Thus, this disembodied image of the claws serves to remind the reader that Prufrock is genuinely trapped in a life that offers him virtually no hope of real connection or wholeness.

The fragmented imagery that pervades "The Love Song of J. Alfred Prufrock" emphasizes and clarifies Prufrock's vision of the world as disconnected and dis-jointed. The fact that Prufrock thinks of people in terms of their individual component parts (specifically, eyes and arms) suggests his lack of understanding of people as whole and complete beings. This reflects his vision of himself as a fragmentary self, culminating in his wish to be not a whole crab, but merely a pair of disembodied claws. By use of these troubling images Eliot infuses the poem with the pain of Prufrock's self-awareness and his confusion at the lack of wholeness he feels, in his world.

Hart's essay suggests a number of useful guidelines for analytic papers:

1. Only those points related to the thesis are included. In another type of paper the significance of Eliot's epigraph from Dante, for example, might have been more important than the imagery.
2. The analysis keeps the images in focus while at the same time indicating how they are significant in revealing Prufrock's character.
3. The title is a useful lead into the paper; it provides a sense of what the topic is.
4. The introductory paragraph is direct and clearly indicates the paper will argue that the images serve to reveal Prufrock's character.
5. Brief quotations are deftly incorporated into the text of the paper to illustrate points. We are told what we need to know about the poem as evidence is provided to support ideas. There is no unnecessary summary.
6. The paragraphs are well developed, unified, and coherent. They flow naturally from one to another. Notice, for example, the smooth transition worked into the final sentence of the third paragraph and the first sentence of the fourth paragraph.
7. Hart makes excellent use of her careful reading and notes by finding revealing connections among the details she has observed.
8. As events in the poem are described, the present tense is used. This avoids awkward tense shifts and lends an immediacy to the discussion.
9. The concluding paragraph establishes the significance of why the images should be seen as a reflection of Prufrock's character and provides a sense of closure by relating the images of Prufrock's disjointed world with the images of his fragmentary self.
10. In short, Hart has demonstrated that she has read the work closely, has understood the function of the images in the revelation of Prufrock's sensibilities, and has argued her thesis convincingly by using evidence from the poem.

Comparison and Contrast

Another essay assignment in literature courses often combined with analytic topics is the type that requires you to write about similarities and differences between or within works. You might be asked to discuss "How Sounds Express Meanings in May Swenson's 'A Nosty Fright' and Lewis Carroll's 'Jabberwocky,'" or "Love and Hate in Sylvia Plath's 'Daddy.'" A *comparison* of either topic would emphasize their similarities, while a *contrast* would stress their differences. It is possible, of course, to include both perspectives in a paper if you find significant likenesses and differences. A comparison of Andrew Marvell's "To His Coy Mistress" and Richard Wilbur's "A Late Aubade" would, for example, yield similarities, because each poem describes a man urging his lover to make the most of their precious time together; however, important differences also exist in the tone and theme of each poem that would constitute a contrast. (You should, incidentally, be aware that the term *comparison* is sometimes used inclusively to refer to both similarities and differences. If you are assigned a comparison of two works, be sure that you understand what your instructor's expectations are; you may be required to include both approaches in the essay.)

When you choose your own topic, the paper will be more successful — more manageable — if you write on works that can be meaningfully related to each other. Although Robert Herrick's "To the Virgins, to Make Much of Time" and T. S. Eliot's "The Love Song of J. Alfred Prufrock" both have something to do with hesitation, the likelihood of anyone making a connection between the two that reveals something interesting and important is remote — though perhaps not impossible if the topic were conceived imaginatively and tactfully. Choose a topic that encourages you to ask significant questions about each work; the purpose of a comparison or contrast is to understand the works more clearly for having examined them together.

Choose works to compare or contrast that intersect with each other in some significant way. They may, for example, be written by the same author or about the same subject. Perhaps you can compare their use of some technique, such as irony or point of view. Regardless of the specific topic, be sure to have a thesis that allows you to organize your paper around a central idea that argues a point about the two works. If you merely draw up a list of similarities or differences without a thesis in mind, your paper will be little more than a series of observations with no apparent purpose. Keep in the foreground of your thinking what the comparison or contrast reveals about the works.

There is no single way to organize comparative papers since each topic is likely to have its own particular issues to resolve, but it is useful to be aware of two basic patterns that can be helpful with a comparison, a contrast, or a combination of both. One method that can be effective for relatively short papers consists of dividing the paper in half, first discussing one work and then the other. Here, for example, is a partial informal outline for a discussion of Hughes's "Un-American Investigators" and Laviera's "AmeRícan"; the topic is a comparison and contrast:

```
"Two Views of America by Hughes and Laviera"

1. "Un-American Investigators"
   a. Diction
   b. Images
   c. Allusions
   d. Themes
2. "AmeRícan"
   a. Diction
   b. Images
   c. Allusions
   d. Themes
```

This organizational strategy can be effective provided that the second part of the paper combines the discussion of "AmeRícan" with references to "Un-American Investigators" so that the thesis is made clear and the paper unified without being repetitive. If the two poems were treated entirely separately, then the discussion would be merely parallel rather than integrated. In a lengthy paper, this organization probably would not work well because a reader would have difficulty remembering the points made in the first half as he or she reads on.

Thus for a longer paper it is usually better to create a more integrated structure that discusses both works as you take up each item in your outline. Shown here in partial outline is the second basic pattern using the elements just cited.

```
1. Diction
   a. "Un-American Investigators"
   b. "AmeRícan"
2. Images
   a. "Un-American Investigators"
   b. "AmeRícan"
3. Allusions
   a. "Un-American Investigators"
   b. "AmeRícan"
4. Themes
   a. "Un-American Investigators"
   b. "AmeRícan"
```

This pattern allows you to discuss any number of topics without requiring that your reader recall what you first said about the diction of "Un-American Investigators" before you discuss the diction of "AmeRícan" many pages later. However you structure your comparison or contrast paper, make certain that a reader can follow its elements and keep track of its thesis.

A SAMPLE COMPARISON
MARVELL AND ACKERMAN SEIZE THE DAY

The following paper is in response to an assignment that required a comparison and contrast — about 1,000 words — of two assigned poems. The student chose to write an analysis of two very different *carpe diem* poems.

Although these two poems are fairly lengthy, Stephanie Smith's brief analysis of them is satisfying because she focuses on the male and female *carpe diem* voices of Andrew Marvell's "To His Coy Mistress" (p. 65) and

Diane Ackerman's "A Fine, a Private Place" (p. 69). After introducing the topic in the first paragraph, she takes up the two poems in a pattern similar to the first outline suggested for "Two Views of America by Hughes and Laviera." Notice how Smith works in subsequent references to Marvell's poem as she discusses Ackerman's so that her treatment is integrated and we are reminded why she is comparing and contrasting the two works. Her final paragraph sums up her points without being repetitive and reiterates the thesis with which she began.

Stephanie Smith

English 109-10

Professor Monroe

April 2, 20--

Marvell and Ackerman Seize the Day

In her 1983 poem "A Fine, a Private Place," Diane
Ackerman never mentions Andrew Marvell's 1681 poem "To
His Coy Mistress." However, her one-line allusion to
Marvell's famous argument to his lover is all the refer-
ence she needs. Through a contemporary lens, she firmly
qualifies Marvell's seventeenth-century masculine per-
spective. Marvell's speaker attempts to woo a young woman
and convince her to have sexual relations with him. His
seize-the-day rhetoric argues that "his mistress" should
let down her conventional purity and enjoy the moment,
his logic being that we are grave-bound anyway, so why
not? Although his poetic pleading is effective, both
stylistically and argumentatively, Marvell's speaker ob-
viously assumes that the coy mistress will succumb to his
grasps at her sexuality. Further, and most important for
Ackerman, the speaker takes for granted that the female
must be persuaded to love. His smooth talk leaves no room
for a feminine perspective, be it a slap in the face or a
sharing of his carpe diem attitudes. Ackerman accommo-
dates Marvell's masculine speaker but also deftly takes
poetic license in the cause of female freedom and sensu-
ously lays out her own fine and private place. Through
describing a personal sexual encounter both sensually and
erotically, Ackerman's female speaker demonstrates that
women have just as many lustful urges as the men who
would seduce them; she presents sex as neither solely a
male quest nor a female sacrifice. "A Fine, a Private

Place" takes a female perspective on sex, and enthusias-
tically enjoys the pleasure of it.

"To His Coy Mistress" is in a regular rhyme scheme,
as each line rhymes with the next--almost like a compila-
tion of couplets. And this, accompanied by traditional
iambic tetrameter, lays the foundation for a forcefully
flowing speech, a command for the couple to just do it.
By the end of the poem the speaker seems to expect his
mistress to capitulate. Marvell's speaker declares at the
start that if eternity were upon them, he would not mind
putting sex aside and paying her unending homage. "Had we
but world enough, and time, / This coyness, lady, were no
crime. / We would sit down, and think which way / To
walk, and pass our long love's day" (lines 1-4). He pro-
claims he would love her "ten years before the Flood" (8)
and concedes that she "should, if you please, refuse /
Till the conversion of the Jews" (9-10). This eternal
love-land expands as Marvell asserts that his "vegetable
love should grow / Vaster than empires, and more slow"
(11-12). Every part of her body would be admired for an
entire "age" because "lady, you deserve this state, / Nor
would I love at lower rate" (19-20). He would willingly
wait but, alas, circumstances won't let him. She'll have
to settle for the here and now, and he must show her that
life is not an eternity but rather an alarm clock.

The speaker laments that "at my back I always hear /
Time's wingèd chariot hurrying near" (21-22). He then
cleverly draws a picture of what exactly eternity does
have in store for them, namely barren "Deserts" where her
"beauty shall no more be found" (25) while "worms shall
try / That long preserved virginity" (27-28) and her
"quaint honor turn to dust" (29). This death imagery is

meant to frighten her for not having lived enough. He astutely concedes that "The grave's a fine and private place, / But none, I think, do there embrace" (31-32), thereby making even more vivid the nightmare he has just laid before her. Although he must make his grim argument, he does not want to dampen the mood, so he quickly returns to her fair features.

"Now," the speaker proclaims, "while the youthful hue / Sits on thy skin like morning dew, / And while thy willing soul transpires / At every pore with instant fires, / Now let us sport us while we may" (33-37). The speaker has already made the decision for her. Through sex, their energies will become one--they will "roll" their "strength" and "sweetness up into one ball" (41) as they "tear" their "pleasures with rough strife" (43). If the two of them cannot have eternity and make the "sun / Stand still" (45-46), then they will seize the day, combine and celebrate their humanity, and "make [the sun] run" (46). The speaker makes a vivid case in favor of living for the moment. His elaborate images of the devotion his mistress deserves, the inevitability of death, and the vivaciousness of human life are compelling. Three hundred years later, however, Diane Ackerman demonstrates that women no longer need this lesson, because they share the same desires.

Ackerman's title is taken directly from "To His Coy Mistress." This poet's fine and private place is not the grave, as it was in Marvell's poetic persuasion, but rather her underwater sexual encounter. Ackerman's familiarity with Marvell informs us that she knows about death and its implications. More importantly, her speaker needs no rationale to live fully, she just does. She has sex on her own, willingly, knowingly, and thoroughly.

Smith 4

Unlike "To His Coy Mistress," the poem has no rhyme scheme and has little meter or conventional form. The free verse tells the sexual story in an unconfined, open way. The poem flows together with sensual, sexual images drawn from the mystical, vibrant, undersea world. The speaker and her lover float "under the blue horizon / where long sea fingers / parted like beads / hitched in the doorway / of an opium den" (2-6). Whereas Marvell's lovers race against time, Ackerman's seem to bathe in it. Within this sultry setting the "canyons mazed the deep / reef with hollows, / cul-de-sacs, and narrow boudoirs" (7-10) that evoke erotic images. Her lover's "stroking her arm / with a marine feather / slobbery as aloe pulp" (12-14) constitutes foreplay, and when "the octopus / in his swimsuit / stretch[es] one tentacle / ripple[s] its silky bag" (15-18), she becomes a willing partner. In this "lusty dream" (58), "her hips rolled" (59), "her eyes swam / and chest began to heave" (61-62), and the sea also becomes a willing partner in their love-making as the underwater waves help "drive [his brine] / through petals / delicate as anemone veils / to the dark purpose / of a conch-shaped womb" (68-72).

After "panting ebbed" (75), they return to "shallower realms, / heading back toward / the boat's even keel" (81-83), away from the sensual, wild, sea-world in which they reveled. However, the speaker has not literally or figuratively exhausted the waters yet. The "ocean still petted her / cell by cell, murmuring / along her legs and neck / caressing her / with pale, endless arms" (84-88). Though she emerges from the water and the encounter, the experience stays with her as a satisfying memory.

Her sensual memories of the encounter allow her to

savor the moment, in contrast to Marvell's speaker, whose desperate, urgent tone is filled with tension rather than the relief of consummation. In the final section of the poem (106-15), we see that the speaker's sexual encounter is an experience that stays with her "miles / and fathoms away." The erotic language of the sea is in her own voice as she looks out at "minnow snowflakes" while "holding a sponge / idly under [a] tap-gush." As water seems to cascade all around her, the memory of her underwater experience surfaces in the sensuous image of "sinking her teeth / into the cleft / of a voluptuous peach." Ackerman's subject does not have to be persuaded by an excited man to be a sexual being; her sexuality seeps into every day of her life, and we marvel at the depth of her sensuality. Unlike Marvell's speaker, who remains eternally poised to "tear our pleasures," Ackerman's speaker is steeped in those pleasures.

21

The Literary
Research Paper

A close reading of a primary source such as a short story, poem, or play can give insights into a work's themes and effects, but sometimes you will want to know more. A published commentary by a critic who knows the work well and is familiar with the author's life and times can provide insights that otherwise may not be available. Such comments and interpretations — known as *secondary sources* — are, of course, not a substitute for the work itself, but they often can take you into a work further than if you made the journey by yourself.

After imagination, good sense, and energy, perhaps the next most important quality for writing a research paper is the ability to organize material. A research paper on a literary topic requires a writer to take account of quite a lot at once: the text, ideas, sources, and documentation techniques all make demands on one's efforts to present a topic clearly and convincingly.

The following list should give you a sense of what goes into creating a research paper. Although some steps on the list can be folded into one another, they offer an overview of the work that will involve you.

1. Choosing a topic
2. Finding sources
3. Evaluating sources
4. Taking notes
5. Developing a thesis
6. Organizing an outline
7. Writing drafts
8. Revising
9. Documenting sources
10. Preparing the final draft and proofreading

Even if you have never written a research paper, you most likely have already had experience choosing a topic, developing a thesis, organizing an outline, and writing a draft that you then revised, proofread, and handed in. Those skills represent six of the ten items on the list. This chapter briefly reviews some of these steps and focuses on the remaining tasks, unique to research paper assignments.

CHOOSING A TOPIC

Chapter 20 discussed the importance of reading a work closely and taking careful notes as a means of generating topics for writing about literature. If you know a work well and record your understanding of it in notes, you'll have impressions and ideas to choose from for potential topics. You may find it useful to review the information on pages 520–522 before reading the advice about putting together a research paper in this chapter.

The student author of the sample research paper "Individual and Community in 'Mending Wall'" (p. 575) was asked to write a five-page paper that demonstrated some familiarity with published critical perspectives on a Robert Frost poem of her choice. Before looking into critical discussions of the poem, she read "Mending Wall" several times, taking notes and making comments in the margin of her textbook on each reading.

What prompted her choice of "Mending Wall" was a class discussion that focused on the poem's speaker's questioning the value and necessity of the wall in contrast to his neighbor's insistence upon it. At one point, however, the boundaries of the discussion opened up to the possibility that the wall is important to both characters in the poem rather than only the neighbor. It is, after all, the speaker, not the neighbor, who repairs the damage to the wall caused by hunters and who initiates the rebuilding of the wall. Why would he do that if he wanted the wall down? Only after having thoroughly examined the poem did the student go to the library to see what professional critics had to say about this question.

FINDING SOURCES

Whether your college library is large or small, its reference librarians can usually help you locate secondary sources about a particular work or author. Unless you choose a very recently published poem, play, or essay about which little or nothing has been written, you should be able to find out more about a literary work efficiently and quickly. Even if a work has been published recently, you can probably find relevant information on the Internet (see Electronic Sources, p. 560). Here are some useful reference sources that can help you to establish both an overview of a potential topic and a list of relevant books and articles.

Annotated List of References

American Writers. 4 vols. New York: Scribner's, 1979–87. Chronological essays offer biography and criticism of major American writers.

Baker, Nancy L., and Nancy Huling. *A Research Guide for Undergraduate Students: English and American Literature.* 4th ed. New York: MLA, 1995. Especially designed for students; a useful guide to reference sources.

Bryer, Jackson, ed. *Sixteen Modern American Authors: A Survey of Research and Criticism.* New York: Norton, 1973. Extensive bibliographic essays on Sherwood Anderson, Willa Cather, Hart Crane, Theodore Dreiser, T. S. Eliot, William Faulkner, F. Scott Fitzgerald, Robert Frost, Ernest Hemingway, Eugene O'Neill, Ezra Pound, Edwin Arlington Robinson, John Steinbeck, Wallace Stevens, William Carlos Williams, and Thomas Wolfe.

Contemporary Literary Criticism. 106 vols. to date. Detroit: Gale, 1973–. Brief biographies of contemporary authors along with excerpts from reviews and criticism of their work.

Corse, Larry B., and Sandra B. Corse. *Articles on American and British Literature: An Index to Selected Periodicals, 1950–1977.* Athens, OH: Swallow, 1981. Specifically designed for students using small college libraries.

Dictionary of Literary Biography. Detroit: Gale, 1978–. A multivolume series in progress of American, British, and world writers that provides useful biographical and critical overviews.

Eddleman, Floyd E., ed. *American Drama Criticism: Interpretations, 1890–1977.* 2nd ed. Hamden, CT: Shoe String, 1979. Supplement 1984.

Elliot, Emory, et al. *Columbia Literary History of the United States.* New York: Columbia UP, 1988. This updates the discussions in Spiller (p. 560) and reflects recent changes in the canon.

Harner, James L. *Literary Research Guide: A Guide to Reference Sources for the Study of Literature in English and Related Topics.* 3rd ed. New York: MLA, 1998. A selective but extensive annotated guide to important bibliographies, abstracts, databases, histories, surveys, dictionaries, encyclopedias, and handbooks; an invaluable research tool with extensive, useful indexes.

Holman, C. Hugh, and William Harmon. *A Handbook to Literature.* 8th ed. New York: Macmillan, 1999. A thorough dictionary of literary terms that also provides brief, clear overviews of literary movements such as Romanticism.

Kuntz, Joseph M., and Nancy C. Martinez. *Poetry Explication: A Checklist of Interpretation since 1925 of British and American Poems Past and Present.* Boston: Hall, 1980.

MLA International Bibliography of Books and Articles on Modern Language and Literature. New York: MLA, 1921–. Compiled annually; a major source for articles and books. Also available online and on CD-ROM.

The New Cambridge Bibliography of English Literature. 5 vols. Cambridge, Eng.: Cambridge UP, 1967–77. An important source on the literature from A.D. 600 to 1950.

Ousby, Ian, ed. *The Cambridge Guide to English Literature.* 2nd ed. Cambridge, Eng.: Cambridge UP, 1994. A valuable overview.

The Oxford History of English Literature. 13 vols. Oxford, Eng.: Oxford UP, 1945–, in progress. The most comprehensive literary history.

The Penguin Companion to World Literature. 4 vols. New York: McGraw-Hill, 1969–71. Covers classical, Asian, African, European, English, and American literature.

Preminger, Alex, and T. V. F. Brogan, eds. *The New Princeton Encyclopedia of Poetry and Poetics.* Princeton: Princeton UP, 1993. Includes entries on technical terms and poetic movements.

Rees, Robert, and Earl N. Harbert. *Fifteen American Authors before 1900: Bibliographic Essays on Research and Criticism.* Madison: U of Wisconsin P, 1971. Among the writers covered are Stephen Crane and Emily Dickinson.

Spiller, Robert E., et al. *Literary History of the United States.* 4th ed. 2 vols. New York: Macmillan, 1974. Coverage of literary movements and individual writers from colonial times to the 1960s.

Walker, Warren S. *Twentieth-Century Short Story Explication.* 3rd ed. Hamden, CT: Shoe String, 1977. A bibliography of criticism on short stories written since 1800; supplements appear every few years.

These sources are available in the reference sections of most college libraries; ask a reference librarian to help you locate them or to help you use their electronic resources.

Electronic Sources

Researchers can locate materials in a variety of sources, including card catalogs, specialized encyclopedias, bibliographies, and indexes to periodicals. Most libraries now also provide computer searches that are linked to a database of the libraries' holdings; you can even access many of these databases from home. This can be an efficient way to establish a bibliography on a specific topic. If your library has such a service, consult a reference librarian about how to use it and to determine whether it is feasible for your topic. If a computer service is impractical, you can still collect the same information from printed sources.

In addition to the many electronic databases ranging from your library's computerized holdings to the many specialized CD-ROMs available, such as *MLA International Bibliography* (a major source for articles and books on literary topics), the Internet also connects millions of sites with primary sources (the full texts of stories, poems, plays, and essays) and secondary sources (biography or criticism). If you have not had practice with research on the Web, it is a good idea to get guidance from your instructor or a librarian. Browsing on the Net can be absorbing as well as informative, but unless you have plenty of time to spare, don't wait until the last minute to locate your electronic sources. You might find yourself trying to find reliable, professional sources among thousands of sites if you enter an unqualified entry such as "Robert Frost." Once you are familiar with the Net, however, you'll find its research potential both fascinating and rewarding.

Do remember that your own college library offers a broad range of electronic sources. If you're feeling uncertain, intimidated, and profoundly unplugged, your reference librarians are there to help you to get started. Once you take advantage of their advice and tutorials, you'll soon find that negotiating the World Wide Web can be an efficient means of researching almost any subject.

Online Resources for Research and Writing

The details you'll need to conduct research on the Web go beyond the scope of this chapter, but Bedford/St. Martin's offers several online resources for researching and writing about literature that can help you find what you need on the Web — and then use it once you find it. Visit **<www.bedfordstmartins.com/literature>,** and explore the resources we offer to help you research online.

Citing sources correctly in a final paper is often a challenge, and the Web has made it even more complex. ***Research and Documentation Online,*** the online version of the popular booklet *Research and Documentation in the Electronic Age,* by Diana Hacker, provides clear, authoritative advice on documentation in every discipline. It also covers conducting library and online research and includes links to Internet research sources.

The English Research Room is a good starting place for any research project, large or small. *Research Web guides* will answer questions you may have about doing research, conducting electronic searches, using the Web and other online resources, and evaluating and citing sources. *Interactive tutorials* give you the opportunity to practice common electronic search techniques in a live environment. *Research links* make it easy to find hundreds of useful research sites, including search engines and reference sites.

Organized alphabetically by author within five genres, **LitLinks** offers links to sites about many of the authors in this book. Clear, concise annotations and links to more than five hundred professionally maintained sites help you browse with direction, whether you're looking for a favorite text, additional biographical or critical information about an author, critical articles, or conversation with other students and scholars.

Once you're on the Web — or in the library — ***Research Assistant,*** a standalone application, can help you manage your research sources. Functioning as a smart file cabinet, *Research Assistant* helps you collect, evaluate, and cite your sources. It works not only with text but also with graphics, audio clips, and video clips. If you're writing a paper, *Research Assistant* will help you sort and organize your sources, moving you from researching into writing.

EVALUATING SOURCES AND TAKING NOTES

Evaluate your sources for their reliability and the quality of their evidence. Check to see if an article or book has been superseded by later studies; try to use up-to-date sources. A popular magazine article will probably not be as authoritative as an article in a scholarly journal. Sources that are well documented with primary and secondary materials usually indicate that the author has done his or her homework. Books printed by university presses and established trade presses are preferable to books privately printed. But there are always exceptions. If you are uncertain about how to assess a book, try to find out something about the author. Are there any other books listed in the catalog that indicate the author's expertise? What do book reviews say about the work? Three valuable indexes to book reviews of literary studies are *Book Review Digest, Book Review Index,* and *Index to Book Reviews in the Humanities.* Your reference librarian can show you how to use these important tools for evaluating books. Reviews can be a quick means to get a broad perspective on writers and their works because reviewers often survey previous approaches to the topic under discussion.

A cautionary note: assessing online sources can be more problematic than evaluating print sources because anyone with a computer and online access can publish on the Internet. Be sure to determine the nature of your sources and their authority. Is the site the work of a professional or an amateur? Is the information likely to be reliable? Is it biased? Is it documented? Before placing your trust in an Internet source, make sure that it warrants your confidence.

As you prepare a list of reliable sources relevant to your topic, record the necessary bibliographic information so that it will be available when

Lynen, John F. The Pastoral
    Art of Robert Frost.
New Haven: Yale UP,
1960.

Sample bibliography card for a book.

you make up the list of works cited for your paper. (See the sample bibliography card on page 562.) For a book include the author, complete title, place of publication, publisher, and date. For an article include author, complete title, name of periodical, volume number, date of issue, and page numbers. For an Internet source, include the author, complete title, database title, periodical or site name, date of posting of the site (or last update), name of institution or organization, date when you accessed the source, and the network address (URL).

Once you have assembled a tentative bibliography, you will need to take notes on your readings. If you are not using a word processor, use 3 × 5-, 4 × 6-, or 5 × 8-inch cards for note taking. They are easy to manipulate and can be readily sorted later on when you establish subheadings for your paper. Be sure to keep track of where the information comes from by writing the author's name and page number on each notecard. If you use more than one work by the same author include a brief title as well as the author's name. (See the illustration of the sample notecard below.)

The sample notecard records the source of information (the complete publishing information is on the bibliography card) and provides a heading that will allow easy sorting later on. Notice that the information is summarized rather than quoted in large chunks. The student also includes a short note asking herself if Lynen's reading could be expanded upon.

Notecards can combine quotations, paraphrases, and summaries; you can also use them to cite your own ideas and give them headings so that you don't lose track of them. As you take notes try to record only points relevant to your topic, though, inevitably, you'll end up not using some of your notes.

Symbolic value of the wall   Lynen 29

    Lynen describes the wall as
"the symbol for all kinds of
man-made barriers."

[Do these barriers have any
positive value?]

Sample notecard.

DEVELOPING A THESIS AND ORGANIZING THE PAPER

As the notes on "Mending Wall" accumulated, the student sorted them into topics including

1. Publication history of the poem

2. Frost's experiences as a farmer

3. Critics' readings of the poem

4. The speaker's attitude toward the wall

5. The neighbor's attitude toward the wall

6. Mythic elements in the poem

7. Does the wall have any positive value?

8. How do the speaker and neighbor characterize themselves?

9. Humor in the poem

10. Frost as a regional poet

The student quickly saw that items 1, 2, 6, and 10 were not directly related to her topic concerning why the speaker initiates the rebuilding of the wall. The remaining numbers (3–5, 7–9) are the topics taken up in the paper. The student had begun her reading of secondary sources with a tentative thesis that stemmed from her question about why the poem's speaker helps his neighbor to rebuild the wall. That "why" shaped itself into the expectation that she would have a thesis something like this: "The speaker helps to rebuild the wall because. . . ."

She assumed she would find information that indicated some specific reason. But the more she read the more she discovered that there was no single explanation provided by the poem or by critics' readings of the poem. Instead, through the insights provided by her sources, she began to see that the wall had several important functions in the poem. The perspective she developed into her thesis — that the wall "provided a foundation upon which the men build a personal sense of identity" — allowed her to incorporate a number of the critics' insights into her paper in order to shed light on why the speaker helps to rebuild the wall.

Because the assignment was relatively brief, the student did not write up a formal outline but instead organized her stacks of usable notecards and proceeded to write the first draft from them.

REVISING

After writing your first draft, you should review the advice and revision checklist on p. 535 so that you can read your paper with an objective eye. Two days after writing her next-to-last draft, the writer of "Individuality and Community in 'Mending Wall'" realized that she had allotted too much space for critical discussions of the humor in the poem that were not directly related to her approach. She realized that it was not essential to point out and discuss the puns in the poem; hence she corrected this by simply deleting most references to the poem's humor. The point is that she saw this herself after she took some time to approach the paper from a fresh perspective.

DOCUMENTING SOURCES

You must acknowledge the use of a source when you (1) quote someone's exact words, (2) summarize or borrow someone's opinions or ideas, or (3) use information and facts that are not considered to be common knowledge. The purpose of this documentation is to acknowledge your sources, to demonstrate that you are familiar with what others have thought about the topic, and to provide your reader access to the same sources. If your paper is not adequately documented, it will be vulnerable to a charge of *plagiarism* — the presentation of someone else's work as your own. Conscious plagiarism is easy to avoid; honesty takes care of that for most people. However, there is a more problematic form of plagiarism that is often inadvertent. Whether inadequate documentation is conscious or not, plagiarism is a serious matter and must be avoided. Papers can be evaluated only by what is on the page, not by their writers' intentions.

Let's look more closely at what constitutes plagiarism. Consider the following passage quoted from A. R. Coulthard, "Frost's 'Mending Wall,'" *Explicator* 45 (Winter 1987): 40:

> "Mending Wall" has many of the features of an "easy" poem aimed at high-minded readers. Its central symbol is the accessible stone wall to represent separation, and it appears to oppose isolating barriers and favor love and trust, the stuff of Golden Treasury of Inspirational Verse.

Now read this plagiarized version:

> "Mending Wall" is an easy poem that appeals to high-minded readers who take inspiration from its symbolism of the stone wall, which seems to oppose isolating barriers and support trusting love.

Though the writer has shortened the passage and made some changes in the wording, this paragraph is basically the same as Coulthard's. Indeed, several of his phrases are lifted almost intact. (Notice, however, that the plagiarized version seems to have missed Coulthard's irony and, therefore, misinterpreted and misrepresented the passage.) Even if a parenthetical reference had been included at the end of the passage and the source included in "Works Cited," the language of this passage would still be plagiarism because it is presented as the writer's own. Both language and ideas must be acknowledged.

Here is an adequately documented version of the passage:

```
A. R. Coulthard points out that "high-minded readers" mis-
takenly assume that "Mending Wall" is a simple inspirational
poem that uses the symbolic wall to reject isolationism and
to support, instead, a sense of human community (40).
```

This passage makes absolutely clear that the observation is Coulthard's, and it is written in the student's own language with the exception of one quoted phrase. Had Coulthard not been named in the passage, the parenthetical reference would have included his name: (Coulthard 40).

Some mention should be made of the notion of common knowledge before we turn to the standard format for documenting sources. Observations and facts that are widely known and routinely included in many of your sources do not require documentation. It is not necessary to cite a source for the fact that Alfred, Lord Tennyson, was born in 1809 or that Frost writes about New England. Sometimes it will be difficult for you to determine what common knowledge is for a topic that you know little about. If you are in doubt, the best strategy is to supply a reference.

There are two basic ways to document sources. Traditionally, sources have been cited in footnotes at the bottom of each page or in endnotes grouped together at the end of the paper. Here is how a portion of the sample paper on "Mending Wall" would look if footnotes were used instead of parenthetical documentation:

```
It remains one of Frost's more popular poems, and, as
Douglas Wilson notes, "one of the most famous in all of
American poetry."¹

    ¹Douglas L. Wilson, "The Other Side of the Wall,"
Iowa Review 10 (Winter 1979): 65.
```

Unlike endnotes, which are double spaced throughout under the title of "Notes" on separate pages at the end of the paper, footnotes appear four spaces below the text. They are single spaced with double spaces between notes.

No doubt you will have encountered these documentation methods in your reading. A different style is recommended, however, in the Modern Language Association's *MLA Handbook for Writers of Research Papers,* 5th ed. (1999). The MLA style employs parenthetical references within the text of the paper; these are keyed to an alphabetical list of works cited at the end of the paper. This method is designed to be less distracting for the reader.

Unless you are instructed to follow the footnote or endnote style for documentation, use the parenthetical method explained in the next section.

The List of Works Cited

Items in the list of works cited are arranged alphabetically according to the author's last name and indented five spaces after the first line. This allows the reader to locate quickly the complete bibliographic information for the author's name cited within the parenthetical reference in the text. The following are common entries for literature papers and should be used as models. If some of your sources are of a different nature, consult the *MLA Handbook for Writers of Research Papers*, 5th ed. (1999); many of the bibliographic possibilities you are likely to need are included in this source. For the latest updates, check MLA's Web site at <http://www.mla.org>.

A BOOK BY ONE AUTHOR

Hendrickson, Robert. The Literary Life and Other
        Curiosities. New York: Viking, 1981.

Notice that the author's name is in reverse order. This information, along with the full title, place of publication, publisher, and date should be taken from the title and copyright pages of the book. The title is underlined to indicate italics and is also followed by a period. If the city of publication is well known, it is unnecessary to include the state. Use the publication date on the title page; if none appears there use the copyright date (after ©) on the back of the title page.

A BOOK BY TWO AUTHORS

Horton, Rod W., and Herbert W. Edwards. Backgrounds of
        American Literary Thought. 3rd ed. Englewood Cliffs:
        Prentice, 1974.

Only the first author's name is given in reverse order. The edition number appears after the title.

A BOOK WITH MORE THAN THREE AUTHORS

Gates, Henry Louis, Jr., et al., eds. The Norton Anthology
        of African American Literature. New York: Norton, 1997.

The abbreviation *et al.* means "and others." It is used to avoid having to list all fourteen editors of this work.

A WORK IN A COLLECTION BY THE SAME AUTHOR

O'Connor, Flannery. "Greenleaf." The Complete Stories. By
    O'Connor. New York: Farrar, 1971. 311-34.

Page numbers are given because the reference is to only a single story in the collection.

A WORK IN A COLLECTION BY DIFFERENT WRITERS

Frost, Robert. "Design." Poetry: An Introduction. 3rd ed.
    Ed. Michael Meyer. Boston: Bedford/St. Martin's,
    2001. 356.

A TRANSLATED BOOK

Grass, Günter. The Tin Drum. Trans. Ralph Manheim. New York:
    Vintage-Random, 1962.

AN INTRODUCTION, PREFACE, FOREWORD, OR AFTERWORD

Johnson, Thomas H. Introduction. Final Harvest: Emily
    Dickinson's Poems. By Emily Dickinson. Boston: Little,
    Brown, 1961. vii-xiv.

This cites the introduction by Johnson. Notice that a colon is used between the book's main title and subtitle. To cite a poem in this book use this method:

Dickinson, Emily. "A Tooth upon Our Peace." Final Harvest:
    Emily Dickinson's Poems. Ed. Thomas H. Johnson.
    Boston: Little, Brown, 1961. 110.

AN ENCYCLOPEDIA

"Wordsworth, William." The New Encyclopedia Britannica.
    1984 ed.

Because this encyclopedia is organized alphabetically, no page number or other information is given, only the edition number (if available) and date.

AN ARTICLE IN A MAGAZINE

Morrow, Lance. "Pressing the Germy Flesh." Time 8 Nov.
    1999: 164.

The citation for an unsigned article would begin with the title and be alphabetized by the first word of the title other than "a," "an," or "the."

AN ARTICLE IN A SCHOLARLY JOURNAL WITH
CONTINUOUS PAGINATION BEYOND A SINGLE ISSUE

Mahar, William J. "Black English in Early Blackface
    Minstrelsy: A New Interpretation of the Sources of
    Minstrel Show Dialect." American Quarterly 37 (1985):
    260-85.

Because this journal uses continuous pagination instead of separate pagination for each issue, it is not necessary to include the month, season, or number of the issue. Only one of the quarterly issues will have pages numbered 260-85. If you are not certain whether a journal's pages are numbered continuously throughout a volume, supply the month, season, or issue number, as in the next entry.

AN ARTICLE IN A SCHOLARLY JOURNAL WITH
SEPARATE PAGINATION FOR EACH ISSUE

Updike, John. "The Cultural Situation of the American
    Writer." American Studies International 15 (Spring
    1977): 19-28.

By noting the spring issue, the entry saves a reader looking through each issue of the 1977 volume for the correct article on pages 19-28.

AN ARTICLE IN A NEWSPAPER

Ziegler, Philip. "The Lure of Gossip, the Rules of History."
    New York Times 23 Feb. 1986: sec. 7: 1+.

A LECTURE

Tilton, Robert. "The Beginnings of American Studies."
    English 270 class lecture. University of Connecticut,
    Storrs, 12 Mar. 2000.

LETTER, E-MAIL, OR INTERVIEW

Vellenga, Carolyn. Letter to the author. 9 Oct. 1999.
Harter, Stephen P. E-mail to the author. 28 Dec. 1999.
McConagha, Bill. Personal interview [or Telephone
    interview]. 4 March 1998.

If a source appears in print as well as in an electronic format, provide the same publication information you would for printed sources — the title of the electronic source, the medium (such as "CD-ROM"), the name of the distributor, and the date of publication. If it does not appear in print form, or if you don't have all or some of the information, provide as much as you have along with the date of access and the electronic address. You need to provide all the information necessary for your readers to find the source themselves.

CD-ROM Issued Periodically

```
Aaron, Belèn V. "The Death of Theory." Scholarly Book
     Reviews 4.3 (1997): 146-47. ERIC. CD-ROM. Silver-
     Platter. Dec. 1997.
```

CD-ROM Issued in a Single Edition

```
Sideman, Bob, and Donald Sheehy. "The Risk of Spirit."
     Robert Frost: Poems, Life, Legacy. CD-ROM. Vers. 1.0.
     New York: Holt, 1997.
```

Electronic Web Site

```
Cody, David. "Dickens: A Brief Biography." World Wide Web.
     13 Feb. 1998. <http://www.stg.brown.edu/projects/
     hypertext/landow/victorian/dickens/dickensbio1.html>.
```

Electronic Newsgroup

```
Kathman, David. "Shakespeare's Literacy--or Lack of." 3 Mar.
     1998. Newsgroup. <humanities.lit.authors.shakespeare>.
```

Parenthetical References

A list of works cited is not an adequate indication of how you have used sources in your paper. You must also provide the precise location of quotations and other information by using parenthetical references within the text of the paper. You do this by citing the author's name (or the source's title if the work is anonymous) and the page number.

```
Collins points out that "Nabokov was misunderstood by early
reviewers of his work" (28).
```

or

```
Nabokov's first critics misinterpreted his stories
(Collins 28).
```

Either way a reader will find the complete bibliographic entry in the list of works cited under Collins's name and know that the information cited in the paper appears on page 28. Notice that the end punctuation comes after the parentheses.

If you have listed more than one work by the same author, you would add a brief title to the parenthetical reference to distinguish between them. You could also include the full title in your text.

```
Nabokov's first critics misinterpreted his stories (Collins
"Early Reviews" 28).
```

or

```
Collins points out in "Early Reviews of Nabokov's Fiction"
that his early work was misinterpreted by reviewers (28).
```

There can be many variations on what is included in a parenthetical reference, depending on the nature of the entry in the list of works cited. But the general principle is simple enough: provide enough parenthetical information for a reader to find the work in "Works Cited." Examine the sample research paper for more examples of works cited and strategies for including parenthetical references. If you are puzzled by a given situation, ask your reference librarian to show you the *MLA Handbook*.

Incorporating Secondary Sources

The following questions can help you to incorporate materials from critical or biographical essays into your own writing about a literary work. You may initially feel intimidated by the prospect of responding to the arguments of professional writers in your own paper. However, the process will not defeat you if you have clearly formulated your own response to the literary work and are able to distinguish it from the critics' perspectives. Reading what other people have said about a work can help you to develop your own ideas—perhaps, to cite just two examples, by using them as supporting evidence or by arguing with them in order to clarify or qualify their points about the literary work. As you write and discover how to advance your thesis, you'll find yourself participating in a dialogue with the critics. This sort of conversation will help you to improve your thinking and hone your argument.

Keep in mind that the work of professional critics is a means of enriching your understanding of a literary work rather than a substitution for your own analysis and interpretation of that work. Quoting, paraphrasing, or summarizing someone else's perspective does not relieve you of the obligation of choosing a topic, organizing information, developing a thesis, and arguing your point of view by citing sufficient evidence from the text you are examining. These matters are discussed in further detail in Chapter 20. You should also be familiar with the methods for documenting sources that are explained in this chapter; and keep in mind how important it is to avoid plagiarism.

No doubt you won't find everything you read about a work equally useful: some critics' arguments won't address your own areas of concern; some will be too difficult for you to get a handle on; and some will seem wrong-headed. However, much of the criticism you read will serve to make a literary work more accessible and interesting to you, and disagreeing with others' arguments will often help you to develop your own ideas about a work. When you use the work of critics in your own writing, you should consider the following questions. Responding to these questions will help you to ensure that you have a clear understanding of what a critic is arguing about a work, to what extent you agree with that argument, and how you plan to incorporate and respond to the critic's reading in your own paper. The more questions you can ask yourself in response to this list or as a result of your own reading, the more you'll be able to think critically about how you are approaching both the critics and the literary work under consideration.

Questions for Incorporating Secondary Sources

1. Have you read the poem carefully and taken notes of your own impressions before reading any critical perspectives so that your initial insights are not lost to the arguments made by the critics? Have you articulated your own responses to the work in a journal entry prior to reading the critics?
2. Are you sufficiently familiar with the poem that you can determine the accuracy, fairness, and thoroughness of the critic's use of evidence from the work?
3. Have you read the critic's piece carefully? Try summarizing the critic's argument in a brief paragraph. Do you understand the nature and purpose of the critic's argument? Which passages are especially helpful to you? Which seem unclear? Why?
4. Is the critic's reading of the poem similar to or different from your own reading? Why do you agree or disagree? What generational, historical, cultural, or biographical considerations might help to account for any differences between the critic's responses and your own?
5. How has your reading of the critic influenced your understanding of the poem? Do issues that previously seemed unimportant now seem significant? What are these issues, and how does a consideration of them affect your reading of the work?

6. Are you too quickly revising or even discarding your own reading because the critic's perspective seems so polished and persuasive? Are you making use of your reading notes and the responses in your journal entries?

7. How would you classify the critic's approach? Through what kind of lens does the critic view the poem? Is the critical approach formalist, biographical, psychological, historical, mythological, reader-response, deconstructionist, or some combination of these or possibly other strategies? (For a discussion of these approaches, see Chapter 19, "Critical Strategies for Reading.")

8. What biases, if any, can you detect in the critic's approach? How might, for example, a southern critic's reading of "Mending Wall" differ from a northern critic's?

9. Can you determine how other critics have responded to the critic's work? Is the critic's work cited and taken seriously in other critics' books and articles? Is the work dated by having been superseded by subsequent studies?

10. Are any passages or topics that you deem important left out by the critic? Do these omissions qualify or refute the critic's argument?

11. What judgments does the critic seem to make about the work? Is the work regarded, for example, as significant, unified, representative, trivial, inept, or irresponsible? Do you agree with these judgments? If not, can you develop and support a thesis about your difference of opinion?

12. What important disagreements do critics reveal in their approaches to the work? Do you find one perspective more convincing than another? Why? Is there a way of resolving their conflicting views that could serve as a thesis for your paper?

13. Can you extend or qualify the critic's argument to matters in the literary text that are not covered by the critic's perspective? Will this allow you to develop your own topic while acknowledging the critic's useful insights?

14. Have you quoted, paraphrased, or summarized the critic accurately and fairly? Have you avoided misrepresenting the critic's arguments in any way?

15. Are the critic's words, ideas, opinions, and insights adequately acknowledged and documented in the correct format? Do you understand the difference between common knowledge and plagiarism? Have you avoided quoting excessively? Are the quotations smoothly integrated into your own text?

16. Are you certain that your incorporation of the critic's work is for the purpose of developing your paper's thesis rather than for name-dropping or padding your paper? How can you explain to yourself why the critic's work is useful for your argument?

A SAMPLE RESEARCH PAPER

Individuality and Community in Frost's "Mowing" and "Mending Wall"

As you read the paper by Stephanie Tobin (following) on Robert Frost's "Mowing" (p. 341) and "Mending Wall" (p. 342), pay special attention to how she documents outside sources and incorporates other people's ideas into her own argument. How strong do you think her final thesis is? Is it effectively supported by the sources? Has she integrated the sources fully into the paper? How does the paper enhance your understanding of the two poems?

Stephanie's paper follows the format described in the *MLA Handbook for Writers of Research Papers,* 5th ed. This format is discussed in the preceding section on documentation in this chapter (p. 565) and in Chapter 20 in the section on manuscript form (p. 536). Though the sample paper is short, it illustrates many of the techniques and strategies useful for writing an essay that includes secondary sources — including a CD-ROM, a Web site, books, and journals.

Stephanie Tobin

Professor Bass

Poetry 100

November 19, 20--

Individuality and Community in

Frost's "Mowing" and "Mending Wall"

We think of Robert Frost as a poet of New England
who provides portraits of the rural landscape and commu-
nities. But it was not until Frost's second book, North
of Boston (1914), that he truly gave voice to a commu-
nity--in dramatic monologues, dialogues, and narrative
poems. The poems in his first book, A Boy's Will (1913),
are mainly personal lyrics in which the poet encounters
the world and defines it for himself through the writing
of poetry, establishing both an individual perspective
and an aesthetic. A poem from the first book, "Mowing,"
illustrates the theme of individualism, against which a
poem from the second book, "Mending Wall," can be seen
as a widening of the thematic lens to include other
perspectives.

In A Boy's Will, Frost explores the idea of man as a
solitary creature, alone, at work in the natural world.
Poems such as "Mowing" capture the essence of this per-
spective in the very first lines: "There was never a
sound beside the wood but one, / And that was my long
scythe whispering to the ground" (lines 1-2). Jay Parini
describes "Mowing" as a poem in which the "poet culti-
vates a private motion" (121)--the motions both of farm
work, done to support oneself, and the motion of the in-
dividual mind expressed in the poem as it moves down the
page. The sense of privacy and of individually defined
world captured in "Mowing" is central to the book itself.

The dramatic change in perspective evident in North
of Boston illustrates Frost's development as a writer.

Although the second collection was published just one year later, Frost expresses a different perception and understanding of human nature in North of Boston. W. S. Braithwaite wrote in 1915, in a review of the two books, that A Boy's Will and North of Boston "represent a divergent period of development. The earlier book expresses an individuality, the later interprets a community" (2). The focus on community is best demonstrated by the poem "Mending Wall," which presents the reader with an image of two men, separated literally and metaphorically by a wall, yet joined by their dedication to the task they must undertake and the basic human need for boundaries that compels them. The speaker in "Mending Wall" does not forfeit his own individuality, but rather comes to understand it more fully in the context of the society in which he lives, with its traditions and requirements, some of which he tries to see as a game: "Oh, just another kind of outdoor game, / One on a side" (21-22), while still allowing for deeper implications.

Individuality can be defined by one's differences from others, as well as by the creative work of defining, and self-defining, done in poetry. Frost's own experience of life in New England helped shape the perspectives of both individualism and community exemplified in his first two books. When Frost wrote "Mowing" his perspective on life in New England leaned more toward isolation than community. The first few years of farm life were arduous and lonely, and the stark environment provided an atmosphere far more suitable for self-realization than socialization. Prior to the publication of A Boy's Will, Frost had spent "five years of self-enforced solitude" (Meyers 99). "Mowing," which Frost considered to be the best poem in the collection, exemplifies this feeling of isolation and the need for self-exploration. While the poem is, in the literal sense, about the act of cutting grass in order to make hay, it is metaphorically rooted in the idea that man finds meaning and beauty in the world, alone. Parini suggests that the idea that "a man's complete meaning is derived alone, at work[. . .]is a consistent theme in Frost and one that could be explored at length in all his work" (14).

"Mowing" begins with the speaker's observation of the silence that surrounds him as he works. The only sound is the hushed whisper of his scythe as he mows. He writes, "What was it it whispered? I knew not well my-self" (3). The possibility that its meaning could be found in some fanciful imagination of the task is dismissed: "It was no dream of the gift of idle hours, / or easy gold at the hand of fay or elf" (7-8). For Frost, an exaggeration of the action would imply that meaning cannot be found in objective reality, an idea continually argued by his poems.

Instead, this poem asserts a faith in nature as it is, and in the labor necessary to support and define one-self--labor in the natural world, and in the making of poems. This idea is brought forth in the next line: "Anything more than the truth would have seemed to weak / To the earnest love that laid the swale in rows" (9-10). Whether the "fact" that is the "sweetest dream that labour knows" (13) is the actual act of cutting the grass or the verse that is inspired by the simple action, it is something that must be achieved in solitude.

This faith in the work of the individual demonstrated in A Boy's Will is not lost in North of Boston but is redefined. Meyers writes that North of Boston "signaled Frost's change of emphasis from solitary to social beings" (112). In Frost's dedication to his wife he called North of Boston "This Book of People." The

poems in this collection demonstrate an understanding of
the individual, as well as the community in which he
lives. This shift seems a natural development after a
book in which Frost so carefully established his sense of
self and his particular poetic vision and aims.

"Mending Wall," a poem in <u>North of Boston</u>, illus-
trates Frost's shift in focus from the solitary individ-
ual to the interacting society. In the poem, the speaker
and his neighbor set out to perform the annual task of
mending a wall that divides their properties. From the
very beginning, the speaker's tone--at once humorous and
serious--indicates that the real subject of the poem is
not the mending of the wall, which he describes almost
lightheartedly, but the "mending" of the subtle bound-
aries between the speaker and his neighbor. The poem be-
gins, "Something there is that doesn't love a wall, /
that sends the frozen-ground-swell under it" (1-2), yet
this "something," mentioned twice in the poem, refers to
more than the seasonal frost that "spills the upper boul-
ders in the sun" (3). Peter Stanlis writes in a commen-
tary on "Mending Wall" that "the central theme falls
within the philosophical polarities of the speaker and
his neighbor" (1). The man's statement that "good fences
make good neighbors" (26) implies his belief that
boundaries between people will maintain the peace between
them, but the speaker questions this need for boundaries:
"Before I built a wall I'd ask to know / What I was
walling in or walling out" (31-32). With this he brings
the wall into the figurative realm to decipher its
meaning.

His neighbor feels no need for such analysis. But
while articulating a figurative barrier of noncommunica-
tion, and different values, between the men, the poem is
as much about community as individuality; the wall is

what connects as well as separates them. Marie Borroff argues that "the story told in the poem is not about a one-man rebellion against wall mending but about an attempt to communicate" (66). However individuated the men may perceive themselves to be, the common task they must undertake and the ethos it represents join them in a particular social community, the assumptions of which Frost articulates in this poem by both participating in and questioning them.

For the speaker, the task of mending the wall provides an opportunity for thought and questioning rather than serving a utilitarian purpose. While the tradition unites the men "by marking their claims to private property through mutual respect," it is still a barrier (Stanlis 3). Both joined and separated by the fence, the two neighbors walk together and alone, isolated by the physical boundary but connected by their maintenance of the relationship and tradition that created it. As James R. Dawes points out, these "men can only interact when reassured by the constructed alienation of the wall" (300). They keep the wall in place, and thereby keep in place their separate senses of self.

While the speaker is explicitly and lightheartedly critical of the ritual, it is he who "insists on the yearly ritual, as if civilization depends upon the collective activity of making barriers [. . .]. One senses a profound commitment to the act of creating community in the speaker" (Parini 139). Unwilling to placate his neighbor by performing the task in silence, the speaker makes a playful attempt at communication. Explaining that "My apple trees will never get across / And eat the cones under his pines" (24-25), he asks why the wall is necessary. But rather than contemplate the logic behind the boundary, the neighbor rejects the invitation to

communicate: "He only says, 'Good fences make good neigh-
bors'" (26). By refusing to think about the speaker's
question, and choosing to hide behind his own father's
words, he closes any possible window of communication
between them (Monteiro 127), not crossing the barrier of
the wall literally or psychologically. And even while the
speaker jokes about the wall's uselessness, he keeps his
deeper questions to himself. Rather than threaten the
agreed-upon terms of community, he is complicit in keep-
ing them there in actuality, only privately articulating
and upending them, in poetry.

    Mark Van Doren wrote in 1951 that Robert Frost's
poems "are the work of a man who has never stopped ex-
ploring himself" (2); he never stopped exploring the psy-
chology of others, either. "Mowing," which illustrates
his initial focus on individualism, was only a starting
point in Frost's understanding of his place in the world
as a poet. The change of perspective evident in "Mending
Wall" demonstrates his enriched idea of man as an indi-
vidual within a community. Having established a singular
voice and his own moral aesthetic--"The fact is the
sweetest dream that labour knows" (13)--Frost has the
confidence to incorporate different voices into his poems
and to allow his "facts" and values to encounter those of
others, as the two men in "Mending Wall" do across the
wall, each maintaining his own and the other's sense of
personal identity.

Works Cited

Borroff, Marie. "Robert Frost's New Testament: The Uses
　　of Simplicity." Modern Critical Views: Robert Frost.
　　Ed. Harold Bloom. New York: Chelsea House, 1986.
　　63-83.

Braithwaite, W. S. "A Poet of New England." The Boston
　　Evening Transcript 28 April 1915. From Robert Frost:
　　Poems, Life, Legacy. CD-ROM. New York: Holt, 1997.

Dawes, James R. "Masculinity and Transgression in Robert
　　Frost." American Literature 65 (June 1993): 297-312.

Meyer, Michael. Poetry: An Introduction. 3rd ed. Boston:
　　Bedford/St. Martin's, 2001.

Meyers, Jeffrey. Robert Frost: A Biography. New York:
　　Houghton, 1996.

Monteiro, George. Robert Frost and the New England
　　Renaissance. Lexington: UP of Kentucky, 1988.

Parini, Jay. Robert Frost: A Life. New York: Holt, 1999.

Stanlis, Peter J. "Commentary: Mending Wall." Robert
　　Frost: Poems, Life, Legacy. CD-ROM. New York: Holt,
　　1997.

Van Doren, Mark. "Robert Frost's America." Atlantic-
　　Monthly June 1951. Atlantic Unbound <http://www.
　　theatlantic.com/unbound/poetry/frost/vand.htm>.

22

Taking Essay
Examinations

PREPARING FOR AN ESSAY EXAM

Keep Up with the Reading

The best way to prepare for an examination is to keep up with the reading. If you begin the course with a commitment to completing the reading assignments on time, you will not have to read in a frenzy and cram just days before the test. The readings will be a pleasure, not a frantic ordeal. Moreover, you will find that your instructor's comments and class discussion will make more sense to you and that you'll be able to participate in class discussion. As you prepare for the exam you should be rereading texts rather than reading for the first time. It may not be possible to reread everything but you'll at least be able to scan a familiar text and reread passages that are particularly important.

Take Notes and Annotate the Text

Don't rely exclusively on your memory. The typical literature class includes a hefty amount of reading, so unless you take notes, annotate the text with your own comments, and underline important passages, you're likely to forget material that could be useful for responding to an examination question (see pp. 521–523 for a discussion of these matters). The more you can retrieve from your reading the more prepared you'll be for reviewing significant material for the exam. Your notes can be used to illustrate points that were made in class. By briefly quoting an important phrase or line from the text you can provide supporting evidence that will make your argument convincing. Consider, for example, the difference between writing that "Marvell's speaker in 'To His Coy Mistress' says that they won't be able to love after they die" and writing that "the speaker intones that 'The grave's a fine

582

and private place / But none, I think, do there embrace.'" No one expects you to memorize the entire poem, but recalling a few lines here and there can transform a sleepy generality into an illustrative, persuasive argument.

Anticipate Questions

As you review the readings keep in mind the class discussions and the focus provided by your instructor. Very often class discussions and the instructor's emphasis become the basis for essay questions. You may not see the exact same topics on the exam, but you might find that the matters you've discussed in class will serve as a means of responding to an essay question. If, for example, class discussion of Robert Frost's "Mending Wall" (see p. 342) centered on the poem's rural New England setting, you could use that conservative, traditional setting to answer a question such as "Discuss how the conflicts between the speaker and his neighbor are related to the poem's theme." A discussion of the neighbor's rigidity and his firmly entrenched conservative New England attitudes could be connected to his impulse to rebuild the wall between himself and the poem's speaker. The point is that you'll be well prepared for an essay exam when you can shape the material you've studied so that it is responsive to whatever kinds of reasonable questions you encounter on the exam. Reasonable questions? Yes, your instructor is more likely to offer you an opportunity to demonstrate your familiarity with and understanding of the text than to set a trap that, for instance, demands you discuss how Frost's work experience as an adolescent informs the poem when no mention was ever made of that in class or in your reading.

You can also anticipate questions by considering the generic Questions for Responsive Reading and Writing about poetry (p. 47), and the questions in Arguing about Literature (p. 526), along with the Questions for Writing About an Author in Depth (p. 325). Not all of these questions will necessarily be relevant to every work that you read, but they cover a wide range of concerns that should allow you to organize your reading, note taking, and reviewing so that you're not taken by surprise during the exam.

Studying with a classmate or a small group from class can be a stimulating and fruitful means of discovering and organizing the major topics and themes of the course. This method of brainstorming can be useful not only for studying for exams, but through the semester as a way to understand and review course readings. And, finally, you needn't be shy about asking your instructor what types of questions might appear on the exam and how best to study for them. You may not get a very specific reply but almost any information is more useful than none.

TYPES OF EXAMS

Closed-Book versus Open-Book Exams

Closed-book exams require more memorization and recall than open-book exams, which permit you to use your text and perhaps even your notes to answer questions. Obviously, dates, names, definitions, and other details play less of a role in an open-book exam. An open-book exam requires no less preparation, however, because you'll need to be intimately familiar with the texts and the major ideas, themes, and issues that you've studied in order to quickly and efficiently support your points with relevant, specific evidence. Since every student has the same advantage of having access to the text, preparation remains the key to answering the questions. Some students find open-book exams more difficult than closed-book tests, because they risk spending too much time reading, scanning, and searching for material and not enough time writing a response that draws upon the knowledge and understanding that their reading and studying has provided them. It's best to limit the time you allow yourself to review the text and/or notes, so that you devote an adequate amount of time to getting your ideas down on paper.

Essay Questions

Essay questions generally fall within one of the following categories. If you can recognize quickly what is being asked of you, you will be able to respond to them more efficiently.

1. **Explication.** Explication calls for a line-by-line explanation of a passage of poetry or prose that considers, for example, diction, figures of speech, symbolism, sound, form, and theme in an effort to describe how language creates meaning. (For a more detailed discussion of explication see p. 537.)

2. **Definition.** Defining a term and then applying it to a writer or work is a frequent exam exercise. Consider: "Define *romanticism*. To what extent can Keats's "Ode on a Grecian Urn" (p. 79) be regarded as a romantic poem?" This sort of question requires that you first describe what constitutes a romantic literary work and then explain how "Ode on a Grecian Urn" does (or doesn't) fit the bill.

3. **Analysis.** An analytical question focuses on a particular part of a literary work. You might be asked, for example, to analyze the significance of images in Diane Ackerman's poem "A Fine, a Private Place" (p. 69). This sort of question requires you to discuss not only a specific element of the poem but to explain also how that element contributes to the poem's overall effect. (For a more detailed discussion of analysis, see p. 543.)

4. **Comparison and Contrast.** Comparison and contrast calls for a discussion of the similarities and/or differences between writers, works, or

elements of works, for example, "Compare and contrast the tone of the *carpe diem* arguments made by the speaker in Richard Wilbur's 'A Late Aubade' (p. 68) and in Andrew Marvell's 'To His Coy Mistress' (p. 65)." Despite the nearly three hundred years that separate these two poems in setting and circumstances, a discussion of the tone of the speakers' arguments reveals some intriguing similarities and differences. (For a more detailed discussion of comparison and contrast, see p. 548.)

5. **Discussion of a Critical Perspective.** A brief quotation by a critic about a work is usually designed to stimulate a response that requires you to agree with, disagree with, or qualify a critic's perspective. Usually it is not so important whether you agree or disagree with the critic; what matters is the quality of your argument. Think about how you might wrestle with this assessment of Robert Frost written by Lionel Trilling: "The manifest America of Mr. Frost's poems may be pastoral; the actual America is tragic." With some qualifications (surely not all of Frost's poems are "tragic") this could provide a useful way of talking about a poem such as "Mending Wall" (p. 342).

6. **Imaginative Questions.** To a degree every question requires imagination regardless of whether it's being asked or answered. However, some questions require more imaginative leaps to arrive at the center of an issue than others do. Consider, for example, the intellectual agility needed to respond to this question: "Discuss the speakers' attitudes toward the power of imagination in Emily Dickinson's 'To make a prairie it takes a clover and one bee' (p. 293), Frost's 'Mending Wall' (p. 342), and Philip Larkin's 'A Study of Reading Habits' (p. 22)." As tricky as this thematic triangulation may seem, there is plenty to discuss concerning the speakers' varied, complicated, and contradictory attitudes toward the power of an individual's imagination. Or try a simpler but no less interesting version: "How do you think Frost would review Marvell's 'To His Coy Mistress' and Ackerman's 'A Fine, a Private Place'?" Such questions certainly require detailed, reasoned responses, but they also leave room for creativity and even wit.

STRATEGIES FOR WRITING ESSAY EXAMS

Your hands may be sweaty and your heart pounding as you begin the exam, but as long as you're prepared and you keep in mind some basic strategies for writing essay exams, you should be able to respond to questions with confidence and a genuine sense of accomplishment.

1. Before you begin writing, read through the entire exam. If there are choices to be made, make certain you know how many questions must be answered (for instance, only one out of four, not two). Note how many points each question is worth; spend more time on the two worth forty points each and perhaps leave the twenty-point question for last.

2. Budget your time. If there are short-answer questions do not allow them to absorb you so that you cannot do justice to the longer essay questions. Follow the suggested time limits for each question; if none is offered, then create your own schedule in proportion to the points allotted for each question.

3. Depending upon your own sensibilities, you may want to begin with the easiest or hardest questions. It doesn't really matter which you begin with as long as you pace yourself to avoid running out of time.

4. Be sure that you understand the question. Does it ask you to compare and/or contrast, define, analyze, explicate, or use some other approach? Determine how many elements there are to the question so that you don't inadvertently miss part of the question. Do not spend time copying the question.

5. Make some brief notes about how you plan to answer the question; even a simple list of what you'll need to cover can serve as a useful outline.

6. Address the question; avoid unnecessary summaries or irrelevant asides. Focus on the particular elements enumerated or implied by the question.

7. After beginning the essay, write a clear thesis that describes the major topics you will discuss: "Mending Wall" is typical of Frost's concerns as a writer owing to its treatment of setting, tone, and theme.

8. Support and illustrate your answer with specific, relevant references to the text. The more specificity — the more you demonstrate a familiarity with the text (rather than simply providing a summary) — the better the answer.

9. Don't overlap and repeat responses to questions; your instructor will recognize such padding. If two different questions are about the same work or writer, demonstrate the breadth and depth of your knowledge of the subject.

10. Allow time to proofread and to qualify and to add more supporting material if necessary. At this final stage, too, it's worth remembering that Mark Twain liked to remind his readers that the difference between the right word and the almost right word is the difference between lightning and the lightning bug.

A Collection
of Poems

MAYA ANGELOU (B. 1924)

Africa

1975

Thus she had lain
sugar cane sweet
deserts her hair
golden her feet
mountains her breasts   5
two Niles her tears
Thus she has lain
Black through the years.

Over the white seas
rime white and cold   10
brigands ungentled
icicle bold
took her young daughters
sold her strong sons
churched her with Jesus   15
bled her with guns.
Thus she has lain.

Now she is rising
remember her pain
remember the losses   20
her screams loud and vain
remember her riches
her history slain
now she is striding
although she had lain.   25

ANONYMOUS (TRADITIONAL SCOTTISH BALLAD)

Bonny Barbara Allan   *date unknown*

It was in and about the Martinmas° time,
    When the green leaves were afalling,
That Sir John Graeme, in the West Country,
    Fell in love with Barbara Allan.

He sent his men down through the town,   5
    To the place where she was dwelling:
"Oh haste and come to my master dear,
    Gin° ye be Barbara Allan."   *if*

O hooly,° hooly rose she up,   *slowly*
    To the place where he was lying,   10
And when she drew the curtain by:
    "Young man, I think you're dying."

"O it's I'm sick, and very, very sick,
    And 'tis a' for Barbara Allan." —
"O the better for me ye's never be,   15
    Tho your heart's blood were aspilling."

"O dinna ye mind,° young man," she said,   *don't you remember*
    "When ye was in the tavern adrinking,
That ye made the health° gae round and round,   *toasts*
    And slighted Barbara Allan?"   20

He turned his face unto the wall,
    And death was with him dealing:
"Adieu, adieu, my dear friends all,
    And be kind to Barbara Allan."

And slowly, slowly raise her up,   25
    And slowly, slowly left him,
And sighing said she could not stay,
    Since death of life had reft him.

She had not gane a mile but twa,
    When she heard the dead-bell ringing,   30
And every jow° that the dead-bell geid,   *stroke*
    It cried, "Woe to Barbara Allan!"

"O mother, mother, make my bed!
    O make it saft and narrow!
Since my love died for me today,   35
    I'll die for him tomorrow."

1 *Martinmas:* St. Martin's Day, November 11.

ANONYMOUS

Scottsboro°   *1936*

Paper come out — done strewed de news
Seven po' chillun moan deat' house blues,
Seven po' chillun moanin' deat' house blues.
Seven nappy heads wit' big shiny eye
All boun' in jail and framed to die,   5
All boun' in jail and framed to die.

Messin' white woman — snake lyin' tale
Hang and burn and jail wit' no bail.
Dat hang and burn and jail wit' no bail.
Worse ol' crime in white folks' lan'   10

Scottsboro: This blues song refers to the 1931 arrest of nine black youths in Scottsboro, Alabama, who were charged with raping two white women. All nine were acquitted after several trials, but a few of them had already been sentenced to death when this song was written.

Black skin coverin' po' workin' man,
Black skin coverin' po' workin' man.

Judge and jury — all in de stan'
Lawd, biggety name for same lynchin' ban'
Lawd, biggety name for same lynchin' ban'.   15
White folks and nigger in great co't house
Like cat down cellar wit' nohole mouse.
Like cat down cellar wit' nohole mouse.

W. H. AUDEN (1907–1973)

The Unknown Citizen   *1940*

(To JS/07/M/378
This Marble Monument
Is Erected by the State)

He was found by the Bureau of Statistics to be
One against whom there was no official complaint,
And all the reports on his conduct agree
That, in the modern sense of an old-fashioned word, he was a saint,
For in everything he did he served the Greater Community.   5
Except for the War till the day he retired
He worked in a factory and never got fired,
But satisfied his employers, Fudge Motors Inc.
Yet he wasn't a scab or odd in his views,
For his Union reports that he paid his dues,   10
(Our report on his Union shows it was sound)
And our Social Psychology workers found
That he was popular with his mates and liked a drink.
The Press are convinced that he bought a paper every day
And that his reactions to advertisements were normal in every way. 15
Policies taken out in his name prove that he was fully insured,
And his Health-card shows he was once in hospital but left it cured.
Both Producers Research and High-Grade Living declare
He was fully sensible to the advantages of the Installment Plan
And had everything necessary to the Modern Man,   20
A phonograph, radio, car and a frigidaire.
Our researchers into Public Opinion are content
That he held the proper opinions for the time of year;
When there was peace, he was for peace; when there was war, he went.
He was married and added five children to the population,   25
Which our Eugenist says was the right number for a parent of his generation,
And our teachers report that he never interfered with their education.
Was he free? Was he happy? The question is absurd:
Had anything been wrong, we should certainly have heard.

MARGARET AVISON (B. 1918)

Tennis

Service is joy, to see or swing. Allow
All tumult to subside. Then tensest winds
Buffet, brace, viol° and sweeping bow.
Courts are for love and volley. No one minds
The cruel ellipse of service and return,   5
Dancing white galliardes° at tape or net
Till point, on the wire's tip, or the long burn-
ing arc to nethercourt° marks game and set.
Purpose apart, perched like an umpire, dozes,
Dreams golden balls whirring through indigo.   10
Clay blurs the whitewash but day still encloses
The albinos, bonded in their flick and flow.
Playing in musicked gravity, the pair
Score liquid Euclids° in foolscaps of air.

3 *viol:* A stringed musical instrument.   6 *galliardes:* Spirited dance movements.   8 *nethercourt:* Down court.   14 *Euclids:* Geometric shapes.

WILLIAM BLAKE (1757–1827)

The Garden of Love

I went to the Garden of Love,
And saw what I never had seen:
A Chapel was built in the midst,
Where I used to play on the green.

And the gates of this Chapel were shut,   5
And "Thou shalt not" writ over the door;
So I turned to the Garden of Love
That so many sweet flowers bore;

And I saw it was filled with graves,
And tomb-stones where flowers should be;   10
And Priests in black gowns were walking their rounds,
And binding with briars my joys and desires.

WILLIAM BLAKE (1757–1827)

Infant Sorrow

My mother groand! my father wept.
Into the dangerous world I leapt:

Helpless naked piping loud:
Like a fiend hid in a cloud.

Struggling in my fathers hands:
Striving against my swadling bands
Bound and weary I thought best
To sulk upon my mothers breast.

ROBERT BLY (B. 1926)

Snowfall in the Afternoon   *1962*

1
The grass is half-covered with snow.
It was the sort of snowfall that starts in late afternoon.
And now the little houses of the grass are growing dark.

2
If I reached my hands down, near the earth,
I could take handfuls of darkness!   5
A darkness was always there, which we never noticed.

3
As the snow grows heavier, the cornstalks fade farther away,
And the barn moves nearer to the house.
The barn moves all alone in the growing storm.

4
The barn is full of corn, and moving toward us now,   10
Like a hulk blown toward us in a storm at sea;
All the sailors on deck have been blind for many years.

LOUISE BOGAN (1897–1970)

Women   *1923*

Women have no wilderness in them,
They are provident instead,
Content in the tight hot cell of their hearts
To eat dusty bread.

They do not see cattle cropping red winter grass,   5
They do not hear
Snow water going down under culverts
Shallow and clear.

They wait, when they should turn to journeys,
They stiffen, when they should bend.   10

They use against themselves that benevolence
To which no man is friend.

They cannot think of so many crops to a field
Or of clean wood cleft by an axe.
Their love is an eager meaninglessness   15
Too tense, or too lax.

They hear in every whisper that speaks to them
A shout and a cry.
As like as not, when they take life over their door-sills
They should let it go by.   20

ROO BORSON (B. 1952)

Talk   *1981*

The shops, the streets are full of old men
who can't think of a thing to say anymore.
Sometimes, looking at a girl, it
almost occurs to them, but they can't make it out,
they go pawing toward it through the fog.   5

The young men are still jostling shoulders
as they walk along, tussling at one another with words.
They're excited by talk, they can still see the danger.
The old women, thrifty with words,
haggling for oranges, their mouths   10
take bites out of the air. They know the value of oranges.
They had to learn everything
on their own.

The young women are the worst off, no one has bothered
to show them things.   15
You can see their minds on their faces,
they are like little lakes before a storm.
They don't know it's confusion that makes them sad.
It's lucky in a way though, because the young men take
a look of confusion for inscrutability, and this   20
excites them and makes them want to own
this face they don't understand,
something to be tinkered with at their leisure.

ANNE BRADSTREET (C. 1612–1672)

Before the Birth of One of Her Children   *1678*

All things within this fading world hath end,
Adversity doth still our joys attend;
No ties so strong, no friends so dear and sweet,

But with death's parting blow is sure to meet.
The sentence past is most irrevocable,   5
A common thing, yet oh, inevitable.
How soon, my Dear, death may my steps attend,
How soon't may be thy lot to lose thy friend,
We both are ignorant, yet love bids me
These farewell lines to recommend to thee,   10
That when that knot's untied that made us one,
I may seem thine, who is effect am none.
And if I see not half my days that's due,
What nature would, God grant to yours and you;
The many faults that well you know I have   15
Let be interred in my oblivious grave;
If any worth or virtue were in me,
Let that live freshly in thy memory
And when thou feel'st no grief, as I no harms,
Yet love thy dead, who long lay in thine arms,   20
And when thy loss shall be repaid with gains
Look to my little babes, my dear remains.
And if thou love thyself, or loved'st me,
These O protect from stepdame's° injury.   *stepmother's*
And if chance to thine eyes shall bring this verse,   25
With some sad sighs honor my absent hearse;
And kiss this paper for thy love's dear sake,
Who with salt tears this last farewell did take.

GWENDOLYN BROOKS (1917–2000)

The Mother   *1945*

Abortions will not let you forget.
You remember the children you got that you did not get,
The damp small pulps with a little or with no hair,
The singers and workers that never handled the air.
You will never neglect or beat   5
Them, or silence or buy with a sweet.
You will never wind up the sucking-thumb
Or scuttle off ghosts that come.
You will never leave them, controlling your luscious sigh,
Return for a snack of them, with gobbling mother-eye.   10

I have heard in the voices of the wind the voices of my dim
          killed children
I have contracted. I have eased
My dim dears at the breasts they could never suck.
I have said, Sweets, if I sinned, if I seized
Your luck   15
And your lives from your unfinished reach,
If I stole your births and your names,

Your straight baby tears and your games,
Your stilted or lovely loves, your tumults, your marriages, aches,
    and your deaths,
If I poisoned the beginnings of your breaths,   20
Believe that even in my deliberateness I was not deliberate.
Though why should I whine,
Whine that the crime was other than mine? —
Since anyhow you are dead.
Or rather, or instead,   25
You were never made.

But that too, I am afraid,
Is faulty: oh, what shall I say, how is the truth to be said?
You were born, you had body, you died.
It is just that you never giggled or planned or cried.   30

Believe me, I loved you all.
Believe me, I knew you, though faintly, and I loved, I loved you
All.

ROBERT BROWNING (1812–1889)

Home-Thoughts, from Abroad   *1845*

1
Oh, to be in England
Now that April's there,
And whoever wakes in England
Sees, some morning, unaware,
That the lowest boughs and the brushwood sheaf   5
Round the elm-tree bole are in tiny leaf,
While the chaffinch sings on the orchard bough
In England — now!

2
And after April, when May follows,
And the whitethroat° builds, and all the swallows!   *sparrow*   10
Hark, where my blossomed pear-tree in the hedge
Leans to the field and scatters on the clover
Blossoms and dewdrops — at the bent spray's edge —
That's the wise thrush; he sings each song twice over,
Lest you should think he never could recapture   15
The first fine careless rapture!
And though the fields look rough with hoary dew
All will be gay when noontide wakes anew
The buttercups, the little children's dower
— Far brighter than this gaudy melon-flower!   20

ROBERT BROWNING (1812–1889)
Meeting at Night

1845

The gray sea and the long black land;
And the yellow half-moon large and low;
And the startled little waves that leap
In firey ringlets from their sleep,
As I gain the cove with pushing prow,   5
And quench its speed i' the slushy sand.

Then a mile of warm sea-scented beach;
Three fields to cross till a farm appears;
A tap at the pane, the quick sharp scratch
And blue spurt of a lighted match,   10
And a voice less loud, through its joys and fears,
Than the two hearts beating each to each!

ROBERT BROWNING (1812–1889)
Parting at Morning

1845

Round the cape of a sudden came the sea,
And the sun looked over the mountain's rim:
And straight was a path of gold for him,
And the need of a world of men for me.

GEORGE GORDON, LORD BYRON (1788–1824)
She Walks in Beauty

1814

From Hebrew Melodies

I
She walks in Beauty, like the night
    Of cloudless climes and starry skies;
And all that's best of dark and bright
    Meet in her aspect and her eyes:
Thus mellowed to that tender light   5
    Which Heaven to gaudy day denies.

II
One shade the more, one ray the less,
    Had half impaired the nameless grace
Which waves in every raven tress,
    Or softly lightens o'er her face;   10
Where thoughts serenely sweet express,
    How pure, how dear their dwelling-place.

III
And on that cheek, and o'er that brow,
    So soft, so calm, yet eloquent,
The smiles that win, the tints that glow,   15
    But tell of days in goodness spent,
A mind at peace with all below,
    A heart whose love is innocent!

SAMUEL TAYLOR COLERIDGE (1772–1834)

Sonnet to the River Otter

1797

Dear native brook! wild streamlet of the West!
   How many various-fated years have past,
   What happy, and what mournful hours, since last
I skimmed the smooth thin stone along thy breast,
Numbering its light leaps! yet so deep imprest   5
Sink the sweet scenes of childhood, that mine eyes
   I never shut amid the sunny ray,
But straight with all their tints thy waters rise,
   Thy crossing plank, thy marge with willows gray,
And bedded sand that, veined with various dyes,   10
Gleamed through thy bright transparence! On my way,
   Visions of childhood! oft have ye beguiled
Lone manhood's cares, yet waking fondest sighs:
   Ah! that once more I were a careless child!

SAMUEL TAYLOR COLERIDGE (1772–1834)

Kubla Khan: or, a Vision in a Dream°

1798

In Xanadu did Kubla Khan°
    A stately pleasure-dome decree:
Where Alph, the sacred river, ran
Through caverns measureless to man
    Down to a sunless sea.   5

So twice five miles of fertile ground
With walls and towers were girdled round:
And here were gardens bright with sinuous rills
Where blossomed many an incense-bearing tree;

Vision in a Dream: This poem came to Coleridge in an opium-induced dream, but he was in-
terrupted by a visitor while writing it down. He was later unable to remember the rest of the
poem.

1 *Kubla Khan:* The historical Kublai Khan (1216–1294, grandson of Genghis Khan) was the
founder of the Mongol dynasty in China.

And there were forests ancient as the hills,   10
Enfolding sunny spots of greenery.

But oh! that deep romantic chasm which slanted
Down the green hill athwart a cedarn cover!°
A savage place! as holy and enchanted
As e'er beneath a waning moon was haunted   15
By woman wailing for her demon-lover!
And from this chasm, with ceaseless turmoil seething,
As if this earth in fast thick pants were breathing,
A mighty fountain momently was forced,
Amid whose swift half-intermitted burst   20
Huge fragments vaulted like rebounding hail,
Of chaffy grain beneath the thresher's flail:
And 'mid these dancing rocks at once and ever
It flung up momently the sacred river.
Five miles meandering with a mazy motion   25
Through wood and dale the sacred river ran,
Then reached the caverns measureless to man,
And sank in tumult to a lifeless ocean:
And 'mid this tumult Kubla heard from far
Ancestral voices prophesying war!   30
      The shadow of the dome of pleasure
      Floated midway on the waves;
      Where was heard the mingled measure
      From the fountain and the caves.
It was a miracle of rare device,   35
A sunny pleasure-dome with caves of ice!

      A damsel with a dulcimer
      In a vision once I saw:
      It was an Abyssinian maid,
      And on her dulcimer she played,   40
      Singing of Mount Abora.
      Could I revive within me
      Her symphony and song,
      To such a deep delight 'twould win me,
That with music loud and long,   45
I would build that dome in air,
That sunny dome! those caves of ice!
And all who heard should see them there,
And all should cry, Beware! Beware!
His flashing eyes, his floating hair!   50
Weave a circle round him thrice,
And close your eyes with holy dread,
For he on honey-dew hath fed,
And drunk the milk of Paradise.

13 *athwart . . . cover:* Spanning a grove of cedar trees.

PAM CROW (B. 1957)

Meat Science   *1998*

I'm remembering the time
you sat on a roof in Wisconsin
to get away for a smoke,
and a drunk senior stumbled
to the edge of the roof to take a piss   5
then folded his body down next to yours.
Below, a faint sound of drums
and bass throbbed through the house.
"Pigs," said the boy, "are as smart
as we are. Smarter. If you don't   10
believe me, look into a pig's eyes
sometime. You'll see
what I'm talking about."
His hair was yellow, freshly shorn,
his eyes were blue.   15
He had graduated that morning
with a bachelor's degree in Meat Science.

You learned all about pigs that night,
feeding, breeding, slaughter. "With this degree
I can go anywhere: Oscar Meyer, Hormel . . ."   20
You both looked at the stars, remarked
how the moon glowed, a thin, cool dime
on such a warm night. "I shook hands
with my father this morning. Mom took
a picture of me in my cap and gown."   25
You couldn't remember the particular
breed of pig he had raised, but it had
velvet ears the size of a man's hand.
Each year there was the day his father
killed a bottle of Jim Beam. Maybe   30
there was a sickness in the weaning
pigs, or a shortfall in production.
He ran to the barn as fast
as he could, his father bellowing
behind him, swinging a black belt   35
from one clenched fist.
The boy dove into the pigs' pen
and was hidden by quiet sows,
their ears a cover for his face.
You sat blowing smoke   40
at the stars all night long,
while the boy drank, and cried,
and shaped his story
into something he could hold.

VICTOR HERNÁNDEZ CRUZ (B. 1949)

Anonymous

1982

And if I lived in those olden times
With a funny name like Choicer or
Henry Howard, Earl of Surrey, what chimes!
I would spend my time in search of rhymes
Make sure the measurement termination surprise   5
In the court of kings snapping till woo sunrise
Plus always be using the words *alas* and *hath*
And not even knowing that that was my path
Just think on the Lower East Side of Manhattan
It would have been like living in satin   10
Alas! The projects hath not covered the river
Thou see-est vision to make thee quiver
Hath I been delivered to that "wildernesse"
So past
I would have been the last one in the   15
Dance to go
Taking note the minuet so slow
All admire my taste
Within thou *mambo* of much more haste.

COUNTEE CULLEN (1903–1946)

Yet Do I Marvel

1925

I doubt not God is good, well-meaning, kind,
And did He stoop to quibble could tell why
The little buried mole continues blind,
Why flesh that mirrors Him must some day die,
Make plain the reason tortured Tantalus   5
Is baited by the fickle fruit, declare
If merely brute caprice dooms Sisyphus
To struggle up a never-ending stair.
Inscrutable His ways are, and immune
To catechism by a mind too strewn   10
With petty cares to slightly understand
What awful brain compels His awful hand.
Yet do I marvel at this curious thing:
To make a poet black, and bid him sing!

E. E. CUMMINGS (1894–1962)

Buffalo Bill 's°

Buffalo Bill 's
defunct
    who used to
    ride a watersmooth-silver
                  stallion 5
and break onetwothreefourfive pigeonsjustlikethat
                Jesus
he was a handsome man
          and what i want to know is
how do you like your blueeyed boy 10
Mister Death

Buffalo Bill: William Frederick Cody (1846–1917) was an American frontier scout and Indian killer turned international circus showman with his Wild West show, which employed Sitting Bull and Annie Oakley.

MARY DI MICHELE (B. 1949)

As in the Beginning

A man has two hands and when one
gets caught on the belt and his fingers
are amputated and then patched
he cannot work. His hands are insured
however so he gets some money 5
for the work his hands have done before.
If he loses a finger he gets a flat sum
of $250 for each digit &/or $100 for a joint
missing for the rest of his stay on earth,
like an empty stool at a beggar's banquet. 10
When the hands are my father's hands
it makes me cry although my pen must keep scratching
its head across the page of another night.
To you my father is a stranger
and perhaps you think the insurance paid is enough. 15

Give me my father's hands when they are not broken
and swollen,
give me my father's hands, young again,
and holding the hands of my mother,
give me my father's hands still brown and uncallused, 20
beautiful hands that broke bread for us at table,
hands as smooth as marble and naked as the morning,
give me hands without a number tattooed at the wrist,
without the copper sweat of clinging change,
give my father's hands as they were in the beginning, 25

whole,
open,
warm
and without fear.

GREGORY DJANIKIAN (B. 1949)

When I First Saw Snow

Tarrytown, N.Y.

Bing Crosby was singing "White Christmas"
    on the radio, we were staying at my aunt's house
    waiting for papers, my father was looking for a job.
We had trimmed the tree the night before,
    sap had run on my fingers and for the first time   5
    I was smelling pine wherever I went.
Anais, my cousin, was upstairs in her room
    listening to Danny and the Juniors.
Haigo was playing Monopoly with Lucy, his sister,
    Buzzy, the boy next door, had eyes for her   10
    and there was a rattle of dice, a shuffling
    of Boardwalk, Park Place, Marvin Gardens.
There were red bows on the Christmas tree.
It had snowed all night.
My boot buckles were clinking like small bells   15
    as I thumped to the door and out
    onto the gray planks of the porch dusted with snow.
The world was immaculate, new,
    even the trees had changed color,
    and when I touched the snow on the railing   20
    I didn't know what I had touched, ice or fire.
I heard, "I'm dreaming . . ."
I heard, "At the hop, hop, hop . . . oh, baby."
I heard "B & O" and the train in my imagination
    was whistling through the great plains.   25
And I was stepping off,
I was falling deeply into America.

JOHN DONNE (1572–1631)

The Apparition

When by thy scorn, O murderess, I am dead,
    And that thou thinkst thee free
From all solicitation from me,
Then shall my ghost come to thy bed,
And thee, feigned vestal, in worse arms shall see;   5
Then thy sick taper° will begin to wink,   *candle*

And he, whose thou art then, being tired before,
Will, if thou stir, or pinch to wake him, think
      Thou call'st for more,
And in false sleep will from thee shrink.   10
And then, poor aspen wretch, neglected, thou,
Bathed in a cold quicksilver sweat, wilt lie
      A verier° ghost than I.   *truer*
What I will say, I will not tell thee now,
Lest that preserve thee; and since my love is spent,   15
I had rather thou shouldst painfully repent,
Than by my threatenings rest still innocent.

JOHN DONNE (1572–1631)

Batter My Heart   *1610*

Batter my heart, three-personed God; for You
As yet but knock, breathe, shine, and seek to mend;
That I may rise and stand, o'erthrow me, and bend
Your force, to break, blow, burn, and make me new.
I, like an usurped town, to another due,   5
Labor to admit You, but Oh, to no end!
Reason, Your viceroy in me, me should defend,
But is captived, and proves weak or untrue.
Yet dearly I love You, and would be loved fain.
But am betrothed unto Your enemy: 10
Divorce me, untie, or break that knot again,
Take me to You, imprison me, for I,
Except You enthrall me, never shall be free,
Nor ever chaste, except You ravish me.

JOHN DONNE (1572–1631)

The Flea   *1633*

Mark but this flea, and mark in this°
How little that which thou deny'st me is;
It sucked me first, and now sucks thee,
And in this flea our two bloods mingled be;
Thou know'st that this cannot be said   5
A sin, nor shame, nor loss of maidenhead,
      Yet this enjoys before it woo,
        And pampered swells with one blood made of two,
        And this, alas, is more than we would do.°

Oh stay, three lives in one flea spare,   10
Where we almost, yea more than, married are.

1 *mark in this:* Take note of the moral lesson in this object.   9 *more than we would do:* That is, if we do not join our blood in conceiving a child.

This flea is you and I, and this
Our marriage bed, and marriage temple is;
Though parents grudge, and you, we're met
And cloistered in these living walls of jet.   15
        Though use° make you apt to kill me,   *habit*
        Let not to that, self-murder added be,
        And sacrilege, three sins in killing three.

Cruel and sudden, hast thou since
Purpled thy nail in blood of innocence?   20
Wherein could this flea guilty be,
Except in that drop which it sucked from thee?
Yet thou triumph'st, and say'st that thou
Find'st not thyself, nor me, the weaker now;
        'Tis true; then learn how false, fears be;   25
        Just so much honor, when thou yield'st to me,
        Will waste, as this flea's death took life from thee.

DAVID DONNELL (B. 1939)

The Canadian Prairie's View of Literature   *1983*

First of all it has to be anecdotal; ideas don't exist;
themes struggle dimly out of accrued material like the shadow
of a slow caterpillar struggling out of a large cocoon;
even this image itself is somewhat urban inasmuch is it suggests
the tree-bordered streets of small southern Ontario towns;   5
towns are alright; Ontario towns are urban; French towns are European;
the action should take place on a farm between April and October;
nature is quiet during winter; when it snows, there's a lot of it;
the poem shimmers in the school-teacher's head like an image
of being somewhere else without a railway ticket to return;   10
the novel shifts its haunches in the hot reporter's head
and surveys the possible relationship between different farms;
sometimes the action happens in the beverage rooms and cheap
hotels area of a small town that has boomed into a new city;
Indians and Metis appear in the novel wearing the marks   15
of their alienation like a sullen confusion of the weather;
the town drunk appears looking haggard and the town mayor
out ward-heeling and smelling women's hands buys him a drink;
a woman gets married and another woman has a child;
the child is not old enough to plow a field and therefore   20
does not become a focus of interest except as another mouth;
they sit around with corn shucks in the head and wonder
who they should vote for, the question puzzles them,
vote for the one with the cracked shoes, he's a good boy,
or the one who jumped over six barrels at a local dance;   25
the fewer buildings they have, the more nationalistic they become
like a man who has stolen all his life accused of cheating;
above all, they dislike the east which at least gives them form

and allows their musings and discontents to flower into rancour;
musing and rancorous, I turn down the small side streets of Galt,   30
Ontario, afternoon light, aged twelve, past South Water Street,
not quite like Rimbaud leaving Charleville,
my hands in my windbreaker pockets like white stones,
and promise myself once again that when I get to the city
everything will happen, I will learn all of its history   35
and become the best writer they have ever dreamed of,
I'll make them laugh and I'll even make them cry,
I'll drink their whiskey and make love to all their wives,
the words tumbling out of my mouth as articulate as the young Hector,
the corn under my shirt awkward a little rough light brown dry   40
and making me itch at times

GEORGE ELIOT (MARY ANN EVANS / 1819–1880)

In a London Drawingroom   *1865*

The sky is cloudy, yellowed by the smoke.
For view there are the houses opposite,
Cutting the sky with one long line of wall
Like solid fog: far as the eye can stretch
Monotony of surface and of form   5
Without a break to hang a guess upon.
No bird can make a shadow as it flies,
For all its shadow, as in ways o'erhung
By thickest canvas, where the golden rays
Are clothed in hemp. No figure lingering   10
Pauses to feed the hunger of the eye
Or rest a little on the lap of life.
All hurry on and look upon the ground
Or glance unmarking at the passersby.
The wheels are hurrying, too, cabs, carriages   15
All closed, in multiplied identity.
The world seems one huge prison-house and court
Where men are punished at the slightest cost,
With lowest rate of color, warmth, and joy.

THOMAS HARDY (1840–1928)

Hap   *1866*

If but some vengeful god would call to me
From up the sky, and laugh: "Thou suffering thing,
Know that thy sorrow is my ecstasy,
That thy love's loss is my hate's profiting!"

Then would I bear it, clench myself, and die,   5
Steeled by the sense of ire unmerited;

Half-eased in that a Powerfuller than I
Had willed and meted me the tears I shed.

But not so. How arrives it joy lies slain,
And why unblooms the best hope ever sown?   10
—Crass Casualty obstructs the sun and rain,
And dicing Time for gladness casts a moan. . . .
These purblind Doomsters had as readily strown
Blisses about my pilgrimage as pain.

THOMAS HARDY (1840–1928)

In Time of "The Breaking of Nations"°   *1915*

1
Only a man harrowing clods
    In a slow silent walk
With an old horse that stumbles and nods
    Half asleep as they stalk.

2
Only thin smoke without flame   5
    From the heaps of couch-grass;
Yet this will go onward the same
    Though Dynasties pass.

3
Yonder a maid and her wight°   *man*
    Come whispering by: 10
War's annals will cloud into night
    Ere their story die.

The Breaking of Nations: See Jeremiah 51:20: "Thou art my battle axe and weapons of war: for with thee will I break in pieces the nations, and with thee will I destroy kingdoms."

JOY HARJO (B. 1951)

Fishing   *1991*

This is the longest day of the year, on the Illinois River or a similar river in
the same place. Cicadas are part of the song as they praise their invisible
ancestors while fish blinking back the relentless sun in Oklahoma circle in
the muggy river of life. They dare the fisher to come and get them. Fish too
anticipate the game of fishing. Their ancestors perfected the moves, sent   5
down stories that appear as electrical impulse when sunlight hits water.
The hook carries great symbology in the coming of age, and is crucial to
the making of warriors. The greatest warriors are those who dangle a
human for hours on a string, break sacred water for the profanity of air
then snap fiercely back into pearly molecules that describe fishness. They   10
smell me as I walk the banks with fishing pole, nightcrawlers and a
promise I made to that old friend Louis to fish with him this summer. This

is the only place I can keep that promise, inside a poem as familiar to him
as the banks of his favorite fishing place. I try not to let the fish see me see
them as they look for his tracks on the soft earth made of fossils and ashes.   15
I hear the burble of fish talk: When is that old Creek coming back? He
was the one we loved to tease most, we liked his songs and once in awhile
he gave us a good run. Last night I dreamed I tried to die, I was going to
look for Louis. It was rather comical. I worked hard to muster my last
breath, then lay down in the summer, along the banks of the last mythic   20
river, my pole and tackle box next to me. What I thought was my last
breath floated off as a cloud making an umbrella of grief over my relatives.
How embarrassing when the next breath came, and then the next. I reeled
in one after another, as if I'd caught a bucket of suckers instead of bass. I
guess it wasn't my time, I explained, and went fishing anyway as a liar   25
and I know most fishers to be liars most of the time. Even Louis when it
came to fishing, or even dying. The leap between the sacred and profane is
as thin as a fishing line, and is part of the mystery on this river of life, as is
the way our people continue to make warriors in the strangest of times. I
save this part of the poem for the fish camp next to the oldest spirits whose   30
dogs bark to greet visitors. It's near Louis's favorite spot where the
wisest and fattest fish laze. I'll meet him there.

FRANCES E. W. HARPER (1825–1911)

Learning to Read   *1872*

Very soon the Yankee teachers
   Came down and set up school;
But oh! how the Rebs did hate it, —
   It was agin' their rule

Our masters always tried to hide   5
   Book learning from our eyes;
Knowledge did'nt agree with slavery —
   'Twould make us all too wise.

But some of us would try to steal
   A little from the book,   10
And put the words together,
   And learn by hook or crook.

I remember Uncle Caldwell,
   Who took pot-liquor fat
And greased the pages of his book,   15
   And hid it in his hat.

And had his master ever seen
   The leaves upon his head,
He'd have thought them greasy papers,
   But nothing to be read.   20

And there was Mr. Turner's Ben
   Who heard the children spell,

And picked the words right up by heart,
  And learned to read 'em well.

Well the Northern folks kept sending   25
  The Yankee teachers down
And they stood right up and helped us,
  Though Rebs did sneer and frown,

And, I longed to read my Bible,
  For precious words it said;   30
But when I begun to learn it,
  Folks just shook their heads,

And said there is no use trying,
  Oh! Chloe, you're too late;
But as I was rising sixty,   35
  I had no time to wait.

So I got a pair of glasses,
  And straight to work I went,
And never stopped till I could read
  The hymns and Testament.   40

Then I got a little cabin —
  A place to call my own —
And I felt as independent
  As the queen upon her throne.

Anthony Hecht (b. 1923)

The Dover Bitch°   *1968*

A Criticism of Life

So there stood Matthew Arnold and this girl
With the cliffs of England crumbling away behind them,
And he said to her, "Try to be true to me,
And I'll do the same for you, for things are bad
All over, etc., etc."   5
Well now, I knew this girl. It's true she had read
Sophocles in a fairly good translation
And caught that bitter allusion to the sea,°
But all the time he was talking she had in mind
The notion of what his whiskers would feel like   10
On the back of her neck. She told me later on
That after a while she got to looking out
At the lights across the channel, and really felt sad,
Thinking of all the wine and enormous beds

The Dover Bitch: A parody of Arnold's poem "Dover Beach" (see p. 95).   8 *allusion to the sea:*
Lines 9–18 in "Dover Beach" refer to Sophocles' *Antigone*, lines 583–591.

And blandishments in French and the perfumes.   15
And then she got really angry. To have been brought
All the way down from London, and then be addressed
As a sort of mournful cosmic last resort
Is really tough on a girl, and she was pretty.
Anyway, she watched him pace the room   20
And finger his watch-chain and seem to sweat a bit,
And then she said one or two unprintable things.
But you mustn't judge her by that. What I mean to say is,
She's really all right. I still see her once in a while
And she always treats me right. We have a drink   25
And I give her a good time, and perhaps it's a year
Before I see her again, but there she is,
Running to fat, but dependable as they come.
And sometimes I bring her a bottle of *Nuit d'Amour.*

GEORGE HERBERT (1593–1633)

The Collar   *1633*

I struck the board° and cried, "No more;	*table*
I will abroad!	
What? shall I ever sigh and pine?	
My lines and life are free, free as the road,	
Loose as the wind, as large as store.°	5
Shall I be still in suit?°	*serving another*
Have I no harvest but a thorn	
To let me blood, and not restore	
What I have lost with cordial° fruit?	*restorative*
Sure there was wine	10
Before my sighs did dry it; there was corn	
Before my tears did drown it.	
Is the year only lost to me?	
Have I no bays° to crown it,	*triumphal wreaths*
No flowers, no garlands gay? All blasted?	15
All wasted?	
Not so, my heart; but there is fruit,	
And thou hast hands.	
Recover all thy sigh-blown age	
On double pleasures: leave thy cold dispute	20
Of what is fit, and not. Forsake thy cage,	
Thy rope of sands,	
Which petty thoughts have made, and made to thee	
Good cable, to enforce and draw,	
And be thy law,	25
While thou didst wink and wouldst not see.	
Away! take heed;	

5 *store:* A storehouse or warehouse.

I will abroad.
Call in thy death's-head° there; tie up thy fears.
      He that forbears   30
        To suit and serve his need,
        Deserves his load."
But as I raved and grew more fierce and wild
        At every word,
Methought I heard one calling, *Child!*   35
        And I replied, *My Lord.*

29 *death's-head:* A skull, reminder of mortality.

LINDA HOGAN (b. 1947)

Song for My Name

1979

Before sunrise
think of brushing out an old woman's
dark braids.
Think of your hands,
fingertips on the soft hair.   5

If you have this name,
your grandfather's dark hands
lead horses toward the wagon
and a cloud of dust follows,
ghost of silence.   10

That name is full of women
with black hair
and men with eyes like night.
It means no money
tomorrow.   15

Such a name my mother loves
while she works gently
in the small house.
She is a white dove
and in her own land   20
the mornings are pale,
birds sing into the white curtains
and show off their soft breasts.

If you have a name like this,
there's never enough water.   25
There is too much heat.
When lightning strikes, rain
refuses to follow.
It's my name,
that of a woman living   30
between the white moon

and the red sun, waiting to leave.
It's the name that goes with me
back to earth
no one else can touch.   35

M. Carl Holman (1919–1988)

Mr. Z   1967

Taught early that his mother's skin was the sign of error,
He dressed and spoke the perfect part of honor;
Won scholarships, attended the best schools,
Disclaimed kinship with jazz and spirituals;
Chose prudent, raceless views for each situation,   5
Or when he could not cleanly skirt dissension,
Faced up to the dilemma, firmly seized
Whatever ground was Anglo-Saxonized.

In diet, too, his practice was exemplary:
Of pork in its profane forms he was wary;   10
Expert in vintage wines, sauces and salads,
His palate shrank from cornbread, yams and collards.

He was as careful whom he chose to kiss:
His bride had somewhere lost her Jewishness,
But kept her blue eyes; an Episcopalian   15
Prelate proclaimed them matched chameleon.
Choosing the right addresses, here, abroad,
They shunned those places where they might be barred;
Even less anxious to be asked to dine
Where hosts catered to kosher accent or exotic skin.   20

And so he climbed, unclogged by ethnic weights,
An airborne plant, flourishing without roots.
Not one false note was struck — until he died:
His subtly grieving widow could have flayed
The obit writers, ringing crude changes on a clumsy phrase: 25
"One of the most distinguished members of his race."

Gerard Manley Hopkins (1844–1889)

Hurrahing in Harvest   1877

Summer ends now; now, barbarous in beauty, the stooks° arise   *sheaves*
    Around; up above, what wind-walks! what lovely behaviour
    Of silk-sack clouds! has wilder, wilful-wavier
Meal-drift moulded ever and melted across skies?

I walk, I lift up, I lift up heart, eyes,   5
    Down all that glory in the heavens to glean our Saviour;

And, eyes, heart, what looks, what lips yet gave you a
Rapturous love's greeting of realer, of rounder replies?

And the azurous hung hills are his world-wielding shoulder
    Majestic — as a stallion stalwart, very-violet-sweet! —   10
These things, these things were here and but the beholder
    Wanting; which two when they once meet,
The heart rears wings bold and bolder
    And hurls for him, O half hurls earth for him off under his feet.

GERARD MANLEY HOPKINS (1844–1889)

Pied Beauty   *1877*

Glory be to God for dappled things —
    For skies of couple-color as a brinded cow;
        For rose moles all in stipple upon trout that swim;
Fresh-firecoal chestnut-falls;° finches' wings;   *fallen chestnut*
    Landscape plotted and pieced — fold, fallow, and plow;   5
        And all trades, their gear and tackle and trim.

All things counter, original, spare, strange;
    Whatever is fickle, freckled (who knows how?)
        With swift, slow; sweet, sour; adazzle, dim;
He fathers-forth whose beauty is past change: 10
        Praise him.

GERARD MANLEY HOPKINS (1844–1889)

The Windhover°   *1877*

To Christ Our Lord

I caught this morning morning's minion,° king-   *favorite*
    dom of daylight's dauphin, dapple-dawn-drawn Falcon, in his riding
        Of the rolling level underneath him steady air, and striding
High there, how he rung upon the rein of a wimpling wing
In his ecstasy! then off, off forth on swing,   5
    As a skate's heel sweeps smooth on a bow-bend: the hurl and gliding
    Rebuffed the big wind. My heart in hiding
Stirred for a bird, — the achieve of, the mastery of the thing!

Brute beauty and valour and act, oh, air, pride, plume, here
    Buckle!° AND the fire that breaks from thee then, a billion   10
Times told lovelier, more dangerous, O my chevalier!

    No wonder of it: shéer plód makes plough down sillion°   *furrow*
Shine, and blue-bleak embers, ah my dear,
    Fall, gall themselves, and gash gold-vermilion.

The Windhover: "A name for the kestrel [a kind of small hawk], from its habit of hovering or hanging with its head to the wind" [*OED*].   10 *Buckle:* To join, to equip for battle, to crumple.

A. E. HOUSMAN (1859–1936)

Is my team ploughing

1896

"Is my team ploughing,
  That I was used to drive
And hear the harness jingle
  When I was man alive?"

Ay, the horses trample,   5
  The harness jingles now;
No change though you lie under
  The land you used to plough.

"Is football playing
  Along the river shore,   10
With lads to chase the leather,
  Now I stand up no more?"

Ay, the ball is flying,
  The lads play heart and soul;
The goal stands up, the keeper   15
  Stands up to keep the goal.

"Is my girl happy,
  That I thought hard to leave,
And has she tired of weeping
  As she lies down at eve?"   20

Ay, she lies down lightly,
  She lies not down to weep:
Your girl is well contented.
  Be still, my lad, and sleep.

"Is my friend hearty,   25
  Now I am thin and pine,
And has he found to sleep in
  A better bed than mine?"

Yes, lad, I lie easy,
  I lie as lads would choose;   30
I cheer a dead man's sweetheart,
  Never ask me whose.

A. E. HOUSMAN (1859–1936)

To an Athlete Dying Young

1896

The time you won your town the race
We chaired° you through the marketplace;

2 *chaired:* Carried on the shoulders in triumphal parade.

Man and boy stood cheering by,
And home we brought you shoulder-high.

Today, the road all runners come,   5
Shoulder-high we bring you home,
And set you at your threshold down,
Townsman of a stiller town.

Smart lad, to slip betimes away
From fields where glory does not stay,   10
And early though the laurel° grows
It withers quicker than the rose.

Eyes the shady night has shut
Cannot see the record cut,
And silence sounds no worse than cheers   15
After earth has stopped the ears:

Now you will not swell the rout
Of lads that wore their honors out,
Runners whom renown outran
And the name died before the man.   20

To set, before its echoes fade,
The fleet foot on the sill of shade,
And hold to the low lintel up
The still-defended challenge-cup.

And round that early-laureled head   25
Will flock to gaze the strengthless dead,
And find unwithered on its curls
The garland briefer than a girl's.

11 *laurel:* Flowering shrub traditionally used to fashion wreaths of honor.

RODNEY JONES (B. 1950)

TV   *1996*

All the preachers claimed it was Satan.
Now the first sets seem more venerable
Than Abraham or Williamsburg
Or the avant garde. Back then nothing,

Not even the bomb, had ever looked so new.   5
It seemed almost heretical watching it
When we visited relatives in the city,
Secretly delighting, but saying later,

After church, probably it would not last,
It would destroy things: standards   10
And the sacredness of words in books.
It was well into the age of color,

Korea and Little Rock long past,
Before anyone got one. Suddenly some
Of them in the next valley had one.   15
You would know them by their lights

Burning late at night, and the recentness
And distance of events entering their talk,
But not one in our valley; for a long time
No one had one, so when the first one   20

Arrived in the van from the furniture store
And the men had set the box on the lawn,
At first we stood back from it, circling it
As they raised its antenna and staked in

The guy-wires before taking it in the door,   25
And I seem to recall a kind of blue light
Flickering from inside and then a woman
Calling out that they had got it tuned in —

A little fuzzy, a ghost picture, but something
That would stay with us, the way we hurried   30
Down the dirt road, the stars, the silence,
Then everyone disappearing into the houses.

BEN JONSON (1573–1637)

On My First Son   *1603*

Farewell, thou child of my right hand,° and joy.
My sin was too much hope of thee, loved boy;
Seven years thou wert lent to me, and I thee pay,
Exacted by thy fate, on the just day.°   *his birthday*
Oh, could I lose all father° now. For why   *fatherhood* 5
Will man lament the state he should envy? —
To have so soon 'scaped world's and flesh's rage,
And, if no other misery, yet age.
Rest in soft peace, and asked, say, "Here doth lie
Ben Jonson his best piece of poetry,"   10
For whose sake henceforth all his vows be such
As what he loves may never like too much.

1 *child of my right hand:* This phrase translates the Hebrew name "Benjamin," Jonson's son.

BEN JONSON (1573–1637)

To Celia   *1616*

Drink to me only with thine eyes,
    And I will pledge with mine;

Or leave a kiss but in the cup,
    And I'll not ask for wine.
The thirst that from the soul doth rise   5
    Doth ask a drink divine;
But might I of Jove's nectar sup,
    I would not change for thine.

I sent thee late a rosy wreath,
    Not so much honoring thee   10
As giving it a hope that there
    It could not withered be.
But thou thereon didst only breathe,
    And sent'st it back to me;
Since when it grows, and smells, I swear,   15
    Not of itself but thee.

JOHN KEATS (1795–1821)
To One Who Has Been Long in City Pent   *1816*

To one who has been long in city pent,
    'Tis very sweet to look into the fair
    And open face of heaven, — to breathe a prayer
Full in the smile of the blue firmament.
Who is more happy, when, with heart's content,   5
    Fatigued he sinks into some pleasant lair
    Of wavy grass, and reads a debonair
And gentle tale of love and languishment?

Returning home at evening, with an ear
    Catching the notes of Philomel,° — an eye   *A nightingale* 10
Watching the sailing cloudlet's bright career,
    He mourns that day so soon has glided by:
E'en like the passage of an angel's tear
    That falls through the clear ether silently.

JOHN KEATS (1795–1821)
Written in Disgust of Vulgar Superstition   *1816*

The church bells toll a melancholy round,
    Calling the people to some other prayers,
    Some other gloominess, more dreadful cares,
More hearkening to the sermon's horrid sound.
Surely the mind of man is closely bound   5
    In some black spell; seeing that each one tears
    Himself from fireside joys, and Lydian airs,
And converse high of those with glory crown'd.

Still, still they toll, and I should feel a damp—
    A chill as from a tomb, did I not know   10
That they are going like an outburnt lamp;
    That 'tis their sighing, wailing ere they go
    Into oblivion;—that fresh flowers will grow,
And many glories of immortal stamp.

JOHN KEATS (1795–1821)

When I have fears that I may cease to be   *1818*

When I have fears that I may cease to be
    Before my pen has gleaned my teeming brain,
Before high-piled books, in charactery,°   *print*
    Hold like rich garners the full ripened grain;
When I behold, upon the night's starred face,   5
    Huge cloudy symbols of a high romance,
And think that I may never live to trace
    Their shadows, with the magic hand of chance;
And when I feel, fair creature of an hour,
    That I shall never look upon thee more,   10
Never have relish in the faery° power   *magic*
    Of unreflecting love;—then on the shore
Of the wide world I stand alone, and think
Till love and fame to nothingness do sink.

JOHN KEATS (1795–1821)

La Belle Dame sans Merci°   *1819*

O what can ail thee, knight-at-arms,
    Alone and palely loitering?
The sedge has withered from the lake,
    And no birds sing.

O what can ail thee, knight-at-arms,   5
    So haggard and so woe-begone?
The squirrel's granary is full,
    And the harvest's done.

I see a lily on thy brow,
    With anguish moist and fever dew,   10
And on thy cheeks a fading rose
    Fast withereth too.

I met a lady in the meads,
    Full beautiful—a faery's child,

La Belle Dame sans Merci: This title is borrowed from a medieval poem and means "The Beautiful Lady without Mercy."

Her hair was long, her foot was light,   15
    And her eyes were wild.

I made a garland for her head,
    And bracelets too, and fragrant zone;°   *belt*
She looked at me as she did love,
    And made sweet moan.   20

I set her on my pacing steed,
    And nothing else saw all day long,
For sidelong would she bend, and sing
    A faery's song.

She found me roots of relish sweet,   25
    And honey wild, and manna dew,
And sure in language strange she said,
    "I love thee true."

She took me to her elfin grot,
    And there she wept, and sighed full sore,   30
And there I shut her wild wild eyes
    With kisses four.

And there she lullèd me asleep,
    And there I dreamed — Ah! woe betide!
The latest° dream I ever dreamed   *last*   35
    On the cold hill side.

I saw pale kings and princes too,
    Pale warriors, death-pale were they all;
They cried — "La Belle Dame sans Merci
    Hath thee in thrall!"   40

I saw their starved lips in the gloam,
    With horrid warning gapèd wide,
And I awoke and found me here,
    On the cold hill's side.

And this is why I sojourn here,   45
    Alone and palely loitering,
Though the sedge has withered from the lake,
    And no birds sing.

WILLYCE KIM (B. 1946)

In This Heat   *1986*

In this heat
we gather ourselves
and hold together
day folding into night
we press for darkness   5
as if the heat

would steal away
like some errant ship,
vanquished by moon
and stars,   10
we close our eyes
the night half-swollen
with the whispers
of the day.
Out, across the way   15
a dog barks.
Yesterday,
a Chinese girl
with skin the color
of dragon's eyes   20
and hair as fine
as my beloved's
killed herself.
She answered an ad
in one of the dailies   25
and was raped
during the long interview.
No one believed her.
You know the old story.
Tonight I hold your   30
hands between my palms.
Afraid of yesterday.
Uncertain of tomorrow.
Outside the moon pales
against the window   35
as shadows lap across
the sky.
Sleep flutters
like burning incense.
We curl into darkness   40
and are gone.

ETHERIDGE KNIGHT (B. 1931)

A Watts Mother Mourns while Boiling Beans   *1973*

The blooming flower of my life is roaming
in the night, and I think surely
that never since he was born
have I been free from fright.
My boy is bold, and his blood   5
grows quickly hot even now
he could be crawling in the street
bleeding out his life, likely as not.
Come home, my bold and restless son. — Stop
my heart's yearning! But I must quit   10

this thinking — my husband is coming
and the beans are burning.

PHILIP LARKIN (1922–1985)

This Be the Verse   *1974*

They fuck you up, your mum and dad.
    They may not mean to, but they do.
They fill you with the faults they had
    And add some extras, just for you.

But they were fucked up in their turn   5
    By fools in old-style hats and coats,
Who half the time were soppy-stern
    And half at one another's throats.

Man hands on misery to man.
    It deepens like a coastal shelf.   10
Get out as early as you can,
    And don't have any kids yourself.

LI-YOUNG LEE (B. 1957)

Eating Together   *1986*

In the steamer is the trout
seasoned with slivers of ginger,
two sprigs of green onion, and sesame oil.
We shall eat it with rice for lunch,
brothers, sister, my mother who will   5
taste the sweetest meat of the head,
holding it between her fingers
deftly, the way my father did
weeks ago. Then he lay down
to sleep like a snow-covered road   10
winding through pines older than him,
without any travelers, and lonely for no one.

RACHEL LODEN (B. 1948)

We Are Sorry to Say   *1999*

that the decision has gone against
these poems. It just up and went

against them, like an enormous rearing
horse, a careening locomotive, and we

tried to get out of the way. We still
wake up screaming. Frankly   5

the decision scares us
more than a little. We think it wears

a muscle shirt and is named Bluto,
but who really knows? All we want   10

is peace and quiet, maybe a cottage
in the Hamptons, some sort of tonic

for our splintered nerves. That's what
we want, but there are sparrows

on the roof. And white roiling seas   15
of manuscripts that curse

and shriek, and tender envelopes
that bleed hysterically when opened.

Henry Wadsworth Longfellow (1807–1882)

Snow-Flakes   *1863*

Out of the bosom of the Air,
   Out of the cloud-folds of her garments shaken,
Over the woodlands brown and bare
   Over the harvest-fields forsaken,
     Silent, and soft, and slow   5
     Descends the snow.

Even as our cloudy fancies take
   Suddenly shape in some divine expression,
Even as the troubled heart doth make
In the white countenance confession,   10
     The troubled sky reveals
     The grief it feels.

This is the poem of the air,
   Slowly in silent syllables recorded;
This is the secret of despair,   15
   Long in its cloudy bosom hoarded,
     Now whispered and revealed
     To wood and field.

Audre Lorde (1934–1992)

Hanging Fire   *1978*

I am fourteen
and my skin has betrayed me
the boy I cannot live without

still sucks his thumb
in secret   5
how come my knees are
always so ashy
what if I die
before morning
and momma's in the bedroom   10
with the door closed.

I have to learn how to dance
in time for the next party
my room is too small for me
suppose I die before graduation   15
they will sing sad melodies
but finally
tell the truth about me
There is nothing I want to do
and too much   20
that has to be done
and momma's in the bedroom
with the door closed.

Nobody even stops to think
about my side of it   25
I should have been on Math Team
my marks were better than his
why do I have to be
the one
wearing braces   30
I have nothing to wear tomorrow
will I live long enough
to grow up
and momma's in the bedroom
with the door closed.   35

ROBERT LOWELL (1917–1977)

For Sale   *1959*

Poor sheepish plaything,
organized with prodigal animosity,
lived in just a year —
my Father's cottage at Beverly Farms
was on the market the month he died.   5
Empty, open, intimate,
its town-house furniture
had an on tiptoe air
of waiting for the mover
on the heels of the undertaker.   10
Ready, afraid
of living alone till eighty,

Mother mooned in a window,
as if she had stayed on a train
one stop past her destination.   15

ARCHIBALD MACLEISH (1892–1982)

Ars Poetica   *1926*

A poem should be palpable and mute
As a globed fruit,

Dumb
As old medallions to the thumb,

Silent as the sleeve-worn stone   5
Of casement ledges where the moss has grown —

A poem should be wordless
As the flight of birds.

A poem should be motionless in time
As the moon climbs,   10

Leaving, as the moon releases
Twig by twig the night-entangled trees,

Leaving, as the moon behind the winter leaves,
Memory by memory the mind —

A poem should be motionless in time   15
As the moon climbs.

A poem should be equal to:
Not true.

For all the history of grief
An empty doorway and a maple leaf.   20

For love
The leaning grasses and two lights above the sea —

A poem should not mean
But be.

CLEOPATRA MATHIS (B. 1947)

What to Tip the Boatman?   *1999*

Delicate — the way at three she touched
her hands tip to tip, each finger a rib
framing the teepee of her hands.
So tentative that joining, taking
tender hold of her body, as if the ballast   5

of her selfhood rested there. Already
she could thread tiny beads through the eye
and onto string, correctly placing
each letter of her name, sorting
thin black lines to make an alphabet,   10
the needle just so in her little hand.
She loved that necklace less
than cat's cradle, a game to weave
the strand through forefinger, ring finger, pinkie.
She could lace a basket, a boat   15
that could even carry water. What to tip
the boatman? I asked, trying to amuse her
with church and steeple turned to my empty palm.
Naptime, she'd lie there making shapes
above her, signing the air.   20

Later I saw the light touch of those twinned
fingertips had become her way
of holding still, keeping balance.
She had reached home before I did, finding
no mother at the bus stop, and entered   25
the silenced house for the first time alone.
Ancient, venerable, the whole place
waited, a relative with smells and creaks
she hesitated to greet. When I found her
she had made her way to the formal great room,   30
polite center of the hectic house where even
the clock's old thud gave back the heart
of simple waiting. Good guest, a shadow
on the rose Victorian settee, she sat,
her hands precise before her, an offering.   35

W. S. MERWIN (B. 1927)

For the Anniversary of My Death   *1967*

Every year without knowing it I have passed the day
When the last fires will wave to me
And the silence will set out
Tireless traveller
Like the beam of a lightless star   5

Then I will no longer
Find myself in life as in a strange garment
Surprised at the earth
And the love of one woman
And the shamelessness of men   10
As today writing after three days of rain
Hearing the wren sing and the falling cease
And bowing not knowing to what

EDNA ST. VINCENT MILLAY (1892–1950)

I, Being Born a Woman and Distressed   *1923*

I, being born a woman and distressed
By all the needs and notions of my kind,
Am urged by your propinquity to find
Your person fair, and feel a certain zest
To bear your body's weight upon my breast: 5
So subtly is the fume of life designed,
To clarify the pulse and cloud the mind,
And leave me once again undone, possessed.
Think not for this, however, the poor treason
Of my stout blood against my staggering brain,   10
I shall remember you with love, or season
My scorn with pity, — let me make it plain:
I find this frenzy insufficient reason
For conversation when we meet again.

JOHN MILTON (1608–1674)

On the Late Massacre in Piedmont°   *1655*

Avenge, O Lord, thy slaughtered saints, whose bones
    Lie scattered on the Alpine mountains cold;
    Even them who kept thy truth so pure of old,
When all our fathers worshiped stocks and stones,°
Forget not: in thy book record their groans   5
    Who were thy sheep, and in their ancient fold
    Slain by the bloody Piedmontese, that rolled
Mother with infant down the rocks.° Their moans
The vales redoubled to the hills, and they
    To heaven. Their martyred blood and ashes sow   10
O'er all the Italian fields, where still doth sway
    The triple Tyrant;° that from these may grow
    A hundredfold, who, having learnt thy way,
Early may fly the Babylonian woe.°

On the Late Massacre . . . : Milton's protest against the treatment of the Waldenses, members of a Puritan sect living in the Piedmont region of northwest Italy, was not limited to this sonnet. It is thought that he wrote Cromwell's appeals to the duke of Savoy and to others to end the persecution.

4 *When . . . stones:* In Milton's Protestant view, English Catholics had worshiped their stone and wooden statues in the twelfth century, when the Waldensian sect was formed.

5–8 *in thy book . . . rocks:* On Easter Day, 1655, 1,700 members of the Waldensian sect were massacred in Piedmont by the duke of Savoy's forces.

12 *triple Tyrant:* The Pope, with his three-crowned tiara, has authority on earth and in Heaven and Hell.

14 *Babylonian woe:* The destruction of Babylon, symbol of vice and corruption, at the end of the world (see Rev. 17–18). Protestants interpreted the "Whore of Babylon" as the Roman Catholic Church.

JOHN MILTON (1608 1674)

When I consider how my light is spent   c. 1655

When I consider how my light is spent,°
    Ere half my days in this dark world and wide,
    And that one talent° which is death to hide
Lodged with me useless, though my soul more bent
To serve therewith my Maker, and present   5
    My true account, lest He returning chide;
    "Doth God exact day-labor, light denied?"
I fondly° ask. But Patience, to prevent   *foolishly*
That murmur, soon replies, "God doth not need
    Either man's work or His own gifts. Who best   10
    Bear His mild yoke, they serve Him best. His state
Is kingly: thousands at His bidding speed,
    And post o'er land and ocean without rest;
    They also serve who only stand and wait."

1 *how my light is spent:* Milton had been totally blind since 1651.   3 *that one talent:* Refers to Jesus' parable of the talents (units of money), in which a servant entrusted with a talent buries it rather than invests it and is punished on his master's return (Matt. 25:14-30).

N. SCOTT MOMADAY (B. 1934)

Crows in a Winter Composition   1976

This morning the snow,
The soft distances
Beyond the trees
In which nothing appeared —
Nothing appeared.   5
The several silences,
Imposed one upon another,
Were unintelligible.

I was therefore ill at ease
When the crows came down,   10
Whirling down and calling,
Into the yard below
And stood in a mindless manner
On the gray, luminous crust,
Altogether definite, composed,   15
In the bright enmity of my regard,
In the hard nature of crows.

MARIANNE MOORE (1887–1972)

Poetry   *1921*

I, too, dislike it: there are things that are important beyond all this fiddle.
    Reading it, however, with a perfect contempt for it, one discovers in it
    after all, a place for the genuine.
        Hands that can grasp, eyes
           that can dilate, hair that can rise   5
               if it must, these things are important not because a

high-sounding interpretation can be put upon them but because they are
    useful. When they become so derivative as to become unintelligible,
    the same thing may be said for all of us, that we
        do not admire what   10
        we cannot understand: the bat
           holding on upside down or in quest of something to

eat, elephants pushing, a wild horse taking a roll, a tireless wolf under
    a tree, the immovable critic twitching his skin like a horse that feels a
    flea, the base-   15
ball fan, the statistician —
        nor is it valid
           to discriminate against "business documents and

school-books"; all these phenomena are important. One must make a
    distinction
however: when dragged into prominence by half poets, the result is
    not poetry,
    nor till the poets among us can be   20
        "literalists of
        the imagination" — above
           insolence and triviality and can present

for inspection, "imaginary gardens with real toads in them," shall we have
    it. In the meantime, if you demand on the one hand,   25
    the raw material of poetry in
        all its rawness and
        that which is on the other hand
           genuine, you are interested in poetry.

PAT MORA (B. 1942)

Another Brown Man   *1995*

Startling as blood
from a pinprick,
my tears, pull
me to him, away from hipsway,
drumbeats, música cubana.   5

His hands, like yours,
the color of tobacco
he smooths, cuts, rolls,
another brown man,
hands and humor busy. Like yours.   10

His chuckles curl with his cigar smoke,
he teases to girls in nearby shops,
"Oye, linda,"
banter familiar as the work,
rhythm I remember.   15

        You stopped breathing
        once this year. Your body,
        solid as an álamo,
        we can never trust again.
        It practiced stillness.   20

I stare at him, hover
near music I once knew,
listen, hear you
whose voice alone
pricks my tears.   25

I turn, and he's gone,
light off, cigar rolling done for the day,
his spot bare under the palm trees,
only a shadow.
Like yours.   30

ROBERT MORGAN (B. 1944)

Wind from a Waterfall   1999

The air around a waterfall
is thrilling. Gusts and downdrafts prowl
from out of mist, and rainbow air
will seem to pour right off the roar.
But take one step and feel the breeze   5
reverse and veer away in craze
of air around the plunge, perform
a theater of tumbling foam
in knots, a hundred whips and currents,
as tons of milk and spray condense   10
in atmospheres pushed down that must
escape across the bottom forced
to circulate as eddies, spin
of backwash, pocket, conflagration.
And as above a witch's cauldron   15
the air goes wild and darts, is torn

by fits and swoops of jubilation,
then whispers, barks, in Pentecost
and song, of families long lost
from far upstream and still stirred up   20
by heavy tongue from river's lip.

SARAH MORGAN BRYAN PIATT (1836–1919)

A New Thanksgiving   *1910*

For war, plague, pestilence, flood, famine, fire,
    For Christ discrowned, for false gods set on high;
For fools, whose hands must have their hearts' desire,
    We thank Thee — in the darkness — and so die.

For shipwreck: Oh, the sob of strangling seas! —   5
    No matter. For the snake that charms the dove;
And (is it not the bitterest of all these?)
    We thank Thee — in our blind faith — even for Love.

For breaking hearts; for all that breaks the heart;
    For Death, the one thing after all the rest,   10
We thank Thee, O our Father! Thou who art,
    And wast, and shalt be — knowing these are best.

SYLVIA PLATH (1932–1963)

Daddy   *1962*

You do not do, you do not do
Any more, black shoe
In which I have lived like a foot
For thirty years, poor and white,
Barely daring to breathe or Achoo.   5

Daddy, I have had to kill you.
You died before I had time —
Marble-heavy, a bag full of God,
Ghastly statue with one gray toe
Big as a Frisco seal   10

And a head in the freakish Atlantic
Where it pours bean green over blue
In the waters off beautiful Nauset.°   *Cape Cod inlet*
I used to pray to recover you.
Ach, du.°   *Oh, you*   15

In the German tongue, in the Polish Town°
Scraped flat by the roller

16 *Polish Town:* Refers to Otto Plath's birthplace, Granbow.

Of wars, wars, wars.
But the name of the town is common.
My Polack friend   20

Says there are a dozen or two.
So I never could tell where you
Put your foot, your root,
I never could talk to you.
The tongue stuck in my jaw.   25

It stuck in a barb wire snare.
Ich, ich, ich, ich,°   *I, I, I, I,*
I could hardly speak.
I thought every German was you.
And the language obscene   30

An engine, an engine
Chuffing me off like a Jew.
A Jew to Dachau, Auschwitz, Belsen.°
I began to talk like a Jew.
I think I may well be a Jew.   35

The snows of the Tyrol, the clear beer of Vienna
Are not very pure or true.
With my gypsy-ancestress and my weird luck
And my Taroc° pack and my Taroc pack
I may be a bit of a Jew.   40

I have always been scared of *you,*
With your Luftwaffe,° your gobbledygoo.
And your neat mustache
And your Aryan eye, bright blue.
Panzer-man, panzer-man,° O You —   45

Not God but a swastika
So black no sky could squeak through.
Every woman adores a Fascist,
The boot in the face, the brute
Brute heart of a brute like you.   50

You stand at the blackboard, daddy,
In the picture I have of you,
A cleft in your chin instead of your foot
But no less a devil for that, no not
Any less the black man who   55

Bit my pretty red heart in two.
I was ten when they buried you.

33 *Dachau . . . Belsen:* Nazi death camps in World War II.

39 *Taroc:* Or *Tarot,* a pack of cards used to tell fortunes. It is said to have originated among the early Jewish Cabalists and to have been transmitted to European Gypsies during the Middle Ages.

42 *Luftwaffe:* World War II German air force.

45 *panzer-man:* A member of the panzer division of the German army in World War II, which used armored vehicles and was organized for rapid attack.

At twenty I tried to die
And get back, back, back to you.
I thought even the bones would do   60

But they pulled me out of the sack,
And they stuck me together with glue.
And then I knew what to do.
I made a model of you,
A man in black with a Meinkampf° look   65

And a love of the rack and the screw.
And I said I do, I do.
So daddy, I'm finally through.
The black telephone's off at the root,
The voices just can't worm through.   70

If I've killed one man, I've killed two —
The vampire who said he was you
And drank my blood for a year,
Seven years, if you want to know.
Daddy, you can lie back now.   75

There's a stake in your fat black heart
And the villagers never liked you.
They are dancing and stamping on you.
They always *knew* it was you.
Daddy, daddy, you bastard, I'm through.   80

65 *Meinkampf:* An allusion to Hitler's autobiography (*My Struggle*).

Sir Walter Ralegh (1554–1618)

The Nymph's Reply to the Shepherd   *1600*

If all the world and love were young,
And truth in every shepherd's tongue,
These pretty pleasures might me move
To live with thee and be thy love.

Time drives the flocks from field to fold,   5
When rivers rage and rocks grow cold,
And Philomel° becometh dumb;   *nightingale*
The rest complains of cares to come.

The flowers do fade, and wanton fields
To wayward winter reckoning yields;   10
A honey tongue, a heart of gall,
Is fancy's spring, but sorrow's fall.

Thy gowns, thy shoes, thy beds of roses,
Thy cap, thy kirtle, and thy posies
Soon break, soon wither, soon forgotten —
In folly ripe, in reason rotten.   15

Thy belt of straw and ivy buds,
Thy coral clasps and amber studs,
All these in me no means can move
To come to thee and be thy love.   20

But could youth last and love still breed,
Had joys no date° nor age no need,   end
Then these delights my mind might move
To live with thee and be thy love.

ADRIENNE RICH (B. 1929)

Living in Sin   1955

She had thought the studio would keep itself;
no dust upon the furniture of love.
Half heresy, to wish the taps less vocal,
the panes relieved of grime. A plate of pears,
a piano with a Persian shawl, a cat   5
stalking the picturesque amusing mouse
had risen at his urging.
Not that at five each separate stair would writhe
under the milkman's tramp; that morning light
so coldly would delineate the scraps   10
of last night's cheese and three sepulchral bottles;
that on the kitchen shelf among the saucers
a pair of beetle-eyes would fix her own —
envoy from some black village in the mouldings . . .
Meanwhile, he, with a yawn,   15
sounded a dozen notes upon the keyboard,
declared it out of tune, shrugged at the mirror,
rubbed at his beard, went out for cigarettes;
while she, jeered by the minor demons,
pulled back the sheets and made the bed and found   20
a towel to dust the table-top,
and let the coffee-pot boil over on the stove.
By evening she was back in love again,
though not so wholly but throughout the night
she woke sometimes to feel the daylight coming   25
like a relentless milkman up the stairs.

CHRISTINA GEORGINA ROSSETTI (1830–1894)

Some Ladies Dress in Muslin Full and White   c. 1848

Some ladies dress in muslin full and white,
Some gentlemen in cloth succinct and black;
Some patronise a dog-cart, some a hack,

Some think a painted clarence only right.
Youth is not always such a pleasing sight: 5
Witness a man with tassels on his back;
Or woman in a great-coat like a sack,
Towering above her sex with horrid height.
If all the world were water fit to drown,
There are some whom you would not teach to swim,   10
Rather enjoying if you saw them sink:
Certain old ladies dressed in girlish pink,
With roses and geraniums on their gown.
Go to the basin, poke them o'er the rim —

CHRISTINA GEORGINA ROSSETTI (1830–1894)

Promises Like Pie-Crust°   1896

Promise me no promises,
    So will I not promise you;
Keep we both our liberties,
    Never false and never true:
Let us hold the die uncast,   5
    Free to come as free to go;
For I cannot know your past,
    And of mine what can you know?

You, so warm, may once have been
    Warmer towards another one;   10
I, so cold, may once have seen
    Sunlight, once have felt the sun:
Who shall show us if it was
    Thus indeed in time of old?
Fades the image from the glass   15
    And the fortune is not told.

If you promised, you might grieve
    For lost liberty again;
If I promised, I believe
    I should fret to break the chain: 20
Let us be the friends we were,
    Nothing more but nothing less;
Many thrive on frugal fare
    Who would perish of excess.

Pie-Crust: An old English proverb: "Promises are like pie-crust, made to be broken."

WILLIAM SHAKESPEARE (1564–1616)
That time of year thou mayst in me behold   1609

That time of year thou mayst in me behold
When yellow leaves, or none, or few, do hang
Upon those boughs which shake against the cold,
Bare ruined choirs, where late the sweet birds sang.
In me thou see'st the twilight of such day   5
As after sunset fadeth in the west;
Which by and by black night doth take away,
Death's second self,° that seals up all in rest.   *sleep*
In me thou see'st the glowing of such fire,
That on the ashes of his youth doth lie,   10
As the deathbed whereon it must expire,
Consumed with that which it was nourished by.
    This thou perceiv'st, which makes thy love more strong,
    To love that well which thou must leave ere long.

WILLIAM SHAKESPEARE (1564–1616)
When forty winters shall besiege thy brow   1609

When forty winters shall besiege thy brow
And dig deep trenches in thy beauty's field,
Thy youth's proud livery, so gazed on now,
Will be a tattered weed,° of small worth held.   *garment*
Then being asked where all thy beauty lies,   5
Where all the treasure of thy lusty days,
To say within thine own deep-sunken eyes
Were an all-eating shame and thriftless praise.
How much more praise deserved thy beauty's use
If thou couldst answer, "This fair child of mine   10
Shall sum my count and make my old excuse,"
Proving his beauty by succession thine.
    This were to be new made when thou art old,
    And see thy blood warm when thou feel'st it cold.

WILLIAM SHAKESPEARE (1564–1616)
When, in disgrace with Fortune and men's eyes   1609

When, in disgrace with Fortune and men's eyes,
I all alone beweep my outcast state,
And trouble deaf heaven with my bootless cries,
And look upon myself and curse my fate,
Wishing me like to one more rich in hope,   5

Featured like him, like him with friends possessed,
Desiring this man's art, and that man's scope,
With what I most enjoy contented least,
Yet in these thoughts myself almost despising,
Haply I think on thee, and then my state,   10
Like to the lark at break of day arising
From sullen earth, sings hymns at heaven's gate;
  For thy sweet love remembered such wealth brings
  That then I scorn to change my state with kings.

PERCY BYSSHE SHELLEY (1792–1822)

Ozymandias°   *1818*

I met a traveler from an antique land
Who said: Two vast and trunkless legs of stone
Stand in the desert. . . . Near them, on the sand,
Half sunk, a shattered visage lies, whose frown,
And wrinkled lip, and sneer of cold command,   5
Tell that its sculptor well those passions read
Which yet survive, stamped on these lifeless things,
The hand that mocked them, and the heart that fed:
And on the pedestal these words appear:
"My name is Ozymandias, King of Kings: 10
Look on my works, ye Mighty, and despair!"
Nothing beside remains. Round the decay
Of that colossal wreck, boundless and bare
The lone and level sands stretch far away.

Ozymandias: Greek name for Ramses II, pharaoh of Egypt for sixty-seven years during the thirteenth century B.C. His colossal statue lies prostrate in the sands of Luxor. Napoleon's soldiers measured it (56 feet long, ear 3¾ feet long, weight 1,000 tons). Its inscription, according to the Greek historian Diodorus Siculus, was "I am Ozymandias, King of Kings; if anyone wishes to know what I am and where I lie, let him surpass me in some of my exploits."

PERCY BYSSHE SHELLEY (1792–1822)

Sonnet: Lift not the painted veil   *1818*

Lift not the painted veil which those who live
Call Life: though unreal shapes be pictured there,
And it but mimic all we would believe
With colours idly spread, — behind, lurk Fear
And Hope, twin Destinies; who ever weave   5
Their shadows, o'er the chasm, sightless and drear.
I knew one who had lifted it — he sought,
For his lost heart was tender, things to love,
But found them not, alas! nor was there aught

The world contains, the which he could approve.   10
Through the unheeding many he did move,
A splendour among shadows, a bright blot
Upon this gloomy scene, a Spirit that strove
For truth, and like the Preacher° found it not.

14 *Preacher:* The preacher of Ecclesiastes who insists that "all is vanity."

SIR PHILIP SIDNEY (1554–1586)

Loving in Truth, and Fain in Verse My Love to Show   *1591*

Loving in truth, and fain in verse my love to show,
That she, dear she, might take some pleasure of my pain,
Pleasure might cause her read, reading might make her know,
Knowledge might pity win, and pity grace obtain,
I sought fit words to paint the blackest face of woe,   5
Studying inventions fine, her wits to entertain,
Oft turning others' leaves, to see if thence would flow
Some fresh and fruitful showers upon my sunburnt brain.
But words came halting forth, wanting Invention's stay;
Invention, Nature's child, fled step-dame° Study's blows;   *stepmother* 10
And others' feet still seemed but strangers in my way.
Thus great with child to speak, and helpless in my throes,
Biting my truant pen, beating myself for spite:
"Fool," said my Muse to me, "look in thy heart and write."

GARY SOTO (B. 1952)

Black Hair   *1985*

At eight I was brilliant with my body.
In July, that ring of heat
We all jumped through, I sat in the bleachers
Of Romain Playground, in the lengthening
Shade that rose from our dirty feet.   5
The game before us was more than baseball.
It was a figure — Hector Moreno
Quick and hard with turned muscles,
His crouch the one I assumed before an altar
Of worn baseball cards, in my room.   10
I came here because I was Mexican, a stick
Of brown light in love with those
Who could do it — the triple and hard slide,
The gloves eating balls into double plays.
What could I do with 50 pounds, my shyness,   15

My black torch of hair, about to go out?
Father was dead, his face no longer
Hanging over the table or our sleep,
And mother was the terror of mouths
Twisting hurt by butter knives.   20

In the bleachers I was brilliant with my body,
Waving players in and stomping my feet,
Growing sweaty in the presence of white shirts.
I chewed sunflower seeds. I drank water
And bit my arm through the late innings.   25
When Hector lined balls into deep
Center, in my mind I rounded the bases
With him, my face flared, my hair lifting
Beautifully, because we were coming home
To the arms of brown people.   30

WALLACE STEVENS (1879–1955)

The Emperor of Ice-Cream   *1923*

Call the roller of big cigars,
The muscular one, and bid him whip
In kitchen cups concupiscent curds.°
Let the wenches dawdle in such dress
As they are used to wear, and let the boys   5
Bring flowers in last month's newspapers.
Let be be finale of seem.°
The only emperor is the emperor of ice-cream.

Take from the dresser of deal,
Lacking the three glass knobs, that sheet   10
On which she embroidered fantails once
And spread it so as to cover her face.
If her horny feet protrude, they come
To show how cold she is, and dumb.
Let the lamp affix its beam.   15
The only emperor is the emperor of ice-cream.

3 *concupiscent curds:* "The words 'concupiscent curds' have no genealogy; they are merely expressive: at least, I hope they are expressive. They express the concupiscence of life, but, by contrast with the things in relation in the poem, they express or accentuate life's destitution, and it is this that gives them something more than a cheap lustre" (Wallace Stevens, *Letters* [New York: Knopf, 1960], p. 500).

7 *Let . . . seem:* "The true sense of 'Let be be finale of seem' is let being become the conclusion or denouement of appearing to be: in short, ice cream is an absolute good. The poem is obviously not about ice cream, but about being as distinguished from seeming to be" (*Letters,* p. 341).

Alfred, Lord Tennyson (1809–1892)

Ulysses°   1833

It little profits that an idle king,
By this still hearth, among these barren crags,
Matched with an agèd wife,° I mete and dole   Penelope
Unequal laws unto a savage race,
That hoard, and sleep, and feed, and know not me.   5
   I cannot rest from travel; I will drink
Life to the lees. All times I have enjoyed
Greatly, have suffered greatly, both with those
That loved me, and alone; on shore, and when
Through scudding drifts the rainy Hyades°   10
Vexed the dim sea. I am become a name;
For always roaming with a hungry heart
Much have I seen and known — cities of men
And manners, climates, councils, governments,
Myself not least, but honored of them all —   15
And drunk delight of battle with my peers,
Far on the ringing plains of windy Troy.
I am a part of all that I have met;
Yet all experience is an arch wherethrough
Gleams that untraveled world, whose margin fades   20
For ever and for ever when I move.
How dull it is to pause, to make an end,
To rust unburnished, not to shine in use!
As though to breathe were life. Life piled on life
Were all too little, and of one to me   25
Little remains; but every hour is saved
From that eternal silence, something more,
A bringer of new things; and vile it were
For some three suns to store and hoard myself,
And this gray spirit yearning in desire   30
To follow knowledge like a sinking star,
Beyond the utmost bound of human thought.

   This is my son, mine own Telemachus,
To whom I leave the scepter and the isle —
Well-loved of me, discerning to fulfill   35
This labor, by slow prudence to make mild
A rugged people, and through soft degrees
Subdue them to the useful and the good.
Most blameless is he, centered in the sphere
Of common duties, decent not to fail   40
In offices of tenderness, and pay

Ulysses: Ulysses, the hero of Homer's epic poem the *Odyssey,* is presented by Dante in *The Inferno,* XXVI, as restless after his return to Ithaca, and eager for new adventures. 10 *Hyades:* Five stars in the constellation Taurus, supposed by the ancients to predict rain when they rose with the sun.

Meet adoration to my household gods,
When I am gone. He works his work, I mine.

    There lies the port; the vessel puffs her sail:
There gloom the dark, broad seas. My mariners,   45
Souls that have toiled, and wrought, and thought with me —
That ever with a frolic welcome took
The thunder and the sunshine, and opposed
Free hearts, free foreheads — you and I are old;
Old age hath yet his honor and his toil.   50
Death closes all; but something ere the end,
Some work of noble note, may yet be done,
Not unbecoming men that strove with Gods.
The lights begin to twinkle from the rocks;
The long day wanes; the slow moon climbs; the deep   55
Moans round with many voices. Come, my friends.
'Tis not too late to seek a newer world.
Push off, and sitting well in order smite
The sounding furrows; for my purpose holds
To sail beyond the sunset, and the baths   60
Of all the western stars, until I die.
It may be that the gulfs will wash us down;
It may be we shall touch the Happy Isles,°
And see the great Achilles,° whom we knew.
Though much is taken, much abides; and though   65
We are not now that strength which in old days
Moved earth and heaven, that which we are, we are:
One equal temper of heroic hearts,
Made weak by time and fate, but strong in will
To strive, to seek, to find, and not to yield.   70

63 *Happy Isles:* Elysium, the home after death of heroes and others favored by the gods. It
was thought by the ancients to lie beyond the sunset in the uncharted Atlantic.
64 *Achilles:* The hero of Homer's *Iliad.*

ALFRED, LORD TENNYSON (1809–1892)

Tears, Idle Tears   *1847*

    Tears, idle tears, I know not what they mean,
Tears from the depth of some divine despair
Rise in the heart, and gather to the eyes,
In looking on the happy Autumn-fields,
And thinking of the days that are no more.   5

    Fresh as the first beam glittering on a sail,
That brings our friends up from the underworld,
Sad as the last which reddens over one

That sinks with all we love below the verge;
So sad, so fresh, the days that are no more.   10

    Ah, sad and strange as in dark summer dawns
The earliest pipe of half-awaken'd birds
To dying ears, when unto dying eyes
The casement° slowly grows a glimmering square;   *window*
So sad, so strange, the days that are no more.   15

    Dear as remember'd kisses after death,
And sweet as those by hopeless fancy feign'd
On lips that are for others; deep as love,
Deep as first love, and wild with all regret;
O Death in Life, the days that are no more.   20

ROBERT WALLACE (B. 1932)

The Double-Play   *1961*

In his sea lit
distance, the pitcher winding
like a clock about to chime comes down with

the ball, hit
sharply, under the artificial   5
banks of arc-lights, bounds like a vanishing string

over the green
to the shortstop magically
scoops to his right whirling above his invisible

shadows   10
in the dust redirects
its flight to the running poised second baseman

pirouettes
leaping, above the slide, to throw
from mid-air, across the colored tightened interval,   15

to the leaning-
out first baseman ends the dance
drawing it disappearing into his long brown glove

stretches. What
is too swift for deception   20
is final, lost, among the loosened figures

jogging off the field
(the pitcher walks), casual
in the space where the poem has happened.

PHILLIS WHEATLEY (1753?–1784)

On Being Brought from Africa to America

1773

'Twas mercy brought me from my pagan land,
Taught my benighted soul to understand
That there's a God — that there's a Saviour too;
Once I redemption neither sought nor knew.
Some view our sable race with scornful eye —
'Their color is a diabolic dye.'
Remember, Christians, Negroes black as Cain
May be refined, and join the angelic train.

WALT WHITMAN (1819–1892)

One's-Self I Sing

1867

One's-Self I sing, a simple separate person,
Yet utter the word Democratic, the word En-Masse.

Of physiology from top to toe I sing,
Not physiognomy alone nor brain alone is worthy for the Muse, I say the
    Form complete is worthier far,
The Female equally with the Male I sing.

Of Life immense in passion, pulse, and power,
Cheerful, for freest action formed under the laws divine,
The Modern Man I sing.

WALT WHITMAN (1819–1892)

When I Heard the Learn'd Astronomer

1865

When I heard the learn'd astronomer,
When the proofs, the figures, were ranged in columns before me,
When I was shown the charts and diagrams, to add, divide, and measure them,
When I sitting heard the astronomer where he lectured with much applause
    in the lecture-room,
How soon unaccountable I became tired and sick,
Till rising and gliding out I wandered off by myself,
In the mystical moist night-air, and from time to time,
Looked up in perfect silence at the stars.

RICHARD WILBUR (B. 1921)

Love Calls Us to the Things of This World°

1956

      The eyes open to a cry of pulleys,°
And spirited from sleep, the astounded soul
Hangs for a moment bodiless and simple
As false dawn.
            Outside the open window   5
The morning air is all awash with angels.
Some are in bed-sheets, some are in blouses,
Some are in smocks: but truly there they are.
Now they are rising together in calm swells
Of halcyon feeling, filling whatever they wear   10
With the deep joy of their impersonal breathing;
Now they are flying in place, conveying
The terrible speed of their omnipresence, moving
And staying like white water; and now of a sudden
They swoon down into so rapt a quiet   15
That nobody seems to be there.
                  The soul shrinks

              From all that it is about to remember,
From the punctual rape of every blessèd day,
And cries,   20
        "Oh, let there be nothing on earth but laundry,
Nothing but rosy hands in the rising steam
And clear dances done in the sight of heaven."

Yet, as the sun acknowledges
With a warm look the world's hunks and colors,   25
The soul descends once more in bitter love
To accept the waking body, saying now
In a changed voice as the man yawns and rises,

"Bring them down from their ruddy gallows;
Let there be clean linen for the backs of thieves;   30
Let lovers go fresh and sweet to be undone,
And the heaviest nuns walk in a pure floating
Of dark habits,
            keeping their difficult balance."

Loves Calls Us . . . : From St. Augustine's *Commentary on the Psalms.*   1 *pulleys:* Grooved wheels at each end of a laundry line; clothes are hung on the line and advance as the line is moved.

C. K. WILLIAMS (B. 1936)

The Nail

1999

Some dictator or other had gone into exile, and now reports were coming
    about his regime,

the usual crimes, torture, false imprisonment, cruelty and corruption, but
    then a detail:
that the way his henchmen had disposed of enemies was by hammering nails
    into their skulls.
Horror, then, what mind does after horror, after that first feeling that you'll
    never catch your breath,
mind imagines — how not be annihilated by it? — the preliminary tap, feels it
    in the tendons of the hand,   5
feels the way you do with *your* nail when you're fixing something, making
    something, shelves, a bed;
the first light tap to set the slant, and then the slightly harder tap, to embed
    the tip a little more . . .

No, no more: this should be happening in myth, in stone, or paint, not in
    reality, not here;
it should be an emblem of itself, not itself, something that would *mean,* not
    really have to happen,
something to go out, expand in implication from that unmoved mass of
    matter in the breast;   10
as in the image of an anguished face, in grief for us, not us as us, us as in a
    myth, a moral tale,
a way to tell the truth that grief is limitless, a way to tell us we must always
    understand
it's we who do such things, we who set the slant, embed the tip, lift the sledge
    and drive the nail,
drive the nail which is the axis upon which turns the brutal human world
    upon the world.

MILLER WILLIAMS (B. 1930)

Thinking about Bill, Dead of AIDS   *1989*

We did not know the first thing about
how blood surrenders to even the smallest threat
when old allergies turn inside out,

the body rescinding all its normal orders
to all defenders of flesh, betraying the head,   5
pulling its guards back from all its borders.

Thinking of friends afraid to shake your hand,
we think of your hand shaking, your mouth set,
your eyes drained of any reprimand.

Loving, we kissed you, partly to persuade   10
both you and us, seeing what eyes had said,
that we were loving and we were not afraid.

If we had had more, we would have given more.
As it was we stood next to your bed,
stopping, though, to set our smiles at the door.   15

Not because we were less sure at the last.
Only because, not knowing anything yet,
we didn't know what look would hurt you least.

WILLIAM CARLOS WILLIAMS (1883–1963)

Spring and All   *1923*

By the road to the contagious hospital
under the surge of the blue
mottled clouds driven from the
northeast — a cold wind. Beyond, the
waste of broad, muddy fields   5
brown with dried weeds, standing and fallen

patches of standing water
and scattering of tall trees

All along the road the reddish
purplish, forked, upstanding, twiggy   10
stuff of bushes and small trees
with dead, brown leaves under them
leafless vines —

Lifeless in appearance, sluggish
dazed spring approaches —   15

They enter the new world naked,
cold, uncertain of all
save that they enter. All about them
the cold, familiar wind —

Now the grass, tomorrow   20
the stiff curl of wildcarrot leaf
One by one objects are defined —
It quickens: clarity, outline of leaf

But now the stark dignity of
entrance — Still, the profound change   25
has come upon them: rooted, they
grip down and begin to awaken

WILLIAM CARLOS WILLIAMS (1883–1963)

This Is Just to Say   *1934*

I have eaten
the plums
that were in
the icebox

and which   5
you were probably
saving
for breakfast

Forgive me
they were delicious   10
so sweet
and so cold

WILLIAM WORDSWORTH (1770–1850)

Lines Written in Early Spring   *1798*

I heard a thousand blended notes,
While in a grove I sate reclined,
In that sweet mood when pleasant thoughts
Bring sad thoughts to the mind.

To her fair works did nature link   5
The human soul that through me ran;
And much it griev'd my heart to think
What man has made of man.

Through primrose-tufts, in that sweet bower,
The periwinkle trail'd its wreathes;   10
And 'tis my faith that every flower
Enjoys the air it breathes.

The birds around me hopp'd and play'd:
Their thoughts I cannot measure,
But the least motion which they made,   15
It seem'd a thrill of pleasure.

The budding twigs spread out their fan,
To catch the breezy air;
And I must think, do all I can,
That there was pleasure there.   20

If I these thoughts may not prevent,
If such be of my creed the plan,
Have I not reason to lament
What man has made of man?

WILLIAM WORDSWORTH (1770–1850)

I Wandered Lonely as a Cloud   *1807*

I wandered lonely as a cloud
That floats on high o'er vales and hills,
When all at once I saw a crowd,
A host, of golden daffodils,

Beside the lake, beneath the trees,   5
Fluttering and dancing in the breeze.

Continuous as the stars that shine
And twinkle on the milky way,
They stretched in never-ending line
Along the margin of a bay;   10
Ten thousand saw I at a glance,
Tossing their heads in sprightly dance.

The waves beside them danced, but they
Outdid the sparkling waves in glee;
A poet could not but be gay,   15
In such a jocund company;
I gazed — and gazed — but little thought
What wealth the show to me had brought:

For oft, when on my couch I lie
In vacant or in pensive mood,   20
They flash upon that inward eye
Which is the bliss of solitude;
And then my heart with pleasure fills,
And dances with the daffodils.

WILLIAM WORDSWORTH (1770–1850)

A Slumber Did My Spirit Seal   *1800*

A slumber did my spirit seal;
  I had no human fears —
She seemed a thing that could not feel
  The touch of earthly years.

No motion has she now, no force;
  She neither hears nor sees;
Rolled round in earth's diurnal course.
  With rocks, and stones, and trees.

WILLIAM WORDSWORTH (1770–1850)

The Solitary Reaper°   *1807*

Behold her, single in the field,
Yon solitary Highland lass!
Reaping and singing by herself;
Stop here, or gently pass!

The Solitary Reaper: Dorothy Wordsworth (William's sister) writes that the poem was suggested by this sentence in Thomas Wilkinson's *Tour of Scotland:* "Passed a female who was reaping alone; she sung in Erse, as she bended over her sickle; the sweetest human voice I ever heard; her strains were tenderly melancholy, and felt delicious, long after they were heard no more."

Alone she cuts and binds the grain,   5
And sings a melancholy strain;
O listen! for the vale profound
Is overflowing with the sound.

No nightingale did ever chaunt
More welcome notes to weary bands   10
Of travelers in some shady haunt
Among Arabian sands.
A voice so thrilling ne'er was heard
In springtime from the cuckoo-bird,
Breaking the silence of the seas   15
Among the farthest Hebrides.

Will no one tell me what she sings? —
Perhaps the plaintive numbers flow
For old, unhappy, far-off things,
And battles long ago.   20
Or is it some more humble lay,
Familiar matter of today?
Some natural sorrow, loss, or pain,
That has been, and may be again?

Whate'er the theme, the maiden sang   25
As if her song could have no ending;
I saw her singing at her work,
And o'er the sickle bending —
I listened, motionless and still;
And, as I mounted up the hill,   30
The music in my heart I bore
Long after it was heard no more.

WILLIAM WORDSWORTH (1770–1850)

Mutability   *1822*

From low to high doth dissolution climb,
And sink from high to low, along a scale
Of awful° notes, whose concord shall not fail;   *awe-filled*
A muscial but melancholy chime,
Which they can hear who meddle not with crime,   5
Nor avarice, nor over-anxious care.
Truth fails not; but her outward forms that bear
The longest date do melt like frosty rime,
That in the morning whitened hill and plain
And is no more; drop like the tower sublime   10
Of yesterday, which royally did wear
His crown of weeds, but could not even sustain
Some casual shout that broke the silent air,
Or the unimaginable touch of Time.

BARON WORMSER (B. 1948)

Shoplifting   *1997*

The store dick lays a hand on your shoulder
Three steps from the exit. He asks what's
In your pockets but it's more like a statement
Than a question. Two candy bars and a roll of film.

Your stomach melts and your heart starts to beat   5
Like when you used to race on the playground.
He tells you to sit down on the bench by the doors.
Usually there are some old people sitting there

Gabbling about bargains but no one's around
This late in the evening. You expect the manager   10
To show up and give you a lecture about kids
Nowadays but he doesn't

And when the cop appears he doesn't say
Anything special beyond you'll have to go to court.
When he gives you the paper he's almost smiling   15
Or he's not there at all, he's not seeing you.

Thoughts, thoughts . . . your head's raw dough
One moment, light as a balloon the next.
They're always playing a song in the background
In these stores that you can't quite identify.   20

Your foot's tapping to the vacant beat
And after the cop leaves and you
Can leave you don't for some minutes.
You don't even own a camera.

MITSUYE YAMADA (B. 1923)

A Bedtime Story   *1976*

Once upon a time,
an old Japanese legend
goes as told
by Papa,
an old woman traveled through   5
many small villages
seeking refuge
for the night.

Each door opened
a sliver   10
in answer to her knock
then closed.
Unable to walk

any further
she wearily climbed a hill 15
found a clearing
and there lay down to rest
a few moments to catch
her breath.

The village town below 20
lay asleep except
for a few starlike lights.
Suddenly the clouds opened
and a full moon came into view
over the town. 25

The old woman sat up
turned toward
the village town
and in supplication
called out 30
Thank you people
of the village,
If it had not been for your
kindness
in refusing me a bed 35
for the night
these humble eyes would never
have seen this
memorable sight.

Papa paused, I waited. 40
In the comfort of our
hilltop home in Seattle
overlooking the valley,
I shouted
"That's the *end?*" 45

WILLIAM BUTLER YEATS (1865–1939)

Crazy Jane Talks with the Bishop   *1933*

I met the Bishop on the road
And much said he and I.
"Those breasts are flat and fallen now,
Those veins must soon be dry;
Live in a heavenly mansion, 5
Not in some foul sty."

"Fair and foul are near of kin,
And fair needs foul," I cried.
"My friends are gone, but that's a truth
Nor grave nor bed denied, 10

Learned in bodily lowliness
And in the heart's pride.

"A woman can be proud and stiff
When on love intent;
But Love has pitched his mansion in   15
The place of excrement;
For nothing can be sole or whole
That has not been rent."

WILLIAM BUTLER YEATS (1865–1939)

Leda and the Swan°   1924

A sudden blow: the great wings beating still
Above the staggering girl, her thighs caressed
By the dark webs, her nape caught in his bill,
He holds her helpless breast upon his breast.

How can those terrified vague fingers push   5
The feathered glory from her loosening thighs?
And how can body, laid in that white rush,
But feel the strange heart beating where it lies?

A shudder in the loins engenders there
The broken wall, the burning roof and tower   10
And Agamemnon dead.
                              Being so caught up,
So mastered by the brute blood of the air,
Did she put on his knowledge with his power
Before the indifferent beak could let her drop?   15

Leda and the Swan: In Greek myth, Zeus in the form of a swan seduced Leda and fathered Helen of Troy (whose abduction started the Trojan War) and Clytemnestra, Agamemnon's wife and murderer. Yeats thought of Zeus's appearance to Leda as a type of annunciation, like the angel appearing to Mary.

WILLIAM BUTLER YEATS (1865–1939)

Sailing to Byzantium°   1927

I
That is no country for old men.° The young
In one another's arms, birds in the trees
— Those dying generations — at their song,

Byzantium: Old name for the modern city of Istanbul, capital of the Eastern Roman Empire, ancient artistic and intellectual center. Yeats uses Byzantium as a symbol for "artificial" (and therefore, deathless) art and beauty, as opposed to the beauty of the natural world, which is bound to time and death.

1 *That ... men:* Ireland, part of the time-bound world.   19 *perne in a gyre:* Bobbin making a spiral pattern.

The salmon-falls, the mackerel-crowded seas
Fish, flesh, or fowl, commend all summer long 5
Whatever is begotten, born and dies.
Caught in that sensual music all neglect
Monuments of unaging intellect.

II
An aged man is but a paltry thing,
A tattered coat upon a stick, unless 10
Soul clap its hands and sing, and louder sing
For every tatter in its mortal dress,
Nor is there singing school but studying
Monuments of its own magnificence;
And therefore I have sailed the seas and come 15
To the holy city of Byzantium.

III
O sages standing in God's holy fire
As in the gold mosaic of a wall,
Come from the holy fire, perne in a gyre,°
And be the singing-masters of my soul. 20
Consume my heart away; sick with desire
And fastened to a dying animal
It knows not what it is; and gather me
Into the artifice of eternity.

IV
Once out of nature I shall never take 25
My bodily form from any natural thing,
But such a form as Grecian goldsmiths make
Of hammered gold and gold enameling
To keep a drowsy Emperor awake;°
Or set upon a golden bough° to sing 30
To lords and ladies of Byzantium
Of what is past, or passing, or to come.

27–29 *such . . . awake:* "I have read somewhere that in the Emperor's palace at Byzantium was a tree made of gold and silver, and artificial birds that sang." [Yeats's note.]

30 *golden bough:* In Greek legend, Aeneas had to pluck a golden bough from a tree in order to descend into Hades. As soon as the bough was plucked, another grew in its place.

WILLIAM BUTLER YEATS (1865–1939)

The Second Coming° 1921

Turning and turning in the widening gyre°
The falcon cannot hear the falconer;

The Second Coming: According to Matthew 24:29–44, Christ will return to earth after a time of tribulation to reward the righteous and establish the millennium of heaven on earth. Yeats saw his troubled time as the end of the Christian era and feared the portents of the new cycle.

1 *gyre:* Widening spiral of a falcon's flight, used by Yeats to describe the cycling of history.

Things fall apart; the center cannot hold;
Mere anarchy is loosed upon the world,
The blood-dimmed tide is loosed, and everywhere   5
The ceremony of innocence is drowned;
The best lack all conviction, while the worst
Are full of passionate intensity.

Surely some revelation is at hand;
Surely the Second Coming is at hand.   10
The Second Coming! Hardly are those words out
When a vast image out of *Spiritus Mundi*°   *Soul of the world*
Troubles my sight: somewhere in sands of the desert
A shape with lion body and the head of a man,
A gaze blank and pitiless as the sun,   15
Is moving its slow thighs, while all about it
Reel shadows of the indignant desert birds.
The darkness drops again; but now I know
That twenty centuries of stony sleep
Were vexed to nightmare by a rocking cradle,   20
And what rough beast, its hour come round at last,
Slouches towards Bethlehem to be born?

WILLIAM BUTLER YEATS (1865–1939)

The Wild Swans at Coole   *1916*

The trees are in their autumn beauty,
The woodland paths are dry,
Under the October twilight the water
Mirrors a still sky;
Upon the brimming water among the stones   5
Are nine-and-fifty swans.

The nineteenth autumn has come upon me
Since I first made my count;
I saw, before I had well finished,
All suddenly mount   10
And scatter wheeling in great broken rings
Upon their clamorous wings.

I have looked upon those brilliant creatures,
And now my heart is sore.
All's changed since I, hearing at twilight,   15
The first time on this shore,
The bell-beat of their wings above my head,
Trod with a lighter tread.

Unwearied still, lover by lover,
They paddle in the cold   20
Companionable streams or climb the air;
Their hearts have not grown old;

Passion or conquest, wander where they will,
Attend upon them still.

But now they drift on the still water,   25
Mysterious, beautiful;
Among what rushes will they build,
By what lake's edge or pool
Delight men's eyes when I awake some day
To find they have flown away?   30

DAVID ZIEROTH (B. 1946)

Time over Earth   1993

Above bank after bank of cloud
and the sudden open hole for rock or snow,
his seat partner
wrestles newspaper into a fold,
and in the cockpit the first officer   5
fights ennui and gazes into the round faces
of his instruments as they cast upon him
their evening glow, their eagerness
to serve. The steward from first class
offers comments from the passengers   10
on the delicacy of the flight,
the sureness of the surge, the persuasiveness
of their arc in and out of heaven.

Meanwhile in seat 16A
the view slips   15
into darkness once more,
forcing the eyes back from the vista.
His worries resurface
in this airy world
of alloy and wine, foam seats and hard-eyed   20
understanding focused in the one-brain
of the crew. A beam, he thinks, will soon
pick them up and lead them down,
and they will stay fastened
to this hope.   25

They rush to smell the new city — or the same one
returned to, which he re-enters
unchanged by time over earth; he knew
the thin light reaching into black
had not touched him   30
when he swept through revolving doors
in no less hurry
than other earthling friends.

Now asleep in his bed
his body still floats   35
across space, trying to arrive
on time, not caught
by the trees reaching up
to tear and throw him open.
Motionless under quilt, on pillow,   40
his eyes repeat all he has seen
and feared to see, each breath
hanging out of his body
in the worst kind of silent air.

AN ALBUM OF WORLD LITERATURE

ANNA AKHMATOVA (RUSSIA / 1889–1966)

Born in Russia, Anna Akhmatova was a poet and translator who was re-
garded as a major modern poet in Russia. Although she was expelled from
the Union of Soviet Writers during Stalin's rule, she was reclaimed by her
country in the 1960s. Her poetry is characterized by its clarity, precision, and
simplicity. Her work is translated in *Complete Poems of Anna Akhmatova* (1990).

Lot's Wife   *1922*

TRANSLATED BY RICHARD WILBUR

The just man followed then his angel guide
Where he strode on the black highway, hulking and bright;
But a wild grief in his wife's bosom cried,
Look back, it is not too late for a last sight

Of the red towers of your native Sodom, the square   5
Where once you sang, the gardens you shall mourn,
And the tall house with empty windows where
You loved your husband and your babes were born.

She turned, and looking on the bitter view
Her eyes were welded shut by mortal pain;   10
Into transparent salt her body grew,
And her quick feet were rooted in the plain.

Who would waste tears upon her? Is she not
The least of our losses, this unhappy wife?
Yet in my heart she will not be forgot   15
Who, for a single glance, gave up her life.

CONNECTIONS TO OTHER SELECTIONS

1. Discuss the use of Biblical allusions in "Lot's Wife" and in William Butler Yeats's "The Second Coming" (p. 653). How is an understanding of the allusions crucial to interpreting each poem?

2. Consider the "unhappy wife" in this poem and in Linda Pastan's "Marks" (p. 132). Discuss how you regard the wife in each poem.

CLARIBEL ALEGRÍA (EL SALVADOR / B. 1924)

Born in Estelí, Nicaragua, Claribel Alegría moved with her family to El Salvador within a year of her birth. A 1948 graduate of George Washington University, she considers herself a Salvadoran, and much of her writing reflects the political upheaval of recent Latin American history. In 1978 she was awarded the Casa de las Americas Prize for her book *I Survive*. A bilingual edition of her major works, *Flowers from the Volcano*, was published in 1982.

I Am Mirror   *1978*

TRANSLATED BY ELECTA ARENAL AND MARSHA GABRIELA DREYER

Water sparkles
on my skin
and I don't feel it
water streams
down my back   5
I don't feel it
I rub myself with a towel
I pinch myself in the arm
I don't feel
frightened I look at myself in the mirror   10
she also pricks herself
I begin to get dressed
stumbling
from the corners
shouts like lightning bolts   15
tortured eyes
scurrying rats
and teeth shoot forth
although I feel nothing
I wander through the streets: 20
children with dirty faces
ask me for charity
child prostitutes
who are not yet fifteen
the streets are paved with pain   25
tanks that approach

raised bayonets
bodies that fall
weeping
finally I feel my arm   30
I am no longer a phantom
I hurt
therefore I exist
I return to watch the scene:
children who run   35
bleeding
women with panic
in their faces
this time it hurts me less
I pinch myself again   40
and already I feel nothing
I simply reflect
what happens at my side
the tanks
are not tanks   45
nor are the shouts
shouts
I am a blank mirror
that nothing penetrates
my surface   50
is hard
is brilliant
is polished
I became a mirror
and I am fleshless   55
scarcely preserving
a vague memory
of pain.

CONNECTIONS TO OTHER SELECTIONS

1. Compare the ways Alegría uses mirror images to reflect life in El Salvador with Plath's concerns in "Mirror" (p. 126).

2. Write an essay comparing the speaker's voice in this poem and that in Blake's "London" (p. 10). How do the speakers evoke emotional responses to what they describe?

YEHUDA AMICHAI (ISRAEL / B. 1924)

A leading contemporary Hebrew poet, Yehuda Amichai was born in Germany in 1924, and later moved with his family to Jerusalem. Amichai fought with the Jewish Brigade of the British Army during World War II and in the War of Independence. After the war, he attended Hebrew University. His first volume of poetry, *Achshav Uve-Yamin HaAharim* ("Now and in Other Days") appeared in 1955 and immediately attracted the interest of the poetry-reading public. Widely read and admired outside his country, his works have been translated into thirty-three languages. His *Collected Poems* appeared in 1963; he is also the author of two novels and a book of short stories. *The Selected Poems of Yehuda Amichai* was published in 1996.

Jerusalem, 1985   *1985*

TRANSLATED BY CHANA BLOCH

Scribbled wishes stuck between the stones
of the Wailing Wall:
bits of crumpled, wadded paper.

And across the way, stuck in an old iron gate
half-hidden by jasmine: 5
"Couldn't make it,
I hope you'll understand."

CONNECTIONS TO OTHER SELECTIONS

1. Consider the use of irony in this poem and in Emily Dickinson's "I know that He exists" (p. 327).
2. Based on the content and style of "Jerusalem, 1985" and Wislawa Szymborska's "Maybe All This" (p. 665), characterize the speaker in each poem. Explain why you think they are more alike or different.

FAIZ AHMED FAIZ (PAKISTAN / 1911–1984)

Born in Pakistan, Faiz Ahmed Faiz served in the British Indian Army during World War II. After the war he became a spokesman for Pakistani and Indian rights by editing the *Pakistani Times* and writing poetry in Urdu. Faiz served several jail sentences for his political activism, spending a considerable amount of time in solitary confinement. His poetry is widely known in India and the subcontinent; a translation of some is available as *Poems by Faiz* (1971).

If You Look at the City from Here   *1971*

TRANSLATED BY NAOMI LAZARD

If you look at the city from here
you see it is laid out in concentric circles,
each circle surrounded by a wall
        exactly like a prison.

Each street is a dog-run for prisoners,   5
no milestones, no destinations, no way out.

If anyone moves too quickly you wonder
why he hasn't been stopped by a shout.
If someone raises his arm
you expect to hear the jangling of chains.   10

If you look at the city from here
there is no one with dignity,
no one fully in control of his senses.
Every young man bears the brand of a criminal,
every young woman the emblem of a slave.   15

You cannot tell whether you see
               a group of revelers or mourners
in the shadows dancing around the distant lamps,
and from here you cannot tell
whether the color streaming down the walls   20
is that of blood or roses.

CONNECTIONS TO OTHER SELECTIONS

1. Compare the treatment of the city in this poem and in Blake's "London" (p. 101).
2. Write an essay on the meaning of confinement in Faiz's poem and in Rilke's "The Panther" (p. 105).

XU GANG (CHINA / B. 1945)

Born in Shanghai, China, Xu Gang served in the army after being drafted in 1962 and began writing poetry in support of the Cultural Revolution. However, after graduating from Beijing University in 1974, he questioned the principles and brutally disruptive consequences of the Cultural Revolution, a disillusionment suggested by "Red Azalea on the Cliff." His collections of poems include *The Flower of Rain, Songs for the Far Away*, and *One Hundred Lyrics*.

Red Azalea on the Cliff   1982

TRANSLATED BY FANG DAI, DENNIS DING, AND EDWARD MORIN

Red azalea, smiling
From the cliffside at me,
You make my heart shudder with fear!
A body could smash and bones splinter in the canyon —
Beauty, always looking on at disaster.   5

But red azalea on the cliff,
That you comb your twigs even in a mountain gale

Calms me down a bit.
Of course you're not wilfully courting danger,
Nor are you at ease with whatever happens to you.   10
You're merely telling me: beauty is nature.

Would anyone like to pick a flower
To give to his love
Or pin to his own lapel?
On the cliff there is no road   15
And no azalea grows where there is a road.
If someone actually reached that azalea,
Then an azalea would surely bloom in his heart.

Red azalea on the cliff,
You smile like the Yellow Mountains,   20
Whose sweetness encloses slyness,
Whose intimacy embraces distance.
You remind us all of our first love.
Sometimes the past years look
Just like the azalea on the cliff.   25

MAY 1982
Yellow Mountain
Revised at Hangzhou

CONNECTION TO ANOTHER SELECTION

1. In an essay explain how beauty is associated with danger in Xu Gang's poem and in Keats's "La Belle Dame sans Merci" (p. 618).

PABLO NERUDA (CHILE / 1904–1973)

Born in Chile, Pablo Neruda insisted all his life on the connection between poetry and politics. He was an activist and a Chilean diplomat in a number of countries during the 1920s and 1930s and remained politically active until his death. Neruda was regarded as a great and influential poet (he was awarded the Nobel Prize in 1971) whose poetry ranged from specific political issues to the yearnings of romantic love. Among his many works are *Twenty Love Poems and a Song of Despair* (1924), *Residence on Earth* (three series, 1925–45), *Spain in the Heart* (1937), *The Captain's Verses* (1952), and *Memorial of Isla Negra* (1964).

Sweetness, Always   1958

TRANSLATED BY ALASTAIR REID

Why such harsh machinery?
Why, to write down the stuff
and people of every day,

must poems be dressed up in gold,
in old and fearful stone?   5
I want verses of felt or feather
which scarcely weigh, mild verses
with the intimacy of beds
where people have loved and dreamed.
I want poems stained   10
by hands and everydayness.

Verses of pastry which melt
into milk and sugar in the mouth,
air and water to drink,
the bites and kisses of love.   15
I long for eatable sonnets,
poems of honey and flour.

Vanity keeps prodding us
to lift ourselves skyward
or to make deep and useless   20
tunnels underground.
So we forget the joyous
love-needs of our bodies.
We forget about pastries.
We are not feeding the world.   25

In Madras a long time since,
I saw a sugary pyramid,
a tower of confectionery—
one level after another,
and in the construction, rubies,   30
and other blushing delights,
medieval and yellow.

Someone dirtied his hands
to cook up so much sweetness.

Brother poets from here   35
and there, from earth and sky,
from Medellín, from Veracruz,
Abyssinia, Antofagasta,
do you know the recipe for honeycombs?

Let's forget all about that stone.   40

Let your poetry fill up
the equinoctial pastry shop
our mouths long to devour—
all the children's mouths
and the poor adults' also.   45
Don't go on without seeing,
relishing, understanding
all these hearts of sugar.

Don't be afraid of sweetness.

With us or without us,   50
sweetness will go on living
and is infinitely alive,
forever being revived,
for it's in a man's mouth,
whether he's eating or singing,   55
that sweetness has its place.

CONNECTIONS TO OTHER SELECTIONS

1. Compare the view of life offered in this poem with that in Frost's "Birches" (p. 347).
2. Write an essay that discusses Kinnell's "Blackberry Eating" (p. 176) and Chasin's "The Word *Plum*" (p. 195) as the sort of "eatable" poetry the speaker calls for in this poem.

OCTAVIO PAZ (MEXICO / 1914–1998)

Born in Mexico City, Octavio Paz studied at the National Autonomous University and in 1943 helped found one of Mexico's most important literary reviews, the *Prodigal Son*. He served in the Mexican diplomatic corps in Paris, New Delhi, and New York. Much of Paz's poetry reflects Hispanic traditions and European modernism as well as Buddhism. In 1990 he received the Nobel Prize for Literature. Paz's major works include *Sun Stone* (1958), *The Violent Season* (1958), *Salamander* (1962), *Blanco* (1966), *Eastern Rampart* (1968), *Renga* (1971), and *Collected Poems, 1957–1987* (1987).

The Street   *1963*

A long silent street.
I walk in blackness and I stumble and fall
and rise, and I walk blind, my feet
stepping on silent stones and dry leaves.
Someone behind me also stepping on stones, leaves: 5
if I slow down, he slows;
if I run, he runs. I turn: nobody.
Everything dark and doorless.
Turning and turning among these corners
which lead forever to the street   10
where nobody waits for, nobody follows me,
where I pursue a man who stumbles
and rises and says when he sees me: nobody.

CONNECTIONS TO OTHER SELECTIONS

1. How does the speaker's anxiety in this poem compare with that in Frost's "Acquainted with the Night" (p. 139)?
2. Write an essay comparing the tone of this poem and that of Hughes's "Lenox Avenue: Midnight" (p. 383).

INDIRA SANT (INDIA / B. 1914)

Born in Pune in the state of Maharashtra, India, Indira Sant began her career as a teacher and a writer of children's fiction. In the 1950s she focused her talent on writing feminist poetry that sympathetically described the hardships endured by Indian mothers, wives, and daughters. Her work has not been widely translated, but the following poem appeared in the journal *Daedalus*.

Household Fires 1989

TRANSLATED BY VINAY DHARWADKER

The daughter's job: without a murmur
to do the chores piling up around the house
until she leaves for work,
to pay her younger brother's fees,
to buy her sister ribbons, 5
to get her father's spectacles changed.
To take the others to the movies on holidays,
to keep back a little and hand over the rest
on payday.

The son's job: fresh savory snacks 10
for the whole household to eat:
to bring back the clothes from the washerman,
to clean and put away the bicycle,
to sing out of key while packing his father's lunch
at the stroke of the hour, 15
to open the door sulkily
whenever someone comes home from the movies,
to wrinkle his brow
when he puts out his hand for money
and is asked instead, "How much? For what?" 20

The younger daughter's job:
to savor the joys of shyness,
to shrink back minute by minute.
The younger son's job:
to choke all the while, grow up slowly 25
in states of wet and dry.

Four children learning in her fold,
her body drained by hardship,
what's left of her? A mass of tatters,
five tongues of flame 30
licking and licking at her on every side,
fanning and fanning the fire in her eyes
till her mind boils over,
gets burned.

CONNECTIONS TO OTHER SELECTIONS

1. Implicit in this poem is the father's presence. Compare the treatment of the father in "Household Fires" and Plath's "Daddy" (p. 630).

2. Write an essay that compares the life described in this poem with Divakaruni's "Indian Movie, New Jersey" (p. 162).

WOLE SOYINKA (NIGERIA / B. 1934)

Born Oluwole Akinwande Soyinka, in the western Nigerian town of Akinwande, Wole Soyinka has embodied in his life and art the contradictions and tensions that can often seem inevitable for the European-educated, English-speaking African writers. Although he has written and published novels and poetry (the following poem is from *A Shuttle in the Crypt* [1972]), Soyinka is most renowned as a playwright whose work embodies his concerns as a political reformer and social critic. His many plays include *The Lion and the Jewel* (1959), *The Strong Bond* (1963), and *Death of the King's Horseman* (1976). His autobiography *The Man Died* (1973) records his experiences as a political prisoner in Nigeria. In 1986 he was awarded the Nobel Prize for Literature.

Future Plans 1972

The meeting is called
To odium: Forgers, framers
Fabricators Inter-
national. Chairman,
A dark horse, a circus nag turned blinkered sprinter   5

Mach Three°
We rate him — one for the Knife°
Two for 'iavelli,° Three —
Breaking speed
Of the truth barrier by a swooping detention decree   10
Projects in view:
Mao Tse Tung° in league
With Chiang Kai. Nkrumah°

6 *Mach Three:* An air speed of three times the speed of sound.   7 *Knife:* Mack the Knife, an unsavory character from *The Threepenny Opera* (1933), by Bertolt Brecht and Kurt Weill.

8 *'iavelli:* Niccolò Machiavelli (1469–1527), an Italian political theorist who described ruthless strategies for gaining power in *The Prince* (1532).

12 *Mao Tse Tung:* Mao Tse-tung (1893–1975), Chinese Communist leader.

13 *Chiang Kai, Nkrumah:* Chiang Kai-shek (1887–1975), Chinese Nationalist leader exiled in Taiwan by Mao Tse-tung; Kwame Nkrumah (1909–1972), first president of Ghana.

Makes a secret
Pact with Verwood, sworn by Hastings Banda.°   15
Proven: Arafat°
In flagrante cum
Golda Meir. Castro° drunk
With Richard Nixon°
Contraceptives stacked beneath the papal bunk . . .   20
                    . . . *and more to come*

15 *Verwood, Hastings Banda:* Hendrick Verwoerd (1901–1966), former prime minister of South
Africa, assassinated in 1966; Hastings Banda (b. 1905), African political leader and first presi-
dent of Malawi.

16 *Arafat:* Yasir Arafat (b. 1929), Palestinian leader.

18 *Golda Meir, Castro:* Golda Meir (1898–1978), former prime minister of Israel; Fidel Castro
(b. 1927), Cuban premier since 1959.

19 *Richard Nixon* (1913–1994): Former U.S. president forced to resign in 1974 due to political
scandal.

CONNECTIONS TO OTHER SELECTIONS

1. Discuss the political satire in "Future Plans" and in Fearing's "AD" (p. 144).

2. Write an essay on whether the leaders alluded to in "Future Plans" are man-
   ifestations of the type of leader described in Thomas's "The Hand That
   Signed the Paper" (p. 120).

WISLAWA SZYMBORSKA (POLAND / B. 1923)

Born in Poland, Wislawa Szymborska has lived in Cracow since the age of
eight. She steadfastly refuses to reveal biographical details of her life, in-
sisting that her poems should speak for themselves. With the exception of
Sounds, Feelings, Thoughts. Seventy Poems by Wislawa Szymborska (1981), trans-
lated and introduced by Magnus J. Krynski and Robert A. Maguire, and *View
with a Grain of Sand: Selected Poems* (1995), translated by Stanislaw Barańczak
and Clare Cavanagh, only some of Szymborska's poems have been translated
into English. Three of her later poetry collections — as yet untranslated — are
There But for the Grace (1972), *A Great Number* (1976), and *The People of the Bridge*
(1986). She was awarded the Nobel Prize in Literature in 1996.

Maybe All This   *1993*

TRANSLATED BY STANISLAW BARAŃCZAK AND CLARE CAVANAGH

Maybe all this
is happening in some lab?
Under one lamp by day
and billions by night?

Maybe we're experimental generations?   5
Poured from one vial to the next,

shaken in test tubes,
not scrutinized by eyes alone,
each of us separately
plucked up by tweezers in the end? 10

Or maybe it's more like this:
No interference?
The changes occur on their own
according to plan?
The graph's needle slowly etches 15
its predictable zigzags?

Maybe thus far we aren't of much interest?
The control monitors aren't usually plugged in?
Only for wars, perferably large ones,
for the odd ascent above our clump of Earth, 20
for major migrations from point A to B?

Maybe just the opposite:
They've got a taste for trivia up there?
Look! on the big screen a little girl
is sewing a button on her sleeve. 25
The radar shrieks,
the staff comes at a run.
What a darling little being
with its tiny heart beating inside it!
How sweet, its solemn 30
threading of the needle!
Someone cries enraptured:
Get the Boss,
tell him he's got to see this for himself!

CONNECTIONS TO OTHER SELECTIONS

1. Discuss the themes of "Maybe All This" and Dickinson's "Apparently with No Surprise." (p. 328).
2. Write an essay on the tone of "Maybe All This" and Robert Frost's "Design" (p. 356).

TOMAS TRANSTROMER (SWEDEN / B. 1931)

Born in Stockholm, Sweden, Tomas Transtromer's work is translated more than any other contemporary Scandinavian poet's. He has worked as a psychologist with juvenile offenders and handicapped persons. His collections of poetry include *Night Vision* (1971), *Windows and Stones: Selected Poems* (1972), *Truth Barriers* (1978), and *Selected Poems* (1981). Among his awards are the Petrarch Prize (1981) and a lifetime subsidy from the government of Sweden.

April and Silence

1991

TRANSLATED BY ROBIN FULTON

Spring lies desolate.
The velvet-dark ditch
crawls by my side
without reflections.

The only thing that shines   5
is yellow flowers.

I am carried in my shadow
like a violin
in its black box.

The only thing I want to say   10
glitters out of reach
like the silver
in a pawnbroker's.

CONNECTIONS TO OTHER SELECTIONS

1. Discuss the description of spring in this poem and in William Carlos
   Williams's "Spring and All" (p. 645).

2. In an essay explain how the dictions used in "April and Silence" and Es-
   pada's "Latin Night at the Pawnshop" (p. 62) contribute to the poems'
   meanings and tone.

AN ALBUM OF CONTEMPORARY POEMS

BILLY COLLINS (B. 1941)

Since the publication of his first book, *The Apple That Astonished Paris* (1988),
Billy Collins (born in New York City in 1941) has established himself as a
prominent voice in contemporary American poetry. His recent books in-
clude *Picnic, Lightning* (1998), *The Art of Drowning* (1995) — a finalist for the
Lenore Marshall Prize — and *Questions about Angels* (1991), selected for the
National Poetry Series and reissued in 1999.

Marginalia

1998

Sometimes the notes are ferocious,
skirmishes against the author
raging along the borders of every page
in tiny black script.
If I could just get my hands on you,   5

Kierkegaard,° or Conor Cruise O'Brien,°
they seem to say,
I would bolt the door and beat some logic into your head.

Other comments are more offhand, dismissive —
"Nonsense." "Please!" "HA!!" —   10
that kind of thing.
I remember once looking up from my reading,
my thumb as a bookmark,
trying to imagine what the person must look like
who wrote "Don't be a ninny"   15
alongside a paragraph in *The Life of Emily Dickinson.*

Students are more modest
needing to leave only their splayed footprints
along the shore of the page.
One scrawls "Metaphor" next to a stanza of Eliot's.°   20
Another notes the presence of "Irony"
fifty times outside the paragraphs of *A Modest Proposal.*°

Or they are fans who cheer from the empty bleachers,
hands cupped around their mouths.
"Absolutely," they shout   25
to Duns Scotus° and James Baldwin.°
"Yes." "Bull's-eye." "My man!"
Check marks, asterisks, and exclamation points
rain down along the sidelines.

And if you have managed to graduate from college   30
without ever having written "Man vs. Nature"
in a margin, perhaps now
is the time to take one step forward.

We have all seized the white perimeter as our own
and reached for a pen if only to show   35
we did not just laze in an armchair turning pages;
we pressed a thought into the wayside,
planted an impression along the verge.

Even Irish monks in their cold scriptoria°
jotted along the borders of the Gospels   40
brief asides about the pains of copying,
a bird singing near their window,
or the sunlight that illuminated their page —

6 *Kierkegaard:* Sören Aaby Kierkegaard (1813–1855), Danish philosopher and theologian.
Conor Cruise O'Brien (b. 1917): Irish historian, critic, and statesman.

20 *Eliot's:* Thomas Stearns Eliot (1888–1965), American-born English poet and critic.   22 *A Modest Proposal:* An essay by English satirist Jonathan Swift (1667–1745).

26 *Duns Scotus* (1265?–1308): Scottish theologian.   *James Baldwin* (1924–1987): African American essayist and novelist.

39 *scriptoria:* Rooms in a monastery used for writing and copying.

anonymous men catching a ride into the future
on a vessel more lasting than themselves.   45

And you have not read Joshua Reynolds,°
they say, until you have read him
enwreathed with Blake's° furious scribbling.

Yet the one I think of most often,
the one that dangles from me like a locket,   50
was written in the copy of *Catcher in the Rye*°
I borrowed from the local library
one slow, hot summer.
I was just beginning high school then,
reading books on a davenport in my parents' living room,   55
and I cannot tell you
how vastly my loneliness was deepened,
how poignant and amplified the world before me seemed,
when I found on one page

a few greasy looking smears   60
and next to them, written in soft pencil —
by a beautiful girl, I could tell,
whom I would never meet —
"Pardon the egg salad stains, but I'm in love."

46 *Joshua Reynolds* (1723–1792): English portrait artist who entertained many of the impor-
tant writers of his time.

48 *Blake's:* William Blake (1757–1827), English mystic and poet.

51 *Catcher in the Rye:* A novel (1951) about adolescence by American author J. D. Salinger
(b. 1919).

CONNECTIONS TO OTHER SELECTIONS

1. Discuss the speaker's response to reading in "Marginalia" and in Philip
   Larkin's "A Study of Reading Habits" (p. 22). How is reading used as a mea-
   sure of each speaker's character?

2. Describe the impact made on the speaker's imagination by what is contem-
   plated in "Marginalia" and in C. K. Williams's "The Nail" (p. 643).

CORNELIUS EADY (B. 1954)

Cornelius Eady, born in Rochester, New York, has taught poetry at several
colleges and universities; he is currently director of the Poetry Center at
the State University of New York at Stony Brook. The recipient of many
fellowships and awards, he has published five books of poetry including
Victims of the Latest Dance Craze (1986) and *The Gathering of My Name* (1991).

The Supremes

1991

We were born to be gray. We went to school,
Sat in rows, ate white bread,
Looked at the floor a lot. In the back
Of our small heads

A long scream. We did what we could,   5
And all we could do was
Turn on each other. How the fat kids suffered!
Not even being jolly could save them.

And then there were the anal retentives,
The terrified brown-noses, the desperately   10
Athletic or popular. This, of course,
Was training. At home

Our parents shook their heads and waited.
We learned of the industrial revolution,
The sectioning of the clock into pie slices.   15
We drank cokes and twiddled our thumbs. In the
Back of our minds

A long scream. We snapped butts in the showers,
Froze out shy girls on the dance floor,
Pin-pointed flaws like radar.   20
Slowly we understood: this was to be the world.

We were born insurance salesmen and secretaries,
Housewives and short order cooks,
Stock room boys and repairmen,
And it wouldn't be a bad life, they promised,   25
In a tone of voice that would force some of us
To reach in self-defense for wigs,
Lipstick,

Sequins.

CONNECTIONS TO OTHER SELECTIONS

1. Discuss the speakers' memories of school in "The Supremes" and in Judy
   Page Heitzman's "The Schoolroom on the Second Floor of the Knitting
   Mill" (p. 446).
2. In an essay compare the themes of "The Supremes" and Dickinson's "From
   all the Jails the Boys and Girls" (p. 442).

MARTÍN ESPADA (B. 1957)

Martín Espada was born in Brooklyn, New York. He has worked as a tenant
lawyer in Boston and now teaches in the English Department at the Uni-
versity of Massachusetts at Amherst. He has been awarded several fellow-

ships including two from the National Endowment for the Arts. His books of poetry include *Rebellion Is the Circle of a Lover's Hand* (1990), *City of Coughing and Dead Radiators* (1993), and *Imagine the Angels of Bread* (1996)

Coca-Cola and Coco Frío   *1993*

On his first visit to Puerto Rico,
island of family folklore,
the fat boy wandered
from table to table
with his mouth open.   5
At every table, some great-aunt
would steer him with cool spotted hands
to a glass of Coca-Cola.
One even sang to him, in all the English
she could remember, a Coca-Cola jingle   10
from the forties. He drank obediently, though
he was bored with this potion, familiar
from soda fountains in Brooklyn.

Then, at a roadside stand off the beach, the fat boy
opened his mouth to coco frío, a coconut   15
chilled, then scalped by a machete
so that a straw could inhale the clear milk.
The boy tilted the green shell overhead
and drooled coconut milk down his chin;
suddenly, Puerto Rico was not Coca-Cola   20
or Brooklyn, and neither was he.

For years afterward, the boy marveled at an island
where the people drank Coca-Cola
and sang jingles from World War II
in a language they did not speak,   25
while so many coconuts in the trees
sagged heavy with milk, swollen
and unsuckled.

CONNECTIONS TO OTHER SELECTIONS

1. Compare what the boy in this poem discovers about Puerto Rico with what the speaker learns in Hughes's "Theme for English B" (p. 442).
2. Write an essay discussing the images used to describe Puerto Rico and the United States in this poem and in Laviera's "AmeRícan" (p. 269).

DEBORAH GARRISON (B. 1965)

Raised in Ann Arbor, Michigan, Deborah Garrison graduated from Brown University and works on the editorial staff of *The New Yorker*. She published a collection of poems, *A Working Girl Can't Win,* in 1998. Her poetry appears regularly in *The New Yorker.*

The Boss   1998

A firecracker, even after middle age
set in, a prince of repression
in his coat and tie, with cynical words

for everything dear to him.
Once I saw a snapshot of the house   5
he lives in, its fence painted

white, the flowers a wife
had planted leaning into the frame
on skinny stalks, shaking little pom-poms

of color, the dazzle all   10
accidental, and I felt
a hot, corrective

sting: our lives would never
intersect. At some point
he got older, trimmer, became   15

the formidable man around the office.
His bearing upright, what hair he has
silver and smooth, he shadows my doorway,

jostling the change in his pocket—
milder now, and mildly vexed.   20
The other day he asked what on earth

was wrong with me, and sat me down
on his big couch, where I cried
for twenty minutes straight,

snuffling, my eyeliner   25
betraying itself in the stained
tears. Impossible to say I was crying

because he had asked. He passed
tissues, at ease with the fearsome
womanly squall that made me alien   30

even to myself. No, it didn't make him
squirm. Across his seventy years,
over his glasses, he eyed me kindly,

and I thought what countless scenes
of tears, of love revealed,   35
he must have known.

DONALD HALL (B. 1928)

Born in New Haven, Connecticut, Donald Hall taught at the University of Michigan and for years has made his living in New Hampshire as a freelance writer of numerous books of poetry as well as literary criticism, essays, and children's books. His collections of poems include *The One Day* (1988), winner of the National Book Critics Award, *The Museum of Clear Ideas* (1993), and *Without* (1998).

Letter with No Address   *1996*

Your daffodils rose up
and collapsed in their yellow
bodies on the hillside
garden above the bricks
you laid out in sand, squatting   5
with pants pegged and face
masked like a beekeeper's
against the black flies.
Buttercups circle the planks
of the old wellhead   10
this May while your silken
gardener's body withers or moulds
in the Proctor graveyard.
I drive and talk to you crying
and come back to this house   15
to talk to your photographs.

There's news to tell you:
Maggie Fisher's pregnant.
I carried myself like an egg
at Abigail's birthday party   20
a week after you died,
as three-year-olds bounced
uproarious on a mattress.
Joyce and I met for lunch
at the mall and strolled weepily   25
through Sears and B. Dalton.

Today it's four weeks
since you lay on our painted bed

and I closed your eyes.
Yesterday I cut irises to set   30
in a pitcher on your grave;
today I brought a carafe
to fill it with fresh water.
I remember the bone-pain,
vomiting, and delirium. I remember   35
the pond afternoons.

              My routine
is established: coffee;
the *Globe;* breakfast;
writing you this letter   40
at my desk. When I go to bed
to sleep after baseball,
Gus follows me into the bedroom
as he used to follow us.
Most of the time he flops   45
down in the parlor
with his head on his paws.

Once a week I drive to Tilton
to see Dick and Nan.
Nan doesn't understand much   50
but she knows you're dead;
I feel her fretting. The tune
of Dick and me talking
seems to console her.

             You know now   55
whether the soul survives death.
Or you don't. When you were dying
you said you didn't fear
punishment. We never dared
to speak of Paradise.   60

At five a.m., when I walk outside,
mist lies thick on hayfields.
By eight, the air is clear,
cool, sunny with the pale yellow
light of mid-May. Kearsarge   65
rises huge and distinct,
each birch and balsam visible.
To the west the waters
of Eagle Pond waver
and flash through popples just   70
leafing out.

             Always the weather,
writing its book of the world,
returns you to me.
Ordinary days were best,   75
when we worked over poems

in our separate rooms.
I remember watching you gaze
out the January window
into the garden of snow   80
and ice, your face rapt
as you imagined burgundy lilies.

Your presence in this house
is almost as enormous
and painful as your absence.   85
Driving home from Tilton,
I remember how you cherished
that vista with its center
the red door of a farmhouse
against green fields.   90
Are you past pity?
If you have consciousness now,
if something I can call
"you" has something
like "consciousness," I doubt   95
you remember the last days.
I play them over and over:
I lift your wasted body
onto the commode, your arms
looped around my neck, aiming   100
your bony bottom so that
it will not bruise on a rail.
Faintly you repeat,
"Momma, Momma."

             You lay   105
astonishing in the long box
while Alice Ling prayed
and sang "Amazing Grace"
a capella. Three times today
I drove to your grave.   110
Sometimes, coming back home
to our circular driveway,
I imagine you've returned
before me, bags of groceries upright
in the back of the Saab,   115
its trunklid delicately raised
as if proposing an encounter,
dog-fashion, with the Honda.

CONNECTIONS TO OTHER SELECTIONS

1. Compare how the speaker copes with grief in "Letter with No Address" with the speaker in Dickinson's "The Bustle in a House" (p. 312).

2. Write an essay on the tone of this poem and Frost's "Home Burial" (p. 343).

JANE HIRSHFIELD (B. 1953)

Born in New York City, Jane Hirshfield is the author of four books of po-
etry, most recently *The Lives of the Heart* (1997), and a collection of essays,
Nine Gates: Entering the Mind of Poetry (1997). She has also edited and co-
translated two collections of poetry by women from the past, *Women in
Praise of the Sacred: Forty-three Centuries of Spiritual Poetry by Women* (1995)
and *The Ink Dark Moon: Poems by Ono no Komachi and Izumi Shikibu, Women
of the Ancient Court of Japan* (1990). Hirshfield's awards include the Poetry
Center Book Award, the Bay Area Book Reviewers Award, Columbia Uni-
versity's Translation Center Award, and fellowships from the Guggenheim
and Rockefeller Foundations.

The Lives of the Heart   1997

Are ligneous, muscular, chemical.
Wear birch-colored feathers,
green tunnels of horse-tail reed.
Wear calcified spirals, Fibonnacian° spheres.
Are edible; are glassy; are clay; blue schist.   5
Can be burned as tallow, as coal,
can be skinned for garnets, for shoes.
Cast shadows or light;
shuffle; snort; cry out in passion.
Are salt, are bitter,   10
tear sweet grass with their teeth.
Step silently into blue needle-fall at dawn.
Thrash in the net until hit.
Rise up as cities, as serpentined magma, as maples,
hiss lava-red into the sea.   15
Leave the strange kiss of their bodies
in Burgess Shale. Can be found, can be lost,
can be carried, broken, sung.
Lie dormant until they are opened by ice,
by drought. Go blind in the service of lace.   20
Are starving, are sated, indifferent, curious, mad.
Are stamped out in plastic, in tin.
Are stubborn, are careful, are slipshod,
are strung on the blue backs of flies
on the black backs of cows.   25
Wander the vacant whale-roads, the white thickets
heavy with slaughter.
Wander the fragrant carpets of alpine flowers.
Not one is not held in the arms of the rest, to blossom.
Not one is not given to ecstasy's lions.   30

4 *Fibonnacian:* An apparent reference to Leonardo Fibonacci (1170–1240), a famous Italian
mathematician.

Not one does not grieve.
Each of them opens and closes, closes and opens
the heavy gate — violent, serene, consenting, suffering it all.

CONNECTIONS TO OTHER SELECTIONS

1. Discuss the use of personification in this poem and Stevens's "Schizophrenia" (p. 129).
2. Write an essay that compares the diction and images of "The Lives of the Heart" and Alice Jones's "The Foot" (p. 208).

LINDA HOGAN (B. 1947)

Born in Denver, Colorado, and raised in Oklahoma, Linda Hogan is a member of the Chickasaw tribe. She was educated at the University of Colorado, where she now teaches creative writing. She has been awarded fellowships from the Guggenheim Foundation and the National Endowment for the Arts and has received an American Book Award. In addition to publishing fiction — her novel *Mean Spirit* appeared in 1989 — she has published several volumes of poetry including *Eclipse* (1985), *Seeing through the Sun* (1985), *Savings* (1988), and *The Book of Medicines* (1993).

Hunger   *1993*

Hunger crosses oceans.
It loses its milk teeth.
It sits on the ship and cries.

Thin, afraid,
it fashioned hooks to catch   5
the passing songs of whales so large
the men grew small
as distant, shrinking lands.
They sat on the ship and cried.

Hunger was the fisherman   10
who said dolphins are like women,
we took them from the sea
and had our way
with them.

Hunger knows we have not yet reached   15
the black and raging depths of anything.

It is the old man
who comes in the night

to cast a line
and wait at the luminous shore.   20

He knows the sea is pregnant
with clear fish
and their shallow pools of eggs
and that the ocean has hidden
signs of its own hunger, 25
lost men and boats
and squid that flew
toward churning light.

Hunger lives in the town
whose walls are made of shells 30
white and shining in the moon,
where people live surrounded
by what they've eaten
to forget that hunger
sits on a ship and cries. 35

And it is a kind of hunger
that brings us to love,
to rocking currents of a secret wave
and the body that wants to live beyond itself
like the destitute men 40
who took the shining dolphins from the sea.
They were like women,
they said,
and had their way
with them, 45
wanting to be inside,
to drink
and be held in
the thin, clear milk of the gods.

CONNECTIONS TO OTHER SELECTIONS

1. Write an essay comparing Hogan's definition of hunger with Dickinson's definition of heaven in "'Heaven'—is what I cannot reach!" (p. 299). Which definition do you find more complete and satisfying? Explain why.

2. Discuss the relation between love and hunger in this poem and in Croft's "Home-Baked Bread" (p. 107).

PHILIP LEVINE (B. 1928)

Immersed in the working-class milieu of Detroit, where he was born in 1928, Philip Levine's work records an America where the "time will never come / nor the ripeness be all." Nonetheless his poems celebrate—quietly, with irony and humor—the stoicism of the human spirit. Levine attended Wayne State University and while there studied with the poet John Berryman. In 1958 he was awarded the prestigious Fellowship in Poetry at Stanford University. Since 1969 he has taught English at California State University in

Fresno and now divides his time between Fresno and New York University. His most recent collections include *What Work Is* (1991), *The Simple Truth* (1994), *Unselected Poems* (1997), *The Return* (1999), and an autobiography, *The Bread of Time* (1994). *Selected Poems* appeared in 1984. He has received two Pulitzer Prizes, two National Book Awards, two National Book Critics Circle Awards, the Lenore Marshall Award, and the Ruth Lilly Award.

Reinventing America   *1999*

The city was huge. A boy of twelve could walk
for hours while the closed houses stared down at him
from early morning to dusk, and he'd get nowhere.
Oh no, I was not that boy. Even at twelve I knew
enough to stay in my own neighborhood,   5
I knew anyone who left might not return.
Boys were animals with animal hungers
I learned early. Better to stay close to home.
I'd try to bum cigarettes from the night workers
as they left the bars in the heavy light of noon   10
or I'd hang around the grocery hoping
one of the beautiful young wives would ask me
to help her carry her shopping bags home.
You're wondering what I was up to. Not much.
The sun rose late in November and set early.   15
At times I thought life was rushing by too fast.
Before I knew it I'd be my half-blind uncle
married to a woman who cried all day long
while in the basement he passed his time working
on short-wave radio calls to anywhere.   20
I'd sneak down and talk to him, Uncle Nathan,
wiry in his boxer's shorts and high-topped boots,
chewing on a cigar, the one dead eye catching
the overhead light while he mused on his life
on the road or at sea. How he loved the whores   25
in the little Western towns or the Latin ports!
He'd hold his hands out to approximate
their perfect breasts. The months in jail had taught him
a man had only his honor and his ass
to protect. "You turn your fist this way," he said,   30
taking my small hand in both of his, "and fire
from the shoulder, so," and he'd extend it out
to the face of an imaginary foe.
Why he'd returned to this I never figured out,
though life was ample here, a grid of crowded blocks   35
of Germans, Wops, Polacks, Jews, wild Irish,
plus some square heads from the Upper Peninsula.
Six bakeries, four barber shops, a five and dime,
twenty beer gardens, a Catholic church with a *shul*

next door where we studied the Talmud-Torah.   40
Wonderful how all the old hatreds bubbled
so quietly on the back burner you could
forget until one day they tore through the pool halls,
the bowling alley, the high school athletic fields
leaving an eye gone, a long fresh, livid scar   45
running to touch a mouth, young hands raw or broken,
boys and girls ashamed of what they were, ashamed
of what they were not. It was merely village life,
exactly what our parents left in Europe
brought to America with pure fidelity.   50

CONNECTIONS TO OTHER SELECTIONS

1. Compare the description of immigrant life in "Reinventing America" with
   that in Tato Laviera's "AmeRícan" (p. 269).
2. What kind of values are associated with village life in Europe in Levine's
   poem? How do those values compare with the values associated with In-
   dian life depicted in the movies in Chitra Banerjee Divakaruni's "Indian
   Movie, New Jersey" (p. 162)?

GAIL MAZUR (B. 1937)

Gail Mazur was born in Cambridge, Massachusetts, and grew up there in
the nearby town of Newton. Her three collections of poetry are *Nightfire*
(1978), *The Pose of Happiness* (1986), and *The Common* (1995). A fourth, titled
They Can't Take That Away From Me, is due in 2001. She has been visiting
professor at the University of Houston and is currently writer-in-residence
at Emerson College in Boston. From 1996 to 1997, she was the Fellow in Po-
etry at the Bunting Institute at Radcliffe College. Mazur founded and has
for many years directed the Blacksmith House Poetry Center in Cam-
bridge, an organization committed to the support of contemporary Amer-
ican poets. She lives in Cambridge and in Provincetown, Massachusetts,
where, with her husband Michael Mazur, she is involved with the Province-
town Fine Arts Work Center.

Snake in the Grass   *1995*

— I'd screamed when it slithered under my hand
as I leaned to pick the first ripe blueberry.
It was noon, a Monday in late July. The sun,
as always, was hot on my shoulders, hot
on the back of my blouse. I'd forgotten   5
the universe wasn't all dead pines and Indian
graves and boarded-up houses, that I wasn't

the only creature left alive in it, that I'd
never found my comfortable place inside it.
I wanted to be someone who doesn't scare,   10
who can't be shaken, so I wanted no witnesses
to this paradigm in the Garden. Then, the snake
slid noiselessly under the rotting porch
of our family cottage. The reduced summer woods,
the wide sky, were stunned and silent. Imagine   15
a silence, all you hear your own scream vanishing.
A second before, you'd knelt to the ground,
humming, and something writhed at your left hand,
wild as migraine, while your right reached
through transparent air to the first sweet berry,   20
treasure of asthmatic childhood's summers.
It isn't death you fear now, or years ago,
it's the sneak attack, the large hand clapped
over your mouth, bad moments that suddenly
come back when you think you're at home   25
in the frayed landcape you've already lost,
and a snake, a *not-you,* invisible, camouflaged
in the famished grass, jolts you out of your dream.
Try being rational and patient:
get into your car, drive down the old road   30
to Dunroamin' Campgrounds. You've got a quarter—
telephone a friend, he'll probably be in
his amber-lit air-conditioned office, reading
student papers. He might say postmodernism's
days are numbered, but he'd like to get away.   35
Tell him not to come down to the Cape.
Tell him about the harmless snake, give him
the scream, how you blushed that one of nature's
creatures should think you're a silly woman.
Embellish a little, laugh at yourself in the hot   40
glass booth. There'll be kids playing volleyball
on the parched field, mosquitoes, mothers
spreading mustard on baloney sandwiches.
— Wouldn't anyone have screamed at the chill
reptilian underhand move of that snake?   45
Wasn't that scream waiting for years?
Can't you relent, can't you love yet
your small bewildering part in this world?

CONNECTIONS TO OTHER SELECTIONS

1. How does this speaker's response to being surprised by a snake compare
   with the speaker's response in Emily Dickinson's "A narrow Fellow in the
   Grass" (p. 2).

2. Compare the theme of this poem with that of Ronald Wallace's "Dogs"
   (p. 685).

ROBERT MORGAN (B. 1944)

Robert Morgan is a poet and novelist who has been widely praised as the poet laureate of Appalachia. Morgan was born and raised in North Carolina in a small and isolated valley in the Blue Ridge Mountains. He earned his B.A. from the University of North Carolina at Chapel Hill and attended the University of North Carolina at Greensboro, where he earned his M.F.A. Morgan has published four books of fiction since 1969, including *The Hinterlands* (1994) and *The Truest Pleasure* (1995). He has been widely published in magazines including *The Atlantic Monthly, The New Republic, Poetry, The Southern Review, The Yale Review, The Carolina Quarterly,* and *The New England Review*. Morgan has also published nine volumes of poetry. In 1971 Morgan began teaching at Cornell University where, since 1992, he has been Kappa Alpha Professor of English. He has won several awards, including four National Endowment for the Art Fellowships, a Guggenheim Fellowship, and has been included in *New Stories from the South* and *Prize Stories: The O. Henry Awards*. His most recent novel, *Gap Creek* (1999), was selected for Oprah's Book Club.

Time's Music   *1996*

Insects in an August field seem
to register the background noise
of space and amplify the twitch
of partners in atoms. The click
of little timepieces, chirp of   5
tiny chisels, as grasshoppers
and crickets effervesce and spread
in the weeds ahead, then wash back
in a wake of crackling music
that sparkles through grass, ticking   10
away the summer, whispering of
frost and stars overhead and chatter
of memory in every bit
of matter, of half-life in
the thick and flick of creation.   15

CONNECTIONS TO OTHER SELECTIONS

1. Discuss the treatment of time in Morgan's poem and in Sophie Cabot Black's "August" (p. 125).
2. Consider Morgan's use of sounds and their effects along with Galway Kinnell's in "Blackberry Eating" (p. 176).

JOAN MURRAY (B. 1945)

Born and raised in New York City, Joan Murray was educated at Hunter College and New York University. She has taught at Lehman College of the City University of New York. Among her awards for poetry are the National Endowment for the Arts and a Pushcart Prize. Her published volumes of poetry include *Egg Tooth* (1975) and *The Same Water* (1990).

Play-By-Play   *1997*

Yaddo°

Would it surprise the young men
playing softball on the hill to hear the women
on the terrace admiring their bodies:
the slim waist of the pitcher, the strength
of the runner's legs, the torso of the catcher   5
rising off his knees to toss the ball back to the mound?
Would it embarrass them
to hear two women, sitting together after dinner,
praising even their futile motions:
the flex of a batter's hips   10
before his missed swing, the wide-spread stride
of a man picked off his base, the intensity
on the new man's face
as he waits on deck and fans the air?

Would it annoy them, the way some women   15
take offense when men caress them with their eyes?
And why should it surprise me that these women,
well past sixty, haven't put aside desire
but sit at ease and in pleasure,
watching the young men move above the rose garden   20
where the marble Naiads
pose and yawn in their fountain?
Who better than these women, with their sweaters
draped across their shoulders, their perspectives
honed from years of lovers, to recognize   25
the beauty that would otherwise
go unnoticed on this hill?
And will it compromise their pleasure
if I sit down at their table to listen
to the play-by-play and see it through their eyes?   30

Would it distract the young men if they realized
that three women laughing softly on the terrace

Yaddo: An artist's colony in Saratoga Springs, New York.

above closed books and half-filled wineglasses
are moving beside them on the field?
Would they want to know how they've been   35
held to the light till some motion or expression
showed the unsuspected loveliness
in a common shape or face?
Wouldn't they have liked to see how they looked
down there, as they stood for a moment at the plate,   40
bathed in the light of perfect expectation,
before their shadows lengthened, before they
walked together up the darkened hill,
so beautiful they would not have
recognized themselves?   45

CONNECTIONS TO OTHER SELECTIONS

1. Compare the voice of the speaker in "Play-By-Play" with that of Acker-
   man's "A Fine, a Private Place" (p. 69).

2. Write an essay on the speaker's gaze in this poem and in Steele's "An
   Aubade" (p. 439).

MARY OLIVER (B. 1935)

Mary Oliver taps the resplendent depths of the natural world and brings
brightness back to share. Born in Cleveland, Ohio, in 1935, Oliver attended
Vassar College. Since then she has taught and been poet-in-residence at
several colleges. Her early collection, *American Primitive* (1983), won the
Pulitzer Prize; other collections include *No Voyage and Other Poems* (1965),
The River Styx, Ohio and Other Poems (1972), *Twelve Moons* (1979), and *Dream
Work* (1986). Her *New and Selected Poems* won the National Book Award. She
currently teaches at Bennington College and lives in Provincetown, Massa-
chusetts, and in Bennington, Vermont.

Seven White Butterflies   *1995*

Seven white butterflies
delicate in a hurry look
how they bang the pages
    of their wings as they fly

to the fields of mustard yellow   5
and orange and plain
gold all eternity
    is in the moment this is what

Blake said Whitman said such
wisdom in the agitated   10

motions of the mind seven
   dancers floating

even as worms toward
paradise see how they banter
and riot and rise   15
   to the trees flutter

lob their white bodies into
the invisible wind weightless
lacy willing
   to deliver themselves unto   20

the universe now each settles
down on a yellow thumb on a
brassy stem now
   all seven are rapidly sipping

from the golden towers who   25
would have thought it could be so easy?

CONNECTIONS TO OTHER SELECTIONS

1. Compare the sounds and rhythms used to describe the movement of butterflies in Oliver's poem with Emily Dickinson's use of sound and rhythm in "A Bird came down the Walk —" (p. 173).

2. Discuss the theme of this poem and of Robert Frost's "Nothing Gold Can Stay" (p. 354).

RONALD WALLACE (B. 1945)

Born in Cedar Rapids, Iowa, Ronald Wallace earned a B.A. at the College of Wooster, and an M.A. and a Ph.D. at the University of Michigan. He has taught in the Department of English at the University of Wisconsin, Madison, since 1972. Among his awards are a Rackham Prize Fellowship and several American Council of Learned Society fellowships. His collections of poems include *People and Dog in the Sun* (1987), *The Makings of Happiness* (1991), and *Time's Fancy* (1994).

Dogs   *1997*

When I was six years old I hit one with
a baseball bat. An accident, of course,
and broke his jaw. They put that dog to sleep,
a euphemism even then I knew
could not excuse me from the lasting wrath   5
of memory's flagellation. My remorse

could dog me as it would, it wouldn't keep
me from the life sentence that I drew:

For I've been barked at, bitten, nipped, knocked flat,
slobbered over, humped, sprayed, beshat,   10
by spaniel, terrier, retriever, bull, and Dane.
But through the years what's given me most pain
of all the dogs I've been the victim of
are those whose slow eyes gazed at me, in love.

CONNECTIONS TO OTHER SELECTIONS

1. Compare this poem's theme with Updike's "Dog's Death" (p. 11).
2. In an essay discuss the strategies used in this sonnet and Shakespeare's "My mistress' eyes are nothing like the sun" (p. 229) to create emotion in the reader.

Glossary of Literary Terms

Accent The emphasis, or STRESS, given a syllable in pronunciation. We say *"syllable"* not *"syllable,"* *"emphasis"* not *"emphasis."* Accents can also be used to emphasize a particular word in a sentence: *Is* she con*tent* with the *con*tents of the *yellow package?* See also METER.

Allegory A narration or description usually restricted to a single meaning because its events, actions, characters, settings, and objects represent specific abstractions or ideas. Although the elements in an allegory may be interesting in themselves, the emphasis tends to be on what they ultimately mean. Characters may be given names such as Hope, Pride, Youth, and Charity; they have few if any personal qualities beyond their abstract meanings. These personifications are not symbols because, for instance, the meaning of a character named Charity is precisely that virtue. See also SYMBOL.

Alliteration The repetition of the same consonant sounds in a sequence of words, usually at the beginning of a word or stressed syllable: *"descending dew drops"*; *"luscious lemons."* Alliteration is based on the sounds of letters, rather than the spelling of words; for example, *"keen"* and *"car"* alliterate, but *"car"* and *"cite"* do not. Used sparingly, alliteration can intensify ideas by emphasizing key words, but when used too self-consciously, it can be distracting, even ridiculous, rather than effective. See also ASSONANCE, CONSONANCE.

Allusion A brief reference to a person, place, thing, event, or idea in history or literature. Allusions conjure up biblical authority, scenes from Shakespeare's plays, historic figures, wars, great love stories, and anything else that might enrich an author's work. Allusions imply reading and cultural experiences shared by the writer and reader, functioning as a kind of shorthand whereby the recalling of something outside the work supplies an emotional or intellectual context, such as a poem about current racial struggles calling up the memory of Abraham Lincoln.

Ambiguity Allows for two or more simultaneous interpretations of a word, phrase, action, or situation, all of which can be supported by the context of a work. Deliberate ambiguity can contribute to the effectiveness and richness of a work. However, unintentional ambiguity obscures meaning and can confuse readers.

Anagram A word or phrase made from the letters of another word or phrase, as "heart" is an anagram of "earth." Anagrams have often been considered merely an exercise of one's ingenuity, but sometimes writers use anagrams to conceal proper names or veiled messages, or to suggest important connections between words, as in "hated" and "death."

Anapestic meter See FOOT.

Apostrophe An address, either to someone who is absent and therefore cannot hear the speaker or to something nonhuman that cannot comprehend. Apostrophe often provides a speaker the opportunity to think aloud.

Approximate rhyme See RHYME.

Archetype A term used to describe universal symbols that evoke deep and sometimes unconscious responses in a reader. In literature, characters, images, and themes that symbolically embody universal meanings and basic human experiences, regardless of when or where they live, are considered archetypes. Common literary archetypes include stories of quests, initiations, scapegoats, descents to the underworld, and ascents to heaven. See also MYTHOLOGICAL CRITICISM.

Assonance The repetition of internal vowel sounds in nearby words that do not end the same, for example, "asl*ee*p under a tr*ee*," or "*ea*ch *e*vening." Similar endings result in rhyme, as in asl*eep* in the d*eep*. Assonance is a strong means of emphasizing important words in a line. See also ALLITERATION, CONSONANCE.

Ballad Traditionally, a ballad is a song, transmitted orally from generation to generation, that tells a story and that eventually is written down. As such, ballads usually cannot be traced to a particular author or group of authors. Typically, ballads are dramatic, condensed, and impersonal narratives, such as "Bonny Barbara Allan." A **literary ballad** is a narrative poem that is written in deliberate imitation of the language, form, and spirit of the traditional ballad, such as Keats's "La Belle Dame sans Merci." See also BALLAD STANZA, QUATRAIN.

Ballad stanza A four-line stanza, known as a QUATRAIN, consisting of alternating eight- and six-syllable lines. Usually only the second and fourth lines rhyme (an *abcb* pattern). Coleridge adopted the ballad stanza in "The Rime of the Ancient Mariner."

All in a hot and copper sky
The bloody Sun, at noon,
Right up above the mast did stand,
No bigger than the Moon.

See also BALLAD, QUATRAIN.

Biographical criticism An approach to literature that suggests that knowledge of the author's life experiences can aid in the understanding of his or her work. While biographical information can sometimes complicate one's interpretation of a work, and some formalist critics (such as the New Critics) disparage the use of the author's biography as a tool for textual interpretation, learning about the life of the author can often enrich a reader's appreciation for that author's work. See also FORMALIST CRITICISM, NEW CRITICISM.

Blank verse Unrhymed iambic pentameter. Blank verse is the English verse form closest to the natural rhythms of English speech and therefore is the most common pattern found in traditional English narrative and dramatic poetry from Shakespeare to the early twentieth century. Shakespeare's plays use blank verse extensively. See also IAMBIC PENTAMETER.

Cacophony Language that is discordant and difficult to pronounce, such as this line from John Updike's "Player Piano": "never my numb plunker fumbles." Cacophony ("bad sound") may be unintentional in the writer's sense of music, or it may be used consciously for deliberate dramatic effect. See also EUPHONY.

Caesura A pause within a line of poetry that contributes to the rhythm of the line. A caesura can occur anywhere within a line and need not be indicated by punctuation. In scanning a line, caesuras are indicated by a double vertical line (‖). See also METER, RHYTHM, SCANSION.

Canon Those works generally considered by scholars, critics, and teachers to be the most important to read and study, which collectively constitute the "masterpieces" of literature. Since the 1960s, the traditional English and American literary canon, consisting mostly of works by white male writers, has been rapidly expanding to include many female writers and writers of varying ethnic backgrounds.

Carpe diem The Latin phrase meaning "seize the day." This is a very common literary theme, especially in lyric poetry, which emphasizes that life is short, time is fleeting, and that one should make the most of present pleasures. Robert Herrick's poem "To the Virgins, to Make Much of Time" employs the *carpe diem* theme.

Cliché An idea or expression that has become tired and trite from overuse, its freshness and clarity having worn off. Clichés often anesthetize readers, and are usually a sign of weak writing. See also SENTIMENTALITY, STOCK RESPONSES.

Colloquial Refers to a type of informal diction that reflects casual, conversational language and often includes slang expressions. See also DICTION.

Connotation Associations and implications that go beyond the literal meaning of a word, which derive from how the word has been commonly used and the associations people make with it. For example, the word *eagle* connotes ideas of liberty and freedom that have little to do with the word's literal meaning. See also DENOTATION.

Consonance A common type of near rhyme that consists of identical consonant sounds preceded by different vowel sounds: *home, same; worth, breath.* See also RHYME.

Contextual symbol See SYMBOL.

Controlling metaphor See METAPHOR.

Convention A characteristic of a literary genre (often unrealistic) that is understood and accepted by readers because it has come, through usage and time, to be recognized as a familiar technique. For example, the use of meter and rhyme are poetic conventions.

Conventional symbol See SYMBOL.

Cosmic irony See IRONY.

Couplet Two consecutive lines of poetry that usually rhyme and have the same meter. A **heroic couplet** is a couplet written in rhymed iambic pentameter.

Cultural criticism An approach to literature that focuses on the historical as well as social, political, and economic contexts of a work. Popular culture — mass produced and consumed cultural artifacts ranging from advertising and popular fiction to television to rock music — is given equal emphasis as "high culture." Cultural critics use widely eclectic strategies such as new historicism, psychology, gender studies, and deconstructionism to analyze not only literary texts but everything from radio talk shows, comic strips, calendar art, commercials, to travel guides and baseball cards. See also HISTORICAL CRITICISM, MARXIST CRITICISM, POSTCOLONIAL CRITICISM.

Dactylic meter See FOOT.

Deconstructionism An approach to literature that suggests that literary works do not yield fixed, single meanings, because language can never say exactly what we intend it to mean. Deconstructionism seeks to destabilize meaning by examining the gaps and ambiguities of the language of a text. Deconstructionists pay close attention to language in order to discover and describe how a variety of possible readings are generated by the elements of a text. See also NEW CRITICISM.

Denotation The dictionary meaning of a word. See also CONNOTATION.

Dialect A type of informational diction. Dialects are spoken by definable groups of people from a particular geographic region, economic group, or social class. Writers use dialect to contrast and express differences in educational, class, social, and regional backgrounds of their characters. See also DICTION.

Diction A writer's choice of words, phrases, sentence structures, and figurative language, which combine to help create meaning. **Formal diction** consists of a dignified, impersonal, and elevated use of language; it follows the rules of syntax exactly and is often characterized by complex words and lofty tone. **Middle diction** maintains correct language usage, but is less elevated than formal diction; it reflects the way most educated people speak. **Informal diction** represents the plain language of everyday use, and often includes idiomatic expressions, slang, contractions, and many simple, common words. **Poetic diction** refers to the way poets sometimes employ an elevated diction that deviates significantly from the common speech and writing of their time, choosing words for their supposedly inherent poetic qualities. Since the eighteenth century, however, poets have been incorporating all kinds of diction in their work and so there is no longer an automatic distinction between the language of a poet and the language of everyday speech. See also DIALECT.

Didactic poetry Poetry designed to teach an ethical, moral, or religious lesson. Michael Wigglesworth's Puritan poem *Day of Doom* is an example of didactic poetry.

Doggerel A derogatory term used to describe poetry whose subject is trite and whose rhythm and sounds are monotonously heavy-handed.

Dramatic irony See IRONY.

Dramatic monologue A type of lyric poem in which a character (the speaker) addresses a distinct but silent audience imagined to be present in the poem in such a way as to reveal a dramatic situation and, often unintentionally, some aspect of his or her temperament or personality. See also LYRIC.

Electra complex The female version of the Oedipus complex. *Electra complex* is a term used to describe the psychological conflict of a daughter's unconscious rivalry with her mother for her father's attention. The name comes from the Greek legend of Electra, who avenged the death of her father, Agamemnon, by plotting the death of her mother. See also OEDIPUS COMPLEX, PSYCHOLOGICAL CRITICISM.

Elegy A mournful, contemplative lyric poem written to commemorate someone who is dead, often ending in a consolation. Tennyson's *In Memoriam*, written on the death of Arthur Hallam, is an elegy. *Elegy* may also refer to a serious meditative poem produced to express the speaker's melancholy thoughts. See also LYRIC.

End rhyme See RHYME.

End-stopped line A poetic line that has a pause at the end. End-stopped lines reflect normal speech patterns and are often marked by punctuation. The first line of Keats's "Endymion" is an example of an end-stopped line; the natural pause coincides with the end of the line, and is marked by a period:

A thing of beauty is a joy forever.

English sonnet See SONNET.

Enjambment In poetry, when one line ends without a pause and continues into the next line for its meaning. This is also called a **run-on line.** The transition between the first two lines of Wordsworth's poem "My Heart Leaps Up" demonstrates enjambment:

My heart leaps up when I behold
　A rainbow in the sky:

Envoy See SESTINA.

Epic A long narrative poem, told in a formal, elevated style, that focuses on a serious subject and chronicles heroic deeds and events important to a culture or nation. Milton's *Paradise Lost*, which attempts to "justify the ways of God to man," is an epic. See also NARRATIVE POEM.

Epigram A brief, pointed, and witty poem that usually makes a satiric or humorous point. Epigrams are most often written in couplets, but take no prescribed form.

Euphony *Euphony* ("good sound") refers to language that is smooth and musically pleasant to the ear. See also CACOPHONY.

Exact rhyme See RHYME.

Extended metaphor See METAPHOR.

Eye rhyme See RHYME.

Falling meter See METER.

Feminine rhyme See RHYME.

Feminist criticism An approach to literature that seeks to correct or supplement what may be regarded as a predominantly male-dominated critical perspective with a feminist consciousness. Feminist criticism places literature in a social context and uses a broad range of disciplines, including history, sociology, psychology, and linguistics, to provide a perspective sensitive to feminist issues. Feminist theories also attempt to understand representation from a woman's point of view and to explain women's writing strategies as specific to their social conditions. See also GENDER CRITICISM.

Figures of speech Ways of using language that deviate from the literal, denotative meanings of words in order to suggest additional meanings or effects. Figures of speech say one thing in terms of something else, such as when an eager funeral director is described as a vulture. See also METAPHOR, SIMILE.

Fixed form A poem that may be categorized by the pattern of its lines, meter, rhythm, or stanzas. A sonnet is a fixed form of poetry because by definition it must have fourteen lines. Other fixed forms include LIMERICK, SESTINA, and VILLANELLE. However, poems written in a fixed form may not always fit into categories precisely, because writers sometimes vary traditional forms to create innovative effects. See also OPEN FORM.

Foot The metrical unit by which a line of poetry is measured. A foot usually consists of one stressed and one or two unstressed syllables. An *iambic foot,* which consists of one unstressed syllable followed by one stressed syllable ("away"), is the most common metrical foot in English poetry. A *trochaic foot* consists of one stressed syllable followed by an unstressed syllable ("lovely"). An *anapestic foot* is two unstressed syllables followed by one stressed one ("understand"). A *dactylic foot* is one stressed syllable followed by two unstressed ones ("desperate"). A *spondee* is a foot consisting of two stressed syllables ("dead set"), but is not a sustained metrical foot and is used mainly for variety or emphasis. See also IAMBIC PENTAMETER, LINE, METER.

Form The overall structure or shape of a work, which frequently follows an established design. Forms may refer to a literary type (narrative form, lyric form) or to patterns of meter, lines, and rhymes (stanza form, verse form). See also FIXED FORM, OPEN FORM.

Formal diction See DICTION.

Formalist criticism An approach to literature that focuses on the formal elements of a work, such as its language, structure, and tone. Formalist critics offer intense examinations of the relationship between form and meaning in a work, emphasizing the subtle complexity in how a work is arranged. Formalists pay special attention to diction, irony, paradox, metaphor, and symbol, as well as larger elements such as plot, characterization, and narrative technique. Formalist critics read literature as an independent work of art rather than as a reflection of the author's state of mind or as a representation of a moment in history. Therefore, anything outside of the work, including historical influences and authorial intent, is generally not examined by formalist critics. See also NEW CRITICISM.

Found poem An unintentional poem discovered in a nonpoetic context, such as a conversation, news story, or advertisement. Found poems serve as reminders that everyday language often contains what can be considered poetry, or that poetry is definable as any text read as a poem.

Free verse Also called *open form poetry*, free verse refers to poems characterized by their nonconformity to established patterns of meter, rhyme, and stanza. Free verse uses elements such as speech patterns, grammar, emphasis, and breath pauses to decide line breaks, and usually does not rhyme. See OPEN FORM.

Gay and lesbian criticism An approach to literature that focuses on how homosexuals are represented in literature, how they read literature, and whether sexuality, as well as gender, is culturally constructed or innate. See also FEMINIST CRITICISM, GENDER CRITICISM.

Gender criticism An approach to literature that explores how ideas about men and women — what is masculine and feminine — can be regarded as socially constructed by particular cultures. Gender criticism expands categories and definitions of what is masculine or feminine and tends to regard sexuality as more complex than merely masculine or feminine, heterosexual or homosexual. See also FEMINIST CRITICISM, GAY AND LESBIAN CRITICISM.

Genre A French word meaning kind or type. The major genres in literature are poetry, fiction, drama, and essays. Genre can also refer to more specific types of literature such as comedy, tragedy, epic poetry, or science fiction.

Haiku A style of lyric poetry borrowed from the Japanese that typically presents an intense emotion or vivid image of nature, which, traditionally, is designed to lead to a spiritual insight. Haiku is a fixed poetic form, consisting of seventeen syllables organized into three unrhymed lines of five, seven, and five syllables. Today, however, many poets vary the syllabic count in their haiku. See also FIXED FORM.

Heroic couplet See COUPLET.

Historical criticism An approach to literature that uses history as a means of understanding a literary work more clearly. Such criticism moves beyond both the facts of an author's personal life and the text itself in order to examine the social and intellectual currents in which the author composed the work. See also CULTURAL CRITICISM, MARXIST CRITICISM, NEW HISTORICISM, POSTCOLONIAL CRITICISM.

Hyperbole A boldly exaggerated statement that adds emphasis without intending to be literally true, as in the statement "He ate everything in the house." Hyperbole (also called *overstatement*) may be used for serious, comic, or ironic effect. See also FIGURES OF SPEECH.

Iambic meter See FOOT.

Iambic pentameter A metrical pattern in poetry that consists of five iambic feet per line. (An iamb, or iambic foot, consists of one unstressed syllable followed by a stressed syllable.) See also FOOT, METER.

Image A word, phrase, or figure of speech (especially a SIMILE or a METAPHOR) that addresses the senses, suggesting mental pictures of sights, sounds, smells, tastes, feelings, or actions. Images offer sensory impressions to the reader and also convey emotions and moods through their verbal pictures. See also FIGURES OF SPEECH.

Implied metaphor See METAPHOR.

Informal diction See DICTION.

Internal rhyme See RHYME.

Irony A literary device that uses contradictory statements or situations to reveal a reality different from what appears to be true. It is ironic for a firehouse to burn down, or for a police station to be burglarized. **Verbal irony** is a figure of speech that occurs when a person says one thing but means the opposite. **Sarcasm** is a strong form of verbal irony that is calculated to hurt someone through, for example, false praise. **Dramatic irony** creates a discrepancy between what a character believes or says and what the reader or audience member knows to be true. **Situational irony** exists when there is an incongruity between what is expected to happen and what actually happens due to forces beyond human comprehension or control. The suicide of the seemingly successful main character in Edwin Arlington Robinson's poem "Richard Cory" is an example of situational irony. **Cosmic irony** occurs when a writer uses God, destiny, or fate to dash the hopes and expectations of a character or of humankind in general. In cosmic irony, a discrepancy exists between what a character aspires to and what universal forces provide. Stephen Crane's poem "A Man Said to the Universe" is a good example of cosmic irony, because the universe acknowledges no obligation to the man's assertion of his own existence.

Italian sonnet See SONNET.

Limerick A light, humorous style of fixed form poetry. Its usual form consists of five lines with the rhyme scheme *aabba;* lines 1, 2, and 5 contain three feet, while lines 3 and 4 usually contain two feet. Limericks range in subject matter from the silly to the obscene, and since Edward Lear popularized them in the nineteenth century, children and adults have enjoyed these comic poems. See also FIXED FORM.

Line A sequence of words printed as a separate entity on the page. In poetry, lines are usually measured by the number of feet they contain. The names for various line lengths are as follows:

monometer: one foot	pentameter: five feet
dimeter: two feet	hexameter: six feet
trimeter: three feet	heptameter: seven feet
tetrameter: four feet	octameter: eight feet

The number of feet in a line, coupled with the name of the foot, describes the metrical qualities of that line. See also END-STOPPED LINE, ENJAMBMENT, FOOT, METER.

Literary ballad See BALLAD.

Literary symbol See SYMBOL.

Litotes See UNDERSTATEMENT.

Lyric A type of brief poem that expresses the personal emotions and thoughts of a single speaker. It is important to realize, however, that although the lyric is uttered in the first person, the speaker is not necessarily the poet. There are many varieties of lyric poetry, including the DRAMATIC MONOLOGUE, ELEGY, HAIKU, ODE, and SONNET forms.

Marxist criticism An approach to literature that focuses on the ideological content of a work — its explicit and implicit assumptions and values about matters such as culture, race, class, and power. Marxist criticism, based largely on the writings of Karl Marx, typically aims at not only revealing and clarifying ideological issues but also correcting social injustices. Some Marxist critics use literature to describe the competing socioeconomic interests that too often advance capitalist interests such as money and power rather than socialist interests such as morality and justice. They argue that literature and literary criticism are essentially political because they either challenge or support economic oppression. Because of this strong emphasis on the political aspects of texts, Marxist criticism focuses more on the content and themes of literature than on its form. See also CULTURAL CRITICISM, HISTORICAL CRITICISM, SOCIOLOGICAL CRITICISM.

Masculine rhyme See RHYME.

Metaphor A metaphor is a figure of speech that makes a comparison between two unlike things, without using the words *like* or *as*. Metaphors assert the identity of dissimilar things, as when Macbeth asserts that life *is* a "brief candle." Metaphors can be subtle and powerful, and can transform people, places, objects, and ideas into whatever the writer imagines them to be. An **implied metaphor** is a more subtle comparison; the terms being compared are not so specifically explained. For example, to describe a stubborn man unwilling to leave, one could say that he was "a mule standing his ground." This is a fairly explicit metaphor; the man is being compared to a mule. But to say that the man "brayed his refusal to leave" is to create an implied metaphor, because the subject (the man) is never overtly identified as a mule. Braying is associated with the mule, a notoriously stubborn creature, and so the comparison between the stubborn man and the mule is sustained. Implied metaphors can slip by inattentive readers who are not sensitive to such carefully chosen, highly concentrated language. An **extended metaphor** is a sustained comparison in which part or all of a poem consists of a series of related metaphors. Robert Francis's poem "Catch" relies on an extended metaphor that compares poetry to playing catch. A **controlling metaphor** runs through an entire work and determines the form or nature of that work. The controlling metaphor in Anne Bradstreet's poem "The Author to Her Book" likens her book to a child. **Synecdoche** is a kind of metaphor in which a part of something is used to signify the whole, as when a gossip is called a "wagging tongue," or when ten ships are called "ten sails." Sometimes, synecdoche refers to the whole being used to signify the part, as in the phrase "Boston won the baseball game." Clearly, the entire city of Boston did not participate in the game; the whole of Boston is being used to signify the individuals who played and won the game. **Metonymy** is a type of metaphor in which something closely associated with a subject is substituted for it. In this way, we speak of the "silver screen" to mean motion pictures, "the crown" to stand for the king, "the White House" to stand for the activities of the president. See also FIGURES OF SPEECH, PERSONIFICATION, SIMILE.

Meter When a rhythmic pattern of stresses recurs in a poem, it is called *meter.* Metrical patterns are determined by the type and number of feet in a line of verse; combining the name of a line length with the name of a foot concisely describes the meter of the line. **Rising meter** refers to metrical feet that move from unstressed to stressed sounds, such as the iambic foot and the anapestic foot. **Falling meter** refers to metrical feet that move from stressed to unstressed sounds, such as the trochaic foot and the dactylic foot. See also ACCENT, FOOT, IAMBIC PENTAMETER, LINE.

Metonymy See METAPHOR.

Middle diction See DICTION.

Mythological criticism An approach to literature that seeks to identify what in a work creates deep universal responses in readers, by paying close attention to the hopes, fears, and expectations of entire cultures. Mythological critics (sometimes called *archetypal critics*) look for underlying, recurrent patterns in literature that reveal universal meanings and basic human experiences for readers regardless of when and where they live. These critics attempt to explain how archetypes (the characters, images, and themes that symbolically embody universal meanings and experiences) are embodied in literary works in order to make larger connections that explain a particular work's lasting appeal. Mythological critics may specialize in areas such as classical literature, philology, anthropology, psychology, and cultural history, but they all emphasize the assumptions and values of various cultures. See also ARCHETYPE.

Narrative poem A poem that tells a story. A narrative poem may be short or long, and the story it relates may be simple or complex. See also BALLAD, EPIC.

Near rhyme See RHYME.

New Criticism An approach to literature made popular between the 1940s and the 1960s that evolved out of formalist criticism. New Critics suggest that detailed analysis of the language of a literary text can uncover important layers of meaning in that work. New Criticism consciously downplays the historical influences, authorial intentions, and social contexts that surround texts in order to focus on explication — extremely close textual analysis. See also FORMALIST CRITICISM.

New historicism An approach to literature that emphasizes the interaction between the historic context of the work and a modern reader's understanding and interpretation of the work. New Historicists attempt to describe the culture of a period by reading many different kinds of texts and paying close attention to many different dimensions of a culture, including political, economic, social, and aesthetic concerns. They regard texts not simply as a reflection of the culture that produced them but also as productive of that culture playing an active role in the social and political conflicts of an age. New Historicism acknowledges and then explores various versions of "history," sensitizing us to the fact that the history on which we choose to focus is colored by being reconstructed from our present circumstances. See also HISTORICAL CRITICISM.

Octave A poetic stanza of eight lines, usually forming one part of a sonnet. See also SONNET, STANZA.

Ode A relatively lengthy lyric poem that often expresses lofty emotions in a dignified style. Odes are characterized by a serious topic, such as truth, art, freedom, justice, or the meaning of life; their tone tends to be formal. There is no prescribed pattern that defines an ode; some odes repeat the same pattern in each stanza, while others introduce a new pattern in each stanza. See also LYRIC.

Oedipus complex A Freudian term derived from Sophocles' tragedy *Oedipus the King*. It describes a psychological complex that is predicated on a boy's unconscious rivalry with his father for his mother's love and his desire to eliminate his father in order to take his father's place with his mother. The female equivalent of this complex is called the *Electra complex*. See also ELECTRA COMPLEX, PSYCHOLOGICAL CRITICISM.

Off rhyme See RHYME.

Onomatopoeia A term referring to the use of a word that resembles the sound it denotes. *Buzz, rattle, bang,* and *sizzle* all reflect onomatopoeia. Onomatopoeia can also consist of more than one word; writers sometimes create lines or whole passages in which the sound of the words helps to convey their meanings.

Open form Sometimes called *free verse*, open form poetry does not conform to established patterns of METER, RHYME, and STANZA. Such poetry derives its rhythmic qualities from the repetition of words, phrases, or grammatical structures, the arrangement of words on the printed page, or by some other means. The poet E. E. Cummings wrote open form poetry; his poems do not have measurable meters, but they do have RHYTHM. See also FIXED FORM.

Organic form Refers to works whose formal characteristics are not rigidly predetermined but follow the movement of thought or emotion being expressed. Such works are said to grow like living organisms, following their own individual patterns rather than external fixed rules that govern, for example, the form of a SONNET.

Overstatement See HYPERBOLE.

Oxymoron A condensed form of paradox in which two contradictory words are used together, as in "sweet sorrow" or "jumbo shrimp." See also PARADOX.

Paradox A statement that initially appears to be contradictory but then, on closer inspection, turns out to make sense. For example, John Donne ends his sonnet "Death, Be Not Proud" with the paradoxical statement "Death, thou shalt die." To solve the paradox, it is necessary to discover the sense that underlies the statement. Paradox is useful in poetry because it arrests a reader's attention by its seemingly stubborn refusal to make sense.

Paraphrase A prose restatement of the central ideas of a poem, in your own language.

Parody A humorous imitation of another, usually serious, work. It can take any fixed or open form, because parodists imitate the tone, language, and shape of the original in order to deflate the subject matter, making the original work seem absurd. Anthony Hecht's poem "Dover Bitch" is a famous parody of Matthew Arnold's well-known "Dover Beach." Parody may also be used as a form of literary criticism to expose the defects in a work. But sometimes parody becomes an affectionate acknowledgment that a well-known work has become both institutionalized in our culture and fair game for some fun. For example, Peter De Vries's "To His Importunate Mistress" gently mocks Andrew Marvell's "To His Coy Mistress."

Persona Literally, a *persona* is a mask. In literature, a *persona* is a speaker created by a writer to tell a story or to speak in a poem. A persona is not a character in a story or narrative, nor does a persona necessarily directly reflect the author's personal voice. A persona is a separate self, created by and distinct from the author, through which he or she speaks.

Personification A form of metaphor in which human characteristics are attributed to nonhuman things. Personification offers the writer a way to give the world life and motion by assigning familiar human behaviors and emotions to animals, inanimate objects, and abstract ideas. For example, in Keats's "Ode on a Grecian Urn," the speaker refers to the urn as an "unravished bride of quietness." See also METAPHOR.

Petrarchan sonnet See SONNET.

Picture poem A type of open form poetry in which the poet arranges the lines of the poem so as to create a particular shape on the page. The shape of the poem embodies its subject; the poem becomes a picture of what the poem is describing. Michael McFee's "In Medias Res" is an example of a picture poem. See also OPEN FORM.

Poetic diction See DICTION.

Postcolonial criticism An approach to literature that focuses on the study of cultural behavior and expression in relationship to the colonized world. Postcolonial criticism refers to the analysis of literary works written by writers from countries and cultures that at one time have been controlled by colonizing powers—such as Indian writers during or after British colonial rule. Postcolonial criticism also refers to the analysis of literary works written about colonial cultures by writers from the colonizing country. Many of these kinds of analyses point out how writers from colonial powers sometimes misrepresent colonized cultures by reflecting more their own values. See also CULTURAL CRITICISM, HISTORICAL CRITICISM, MARXIST CRITICISM.

Prose poem A kind of open form poetry that is printed as prose and represents the most clear opposite of fixed form poetry. Prose poems are densely compact and often make use of striking imagery and figures of speech. See also FIXED FORM, OPEN FORM.

Prosody The overall metrical structure of a poem. See also METER.

Psychological criticism An approach to literature that draws upon psychoanalytic theories, especially those of Sigmund Freud or Jacques Lacan, to understand more fully the text, the writer, and the reader. The basis of this approach is the idea of the existence of a human unconscious—those impulses, desires, and feelings about which a person is unaware but which influence emotions and behavior. Critics use psychological approaches to explore the motivations of characters and the symbolic meanings of events, while biographers speculate about a writer's own motivations — conscious or unconscious — in a literary work. Psychological approaches are also used to describe and analyze the reader's personal responses to a text.

Pun A play on words that relies on a word's having more than one meaning or sounding like another word. Shakespeare and other writers use puns extensively, for serious and comic purposes; in *Romeo and Juliet* (III.i.101), the dying Mercutio puns, "Ask for me tomorrow and you shall find me a grave man." Puns have serious literary uses, but since the eighteenth century, puns have been used almost purely for humorous effect.

Quatrain A four-line stanza. Quatrains are the most common stanzaic form in the English language; they can have various meters and rhyme schemes. See also METER, RHYME, STANZA.

Reader-response criticism An approach to literature that focuses on the reader rather than the work itself, by attempting to describe what goes on in the reader's mind during the reading of a text. Hence, the consciousness of the reader — produced by reading the work — is the actual subject of reader-response criticism. These critics are not after a "correct" reading of the text or what the author presumably intended; instead, they are interested in the reader's individual experience with the text. Thus, there is no single definitive reading of a work, because readers create rather than discover absolute meanings in texts. However, this approach is not a rationale for mistaken or bizarre readings, but an exploration of the possibilities for a plurality of readings. This kind of strategy calls attention to how we read and what influences our readings, and what that reveals about ourselves.

Rhyme The repetition of identical or similar concluding syllables in different words, most often at the ends of lines. Rhyme is predominantly a function of sound rather than spelling; thus, words that end with the same vowel sounds rhyme, for instance, *day, prey, bouquet, weigh,* and words with the same consonant ending rhyme, for instance *vain, feign, rein, lane.* Words do not have to be spelled the same way or look alike to rhyme. In fact, words may look alike but not rhyme at all. This is called **eye rhyme,** as with *bough* and *cough,* or *brow* and *blow.*

End rhyme is the most common form of rhyme in poetry; the rhyme comes at the end of the lines.

> It runs through the reeds
>   And away it proceeds,
> Through meadow and glade,
>   In sun and in shade.

The **rhyme scheme** of a poem describes the pattern of end rhymes. Rhyme schemes are mapped out by noting patterns of rhyme with small letters: the first rhyme sound is designated *a,* the second becomes *b,* the third *c,* and so on. Thus, the rhyme scheme of the stanza above is *aabb.* **Internal rhyme** places at least one of the rhymed words within the line, as in "Dividing and gliding and sliding" or "In mist or cloud, on mast or shroud." **Masculine rhyme** describes the rhyming of single-syllable words, such as *grade* or *shade.* Masculine rhyme also occurs when rhyming words of more than one syllable, when the same sound occurs in a final stressed syllable, as in *defend* and *contend, betray* and *away.* **Feminine rhyme** consists of a rhymed stressed syllable followed by one or more identical unstressed syllables, as in *butter, clutter; gratitude, attitude; quivering, shivering.* All the examples so far have illustrated **exact rhymes,** because they share the same stressed vowel sounds as well as sharing sounds that follow the vowel. In **near rhyme** (also called **off rhyme, slant rhyme,** and **approximate rhyme**), the sounds are almost but not exactly alike. A common form of near rhyme is CONSONANCE, which consists of identical consonant sounds preceded by different vowel sounds: *home, same; worth, breath.*

Rhyme scheme See RHYME.

Rhythm A term used to refer to the recurrence of stressed and unstressed sounds in poetry. Depending on how sounds are arranged, the rhythm of a poem may be fast or slow, choppy or smooth. Poets use rhythm to create pleasurable sound patterns and to reinforce meanings. Rhythm in prose arises from pattern repetitions of sounds and pauses that create looser rhythmic effects. See also METER.

Rising meter See METER.

Run-on line See ENJAMBMENT.

Sarcasm See IRONY.

Satire The literary art of ridiculing a folly or vice in order to expose or correct it. The object of satire is usually some human frailty; people, institutions, ideas, and things are all fair game for satirists. Satire evokes attitudes of amusement, contempt, scorn, or indignation toward its faulty subject in the hope of somehow improving it. See also IRONY, PARODY.

Scansion The process of measuring the stresses in a line of verse to determine the metrical pattern of the line. See also LINE, METER.

Sentimentality A pejorative term used to describe the effort by an author to induce emotional responses in the reader that exceed what the situation warrants. Sentimentality especially pertains to such emotions as pathos and sympathy; it cons readers into falling for the mass murderer who is devoted to stray cats, and it requires that readers do not examine such illogical responses. Clichés and stock responses are the key ingredients of sentimentality in literature. See also CLICHÉ, STOCK RESPONSES.

Sestet A stanza consisting of exactly six lines. See also STANZA.

Sestina A type of fixed form poetry consisting of thirty-six lines of any length divided into six sestets and a three-line concluding stanza called an **envoy.** The six words at the end of the first sestet's lines must also appear at the ends of the other five sestets, in varying order. These six words must also appear in the envoy, where they often resonate important themes. An example of this highly demanding form of poetry is Elizabeth Bishop's "Sestina." See also SESTET.

Setting The physical and social context in which the action of a poem occurs. The major elements of setting are the time, the place, and the social environment that frames the poem. Setting can be used to evoke a mood or atmosphere that will prepare the reader for what is to come, as in Robert Frost's "Home Burial."

Shakespearean sonnet See SONNET.

Simile A common figure of speech that makes an explicit comparison between two things by using words such as *like, as, than, appears,* and *seems:* "A sip of Mrs. Cook's coffee is like a punch in the stomach." The effectiveness of this simile is created by the differences between the two things compared. There would be no simile if the comparison were stated this way: "Mrs. Cook's coffee is as strong as the cafeteria's coffee." This is a literal translation because Mrs. Cook's coffee is compared with something like it — another kind of coffee. See also FIGURES OF SPEECH, METAPHOR.

Situational irony See IRONY.

Slant rhyme See RHYME.

Sociological criticism An approach to literature that examines social groups, relationships, and values as they are manifested in literature. Sociological approaches emphasize the nature and effect of the social forces that shape power relationships between groups or classes of people. Such readings treat literature as either a document reflecting social conditions or a product of those conditions. The former view brings into focus the social milieu; the latter emphasizes the work. Two important forms of sociological criticism are Marxist and feminist approaches. See also FEMINIST CRITICISM, MARXIST CRITICISM.

Sonnet A fixed form of lyric poetry that consists of fourteen lines, usually written in iambic pentameter. There are two basic types of sonnets, the Italian and the English. The **Italian sonnet,** also known as the **Petrarchan sonnet,** is divided into an octave, which typically rhymes *abbaabba,* and a sestet, which may have varying rhyme schemes. Common rhyme patterns in the sestet are *cdecde, cdcdcd,* and *cdccdc.* Very often the octave presents a situation, attitude, or problem that the sestet comments upon or resolves, as in John Keats's "On First Looking into Chapman's Homer." The **English sonnet,** also known as the **Shakespearean sonnet,** is organized into three quatrains and a couplet, which typically rhyme *abab cdcd efef gg.* This rhyme scheme is more suited to English poetry because English has fewer rhyming words than Italian. English sonnets, because of their four-part organization, also have more flexibility with respect to where thematic breaks can occur. Frequently, however, the most pronounced break or turn comes with the concluding couplet, as in Shakespeare's "Shall I compare thee to a summer's day?" See also COUPLET, IAMBIC PENTAMETER, LINE, OCTAVE, QUATRAIN, SESTET.

Speaker The voice used by an author to tell a story or speak a poem. The speaker is often a created identity, and should not automatically be equated with the author's self. See also PERSONA.

Spondee See FOOT.

Stanza In poetry, *stanza* refers to a grouping of lines, set off by a space, that usually has a set pattern of meter and rhyme. See also LINE, METER, RHYME.

Stock responses Predictable, conventional reactions to language, characters, symbols, or situations. The flag, motherhood, puppies, God, and peace are common objects used to elicit stock responses from unsophisticated audiences. See also CLICHÉ, SENTIMENTALITY.

Stress The emphasis, or accent, given a syllable in pronunciation. See also ACCENT.

Style The distinctive and unique manner in which a writer arranges words to achieve particular effects. Style essentially combines the idea to be expressed with the individuality of the author. These arrangements include individual word choices as well as matters such as the length of sentences, their structure, tone, and use of irony. See also DICTION, IRONY, TONE.

Symbol A person, object, image, word, or event that evokes a range of additional meaning beyond and usually more abstract than its literal significance. Symbols are educational devices for evoking complex ideas without having to resort to painstaking explanations that would make a story more like an essay than an experience. **Conventional symbols** have meanings that are widely recognized by a society or culture. Some conventional symbols are the Christian cross, the Star of David, a swastika, or a nation's flag. Writers use conventional symbols to reinforce meanings. E. E. Cummings, for example, emphasizes the spring setting in "in Just—" as a way of suggesting a renewed sense of life. A **literary** or **contextual symbol** can be a setting, character, action, object, name, or anything else in a work that maintains its literal significance while suggesting other meanings. Such symbols go beyond conventional symbols; they gain their symbolic meaning within the context of a specific story. For example, the urn in Keats's "Ode on a Grecian Urn" takes on multiple symbolic meanings in the work, but these meanings do not automatically carry over into other poems about urns. The meanings suggested by Keats's urn are specific to that text; therefore, it becomes a contextual symbol. See also ALLEGORY.

Synecdoche See METAPHOR.

Syntax The ordering of words into meaningful verbal patterns such as phrases, clauses, and sentences. Poets often manipulate syntax, changing conventional word order, to place certain emphasis on particular words. Emily Dickinson, for instance, writes about being surprised by a snake in her poem "A narrow Fellow in the Grass," and includes this line: "His notice sudden is." In addition to the alliterative hissing *s*-sounds here, Dickinson also effectively manipulates the line's syntax so that the verb *is* appears unexpectedly at the end, making the snake's hissing presence all the more "sudden."

Tercet A three-line stanza. See also STANZA, TRIPLET.

Terza rima An interlocking three-line rhyme scheme: *aba, bcb, cdc, ded,* and so on. Dante's *The Divine Comedy* and Frost's "Acquainted with the Night" are written in terza rima. See also RHYME, TERCET.

Theme The central meaning or dominant idea in a literary work. A theme provides a unifying point around which the plot, characters, setting, point of view, symbols, and other elements of a work are organized. It is important not to mistake the theme for the actual subject of the work; the theme refers to the abstract concept that is made concrete through the images, characterization, and action of the text. In nonfiction, however, the theme generally refers to the main topic of the discourse.

Thesis The central idea of an essay. The thesis is a complete sentence (although sometimes it may require more than one sentence) that establishes the topic of the essay in clear, unambiguous language.

Tone The author's implicit attitude toward the reader or the people, places, and events in a work as revealed by the elements of the author's style. Tone may be characterized as serious or ironic, sad or happy, private or public, angry or affectionate, bitter or nostalgic, or any other attitudes and feelings that human beings experience. See also STYLE.

Triplet A tercet in which all three lines rhyme. See also TERCET.

Trochaic meter See FOOT.

Understatement The opposite of hyperbole, *understatement* (or litotes) refers to a figure of speech that says less than is intended. Understatement usually has an ironic effect, and sometimes may be used for comic purposes, as in Mark Twain's statement, "The reports of my death are greatly exaggerated." See also HYPERBOLE, IRONY.

Verbal irony See IRONY.

Verse A generic term used to describe poetic lines composed in a measured rhythmical pattern, that are often, but not necessarily, rhymed. See also LINE, METER, RHYME, RHYTHM.

Villanelle A type of fixed form poetry consisting of nineteen lines of any length divided into six stanzas: five tercets and a concluding quatrain. The first and third lines of the initial tercet rhyme; these rhymes are repeated in each subsequent tercet *(aba)* and in the final two lines of the quatrain *(abaa)*. Line 1 appears in its entirety as lines 6, 12, and 18, while line 3 reappears as lines 9, 15, and 19. Dylan Thomas's "Do not go gentle into that good night" is a villanelle. See also FIXED FORM, QUATRAIN, RHYME, TERCET.

Acknowledgments (continued from p. ii)

Yehuda Amichai. "Jerusalem" from *The Selected Poetry of Yehuda Amichai*, trans./ed. by Bloch, Chana and Stephen Mitchell. Copyright © 1996 by The Regents of the University of California.

A. R. Ammons. "Coward" from *Diversifications* by A. R. Ammons. Copyright ©1975 by A. R. Ammons. Reprinted by permission of W. W. Norton & Co., Inc.

Charles R. Anderson. "Eroticism in 'Wild Nights—Wild Nights!'" from *Emily Dickinson's Poetry: Stairway of Surprise* (Holt, Rhinehart, and Winston, 1960). Reprinted with permission of the estate of Charles R. Anderson.

Maya Angelou. "Africa" from *Oh, Pray My Wings Are Gonna Fit Me Well* by Maya Angelou Copyright © 1975 by Maya Angelou. Reprinted by permission of Random House, Inc.

Richard Armour. "Going to Extremes" from *Light Amour* by Richard Armour. Permission to reprint this material is given courtesy of the family of Richard Armour.

Margaret Atwood. "Bored" and "February" from *Morning in the Burned House* by Margaret Atwood. Copyright © 1995 by Margaret Atwood. Used by permission by McClelland & Stewart, Inc., The Canadian Publishers. "Bored" from *Morning in the Burned House*. Copyright © 1995 by Margaret Atwood. Reprinted by permission of Houghton Mifflin Company. All rights reserved. "February" from *Morning in the Burned House*. Copyright © 1995 by Margaret Atwood. Reprinted by permission of Houghton Mifflin Company. All rights reserved. "February" from *Morning in the Burned House* by Margaret Atwood. Copyright © 1995 by Margaret Atwood. Used by permission, McClelland & Stewart, Inc. The Canadian Publishers. "you fit into me" from *Power Politics* by Margaret Atwood (Toronto: House of Anansi Press, 1971). Reprinted with permission of Stoddart Publishing Co., Limited, Canada.

W. H. Auden. "The Unknown Citizen" from *W.H. Auden: Collected Poems* by W. H. Auden, ed. by Edward Mendelson. Copyright © 1940 and renewed 1968 by W. H. Auden. Reprinted by permission.

Margaret Avison. "Tennis" from *The Dumbfounding* by Margaret Avison. Copyright © 1966 by Margaret Avison. Reprinted by permission of W. W. Norton and Company, Inc.

Jimmy Santiago Baca. "Green Chile" from *Black Mesa Poems*. Copyright © 1989 by Jimmy Santiago Baca. Reprinted by permission of New Directions Publishing Corp.

David Barber. "A Colonial Epitaph Annotated" first appeared in Parnassus, vol. 24, no. 1. Reprinted with permission of the author.

Richard K. Barksdale. "On Censoring 'Ballad of the Landlord'" from *Langston Hughes: The Poet and His Critics* by Richard K. Barksdale. American Library Association, 1977.

Jeanette Barnes. "Battlepiece" reprinted from *Shenandoah: The Washington and Lee University Review*, with the permission of the Editor.

Regina Barreca. "Nighttime Fires" from *The Minnesota Review* (Fall, 1986). Reprinted by permission of the author.

Matsuo Bashō. "Under cherry trees" from *Japanese Haiku*, trans. by Peter Beilenson, Series I, Copyright © 1955-56, Peter Beilenson, Editor. Reprinted by permission of Peter Pauper Press.

Michael L. Baumann. "The 'Overwhelming Question' for Prufrock" excerpted from "Let Us Ask 'What Is It?'" *Arizona Quarterly* 37 (Spring 1981): 47-58.

Paula Bennet. "On 'I heard a Fly buzz—when I died—'" reprinted from *Emily Dickinson: Woman Poet* by Paula Bennet by permission of the University of Iowa Press.

Elizabeth Bishop. "Manners" "Sestina," and "The Fish" from *The Complete Poems 1927–1979* by Elizabeth Bishop. Copyright © 1979, 1983 by Alice Helen Methfessel. Reprinted by permission of Farrar, Straus & Giroux, Inc.

Sophie Cabot Black. "August" copyright © 1994 by Sophie Cabot Black. Reprinted from *The Misunderstanding of Nature* with the permission of Graywolf Press, Saint Paul, Minnesota.

Robert Bly. "Snowbanks North of the House" from *The Man in the Black Coat Turns* by Robert Bly. Copyright © 1981 by Robert Bly. Used by permission of Doubleday, a division of Bantam Doubleday Dell Publishing Group, Inc. "Snowfall in the Afternoon." Reprinted from *Silence in the Snowy Fields*, by Robert Bly, Wesleyan University Press, Middletown, CT, 1962. Copyright © 1962 by Robert Bly. Reprinted with his permission. "On 'Snowbanks North of the House'." Reprinted with permission of the author.

Louise Bogan. "Women" from *The Blue Estuaries*. Copyright © 1923, 1929, 1930,1931, 1933, 1934, 1935, 1936, 1937, 1938, 1941, 1949, 1951, 1952, 1954, 1957, 1958, 1962, 1963, 1964, 1965, 1966, 1967, 1968 by Louise Bogan. Published by the Ecco Press in 1977.

Roo Borson. "Talk" reprinted from *Night walk: Selected Poems*, Oxford University Press, Toronto, 1994. Used by permission of Roo Borson.

Laure-Anne Bosselaar. "The Bumper Sticker" copyright © by Laure-Anne Bosselaar. Reprinted from *The Hour Between Dog and Wolf*, by Laure-Anne Bosselaar, with the permission of BOA Editions, Ltd.

Gwendolyn Brooks. "The Mother," "We Real Cool," and "Sadie and Maude" from *Blacks* (Chicago, IL: Third World Press, 1991). Copyright © 1991 by Gwendolyn Brooks Blakely.

Diane Burns. "Sure You Can Ask Me a Personal Question" from *Riding the One-Eyed Ford* (1981), reprinted in Lavinia Trout ed. *Native American Literature*, NTL Publishing, 1999.

Rosario Castellanos. "Chess" as translated by Maureen Ahern, from *A Rosario Castellanos Reader* by Rosario Castellanos, edited and translated by Maureen Ahern and others. Copyright © 1988. Reprinted with permission of the University of Texas Press and the author.

Keith Casto. "She Don't Bop" from *Light Year '87* Robert Wallace, ed. Brits Press, Cleveland, 1986.

Helen Chasin. "The Word *Plum*" from *Coming Close and Other Poems* by Helen Chasin. Copyright © 1968 by Yale University Press. Reprinted with permission of Yale University Press.

Kelly Cherry. "Alzheimer's" from *Death and Transfiguration*. Copyright © 1997 by Kelly Cherry. Reprinted with permission of Louisiana State University Press.

David Chinitz. "The Romanticization of Africa in the 1920s" from *Rejuvenation through Joy: Langston Hughes, Primitivism, and Jazz.* American Literary History Spring 1997. vol. 9, no. 1, pp. 60-78. Reprinted by permission of Oxford University Press.

Ann Choi. "The Shower" from *The Asian American Literary Reader,* 4, 1991. Used with permission of NTC/Contemporary Publishing Group.

John Ciardi. "Suburban" from *For Instance* by John Ciardi. Copyright © 1979 by Jon Ciardi. Reprinted by permission of W. W. Norton & Company, Inc.

Judith Ortiz Cofer. "Common Ground" is reprinted with permission from the publisher of *Silent Dancing: A Partial Remembrance of a Puerto Rican Childhood* (Houston: Arte Publico Press — University of Houston, 1991).

Michael Collier. "The Barber" from *The Neighbor.* Copyright © 1995 by the University of Chicago Press and Michael Collier. Reprinted with permission of the author.

Billy Collins. "Marginalia" from *Picnic, Lightning,* by Billy Collins. Copyright © 1998. Reprinted by permission of the University of Pittsburgh Press.

Emund Conti. "Pragmatist" from *Light Year '86.* Reprinted by permission of the author.

Herbert R. Coursen Jr. "A Parodic Interpretation of 'Stopping by Woods on a Snowy Evening.'" Excerpted from the "Ghost of Christmas Past: 'Stopping by Woods on a Snowy Evening'" by Herbert R. Coursen Jr., from *College English,* December 1962. Originally published by the National Council of Teachers of English.

Sally Croft. "Home-Baked Bread" from *Light Year '86.* Reprinted by permission of the author.

Pam Crow. "Meat Science" first appeared in *Ploughshares,* Spring 1998, vol. 24, no. 1. Reprinted by permission of the author.

Victor Hernandez Cruz. "Anonymous" from *Rhythm, Content and Flavor.* Copyright © 1969. Reprinted by permission of the author.

Countee Cullen. "On Racial Poetry" reprinted by permission of GRM Associates, Inc., Agents for the Estate of Ida M. Cullen from *Opportunity: A Journal of Negro Life;* February 1926 issue. Copyright © 1926 by *Opportunity* Magazine; copyright renewed 1954 by Ida M. Cullen. "Yet I Do Marvel" reprinted by permission of GRM Associates, Inc., Agents for the Estate of Ida M. Cullen from *Color* by Countee Cullen. Copyright © 1925 by Harper & Brothers; copyright renewed 1953 by Ida M. Cullen.

E. E. Cummings. "Buffalo Bill 's," "in Just-," "l(a," "next to of course god america i," "she being Brand," and "since feeling is first" from *Complete Poems: 1904–1962* by E. E. Cummings, edited by George J. Firmage. Copyright 1923, 1925, 1926, 1931, 1935, 1938, 1939, 1940, 1944, 1945, 1946, 1947, 1948, 1949, 1950, 1951, 1952, 1953, 1954, © 1955, 1956, 1957, 1958, 1959, 1960, 1961, 1962.

Peter De Vries. "To His Importunate Mistress." Reprinted by permission of the Estate of Peter De Vries and the Watkins/Loomis Agency.

Mary di Michele. "As in the Beginning" from *Necessary Sugar.* Originally published by Oberon Press, 1984. Reprinted by permission of the author.

Andrew P. Debicki. "New Criticism and Deconstructionism: Two Attitudes in Teaching Poetry" from *Writing and Reading Differently: Deconstruction and the Teaching of Composition and Literature,* ed. G. Douglas Atkins and Michael L. Johnson. Copyright © 1985 by the Unviversity Press of Kansas. Reprinted by permission.

James Dickey. "Deer Among Cattle" from *Poems, 1957–1967* by James Dickey. Wesleyan UP, 1978. Reprinted by permission of University Press of New England.

Emily Dickinson. "Heaven — is what I cannot reach!," "Faith is a fine invention," "A Bird came down the Walk —," "After great pain a formal feeling comes —," "Apparently with no surprise," "Because I could not stop for Death —," "From all the Jails the Boys and Girls," "I dwell in Possibility —," "I felt a Cleaving in my Mind —," "I heard a Fly buzz—when I died—," "I know that He exists," "I never saw a Moor—," "I read my sentence — steadily," "If I can stop one Heart from breaking," "If I shouldn't be alive," "Much Madness is divinest Sense —," "One need not be a Chamber—to be Haunted—," "Portraits are to daily faces," "Presentiment—is that long Shadow — on the lawn—," "Safe in their Alabaster Chambers —" (1859 version), "Safe in their Alabaster Chambers—" (1861 version), "Some keep the Sabbath going to Church—," "Success is counted sweetest," "Tell all the Truth but tell it slant —," "The Bustle in a House," "The Soul selects her own Society—," "The Thought beneath so slight a film—," "There's a certain Slant of light," "This was a Poet—it Is That," "To make a prairie it takes a clover and one bee," "What Soft—Cherubic Creatures—," "Wild Nights—Wild Nights!," "A loss of something ever felt I—," "How many times these low feet staggered," "I like a look of Agony," "I would not paint—a picture—," "Nature—sometimes sears a Sapling—," "Oh Sumptuous moment," "The Wind begun to knead the Grass—," "These are the days when Birds come back —" reprinted by permission of the publishers and the Trustees of Amherst College from *The poems of Emily Dickinson,* Thomas H. Johnson, ed., Cambridge, Mass.: The Belknap Press of Harvard University Press, copyright © 1951, 1955, 1979, 1983 by the President.

Morris Dickstein. "On the Social Responsibility of the Critic" reprinted by permission of the Modern Language Association of America from *Damaged Literacy. The Decay of Reading.* Originally appeared in *Profession 93.* Copyright © 1993 by the Modern Language Association.

Chitra Banerjee Divakaruni. "Indian Movie New Jersey" from the *Indiana Review,* 1990. Copyright © by Chitra Banerjee Divakaruni. Reprinted by permission of the author.

Gregory Djanikian. "When I First Saw Snow" reprinted from *Gregory Djanikian: Falling Deeply Into America* by permission of Carnegie Mellon University Press. Copyright © 1989 by Gregory Djanikian.

David Donnell. "The Canadian Prairie's View of Literature" from *Settlements* by David Donnell. Used by permission of McClelland & Stewart, Ltd. The Canadian Publishers.

Mark Doty. "Golden Retrievals" from *Sweet Machine* by Mark Doty. Copyright © 1998. Reprinted with permission of HarperCollins Publishers.

Stephen Dunn. "John & Mary" from *Different Hours* by Stephen Dunn. Copyright © 2000 by Stephen Dunn. Used by permission of W. W. Norton & Company, Inc.

Bernard Duyfhuizen. "'To His Coy Mistress': On How a Female Might Respond" excerpted from "Textual Harassment of Marvell's Coy Mistress: The Institutionalization of Masculine Criticism," *College English* (April 1988). Copyright © 1988 by the National Council of Teachers of English.

Cornelius Eady. "The Supremes" reprinted from *Cornelius Eady: The Gathering of My Name* by permission of Carnegie Mellon University Press. Copyright © 1991 by Cornelius Eady.

George Eliot. "In a London Drawingroom" from *George Eliot, Collected Poems*. Reprinted with permission of Skoob Books, Ltd.

James A. Emanuel. "Hughes's Attitudes toward Religion" from "Christ in Alabama: Religion in the Poetry of Langston Hughes" in *Modern Black Poets,* ed. Donald B. Gibson.

Martín Espada. "Coca-Cola and Coca Frío" from *City of Coughing and Dead Radiators* by Martín Espada. Copyright © 1993 by Martín Espada. Reprinted by permission of W. W. Norton & Company, Inc. "Latin Night at the Pawnshop" from *Rebellion is the Circle of a Lover's Hands* by Martín Espada. Curbstone Press, 1990. Reprinted by permission of Curbstone Press, Inc. Distributed by Consortium.

Barbara Everett. "The Problem of Tone in Prufrock" excerpted from "In Search of Prufrock," *Critical Quarterly* 16 (Summer, 1974). Reprinted by permission of Critical Quarterly, Ltd.

Faiz Ahmed Faiz. "If You Look at the City from Here" from *Faiz Ahmed Faiz, The True Subject,* trans. Naomi Lazard. Copyright © 1988 Princeton UP. Reprinted with permission of Princeton University Press.

Blanche Farley. "The Lover Not Taken" from *Light Year '86.* Reprinted by permission of the author.

Kenneth Fearing. "AD" from *New and Collected Poems by Kenneth Fearing* (Indiana University Press, 1956).

Robert Francis. "Catch" copyright © 1950, 1953 by Robert Francis. From *The Orb Weaver,* copyright 1950, 1953 by Robert Francis. Wesleyan University Press. Reprinted by permission of the University Press of New England. "The Pitcher" copyright © 1950, 1953 by Robert Francis. From *The Orb Weaver,* copyright 1950, 1953 by Robert Francis. Wesleyan University Press. Reprinted by permission of the University Press of New England. "On 'Hard' Poetry" reprinted from *The Satirical Rogue of Poetry* by Robert Francis (Amherst: University of Massachusetts Press, 1968), copyright © 1968 by Robert Francis.

Robert Frost. "Acquainted with the Night," "Design," "Fire and Ice," "Neither Out Far nor In Deep," "Nothing Gold Can Stay," "Stopping by Woods on a Snowy Evening," "The Pasture," "The Silken Tent," "A Girl's Garden," "The Investment," "Spring Pools," "The Armful" from *The Poetry of Robert Frost* edited by Edward Connery Lathem, copyright 1936, 1942, 1951, © 1956 by Robert Frost, copyright 1923, 1928, 1969 by Henry Holt and Co., copyright 1964, 1970 by Lesley Frost Ballantine. Reprinted by permission of Henry Holt and Company, LLC. "The Figure a Poem Makes" from *The Selected Prose of Robert Frost,* edited by Hyde Cox and Edward Connery Lathem. Copyright 1946, © 1956, 1959 by Robert Frost. Copyright 1949, 1954, © 1966 by Henry Holt & Co., Inc. Reprinted by permission of Henry Holt & Co., Inc. "On the Living Part of a Poem" from *A Swinger of Birches: A Portrait of Robert Frost* by Sidney Cox. Copyright © 1957 by New York University Press. Reprinted with permission of New York University Press. "On the Way to Read a Poem" from *Poetry and School* by Robert Frost in *The Atlantic Monthly,* June, 1951. Reprinted by permission of the Estate of Robert Frost.

Xu Gang. "Red Azaleas on the Cliff" from *The Red Azalea,* Edited by Edward Morin. Copyright © 1990 University of Hawaii Press. Reprinted with permission.

Deborah Garrison. "The Boss" from *A Working Girl Can't Win* by Deborah Garrison. Copyright © 1998 by Deborah Garrison. Reprinted by permission of Random House, Inc.

Donald B. Gibson. "The Essential Optimism of Hughes and Whitman" excerpt from *The Good Black Poet and the Good Gray Poet: The Poetry of Hughes and Whitman in Langston Hughes — Black Genius: A Critical Evaluation* by Donald B. Gibson. William Morrow, 1971. Reprinted with permission of the author.

Sandra M. Gilbert and Susan Gubar. "On Dickinson's White Dress" excerpted from *The Madwoman in the Attic,* Yale University Press, 1979. Reprinted by permission of Yale University Press.

Sandra M. Gilbert. "Mafioso" reprinted with permission of the author.

Allen Ginsberg. "First Party at Ken Kesey's with Hell's Angels" from *Collected Poems 1947–1980* by Allen Ginsberg. Copyright © 1965 by Allen Ginsberg. Reprinted by permission of HarperCollins Publishers, Inc.

Nikki Giovanni. "Clouds" from *Blues: For All the Changes* by Nikki Giovanni. Copyright © by Nikki Giovanni.

H. D. [Hilda Doolittle]. "Heat" from *Collected Poems, 1912–1944.* Copyright © 1982 by The Estate of Hilda Doolittle. Reprinted by permission of New Directions Publishing Corp.

Rachel Hadas. "The Red Hat" from *Halfway down the Hall: New and Selected Poems.* Copyright © 1998 by Rachel Hadas, Wesleyan University Press by permission of University Press of New England.

Donald Hall. "Letter with No Address." An earlier version of this poem appeared in *Ploughshares,* Winter 1996–97, vol. 22, no. 4, pp. 109–113. Reprinted with permission of the author.

Joy Harjo. "Fishing" from June 21, 1991 Op-Ed page of the *New York Times.* Copyright © 1991 by The New York Times Company. Reprinted by permission.

Jeffrey Harrison. "Horseshoe Contest" first appeared in the *Kenyon Review.* Used with permission of the author.

Robert Hass. "Happiness" from *Sun Under Wood* by Robert Hass. Copyright © 1996 by Robert Hass. Reprinted by permission of HarperCollins Publishers, Inc. "A Story about the Body" from *Human Wishes* by Robert Hass. Copyright © 1989 by Robert Hass. Reprinted by permission of HarperCollins Publishers, Inc.

William Hathaway. "Oh Oh" from *Light Year '86.* This poem was originally published in *The Cincinnati Poetry Review.*

Harriet Hawkins. "Should We Study *King Kong* or *King Lear*?" from "From King Lear to King Kong and Back: Shakespeare in Popular Modern Genres" in "Bad" Shakespeare: Revelations of the Shakespeare Cannon, ed. Maurice Cherney, Fairleigh Dickinson University Press, 1988.

Robert Hayden. "Those Winter Sundays" copyright © 1966 by Robert Hayden, from *Angle of Ascent: New and Selected Poems* by Robert Hayden. Reprinted by permission of Liveright Publishing Corporation.

Seamus Heaney. "Mid-term Break" from *Death of a Naturalist* by Seamus Heaney. Reprinted by permission of Faber & Faber, Ltd. "Mid-term Break" from *Poems 1965–1975* by Seamus Heaney. Copyright © 1980 by Seamus Heaney. Reprinted by permission of Farrar, Straus & Giroux, Inc.

Anthony Hecht. "The Dover Bitch" from *Collected Earlier Poems* by Anthony Hecht. Copyright © 1990 by Anthony D. Hecht. Reprinted by permission of Alfred A. Knopf., Inc.

Judy Page Heitzman. "The Schoolroom on the Second Floor of the Knitting Mill" first appeared in *The New Yorker*, 1992. Reprinted by permission of the author.

William Heyen. "The Trains" from *The Host: Selected Poems 1965–1990*, by William Heyen. Reprinted by permission of Time Being Books. Copyright © 1994 by Time Being Press. All Rights Reserved.

Thomas Wentworth Higginson. "On Meeting Dickinson for the First Time" reprinted by permission of the publishers from *The Letters of Emily Dickinson* edited by Thomas H. Johnson, Cambridge, Mass.: The Belknap Press of Harvard University Press. Copyright © 1958, 1986 by the President and Fellows of Harvard University.

Edward Hirsch. "Fast Break" from *Wild Gratitude* by Edward Hirsch. Reprinted by permission of Alfred A. Knopf, Inc.

Jane Hirshfield. "The Lives of the Heart" from *The Lives of the Heart* published by HarperCollins. Copyright © 1997 by Jane Hirshfield. First appeared in *The Yale Review*, January, 1997, vol 85, no. 1. Used by permission.

Li Ho. "A Beautiful Girl Combs Her Hair" translated by David Young, from *Five T'ang Poets: Field Translation Series #15*. Copyright © 1990 Oberlin College Press. Reprinted by permission of Oberlin College Press.

Linda Hogan. "Hunger" from *The Book of Medicines* by Linda Hogan, Coffee House Press, 1993. Copyright © 1993 by Linda Hogan. Used by permission of the publisher. "Song for My Name" from *Calling Myself Home* by Linda Hogan. Reprinted by permission of Greenfield Review Press.

Jonathan Holden. "Cutting Loose on an August Night" from *The Names of the Rapids*. Copyright © 1985 by Jonathan Holden. Reprinted by permission of the author.

Carl Holman. "Mr. Z." Reprinted by permission of the Carl Holman Estate.

Carolynn Hoy. "In the Summer Kitchen" from *Ariel*, vol. 24.2, April 1993. Reprinted with permission of The Board of Governors, University of Calgary.

Andrew Hudgins. "Seventeen" from *The Glass Hammer*. Copyright © 1994 by Andrew Hudgins. Reprinted by permission of Houghton Mifflin Company. All rights reserved. "Elegy for my Father, Who is Not Dead" from *The Never-Ending*. Copyright © 1991 by Andrew Hudgins. Reprinted by permission of Houghton Mifflin Company. All rights reserved.

Langston Hughes. "Ballad of the Landlord," "Cross," "Danse Africaine," "Dinner Guest: Me," "doorknobs," "Dream Boogie," "Dream Variations," "Formula," "Frederick Douglass: 1817–1895," "Harlem," "I Too," "Jazzonia," "Lenox Avenue: Midnight," "Negro," "Old Walt," "Red Silk Stockings," "Rent-Party Shout: For a Lady Dancer," "The Negro Speaks of Rivers," "The Weary Blues," "Theme for English B," "Un-American Investigators," "Bad Man," "Democracy," "Drum," "Madam and the Census Man," "Mother to Son," "Song for a Dark Girl," and "Uncle Tom," from *Collected Poems* by Langston Hughes. Copyright © 1994 by the Estate of Langston Hughes. Reprinted by permission of Alfred A. Knopf, Inc. "On Harlem Rent Parties" text excerpt from "When the Negro Was in Vogue" from *The Big Sea* by Langston Hughes. Copyright © 1940 by Langston Hughes. Copyright renewed © 1968 by Arna Bontemps and George Houston Bass. Reprinted by permission of Hill and Wang, a division of Farrar, Straus & Giroux, Inc. "On Racial Shame and Pride" excerpt from *The Negro Artist and the Racial Mountain* by Langston Hughes. Reprinted with permission from the June 23, 1926 issue of *The Nation*.

Paul Humphrey. "Blow" from *Light Year '86*. Reprinted with permission of the author.

Mark Jarman. "Unholy Sonnet" from *Questions for Ecclesiastes* by Mark Jarman, Storyline Press, 1997. Reprinted with permission of the author.

Randall Jarrell. "The Death of the Ball Turret Gunner" from *The Complete Poems*. Copyright © 1969 by Mrs. Randall Jarrell. Reprinted by permission of Farrar, Straus & Giroux, Inc.

Onwuchekwa Jemie. "On Universal Poetry" from *Langston Hughes* by Onwuchekwa Jemie. Copyright © 1985 by Columbia University Press.

Alice Jones. "The Foot" from *Anatomy*, Bullnettle Press, San Francisco, 1997. Reprinted by permission of the author. "The Larynx" from *Anatomy*, Bullnettle Press, San Francisco, 1997. Reprinted by permission of the author.

Rodney Jones. "Things that Happen Once." Copyright © 1996. Reprinted by permission of Houghton Mifflin Company.

Donald Justice. "Order in the Streets" from *Loser Weepers* by Donald Justice. Reprinted by permission of the author.

Katherine Kearns. "On the Symbolic Setting of 'Home Burial'" excerpt from "The Place Is the Asylum: Women and Nature in Robert Frost's Poetry" in *American Literature* 59 (May 1987). Copyright © 1991 by Duke University Press. Reprinted by permission of Duke University Press.

Aron Keesbury. "Song to a Waitress." Copyright 1997 by Aron Keesbury, Boston, MA. Reprinted by permission of the author.

Karl Keller. "Robert Frost on Dickinson" from *The Only Kangaroo among the Beauty: Emily Dickinson in America*. Copyright © 1979. The Johns Hopkins University Press.

X. J. Kennedy. "A Visit from St. Sigmund." Copyright © 1993 by X. J. Kennedy. First printed in *Light, The Quarterly of Light Verse*. Reprinted with permission of *Light*.

Jane Kenyon. "The Blue Bowl." Copyright © 1996 by Jane Kenyon. Reprinted from *Otherwise: New & Selected Poems* with the permission of Graywolf Press, Saint Paul, Minnesota. "Surprise" copyright 1996. Reprinted from *Otherwise: New & Selected Poems* with the permission of Graywolf Press, Saint Paul, Minnesota.

Willyce Kim. "In This Heat" from *Asian American Literature*, 2000. Used by permission of NTC/Contemporary Publishing Group.

Maxine Hong Kingston. "Restaurant" from *The Iowa Review* 12 (Spring/Summer, 1981). Reprinted by permission of the author.

Galway Kinnell. "After Making Love We Hear Footsteps" from *Three Books.* Copyright © 1993 by Galway Kinnell. Originally published in *Mortal Acts, Mortal Words* (1980). Reprinted by permission of Houghton Mifflin Company. All rights reserved. "Blackberry Eating" from *Three Books.* Copyright © 1993 by Galway Kinnell. Originally published in *Mortal Acts, Mortal Words* (1980). Reprinted by permission of Houghton Mifflin Company. All rights reserved. "The Deconstruction of Emily Dickinson" from *Imperfect Thirst.* Copyright © 1994 by Galway Kinnell. Reprinted by permission of Houghton Mifflin Company. All rights reserved.

Carolyn Kizer. "After Basho" copyright © 1984 by Carolyn Kizer. Reprinted from *Yin: New Poems,* by Carolyn Kizer, with the permission of BOA Editions, Ltd.

Etheridge Knight. "A Watts Mother Mourns While Boiling Beans" from *Belly Song and Other Poems* by Etheridge Knight. Copyright © 1973 by Broadside Press. Reprinted with their permission.

Ron Koertge. "1989" copyright © 1999 by Ronald Koertge. Reprinted by permission of John Hawkins & Associates, Inc.

Annete Koldny. "On the Commitments of Feminist Criticism" from "Dancing Through the Minefield: Some Observations on the Theory, Practice and Politics of a Feminist Literary Criticism" *Feminist Studies* 6, 1980. Copyright © 1979 by Annette Kolodny: all rights reserved. Reprinted by permission of the author.

Philp Larkin. "A Study of Reading Habits" from *The Whitson Weddings* © 1964 by Philip Larkin. Reprinted by permission of Faber & Faber, Ltd. "A Study of Reading Habits" from *Collected Poems* by Philip Larkin. Copyright © 1988, 1989 by the Estate of Philip Larkin. Reprinted by permission of Farrar, Straus & Giroux, Inc. "This Be the Verse" from *The Whitson Weddings* © 1964 by Philip Larkin. Reprinted by permission of Faber & Faber, Ltd. "This Be the Verse" from *Phillip Larkin, Collected Poems,* ed. Anthony Thwaite © 1988 by the Estate of Philip Larkin.

Richard Lattimore. "Invocation to Aphrodite" (translation of Sappho) from *Greek Lyrics* tr. Richard Lattimore, 2 ed. University of Chicago Press, pp. 38–39. Reprinted by permission of the University of Chicago Press.

Tato Laviera. "AmeRícan" from *AmeRícan.* Copyright © 1985. Reprinted by permission of Arte Publico Press — University of Houston.

Norman Lear. "Meet the Bunkers." "All in the Family" written by Norman Lear from the television series *All in the Family.* "All in the Family" copyright © 1971, Columbia TriStar Television.

Li-Young Lee. "Eating Together" copyright © 1986 by Li-Young Lee. Reprinted from *Rose,* by Li-Young Lee, with the permission of BOA Editions, Ltd.

David Lenson. "On the Contemporary Use of Rhyme" from *The Chronicle of Higher Education* (February 24, 1988).

Denise Levertov. "Gathered at the River" from *A Necessary Poetry.* Copyright © 1997 by Denise Levertov. Reprinted by permission of New Directions Publishing Corp.

Phillip Levine. "Reinventing America" from *The Mercy* by Phillip Levine. Copyright © 1999 by Phillip Levine. Reprinted by permission of Alfred A. Knopf, a division of Random House, Inc.

J. Patrick Lewis. "The Unkindest Cut" *from Light 5* (Spring 1993). Reprinted with permission of the author and *Light.*

Sarah Lindsay. "Aluminum Chlorohydrate" from *Primate Behavior,* copyright © 1997 by Sarah Lindsay. Published with permission of Grove/Atlantic, Inc.

Audre Lorde. "Hanging Fire" from *The Black Unicorn* by Audre Lorde. Copyright © 1978 by Audre Lorde. Reprinted by permission of W. W. Norton & Company, Inc.

Robert Lowell. "For Sale" from *Selected Poems* by Robert Lowell. Copyright © 1976 by Robert Lowell. Reprinted with permission of Farrar, Straus & Giroux.

Thomas Lynch. "Liberty" from *Still Life in Milford* by Thomas Lynch. Copyright © 1998 by Thomas Lynch. Used by permission of W. W. Norton & Company.

Katharyn Howd Machan. "Hazel Tells LaVerne" from *Light Year '85.* Reprinted by permission of the author.

Archibald MacLeish. "Ars Poetica" from *Collected Poems 1917–1982* by Archibald MacLeish. Copyright © 1985 by The Estate of Archibald MacLeish. Reprinted by permission of Houghton Mifflin Company. All rights reserved.

Elaine Magarrell. "The Joy of Cooking" from *Sometime the Cow Kick Your Head, Light Year 88/89.* Reprinted with permission of the author.

Kathy Mangan. "An Arithmetic" first appeared in *Ploughshares.* Reprinted with permission of the author.

Julio Marzan. "The Translator at the Reception for Latin American Writers." Reprinted with permission of the author. "Ethnic Poetry" originally appeared in *Parnassas: Poetry In Review.* Reprinted by permission of the author.

Cleopatra Mathis. "What to Tip the Boatman?" first appeared in *Ploughshares.* Reprinted with permission of the author.

Florence Cassen Mayers. "All-American Sestina." Copyright © 1996 Florence Cassen Mayers, as first published in *The Atlantic Monthly.* Reprinted with permission of the author.

Gail Mazur. "Snake in the Grass" from *The Common,* University of Chicago Press, 1995. Copyright © Gail Mazur. Reprinted with permission of the author.

David T. W. McCord. "Epitaph on a Waiter" from *Odds without Ends* copyright © 1954 by David T. W. McCord. Reprinted by permission of Arthur B. Page, executor of the estate of David McCord.

Michale McFee. "In Medias Res" reprinted from *Colander* by Michael McFee, by permission of the author. Copyright © 1996 by Michael McFee.

Rennie McQuilkin. "The Lighters" reprinted by permission from *The Hudson Review.*

Jay Meek. "Swimmers" first appeared in *Windows,* Carnegie Mellon University Press: Pittsburgh, PA, 1994. Reprinted with permission of the author.

Peter Meinke. "The ABC of Aerobics" from *Night Watch on the Chesapeake*, by Peter Meinke, © 1987. Reprinted by permission of the University of Pittsburgh Press.

James Merrill. "Casual Wear" from *Selected Poems 1946 1985* by James Merrill. Copyright © 1992 by James Merrill. Reprinted by permission of Alfred A. Knopf Inc.

W. S. Merwin. "For the Anniversary of My Death" from *The Lice* by W. S. Merwin, 1970.

Edna St. Vincent Millay. "I will put Chaos into fourteen lines" from *Collected Poems*, HarperCollins. Copyright © 1923, 1951, 1954, 1982 by Edna St. Vincent Millay and Norma Millay Ellis. All rights reserved. Reprinted by permission of Elizabeth Barnett, literary executor.

Janice Mirikitani. "Recipe" excerpted from *Shedding Silence*, copyright © 1987 by Janice Mirikitani. Reprinted by permission of Celestial Arts, P.O. Box 7123, Berkeley, CA 94707.

Elaine Mitchell. "Form" from *Light 9* (Spring 1994). Reprinted by permission of the author.

N. Scott Momaday. "Crows in a Winter Composition" from *In the Presence of the Sun* by N. Scott Momaday. Copyright © 1992 by N. Scott Momaday. Reprinted by permission of St. Martin's Press, LLC.

Marianne Moore "Poetry" reprinted with permission of Simon & Schuster from *Collected Poems of Marianne Moore*. Copyright 1935 by Marianne Moore; copyright renewed © 1963 by Marianne Moore and T. S. Eliot.

Janice Townley Moore. "To a Wasp" first appeared in *Light Year*, Bits Press. Reprinted by permission of the author.

Pat Mora. "Another Brown Man" from *Agua Santa/Holy Water* by Pat Mora. Copyright © 1995 by Pat Mora. Reprinted by permission of Beacon Press, Boston.

Robert Morgan. "Mountain Graveyard" from *Sigodlin*, copyright © 1990 by Robert Morgan. Wesleyan University Press. Reprinted by permission of the University Press of New England. "On the Shape of a Poem" from *Epoch* (Fall/Winter 1983). Reprinted by permission of the author. "Time's Music" from "Poetry and School" by Robert Frost in *The Atlantic Monthly*, June, 1951. Reprinted by permission of the Estate of Robert Frost. "Wind from a Waterfall" from *The Atlantic Monthly*, Sept. 1999. Reprinted by permission of the author.

Robin Morgan. "Invocation" included in *A Hot January: Poems 1996–1999* by Robin Morgan. Copyright © by Robin Morgan. Reprinted by permission of the author.

Paul Muldoon. "Symposium" from *Hay* by Paul Muldoon. Copyright © 1999 by Paul Muldoon. Reprinted with permission of Farrar, Straus & Giroux.

Joan Murray. "Play-By-Play" reprinted by permission from *The Hudson Review*, Vol. XLIX, No. 4 (Winter 1997). Copyright © 1997 by Joan Murray.

Pablo Neruda. "Sweetness Always" from *Extravagaria* by Pablo Neruda, trans. by Alastair Reid. English translation copyright © 1974, by Alastair Reid. Reprinted by permission of Farrar, Straus & Giroux, Inc.

John Frederick Nims "Love Poem" from *Selected Poems*. Copyright © 1982 by the University of Chicago. Reprinted by permission of the Publisher

Alden Nowlan. "The Bull Moose" from *An Exchange of Gifts* by Alden Nowlan. Reprinted with the permission of Stoddart Publishing Co. Limited, Canada

Sharon Olds. "Rite of Passage" from *The Dead and the Living* by Sharon Olds. Copyright © 1983 by Sharon Olds. Reprinted by permission of Alfred A. Knopf., Inc. "Sex without Love" from *The Dead and the Living* by Sharon Olds. Copyright © 1983 by Sharon Olds. Reprinted by permission of Alfred A. Knopf., Inc. "Poem for the Breasts" first appeared in *Ploughshares*. Reprinted with permission of the author.

Mary Oliver. "Seven White Butterflies" from *West Wind* by Mary Oliver. Copyright © 1997 by Mary Oliver. Reprinted by permission of Houghton Mifflin Company. All rights reserved.

Eric Ormsby. "Nose" from *For a Modest God*, Copyright © 1997. Reprinted by permission of ECW Press.

Wilfred Owen. "Dulce et Decorum Est" from *The Collected Poems of Wilfred Owen*. Copyright © 1963 by Chatto & Windus, Ltd. Reprinted by permission of New Directions Publishing Corp.

Sue Owen. "Zero" from *The Book of Winter*, Columbus. Ohio State University Press, 1988. Copyright © 1988 by Sue Owen. Reprinted with permission from the author.

Lisa Parker. "Snapping Beans" from *Parnassus* 1998, vol. 23, no. 1 and 2.

Linda Pastan. "Marks" copyright © 1978 by Linda Pastan from *PM/AM: New and Selected Poems by Linda Pastan*. Reprinted by permission of W. W. Norton & Co., Inc.

Octavio Paz. "The Street" from *Early Poems 1935–1955*. Reprinted with permission of Indiana University Press.

Molly Peacock. "Desire" from *Molly Peacock, Raw Heaven*, Random House, 1984.

Laurence Perrine. "The limerick's never averse" from *A Limerick's always a verse: 200 original limericks* by Laurence Perrine. Copyright © 1990 by Laurence Perrine

Stephen Perry. "Blue Spruce" copyright © 1991 by Stephen Perry. Originally in *The New Yorker*, January 28, 1991, p. 34–35.

Marge Piercy "The Secretary Chant" from *Circles on the Water* by Marge Piercy. Copyright © 1982 by Marge Piercy. Reprinted by permission of Alfred A. Knopf, Inc.

Sylvia Plath. "Daddy" from *The Collected Poems* by Sylvia Plath, ed. Ted Hughes. Reprinted by permission of Faber & Faber, Ltd. "Daddy" from *Ariel* by Sylvia Plath. Copyright © 1963 by Ted Hughes. Reprinted by permission of HarperCollins Publishers, Inc. "Mirror" from *The Collected Poems* by Sylvia Plath, ed. Ted Hughes. Reprinted by permission of Faber & Faber, Ltd. "Mirror" from *Crossing the Water* by Sylvia Plath. Copyright © 1963 by Ted Hughes. Originally appeared in *The New Yorker*. Reprinted by permission of HarperCollins Publishers, Inc. "Mushrooms" from *The Colossus and Other Poems* by Sylvia Plath. Copyright © 1960 by Sylvia Plath. Reprinted by permission of Alfred A. Knopf, Inc.

Ezra Pound. "In a Station of the Metro" from *Personae*. Copyright © 1926 by Ezra Pound. Reprinted by permission of New Directions Publishing Corp.

Jim Powell. "[Artfully adorned Aphrodite, deathless] (translation of Sappho fragment)" from *Sappho A Garland: The Poems and Fragments of Sappho.* Copyright © 1993 by Jim Powell. Reprinted by permission of Farrar, Straus & Giroux, Inc.

Wyatt Prunty. "Elderly Lady Crossing on Green" from *The Run of the House,* page 18. Copyright © 1993. Used by permission of The Johns Hopkins University Press.

Peter Rabinowitz. "On Close Readings" excerpted from *Pedagogy Is Politics: Literary Theory and Critical Thinking,* ed. by Marina-Regina Kecht. Copyright © 1992 by the Board of Trustees of the University of Illinois. Reprinted with permission of the University of Illinois Press.

Henry Reed. "Naming of Parts 'Lessons of War' (1. Naming of the Parts)" from *Henry Reed: Collected Poems,* ed. Jon Stallworthy. Copyright © 1991 by the Executor of Henry Reed's Estate.

Marny Requa. "From an Interview with Julia Alvarez" from "The Politics of Fiction," *Frontera* 5 (1997):n. pdg. World Wide Web. 29 Jan. 1997. Reprinted with permission of Marny Requa.

David S. Reynolds. "Popular Literature and 'Wild Nights — Wild Nights!'" from *Beneath the American Renaissance* by David S. Reynolds, copyright © 1988 by David S. Reynolds.Reprinted by permission of Alfred A. Knopf, Inc.

Oliver Rice. "The Doll House." Reprinted with permission of the author.

Adrienne Rich. "Living in Sin." Copyright © 1993, 1955 by Adrienne Rich, from *Collected Early Poems: 1950–1970* by Adrienne Rich. Reprinted by permission of W. W. Norton & Company, Inc.

Rainer Maria Rilke. "The Panther" from *The Selected Poetry of Rainer Maria Rilke* by Rainer Maria Rilke, edited & translated by Stephen Mitchell copyright © 1982 by Stephen Mitchell. Reprinted by permission of Random House, Inc.

Alberto Ríos. "Seniors" from *Five Indiscretions.* Copyright © 1985 by Alberto Ríos. Reprinted by permission of the author.

Theodore Roethke. "My Papa's Waltz" copyright © 1942 by *Hearst Magazines, Inc.* From *The Collected Poems of Theodore Roethke* by Theodore Roethke. Used by permission of Doubleday, a division of Bantam Doubleday Dell Publishing Group, Inc. "Root Cellar" copyright © 1943 by Modern Poetry Association, Inc. From *The Collected Poems of Theodore Roethke* by Theodore Roethke. Used by permission of Doubleday, a division of Bantam Doubleday Dell Publishing Group, Inc.

Frederik L. Rusch. "Society and Character in 'The Love Song of J. Alfred Prufrock,'" "Approaching Literature through the Social Psychology of Erich Fromm" in *Psychological Perspectives on Literature: Freudian Dissidents and Non-Freudians,* edited by Joseph Natoli. Copyright © 1984. Reprinted by permission of the author.

Kate Rushin. "The Black Back-Ups" from *The Black Back-Ups* by Kate Rushin. Copyright © 1993 by Kate Rushin. Reprinted by permission of Firebrand Books.

Indira Sant. "Household Fires" from *Sixteen Modern Indian Poems* ed. A. K. Ramanujan and Vinay Dharwadker © 1989. Reprinted by permission of *Daedalus, Journal of the American Academy of Arts and Sciences* from the issue entitled "Another India," Fall 1989, vol. 118, no. 4.

Robyn Sarah. "Villanelle for a Cool April" reprinted from *Shenandoah: The Washington and Lee University Review,* with the permission of the editor and author. Copyright 1998 by Robyn Sarah.

Elisabeth Schneider. "Hints of Eliot in Prufrock" reprinted by permission of the Modern Language Association of America from "Prufrock and After: The Theme of Change," PMLA 87 (1982): 1103–1117.

Saundra Sharp. "It's the Law: A Rap Poem" from *Typing in the Dark 1991,* Writers and Readers Publishing, Inc. Reprinted in *African American Literature* 1998. Used by permission of NTC/Contemporary Publishing Group.

Charles Simic. "Filthy Landscape" from *Jackstraws.* Copyright © 1999 by Charles Simic. Reprinted by permission of Harcourt, Inc.

Louis Simpson. "In the Suburbs" from *At the End of the Open Road* by Louis Simpson. Wesleyan UP, 1963. Reprinted by permission of the author.

David R. Slavitt. "Titanic" from *Big Nose* by David R. Slavitt. Copyright © 1983 by David R. Slavitt. Reprinted by permission of Louisiana State University Press.

Ernest Slyman. "Lightning Bugs" from *Sometime the Cow Kick Your Head, Light Year 88/89.* Reprinted by permission of the author.

Patricia Smith. "What It's Like to Be a Black Girl (For Those of You Who Aren't)" reprinted with permission of the author.

David Solway. "Windsurfing" reprinted by permission of the author.

Cathy Song. "The White Porch" from *Picture Bride.* Copyright © 1983 by Yale University Press. Reprinted with permission. "The Youngest Daughter" from *Picture Bride.* Copyright © 1983 by Yale University Press. Reprinted with permission.

Susan Sontag. "Against Interpretation" excerpt from "Against Interpretation" by Susan Sontag from *Against Interpretation* by Susan Sontag. Copyright © 1964; 1966 and copyright renewed © 1994 by Susan Sontag. Reprinted by permission of Farrar, Straus & Giroux, Inc.

Gary Soto. "Behind Grandma's House," "Black Hair," and "Mexicans Begin Jogging" from *New and Selected Works* by Gary Soto. Copyright © 1995, published by Chronicle Books, San Francisco.

Wole Soyinka. "Future Plans" from *A Shuttle in the Crypt* by Wole Soyinka. Copyright © 1972 by Wole Soyinka. Reprinted by permission of Hill and Wang, a division of Farrar, Straus & Giroux, Inc. "Telephone Conversation" from *Ibadan,* volume 10, November 1960, p. 34.

Bruce Springsteen. "The Streets of Philadelphia" reprinted with permission.

William Stafford. "Traveling through the Dark" copyright © 1962, 1998 by the Estate of William Stafford. Reprinted from *The Way It Is: New & Selected Poems* with the permission of Graywolf Press, Saint Paul, Minnesota.

Timothy Steele. "Waiting for the Storm" from *Sapphics Against Anger and Other Poems.* Copyright © 1986 by Timothy Steele. Reprinted with permission of the University of Arkansas Press.

Jim Stevens. "Schizophrenia" originally appeared in *Light: The Quarterly of Light Verse* (Spring 1992). Copyright © 1992 by Jim Stevens.

Wallace Stevens. "The Emperor of Ice-Cream" from *Collected Poems* by Wallace Stevens. Copyright © 1923 and renewed 1951 by Wallace Stevens. Reprinted by permission of Alfred A. Knopf., Inc.

Robert Sward. "A Personal Analysis of 'Love Song of J. Alfred Prufrock'" from *Touchstones: American Poets on a Favorite Poem* eds. Robert Pack and Jay Parini. Middlebury College Press. Published by UP New England.

May Swenson. "A Nosty Fright" from *In Other Words* by May Swenson. Copyright © 1984 by May Swenson. Reprinted by permission of the Estate of May Swenson.

Wislawa Szymborska. "Maybe All This" from *View Within a Grain of Sand.* Copyright © 1993 by Wislawa Szymborska, English translation by Stanislaw Baranczak and Clare Cavanagh. Copyright © 1995 by Harcourt, Inc., reprinted by permission of the publisher.

Diane Thiel. "The Minefield" from *Echolocations,* copyright © 2000 by Diane Thiel. Reprinted with permission of Story Line Press.

Dylan Thomas. "Do not go gentle into that good night" from *Poems of Dylan Thomas.* Copyright 1939 by New Directions Publishing Corporation, 1945 by the Trustees for the Copyrights of Dylan Thomas, 1952 by Dylan Thomas. "Do not go gentle into that good night," from *Poems of Dylan Thomas.* Copyright © 1952 by the Trustees for the Copyrights of Dylan Thomas. Reprinted by permission of New Directions Publishing Corp. "On the Words in Poetry" from *Early Prose Writings.* Copyright © 1972 by the Trustees for the Copyrights of Dylan Thomas. Reprinted by permission of New Directions Publishing Corp. "The Hand That Signed the Paper" from *Poems of Dylan Thomas.* Copyright 1939 by New Directions Publishing Corporation, 1945 by the Trustees for the Copyrights of Dylan Thomas, 1952 by Dylan Thomas. "The Hand That Signed the Paper" from *Poems of Dylan Thomas.* Copyright © 1952 by the Trustees for the Copyrights of Dylan Thomas. Reprinted by permission of New Directions Publishing Corp.

Mabel Loomis Todd. "The Character of Amherst" from *The Years and Hours of Emily Dickinson,* volume 2, by Jay Leda. Copyright © 1960 by Yale University Press.

Tomas Transtromer. "April and Silence" translated by Robin Fulton. Copyright © Robin Fulton and Bloodaxe Books. Reprinted by permission of Bloodaxe Books.

Lionel Trilling. "On Frost as a Terrifying Poet" copyright © 1959 by Lionel Trilling, reprinted by permission of the Wylie Agency, Inc.

John Updike. "Dog's Death" from *Midpoint and Other Poems* by John Updike. Copyright © 1969 by John Updike. Reprinted by permission of Alfred A. Knopf, Inc. "Player Piano" from *Collected Poems 1953–1993* by John Updike. Copyright © 1993 by John Updike. Reprinted by permission of Alfred A. Knopf., Inc.

Mona Van Duyn. "What the Motorcycle Said" from *If It Be Not I* by Mona Van Duyn. Copyright © 1973 by Mona Van Duyn. Reprinted by permission of Alfred A. Knopf, a Division of Random House, Inc.

Richard Wakefield. "In a Poetry Workshop" from *Light* (Winter 1999). Reprinted with permission of *Light.*

Derek Walcott. "The Road Taken" excerpt from "The Road Taken" by Derek Walcott from *Homage to Robert Frost* by Joseph Brodsky, Seamus Heaney, and Derek Walcott. Copyright © 1996 by the Estate of Joseph Brodsky. Reprinted by permission of Farrar, Straus & Giroux, Inc.

Alice Walker. "a woman is not a potted plant" from *Her Blue Body Everything We Know. Earthling Poems, 1965–1990,* copyright © 1991 by Alice Walker, reprinted by permission of Harcourt Brace & Company

Robert Wallace. "The Double-Play" copyright © 1961 by Robert Wallace. From *Views of a Ferris Wheel.* Reprinted by permission of the author. "Dogs" from *The Uses of Adversity,* by Ronald Wallace, copyright © 1998. Reprinted by permission of the University of Pittsburgh Press.

Marilyn Nelson Waniek. "Emily Dickinson's Defunct" from *For the Body* by Marilyn Nelson Waniek. Copyright © 1978 by Marilyn Nelson Waniek. Reprinted by permission of the author.

Richard Wilbur. "A Late Aubade" from *Walking to Sleep: New Poems and Translations.* Copyright © 1968 by Richard Wilbur, originally published in *The New Yorker,* reprinted by permission of Harcourt Brace & Company. "Love Calls Us to the Things of This World" from *Things of This World,* copyright © 1956 and renewed 1984 by Richard Wilbur, reprinted by permission of Harcourt Brace & Company.

William Carlos Williams. "Poem" from *Collected Poems: 1909–1939, Volume I.* Copyright © 1938 by New Directions Publishing Corp. Reprinted by permission of New Directions Publishing Corp. "Spring and All" from *Collected Poems: 1909–1939, Volume I.* Copyright © 1938 by New Directions Publishing Corp. Reprinted by permission of New Directions Publishing Corp. "The Red Wheelbarrow" from *Collected Poems: 1909–1939, Volume I.* Copyright © 1938 by New Directions Publishing Corp. Reprinted by permission of New Directions Publishing Corp. "This Is Just to Say" from *Collected Poems, 1909–1939, Volume I.* Copyright © 1938 by New Directions Publishing Corp. Reprinted by permission of New Directions Publishing Corp.

C. K. Williams. "The Nail" from *Repair* by C. K. Williams. Copyright © 1998 by C. K. Williams. Reprinted with permission of Farrar, Straus & Giroux.

Miller Williams. "Thinking About Bill Dead of AIDS" from *Living on the Surface: New and Selected Poems* by Miller Williams. Copyright © 1972, 1973, 1976, 1979, 1980, 1987, 1988, 1989, by Miller Williams. Reprinted by permission of Louisiana State University Press.

Cynthia Griffin Wolff. "On the Many Voices in Dickinson's Poetry" from *Emily Dickinson* by Cynthia Griffin Wolff. Copyright © 1986 by Cynthia Griffin Wolff. Reprinted by permission of Alfred A. Knopf, Inc.

Baron Wormser. "Shoplifting" is reprinted from *When* by Baron Wormser, published by Sarabande Books, Inc. Copyright © 1997 by Baron Wormser. Reprinted by permission of Sarabande Books and the author.

William Butler Yeats. "Crazy Jane Talks with the Bishop" from *The Poems of W. B. Yeats: A New Edition,* edited by Richard J. Finneran. Copyright 1933 by Macmillan Publishing Company; copyright renewed © 1961 by Bertha Georgie Yeats. "Leda and the Swan" from *The Poems of W. B. Yeats: A New Edition,* edited by Richard J. Finneran. Copyright 1933 by Macmillan Publishing Company; copyright renewed © 1961 by Bertha Georgie Yeats. "Leda and the Swan" reprinted with the permission of Simon & Schuster from *The Poems of W. B. Yeats: A New Edition,* edited by Richard J. Finneran. Copyright 1928 by Macmillan Publishing Company; copyright renewed © 1956 by Bertha Georgie Yeats. "Sailing to Byzantium" from *The Poems of W. B. Yeats: A New Edition,* edited by Richard J. Finneran. Copyright 1933 by Macmillan Publishing Company; copyright renewed © 1961 by Bertha Georgie Yeats. "Sailing to Byzantium" reprinted with the permission of Simon & Schuster from *The Poems of W. B. Yeats: A New Edition,* edited by Richard J. Finneran. Copyright 1928 by Macmillan Publishing Company; copyright renewed © 1956 by Bertha Georgie Yeats. "The Second Coming" reprinted with the permission of Scribner, a Division of Simon & Schuster from *The Collected Poems of W. B. Yeats,* Revised Second Edition edited by Richard J. Finneran. Copyright 1928 by Macmillan Publishing Company; copyright renewed © 1956 by Georgie Yeats. "Crazy Jane Talks with the Bishop" reprinted with the permission of Scribner, a Division of Simon & Schuster from *The Collected Poems of W. B. Yeats,* Revised Second Edition edited by Richard J. Finneran. Copyright 1928 by Macmillan Publishing Company; copyright renewed © 1956 by Georgie Yeats. "The Wild Swans at Coole" reprinted with the permission of Scribner, a Division of Simon & Schuster from *The Collected Poems of W. B. Yeats,* Revised Second Edition edited by Richard J. Finneran. Copyright 1928 by Macmillan Publishing Company; copyright renewed © 1956 by Georgie Yeats.

David Zieroth. "Time over Earth" from *Canadian Literature 138/139,* Fall/Winter, 1993. Reprinted by permission of the author.

Index of First Lines

Index of Authors and Titles

Index of Terms

Boldface numbers refer to the Glossary of Literary Terms